SHOSTAKOVICH RECONSIDERED

SHOSTAKOVICH RECONSIDERED

Written and Edited by
ALLAN B. HO
and
DMITRY FEOFANOV

With an Overture by
VLADIMIR ASHKENAZY

TOCCATA
PRESS

First published in 1998 by Toccata Press;
paperback edition published in 2006

British Library Cataloguing in Publication Data
Shostakovich reconsidered
1. Shostakovich, D. (Dmitrii), 1906–1975—Criticism and interpretation
I. Ho, Allan. II. Feofanov, Dmitry

ISBN-10 0-907689-57-4
ISBN-13 978-0-907689-57-7

Set in 11 on 12 point Imprint by YHT Ltd, London
Printed and bound by SRP Ltd., Exeter

CONTENTS

Theme

Variations on a Theme

Coda

Overture

Vladimir Ashkenazy

I shall never forget the time when my piano teacher told me how she first met Dmitry Shostakovich outside the apartment building in Moscow where both of them lived. He asked if her water supply had been cut off. She answered: 'No, but why do you ask?' He said that his supply had been cut off, but then added that he was sure he knew why. This was soon after the Zhdanov committee's pronouncement on 'formalism', 'modernism' and other sins attributed to a few Soviet composers, Shostakovich among them – and my teacher told me that he looked like a hunted animal, fearing the worst.

This episode was only one of the countless snippets of information that reached us students and teachers of the Conservatory and the musical community in general – information relating to Shostakovich's state of mind and his reaction to what was happening in the country. One must not forget that such things were not – and, indeed, could not ever be – discussed in public, and we knew without a shadow of a doubt that Shostakovich deeply detested the system in which he lived, we knew how much he suffered from it and how helpless he felt about being unable to do anything except express himself through his music.

I and my fellow students had the privilege of attending several first Moscow performances of Shostakovich works (first performances usually being in Leningrad) – and one would have to be deaf not to have heard what he wanted to say. We were literally afraid for him at the premiere of the Tenth Symphony: surely, we thought, even the Party hacks could hear the gloomy helplessness and desperation in it, save for the finale, which we did not understand at the time, thinking that the composer had to put in 'a happy ending' to please the apparatchiks (only later we understood that it wasn't 'a happy ending' at all but a reflection of the ubiquitous trivia that surrounded him, which he was unable to ignore being caught up in it by virtue of his destiny – DSCH dancing against his will in the midst of it). But times were different then, and things were not as bad as they had been. The other monumental work – the First Violin Concerto (Oistrakh was the soloist) – was another indictment of the 'glorious Soviet reality': no light at the end of the tunnel.

Naturally, we lamented Shostakovich's joining the Communist Party, but we knew only too well that he had to do it to afford himself some protection from yet another bout of harassment by the authorities. I was present at the first Moscow performances of what I would call two 'interim' symphonies – Nos. 11 and 12 – which on the face of it seemed to play into the hands of the Party. But No. 11 ('The Year 1905') tells us more about the tragedy of revolution (which was largely not perceived by the Party); and in No. 12 ('The Year 1917', dedicated 'To the Memory of Vladimir Ilyich Lenin') the great composer could not convince himself, let alone his listeners, of the 'humanity' of Ulyanov-Lenin.

Then, in 1962, came the Thirteenth Symphony and with it the strongest and most eloquent condemnation of Soviet 'reality'. This was when Shostakovich's Party ticket came to the rescue. Had he not been a member of the Party, the premiere of the Symphony would in all likelihood have been cancelled outright. But in the circumstances the Central Committee resorted to subterfuge by 'persuading' Mr Nechipaylo (the bass soloist in all the movements of the Symphony) to declare that he was ill on the eve of the premiere. Thanks to the foresight and bravery of Kirill Kondrashin, the conductor of the first performance (Mravinsky was afraid to agree to conduct the piece) who had prepared an understudy, the evening was saved and the Symphony received a tremendous ovation and enormous public acclaim. Unfortunately, I was in the middle of a long concert tour and was not in Moscow at the time, but when I returned a few weeks later the city was still full of excitement from the event – Shostakovich having shown once again what his true convictions were and how determined he was to convey them.

When I read *Testimony*, there was no question in my mind that the real Shostakovich was here in this book. All that we knew about him was now confirmed in print; and there was much more in the same spirit. I personally was happy that the rest of the world would now be able to know the truth. Needless to say, the reaction of official Soviet musicology was predictable; what else would one expect from this totalitarian state, this huge Potemkin village, and what, consequently, would one expect from the Soviet stooges in the West?

I am convinced that without the Soviet denunciation of the book no one would have been asking if it was genuine – and to this day the pointless controversy continues. It is about time that the world ceased to be a victim of totalitarian ideological disinformation. But what I find even more amazing and distressing is that some of the so-called 'experts' on Shostakovich in the West still persist in distorting the facts to suit their arguments, while others show an unacceptable lack of knowledge of the Soviet reality – and I need hardly to emphasise at this stage that without profound (and, I repeat, *profound*) knowledge of what Shostakovich had to live through it is virtually impossible to be a serious and credible analyst of his output.

It is hard to believe that one such 'expert' writes that Shostakovich was ever 'perhaps the Soviet Union's most loyal musical son' – and that in 1994! Is it still possible that this musicologist still cannot shed the skin of an agent of influence of the USSR (and there were thousands of them in the West) or that he simply does not possess enough intelligence for this matter? Neither conclusion is attractive or, indeed, palatable. It is equally impossible to accept the credibility of another 'expert' who writes in his analysis of Shostakovich's Fifth Symphony, discussing the hidden message in it, that 'Shostakovich's original pronouncements on this Symphony at the time of its premiere made no mention of a hidden agenda'. Did this critic expect Shostakovich to put a noose around his neck by stating publicly what he had in mind? Ian MacDonald quite rightly says that 'the idea that he could have openly confessed such an agenda during Stalin's terror [. . .] verges on the surreal'.

This book settles the issue once and for all. I am sure that no one in his sane mind, having read the evidence presented by the authors, will ever ask the question of whether *Testimony* is authentic Shostakovich or not. The answer is that it most definitely is.

Vladimir Ashkenazy

To Solomon Moiseyevich Volkov

INTRODUCTION

Shostakovich Reconsidered is being written over twenty years after Dmitry Shostakovich died. One of us still remembers that hot summer day.

I spent the summer of 1975 on our dacha *near Moscow, as usual. One day, my mother came back from a rehearsal in the city and told us, 'Shostakovich died'.*

I remember seeing Shostakovich on TV several times, attending premieres of his works, always sitting in his own characteristic pose, most often accompanied by his wife Irina Antonovna. As a pianist, and committed Prokofiev enthusiast, I tended to place him in the 'also ran' category: I did not like his First Piano Concerto, dismissed his Second as 'pioneer music',[1] *felt vague respect for the Second Sonata and Preludes and Fugues. As for the Symphonies, despite having heard a few while attending the concerts of my mother's orchestra, their devastating implications fell on deaf ears when it came to impressing a certain teenage pianist, then in the midst of the first romantic crisis of his life.*

Things changed with the Fifteenth. My mother's orchestra premiered the work. She brought a cassette recorder to the rehearsals, and later played it for my father and me in the kitchen of our Moscow apartment. This was the first Shostakovich symphony I learned well, and to this day I consider the Fifteenth one of his greatest works. I attended the premiere and saw the man. An appreciation of others of the Symphonies soon followed.

When my mother brought us the news, I understood that an era had ended. My first impulse was to go to Moscow to attend the funeral, but my parents thought there would be pandemonium at the Conservatory, and their cooler heads prevailed. There were things to do at the dacha, *practising to be done, and*

[1] 'Young Pioneers' was a children's propaganda organisation in the Soviet Union, similar to the Boy and Girl Scouts.

the dog needed attention. I petted him with a heavy heart. (The only other death of a famous musical figure affecting me to a comparable extent was that of Glenn Gould in 1982.) I regret not going to the funeral: had I gone, I would have met one of the main protagonists of the drama that unfolded, although the true significance of such a meeting would have eluded me then.

Since the time of his death, Shostakovich's stature in the history of music has continued to grow. Still, some two decades later and nine since his birth, controversy remains. Aspects of his life, from the authenticity of his memoirs to the true nature of his relationship with the Soviet regime, continue to be debated. Inevitably, this debate colours the understanding of his music.

Even though the meaning of Shostakovich's music is crystal-clear for those 'with ears to listen', as the composer was wont to say, many, especially among those who should know better – musicologists – continue to misinterpret Shostakovich's art. In part, this misinterpretation stems from a regrettable lack of knowledge of the conditions in the Soviet Union during the relevant time period. In part, it stems from outright distortions.

Shostakovich Reconsidered places the composer and his music into proper perspective. It consists of three parts: (1) our 'Theme', 'Shostakovich's *Testimony*: Reply to an Unjust Criticism', a 'trial' of the composer's memoirs;[2] (2) 'Variations on a Theme', a collection of sixteen articles by prominent musicians and scholars, both Western and (post-)Soviet, which supports and amplifies points made in 'Reply', and sheds valuable new light on Shostakovich's works, life and personality; and (3) a 'Coda', which addresses the larger issue of a scandalous academic cover-up in many areas of Shostakovich research.

In 'Shostakovich's *Testimony*: Reply to an Unjust Criticism' we confront the issues surrounding *Testimony*, the Shostakovich memoirs brought to the world's attention by Solomon Volkov – in particular, the question of its authentic-

[2] *Testimony: The Memoirs of Dmitri Shostakovich*, as related to and edited by Solomon Volkov, transl. Antonina W. Bouis, Hamish Hamilton, London/Harper and Row, New York, 1979 (hereafter *Testimony*).

ity and accuracy. *Testimony* is a remarkable document, singly responsible for destroying the commonly accepted image of Shostakovich as a 'Soviet patriot' and Stalin apologist. In spite of the 'unjust criticism' that it is a forgery, it remains one of the most important and influential books in the history of music, a unique historical document of life in Stalin's Russia.

Adopting the format of a trial, we begin with an 'Opening Statement' briefly summarising the impact of *Testimony* as well as the controversies surrounding it. Next, in the 'Cross-Examination', we explore in more detail the often intense reactions elicited by these memoirs, both in the Soviet Union and in the West. We consider the 'official' Soviet response; chronicle the changing views of Maxim Shostakovich, the composer's son (pre- and post-defection); present the first extended comments about *Testimony* and Volkov made by Galina Shostakovich, the composer's daughter; and challenge the conclusions of Western detractors with respect to Volkov's relationship with Shostakovich, the true nature of these memoirs, alleged factual discrepancies, contradictions and omissions, the meanings of Shostakovich's most famous works, and the composer's politics.

In the 'Case for the Defence', we provide a wealth of material corroborating *Testimony*, including unequivocal endorsements from Shostakovich's inner circle and important documentary evidence. Chief among the latter is *Rayok*, the undeniably authentic anti-Stalinist satire, which leaves no doubt about Shostakovich's true feelings toward the regime. By calling attention to numerous heretofore hidden parallels between these works, we demonstrate that *Rayok* and *Testimony* are, in fact, twins in mind and spirit.

Finally, in the 'Closing Argument', we recapitulate the main points of this multidisciplinary discourse on music, history, politics, law, and the psychology of conformism, and place Shostakovich and his *Testimony* into proper perspective. We conclude that, when viewed in perspective, *Testimony* is neither fiction nor an anomaly, but merely the last of many courageous attempts by Shostakovich to speak the truth.

In this first thorough, objective investigation of *Testimony*, we defend the Shostakovich memoirs without pulling any punches. It is not our purpose to try to change the minds of those who made their careers and reputations indicting both *Testimony* and Volkov; such efforts are usually futile. But we do intend to reveal how their research casting doubt on the authenticity of *Testimony* is materially deficient, and does not withstand rigorous cross-examination. We demonstrate that the 'experts' themselves have committed the very sins for which they have castigated Volkov. But unlike the 'experts' we do not hurl insults at those who do not share our views. We do not call their books 'moronic tracts',[3] claim they are 'puppets' of other, sinister, forces,[4] or dismiss them as 'vile trivialisers', 'McCarthyites', and 'Stalinists'.[5] As Shostakovich himself would have said, 'do not dig a hole for another – you might fall into it yourself' (the Russian equivalent of 'what goes around, comes around').

We challenge the critics of Volkov and *Testimony* on numerous grounds. They refuse to accept the authenticity of the book despite the presence of undeniably genuine Shostakovich signatures at the beginning of each chapter (confirmed as such by a handwriting expert as well as the composer's children). They claim that these chapters begin with non-controversial material and, from this premise, weave an elaborate theory of conspiracy and deception. Yet, the 'experts' fail to acknowledge that, in two instances, signatures are found on pages containing some of the most embittered statements in *Testimony*.

Time after time, we raise grave questions concerning the scholarly integrity of Volkov's most prominent critics. We document their 'selective scholarship' – the suppression of data not supporting their thesis. We document their 'vicious abstractions'[6] – quotation out-of-context and distortion of statements susceptible of most innocent interpretation. We

[3] Laurel Fay, paper, meeting of the American Musicological Society, 3 November 1995, New York (hereafter Fay, paper). *Cf.* p. 237, note 444.

[4] Richard Taruskin, 'Public Lies and Unspeakable Truth: Interpreting Shostakovich's Fifth Symphony', *Shostakovich Studies*, ed. David Fanning, Cambridge University Press, Cambridge, 1995, p. 31 (hereafter Taruskin, 'Lies').

[5] *Ibid.*, pp. 52–53.

[6] 'Vicious abstraction' is a species of logical fallacy, where a statement is removed from its context or altered, thereby changing its meaning. *Cf.*

document their lack of perspective – for example, the uncritical acceptance of Soviet denunciations of Volkov and *Testimony* (while failing to note that those who signed such denunciations often had been coerced to do so or had not even read that which they were denouncing).

For the first time in the scholarly literature, we trace the *Testimony* controversy to the KGB, and query whether Volkov's most prominent critics feasted off the 'Soviet platter'. We present uncensored new evaluations by members of Shostakovich's own family – his children Maxim and Galina – who now endorse both *Testimony* and Volkov. We reveal the 'tabloid musicology' style of Volkov's critics and demonstrate that, on occasion, prominent individuals acclaimed as experts prove to be ill-informed in the fields of their expertise. We present startling new information on the genesis of Shostakovich's arguably most (in)famous work – the Seventh Symphony – and consider the deeper meanings of other compositions, including the Fifth, Ninth, Tenth, Eleventh and Fifteenth Symphonies, the Eighth Quartet, and the vocal cycles *Satires* and *From Jewish Folk Poetry*. Finally, we trace Shostakovich's recurring thoughts of emigration (and, implicitly, his internal dissidence) to as early as 1928.

We conclusively disprove the myth that Shostakovich was 'perhaps Soviet Russia's most loyal musical son'.[7]

We surmise that the intensity of adverse reaction by some to Volkov is explained, at least in part, by a deep-seated anti-Semitism and present evidence in support of this hypothesis. We also point out that, contrary to the oft-repeated claims of Volkov's critics, no major, compromising error has yet been found in *Testimony* after almost two decades of intense scrutiny; on the other hand, numerous revelations in *Testimony* have been corroborated repeatedly in the intervening years by both documentary evidence and Shostakovich's contemporaries. (Chief among these is the description of the genesis of the Seventh Symphony as a requiem based on the Psalms

---

Ruggero J. Aldisert, *The Judicial Process*, West Publishing Co., St. Paul, 1976, p. 638, citing William S. and Mabel Lewis Sahakian, 'Material Fallacies of Reasoning', *Ideas of Great Philosophers*, Harper and Row, New York, 1966.

[7] *Cf.* pp. 171–77.

of David, planned before the Nazi invasion. These revelations have now been confirmed by various sources, including Manashir Yakubov, curator of the Shostakovich family archive and Sofiya Khentova, the composer's 'authorised' Russian biographer, respectively.) Finally, over sixteen years after it was first made, and accepted without question by many in the cultural community, we demonstrate that the most serious charge against Volkov – that of plagiarism – is based on inadequate knowledge of Shostakovich and his work, and is without merit.

Based on newly revealed information and textual and musical analyses of Shostakovich's music, we demonstrate that the 'new' Shostakovich,[8] which so shocked the musical establishment when *Testimony* was published, was and is the real Shostakovich. Profane, embittered, deeply disillusioned, taking calculated risks in his struggle with the regime – these attributes the critics found unbelievable, warranting their rejection of *Testimony*: 'a lie from beginning to end'.[9] The critics were wrong. Shostakovich's own *Struggle between Realism and Formalism in Music*, commonly known as *Rayok*, presents all of these, and more. Additional works that amply reveal the extent of Shostakovich's not-so-internal dissidence range from his symphonies to his *Preface to the Complete Edition of My Works and a Brief Reflection Upon this Preface*, *Suite on Verses of Michelangelo* and *From Jewish Folk Poetry*.

We feel compelled to bring this information to the attention of the cultural community because an Orwellian rewriting of history is now going on in Shostakovich research. When *Testimony* appeared, some critics vehemently rejected this 'new' Shostakovich as a falsified image and branded Volkov a liar, plagiarist and forger. Today, the very same people are changing their tune: we never denied, they say, that the overall portrayal of Shostakovich in *Testimony* was on the mark (an admission difficult to evade after the collapse of the Soviet Union); our problem, they say, was

[8] *Cf.* Ian MacDonald, *The New Shostakovich*, Fourth Estate, London/Northeastern University Press, Boston, 1990.

[9] Phillip Bonosky, 'Defaming the Memory of a Famous Composer', *Daily World*, 10 November 1979, p. 12 (hereafter Bonosky).

only with the specifics of the book. Contrary to their belated assertions, however, up to this day the 'experts' have never admitted publicly, for the record, that they were wrong in denying *Testimony*'s 'essential truths' – that Shostakovich was not 'Soviet Russia's most loyal musical son', that his works were gulags in music, that they, the 'experts', were simply wrong.[10] This is why 'Shostakovich's *Testimony*: Reply to an Unjust Criticism' fills a major void in the scholarly literature: nearly twenty years after *Testimony* appeared, the time has come to complete the paradigm shift in Shostakovich studies which *Testimony* inaugurated.

'Variations on a Theme' presents additional evidence that the 'new' Shostakovich in *Testimony* was the real Shostakovich. Several of these articles, including contributions by Timothy L. Jackson, Ian MacDonald and Harlow Robinson, were prepared specially for this publication. Other materials, such as the writings of Andrey Bitov, Galina Drubachevskaya, Lev Lebedinsky, Leo Mazel', Solomon Volkov, Vladimir Zak and Daniil Zhitomirsky, were newly translated and, in many cases, are being made available complete in English for the first time. Finally, pieces that have appeared elsewhere, as in the journal *DSCH*, are here given wider distribution and often include additions and revisions by the original authors.

In 'Variation I' we present materials involving Solomon Volkov and Maxim Shostakovich. Volkov has remained a controversial and unjustly maligned figure ever since *Testimony*, which was 'related to and edited by' him, was published in 1979. His notoriety has not been diminished, as one would have expected, by the appearance of other books related to him by choreographer George Balanchine and violinist Nathan Milstein. First, Volkov himself reminisces with Galina Drubachevskaya, one of his former colleagues at *Sovetskaya Muzyka*, about the arts in Russia and the West, his relationship with Shostakovich, and the writing of *Testimony*, in the process rebutting several of the charges that

[10] In November 1995, Volkov's most prominent critic, Laurel Fay, stated: '*For the record*, I have not found any evidence to change my opinions about the authenticity of those memoirs' (Fay, paper).

have been levelled against him. Volkov then interviews another giant of the music world, Mstislav Rostropovich, who shares his personal memories of Shostakovich, Prokofiev, and Britten.

Maxim Shostakovich, the composer's son, remains an important figure in the controversy surrounding *Testimony*. Initially expressing doubts about these memoirs, his opinion, post-defection, has turned gradually to appreciation. If actions speak louder than words, Maxim's sharing a podium with and complimenting Volkov at a Shostakovich symposium in 1992 reflects their new relationship and mutual respect. Harlow Robinson's transcription of this historic occasion, which also featured the poet Yevgeny Yevtushenko (Shostakovich's collaborator on the Thirteenth Symphony (*Babi Yar*) and *The Execution of Stepan Razin*), is filled with personal and perceptive insights into the composer, his music and milieu. It is followed by informal, but equally informative, notes transcribed by John-Michael Albert during Maxim's six lectures on his father's music presented at the University of Houston in 1990.

In 'Variation II' we include new English translations of six important post-Soviet re-evaluations of Shostakovich, several of which also touch upon *Testimony*. In these articles some of the best-known figures in Soviet music and culture, including the musicologists Lev Lebedinsky, Leo Mazel', Vladimir Zak and Daniil Zhitomirsky, the conductor Kirill Kondrashin and the writer Andrey Bitov, reveal their true opinions of the composer. All concur, for reasons ranging from stylistic and literary analyses to personal remembrances, that *Testimony* is authentic.

In 'Variation III' we present three essays by Ian MacDonald. In his article 'His Misty Youth: The Glivenko Letters and Life in the '20s', MacDonald shows that, by the age of twenty, Shostakovich was already cynical about both Communism and 'Soviet reality' in general. In 'Universal Because Specific: Arguments for a Contextual Approach', MacDonald expands upon ideas deployed in his book *The New Shostakovich* (1990) by arguing that not only does Shostakovich's entire œuvre require re-evaluation in the light of its historical context but that such a specific focus, far from belittling the significance of the music, is an indispensable prerequisite to comprehending its universality.

Finally, in 'Writing About Shostakovich: The Post-Communist Perspective', MacDonald postulates that the failure of Western musicology to perceive the dramatic specificity of Shostakovich's music has exposed a fundamental philosophical flaw in the modern view of what music is or should be. He argues that, because of this, any re-evaluation of Shostakovich's output must logically lead to a fundamental reassessment of the working principles of contemporary music criticism.

In the last 'Variation', we include articles by Ian MacDonald, Semyon Bychkov and Timothy L. Jackson focusing on specific works by Shostakovich. Although, as Maxim points out, 'only a stupid person' could not understand the autobiographical nature of the Eighth Quartet, Volkov is equally correct in noting that 'there are still a lot of these stupid people around'. MacDonald's article, 'The Legend of the Eighth Quartet', concisely sets the record straight, summarising the background for, and true meaning of, this much talked-about but often misunderstood work. Bychkov's interview, 'The Seventh Symphony: Truth or Legend', similarly separates fact from fiction, placing the work into proper perspective, while sharing the valuable personal insights of a performer. Finally, Jackson's article, 'Dmitry Shostakovich: The Composer As Jew', expands upon earlier investigations of this important aspect of Shostakovich's life and music. Jackson explores the early formation and repeated, although sometimes disguised and subtle, manifestations of Shostakovich's 'Jewish identity', shedding new light on landmark works such as the Fifth, Seventh and Fifteenth Symphonies.

The 'Coda' of *Shostakovich Reconsidered* provides a fitting conclusion to a book which moves from the specific (a defence of *Testimony*) to the more universal (a commentary on the deplorable state of Shostakovich research in the West). In 'Naïve Anti-Revisionism: The Academic Misrepresentation of Shostakovich', Ian MacDonald repeatedly dismantles the spurious claims of the leading anti-revisionist writers, such as Laurel Fay, Richard Taruskin and Malcolm Brown, taking them to task for their confused and self-contradictory arguments, absence of human insight and scandalous lack of historical knowledge of Shostakovich's culture and society.

MacDonald again emphasises the importance of reconsidering Shostakovich and his music in proper historical context, while taking into account new evidence, such as that presented earlier in *Shostakovich Reconsidered.* He calls for musicologists – indeed, all proper scholars – to base their research on hard evidence rather than supposition, the whole truth rather than a selective editing of the facts, and general honesty rather than personal or political biases and agendas.

Above all, Shostakovich strove to be honest – in his life, and in his music. To whatever degree he co-operated with the authorities, it was only to save his own life, the lives of his family, and his music. As Lazarus Long put it, '"Cooperate with the inevitable" means "Roll with the punch" – it does not mean stooling for the guards'.[11] And Shostakovich never did. As a real artist, moreover, he was capable of acts of unbelievable, some might say suicidal, courage (such as mocking his would-be executioners in *Rayok*, begun in the wake of the Zhdanov Decree; speaking out for Jews in *From Jewish Folk Poetry* and the Thirteenth Symphony at the height of official anti-Semitic campaigns; or making a poignant commentary on the brutality of power in the Eleventh Symphony, prompting his perceptive son to comment, 'Papa, what if they hang you for this?'[12]).

We have fewer reasons to compromise. Our lives are not endangered, and our biggest enemies are merely complacency and the status quo. They provide a poor excuse for refusing to face the truth. Shostakovich always did, and we owe him at least this much.[13]

Allan B. Ho and Dmitry Feofanov

[11] Robert A. Heinlein, *Expanded Universe*, Ace Books, New York, 1980, p. 417.

[12] Elizabeth Wilson, *Shostakovich: A Life Remembered*, Faber and Faber, London/Princeton University Press, Princeton, 1994, p. 317 (hereafter Wilson).

[13] For additional revelations about Shostakovich's music, life and memoirs, *cf.* Ian MacDonald's website *Music Under Soviet Rule* (http://www.siue.edu/~aho/musov/musov.html).

> In a totalitarian system relations between the artist and the regime are always extremely complex and contradictory. If the artist sets himself against the system, he is put behind bars or simply killed. But if he does not express his disagreement with its dogmas verbally, he is not physically bothered, he is left alone. He is even rewarded from time to time. [. . .] I have always believed that real music has the power to overcome the regime and all its ideological taboos. [. . .] Shostakovich did not wish to rot in prison or a cemetery; he wanted to tell people, through the power of his art, his pain and his hatred of totalitarianism. He wrote all his scores in a Soviet country. He was recognised and given awards there. But in his music he was always honest and uncompromising.

Rodion Shchedrin, letter in *Gramophone*,
Vol. 75, No. 894, November 1997, p. 8.

Acknowledgements

Shostakovich Reconsidered would not have been possible without the assistance of numerous parties. First and foremost, we would like to thank Solomon Moiseyevich Volkov, who gave unprecedented access to his personal archive and, in over a hundred hours of face-to-face and 'phone conversations, answered hundreds of questions about his relationship with Shostakovich and the writing of *Testimony*. Also deserving special mention are our other contributors, translators and colleagues, who lent their expertise in various areas and demonstrated utmost patience as our manuscript gradually took shape, especially Ian MacDonald and Timothy L. Jackson, who offered constant encouragement and innumerable suggestions; Elmer Schönberger, whose early reviews of *Testimony* yielded leads for further investigation; Derek C. Hulme, who shared important background information on Shostakovich's works; Hugh Macdonald and John van der Slice, who early on recognised the significance of this project; Anita Bernstein and Molly Lien of Chicago-Kent College of Law, and Shirley Wilgenbusch, Research Director of the Illinois Appellate Court for the Fourth District, who provided fresh legal insights on many of our arguments; and our own 'distant friend, who must remain nameless' – without your involvement, this book would have been much less complete.

We have also benefitted considerably from the assistance of numerous parties at Southern Illinois University at Edwardsville (SIUE): Therese Dickman, Mary Peters-Grandone, Barbara Zimmermann, Hope Myers, Richard Reilly and Bessie Richards (Lovejoy Library), who located hundreds of pieces of information; Véronique Zaytzeff, Frederick Morrison, Geert Pallemans and Belinda Carstens-Wickham (Department of Foreign Languages and Literature), who translated materials in a variety of languages; Michael Mishra (Department of Music), who proofread our manuscript and provided many valuable suggestions; Ephraim Jones, who typeset the musical examples; Miloš Krstić and Darlene Hatcher, who assisted in bibliographical searches and preparation of the index; and the Graduate School, which provided a Funded University Research Grant and a Research Scholar Award to facilitate completion of this book.

Extracts from the music of Dmitry Shostakovich © G. Schirmer (USA) and Boosey and Hawkes Music Publishers Ltd. (UK), reprinted by permission; extracts from the music of Leonard Bernstein © Warner Bros., copyright renewed; reprinted by permission of Leonard Bernstein Music Publishing Co. L.L.C., Publisher, and Boosey & Hawkes, Inc., Sole Agent. The author and editors express their gratitude to Ms. Zoraya Mendez, Print Licensing Manager, for the grant of permissions.

Special thanks are given to Norman Lebrecht, who recommended our manuscript to Toccata Press, and to Martin Anderson, who expertly guided this text to publication. We also express our deepest gratitude to the following persons and publishers who provided valuable information via interviews and/or granted permission to reproduce copyrighted materials: John-Michael Albert, Vladimir Ashkenazy, Andrey Bitov, Semyon Bychkov, Antonina W. Bouis, Joachim Braun, Susan Brownsberger, Galina Drubachevskaya, Rostislav Dubinsky, Ian Hunter, Timothy L. Jackson, Sofiya Khentova, Frederic Kirchberger, Yury Korev, The Honorable Alex Kozinski, Markus Lång, Norman Lebrecht, Flora Litvinova, Ian MacDonald, Lord Menuhin, Alan Mercer, Ulric Neisser, Harlow Robinson, Rodion Shchedrin, Alisa Shebalin, Galina Shostakovich, Maxim Shostakovich, Elizabeth Valentine, Pierre Vidal, Solomon Volkov, Natalya Vovsi-Mikhoels, Elizabeth Wilson, Manashir Yakubov, Vladimir Zak, the Glinka State Central Museum of Musical Culture; the journals *Daugava*, *Muzykal'naya Academiya*, *Novy Mir* and *Sputnik*; and the publishers Boosey & Hawkes and G. Schirmer. The photographs introducing the 'Theme' and 'Variations' were supplied by David King; that introducing the 'Coda' was taken from Viktor Jusefovich, *David Oistrakh*, Cassell, London, 1979, p. 174, where no copyright holder is acknowledged.

Finally, we wish to acknowledge the oft-mentioned 'experts'. Without their ongoing misinterpretation of Shostakovich and unjust criticisms of his *Testimony*, this book would not have been possible or, indeed, necessary.

THE EDITORS

ALLAN B. HO holds a Ph.D. in musicology and is currently a Professor of Music at Southern Illinois University at Edwardsville. His principal areas of research are Russian/Soviet music, the piano-concerto repertoire, and the works of Liszt.

He has prepared critical and performing editions of Wilhelm Stenhammar's First Piano Concerto (the lost score of which he rediscovered), Grieg's Piano Concerto (in the original version, 1868/72), and Alkan's Concerto, Op. 39 (as orchestrated by Klindworth), which have been recorded on the BIS, Chandos and Naxos labels. He has also been a contributor to various music journals, dictionaries and symposia, and has previously collaborated with Dmitry Feofanov on *Biographical Dictionary of Russian/Soviet Composers* (Greenwood Press, 1989). He may be reached at aho@siue.edu.

DMITRY FEOFANOV holds degrees in both music and law and is currently an attorney with Brooks, Adams and Tarulis in Naperville, Illinois. His research interests include the theory of law and the state, and Russian piano music of the twentieth century.

He shared top honours in the University of Maryland International Piano Competition in 1982, and in 1989–90, in commemoration of the Prokofiev centenary, performed Prokofiev's complete solo piano works in a series of five recitals. He has recorded solo works by Medtner, Rachmaninov and Stanchinsky, as well as the complete piano-and-orchestra works by Alkan. His other publications include four collections of Russian/Soviet piano music for Dover and Carl Fischer, and several articles in music and law journals. He may be reached at alumfeofanov@minna.acc.iit.edu.

THE CONTRIBUTORS

JOHN-MICHAEL ALBERT is on the staff of the Superconductivity Center at the University of Houston. A long-time and knowledgeable enthusiast of Shostakovich's music, he attended Maxim Shostakovich's six lectures on his father's works held at the University of Houston between 7–14 June 1990, during which he transcribed the notes reproduced herein.

ANDREY BITOV is the leading contemporary Russian prose writer and president of the Russian Pen Club. His novels *Pushkin House* and *The Monkey Link* are acclaimed as masterpieces of contemporary Russian literature.

SEMYON BYCHKOV has conducted the world's leading orchestras, including the Berlin Philharmonic, London Philharmonic and Orchestre de Paris. His thorough knowledge of Shostakovich's music and style is evident in his July 1991 conversation with Henrietta Cowling, Assistant Producer, BBC Music and Arts.

GALINA DRUBACHEVSKAYA was a journalist and colleague of Solomon Volkov at *Sovetskaya Muzyka* during the time that *Testimony* was written. She provided first-hand corroboration of how these memoirs came about both in her interview with Volkov and in several conversations with the Editors in the early 1990s.

TIMOTHY L. JACKSON was formerly Assistant Professor of Music at Connecticut College and joins the faculty of the University of North Texas in 1998. He is currently writing *The Music of Richard Strauss* for Yale University Press. Professor Jackson co-edited *Bruckner Studies 1* and *2* and *Sibelius Studies* for Cambridge University Press, and has published numerous articles.

KENNETH KIESLER became Professor of Conducting and Director of the University Orchestras at the University of

Michigan during the 1995–96 season. He is conductor and music director of the St Cecilia Orchestra. He has also conducted the Houston Chamber Orchestra, the Chicago Symphony and many other orchestras in the United States and abroad.

KIRILL KONDRASHIN (1914–81) was a prominent conductor of the Soviet era. He was artistic director of the Moscow Philharmonic from 1960 until 1975. In 1978, he applied for political asylum in Holland, where he conducted the Concertgebouw Orchestra. Highly respected by Shostakovich, whom he first met in 1937, he was asked to premiere the Fourth and Thirteenth Symphonies, *The Execution of Stepan Razin* and the Second Violin Concerto.

LEV LEBEDINSKY (1904–94) was a musicologist and close friend of Shostakovich, especially during the 1950s to early 1960s. He edited the piano score of the second version of *Katerina Izmailova* and also was a collaborator on *Rayok*, Shostakovich's anti-Stalinist satire. He was among the first to openly reveal the hidden meanings of works such as the Eighth Quartet and Eleventh Symphony.

IAN MACDONALD is a music critic and journalist, and the author of *The New Shostakovich* (Fourth Estate, London/ Northeastern University Press, Boston, 1990) and numerous other articles on the composer. His interests and expertise extend from Soviet cultural and political history to the Beatles, about whom he has written a landmark book, *Revolution in the Head* (Fourth Estate, London/Henry Holt, New York, 1994; 2nd edn. 1997).

LEO MAZEL' is a leading Russian music theoretician, who for decades has been one of the most respected and authoritative professors at the Moscow Conservatory. He has contributed enormously to research on and analysis of Shostakovich's music in numerous articles and books on the subject, including *Symphonies of D. D. Shostakovich* (Sovetsky Kompozitor, Moscow, 1960) and *Études on Shostakovich* (Sovetsky Kompozitor, Moscow, 1986).

HARLOW ROBINSON is a Professor in the Department of Foreign Languages and Literatures, Northeastern University, and the author of *Sergei Prokofiev: A Biography* (Viking, New York, 1987) and *The Last Impresario: The Life, Times and Legacy of Sol Hurok* (Viking, New York, 1994/Penguin, Harmondsworth, 1995). He has written widely on Soviet music and culture for many popular and scholarly publications, and is a frequent lecturer for Lincoln Center, the New York Philharmonic and the Metropolitan Opera Guild. He was the co-artistic director of the Salute to Shostakovich Festival.

MSTISLAV ROSTROPOVICH has long been recognised as one of the world's greatest cellists. A close friend of Shostakovich and the dedicatee of several of his works, including the Cello Concertos, he has displayed his deep understanding of the composer's style both as an instrumentalist and as conductor of the National Symphony (Washington, D.C.) and other major orchestras. In 1989 he premiered Shostakovich's anti-Stalinist satire *Rayok*.

MAXIM SHOSTAKOVICH is a distinguished pianist and conductor. He has conducted many of the world's leading orchestras and is particularly noted for his performances and recordings of his father's music. He now resides in New York.

SOLOMON VOLKOV is a music critic, author and journalist, who emigrated to the United States from the USSR in 1976. He collaborated with Shostakovich on *Testimony: The Memoirs of Dmitri Shostakovich, as related to and edited by Solomon Volkov* (Hamish Hamilton, London/Harper & Row, New York, 1979), and also has written *Balanchine's Tchaikovsky*, with George Balanchine (Simon and Schuster, New York, 1985), *From Russia to the West*, with Nathan Milstein (Barrie & Jenkins, London/Henry Holt, Boston, 1990), *St. Petersburg: A Cultural History* (The Free Press, New York, 1995), and many articles on Russian and Soviet music, musicians and culture.

YEVGENY YEVTUSHENKO is a renowned Russian poet, whose works may be enjoyed in *The Collected Poems 1952–1990*, edited by Albert C. Todd (Henry Holt, Boston, 1991). In the 1960s, Shostakovich took an interest in Yevtushenko's texts and set several of them to music in his vocal-symphonic poem *The Execution of Stepan Razin* and *Symphony No. 13* ('Babi Yar').

VLADIMIR ZAK is a prominent Russian musicologist now residing in New York. For many years he was Deputy Chairman of the Commission of Musical Criticism of the Union of Soviet Composers, with a special interest in the folklore elements of twentieth-century music, including works by Prokofiev and Shostakovich.

DANIIL ZHITOMIRSKY (1906–92) was a leading Russian musicologist, and a colleague (and sometimes critic) of Shostakovich for some forty years. After being a proponent of 'Proletarian music' in the 1920s, he became one of the early champions of Shostakovich's works, defending, in particular, the controversial Eighth and Ninth Symphonies against accusations of 'formalism'. Because of this, in the late 1940s he was condemned as one of the 'rootless cosmopolitans'. In 1966, in recognition of his research on the music of Robert Schumann, Zhitomirsky was awarded the International Schumann Award.

THEME

'Reply to an Unjust Criticism' sheds valuable new light not only on the authenticity of Shostakovich's memoirs but also on the efforts of Soviet and some Western sources to mute the truth. Adopting the format of a trial, Ho and Feofanov weigh the evidence and persuasively refute earlier claims that *Testimony* is inaccurate and a forgery. Their arguments are amply supported, sources are thoroughly documented and text is engagingly written for musician and non-musician alike. What makes 'Reply' unique among Shostakovich studies is that it provides detailed answers to the many criticisms leveled at *Testimony* and its editor, Solomon Volkov, during the past seventeen years. At the same time, it raises disturbing new questions about the integrity, expertise and motivations of the critics of these memoirs, who, contrary to the evidence, continue to besmirch Shostakovich as 'perhaps Soviet Russia's most loyal musical son'.

The Honorable Alex Kozinski,
United States Court of Appeals
Ninth Circuit

I have read 'Reply to an Unjust Criticism' and find it admirable, convincing and totally solid in its approach and reasoning. It is riveting reading and reveals human nature in the whole span of the worst and the best and how they fit into each other and how in a certain way the one provokes the other and may even be dependent on each other. It is a wonderful guide to Shostakovich's music.

Lord Menuhin

SHOSTAKOVICH'S *TESTIMONY*: REPLY TO AN UNJUST CRITICISM

Allan B. Ho and Dmitry Feofanov

I. Opening Statement

'Only stupid people couldn't understand that. But there are still a lot of these stupid people around.'

Solomon Volkov,
on the true meaning
of Shostakovich's music.

Since its publication in 1979, *Testimony: The Memoirs of Dmitri Shostakovich*, 'as related to and edited by Solomon Volkov', has remained one of the most important and influential books in the history of music.[1] To date, half a million copies have been printed in some twenty different languages,[2] and the influence of *Testimony* has ranged from being recognised as an immensely important historical document of life in Stalin's Russia[3] to serving as an example of hearsay and its exceptions in the evidence class of a law school.[4]

[1] *Cf.* pp. 34–36.

[2] Galina Drubachevskaya, interviewing Solomon Volkov, 'A Man Has Burned-Up Here', p. 345 (hereafter Drubachevskaya).

[3] *Cf.* pp. 295–96.

[4] Interview with Professor Jacob Corré, Chicago-Kent College of Law, Illinois Institute of Technology, April 1995.

As several writers have noted, the impact of *Testimony* on the musical world has been similar to that of Solzhenitsyn's *Gulag Archipelago* on a more general audience: 'some embraced it, some deplored it, but everyone read it'.[5] When asked, 'Is it true that critics often compare *Testimony* with *Gulag*?', the conductor Kirill Kondrashin, a long-time friend of Shostakovich, confirmed, 'Yes, in the musical world, that is undeniable'.[6] Similar sentiments have been voiced in publications as varied as *The Economist*,[7] *National Review*[8] and *New Republic*,[9] and, more recently, by Igor' Shafarevich:

> [*Testimony*] is a document of amazing depth and force. It does not have material of the same colossal reach as *Gulag Archipelago*, to be sure, but, in a different plane, I think it creates a similarly vivid picture of life in that epoch. It is the history of a man seized by some sort of a monster, injured, barely alive. But thanks to his genius gift, amazing strength of spirit, he keeps all of his creative abilities – and, being a maimed

[5] Terry Teachout, 'The Problem of Shostakovich', *Commentary*, February 1995, p. 47 (hereafter Teachout). Additional parallels may be noted between Solzhenitsyn's literary memoir, *The Oak and the Calf*, and *Testimony*. Both works mix 'high-flown literary rhetoric, cool analysis, colloquial asides, and salty comment [... with] autobiographical content and [a] certain element of gossipy immediacy' (Michael Scammell, *Solzhenitsyn: A Biography*, W. W. Norton, New York, 1984, p. 923); both also have been viciously attacked for their negative portrayal of colleagues and officials, and supposed contradictions (Solzhenitsyn's 'propensity to have his cake and eat it'), omissions, and 'anti-Soviet propaganda' (*cf*. Scammell, pp. 923–30, 986–89, as well as pp. 60–62, 85–86, 143–59 and 177–88, below).

[6] Interview between Kondrashin and Volkov, 22 February 1980 (tape on file with the authors).

[7] '*Testimony* confirms with yet more chapter and verse the "Gulag Archipelago" of Solzhenitsyn [. . .]. It is a horrifying record' ('A Cry from the Tomb', *The Economist*, 273, 27 October 1979, p. 120).

[8] '[*Testimony*] is a tremendous book, Solzhenitsyn's *Gulag* in another version' (Peter P. Witonski, 'Traitor to Art', *National Review*, xxxi/45, 9 November 1979, p. 1410).

[9] 'Rambling and disjointed, *Testimony* is nevertheless one of the most powerful political indictments of the Stalinist era to come along in years – as savage as Solzhenitsyn's *The Gulag Archipelago* or Nadezhda Mandelstam's *Hope Against Hope* [. . .]' (*New Republic*, 181, 10 November 1979, p. 34).

> cripple, still manages to create even more than he would have created had his fate been a happier one.[10]

The surge of interest in Shostakovich's music after 1979 can be attributed, in part, to the composer's memoirs. *Testimony* is, 'arguably, the most widely publicised and controversial book ever written about a composer'.[11] Nearly two decades after its publication, it continues to be the focal point of controversy, causing one critic to write: 'There have been times over the past few years when I've wondered whether some of the disputants value *Testimony* for the light it throws on the music, or the music for the light it throws on *Testimony*'.[12]

Much as Shostakovich and his music were throughout his life, *Testimony* has been alternately praised and criticised. Some Westerners hailed it for its profound insights into the composer's works, personality and life under the Soviet regime:[13]

> An extremely powerful, grim, gripping book and one that will set the record straight ... The memoirs are a serious indictment of past and present Russia, as well as the recollections of a life apparently spent in fear and despair ... *Testimony* is indeed the testimony of a major creator in music. But it is much more than that. The book could have been subtitled 'The Life of the Russian Intellectual Under Stalin'. (Harold C. Schoenberg, *New York Times Book Review*)

> An unexampled picture of some fifty-five years of Soviet musical life .... Now that the memoirs have been published, not one episode of the composer's career can be viewed in the

[10] Igor' R. Shafarevich, 'Shostakovich i Russkoye Soprotivleniye Kommunizmu' ('Shostakovich and The Russian Resistance to Communism'), *Sochineniya v tryokh tomakh* (*Works in Three Volumes*), Feniks, Moscow, 1994, Vol. 2, p. 457 (hereafter Shafarevich). *Cf.* Yevgeny Yevtushenko's analogy of the USSR as the 'mother of cripples' (Harlow Robinson, 'Shostakovich Symposium' (hereafter Robinson), pp. 387 and 399).

[11] Hugh Canning, 'Scores to Settle', *The Sunday Times*, 7 August 1994, p. 7:5 (hereafter Canning).

[12] Stephen Johnson, 'All in a Life', *Gramophone*, Vol. 72, No. 857, October 1994, p. 31 (hereafter Johnson).

[13] The following quotes are presented on the covers of the fourth Limelight edition of *Testimony*, New York, 1992.

> same light as before, not one work of music heard in the same way. (Patricia Blake, *Time*)
>
> The man and musician whose personality beams from these pages is full of the contradictions of flesh and blood and the will to survive. Nobody who gets to know Shostakovich through his *Testimony* will ever hear his music in the naive old way. (Karen Monson, *Chicago Sun-Times*)
>
> No single account portrays so nakedly, so brutally, the crushing hand of Stalin on Russia's cultural and creative life as that of Shostakovich in *Testimony*. This is a gripping, even terrifying attempt by one of the world's great composers to lay bare the torment of his times. (Harrison Salisbury)
>
> *Testimony* is a book of immense power, full of bitterness and heroism, and I do not know of a musician who will not read it with compassion and admiration. These memoirs have afforded me an insight into Shostakovich's thoughts which would otherwise have been quite impossible. (André Previn)
>
> The tragic horror of a trapped genius. (Yehudi Menuhin)
>
> Recipient of an ASCAP/Deems Taylor Award in 1980.
>
> The book of the year. (*The Times* [London])

The Soviets, however, denounced *Testimony* as 'a vile falsification',[14] 'a wretched job', 'a disgraceful concoction', and 'an attempt to blacken our country and Soviet culture'.[15] Soviet contentions were parroted by Western fellow-travellers. Dr Malcolm H. Brown, a prominent authority on Russian/Soviet music, called Volkov a 'liar',[16] Christopher Norris thought *Testimony* just 'too good to be true from an anti-Soviet propaganda viewpoint',[17] and Peter Schaeffer

[14] Tikhon Khrennikov, speech to the Sixth Congress of Composers, in 'Muzyka prinadlezhit narodu' ('Music Belongs to the People'), *Sovetskaya Kul'tura*, 23 November 1979, p. 4 (hereafter 'Muzyka prinadlezhit narodu').

[15] Reported in Daniil Zhitomirsky, 'Shostakovich Ofitsial'ny i Podlinny' ('Shostakovich: The Public and the Private'), *Daugava*, 1990, No. 3, transl. Tatjana M. Marovic (Norbury), Katia Vinogradova and Ian MacDonald (hereafter Zhitomirsky, 'Public and Private').

[16] Malcolm H. Brown, 'Communications', *Notes*, 50/3, March 1994, p. 1210 (hereafter Brown, 'Communications'). *Cf.* p. 243.

[17] *Shostakovich: The Man and His Music*, ed. Christopher Norris, Marion Boyars, London, 1982, p. 9 (hereafter Norris).

dismissed the memoirs as 'yet another all-too-convenient piece of anti-Soviet propaganda [. . .] fouling the atmosphere of peaceful co-existence',[18] asking indignantly:

> Who is this Volkov, what are his credentials, and where is the proof of his claims? Is one readily to accept that this man alone qualified himself on brief acquaintance to receive such confidences as Shostakovich was evidently unwilling to impart to anyone else, including his family and his closest associates?
>
> Is one to take at face value the vilification not only of some of the leading lights of Soviet culture, but also the malice and bitterness with which Shostakovich purportedly speaks of Stanislavsky, Rolland, Shaw, and Feuchtwanger? Finally, is all his life and work, the Symphony on the Siege of Leningrad, on the Year 1906 [*sic*], on the Year 1917, to be taken as an existential lie [. . .]?[19]

Complicating the debate have been the 'defections' of several significant figures, from one side to the other, over the past seventeen years. Dr Richard Taruskin, another specialist in Russian/Soviet music, first lent support to *Testimony*. His letter of recommendation (16 July 1976), which assisted Volkov in obtaining a research fellowship at Columbia University and, in turn, facilitated preparation of *Testimony* for publication, is filled with the most glowing and unequivocal praise:

> I can confidently state that he [Solomon Volkov] is unquestionably the most impressive and accomplished among the Soviet emigré musicians and musicologists whom I have had occasion to meet in the last few years.
>
> Mr. Volkov had already made a mark in the musical life of the USSR at the time of his emigration. He had organized a chamber opera company in Leningrad, and at the time of his leaving he was a senior staff editor of *Sovetskaia muzyka*, the

[18] Peter Schaeffer, 'Shostakovich's *Testimony*: The Whole Truth?', *Books & Arts*, 7 March 1980, p. 29 (hereafter Schaeffer).

[19] *Ibid.*, p. 29. The enumeration of cultural figures allegedly offended in *Testimony* (Stanislavsky, Rolland, Shaw, Feuchtwanger) comes directly from the Soviet press. *Cf.* p. 62.

official organ of the USSR Composers Union. As a critic, he was a recognized authority on the young composers of Leningrad, and a respected and trusted intimate of many of them. He had also served one of them, Valery Arzumanov, as librettist. Mr. Volkov's articles, however, were not mere echoes of an official line [. . .].

As musicologist, Mr. Volkov['s. . .] writings display a lively intelligence and a broad acquaintance with the relevant literature, both Russian and to an extent Western. His competence and training far surpasses that of any musicologist of his generation I have met. [. . .]

Finally, you are probably aware that Mr. Volkov is acting in the capacity of literary executor for the late Dmitri Shostakovich. When it will be time for the preparation of Shostakovich's memoirs for publication, Mr. Volkov will need library access and other advantages of university affiliation. The sponsorship of such a work would reflect credit, I believe, upon the Russian Institute and upon Columbia University generally.

For all these reasons I am happy to endorse most heartily Mr. Volkov's request and application for a research fellowship in the Russian Institute. I would be happy to discuss the matter further with you if you should so desire it, and in general to assist in any way I can.[20]

Later, however, Taruskin became one of *Testimony's* and Volkov's harshest critics. In 1989, he claimed to see what others could (or would) not:

I became an early accomplice in what was, I later realized, a shameful exploitation. [. . .] The book was translated into a dozen languages. It won prizes. It became the subject of symposia. The reception of *Testimony* was the greatest critical scandal I have ever witnessed.

For, as any proper scholar could plainly see, the book was a fraud. Yet even those who could did not want to see. Most, including the author of the standard English-language history of Soviet music, confidently endorsed Volkov's 'ring of authenticity'.[21]

[20] A facsimile of Taruskin's complete letter may be found on p. 300.

[21] Richard Taruskin, 'The Opera and the Dictator', *New Republic*, 200/12, 20 March 1989, p. 34 (hereafter Taruskin, 'Dictator').

Taruskin's new position contrasts strikingly with those of Boris Schwarz, Gerald Abraham and Daniil Zhitomirsky, all of whose credentials as scholars he impugned. Schwarz, alluded to above,[22] acknowledged Soviet and Western criticisms of *Testimony* in his landmark *Music and Musical Life in Soviet Russia, 1917–1981*, but concluded that 'the overall impression is very persuasive'.[23] Abraham, the 'dean' of Western scholars of Russian/Soviet music, while expressing early reservations about *Testimony*,[24] in 1982 pronounced it genuine based on Kirill Kondrashin's wholehearted endorsement and information he had obtained privately from a 'reliable source' in the Soviet Union.[25] Finally, Zhitomirsky, a respected Soviet musicologist and colleague of the composer for thirty years, came to the conclusion diametrically opposed to Taruskin's: 'I'm convinced that no serious scholar of Shostakovich's work – and, in particular, of his life and times – should disregard this source'.[26]

Most significant of all has been the about-face of the composer's son, Maxim Shostakovich. Rejecting *Testimony* in 1979, while still in the Soviet Union,[27] Maxim has, after his defection, acknowledged 'It's true. It's accurate. [. . .] The

[22] I.e., as 'the author of the standard English-language history of Soviet music'. *Cf.* p. 260.

[23] Boris Schwarz, *Music and Musical Life in Soviet Russia, 1917–1981*, enlarged edn., Indiana University Press, Bloomington, 1983, p. 576 (hereafter Schwarz).

[24] In 'Discordant Realities', *The Times Literary Supplement*, 23 November 1979, p. 23, Abraham acknowledges Soviet doubts about the authenticity of the memoirs and concludes, 'for the sake of Shostakovich's memory one would wish they were right. [. . . *Testimony* is] a wretched literary legacy from a man who has left the world a rich musical one.'

[25] Gerald Abraham, 'The Citizen Composer', *The Times Literary Supplement*, 4 June 1982, p. 609 (hereafter Abraham, 'Citizen Composer').

[26] Zhitomirsky, 'Public and Private'.

[27] It is not clear how much of Maxim's rejection came, in fact, from Maxim himself. His tone was more restrained than most of the denunciations sent for signature 'from above'. *Cf.* pp. 84–86.

basis of the book is correct'.[28] If actions speak louder than words, Maxim's decision to collaborate with Volkov on 'On "Late" Shostakovich – A Conversation' in 1988, to praise Ian MacDonald's *The New Shostakovich* (itself partly based on revelations in *Testimony*) in 1990, and to share a podium with and compliment Volkov at a Shostakovich symposium in 1992, can be regarded only as a solid endorsement of the Shostakovich memoirs.[29]

For most of the past eighteen years, Volkov has chosen not to respond to his critics directly and, instead, to use his time more constructively. He collaborated with George Balanchine and Nathan Milstein, both of whom (like Shostakovich) rarely revealed their private sides,[30] on two other insightful books,[31] published a monumental cultural history of St Petersburg,[32] as well as a book and a number of articles on

[28] Ian MacDonald, *The New Shostakovich*, p. 7, quoting Maxim's interview with Michael Berkeley, BBC2, 27 September 1986.

[29] For additional information, *cf*. pp. 111–14

[30] Volkov's gift for getting people to 'open up' is further evident in materials collected from his conversations with Aram Khachaturian, Aleksandr Godunov, Kirill Kondrashin, Yury Lyubimov and Maya Plisetskaya, and his published rare interviews with Mariya Yudina ('Mysli o Muzykal'nom Ispolnitel'stve' ('Thoughts on Musical Performance'), *Muzyka i Zhizn'. Muzyka i Muzykanty Leningrada* (*Music and Life. Music and Musicians of Leningrad*), Sovetsky Kompozitor, Leningrad, 1972, p. 202; reprinted in Mariya Veniaminovna Yudina, *Stat'i, Vospominaniya, Materialy* (*Articles, Reminiscences, Materials*), Sovetsky Kompozitor, Moscow, 1978, p. 299, but with Volkov's name omitted, since he had emigrated in 1976), Leonid Kogan (*Sovetskaya Muzyka*, 1975, No. 1, p. 76; reprinted in Leonid Kogan, *Vospominaniya. Pis'ma. Stat'i. Interv'yu* (*Reminiscences, Letters, Articles, Interview*), Sovetsky Kompozitor, Moscow, 1987, p. 204, again without mention of Volkov), and Lilya Brik, Mayakovsky's long-time lover and a legendary Moscow hostess ('Darf ich Ihnen die "Wolke" widmen?', *Die Zeit*, 30, 22 July 1983, pp. 29–30).

[31] *Balanchine's Tchaikovsky*, transl. Antonina W. Bouis, Simon and Schuster, New York, 1985 (hereafter Volkov, *Balanchine's Tchaikovsky*); *From Russia to the West*, transl. by Antonina W. Bouis, Barrie & Jenkins, London/Henry Holt, New York, 1990 (hereafter Milstein, *From Russia to the West*). The authenticity of these books has never been disputed.

[32] Solomon Volkov, *St Petersburg: A Cultural History*, transl. Antonina W. Bouis, The Free Press, New York, 1995/Sinclair-Stevenson, London 1996 (hereafter Volkov, *St Petersburg*).

Joseph Brodsky[33] and has in hand an important project on Vladimir Horowitz.[34] Volkov's silence, in many ways, is characteristic of Shostakovich himself, who also preferred not to waste time explaining himself to people without ears to listen. According to his friend Isaak Glikman:

> [Shostakovich] read all kinds of absurdities about himself, all kinds of abuse, without ever entering into argument with his opponents. As the ancient Roman moralist Cato the Younger remarked, 'He who knows how to retain his silence when unjustly maligned is equal to the gods'. In this way Dmitri Dmitriyevich was god-like. Truly his silence was eloquent and often brought his noisy critics to a halt.[35]

Unfortunately, Volkov's critics have interpreted *his* silence as 'taking the Fifth',[36] hiding the truth, or worse, confirm-

[33] *Cf.* 'Peizazh poeta' ('Poet's Landscape'), interview of Solomon Volkov with Joseph Brodsky, *Chast' rechi* (*Part of Speech*), 1, New York, 1980, pp. 27–36; 'In Venedig an die Newa denken: Gespräch mit Joseph Brodsky', *Die Welt*, 13 November 1982; 'Venetsiya: glazami stikhotvortsa. Dialog s Iosifom Brodskim' ('Venice in the Eyes of a Poet. Dialogue with Joseph Brodsky'), *Chast' rechi*, 2–3, New York, 1981–82, pp. 175–87; 'Razgovor s Iosifom Brodskim: U. H. Odin' ('Conversation with Iosif Brodsky: W. H. Auden'), a chapter from the book *Conversations with Joseph Brodsky* (The Free Press, New York, 1998), Novy Amerikanets (*New American*), New York, 1982, No. 186, 5–11 September, pp. 25–27; No. 187, 12–18 September, pp. 23–25, No. 188, 19–25 September, pp. 24–26; and No. 189, 26 September–2 October, pp. 24–26; 'Vspominaya Annu Akhmatovu. Razgovor s Iosiform Brodskim' ('Remembering Anna Akhmatova. A Conversation with Joseph Brodsky'), *Kontinent*, 53, 1987, pp. 337–82; and 'Souchastiye voobrazheniya. Razgovor s Iosifom Brodskim' ('Participation of Imagination. A Conversation with Joseph Brodsky'), *Ogonyok*, 1991, No. 7, pp. 7–11. Excerpts from Volkov's 600-page study also have appeared in print: Marianna and Solomon Volkov, *Iosif Brodsky v N'yu-Yorke* (*Joseph Brodsky in New York*), Cultural Center for Soviet Refugees, Inc., New York, 1990; and *Brodsky ob Akhmatovoy: Dialogi s S. Volkovym* (*Brodsky on Akhmatova: Dialogues with S. Volkov*), Nezavisimaya Gazeta, Moscow, 1992.

[34] Volkov's research includes over 25 hours of taped conversations with Horowitz (Drubachevskaya, p. 327).

[35] Wilson, p. 130.

[36] In the American vernacular, an expression referring to the privilege against self-incrimination enshrined in the Fifth Amendment to the US Constitution.

ation of guilt.[37] One is reminded of the trial of cows in *Testimony*:

> [The cows were] being interrogated and specialists in mooing acted as translators. I can imagine how it went. 'Does the enemy of the people admit to such-and-such and so-and-so?' The cow is silent. They stick a spear into its side. It moos and the specialist translates, 'It fully admits culpability in all the acts it performed against the people'.[38]

Like a sacrificial cow, Volkov, too, has been prodded by his critics, damned when he speaks and damned when he doesn't.[39]

Up until 1991, Volkov had 'resigned himself to living with the controversy [surrounding *Testimony*] for the rest of his life'.[40] Recently, however, he has begun to respond to some of the criticisms of himself and of the Shostakovich memoirs, both in print and at various symposia,[41] even if the 'powers that be' sometimes have continued to stifle his message: for example, Volkov's brief written replies to unjust criticisms by Malcolm Brown in *The New York Times* (1979) and

[37] For example, Christopher Norris states that Volkov 'has kept such a low profile since the controversy broke that some commentators question his very existence'. He also cites as grounds for doubting the authenticity of *Testimony* the fact 'that Volkov seemed curiously unwilling to answer the [. . .] charges [against him] or defend his own scholarly integrity' ('The Cold War Revived: Shostakovich and Cultural Politics', *Melos*, 1/4–5, Summer 1993, p. 35). *Cf.* pp. 51–53 regarding charges that the CIA was behind the writing of *Testimony*.

[38] *Testimony*, pp. 94/124–25. Page references to *Testimony* will be given here in this double form, with those of the UK edition (Hamish Hamilton) preceding those of the US edition (Harper and Row). Except in spelling, the translations here follow the Harper and Row edition, preferred by Bouis herself (letter to the authors, 8 October 1997). Some minor modifications, not by Bouis, were made in the Hamish Hamilton edition.

[39] Volkov quickly realised the futility of responding to his interrogators, especially the so-called 'specialists'. *Cf.* Robert Heinlein: 'I learned years ago never to argue with a specialist: you can't win. But I also learned that the history of progress is a long, long list of specialists who were dead wrong when they were most certain' (*Stranger in a Strange Land*, 1961; reprinted Ace Books, New York, 1991, p. 279).

[40] William Littler, 'Editor of Shostakovich Book Talks About the Man', *Toronto Star*, 19 February 1991, p. D4 (hereafter Littler).

[41] *Cf.* Drubachevskaya, pp. 315–58, and Robinson, pp. 373–99.

Richard Taruskin in *Atlantic Monthly* (1995) were never printed by these periodicals and appear here for the first time.[42]

The present authors also have benefitted enormously from Volkov's willingness to answer hundreds of questions about the text of *Testimony* and his meetings with Shostakovich, during over a hundred hours of face-to-face and 'phone conversations in 1993–97.[43] These answers, in turn, became leads for further investigation and independent confirmation. Significantly, for two decades Volkov has remained entirely consistent in his explanation of how *Testimony* came about. He adamantly denies using any secondary sources and asserts that *Testimony* is the direct result of dozens of meetings with Shostakovich over the four-year period 1971–74.[44] In *Muzykal'naya Akademiya*, he adds:

> Looking back now, after almost twenty years, I feel that I have fulfilled my role and I have a perfectly clean conscience about any debt to Dmitry Dmitriyevich Shostakovich. I have accomplished everything we agreed to. As for the effect produced by my book, it is possible that he, a genius, had foreseen it, but as for me, I could never have imagined it.[45]

[42] *Cf.* pp. 301–2.

[43] It might be asked why Volkov should open up to us when he would not even confide in 'America's most brilliant musicologist' (Taruskin) or the 'leading Western expert on [Shostakovich's] life and career' (Fay). In fact, we have had an thirteen-year relationship with Volkov. We came to know him when he was perhaps most *persona non grata*. In 1985, when we asked Volkov to contribute an article on Shostakovich to our *Biographical Dictionary of Russian/Soviet Composers* (Greenwood Press, 1989) he replied at once, 'I'd be happy to do so'.

By not denouncing Volkov (even after being criticised for not having done so), we began to earn the trust which later made this 'Reply' possible. Interestingly, our own relationship with Volkov parallels that between Volkov and Shostakovich (*cf.* pp. 78–79, note 113, and p. 133).

[44] He reiterates this in Solomon Volkov, 'Universal Messages: Reflections in Conversation with Günter Wolter', *Tempo*, No. 200, April 1997, p. 14 (hereafter Volkov, 'Universal'): 'In *Testimony* I only used what Shostakovich told me in conversation. These musicologists [who speculate that I partly used old manuscripts from Shostakovich] got it all wrong. First they said: "*Testimony* is untrue, Shostakovich didn't say it!" Then they changed the tune: "Shostakovich already said it elsewhere!" You can't have your cake and eat it too'.

[45] Drubachevskaya, p. 324.

The twentieth anniversary of Shostakovich's death (1995) and ninetieth anniversary of his birth (1996) provide an opportune time to reconsider the importance of *Testimony*, as well as the controversies surrounding it. *Testimony* now has been in print sufficiently long to have been subjected to the most intense critical scrutiny; additionally, the fall of the Soviet regime in August 1991 has provided a window of opportunity for Shostakovich's family, friends and colleagues to express themselves, without their earlier fears of reprisal. After almost two decades of scrutiny, no compromising error, no fatal flaw has been found that undermines the authenticity of *Testimony*. To the contrary, a wealth of evidence has emerged since 1979 that conclusively corroborates it.

The book at hand is the most extensive and thoroughly documented examination of the controversies surrounding the Shostakovich memoirs. Its title, 'Reply to an Unjust Criticism', is a paraphrase of 'A Soviet Artist's Creative Reply to a Just Criticism', the subtitle coined by a journalist in *Vechernyaya Moskva*[46] that once, erroneously, was thought to be Shostakovich's own description of his Fifth Symphony. The unjust criticism alluded to is that *Testimony* is a forgery. A thorough, objective, independent evaluation of the evidence reveals that the attacks on Volkov and the Shostakovich memoirs are unjust. Soviet contentions, needless to say, were often determined by the propaganda requirements of the state; unfortunately, they have been repeated by some Western commentators without any qualification. In addition, several of Malcolm Brown's and Richard Taruskin's assertions are based on the flimsiest of evidence, including gossip and rumour.[47] Even Dr Laurel E. Fay's article 'Shostakovich versus Volkov: Whose *Testimony*?'[48] – much lauded, often quoted, but never seriously challenged – withers under cross-examination, revealing, at

[46] 'Moy tvorchesky otvet' ('My Artistic Reply'), *Vechernyaya Moskva* (*Moscow Evening Paper*), 25 January 1938, p. 3.

[47] *Cf*. pp. 126–28.

[48] Laurel E. Fay, 'Shostakovich versus Volkov: Whose *Testimony*?', *Russian Review*, 39/4, October 1980, pp. 484–93 (hereafter Fay).

best, the author's naïveté of her subject matter and, at worst, her willingness to conceal and distort pertinent evidence.

Since the prosecution's case-in-chief has been made elsewhere, cross-examination of witnesses and their evidence follows directly. Part II considers the views of Shostakovich's 'friends and family'[49] as well as the criticisms of scholars such as Fay, Taruskin and Brown. Part III presents a wealth of evidence corroborating *Testimony*, including endorsements from the composer's inner circle, and documentary, historical and musical evidence. The defence concludes that the prosecution has failed to prove its case by even a preponderance of the evidence, and anticipates that the jury of readers will return a resounding 'Not Guilty' verdict in favour of Volkov and *Testimony*.

[49] A popular advertising slogan in the United States, this phrase also calls to mind Solzhenitsyn's description of the Stalin era, when 'the people became their own enemies, but, on the other hand, acquired the best friend'.

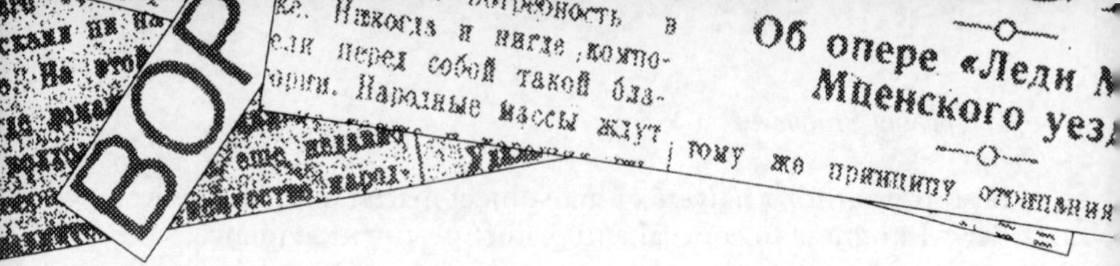

II. Cross-Examination

A. 'Friends and Family': The Official Response

1. Death and Rehabilitation[1]

Following Shostakovich's death on 9 August 1975, Soviet newspapers reported:

> In his sixty-ninth year, the great composer of our times passed away – Dmitri Dmitrievich Shostakovich, Deputy of the Supreme Soviet of the U.S.S.R., laureate of the Lenin and State prizes of the U.S.S.R. A faithful son of the Communist Party, an eminent public and state figure, citizen artist D. D. Shostakovich devoted his entire life to the development of Soviet music, reaffirming the ideals of socialist humanism and internationalism [. . .].[2]

This 'official' obituary was signed by Leonid Brezhnev, Andrey Eshpai, Dmitry Kabalevsky, Kara Karayev, Aram Khachaturian, Tikhon Khrennikov, Kirill Kondrashin, Yevgeny Mravinsky and Georgy Sviridov, among others. At the memorial service, Khrennikov noted: 'When Shostakovich and I were in California he proudly declared to the journalists that "first and foremost he was a communist"'.[3]

[1] The Soviet equivalent of 'Death and Transfiguration'.

[2] *Testimony*, pp. xvi/xix–xx, and Grigory Shneyerson (ed.), *D. Shostakovich: stat'i i materialy* (*D. Shostakovich: Articles and Materials*), Sovetsky Kompozitor, Moscow, 1976, p. 6 (hereafter *D. Shostakovich: Articles and Materials*).

[3] Wilson, p. 475; *cf*. p. 68.

Western obituaries followed suit: Shostakovich was described as 'a committed believer in Communism and Soviet power' in *The Times* (London) and 'a committed Communist who accepted sometimes harsh ideological criticism' in *The New York Times*.[4]

Shostakovich, no doubt, expected this 'posthumous rehabilitation' and probably intended *Testimony*, as well as his recently discovered *Rayok*, to be a counterbalance.[5] He had witnessed Stravinsky's 'change' from 'bourgeois formalist' in the 1940s to 'Russian patriot' twenty years later, and had himself experienced rehabilitation many times, after 1936, 1948 and the like. These observations, no doubt, prompted him to comment, sarcastically, in *Testimony*:

> I like the word 'rehabilitation'. And I'm even more impressed when I hear about 'posthumous rehabilitation'. But that's nothing new either. A general complained to Nicholas I that some hussar had abducted his daughter. They even got married, but the general was against the marriage. After some thought, the emperor proclaimed: 'I decree the marriage annulled, and she is to be considered a virgin'.
>
> Somehow I still don't feel like a virgin.[6]

Shostakovich's 'posthumous rehabilitation' proceeded on schedule until 31 October 1979, when *Testimony* was released.[7] *Testimony* irrevocably altered the image of the composer, revealing a bitter man, bent, but not broken. This 'new' Shostakovich, a closet dissident rather than political

[4] *Testimony*, p. xxxiv/xli.

[5] *Cf*. Kondrashin's opinion, p. 234.

[6] *Testimony*, p. 116/153.

[7] Fay, p. 493, asks, 'Why did it take more than three years, after Volkov's emigration, to have the book translated and published?' Actually, this was not an inordinate amount of time for this material to be published. Volkov has stated previously that the manuscript arrived piecemeal by various couriers after his emigration, then had to be reassembled and translated; Erwin A. Glikes, the head of Harper and Row's trade-book department, and Ann Harris, the book's editor, also have explained that 'secret negotiations for the manuscript and its authentication by musical and political authorities took more than two years' (Herbert Mitgang, 'Shostakovich Memoir, Smuggled Out, Is Due', *The New York Times*, 10 September 1979, p. C14) (hereafter Mitgang, 'Shostakovich Memoir').

toady, elicited a swift and predictable response. Within days, remarkably uniform denunciations had come from Shostakovich's 'friends and family', and, within a year, at least three books had been printed to restore the 'pure' image of the composer sullied by 'the dirty hands of a certain Solomon Volkov':[8] Sofiya Khentova's *Shostakovich in Petrograd-Leningrad*, Lev Danilevich's *Shostakovich: Life and Works* and Mikhail Yakovlev's *D. Shostakovich on Himself and His Times.*[9] Unfortunately for the Soviets, silencing Shostakovich's testimony from the grave was as difficult as unringing the proverbial bell or forgetting about pink elephants.

2. The KGB Connection

The role of the KGB both in the anti-*Testimony* campaign and in Shostakovich's life in general is an important topic which only now is beginning to be explored. The KGB's involvement in 'the *Testimony* Affair' was first revealed in 1976, when a meeting between the KGB and Irina Shostakovich was reported in *A Chronicle of Current Events*, an

[8] 'Zhalkaya poddelka' ('Pitiful Forgery'), *Literaturnaya Gazeta*, 14 November 1979, p. 8. *Cf.* pp. 60–61. In part, the viciousness of these attacks on Volkov was no doubt due to his Jewish origins and Jewish name and patronymic.

[9] *Shostakovich v Petrograde-Leningrade*, Lenizdat, Leningrad, 1979 (hereafter Khentova, *Shostakovich in Petrograd-Leningrad*); *Shostakovich: zhizn' i tvorchestvo*, Sovetsky Kompozitor, Moscow, 1980; and *D. Shostakovich o vremeni i o sebe*, Sovetsky Kompozitor, Moscow, 1980, all reviewed by Seppo Heikinheimo in 'Shostakovich's Memoirs: The Party Line', *Musical America*, November 1981, pp. 20–22 (hereafter Heikinheimo, 'Memoirs'). One could also add to this list Dmitri and Ludmilla Sollertinsky's *Pages from the Life of Dmitri Shostakovich*, Harcourt Brace Jovanovich, New York, 1980/Robert Hale, London, 1981 which 'glosses over Shostakovich's troubles with the Soviet ideologists, does not even mention the Zhdanov Decree of 1948 (in which Shostakovich, Prokofiev and other leading Soviet composers were condemned), [. . .] and in many respects is a contemptible book [. . .] because it is merely a reflection of current Soviet hagiography, [. . . a] portrait of Shostakovich as a Soviet Boy Scout [that] is in complete disagreement with everything we know about the man' (Harold C. Schonberg, 'A Hero of the State', *The New York Times*, 21 September 1980, Section 7, p. 12).

authoritative samizdat summary of news in the Soviet Union:[10]

> Moscow. KGB officials talked with I. A. Shostakovich (the composer's widow) concerning D. D. Shostakovich's memoirs, which he had dictated during the last four years of his life (when he was already gravely ill) to the musicologist S. Volkov.
>
> She was told that information concerning the memoirs had appeared in the West [. . .]. On the advice of the KGB, I. A. Shostakovich asked Volkov to let her read the memoirs before publication. Volkov replied that he had no copies, but would gladly comply with her request abroad. A week later (in the beginning of March), Volkov was given permission to emigrate, for which he had waited the whole year.[11]

Unable to gain access to *Testimony* through Irina or to halt the book's publication through legal means,[12] the KGB then concentrated its efforts on locating the manuscript and discrediting both the text and Volkov. The original manuscript, with the composer's inscription 'Chital [Read]. D. Shostakovich' on the first page of each chapter,[13] is now in a vault in Switzerland. As Volkov explains:

> I had to put it there because there was a real hunt for it all these years. At first, when we were living at a hotel [in New

[10] *A Chronicle of Current Events* has been described as 'one of the most important documents ever to come out of the Soviet Union. An unofficial Moscow journal, its significance can perhaps be compared, in recent years, only with Khrushchev's "secret speech" of 1956 [. . .]' (*Uncensored Russia. Protest and Dissent in the Soviet Union*, ed. and transl. Peter Reddaway, American Heritage Press, New York, 1972, p. 15).

[11] *A Chronicle of Current Events*, Khronika Press, New York, 1976, pp. 80–81. Also, *cf.* pp. 77–78. Volkov categorically denies giving an account of this meeting to *A Chronicle of Current Events*. Only one other person was present besides Volkov and Irina Shostakovich: Boris Tishchenko. Volkov believes that Tishchenko probably was the source.

[12] Erwin A. Glikes of Harper and Row stated that VAAP, the Soviet copyright agency, made the claim not that *Testimony* was a forgery but that the book 'belonged to Mrs. Shostakovich' (Mitgang, 'Shostakovich Memoir', p. C14).

[13] *Cf.* pp. 209–16.

> York City], there were several rather crude moves to snatch it. And even on my way to the States, my suitcases had been ripped open and all the manuscripts (others) crumpled and twisted, and the photographs torn in two.[14]

While the manuscript hunt continued, Vasily Sitnikov, deputy president of VAAP (the Soviet copyright agency), characterised *Testimony* as 'a lie from beginning to end' and asserted that Volkov and Shostakovich had had only four meetings.[15] Even Soviet officials, apparently, found it difficult to claim fewer meetings, since four photographs of Volkov with Shostakovich, taken at different times, are reproduced in *Testimony*.[16] That Sitnikov's statements were cheerfully repeated in the American communist press is not surprising.[17] What is surprising is that these assertions were accepted by scholars and reputable news organisations, sometimes second- or third-hand, without due consideration of the source.[18] In particular, no one mentioned that Vasily Romanovich Sitnikov, then associated with VAAP, was also

[14] Drubachevskaya, p. 321. In a conversation with the authors in August 1995, Volkov explained that he does not even keep a copy of the manuscript with him in New York, since the hunt continues, this time not for ideological reasons, but because of monetary considerations. The manuscript is a valuable property, just as is a Cézanne or a Renoir.

[15] Bonosky, p. 12. Sitnikov also charged that the title of the book had been changed from *Testimony of Guilt* to *Testimony* at the request of the Shostakovich family. Edward Miller, vice-president of Harper and Row, responded that 'if the title had been changed at some point the move had nothing to do with the family' (Evans, 'Moscow', *Reuters Ltd.*, 7 November 1979 (hereafter Evans, 'Moscow'; available in LEXIS, News Library, Archiv file). *Cf.* pp. 233–36.

[16] *Cf.* three photos between pp. 142 and 143/the frontispiece and two photos between pp. 182 and 183. The fourth photograph appears on the dust jacket of the first edition and is reproduced on p. 303.

[17] Bonosky, p. 12. Bonosky, on p. 5 of the preface to his book *Two Cultures*, Progress Publishers, Moscow, 1978, is described by A. S. Mulyarchik as an 'active member of the communist party of the USA, lately working as a correspondent of the party newspaper *Daily World*'.

[18] *Cf.*, for example, Robert Evans, 'Moscow', 7 and 16 November 1979. Evans notes that 'correspondents from non-Communist news organizations were not invited to the meeting' with Sitnikov.

Sitnikov, the deputy chief of the KGB *disinformation* department.[19] Sitnikov's KGB duties included the planting of fraudulent information in the West, often through newspapers secretly sponsored by the Soviets.[20]

A little noticed facet of the Soviet reaction to *Testimony* was the treatment of these memoirs as the handiwork of

[19] The authors were first alerted to Sitnikov's KGB connection by Volkov, who, in turn, had learned about it from Maxim Shostakovich. Maxim had had personal contact with Sitnikov in 1979 (*cf*. p. 84). As for VAAP, Boris Pankin, the organisation's chairman, now reveals that it

> was born as a result of the USSR joining the Geneva convention for the protection of the rights of authors. This joining occurred under strong pressure from the West, where, especially in the US, they considered this measure necessary, in view of the conclusion of preparations to the famous Helsinki meeting of 1975. Yielding on one point, the party authorities were sure that they would be able to gain on the other. It was not the first time for them. If we accepted the supremacy of international law over the national, let's turn it in practice into its opposite. 'The rules of the game' for VAAP really were created so that it could fulfill the role of *okhranka* [secret police].
>
> Boris Pankin, *100 Oborvannykh Dney (100 Days That Were Cut Short)*, Sovershenno Sekretno, Moscow, 1993, p. 197.

The well-known Soviet writers Anatoly Rybakov and Edvard Radzinsky, in conversations with Volkov, also confirmed that Sitnikov worked for VAAP in the capacity of overseer of all cultural exchanges with the West.

[20] Sitnikov was identified as a KGB colonel as early as 1959, in Peter Deriabin and Frank Gibney's *The Secret World*, Doubleday, New York, p. 249. His dual role in the KGB and VAAP was further clarified in the revised edition, Ballantine Books, New York, 1982, pp. 339–40. Sitnikov's disinformation was circulated around the world in the communist press, including, in addition to the *Daily World*, *l'Unità* (*cf*. the article by Carlo Benedetti, 20 October 1979). Sitnikov himself later came into prominence in the West in connection with the '*Ethnos* Affair', which revealed that the allegedly independent Greek newspaper, *Ethnos*, was, in fact, financed by the Soviets. He has since been described as a 'top KGB official' ('Court Cuts Sentence on Writer Who Linked Greek Paper With KGB', *Reuters North European Service*, 26 May 1984), a 'leading Soviet agent of disinformation operating in Europe' (Sir James Goldsmith, 'Soviet Active Measures v. the Free Press', *Heritage Foundation Reports*, No. 465, 28 October 1985, pp. 43 *et seq*.), 'deputy director of the KGB's disinformation department' (Fergus M. Bordewich, 'Democracy Adrift', *Atlantic*, 256/6, December 1985, p. 40), a 'KGB colonel (responsible for disinformation) and deputy chairman of VAAP' ('A Soviet Mouthpiece or a

Western security services.[21] Immediately after its publication, Tikhon Khrennikov, the chairman of the Composers' Union, in a speech to the Congress of the Union (20 November 1979, Moscow), attacked the book as an attempt at ideological subversion:

> We must continue the uncompromising struggle with (to us) foreign ideology in the arts and cultural-social life – through our art and through our polemical word. It is especially important now, when music, through the efforts of old and new 'sovietologists', is being used in the interests of political business, in unseemly speculations. Some, in their attempts to blacken and distort the past and present of Soviet music, engage in malicious fabrications, which are well compensated by the owners of the yellow press. One example of this is the advertising racket created around the book entitled 'Reminiscences of Shostakovich' – this vile falsification,

---

Part of the Free Press?', *The Economist*, 303/7494, 18 April 1987, pp. 21–22), and 'deputy director of the copyright office and simultaneously deputy director of the KGB's Disinformation Department, specializing in disinformation operations against NATO' (Michael Ledeen, 'The New Cold War Revisionism', *American Spectator*, 28, June 1995, p. 29). Ilya Dzhirkvelof, a former 'KGB officer, Deputy General Secretary of the Soviet Journalists' Union (a KGB post), member of the party elite Nomenclatura, and editor of Tass', also has confirmed Sitnikov's long standing KGB connection ('Soviet Mouthpiece', p. 22).

Among the 'revelations' reported by *Ethnos* on behalf of its Soviet handlers were: (1) that 'the Soviets were only trying to liberate Afghanistan'; (2) that Chernobyl was the 'result of America's arms race'; (3) that the Berlin Wall was put up to 'protect Eastern Europe from West German aggression'; and (4) that 'Solidarity in Poland worked for the CIA'. The 'working for the CIA' accusation was a standard Soviet ploy applied, among others, to Volkov and Solzhenitsyn (*cf.* pp. 51, 52, note 21, and p. 53). For example, Bonosky, p. 12, noted in the *Daily World* that 'Volkov is now listed at the Russian Institute at Columbia University as a "researcher" – a euphemism for "working for the CIA"'.

[21] Similar accusations were levelled against the books of Alexander Solzhenitsyn, including the charge of plagiarism:

> [Solzhenitsyn was] an obscure man with a pathological urge for fame, [. . . who] fitted into every element of [the] formula for producing a 'prominent author' as part of CIA subversion against the Soviet Union. [He] essentially [. . .] only popularises anticommunist doctrines and, in his zeal, does not even take the trouble to alter them but usually merely plagiarises.
>
> Nikolay Yakovlev, *CIA's Target – The USSR*, 2nd edn., Progress Publishers, Moscow, 1984, pp. 159–64.

> concocted by one of the renegades who left our country. To rebuff these propaganda intrigues is the duty of everyone who values the achievements and fate of Soviet art, its progressive ideals.[22]

That this attack had been coordinated with Soviet 'higher-ups' is evident from the speech of the Deputy Minister of Culture, Vasily Kukharsky, who, at the same Congress, also declared *Testimony* a product of the malicious schemes of Western 'organs' (the Soviet euphemism for the CIA):

> The ideological struggle of the two worlds became more fierce. [. . .] our times are complex, culture and the arts are more actively included as targets of attacks of anti-Sovietism. One after another follow the attempts of Western politicians to subject cultural exchanges with the Soviet Union to strict control of their organs, to wreck certain Soviet cultural actions in their countries [. . .]. Through falsification, they try to defile the names of the classics of Russian and Soviet culture dear to every Soviet man. That was the role meant to be played by the recently concocted, repugnant movie about P. I. Tchaikovsky.[23] And now – the so-called 'memoirs' of D. D. Shostakovich, a vile attempt to rouse distrust in cultural relations, to portray double-facedness and petty animosity as a supposedly characteristic behaviour of a Soviet artist.[24]

Recently, A. V. Bogdanova has provided an enlightening 'behind-the-scenes' glimpse of Soviet practices in general and of the '*Testimony* affair' specifically. Relying on documents from the archives of the Central Committee of the CPSU, primarily the Repository Centre of Contemporary Documentation,[25] she concludes that

[22] Tikhon Khrennikov, 'Velikaya missiya sovetskoy muzyki' ('The Great Mission of Soviet Music'), *Sovetskaya Muzyka*, 1980, No. 1, pp. 27–28.

[23] Kukharsky here refers to *The Music Lovers*, MGM/United Artists, 1970, directed by Ken Russell.

[24] 'Velikaya missiya sovetskoy muzyki. Shestoy s'yezd kompozitorov SSSR. Iz vystupleny delegatov' ('Great Mission of Soviet Music. The Sixth Congress of Composers of the USSR. From Speeches of the Delegates'), *Sovetskaya Muzyka*, 1980, No. 3, p. 71.

[25] Alla Vladimirovna Bogdanova, *Muzyka i vlast' (poststalinsky period)* (*Music and the Regime (Post-Stalin Period)*), Naslediye, Moscow, 1995, p. 18.

> Any story or situation became known to society in a distorted, false light, if it could be used for propaganda. The informational vacuum was filled by cleverly directed rumors, slander and innuendo. Such methods had an important role in the creation of certain social stereotypes and beliefs. These ideas were transmitted by the mass media, but their 'brain' was the KGB.[26]

As an example, she quotes from a memorandum of the Department of Culture of the Central Committee ('On measures for propaganda and protection of the artistic legacy of D. D. Shostakovich', 14 December 1978), which reveals the coordinated, careful orchestration of the attacks on *Testimony*:

> 'It is suggested that the Ministry of Culture of the USSR and the Union of Composers of the USSR, together with other organisations, take measures to expose the provocation of the American publishing house Harper and Row. [...] If the American publisher refuses to discuss this question with VAAP, and publishes the 'memoirs' distorting the civic and artistic nature of D. D. Shostakovich, it is suggested, through soviet and foreign organs of mass media, to describe the publication as an anti-soviet forgery, discrediting the name of the great composer.'[27]

The '*Testimony*-as-anti-Soviet-forgery' line was obligingly parroted by some Western commentators. For example, Christopher Norris in 1986 stated that

> [*Testimony* was] a veritable gift for the purposes of cold war cultural propaganda. As Volkov presents it, there is a smattering undertow of cryptic anti-soviet comments to just about any major work in the Shostakovich canon.[28]

In part, the KGB was even successful in blaming Volkov and *Testimony* for 'fouling the atmosphere of peaceful co-existence'.[29] Volkov's most prominent critic, Laurel Fay,

[26] Bogdanova, pp. 19–20.

[27] Bogdanova, p. 376.

[28] *The Times Literary Supplement*, 5 June 1986, p. 606. In the same article, Norris refers to Volkov as a Shostakovich student – a claim that has never been made by Volkov.

[29] Schaeffer, p. 29.

seems to agree with this assessment, since she quotes Schaeffer's words at length in her 'conclusive' article without saying he was wrong.[30] Significantly, Fay nowhere mentions the Soviet invasion of Afghanistan, which resulted in severe repercussions for US-USSR relations – the recall of the US ambassador from the USSR, delay in ratification of the SALT II Treaty, embargo on wheat and high-technology exports to the USSR, suspension of Soviet fishing privileges, and exile of academician Andrey Sakharov[31] – all of which were much more detrimental to peaceful co-existence than Shostakovich and his *Testimony*.

According to reliable sources,[32] another response of the KGB to *Testimony* was the establishment of a commission to collect compromising materials on Volkov. This commission was overseen by musicologist Grigory Shneyerson, a figure well known among the Soviet music establishment as having close ties to the KGB.[33] Were these 'compromising

[30] Fay, p. 487.

[31] *The 20th Century, An Almanac*, World Almanac Publications, New York, 1985, p. 460.

[32] Apparently, the personnel in today's Russia differs little from that in old Soviet times. We have encountered several instances in which, because of fear, sources have asked not to be identified by name. The KGB itself has undergone a resurgence of sorts. One human-rights advocate, Vladimir Oiven, Vice-Chairman of the Glasnost Fund, observes that '[t]he KGB is being reconstituted almost entirely [. . .]. The old functions are being given back to them, in a formal way, codified by law' (Jean MacKenzie and Leonid Bershidsky, 'Analysts Fear KGB Comeback', *Moscow Times*, 9 April 1995, international edn., p. 12). On this and other violations of the Russian Constitution by the Yeltsin government, *cf.* Molly Warner Lien and Dmitry Feofanov, 'One Step Ahead, Two Steps Behind, and Who is to Blame? Extraconstitutional Apologetics and the Russian Experiment', unpublished manuscript on file with the authors.

[33] Certain posts in 'creative unions' were automatically KGB posts, including that of 'executive secretary' held by Shneyerson (Gennadi Kostyrchenko, *V plenu u krasnogo faraona* (*In the Captivity of the Red Pharaoh*), p. 41, transl. into English as *Out of the Red Shadows: Anti-Semitism in Stalin's Russia*, Prometheus Books, Amherst, New York, 1995; hereafter Kostyrchenko). From 1931, Shneyerson occupied a number of executive positions, in the Composers' Union, etc. (B. Bernandt, I. M. Yampol'sky, T. Ye. Kiselyova, *Kto pisal o muzyke, Bio-bibliografichesky slovar' muzykal'nykh kritikov i lits, pisavshikh o muzyke v dorevolyutsionnoy Rossii i SSSR* (*Who Wrote About Music, a Bio-Bibliographical Dictionary of Music Critics and People Who Wrote About Music in Pre-Revolutionary*

materials' – collected by, and for, the KGB – handed on a 'Soviet platter' to any conscious or unconscious agent of Soviet influence interested in maintaining the status-quo image of Shostakovich? Exactly how these materials were used must be left for future investigation, when open access to KGB files becomes available. It is nonetheless a matter of record that Soviet pressure and a campaign of vilification resulted in the withdrawal of an invitation for Volkov to write the programme notes for a new production of *Boris Godunov* at La Scala[34] as well as the cancellation of a planned visit by Volkov to Finland.[35]

Russia and the USSR), Sovetsky Kompozitor, Moscow, 1989, Vol. 4, pp. 30–31; hereafter Bernandt, Yampol'sky). Since he oversaw the contacts of Soviet composers with the West, he also had to be in close contact with the KGB.

In print, Shneyerson consistently parroted the official line, being one of its most reactionary representatives. Thus, in 1960 (i.e., in the midst of Khrushchev's Thaw) he characterised Stravinsky as 'one of the biggest cynics of modern art, a man for whom there is nothing sacred either in music or in social life [. . .] a man without a motherland, with no roots other than financial ones in the soil of the American reality [. . .]'. Shneyerson was indignant that Stravinsky dared to 'oppose, in his persona of a political and ideological renegade, the mighty flourishing of culture of the great country of socialism' (Grigory Shneyerson, *O Muzyke Zhivoy i Myortvoy* (*On Music Alive and Dead*), Sovetsky Kompozitor, Moscow, 1960, p. 157).

[34] Volkov's essay was later published as 'Questo Boris è uno specchio oscuro' in *L'Europeo*, 35, 13 December 1979, p. 137, accompanied by an interview with Volkov about the La Scala scandal and the Soviet campaign of pressure (Oliviero Spinelli, 'Alla Scala sale al podio il Maestro Kgb', pp. 134–42). In a related editorial, '"Klop" lopnul' ('The "Bed-Bug" Blew Up'), *Literaturnaya Gazeta*, 19 December 1979, p. 9 (hereafter 'The "Bed-Bug"'), the Soviets mocked Volkov viciously:

> How many words did he [the 'bed-bug'] find to cry when he found out that the Milan theatre, La Scala, which had contracted him to write the notes for the new production of *Boris Godunov*, withdrew its proposal after the adventurer was exposed in the Soviet press. Therefore, the 'bed-bug' will not crawl over the score of Musorgsky. And this is good! [. . .] The decision of the Milan theatre became an absolutely natural finale to this pitiful farce: the 'bed-bug' is squashed. What is left as a result? No answer is needed. But the bad smell remaining after the destruction of the 'bed-bug', thank god, is being diffused quickly [. . .].

[35] Conversation between Volkov and the authors, August 1995.

It should be mentioned that Shneyerson's 'close ties' to the KGB were nothing unusual: in fact, many prominent figures either worked for, or were approached to be recruited by, the secret police.[36] The soprano Galina Vishnevskaya notes:

> In December of 1937, *Pravda* published Mikoyan's report on the twentieth anniversary of the secret police, the Cheka-NKVD [predecessors of the KGB]. It was published for good reason: in that report, Mikoyan issued a new slogan that articulated the Party's goal, '*That every citizen of the USSR be an NKVD* agent'.[37]

'We need only recall the "side-job" of the famous tenor Nelepp', she goes on to say, 'and he was not alone in this [. . .]'.[38] For example, ballerina Maya Plisetskaya reports that the KGB tried to recruit her to be 'friends' with Robert F. Kennedy in 1966,[39] and pianists Vladimir Ashkenazy[40] and Andrey Gavrilov[41] similarly acknowledge being coerced into involvement with the secret police. Others alleged to have

[36] Sensational exposés of major cultural figures as KGB agents have appeared recently. For example, even Pavel Luknitsky, Akhmatova's friend, submitted reports on her (*cf*. 'Arestovannaya literatura' ('Arrested Literature'), *Gosudarstvennaya bezopasnost i demokratiya* (*State Security and Democracy*), Moscow, 1992, Vol. 3, p. 37).

[37] Galina Vishnevskaya, *Galina: A Russian Story*, transl. Guy Daniels, Harcourt Brace Jovanovich, New York, 1984/Hodder and Stoughton, London, 1985, p. 214 (hereafter Vishnevskaya, *Galina*).

[38] Galina Vishnevskaya, *Galina. Istoriya Zhizni* (*Galina. Life History*), La Presse Libre/Kontinent, Paris, 1985, p. 501; not included in the English version.

[39] *Maya Plisetskaya*, Novosti, Moscow, 1994, p. 329. Plisetskaya also mentions being placed under surveillance (pp. 185, 204, 331), having to secure KGB permission to travel abroad (pp. 189, 238, 366–67, 450), being 'escorted' while abroad (p. 262), and having to deal with Western stoolies (p. 304) and impresarios (pp. 271–72) in cahoots with the KGB.

[40] Jasper Parrott with Vladimir Ashkenazy, *Beyond Frontiers*, Collins, London, 1984/Atheneum, New York, 1985, pp. 77–84, 204–5 (hereafter Parrott and Ashkenazy).

[41] Andrey Gavrilov, 'Feeling of Regained Freedom', *Ogonyok*, 49, December 1989, pp. 5, 26.

been working for the 'organs' include the violinist Leonid Kogan,[42] violist Dmitry Shebalin[43] and conductor Yury Simonov.[44]

Given these hidden (and ever-changing) ties between the KGB and members of the artistic elite, it is not surprising that Shostakovich remained guarded in his speech, not knowing for certain who, at any given time, was an agent.[45] Shostakovich's awareness of the KGB's infiltration of even his inner circle of 'friends' and 'students' can now be documented. His son stated in 1990: 'There was total infiltration of society by informers. Shostakovich was afraid to speak to friends, to his wife, to himself'.[46] Khentova confirms Shostakovich's awareness:

> Shostakovich always naïvely attempted to protect himself. It was fashionable for the executioners to patronise literature and the arts. Yagoda went to Kor'kov; Isaak Babel', Boris Pil'nyak were friends with the executioners. An important worker at the MVD (Ministry of Internal Affairs) Slava Dombrovsky and his wife came to see Shostakovich; when the couple appeared, Shostakovich warned the other guests at the

[42] Mentioned by Mstislav Rostropovich in *The New York Post*, 11 July 1978, p. 1, and in Parrott and Ashkenazy, p. 204.

[43] Rostislav Dubinsky, *Stormy Applause: Making Music in a Worker's State*, Hutchison, London/Hill and Wang, New York, 1989, p. 234 (hereafter Dubinsky).

[44] Mentioned by Mstislav Rostropovich in *The New York Post*, 11 July 1978, p. 1.

[45] Infiltration of the family and friends of major Soviet public figures was standard in the former USSR. For numerous examples of this practice as applied to Soviet writers, *cf.* Vitaly Shentalinsky, *The KGB's Literary Archive*, transl. John Crowfoot, with an introduction by Robert Conquest, Harvill Press, London, 1995. A classic instance was the writer Maxim Gorky, for years informed on by his mistress Moura Budberg, his secretary Pyotr Kryuchkov, his daughter-in-law Nadya Peshkova, and 'numerous cooks, chauffeurs, librarians, gardeners and cleaners' (Shentalinsky, pp. 252–54).

[46] John-Michael Albert, notes from Maxim Shostakovich's 'Six Lectures on the Shostakovich Symphonies', p. 413, (hereafter Albert).

> door: 'Bite your tongue' [literally, 'keep your mouth under lock'].[47]

Gavriil Glikman, the brother of Isaak, also recalls that when, in 1960, he organised a series of private showings of his modernist art, often with an anti-Soviet content:

> I was surprised (and later amazed) that one young composer [Shostakovich's pupil Vladislav Uspensky], who was married to the daughter of a famous chess player [grandmaster Mark Taimanov], punctually came to all of my showings. Of course, everything became clear after Dmitry Dmitriyevich trustfully told me: 'Be particularly careful with him. He is connected with the organs'. Here I finally understood my naïve trust.[48]

The KGB's supervision of the Shostakovich family continued long after the composer's death, in part because of 'the *Testimony* Affair'. Khentova points out:

> Conditions even nine years after his death were supervised by the organs of the state security: the agent in charge, alias 'Sinyagin', even in 1984 sent reports regarding the happenings in Shostakovich's family.[49]

In view of this ongoing surveillance, it is not surprising that the composer's family, friends and colleagues also adopted the Party line. Maxim Shostakovich's denunciation of *Testimony*[50] was delivered at VAAP, in the presence of the above-mentioned Vasily Sitnikov; furthermore, even after Maxim defected in 1981, the safety of his loved ones (notably his sister Galina and his first wife, Yelena – the mother of his son Dmitry Maksimovich) remained a legitimate concern. Khentova states:

[47] Sofiya Khentova, 'Shostakovich: Legendy i Pravda' ('Shostakovich: Legends and the Truth'), *Novoye Russkoye Slovo* (*New Russian Word*), 7 July 1989, p. 6; reprinted from *Vecherny Leningrad* (*Evening Leningrad*), 15–19 May 1989 (hereafter Khentova, 'Shostakovich: Legends and the Truth').

[48] Gavriil Glikman, 'Shostakovich As I Knew Him', *Kontinent*, 37, 1983, p. 381 (hereafter G. Glikman, 'Shostakovich As I Knew Him').

[49] Sofiya Khentova, *Udivitel'ny Shostakovich* (*Amazing Shostakovich*), Variant, St. Petersburg, 1993, pp. 169–170 (hereafter Khentova, *Amazing Shostakovich*).

[50] *Cf.* p. 84.

The defection of the son and grandson of Shostakovich inevitably endangered the position of the other relatives. Old enemies of Shostakovich, those who envied his fame, raised their heads in the hope of prohibitions and prosecutions once more.[51]

3. 'Les Six Soviétiques'

Among the earliest Soviet denunciations of *Testimony* was that printed in the Moscow weekly *Literaturnaya Gazeta* on 14 November 1979. This attack consisted of three parts: 'Klop', an editorial, which savagely blasted Volkov, describing him as a 'bedbug' who attached himself to the composer; 'Ofitsial'noye dos'ye' ('Official file'), a summary of communications between Harper & Row and VAAP, which documented the Soviets' unsuccessful legal attempts to block publication; and 'Zhalkaya poddelka' ('Pitiful forgery'), a letter to the editor signed by six Soviet composers (Veniamin Basner, Kara Karayev, Karen Khachaturian, Yury Levitin, Boris Tishchenko and Moisey Vainberg), all of whom had known Shostakovich and declared that they did not believe him to be the true author of the memoirs.[52] 'Pitiful Forgery', the most important of these materials, states:

[51] Khentova, *Amazing Shostakovich*, p. 169. Immediately after his defection in 1981, Maxim stated: 'Of course we were afraid that the book might have serious consequences for our family' (Norbert Kuchinke and Felix Schmidt, 'Shostakovich: Why I Fled From Russia', transl. Gillian Macdonald, *The Sunday Times*, 17 May 1981, p. 35A; hereafter Kuchinke and Schmidt). Volkov added (in conversation with the authors, August 1995):

> The members of Shostakovich's inner circle, including his immediate family, were placed in an awkward situation by the publication of *Testimony*, which could have affected their official standing and real privileges (dachas, perks, etc.). They also faced a moral dilemma, because they could not imitate Shostakovich – go along with the authorities outwardly, but be a hidden dissident. *Testimony* denied them of a moral fig leaf. Shostakovich had had his say, but what about them? Their position as conformists was revealed. And today, their main motivation, besides quite understandable jealousy, is the defence of their own image.

[52] 'Klop', 'Ofitsial'noye dos'ye', and 'Zhalkaya poddelka', *Literaturnaya Gazeta*, 14 November 1979, p. 8.

With pain and outrage we have become acquainted with a book, published in New York by the publishing house 'Harper and Row' as D. D. Shostakovich's 'memoirs'.

The noble and pure image of our great compatriot and great composer, Dmitry Dmitriyevich Shostakovich, was touched by the dirty hands of a certain Solomon Volkov.

It is absolutely clear to us, pupils of Dmitry Shostakovich and people who knew him intimately and associated with him constantly, that this book has nothing to do with the real reminiscences of D. D. Shostakovich. Much, very much, of what is written in the book was invented by its real author – S. Volkov.

Even the true statements of Dmitry Dmitriyevich, well known, and published more than once, are falsified and distorted.

Knowing Dmitry Dmitriyevich's characteristic tact and politeness, one cannot even imagine him having said all those rude words and making deadly remarks about noted composers, musicians and writers, both Soviet and foreign, remarks of which there are so many in the book. Emerging from all these inventions is the figure of the real writer of the 'memoirs', a malicious renegade who has set himself the aim of denigrating the image of the great composer and reducing it to his own low level.

[. . .] people who knew our teacher are struck by Volkov's monstrous attempt to draw a portrait of 'another' Shostakovich. One lie here is piled upon another. [. . .] The author's ultimate goal was to try with this sinister transformation to separate Shostakovich from Soviet music and Soviet music from Shostakovich.

[. . .] By his example, Dmitry Shostakovich taught people to be kind, honest and decent in their relations with other people and to reject totally double-dealing and falsehood.

But no lie concocted by the dirty hands of dealers and rascals can distort the noble portrait of the great composer, an ardent patriot of his Motherland. The attempt to distort his work and life is hopeless. Shostakovich's music itself refutes any falsifications of this kind.[53]

[53] 'Zhalkaya Poddelka. O tak nazyvayemykh "memuarakh" D. D. Shostakovicha' ('Pitiful Forgery. Concerning the So-called "Memoirs" of D. D. Shostakovich', *Literaturnaya Gazeta*, 14 November 1979, p. 8, and *BBC Summary of World Broadcasts*, 16 November 1979, SU/6273/A1/1 (available in LEXIS, News Library, Archiv file); hereafter 'Pitiful Forgery').

Literaturnaya Gazeta further editorialised:

> If we are to believe Volkov, Shostakovich, the modest, reserved man of goodwill his contemporaries knew was an envious misanthrope who denigrated his colleagues with unconcealed malice. The man created by the imagination of a philistine-renegade permits himself to defame Sergei Prokofiev, Reinhold Glière, Vladimir Mayakovsky and Yevgeny Mravinsky, whose friendship and co-operation Shostakovich treasured, as he himself admitted more than once. With a similar bitterness Volkov's 'Shostakovich' opines about Stanislavsky, Rolland, Shaw, Feuchtwanger.[54] [...] It is utterly impossible for upright people to imagine a man hating his society and vilifying the best masters of its culture, accepting gratefully with all his heart a tribute of recognition from this society (and all these masters), joining the Communist Party, and devoting his time to his duties as a Deputy and other public duties (and devoting it generously, as everybody well knows). [...] The publisher claims that, on Volkov's manuscript, it discovered notes of Shostakovich: 'Read'. However, a man who distorted the entire life of the composer would not stop at doing something similar with the composer's 'visas'. Dirty fingerprints of Volkov – that is what we can easily find on the pages of the manuscript! And they, these fingerprints, are certainly genuine.[55]

[54] *Cf*. Schaeffer's roster of names on p. 37.

[55] 'Klop' 'The Bedbug', *Literaturnaya Gazeta*, 14 November 1979, p. 8, and *BBC Summary of World Broadcasts*, 16 November 1979, SU/6273/A1/1 (available in LEXIS, News Library, Archiv file).

The attribution of 'unacceptable' comments in *Testimony* to Volkov was not unusual. The Soviets also preferred a 'sanitised' Stravinsky:

> In a collection of dialogues between Stravinsky and Robert Craft, published in the Soviet Union, not only are the relatively harmless political remarks eliminated but also those that might interfere with creating 'the correct' image of Stravinsky, the true Russian patriot. How is this censorship justified? Where Stravinsky says the acceptable, he speaks in his own voice. But when he goes astray, in the opinion of the Soviet censor, then obviously the words were put in his mouth by the 'tendentious' Mr. Craft. Stravinsky's statement from his Harvard lectures (published as *Poetics of Music*) is still unknown to his compatriots: 'We see Russia falling back into an attitude of the worst sort of nationalism and popular chauvinism which once more separates it radically from European culture'. As Professor [Mikhail] Druskin [author of the latest Soviet biography

Unfortunately, Western scholars often have accepted these denunciations with little or no qualification. Like so many such documents, 'Pitiful Forgery' and 'The Bedbug' present only one – the Soviet – side of the issue, full of lies, distortions and innuendoes worthy of the Orwellian 'Ministry of Truth'. First, the reference to 'a certain Solomon Volkov' in the opening paragraph suggests that the signers did not know Volkov. In fact, three of them (Basner, Karayev and Tishchenko) were personally acquainted with Volkov;[56] Karen Khachaturian knew him from his work at *Sovetskaya Muzyka*, and the others probably were at least familiar with his name from his membership in the Composers' Union and his well-known book *Young Composers of Leningrad*.[57] Second, Volkov's earlier associations with Shostakovich are completely ignored, including the preface the composer had written for Volkov's *Young Composers of Leningrad*.[58]

---

and well-known 'Stravinskiologist'] explains, the author of these words is surely not Stravinsky, but 'some malicious emigre, incompetent in questions of music'.

Solomon Volkov, 'Soviet Schizophrenia toward Stravinsky: Razing His House at Centennial Time', *The New York Times*, 26 June 1982, Section 1, p. 25.

[56] For more on Tishchenko's relations with Volkov, *cf.* pp. 67–72 and 304–6.

[57] Solomon Volkov, *Molodyye Kompozitory Leningrada*, Sovetsky Kompozitor, Leningrad, 1971. Conversation between Volkov and the authors, August 1995.

[58] Also typical of 'Ministry of Truth' reporting, Shostakovich's preface to Volkov's book has been reprinted at least four times, but without mention of Volkov: *cf.* Mikhail Yakovlev's *D. Shostakovich o vremeni i o sebe, 1926–1975* (*D. Shostakovich About His Time and Himself, 1926–1975*), pp. 332–33 (cited without attribution from 'Knizhnoye obozreniye' ('Book Review'), 5 February 1972, p. 374); Lev Grigoryev and Yakov Platek, compilers, *Shostakovich: About Himself and His Times*, transl. Angus and Neilian Roxburgh, Progress Publishers, Moscow, 1981, pp. 305–6 (hereafter Grigoryev and Platek); Sofiya Khentova, *Shostakovich in Petrograd-Leningrad*, pp. 233–34 (in which this material is described as a 'substantial article' rather than a preface); and Sofiya Khentova, *Shostakovich. Zhizn' i tvorchestvo* (*Shostakovich. Life and Work*), Sovetsky Kompozitor, Leningrad, 1986, Vol. 2, pp. 386–87 (which in note 1, p. 387, cites the previous Khentova book as the source! (hereafter Khentova, *Shostakovich*)).

Finally, no mention is made that in musicians' circles it was generally known that Volkov had been meeting with Shostakovich to work on the latter's memoirs;[59] that several of Shostakovich's friends and colleagues, including Boris Chaikovsky, Rodion Shchedrin, Georgy Sviridov and Galina Ustvol'skaya, had refused to sign the denunciation;[60] and that others had done so only under pressure or for personal reasons. For example, Kara Karayev, undergoing treatment for a heart condition, had been ordered to sign or be kicked out of the hospital.[61]

Some scholars also have given 'Pitiful Forgery' and 'The Bedbug' undue weight by considering them in isolation. It is well known, however, that denunciations were a common practice in the Soviet Union, and often the signers neither read nor agreed with that which they had 'endorsed'.[62] Volkov acknowledges, 'It is sad to see the people react at command and denounce in a uniform way a book they have

[59] Elmer Schönberger, '"Er is niets dat mij ook maar enigszins aan de authenticiteit van het boek doet twijfelen" – Mark Lubotski over de memoires van Dmitri Sjostakovitsj' ('There is nothing which makes me doubt at all the authenticity of the book – Mark Lubotsky about the Shostakovich memoirs'), *Vrij Nederland*, 40/50, 15 December 1979, p. 21 (hereafter Schönberger, 'Lubotsky'). Rostislav Dubinsky also recalled Volkov telling him and other members of the Borodin Quartet in 1974 (i.e., while Volkov was still in the USSR and Shostakovich was still alive) that 'Shostakovich had "started talking", and that he [Volkov] would carefully write everything down, then when they would get together again next time, Shostakovich would read and approve it, and so forth' (conversation between Dubinsky and the authors, 28 April 1997). Also *cf*. pp. 251.

[60] Vladimir Zak, 'Shostakovich's Idioms', p. 504 (hereafter Zak), with a hitherto unpublished addendum to his article in *Yevreysky Mir* (*Jewish World*), 50/6, 7 May 1993. Also, a conversation between Volkov and the authors, August 1995.

[61] Phone conversation between Rodion Shchedrin and the authors, October 1992. *Cf*. also Tishchenko's explanation to Volkov in New York (p. 69, note 84). Furthermore, the denunciation of still another member of 'Les Six Soviétiques' may have been prompted by the unflattering revelations about this 'acquaintance' in *Testimony*, pp. 93–94/124–25 (conversation between Volkov and the authors, November 1997).

[62] In recent interviews on the BBC and (US) National Public Radio, May 1996, even Khrennikov has admitted participating in such practices.

not read, movies they have not seen, and positions and events they have not come to know by themselves'.[63] Alas, even Shostakovich signed many such documents, including a letter denouncing Andrey Sakharov, which also had been 'approved' by Kabalevsky, Khachaturian, Khrennikov, Shchedrin and Sviridov.[64] When Rostropovich expressed surprise over some of these materials, Shostakovich responded: 'Look, Slava, I never read these things on principle'.[65] The composer also told Flora Litvinova: 'When somebody starts pestering me, I have only one thought in mind – get rid of him as quickly as possible, and to achieve that I am prepared to sign anything!'[66] He said the same to Yury Lyubimov: 'I'd sign anything even if they hand it to me upside down. All I want is to be left alone'.[67] Shostakovich's friends understood the 'significance' of these official writings. Basner, one of the signatories of 'Pitiful Forgery', notes: 'One should [. . .] discount the articles and statements that Dmitri Dmitriyevich "signed"; we knew that they were meaningless acts to him, but served him as a public shield. His many courageous actions were taken in private'.[68] Vishnevskaya adds:

> Once he had made his decision, Shostakovich unabashedly followed the rules of the game. He made statements in the press and at meetings; he signed 'letters of protest' that, as he himself said, he never read. He didn't worry about what people would say of him, because he knew the time would come when the verbiage would fade away, when only his music would remain. And his music would speak more vividly than any words. His only real life was his art, and into it

[63] Herbert Mitgang, 'Shostakovich Author Responds to Criticism', *The New York Times*, 22 November 1979, Section 3, p. 21 (hereafter Mitgang, 'Shostakovich Author').

[64] *Pravda*, 3 September 1973; Wilson, p. 429.

[65] Heikinheimo, 'Memoirs', p. 22; quotation originally in *Helsingin Sanomat*, 12 May 1979.

[66] Wilson, p. 162.

[67] *Ibid.*, p. 183.

[68] *Ibid.*, p. 123.

he admitted no one. It was his temple: when he entered it, he threw off his mask and was what he was.[69]

The lack of specificity in 'Pitiful Forgery' and 'The Bedbug', as well as their uniformity with other Soviet statements and sometimes bizarre focus,[70] suggests that their (real) authors, too, had not actually read that which they were criticising. *Testimony* had been published in English in the United States only two weeks earlier. It is unlikely that the six signatories of 'Pitiful Forgery' even had access to the published book by 14 November 1979 and were able to read it. Significantly, Maxim Shostakovich qualified his own initial statements by admitting that the Shostakovich family itself had heard only fragments of the text broadcast on Western radio. Moreover, according to Volkov's recollection, none of 'Les Six Soviétiques' was fluent enough in English to have read the book for himself.[71] Indeed, the situation was probably similar to that surrounding Pasternak's *Dr Zhivago*. Vishnevskaya recalls that 'no one had read Pasternak's novel', yet, in letters to the editor, Soviet citizens proceeded 'to criticize the unread book and even demand that the author be publicly humiliated, be accountable to "the people"'.[72] Both she and her husband, Rostropovich, were

[69] Vishnevskaya, *Galina*, p. 399.

[70] In particular, Reinhold Glière is listed among those said to have been 'defame[d]', yet he is mentioned in only three paragraphs in *Testimony* (all at the beginning of the memoirs, on p. 30/42). Shostakovich's harshest comment is 'Glière wasn't a bad fellow, but he was a mediocre composer', an assessment many musicians would share and one which is perfectly understandable given Shostakovich's own high standards. Certainly this criticism does not constitute defamation and is not even as harsh as statements about many other figures in *Testimony*.

[71] *Cf*. p. 84. Indeed, when contacted by the authors on 13 December 1997, Karen Khachaturian, one of the two living signatories of 'Pitiful Forgery', confirmed that he does not read English; he also stated that he was aware of the Volkov-Shostakovich meetings and that the overall image of Shostakovich in *Testimony* is correct ('based on the facts').

[72] Vishnevskaya, *Galina*, p. 245. Chess champion Garri Kasparov fought back when a similar campaign was launched against his own book, *Unlimited Fight*, Fizkul'tura i Sport, Moscow, 1989, p. 5: 'One could ask: if the book is not published in Russian, no one read it, then how can it be discussed seriously, or even denounced?'

personally approached by Party officials to join in these attacks. Vishnevskaya responded:

> 'But how can I sign a letter criticizing *Dr. Zhivago* if I haven't read it?' 'None of us has read it.' 'Well, I want it given to me to read.' 'But we don't have the book. It's banned.' 'Then I won't sign.'[73]

Similarly, Rostropovich, when requested to give a speech criticising Pasternak, answered: 'But I haven't read the book! How can I criticize it?' 'Nobody has read it! Just say a few words – you're so quick-witted'.[74] On another occasion, Vishnevskaya was asked to persuade Rostropovich to sign a letter denouncing Sakharov. Her refusal shocked her solicitors, who noted, matter-of-factly: 'What's so unusual about it? Who pays attention to those letters? Everybody does it.'[75]

Dubinsky notes that 'the new, worldly Communist soon learned that if he paid membership dues on time, attended without question all Party meetings, said only what was printed in *Pravda*, and never voiced his own opinion, he could survive and even make a nice living'.[76] This was confirmed when he asked a schoolmate with a promising career as a violinist why he had joined the Party: 'He answered frankly that he had been advised. I then asked him what his own opinion was. He smiled. "I certainly have an opinion of my own, only now I don't agree with it."'[77] In view of these Soviet tendencies to 'denounce first, read later' and to toe the 'Party line', the value of 'Pitiful Forgery' as evidence is pitiful.

4. Tishinka and Tishchenko

Testimony has been attacked not only in print but also on the podium. Tikhon Khrennikov, immortalised in *Rayok* as

[73] Vishnevskaya, *Galina*, p. 248.

[74] *Ibid.*, p. 248.

[75] *Ibid.*, p. 445.

[76] Dubinsky, p. 8.

[77] *Ibid.*, p. 8.

'Tishinka',[78] speaking before the Sixth Congress of Composers, branded the work 'a vile falsification, concocted by one of the renegades who have forsaken our country'.[79] In addition, Boris Tishchenko, in a speech to an editorial conference of the newspaper *Sovetskaya Kul'tura*, declared:

> I am prepared to take an oath on the Bible that this book [*Testimony*] is a forgery. I happened to be at the meeting between Shostakovich and the author of the book. Shostakovich said to me: 'You see, he insists on a meeting, and I would like you to be present too'. This is the reason I was there. What Shostakovich had to say would fill a thin notebook, but the volume published in the West contains some 400 pages.[80]

Khrennikov's rejection of *Testimony* is understandable, since the former all-powerful,[81] Stalin-appointed chairman of the Composers' Union has always maintained, contrary to the memoirs and other evidence, that Shostakovich was a 'loyal son'. In an interview in 1986, he stated:

> When Shostakovich, Kabalevsky, and I were in Los Angeles in 1959, at a press conference at the Ambassador Hotel, [. . .] he told them [the journalists] that he was a Communist and that he considered the party of the Bolsheviks to be the most progressive force in the world. 'I have always listened to it and will continue to do so.'[82]

[78] Shostakovich's denigrating name for Tikhon Khrennikov in his anti-Stalinist satire *Rayok*; used in place of the usual diminutive, 'Tisha'; also means 'little silence'. For more on *Rayok*, *cf*. pp. 271–86.

[79] Fay, p. 485; also *cf*. p. 52.

[80] Ian MacDonald, 'A Reply to Messrs Norris and Brown', *Melos*, 1/4–5, Summer 1993, p. 47 (hereafter Ian MacDonald, 'Reply'); transl. from Boris Tishchenko, 'Briefly on Important Issues', *Music in the USSR*, July/September 1989, p. 35. In truth, although the *manuscript* has 404 pages, the Harper and Row and Hamish Hamilton editions have around 300 pages only, including the prefatory material and index.

[81] According to recent information, Khrennikov retains considerable power over the artistic elite, despite the changes in the former Soviet Union.

[82] Joel W. Spiegelman, 'The Czar of Soviet Music', *High Fidelity*, 36/3, March 1986, p. 55. Also *cf*. *D. Shostakovich: Articles and Materials*, p. 7, and *Tak Eto Bylo: Tikhon Khrennikov o Vremeni i o Sebe* (*The Way It Was: Tikhon Khrennikov About the Time and Himself*), as related to and edited by V. Rubtsova, Muzyka, Moscow, 1994, pp. 170–71.

It is also not surprising that Khrennikov would denounce a book in which he himself is the butt of some of Shostakovich's most vicious and earthy remarks. Recall the following passage:

> Suddenly Stalin raised his head and peered at Khrennikov. As the people say, 'he put his eye on him'. [. . . Khrennikov] felt a warm mass under him, which scared him even more. He jumped up and backed toward the door [. . .] all the way to the reception area, where he was grabbed by two hearty male nurses, who were specially trained and knew what to do. They dragged Khrennikov off to a special room, where they undressed him and cleaned him up and put him down on a cot to get his breath. They cleaned his trousers in the meantime. [. . .] To shit in your pants in front of the leader and teacher is not something that everyone achieves, it's a kind of honour, a higher delight and a higher degree of adulation.[83]

In contrast, Tishchenko's criticisms have surprised even Volkov.[84] According to the latter, Shostakovich's favourite

[83] *Testimony*, pp. 196–97/253–54.

[84] Ian MacDonald, who has spoken to Volkov on this matter, comments: [Tishchenko's] antipathy to Solomon Volkov partly involves a rivalry about which Volkov prefers to remain silent. It may surprise some commentators to learn that, in spite of their public disagreements, Volkov and Tishchenko remained on sufficiently friendly terms to have met in New York and discussed *Testimony* as recently as 1992. Volkov has conveyed to me some remarkable facts about this meeting (letter, 23 October 1992), but wishes me not to disclose them. The explanation for Tishchenko's denial of *Testimony* in 1979 is hinted at in his speech of October 1988, reported in *Sovetskaya Kul'tura*, 15 October 1988, p. 8, and *Music in the USSR*, July/September 1989, p. 35: 'Following the article in *Literaturnaya gazeta* ['Pitiful Forgery' (1979)], the Composers' Union received a cable addressed to me: "My congratulations on your joining the ranks of Soviet composers. Solomon Volkov". I cabled back: "I am with those who write symphonies, not with those who write pseudo memoirs. If we meet, we'll talk man to man".' Tishchenko could not speak freely in a cable and so had to wait until he met Volkov in New York in 1992 to say his piece. The gist of this was that his overriding impulse in 1979 had been to defend the best interests of the Shostakovich family as he perceived them then (*vis-à-vis* serious threats from the Soviet authorities). Hence he allowed himself to be manipulated by Vasily Sitnikov, the KGB general in charge of the disinformation campaign against *Testimony*. Choosing not to acquire freedom of speech by emigrating, Tishchenko was unable thereafter to disassociate himself from this campaign. Volkov and

pupil was aware both of the writing of *Testimony* and of some of the controversial views contained therein. Tishchenko interceded on Volkov's behalf when Shostakovich initially had doubts about working on his memoirs and Volkov confirms that Tishchenko *was* present at the first meeting for this project:

> Dmitry Dmitriyevich wanted moral support. Tishchenko did come to the first meeting, sat in the corner and listened. After a while – he left. (Everyone was talking without him). He was not present at any other meetings.[85]

Although Tishchenko was not privy to the dozens of other meetings between Volkov and Shostakovich over the next four years (and, hence, has no idea how enough material could have been obtained for a '400-page volume'), he *was* aware that work on the memoirs had continued. For example, it was to Tishchenko that Shostakovich later described Volkov as 'the most intelligent man of the new generation'.[86] This appraisal was then relayed by Tishchenko to Volkov, with Marianna Volkov and Mikhail Byalik present. It was also through Tishchenko that Shostakovich, upon completion of the manuscript, requested confirmation that *Testimony* would be published only after his [Shostakovich's] death. This Volkov did in a letter. Finally, Volkov claims that

---

Tishchenko broke off relations around 1996 as a result of Tishchenko's anger over Volkov's claim that he refused to permit his Requiem of 1966 (on Anna Akhmatova's cycle about Stalin's Terror of 1935–39) to be performed in the West because of his 'fear of open confrontation with the authorities, which would lead to a loss of the privileges he enjoyed' (Volkov, *St Petersburg: A Cultural History*, pp. 487–88).

Tishchenko's current animosity towards Volkov is evident in *Pis'ma Dmitrya Dmitriyevicha Shostakovicha Borisu Tishchenko* (*Letters of Dmitry Dmitriyevich Shostakovich to Boris Tishchenko*), Kompozitor, St Petersburg, 1997, pp. 48–49 (hereafter Tishchenko, *Letters*), in which Tishchenko seems completely oblivious to any of the new evidence corroborating *Testimony* and bases his attacks on the opinion of Irina Shostakovich and the early criticisms of Maxim. Tishchenko's conclusion that *Testimony* is 'a book of Volkov about Volkov' is ridiculous.

[85] Conversations between Volkov and the authors, August 1995.

[86] Quoted in *Testimony*, p. xii/xvi. This appraisal is consistent with the one Shostakovich gave to Flora Litvinova (*cf*. p. 251).

the content of *Testimony* is no surprise for Tishchenko, since the latter told him that he has (or had) 'a number of letters in which Dmitry Dmitriyevich's non-conformist views were expressed quite clearly'.[87]

Tishchenko's hidden role in *Testimony* (convincing Shostakovich to proceed with the project, then serving occasionally as a go-between) has been acknowledged previously by Volkov, who confirms that Tishchenko is the unnamed friend alluded to at the end of his Preface (1979): 'And finally, I thank you, my distant friend who must remain nameless – without your constant involvement and encouragement, this book would not exist'.[88] Volkov again expressed his gratitude to Tishchenko in his article 'Requiem for a Friend' (1980):

> *Testimony* was hard work, sometimes unbearably hard. Without the help of my friend I would never have completed that work. He was Shostakovich's pupil, the favorite one. He realized how important it was for the aging master to have a chance to shout the truth about himself to the world before he died. He did everything he could to make this possible.[89]

Volkov's claim of an earlier friendship with Tishchenko has been denied by the latter[90] but can be readily docu-

[87] Conversations between Volkov and the authors, December 1995. The photograph reproduced on p. 304 shows Tishchenko and Volkov with the letters spread on the table. Forty-two of these, dating from 5 May 1963 to 27 July 1975 were published in 1997 (*cf.* Tishchenko, *Letters*); several corroborate aspects of *Testimony*. That Shostakovich's letters could be, to put it mildly, 'non-conformist' is amply demonstrated in Isaak Glikman, *Pi'sma k drugu* (*Letters to a Friend*), DSCH, Moscow/Kompozitor, St Petersburg, 1993 (hereafter I. Glikman, *Letters to a Friend*).

[88] *Testimony*, p. xv/xviii. Volkov did not identify Tishchenko in his Preface in order to protect his friend with anonymity. The latter, he notes, feared 'open confrontation with the authorities, which would lead to a loss of the privileges he enjoyed'. For example, Tishchenko's Requiem, based on Akhmatova's poem, was completed in 1966, but withheld from performance (even in the West) by the composer, because its 'anti-Stalinist text [. . .] was still strictly taboo' (Volkov, *St Petersburg*, p. 487).

[89] Solomon Volkov, 'Requiem for a Friend', *Ovation*, 1/6, July 1980, p. 15.

[90] Tishchenko referred to 'a certain Solomon Volkov' in 'Pitiful Forgery' (*cf.* p. 61). More recently, when asked to comment on 'the book [*Testimony*] by Solomon Volkov', Tishchenko's curt response was: 'I think it is unethical to mention this name in the conversation about Shostakovich'

mented. For example, three photographs of Volkov and Tishchenko together, in Tishchenko's apartment,[91] are reproduced in the Appendix, along with two handwritten notes from Tishchenko to Volkov. The first note was given to Volkov when Tishchenko left the above-mentioned meeting with Shostakovich: 'Mon! I am at the sea by the old boat'.[92] The second is an inscription on the score of Tishchenko's *Concerto for Cello, 17 Winds, Percussion and Harmonium*:

> Dear Monchik! Thank you for your work – for the book already published [*Young Composers of Leningrad*], and especially for those that have not yet appeared, on which you are working presently, and I am happy to be present at this moment. We will have a lot to reminisce about. Yours B. 9 IV 72. Happy Victory Day![93]

Tishchenko's use of familiar forms of the name 'Solomon' ('Mon' and 'Monchik') suggests the closeness of their friendship. Furthermore, his mention of books 'that have not yet appeared, on which you are working presently' is a clear reference to Volkov's only book-in-progress in April 1972, *Testimony*.

5. Yakubov and Sabinina

Among the Russian scholars who have questioned the authenticity of *Testimony* are Manashir Yakubov, curator of the Shostakovich family archive, and Marina Sabinina. In an interview published in 1993, Yakubov states:

> Volkov begged Boris Tishchenko to bring him into the Shostakovich's place. As a pretext, Volkov said that he wanted to

---

(Irina Nikolska, 'Dmitry Shostakovich' (interviews with Marina Sabinina, Izrael Nesteyev (Nest'yev), Valentin Berlinsky, Ivan Martynov, Lev Lebedinsky, Boris Tishchenko, Vera Volkova and Manashir Yakubov), *Melos*, 1/4–5, Summer 1993, p. 80; hereafter Nikolska).

[91] Reproduced on p. 304–5.

[92] Reproduced on p. 306.

[93] Reproduced on p. 306. Tishchenko expressed gratitude to Volkov because *Young Composers of Leningrad* was the first book to devote a chapter to him. *Cf.* Volkov, 'Universal', p. 15.

> find out some information about young Leningrad composers including Shostakovich's students for the purpose of his book.
>
> [*Testimony*] has not been published in Russia yet and probably never will be. [...] Volkov is afraid because this book is not completely authentic. He told me that he had met Shostakovich only three times but it is impossible to write such a big book only on the basis of three meetings. [...] I think that Volkov was informed by such an irritating and spiteful person as Lev Lebedinsky.[94]

Yakubov clearly has confused Volkov's earlier meetings with Shostakovich for the book *Young Composers of Leningrad* with those for *Testimony*. According to Volkov, even then he never 'begged' Tishchenko to bring him to Shostakovich's place to find out about young Leningrad composers. In fact, that book had already been completed and Shostakovich had written its preface *before* Tishchenko became involved. It was only after the editors severely cut Shostakovich's text, leaving mention of only three composers, that Volkov asked Tishchenko for help: Shostakovich, upset over the cuts, did not want his preface published; Tishchenko convinced him to publish it.[95]

Volkov also categorically denies telling Yakubov 'he had met Shostakovich only three times' and re-affirms that dozens of conversations took place over a four-year period. Furthermore, he claims that 'when the journal *Banner* wanted to publish excerpts from the Russian text of *Testimony*, it was Yakubov who said "over my dead body". So when someone *wanted* to publish it, Yakubov did not want it. And now that he knows that the publishing industry in Russia is in a state of chaos and uncertainty, he blames me for not publishing it'.[96] Finally, Yakubov provides no evidence that Lebedinsky had a hand in *Testimony*. The latter never

[94] Nikolska, pp. 83, 85.

[95] Conversations between Volkov and the authors, August 1995.

[96] Conversations between Volkov and the authors, August 1995. On the publication of the original text, *cf*. pp. 216–18.

The relationship between Yakubov and Volkov has deteriorated significantly since the latter's emigration in 1976 and the publication of *Testimony* in 1979. For example, in an earlier inscription to Volkov,

claimed such participation,[97] even though he had many opportunities to do so and openly acknowledged his involvement in other projects, such as writing the libretto for

---

Yakubov wrote: 'To dear Solomon Volkov (Solomon's Wolf!) [a play on words – 'Volk' in Russian means wolf] with love and good feelings from Manashir 22 January 1975' (reproduced on p. 307). However, Volkov asserts that, despite externally cordial relations, any kind of frank discussion with Yakubov at that time was highly unlikely, since the latter was viewed in the Moscow musical community with a certain suspicion, due to his unusual career in the ranks of the Soviet musical bureaucracy. From the end of 1967 to the beginning of 1971, Yakubov, then in his thirties, served as the head of the musical division of the Committee for Lenin and State prizes, the unofficial part of the Council of Ministers of the USSR – that is, of the Soviet government. As proof, Volkov cites *Sovetskaya Muzykal'naya Entsiklopediya* (*Soviet Musical Encyclopedia*), Sovetskaya Entsiklopediya, Moscow, 1982, Vol. 6, p. 999. Such an appointment signalled a close connection with 'official circles'. For example, Vasily Kukharsky, a notorious Soviet cultural bureaucrat, served on the same committee in 1957–60, just before moving to a position in the cultural division of the Central Committee of the Communist Party, and then to an appointment as the Deputy Minister of Culture of the USSR (L. Grigor'yev and Ya. Platek, *Sovetskiye kompozitory i muzykovedy, spravochnik v 3 tomakh* (*Soviet Composers and Musicologists, Dictionary in 3 Volumes*), Sovetsky Kompozitor, Moscow, 1981, Vol. 2, p. 127; also *cf.* p. 53). Volkov points out that his apprehensions about Yakubov were heightened when the latter, after the death of Shostakovich, was appointed to the politically charged position of curator of the Shostakovich archive. It is curious, Volkov emphasises, that such an important position was given to a musicologist who, from the beginning of his professional career till Shostakovich's death, had not published a single article about Shostakovich or his *œuvre* (*cf.* Bernandt, Yampol'sky, Vol. 4, pp. 86–87). Volkov points out that in those years Yakubov was known mainly as a specialist in Prokofiev's works. His appointment as curator of the Shostakovich archive is, in Volkov's opinion, tantamount to the appointment of a Tolstoy specialist as head of the Dostoyevsky archives (conversation between Volkov and the authors, December 1995).

Yakubov himself seems to corroborate Volkov's statements. In his interview with Nikolska, he admits he knew Shostakovich personally only 'from 1969', and that his writings on the composer, before the latter's death in 1975, consisted of notes for one Melodiya recording and an unidentified 'something' (Nikolska, p. 86).

[97] Nikolska, in her interview with Lebedinsky, p. 78, notes: '(My interlocutor allegedly hints at his own participation in [the] creation of Volkov's book. Irina Nikolska)'. This, however, is not a clear admission on Lebedinsky's part, but an interpretive aside by Nikolska, as indicated by the latter's 'triple hedging' (i.e., parentheses and use of the words 'allegedly' and 'hints').

Rayok.[98] In fact, Lebedinsky was surprised to find in *Testimony* certain details that only he and the composer would know. For him, this was proof positive of its authenticity.[99]

Marina Sabinina also has suggested that Volkov received assistance from others: 'I do not think that everything that was published by Volkov comes directly from Shostakovich. Probably the book was written on the basis of other publications. Volkov could obtain information from the master's students'.[100] Again, however, no proof is provided, and it is significant that no Shostakovich family member, friend, colleague or student has ever admitted having talks with Volkov that could have yielded the 300-page memoirs.[101]

98 *Cf.* p. 272, note 7.

99 Nikolska, p. 78. *Cf.* p. 240.

100 Nikolska, p. 68. Ironically (*cf.* p. 68), Robert Craft hypothesised that 'the book owes much to Boris Tishchenko, Shostakovich's favorite pupil [. . .]' ('Testaments from Shostakovich and Prokofiev', *Present Perspectives*, Alfred A. Knopf, New York, 1984, p. 80 (hereafter Craft, 'Testaments'); from 'Notes from the Composer', *New York Review of Books*, 24 January 1980, p. 9). Sabinina's statement that 'she found Volkov exceedingly conceited, rude, bad-mannered, disagreeable' is, by her own admission, based only on an 'extremely superficial acquaintance' (Nikolska, p. 68). Volkov, for his part, says that he does not know Sabinina personally but does know her book of 1959 (conversations between Volkov and the authors, August 1995), in which, despite the 1958 'correction' of the famous Zhdanov Decree of 1948, Sabinina: (1) labels many of Shostakovich's major works 'formalist' and dispenses indiscriminate 'Soviet-style' criticism of the First Piano Sonata, *Aphorisms*, *The Nose*, Second and Third Symphonies, all three ballets, *Lady Macbeth*, First Piano Concerto, Preludes, Op. 34, and Cello Sonata; (2) finds it difficult to call *The Nose* a real opera, because 'it does not have singing, natural human emotions, or living personages', but has no problem with *Moscow-Cheryomushki*, which is 'full of simple and tender melodies, cheerful and healthful laughter, and acutely satirical'; and (3) describes Shostakovich's music as the 'art of the era of the struggle of the oppressed peoples against their colonial oppressor [. . .]' (Marina Sabinina, *Dmitry Shostakovich*, Znaniye, Moscow, 1959, pp. 9, 27 and 25, respectively).

101 Nikolska, p. 23. The animosity of Yakubov and Sabinina toward Volkov may stem from jealousy. Sabinina, in particular, is in a rather poor position to be casting stones at others, given her role in the 'Vospominaniya' ('Reminiscences') section of Vissarion Shebalin's *Literaturnoye nalslediye* (*Literary Heritage*), Sovetsky Kompozitor, Moscow, 1975)

6. Irina and Galina

Yakubov's assertion that Volkov and Shostakovich met only three times (which he misattributes to Volkov![102]) can actually be traced back to the earliest denunciations. In November 1979, the composer's widow, Irina Antonovna, stated:

> Volkov saw Dmitrich three or maybe four times. He was never an intimate friend of the family – he never had dinner with us here, for instance. I don't see how he could have gathered enough material from Dmitrich for such a thick book. [. . .] He agreed to see Volkov first as a favor to his friend Boris Tishchenko, and two of the meetings he had took place in his presence. He may have met him at other times, but only briefly, at concerts, rehearsals, and so on.[103]

She goes on to say that Volkov told them he was preparing a 'biographical essay' for *Sovetskaya Muzyka* and that it was the practice of this journal that Shostakovich initial any article about him. Therefore, 'he was always coming up to Dmitrich with pictures taken by his wife and asking him to autograph them'. She also notes that no essay was ever published and that, before his emigration in 1976, Volkov never responded to requests from the family to see the manuscript.[104]

In answering Irina's charges, Volkov denies ever saying that he was working on a 'biographical essay' on Shostakovich. Furthermore, he claims that her statement about photographs is completely false: that his wife never took any photographs of Shostakovich, that he was not 'always coming up to Dmitrich' for him to autograph these non-existent pictures, and that the only signed photo he has is that

---

(hereafter Shebalin, 'Reminiscences'), which, according to its preface, pp. 3–4, was only '*in large part* read and authorised' by Shebalin (emphasis added).

[102] *Cf.* p. 73.

[103] Quoted in Craig R. Whitney, 'Shostakovich Memoir a Shock to Kin', *The New York Times*, 13 November 1979, p. C7 (hereafter Whitney). Also *cf.* pp. 00 concerning Sitnikov and KGB disinformation.

[104] Whitney, p. C7.

reproduced as the frontispiece of the US edition of *Testimony*.[105] Next, he rejects Irina's surprise at how 'such a thick book' came about, noting that it was Irina herself who actually returned the chapters to him after they had been read and signed by Shostakovich.[106] Significantly, in a statement to the Central Committee on 22 November 1978, Irina acknowledged that she and others were well aware of *Testimony*. According to the 'Minutes of a meeting in VAAP with the widow of the composer – I. A. Shostakovich' (preserved in the archives of the Central Committee):

> I. A. Shostakovich was asked why she did not appeal then to VAAP for purposes of preventing the undesirable publication abroad. She replied: 'Everyone whom this [*Testimony*] concerned knew about it. The journal *Sovetskaya Muzyka* knew about it as well'.[107]

The Central Committee itself appears to have had no doubt that Shostakovich had worked on his memoirs with Volkov. Its archives include a number of documents that precede the publication of *Testimony*, some of which, according to Bogdanova, give a detailed description of how Shostakovich 'recounted his autobiography to the soviet musicologist S. M. Volkov, who represented the journal *Sovetskaya Muzyka*'.[108] Finally, Volkov points out that he did respond to Irina's request to examine the memoirs, telling her that he would show her the manuscript, but only outside of the Soviet Union, when they were no longer hostages.[109] This offer is corroborated by the article about their meeting in *A*

[105] Reproduced between pp. 142 and 143 of the UK edition. This photograph was taken by Il'ya Shapiro, a free-lance photographer at *Sovetskaya Muzyka*. The other photographs in *Testimony* of Volkov with Shostakovich were taken by Boris Karnaukhov, a photographer at the Leningrad Conservatory (1965); Valentin Polukhin, a photographer at the Moscow Chamber Theatre, in which *The Nose* was being rehearsed (16 October 1975); and Semyon Khenkin, a staff photographer at *Sovetskaya Muzyka* (*cf*. p. 303).

[106] Conversation between Volkov and the authors, July 1995.

[107] Bogdanova, p. 373. *Cf*. also the testimonies of Galina Drubachevskaya and Yury Korev, pp. 136–37.

[108] Bogdanova, p. 373.

[109] Conversation between Volkov and the authors, August 1995.

Chronicle of Currents Events (published in 1976):[110] 'I. A. Shostakovich asked Volkov to let her read the memoirs before publication. Volkov replied that he had no copies, but he would gladly comply with her request abroad'.[111]

Volkov openly admits that he was never an intimate friend of the composer – the type that would have dinner with the family[112] – and, in *Muzykal'naya Akademiya*, also rejects Tishchenko's oft-repeated claim that he has 'pose[d] as a friend of Shostakovich':

> I have never once said such a thing! This is absolute nonsense! I never claimed I was a friend of Balanchine nor a friend of Milstein. I was a collaborator in their projects. They had faith in me. My task was not to let them down.[113]

[110] *Cf.* p. 49.

[111] In Drubachevskaya, p. 322, Volkov quotes Irina saying 'the KGB instructed me to ask you for the manuscript'. Volkov's response was 'that as long as I was a hostage, I would show her nothing, but if we could meet outside the USSR, then I would show her the manuscript'. He notes, 'Now that we are on equal footing, she never came, and never asked me to see anything [. . .]'.

[112] Krzysztof Meyer notes that, although many considered themselves his friends, in his whole life Shostakovich had only a few real friends: apart from Sollertinsky, there were undoubtedly Isaak Glikman and Leo Arnshtam; of course, he had a group of devoted musicians who could also be regarded as his friends – the Beethoven Quartet, David Oistrakh, Mstislav Rostropovich, Moisei Vainberg – but these were, mainly, artistic friendships ('Recollection of a Man', *Melos*, 1/4–5, Summer 1993, p. 52). In addition, Edison Denisov, in his diary for 2 December 1953, quoted Shostakovich as saying: 'I do not like either too friendly or too hostile relationships between people' (Detlef Gojowy, 'Dmitry Schostakowitsch: Briefe an Edison Denissow', *Musik des Ostens*, 10, Bärenreiter, Kassel, 1986, p. 202).

[113] Drubachevskaya, p. 328, and Volkov, 'Universal', p. 18. The question often was asked, 'How could Shostakovich have opened up to some drop-out violinist, some insignificant little reporter, when he had not even confided in his best friends?' (Drubachevskaya, p. 316). Closeness to the composer, however, is no guarantee of a successful collaboration. Wilson notes that 'the gift of observation and sensitive perception is by no means the exclusive right of close friends' (Wilson, p. xiii), and even Yakubov acknowledges that 'Shostakovich may have revealed to Volkov more than he did to his own friends. One is provoked to say this or that depending on the individuality of the person one communicates with' (Nikolska, p. 84). In addition, Shostakovich's family and intimate friends actually may have been *too* close to notate these tell-all memoirs without censoring or second-

At the same time, Volkov refutes Irina's assertion that his meetings with Shostakovich were rare:

> Irina Shostakovich's statement that I only saw Shostakovich three or four times is not true. I had a 15-year relationship with him. My personal acquaintance began in 1960, when I was the first to review his Eighth Quartet in a Leningrad newspaper.[114] [. . .] Over the next few years, I wrote several other articles about his music. I came to know him when he was perhaps most dissatisfied with himself. Later, when I began to work on a book about young Leningrad composers, I wrote to him and requested a preface. He replied at once, 'I'll be happy to meet with you'.[115]

Although Shostakovich's preface was included in *Young Composers of Leningrad*, it had been cut severely and dealt only with the present. According to Volkov, this upset the composer and provided the 'final powerful impetus for him to give the world his version of the events that had unfolded around him in the course of half a century'.[116] 'We met and talked more and more frequently', Volkov says, both in Shostakovich's cottage near Leningrad, where the Composers' Union had a resort, and in Moscow, where Volkov was a senior editor of *Sovetskaya Muzyka*.[117] The latter proved convenient since Shostakovich lived on the sixth floor of the building on Nezhdanova Street that also housed the

---

guessing the composer: 'Do you really want to say that about Stalin and Prokofiev?' This problem is evident in Isaak Glikman's *Letters to a Friend*, in which 'to protect the memory of his most cherished friend, and to protect what *he* knows to be the meaning of his friend's words, the editor interposed himself often and clumsily (and, alas, familiarly) between the reader and the text' (Richard Taruskin, 'Who Was Shostakovich?', *Atlantic Monthly*, 275/2, February 1995, p. 63) (hereafter Taruskin, 'Who'). A friend probably would not have obtained as much from Shostakovich. This distance allowed Volkov to do the book.

[114] 'Novy kvartet D. Shostakovicha' ('New Quartet of D. Shostakovich'), *Smena* (*Change*), 7 October 1960, and Ye. Sadovnikov, ed., *D. Shostakovich. Notografichesky i bibliografichesky spravochnik* (*D. Shostakovich. Musical and Bibliographical Dictionary*), Muzyka, Moscow, 1965, p. 256.

[115] Mitgang, 'Shostakovich Author', p. 21.

[116] *Testimony*, p. xii/xv.

[117] Mitgang, 'Shostakovich Author', p. 21.

offices of the music journal.[118] Volkov remembers that whenever Shostakovich wanted to work 'he would just call me and in two minutes I would be upstairs with him'.[119]

Given the manner in which Volkov and Shostakovich met, always on the spur of the moment, it is not surprising that an accurate tally was not kept, even by the KGB. In fact, the number of meetings acknowledged by Soviet sources themselves has been contradictory. Tishchenko, as noted above, claimed to be at *the* meeting between Volkov and Shostakovich, whereas Irina says he was at two. Even Irina's total of three or four meetings (the number Vasily Sitnikov admitted took place in spring 1973 alone[120]) has been contradicted by 'other observers [who] assert that, in the last years, meetings were frequent'.[121] Notable among the latter is Flora Litvinova, Shostakovich's long-time friend, who recalls the composer himself telling her that he had been meeting 'constantly' with a young Leningrad musicologist to 'tell him *everything* I remember about my works and myself'.[122]

Today, Irina remains the only member of Shostakovich's immediate family who openly denounces Volkov and rejects *Testimony*.[123] When asked in October 1996 whether she had changed her 'opinion on this subject', she stated unequivocally: 'No, I haven't at all changed my opinion regarding Volkov';[124] furthermore, during a Shostakovich conference at

[118] Meyer, p. 54.

[119] Robinson, p. 392.

[120] Evans, 'Moscow', 7 November 1979, and Bonosky, p. 12.

[121] Craft, 'Testaments', p. 80. Among those 'in the know' were Galina Drubachevskaya, Yury Korev and Mark Lubotsky (*cf.* pp. 136–37 and 217).

[122] Flora Litvinova, 'Vspominaya Shostakovicha' ('Remembering Shostakovich'), *Znamya* (*Banner*), 12, December 1996, pp. 168–69 (hereafter Litvinova). *Cf.* p. 251 for the complete passage. Clearly, it would have taken Shostakovich more than the three or four meetings acknowledged by Irina to tell Volkov 'everything' that his phenomenal photographic memory had recorded over sixty eventful years of life.

[123] *Cf.* the recent endorsements of *Testimony* by Galina and Maxim Shostakovich, pp. 83–84 and 112–14.

[124] Irina Shostakovich, 'Remembering Shostakovich', *DSCH Journal*, No. 6, Winter 1996, p. 4 (hereafter Irina Shostakovich, 'Remembering Shostakovich').

California State University, Long Beach (18 February 1996), she dismissed the Shostakovich memoirs as inaccurate and as a 'book that belongs to yesterday', reiterating that

> [Volkov] hadn't been acquainted with [Shostakovich] for a long time. So he hadn't given an adequate kind of reflection of what he had learned in three of his two-hour conversations. He added lots of his own material and kind of narrated it on Shostakovich's behalf. So always next to Shostakovich's voice you can hear a stranger's voice.[125]

Irina's criticisms are suspect for several reasons. Immediately following her statement in California, she seemed to admit that she had not read *Testimony* in its entirety, because 'this book hasn't been published in Russian. But I came across a few excerpts, in [reverse] translation'.[126] Irina, it should be noted, does not know English (her remarks at the conference were translated). She has never admitted having access to the complete Russian text of *Testimony*: indeed, she has always maintained that the latter has been withheld from her by Volkov. Are Irina's statements based merely on 'a few excerpts, in [reverse] translation', and whatever else others have told her about the book, or on a careful, detailed, personal study of the entire text? Apparently, denounce first, read later.[127]

Irina's claim to often hear a 'stranger's voice' in *Testimony* was not supported by any examples and, in fact, has recently been contradicted by Galina and Maxim Shostakovich, both of whom knew their father for a considerably longer time than did Irina, who married the composer only in 1962, after a brief courtship. Indeed, compared to Shostakovich's children, it is Irina who 'hadn't been acquainted with [the

[125] Response by Irina Shostakovich to the question 'What is your personal view of Solomon Volkov's *Testimony*?', transl. Sofiya Krapkova, California State University, Long Beach, 18 February 1996 (hereafter Irina Shostakovich, conference); tape on file with the authors. The authors wish to thank Kristine Forney and Jonathan Pusey for recording this conference and making this material available to researchers.

[126] Irina Shostakovich, conference.

[127] This appears to be the *modus operandi* of many people criticising *Testimony*. Even English-speaking 'experts', such as Brown, Fay, and Norris, in their attacks seem to have difficulty reading plain English: *cf*. pp. 100–2; 128–129, 150–51; and 247–50 respectively.

composer] for a long time'. Both Galina and Maxim recognise in *Testimony* the composer's voice,[128] and Galina Shostakovich specifically mentions that not only the choice of words, but even the way they are put together reminds her of her father.[129] Galina also implicitly questions Irina's assertion regarding the 'stranger's voice', by inquiring exactly which part of *Testimony* is a 'lie'.[130]

Another of Irina's statements is contradicted not only by Maxim Shostakovich and Dmitry Dmitriyevich himself,[131] but by Irina on an earlier occasion. Asked in October 1996 'Did Shostakovich ever think of writing his own memoirs?', Irina responded, 'No. But I hope my chronological list of Shostakovich's life [referring to a day-by-day chronicle she hopes to publish in the future] will serve as much a purpose as this might have done'.[132] Only nine months earlier, however, Irina, at the aforementioned Shostakovich conference in California, had asserted just the opposite:

> You know, it probably will be of interest to you if I tell you that Dmitry Dmitriyevich, over his last years, came back to his life experience, and he more and more wanted to write his *memoirs*. He asked me [for] a telephone book and wanted to write the names of all the people he wanted to write about. And he found an epigram or motto for his memoirs. And that was a quotation from Balzac. I have it written in his own hand. And I would like the interpreter to read it for you: 'In every profession there are true artists who possess invincible pride, aesthetic sensibility, and indestructive stalwartness. Their conscience can never be bought or sold. These writers and artists will be faithful to their art even on the steps of their scaffold'.[133]

[128] For Maxim's statement, *cf*. p. 112.

[129] *Cf*. p. 83.

[130] *Cf*. p. 83.

[131] *Cf*. pp. 85 and 138–39.

[132] Irina Shostakovich, 'Remembering Shostakovich', p. 5.

[133] Irina Shostakovich, conference; emphasis added. In fact, this quote from Balzac aptly describes the courageous and, at times, shocking truthfulness of *Testimony*.

One wonders, just which Irina are we to believe? Obviously, blind acceptance of her opinions is neither warranted nor wise.

Unlike Irina and Maxim, the composer's daughter, Galina Dmitriyevna, has maintained a low profile throughout the *Testimony* debate. Galina's silence is unfortunate since she, born in 1936, is in a better position to verify many of the details in *Testimony* than is Irina, who, as mentioned previously, married the composer only in 1962 (and, apparently, did not enjoy his complete confidence[134]). According to Volkov, Galina told him privately in 1988 that 'she completely supported *Testimony*'.[135] Galina elaborated on this opinion in October 1995, when contacted in Paris:

> I am an admirer of Volkov. There is nothing false there [in *Testimony*]. Definitely the style of speech is Shostakovich's – not only the choice of words, but also the way they are put together. Maxim has shown me parts of the manuscript. There is no question that the signatures ['Chital. D. Shostakovich' at the beginning of each chapter] are his [Shostakovich's]. Shostakovich did sign some stupid articles about inconsequential subjects without reading them, but he would not have signed something this big and important without reading it.
>
> Everybody says that this book is only half truth. But I have never figured out which half is the lie. This book is an outpouring of the soul. It represents, fairly and accurately, Shostakovich's political views, although there is too much 'kitchen talk' and anecdotes.[136]

The few published remarks attributed to Galina about her

[134] Maxim indicated that Shostakovich remained guarded in his words and acts till his death, not speaking candidly even to his wife. *Cf*. p. 58.

[135] Conversation between Volkov and the authors, August 1995.

[136] Conversation between Galina and the authors, 15 October 1995. This statement completely contradicts Sitnikov's assertion in 1979 that Galina [with Maxim and Irina] had

> denounced the book as a forgery and [. . .] called Solomon Volkov an imposter who deliberately created a fraudulent version of the composer's character and ideas in an attempt to compromise not only Shostakovich's honor but also as part of the ongoing 'dirty war' against the Soviet Union.

Bonosky, p. 12.

father also support the image of the 'new' Shostakovich in *Testimony*. For example, Galina corroborates the suggestion that the Eighth Quartet is about Shostakovich himself, an idea first advanced publicly in *Testimony*.[137] She also confirms that her father never mentioned witnessing Lenin's arrival in Petrograd, which is consistent with Shostakovich's statement in *Testimony*, 'They say the major event in my life was the march down to the Finland Station [. . .]. But I don't remember a thing'.[138] Finally, she acknowledges being present when Lebedinsky and her father collaborated on *Rayok*, a work which vividly underscores the anti-Stalinist sentiments in *Testimony*.[139]

7. Maxim Shostakovich: Then

Maxim's initial reaction to *Testimony* was somewhat different from those mentioned above. He characterised the book's publication as a shock, 'like learning about your own death from the newspaper', admitted that the Shostakovich family only had heard the fragments of the text broadcast by Western radio stations, and stated, 'Until I can read the book and judge for myself how much of it is genuinely my father's, I don't want to say anything about it'.[140] Only a few days later, however, Maxim's position changed. At a press conference at VAAP, with Vasily Sitnikov at his side,[141] he claimed that the 'book just published in the West as his father's memoirs was largely a compilation of rumours and anecdotes collected third hand' and that 'the compiler of the book, *Testimony*, had met his father only four times and for no more than two

[137] Leo Mazel', p. 490, note 8 (hereafter Mazel').

[138] Wilson, p. 19, and *Testimony*, p. 4/7.

[139] Lev Lebedinsky, 'The Origin of Shostakovich's *Rayok*', *Tempo*, No. 173, June 1990 (hereafter Lebedinsky, 'Rayok'), pp. 31–32; from *Ekho Planety* (*Echo of the Planet*), 16, 1989.

[140] Whitney, p. C7.

[141] *BBC Summary of World Broadcasts*, 26 November 1979, SU/6281/C/2 (available in LEXIS, News Library, Archiv file).

hours each time'.[142] This was followed by an even lengthier response:

> I've read the recently published book, *Testimony: the memoirs of Dmitri Shostakovich*, as related to and edited by Solomon Volkov. I find that much in it comes from the author himself [meaning Volkov]. The book is a collection of rumours and conversations with other people in the author's interpretation, but all are credited to Shostakovich. Much of it is a rehash of stories that Shostakovich is supposed to have heard from others. There is much that is contradictory in the history of the writing of this book. As far as I know, Volkov told my father that the magazine *Sovetskaya Muzyka* had asked him to do a series of interviews with him, that is, my father. Later it appeared there had been no such assignment.
>
> Let me say that Shostakovich was himself planning to write his memoirs. He even asked me to buy him an address book type of notebook to facilitate the writing. But he never got round to it. I hardly think he would have asked someone else to do what he himself intended to do. He wouldn't think of writing a melody and asking someone else to orchestrate it, which is what Volkov's book amounts to. Further, I can say that Shostakovich was strongly opposed to the publication of private conversations and personal correspondence. Unfortunately, he never kept letters or messages that were addressed to him, and he expressed [*sic*] his relatives and friends to reciprocate.
>
> [. . .] The choice of names Shostakovich is supposed to have mentioned is most strange. He never speaks of many people who were very close to him: his pupils Kara Karayev, Oistrakh, Oborin, the members of the Beethoven String Quartet, Samosud, Benjamin Britten. And there is no mention of many high points in his biography, say the premieres, the productions and so on. Much of the book is given over to conversations about distinguished musicians, and in nearly every case, Shostakovich is depicted as highly critical. Again and again, the author has Shostakovich speaking contemptuously and in the most unfriendly way of Sergey Prokofiev. Actually, my father was a great admirer of Prokofiev and often expressed his admiration . . .

[142] Evans, 'Moscow', 16 November 1979. Also *cf.* pp. 50, 68, 73, 75 and 88, note 153.

> Volkov's book also has Shostakovich speaking most critically about the conducting of Yevgeny Mravinski, his colleague and friend, whom my father is supposed to have accused of a total lack of understanding of his music, though in reality my father considered Mravinski's interpretations ideal. Volkov claims Shostakovich said he hated Toscanini. True, my father did not like Arturo Toscanini's interpretation of his Seventh Symphony[143] but on the whole he had great respect for the maestro, and it was not in keeping with my father's character to express [himself] violently. He was modest and tactful.
>
> [. . . My] father always did all he could to help his friends. He wrote many letters in defence of people who had been treated unjustly. He responded to the slightest show of talent and always wished his colleagues the best.
>
> [. . .] And Shostakovich the humanist goes beyond expressing his attitude towards Stalin to expressing his attitude towards tyranny in general. In reflecting in his music the revolutions and wars the Soviet people lived through he rises to statements about world collisions. And Shostakovich put on a pedestal the cause of defending human dignity. All of this is lacking in Volkov's book, unfortunately . . .[144]

In responding to these denunciations, Volkov doubts Maxim's 'shock' in 1979 over the publication of *Testimony*. He states that right after he [Volkov] applied for emigration in 1975, he 'met with Maxim specially and discussed the matter thoroughly. Maxim knew about the memoirs even before that, and at his father's funeral came over and embraced me, saying "Thank you for everything"'.[145] Volkov also questions Maxim's claim that he 'read' *Testimony*, noting that in 1979 the latter did not know English well enough to do so, and he denies ever telling Shostakovich that '*Sovetskaya Muzyka* had asked him to do a series of interviews with him'.[146] Yury Korev, the chief editor of *Sovetskaya Muzyka*

[143] *Cf.* p. 109, note 233.

[144] *BBC Summary of World Broadcasts*, 26 November 1979, SU/6281/C/2 (available in LEXIS, News Library, Archiv file). In fact, Shostakovich speaks out repeatedly in *Testimony* in defence of human dignity.

[145] Conversations between Volkov and the authors, July and August 1995.

[146] Conversations between Volkov and the authors, July and August 1995.

at the time, confirms that Volkov often mentioned working on Shostakovich's memoirs and that only later did the journal become interested in publishing this material.[147] Finally, Volkov points out that defending the image of a family member is not unique to the Soviets:[148] Nijinsky's widow withheld various parts of his diary;[149] Freud's daughter attempted to stifle any materials that changed the dogmatic image of her father;[150] Berg's widow suppressed the 'secret programme' (including references to the name of Berg's lover, Hanna Fuchs-Robettin) in his *Lyric Suite*;[151] and

[147] Interview with Yury Korev, March 1995. *Cf.* pp. 137–38.

[148] Immediately after his defection in 1981, Maxim stated: '[W]hat worried us more was [that] the personality and integrity of my father would be wronged by the so-called memoirs' (Kuchinke and Schmidt, p. 35A).

[149] *Cf.* Jennifer Dunning, 'Nijinsky Diaries: A Giant's Ardent Effusions', *The New York Times*, 7 September 1995, p. C17:

> [. . .] the version [of Nijinsky's diary] his wife, Romola, published in 1936 was heavily edited and a later version, published in 1953, was even more bowdlerized. [. . .] Diaghilev was Nijinsky's lover, a relationship that Romola Nijinsky denied but that is made clear in the diaries. [. . .] She deleted about a third of the diary, including references to Diaghilev, comments about her that she felt were harsh [. . .].

[150] *Cf.* Robert Stewart, 'I Am Not That Psychoanalytical Superman', *The New York Times*, 6 March 1994, Section 7, p. 1:

> for decades, family members [. . .] denied permission. Freud's daughter Anna was the most adamant; in her role as 'father's keeper', she decided [what] material was too sensitive and should remain private.

[151] *Cf.* George Perle, 'The Secret Program of the *Lyric Suite*', *International Alban Berg Society Newsletter*, June 1977, pp. 4–12; and David Gable and Robert P. Morgan (eds.), *Alban Berg: Historical and Analytical Perspectives*, Clarendon Press, Oxford, 1991, p. 14, in which Douglas Jarman states:

> We had previously known Helene Berg to be an active guardian of her husband's posthumous reputation (her continued refusal to publish, or even to permit to be seen, the material of Act III of *Lulu* had demonstrated how jealously she protected this right); what we had not realized before the revelation of the *Lyric Suite* programme was the extent to which Frau Berg had been willing to censor material, to suppress documents, and to fabricate information in order to project an idealized picture of Berg's life and personality.

Jung's relatives tried to stop publication of a controversial book on Jung.[152]

a. Motive and Opportunity

As can be seen above, Maxim's criticism of *Testimony* rested on four main points: (1) that Volkov only had four meetings with his father (i.e., insufficient contact for a 300-page book); (2) that his father intended to write his memoirs himself and would not have asked anyone for assistance; (3) that several important names and events are not mentioned; and (4) that colleagues who are mentioned are spoken of in a critical, contemptuous, unfriendly manner at odds with his own memory of his father. The first point, that Volkov and Shostakovich met only four times, has been addressed previously.[153] Maxim, like Irina and Yakubov, was not a witness to these meetings, but was merely restating 'facts' provided by official sources. The second point, however, is both new and significant, because it acknowledges that Shostakovich intended to write his memoirs. Unfortunately, Maxim's conclusion, that his father would not have sought assistance, is completely flawed. Given Shostakovich's crippling hand problems in the 1960s–70s,[154] it is understandable that he

[152] According to Dinitia Smith, 'Scholar Who Says Jung Lied Is at War With Descendants', *The New York Times*, 3 June 1995, Section 1, p. 1, Jung's papers at the Library of Congress are controlled by his family, which denied access to Richard Noll, a scholar who proved that Jung falsified data. Princeton University Press later withdrew from circulation Noll's *The Jung Cult: Origins of A Charismatic Movement*, a prize-winning book critical of Jung, and stopped publication of *Mysteria: Jung and the Ancient Mysteries*, a collection of Jung's writings edited and introduced by Noll.

[153] *Cf*. p. 50. Immediately after his defection in 1981, Maxim expanded the number of meetings to possibly 'six times' (Kuchinke and Schmidt, p. 35A). Later, in a conversation with the authors on 19 April 1997, he admitted that he doesn't know how many meetings took place because, at the time, he was no longer living with his father (*cf*. p. 114).

[154] Mentioned in *Testimony*, pp. 115/152, 177/228 and 214/275, and in four letters to Marietta Shaginyan written before and during work on his memoirs: 'My letters are short and slight because of my bad right hand. I have not yet learned to write with my left hand and cannot type' (3 December 1968); 'My right hand is working very badly. So badly I have begun training my left hand, but any success in this is negligible'

would not write a 300-page memoir himself. Furthermore, although Shostakovich did insist that a composer orchestrate his own works,[155] he openly admitted that he was not a writer, did not like writing,[156] and that many of the articles and speeches attributed to him actually were written by others. The latter has been confirmed by Maxim himself in an interview with Boris Schwarz[157] and by numerous friends and colleagues, such as Zhitomirsky:

> There are dozens of speeches and articles catalogued in *D. D. Shostakovich: Musicological and Bibliographical Guide* (Moscow, 1965) as having been published under his name, including a large number that were political and propagandist [. . .]. It was a secret to no one that these and such-like articles were written by professional journalists, and only signed by the supposed author. This was a regular, everyday technique employed for 'speeches by famous people'.
>
> [. . .] Dmitri Dmitriyevich was reconciled to these falsifications not through indolence, and obviously not through moral indifference. Rather I think that he abdicated any real responsibility for these publications for serious reasons. He regarded the official press (and indeed, there was no alternative press) with scepticism as a dismal establishment. His attitude seemed to be, 'Let them write whatever they want. After all, I know its worth. Nobody cares in essence what I am and what I think. Moreover, it would be stupid and highly undesirable to let them see *what* I really am . . .'[158]

Maxim's third point, that important names and events are missing in *Testimony*, is not surprising, since memoirs are always selective, and Shostakovich states at the beginning

---

(10 January 1974); 'My right hand is working badly' (5 March 1974); 'Forgive me writing so little, my right hand is working very badly' (12 April 1974) (all from Shaginyan, 'Fifty Letters from Dmitri Shostakovich', *Soviet Literature*, 1984, No. 1, pp. 92, 98–99) (hereafter Shaginyan). Also *cf*. pp. 140 and 210.

[155] *Cf*. pp. 102–4.

[156] Wilson, p. 432. *Cf*. pp. 139–40.

[157] Schwarz, p. 645. *Cf*. p. 82.

[158] Wilson, pp. 328–29. Wilson notes that 'it is well known that Shostakovich rarely wrote the articles published under his name; certainly this was true after 1936' (p. xiv). *Cf*. Shostakovich's plea to Isaak Glikman: 'I'm asking you to help in writing a preface to a book about Richter' (Glikman, *Letters to a Friend*, p. 156). Zhitomirsky also acknowledges 'collaborating'

'These are not memoirs about myself. These are memoirs about other people'.[159] Accordingly, personal 'high points [. . .], premieres, productions, and so on' go unmentioned, along with equally important details of his family life (marriages, births of his children, and the like). Volkov has previously explained why Oistrakh and other friends do not appear:

> [. . .] these were unusual memoirs: the book turned out to be an elucidation of his political stand, but began as a simple conversation about those who, at the time, were no longer among us – Misha Sokolovsky, Meyerhold and Zoshchenko. He had considered it important to give their memory its due. As for Oistrakh, Rostropovich and the others dear to his heart, he had already written enough about them in the press.[160]

Maxim's final point, that the statements about colleagues in *Testimony* are distorted, is contradicted by a wealth of evidence. Although these assessments may not seem just at first glance, in fact, they accurately reflect the composer's views, as expressed in his letters and private conversations.[161]

---

with (i.e., ghost-writing for) Shostakovich on four occasions, but states that the composer could write 'without any assistance and in quite an interesting manner' on topics of great interest or importance to him, as in 'his reminiscences of Sollertinsky and his long review of the movie about Rimsky-Korsakov' (Daniil Zhitomirsky, 'Shostakovich', pp. 430–32, below) (hereafter Zhitomirsky, 'Shostakovich').

[159] *Testimony*, p. 1/3. He reiterates this focus on pp. 87–88/116: 'I think I'm talking too much about myself, and these memoirs are not about me, they're about others. I want to talk about others first and about me tangentially.'

[160] Drubachevskaya, pp. 323–24.

[161] According to Lebedinsky, Shostakovich 'wasn't in the habit of sharing his deepest thoughts [. . . with] his son' (Wilson, p. 317). Kurt Sanderling explains:

> To him [Maxim] he [Shostakovich] said the least, for a very simple reason. You see, the education of children under a dictatorship is a very complicated affair. On the one hand, you have to teach them to be critical of what is happening politically-speaking, and on the other hand you have to make them understand that one has to be careful when discussing such matters. And I think he told him a lot less than he told, for example, his friends, because quite simply he didn't want to put him in any danger.
>
> 'Performers on Shostakovich: Kurt Sanderling', *DSCH Journal*, No. 6, Winter 1996, p. 14 (hereafter Sanderling).

What actually may have shocked Maxim in 1979 was the truthfulness and multi-dimensionality of the portraits in *Testimony*, which contrast strikingly with the one-sided official images in the Soviet literature.[162]

Among the figures whom Maxim claims are inaccurately portrayed in *Testimony* are Prokofiev, Mravinsky and Toscanini. His contentions are addressed below.

b. Prokofiev and Pogrebov

Although Maxim, in 1979, claimed that his father 'was a great admirer of Prokofiev, often expressed his admiration', and would not have spoken about him 'contemptuously and

[162] Both Shostakovich and Volkov have commented on the Soviet Union's 'sanitised' images. The composer notes:

> A man dies and they want to serve him up to posterity. Serve him, so to speak, trussed up for our dear descendants at the table. [. . .] The deceased, as you know, have the inconvenient habit of cooling off too slowly; they're burning hot. So they are turned into aspics by pouring memories over them – the best form of gelatine.
>
> *Testimony*, p. 21/30.

His own practice, he says, differs:

> I'm trying to remember the people I knew without the gelatine. I don't pour aspic over them, I'm not trying to turn them into a tasty dish. I know that a tasty dish is easier to swallow and easier to digest. You know where it ends up.
>
> *Testimony*, pp. 21–22/30.

Volkov adds:

> In Russia [. . .] we have no substantial, comprehensive and well documented biographies that take into account reminiscences by contemporaries; biographies that provide a picture of the whole person, with his sweat and tears, and contradictions. What we have are highly discreet booklets in which facts are made to support basic theses. Why? Because of our hypocrisy. Because if we were to write the whole truth, the idol would cease to be an idol. The authorisation to criticise geniuses was granted only from higher up. Then it was possible to spit on them to your heart's content. [. . .] All research should be based only on facts. For example, the fact that Musorgsky hated Tchaikovsky and that, in his letters, he called him derisively Sadyk-Pasha, was painted over. As for Tchaikovsky, the nice, mild mannered, and polite Pyotr Ilyich, who loved everyone, wrote his brother: 'with all my heart I send Musorgsky's music to hell, since it is a foul caricature of music'. It is so convenient to forget the simple fact, and it has been forgotten, that creative people permit themselves to attack one another brutally.
>
> Drubachevskaya, pp. 332–33 and 335.

in a most unfriendly way',[163] evidence suggests that the true relationship between these titans of Soviet music was as uneasy as that portrayed in *Testimony*. There Shostakovich admits:

> Prokofiev and I never did become friends, probably because Prokofiev was not inclined toward friendly relations in general. He was a hard man and didn't seem interested in anything other than himself and his music. I hate being patted on the head. Prokofiev didn't like it either, but he allowed himself to be quite condescending to others.[164]

Elaborating on this condescension, he adds: 'I don't think Prokofiev ever treated me seriously as a composer. He considered only Stravinsky a rival and never missed a chance to take a shot at him'.[165] Oleg Prokofiev, who agreed with Maxim in 1979,[166] now confirms the uneasiness of the Prokofiev-Shostakovich relationship:

> [. . .] in a way my father and Shostakovich were 'in different camps' [. . .]. [Even in 1949, when] my father and Shostakovich found themselves 'in the same boat' – and a rather sinking one at that – their relationship was not an easy one. There was neither friendship nor natural communication between them. When one reads the few letters that they exchanged, one is struck by a mixture of polite respect and indifference (each of them ignores all the 'friendly remarks' about their music).[167]

Speaking about Shostakovich in particular, Volkov concludes:

> I do not trust people who called themselves his friends, but who would say with a saccharine lisp what a good man Dmitry Dmitriyevich was, what a gentle man he was: they are either lying or are incapable of understanding him, or never had any serious relations with him.
>
> *Ibid.*, p. 325.

[163] *Cf.* p. 85.

[164] *Testimony*, p. 25/34.

[165] *Ibid.*, p. 26/36.

[166] George Steiner, 'Books: Marche Funebre', *The New Yorker*, 24 March 1980, p. 132 (hereafter Steiner).

[167] Wilson, p. 399. Prokofiev kept copies of virtually all his letters (both to and from correspondents), yet only three letters from Prokofiev to Shostakovich and four from Shostakovich to Prokofiev are known to exist. Two of these are extremely brief; the others mix praise for individual works with specific criticisms (*cf.* 'Prokofiev's Correspondence with Stravinsky and

Zhitomirsky similarly notes: 'I never saw any mutual curiosity expressed by either one of them, although as composers they held each other in high esteem. Psychologically they were totally different people.'[168]

Shostakovich's portrait of Prokofiev the man is often harsh, but understandable. Prokofiev, by many accounts, was not the most likable of persons.[169] Accordingly, he is described in *Testimony* as a musical 'snob',[170] who 'always had a

---

Shostakovich', *Slavonic and Western Music: Essays for Gerald Abraham*, transl. Natalia Rodriguez and Malcolm H. Brown, UMI Research Press, Ann Arbor, 1985, pp. 271–92) (hereafter Rodriguez and Brown).

[168] Zhitomirsky, 'Shostakovich', p. 460. From the start, there was apparently no 'connection' between these composers. Shneyerson reported the following dialogue from their first meeting in Ivanovo:

> *Prokofiev*: You know that I am working very hard here on my Sixth Symphony. I wrote the first movement (a detailed description of the form followed), now I am writing the second with three themes, and the third one will probably be in a sonata form. I feel like I need to compensate for the lack of sonata features in the preceding movements.
>
> *Shostakovich*: Is the weather always like this in these parts?
>
> Zhitomirsky, 'Shostakovich', p. 460.

[169] Lina Prokofiev attributed Stravinsky's unkind remarks about her husband to a misunderstanding of Prokofiev's 'prankishness' and 'wit'. She concluded, 'Of course Prokofiev was too much of a tease and did things without thinking and Stravinsky was too touchy, seeing harm when it was not really meant. It was a sort of overlapping of extreme reaction in both directions' (Rodriguez and Brown, pp. 280–81). Balanchine, however, also recalled unpleasant memories of Prokofiev. Balanchine had worked on Prokofiev's *Prodigal Son* for a long time and needed some money just to survive. He went to see the composer, who started shouting: 'What did you ever do? It's all nonsense, what you did! *The Prodigal Son* is mine! Why should you be paid? Who are you? Get out of here! I won't give you anything!' Balanchine concluded, 'A terrible man, that Prokofiev. He could have said, "You know, my dear man, *golubchik*, I need money myself now, I can't share with you". Or something like that. No – he had to shout at me as if I were a boy. I apologized, bowed, and left quietly' (Volkov, *Balanchine's Tchaikovsky*, p. 211). On Horowitz's similar recollections of Prokofiev, *cf*. Harold C. Schonberg, *Horowitz: His Life and Music*, Simon and Schuster, New York, 1992, pp. 88–89.

[170] Shostakovich states:

> I don't renounce my interest in gypsy songs. I don't see anything shameful in it, as opposed to, say, Prokofiev, who pretended to be enraged when he heard such music. He probably had a better education than I did. But at least I'm not a snob.
>
> *Testimony*, p. 3/6.

chip on his shoulder' and 'was always afraid that he was being overlooked – cheated out of his prizes, orders, and titles'.[171] All of these attitudes conflicted with Shostakovich's own and, no doubt, impeded their friendship. In fact, Shostakovich stresses his lack of snobbery ('I love all music – from Bach to Offenbach [. . . and] like listening to any music, including bad music')[172] and says about awards, simply, 'I like honorary degrees. They're quite decorative and they look good on the wall'.[173]

Shostakovich's appraisal of Prokofiev the composer is more complex, though equally understandable. He, undoubtedly, admired many of Prokofiev's works,[174] and told

---

Volkov adds:

> When the Bolshoi Theatre choreographer, Leonid Lavrovsky, had to extract from Prokofiev a gypsy passage for *The Tale of the Stone Flower*, he brought a pianist with him to the composer's dacha. The pianist proceeded to play all sorts of gypsy tunes. Sergey Sergeyevich was horrified: 'Close the windows! I won't allow such sounds coming from Prokofiev's dacha!' He was very critical of such tunes. As for Dmitry Dmitriyevich Shostakovich, to the contrary, he was quite tolerant in this regard.
>
> Solomon Volkov, 'Tradition Returns: Rostropovich's Symbolism' (hereafter Volkov: 'Tradition Returns'), p. 361.

Shostakovich's love of gypsy songs is also mentioned in a letter to Tishchenko (30 August 1967; Tishchenko, *Letters*, p. 30).

171 *Testimony*, pp. 26–27/36–37.

172 *Ibid.*, p. 131/171. The phrase 'from Bach to Offenbach' was often used by Shostakovich to describe his unusually wide musical tastes (*cf.* Grigoryev and Platek, pp. 272 and 285). Even Tishchenko confirms that Shostakovich used to say: 'I am omnivorous. I like any music from Bach to Offenbach' (Nikolska, p. 79).

173 *Testimony*, p. 129/169. Meyer noticed on his second visit (March 1968) to Shostakovich's flat that the walls were decorated with a poster from a concert devoted to his music and framed diplomas of honorary doctorates (Meyer, p. 57).

For other differences in the backgrounds and personalities of Shostakovich and Prokofiev, *cf.* Harlow Robinson, *Sergei Prokofiev: A Biography*, Viking, New York, 1987, pp. 288, 341 (hereafter Robinson, *Prokofiev*).

174 *Cf.* Grigoryev and Platek, pp. 117, 122, 142, 148, 157, 192–93, 200, 205, 211 and 330. Shostakovich's letters to Prokofiev also include praise for the latter's Sixth Piano Sonata (14 January 1941) and Seventh Symphony (12 October 1952), as well as isolated parts of *Alexander Nevsky* (14 January 1941) and *War and Peace* (4 May 1941).

Rostropovich that the latter's *Symphony-Concerto*, Op. 125, had inspired his own his First Cello Concerto;[175] he also loved Prokofiev's opera *Betrothal in a Monastery* and valued *War and Peace* sufficiently to orchestrate a fragment from the last act for the 1969 Bolshoi Theatre production.[176] At the same time, 'Shostakovich regarded Prokofiev as an uneven composer'[177] and often 'was critical of him'.[178] In his unpublished letter to 'Ronya' [Vissarion Shebalin] of 1 October 1940, he wrote, 'I bought 7 songs Op. 79 of S. Prokofiev. My god, what awful stuff! How sad that he is capable of this. D. Sh.'[179] On 23 January 1941 he added, 'The other day heard Alexander Nevsky of Prokofiev. Did not like it. D. Sh.'[180] Volkov also recalls that

> In our conversations, Shostakovich did speak of his grudges against Prokofiev, including the one that Prokofiev did not understand his music: Prokofiev did not like something about the tremolos of the Fifth Symphony [. . .]. Several years later, after I was already in the States, I read letters from Prokofiev to Shostakovich which had been published in the Soviet

[175] Wilson, p. 323.

[176] *Ibid*., p. 398; also *cf*. p. 94, note 174. Maxim recalls his father insisting that he hear *War and Peace*, 'a masterpiece of true genius' (Albert, p. 402).

[177] Wilson, p. 398.

[178] Nikolska, p. 79 (quoting Lebedinsky).

[179] RGALI, fond 2012, op. 1, ed. khr. 188.

[180] Aleksey Nikolayev (ed.), 'Eto byl zamenchatel'ny drug' ('He was a wonderful friend'), letters to Shebalin, *Sovetskaya Muzyka*, 1982, No. 7, p. 79. This opinion also was expressed directly to Prokofiev:

> I recently heard Stasevich perform your Alexander Nevsky. Despite a whole series of wonderful moments, I didn't like the work as a whole. It seems to me that artistic norms of some sort have been breached in it. There's too much physically loud, illustrative music. It seemed to me in particular that many sections end before they get started. The beginning of the battle [on the ice] and the entire song for low female voice made a powerful impression on me. Unfortunately, I can't say the same thing about the rest of it.
>
> Letter of 14 January 1941; Rodriguez and Brown, p. 283.

Shostakovich also criticised Prokofiev's music to Eisenstein's film *Ivan the Terrible* (Khentova, 'Shostakovich: Legends and the Truth', p. 6).

> Union. And what did I see in those letters? That very same criticism of tremolos.[181]

Prokofiev, of course, more than reciprocated. In *Testimony*, Shostakovich notes that 'in his lengthy correspondence with Miaskovsky, Prokofiev makes quite a few disparaging remarks about me'.[182] Prokofiev also expressed his low opinion of his colleague in a letter to Vladimir Dukelsky (Vernon Duke) (29 September 1935): 'Shostakovich is talented but somehow unprincipled, and, like some of our other friends, has no gift for melody. By the way, they make too much of him here'.[183] Finally, Prokofiev openly criticised several of Shostakovich's works, including his Sixth Symphony and *Lady Macbeth*, the crude eroticism of which he found repulsive,[184] the Piano Quintet, which won the Stalin Prize in 1941[185] (and, perhaps, 'cheated him out of a medal') and the Eighth Symphony, which he asserted would be better if it did not have the second and fourth movements – then 'I am sure there would be much less arguments about this symphony'.[186]

In view of Prokofiev's condescension towards Shostakovich, it is understandable that the latter would not praise his

[181] Drubachevskaya, p. 339. *Cf.* Prokofiev's letter of 5 June 1938 (Rodriguez and Brown, p. 282).

[182] *Testimony*, p. 27/37. *Cf.* S. S. Prokofiev and N. Ya. Myaskovsky, *Pis'ma* (*Letters*), Sovetsky Kompozitor, Moscow, 1977 (hereafter Prokofiev and Myaskovsky, *Letters*).

Irina Shostakovich has confirmed her husband's awareness of these letters: 'After his [Prokofiev's] death, he [Shostakovich] took a very active part in the publication of his [Prokofiev's] correspondence with Myaskovsky' (Irina Shostakovich, conference).

[183] Robinson, *Prokofiev*, p. 307. Also *cf.* Boris Schwarz and Laurel E. Fay, 'Shostakovich', *New Grove Russian Masters 2*, Macmillan, London/ W. W. Norton, New York, 1986, p. 187 (hereafter Schwarz and Fay).

[184] Grigory Pantielyev, 'Prokof'yev: Razmyshleniya, Svidetel'stva, Spory. Beseda s Gennadiyem Rozhdestvenskim' ('Prokofiev: Thoughts, Testimonies, Arguments. A Talk with Gennady Rozhdestvensky'), *Sovetskaya Muzyka*, 1991, No. 4, p. 12 (hereafter Pantielyev, 'Prokofiev').

[185] Schwarz and Fay, p. 187.

[186] Marina Rakhmanova, 'Poslesloviye' ('Afterword [to Prokofiev's Report]'), *Sovetskaya Muzyka*, 1991, No. 4, p. 102 (hereafter Rakhmanova, 'Afterword').

rival's works too strongly in *Testimony*. Yet Shostakovich does not denounce Prokofiev's compositions; he merely notes that his enthusiasm for them has dwindled:

> It's quite strange, but my tastes keep changing, and rather radically. Things that I liked quite recently I now like less, considerably less, and some I don't like at all. [. . .] And it's the same with Prokofiev. So many of his works that I liked once upon a time seem duller now.[187]

He explains further:

> I'm rather cool about Prokofiev's music now and listen to his compositions without any particular pleasure. I suppose *The Gamblers* is the opera of his that I like most, but even it has too many superficial, random effects. Prokofiev sacrificed essential things too often for a flashy effect. You see it in *The Flaming Angel* and in *War and Peace*. I listen and remain unmoved. That's how things are now. Once it was different; but this was a long time ago. And then my infatuation with Mahler pushed Stravinsky and certainly Prokofiev into the background.'[188]

Significantly, Prokofiev is not singled out for scorn. Elsewhere in *Testimony* Shostakovich admits a similar change in his attitudes toward Liszt, Wagner, Hindemith, Křenek, Milhaud and others.[189]

[187] *Testimony*, p. 25/35.

[188] *Ibid.*, p. 27/38. Irina Shostakovich seemed to corroborate a change in Shostakovich's attitude towards Prokofiev in her response to the question 'Could you comment on the relationship between Shostakovich and Prokofiev?' She noted that 'in his youth, when Dmitry Dmitriyevich began his music classes and started composing, Prokofiev used to be his favorite composer'. She then described their later relationship (after Prokofiev returned to Russia) as 'very respectful and correct' (Irina Shostakovich, conference).

[189] Consider the following passages in *Testimony*:

> Studying Mahler changed many things in my tastes as a composer. Mahler and Berg are my favorite composers even today, as opposed to Hindemith, say, or Křenek and Milhaud, whom I liked when I was young but cooled toward rapidly [p. 30/42].
>
> Liszt is a very verbose composer. In my youth I played a lot of Liszt but then I cooled toward him completely, even from the point of view of sheer pianism. My first solo recital had a mixed programme, but my second was all Liszt. But then I grew tired of Liszt – too many notes [p. 38/51].

Shostakovich's criticism of Prokofiev's orchestration also may seem unfair at first glance.[190] When viewed in perspective, however, even this attitude rings true. In the specific areas of craftsmanship where he himself was exceptionally talented, Shostakovich often found fault with others less gifted. Orchestration was one such area[191] and Shostakovich felt quite strongly about it. He says: 'Scriabin knew as much about orchestration as a pig about oranges. Personally, I think all of Scriabin's symphonic poems – the "Divine", and the "Ecstasy", and "Prometheus" – are gibberish'.[192] He

---

> I felt differently toward Wagner at different stages of my life. He wrote some pages of genius, and a lot of very good music, and a lot of average music [p. 97–98/129].
>
> There's no great interest in listening to it [Hindemith's music]. Yet once his works had a great impact on me [p. 173/224].

Similar changes in taste are documented in Shaginyan's notes (pp. 71–72) from her talk with Shostakovich (20 December [1940]):

> His favourite composers:
> 1. Before the Conservatoire, Chopin.
> 2. Afterwards: Glinka, Borodin, Rimsky-Korsakov, Tchaikovsky.
> Now – Mussorgsky.
> Dislikes Scriabin. Indifferent to N. K. Metner.
> Further: Bach, Mozart, Beethoven, Schumann, Schubert, Liszt, Verdi, Mahler. (Does not like Milhaud).
> Wagner – Die Meistersingers.

Also *cf.* p. 180.

190 For example, Phillip Ramey describes Shostakovich's criticism of Prokofiev's orchestration as 'peculiar', 'tired old gossip', the result of 'personal vindictiveness', and, ultimately, 'nonsense' ('Do They Prove a Case?', *Ovation*, 1/1, February 1980, p. 23) (hereafter Ramey).

191 The ease with which Shostakovich orchestrated was well known to his friends and colleagues. He orchestrated Youman's 'Tea for Two' from memory, in 45 minutes, on a wager with Malko (*Testimony*, pp. 51–52/69; Solomon Volkov, 'Dmitri Shostakovitch and "Tea for Two"', *Musical Quarterly*, lxiv/2, 1978, p. 224) (hereafter Volkov, 'Tea for Two'), and wrote his famous *Festive Overture* before Lebedinsky's very eyes, dispatching the still wet pages, one after another, to the copyists an hour or so later (Wilson, p. 264). According to Lebedinsky, with 'his insane technique he [Shostakovich] could do anything. He could have written an opera in three days' (Wilson, p. 346).

192 *Testimony*, pp. 28–29/40. Shostakovich criticised Skryabin's orchestral works, such as the *Poem of Ecstasy*, as early as 1924. *Cf.* Ian MacDonald, 'His Misty Youth: The Glivenko Letters and Life in the '20s', p. 537, note 15 (hereafter Ian MacDonald, 'Glivenko').

also notes that Musorgsky's music 'strives for "new shores", as they say – musical dramaturgy, musical dynamics, language, imagery. But his orchestral technique drags him back to the old shores'.[193]

Prokofiev, by far, receives the harshest criticism, probably due to his unwillingness to take orchestration seriously and to polish his craft through practice. Shostakovich notes that Prokofiev, as a student of Rimsky-Korsakov, made light of his orchestration assignments and, thus, 'never did learn to orchestrate properly'.[194] Significantly, even Prokofiev admits, in 'Yunyye gody' ('Youthful years'), that at the end of the academic year in 1908, following two years of study with Rimsky-Korsakov, he 'barely passed' an exam in orchestration.[195] Maxim, in contradiction of his earlier statement, now also recalls his father, on at least one occasion, 'complaining about [Prokofiev's] orchestration, using tuba and viola in such-and-such a composition'.[196] Furthermore, Shostakovich's criticism in *Testimony* is entirely consistent with his response to Prokofiev's charge at a Composers' Plenum in 1944 that his Eighth Symphony lacked 'a clear, melodic line': 'Melodiousness is a gift from God', Shostakovich said, 'as for orchestration, one can take lessons in that'.[197]

Besides noting that 'orchestration was not Prokofiev's forte', Shostakovich points out:

> [it] was always work for him, and hard work, which Prokofiev always tried to palm off on someone else. The Bolshoi treated his ballets barbarically. It should be known that their

[193] *Testimony*, p. 179/231. This reference to 'new shores' stems from Musorgsky's letter to Vladimir Stasov (18 October 1872), which Shostakovich had previously quoted in an article in *Pravda*, 17 June 1956: 'Onward to new shores! Fearlessly through storms, sandbanks and reefs, onward to new shores!' (Grigoryev and Platek, p. 174).

[194] *Testimony*, p. 20/28.

[195] *Leningradskaya konservatoriya v vospominaniyakh 1862–1962* (*Leningrad Conservatory in Reminiscences 1862–1962*), Gosudarstvennoye muzykal'noye izdatel'stvo, Leningrad, 1962, p. 63 (cited in Robinson, *Prokofiev*, p. 47).

[196] Albert, p. 402.

[197] Wilson, p. 175, and Drubachevskaya, p. 331.

production of *Romeo and Juliet* has Pogrebov as Prokofiev's co-composer. *The Stone Flower* too.[198]

Malcolm Brown, an expert on Prokofiev, has questioned the validity of Shostakovich's statement by questioning the very existence of Pogrebov. Brown writes: 'I have the program booklet of the Bolshoi Ballet's production of *Romeo and Juliet*, and nowhere do I see the name of Pogrebov'.[199] He admits, however, that 'conceivably *someone* has "touched up" Prokofiev's orchestration to help the dancers hear the orchestra even more distinctly from the cavernous stage of the Bolshoi' [emphasis added].[200]

Brown's first mistake is jumping to the conclusion that, according to *Testimony*, Pogrebov's name is mentioned in the Bolshoi's programme booklet. *Testimony*, of course, says nothing of the sort. It merely states that the Bolshoi's 'production of *Romeo and Juliet* has Pogrebov as Prokofiev's co-composer'.[201] This distinction is pointed out by Volkov in his response to Brown, submitted as a 'letter to the editor' to *The New York Times*, but never published.[202] The very fact that proper credit often was not given for the orchestration in Prokofiev's works seems to have irritated Shostakovich. For example, in an earlier speech to the Artistic Council of the Arts Committee (16 November 1945), he sarcastically called special attention to the unacknowledged orchestration (by Pogrebov, according to Rozhdestvensky) in Prokofiev's *Cinderella*:

> The stage-bill does not say who took part in the orchestration and even the re-orchestration in the theatre. This is good work, I was not shocked by it. But in this case I am surprised

[198] *Testimony*, p. 26/37.

[199] Malcolm H. Brown, 'Letters: Shostakovich', *The New York Times Book Review*, 9 December 1979, Section 7, p. 37 (hereafter Brown, 'Letters').

[200] *Ibid*., p. 37.

[201] *Testimony*, p. 26/37.

[202] *Cf*. Appendix, Exhibit 2, p. 301. In this response (18 December 1979), Volkov also disputes Brown's claim that 'many' of Prokofiev's letters to Pavel Lamm had been published, noting that only three (all written between June and November 1942) had thus far been printed.

> that Prokofiev, such an outstanding master of orchestration, could not orchestrate himself.[203]

Brown's second mistake is questioning Pogrebov's activities without checking his facts. Actually, this in-house orchestrator is well remembered by old-time members of the Bolshoi, such as Abram Gurfinkel and Daniil Shindaryov, both of whom confirm that Boris Pogrebov re-orchestrated Prokofiev's and other composers' ballets to make them easier to coordinate with the dancers.[204] Furthermore, Gennady Rozhdestvensky, a frequent conductor at the Bolshoi, states explicitly in an article in *Sovetskaya Muzyka* in 1973 (i.e., six years before Brown's denial) 'that not only did Pogrebov participate in the orchestration of the Bolshoi's production of *Romeo and Juliet*, but that the scores used in the productions of two other Prokofiev ballets, *The Stone Flower* and *Cinderella*, are not the composer's own'.[205] In 1991, Rozhdestvensky again wrote about Pogrebov:

> He was a member of the Bolshoi orchestra, played cymbals, and was extraordinary in the best sense of the word, a craftsman in the area of orchestration. He always did what he was

[203] 'S. S. Prokof'yev glazami sovremennikov: 'Etot balet budet zhit' . . . 'Stenogramma obsuzhdeniya Zolushki. Stenogramma zasedaniya Khudozhetvennogo soveta po teatru i dramaturgii Komiteta po delam iskusstv pri SNK SSSR. 16 Nov. 1945'. ('S. S. Prokofiev in the eyes of his contemporaries. Minutes of the discussion of *Cinderella*'), *Sovetskaya Muzyka*, 1991, No. 11, p. 81.

[204] Conversations between Gurfinkel, Shindaryov and the authors, Spring 1995.

[205] Rozhdestvensky's letter to the editor, 'O sud'be baleta S. Prokof'yeva Romeo i Dzhul'yetta', 'On the Fate of S. Prokofiev's Ballet *Romeo and Juliet*'), *Sovetskaya Muzyka*, 1973, No. 12, pp. 56–58, is an attack on Lavrovsky's 1946 production at the Bolshoi, which he proposes be abandoned. One of the faults Rozhdestvensky attributes to Lavrovsky is assigning Pogrebov to re-orchestrate things: '[Lavrovsky] enlisted the artist of the orchestra, B. Pogrebov, to re-orchestrate *totally* the first half of the second act [of *Romeo and Juliet*], and a number of fragments throughout the entire ballet' (p. 56; emphasis in the original); 'Lavrovsky used the same dubious method of work on *The Tale of the Stone Flower*, which was completely re-orchestrated by the same B. Pogrebov. Lavrovsky's example was followed, regretfully, by P. Zakharov in regard to the score of *Cinderella*' [i.e., Pogrebov was again enlisted] (p. 56, note 3).

> told to do. [... Pogrebov re-orchestrated the entire *Cinderella*] from A to Z. [...] *Tale of the Stone Flower* is Pogrebov completely.[206]

Rozhdestvensky goes on to say that on the same day that his earlier article about the impropriety of Pogrebov's orchestrations was published, 'Shostakovich called me. This was unheard of. He said that he was glad to read my article, and hung up'.[207] This statement confirms Shostakovich's awareness of Pogrebov and suggests agreement with Rozhdestvensky's position. In *Testimony*, too, Shostakovich asserts that the Bolshoi treated Prokofiev's ballets 'barbarically', using Pogrebov's orchestrations of *Romeo and Juliet* and *The Tale of the Stone Flower.*[208]

Although Brown has attempted to defend Prokofiev's working habits by noting that the composer provided detailed instructions for his assistants,[209] 'short scoring' clearly was not enough for Shostakovich. Shostakovich strongly believed that composers must do their own orchestration from beginning to end. In *Testimony*, he notes his 'deep conviction that a composer cannot entrust the orchestration of his works to anyone else',[210] states that writing symphonies and orchestrating them are 'one and the same, so far as I'm concerned',[211] and chides those who require assistance of any sort. He points out, 'there are "great masters"

[206] Pantielyev, 'Prokofiev', p. 15. *Cf. Testimony*, p. 26/37: 'A striking man, that Pogrebov, a percussionist and hussar of orchestration. He orchestrated with hellish speed and solidity'.

[207] Pantielyev, 'Prokofiev', p. 16.

[208] The fact that Prokofiev used assistants to orchestrate his works was not unknown in Shostakovich's lifetime, nor was Shostakovich's criticism of this practice. *Cf.* p. 103, note 212, and Semyon Shlifshtein, *S. S. Prokof'yev: Notografichesky Spravochnik* (*S. S. Prokofiev: Catalogue of Works*), Sovetsky Kompozitor, Moscow, 1962 (hereafter Shlifshtein), pp. 78, 93, 103, 116 and 133, concerning the orchestrations for *Semyon Kotko*, *Suite 1941*, *Ballad about the Boy* and *Story of a Real Man.*

[209] Brown, 'Letters', p. 37.

[210] *Testimony*, p. 204/262.

[211] *Testimony*, p. 171/221. This opinion may sound like hyperbole, but was repeated by Shostakovich throughout his life. In 1943 he wrote, 'I have the utmost respect for Chaikovsky as an orchestrator, for he seldom wrote music and then orchestrated it, but wrote it directly for the orchestra,

[such as Prokofiev] who keep a staff of secretaries to orchestrate their epochal opuses. I never could understand that way of increasing "productivity".'[212] He further acknowledges:

> You can always tape something and then let others orchestrate it for you. I know one such 'talented' man [Oleg Karavaichuk] who behaves in just this ugly manner – he's lazy, I suppose. [. . .] Of course, composing by tape recorder is a special taste, like licking rubber boots, and I not only eschew such perversion, I don't even like composing at the piano.[213]

---

thinking orchestrally as it were' (Grigoryev and Platek, p. 106). Shostakovich re-emphasised this in 1958:

> I am reminded of something Rimsky-Korsakov once said: 'How wrong people are when they say that such-and-such a composer is a master of instrumentation, or that some orchestral work has been well orchestrated. After all, instrumentation is part of the essence of the composition itself.' It could be put no better than that! It is precisely the 'essence of the composition itself' that the composer expresses in his orchestration [. . .].
>
> Grigoryev and Platek, pp. 196–97.

[212] *Testimony*, p. 177/228. Besides Pogrebov, Pavel Lamm also helped orchestrate many of Prokofiev's works, including *Betrothal in a Monastery, Ivan the Terrible, Russian Overture, Ode to the End of the War, Cinderella Suite*, Op. 108, and *Alexander Nevsky* (*cf. Avtografy S. S. Prokof'yeva v Fondakh Gosudarstvennogo tsentral'nogo muzeya muzykal'noy kul'tury im. M. I. Glinki, Spravochnik* (*S. S. Prokofiev's Autographs in the Fonds of the State Central Museum of Culture, named after M. I. Glinka, Catalogue*), Sovetsky Kompozitor, Moscow, 1977, p. 6). Rostropovich, too, acknowledges that 'Prokofiev would sometimes entrust me with his scores in their piano version while asking me to transcribe them into their definitive form [... from] very precise indications in parentheses [. . .]' (*Mstislav Rostropovich and Galina Vishnevskaya: Conversations with Claude Samuel*, transl. E. Thomas Glasow, Amadeus Press, Portland, 1995, p. 39; hereafter *Rostropovich and Vishnevskaya*). On one occasion, Prokofiev even asked him to help compose some cello passages for his *Symphony-Concerto*. When Rostropovich failed to do so, Prokofiev fumed: 'Young man, you don't even have Brahms's talent! Brahms at least produced a mass of notebooks with exercises for the piano. But you, you are incapable of giving me some sixteen measures.' Rostropovich thought to himself, 'how can I go on, if I don't even have Brahms' talent' (Volkov, 'Tradition Returns', p. 361).

[213] *Testimony*, pp. 176–77/228. In contrast, Shostakovich introduced Krzysztof Meyer to Andrey Eshpai with the following words: 'He is a very talented composer, he even knows how to orchestrate all by himself' (Wilson, p. 463).

All of these statements are consistent with a speech given by Shostakovich during the war, in which he criticised Prokofiev's *Suite 1941* and *Ballad about the Boy*. Knowing that both works had involved assistants,[214] Shostakovich pointedly noted:

> One should complete things, one should finish them. You cannot turn out unfinished production. A master must turn out his works finished to the extent of perfection, or close to this degree of perfection.[215]

Yevgeny Chukovsky, Shostakovich's son-in-law, confirms the composer's adamant belief that one must notate one's music oneself: 'Maxim asked him once, "Papa, why are you writing out the parts when the score is there? Anyone who knows how to read and write music could do that for you." Dmitri Dmitriyevich replied, "Everyone should do his own work from beginning to end"'.[216] For Shostakovich, a composer too lazy to realise his own orchestration was like a mother unwilling to carry her child to term.

Volkov, too, has emphasised the importance of viewing the Prokofiev-Shostakovich relationship in perspective, as a constantly changing one:

> I kept being told: 'see, Shostakovich did say good things about Prokofiev at that time and in that place'. In other words, people wanted to believe that if he had once said something about someone, it was an opinion written in stone. But things do change. The year 1948 was one thing. That was when they both were in the same boat. The year 1954 was another: then it was necessary to rehabilitate Prokofiev, and Shostakovich did everything in his power to see that he was awarded the Lenin Prize posthumously. It was still another thing when Prokofiev became a universally recognised composer and it was possible to remember offences inflicted in youth or at a later, mature period of one's life. In his youth,

[214] Shlifshtein, pp. 93 and 103, notes that both works are 'in piano score with indications [by Prokofiev] for orchestration'.

[215] D. Shostakovich, 'Sovetskaya muzyka v dni voiny' ('Soviet Music during the Days of the War'), *Sovetskaya Muzyka*, 1975, No. 11, p. 69. According to Marina Rakhmanova (Rakhmanova, 'Afterword', p. 102), this text was considered too 'bold' to be published earlier, despite the desire of Shostakovich himself.

[216] Wilson, p. 288.

> Dmitry Dmitriyevich could adore Prokofiev and be under his influence. However, later on, and this is quite obvious, they both found themselves laying a claim to a position of certain importance. At present, it seems that we somehow forget the following fact: Shostakovich was the first of them to receive the Stalin Prize in music, while Prokofiev was granted the same prize two or three years later. A biographer's task is to establish what the atmosphere was in 1943 or 1944, why things happened the way they did, and restore the true context of events.[217]

c. Mravinsky and Toscanini

Although Maxim also questioned the portrayals in *Testimony* of Mravinsky and Toscanini, Shostakovich's criticism of these figures again makes sense when viewed in perspective. Shostakovich's surprise 'that the man who considers himself its greatest interpreter does not understand my music'[218] seems to have been elicited, in part, by Mravinsky's 1966 memoirs,[219] published shortly before work on *Testimony* began. For example, Mravinsky writes about the Fifth Symphony:

> Shostakovich makes a great effort to make the finale the authentic confirmation of an objectively affirmative conclusion. But in my view this confirmation is achieved to a large extent by external devices; somewhere in the middle of the movement the quick tempo spends itself and the music seemingly leans against some sort of obstacle, following which the composer leads it out of the cul-de-sac, subjecting it to a big dynamic build-up, applying an 'induction coil'.[220]

In *Testimony*, Shostakovich emphatically disagrees:

> He [Mravinsky] says that I wanted to write exultant finales [. . .] but I couldn't manage it. It never occurred to this man that I never thought about any exultant finales, for what

[217] Drubachevskaya, pp. 339–40.

[218] *Testimony*, p. 140/183.

[219] Yevgeny Mravinsky, 'Tridsat' let s muzykoy Shostakovicha' ('Thirty Years with Shostakovich's Music'), *Dmitry Shostakovich*, ed. Gili Ordzhonikidze *et al.*, Sovetsky Kompozitor, Moscow, 1967, pp. 103–16 (hereafter Mravinsky).

[220] Mravinsky, as transl. in Taruskin, 'Lies', p. 45.

> exultation could there be? I think it is clear to everyone what happens in the Fifth. The rejoicing is forced, created under threat [...]. You have to be a complete oaf not to hear that.[221]

Shostakovich did, at one time, find Mravinsky's interpretations 'authentic', 'supreme', 'perfect' and 'wonderful'.[222] However, the rift that occurred in 1962 over Shostakovich's Thirteenth Symphony further separated them in the years immediately preceding *Testimony*. Shostakovich was extremely loyal to the first performers of his music: the Beethoven Quartet routinely premiered his string quartets, even when other ensembles, such as the young Borodin Quartet, could have done the works more justice; similarly, Vishnevskaya often was called upon to introduce song cycles, Rostropovich cello works, and Mravinsky the symphonies.[223] In return, Shostakovich expected equal loyalty from his performers. Mravinsky, however, declined to premiere the Thirteenth Symphony, feebly excusing himself by saying that he forgot to take the score with him on vacation and that he 'never conducted choral works, and this symphony called for a bass soloist and male choir'.[224] The real reason for Mravinsky's retreat has been noted by Kondrashin, who stepped-in to premiere this tribute to the Jewish victims of Babi Yar at a time of intense anti-Semitism in the USSR: 'Mravinsky had been advised from above not to perform the symphony, and he withdrew like a coward. Shostakovich was very hurt'.[225] This assessment has been confirmed by many others. Meyer notes that Shostakovich's friendship with Mravinsky was irrevocably broken in the early 1960s[226] and Yakubov acknowledges:

> Dmitry Dmitriyevich did not forgive him. [...] Probably their relations were never the same again. The *Thirteenth*

221 *Testimony*, p. 140/183.

222 Wilson, p. 138; *cf*. also Grigoryev and Platek, pp. 74 and 98.

223 Wilson, pp. 246 and 369.

224 *Ibid*., p. 368; the second excuse was expressed by (or through) his wife, Inna Serikova. *Cf*. also p. 229.

225 *Ibid*., p. 358.

226 Meyer, p. 52.

> *Symphony* was followed by the *14th* and *15th Symphonies*. Shostakovich did not ask Mravinsky to conduct them.[227]

Rostropovich concludes:

> Although Shostakovich later made his peace with Mravinsky, I nevertheless believe that he despised him as a human being for his cowardice in the whole affair of the Thirteenth Symphony. There was no excuse for such behaviour. Mravinsky must have understood what a brilliant work the Thirteenth Symphony was, as well as its importance to Shostakovich.
>
> [. . .] I think that, after the affair of the Thirteenth Symphony, Mravinsky was left with a feeling of extreme awkwardness towards Shostakovich, and he virtually stopped performing his new works. He never conducted the Thirteenth or Fourteenth Symphonies, and only much later conducted the Fifteenth on one or two occasions.
>
> [. . .] As far as Mravinsky was concerned, Dmitri Dmitriyevich would have trusted him with all of his works till the end of his days if Mravinsky had not proved himself to be such an unprincipled turncoat.[228]

In contrast to the relationship between Mravinsky and Shostakovich, which deteriorated significantly in the years

[227] Nikolska, p. 86.

[228] Wilson, pp. 368–69. Mravinsky also withdrew from conducting Shostakovich's Second Cello Concerto just two weeks before the premiere, saying 'he hadn't had time to learn the score'. This concert was to be in honour of the composer's sixtieth birthday.

Kurt Sanderling, Mravinsky's assistant for twenty years with the Leningrad Philharmonic, recently has offered an explanation for the latter's actions, portraying him in a more favourable light. He believes that Mravinsky

> was afraid for the choir and soloist and the possible problems that might have arisen by their playing [the Thirteenth Symphony]. I don't think – and I knew him very well – that he was afraid himself of political consequences. As for the conflict surrounding the 2nd Cello Concerto – at that time the Leningrad orchestra was just about to perform abroad – and this meant [. . .] that for 2 or 3 weeks there were rehearsals only of those works which were due to be played during the concerts abroad. Mravinsky was not willing, at this time – indeed he was not capable – of thinking about several works at a time. And so, for Mravinsky, the question would have been: to go on tour with the Leningrad orchestra or not to perform the work at that special moment. In my opinion, when Shostakovich had fin-

preceding *Testimony*, that between the composer and Toscanini was never close or particularly amiable. Each figure is rarely mentioned in books about the other and passing remarks are usually disparaging. In *Testimony*, Shostakovich admits:

> I hate Toscanini. I've never heard him in a concert hall, but I've heard enough of his recordings. What he does to music is terrible, in my opinion. He chops it up into hash and then pours a disgusting sauce over it. Toscanini 'honoured' me by conducting my symphonies. I heard those records too, and they're worthless. [. . .] Toscanini sent me his recording of my Seventh Symphony and hearing it made me very angry. Everything is wrong. The spirit and the character and the tempos. It's a lousy hack job.
>
> I've read about Toscanini's conducting style and his manner of conducting a rehearsal. The people who describe this disgraceful behaviour are for some reason delighted by it. I simply can't understand what they find delightful.
>
> I think it's outrageous, not delightful. He screams and curses the musicians and makes scenes in the most shameless manner. The poor musicians have to put up with all this nonsense or be fired. And they even begin to see 'something' in it.
>
> [. . .] Conductors are too often rude and conceited tyrants.[229]

Viewed in perspective, these comments, again, ring true. Shostakovich's treatment of fellow musicians was antithetical to Toscanini's. Shostakovich granted performers a certain leeway in interpreting his music and remained courteous, even in disagreement;[230] Toscanini, on the other hand,

---

> ished a new work, everything else had to follow. But, that was a difficult, personal decision – and I don't blame Mravinsky for it.
>
> Sanderling, p. 13.

229 *Testimony*, p. 17/24. Toscanini recorded Shostakovich's Seventh Symphony in 1942 and First Symphony in 1944. Both are now available on compact disc as RCA 60293 and 60323, respectively.

230 *Cf.* p. 109, note 233, pp. 263–64 and Shostakovich's hand-written letter to Serge Koussevitsky (Moscow, 10 February 1945; discovered by Richard Pleak in the Koussevitsky Collection, Library of Congress) regarding Koussevitsky's recording of the Eighth Symphony. There Shostakovich writes:

> I couldn't agree with some passages, but I don't want to force my

dictated his views in a tyrannical manner distasteful to the composer.[231] Shostakovich's negative reaction to Toscanini's recording of his Seventh Symphony has been confirmed by Maxim,[232] Lev Arnshtam and others;[233] it is also understandable that he would expand upon this criticism in the 1970s given the conductor's open and well-documented rebukes of the composer. For example, in a letter to Leopold Stokowski, Toscanini noted 'I renounced to be the first interpreter of the Shostakovich Fifth Symphony because of my scant interest in it'.[234] He also repeatedly criticised the Seventh Symphony, which he had premiered in the United States in 1942 for political reasons rather than love of the music:

> point of view on you. I'm a sincere supporter of individual renditions, and even when I'm not in total agreement with a performer's conception of a work, I'm nervous of insisting on my views. Yet, so long as my remarks aren't completely antipathetic to your thoughts, I ask you very strongly to take them into consideration in the future. [A list of specific suggestions follows.]

[231] *Testimony*, p. 17/24.

[232] *Cf.* p. 86.

[233] About Toscanini's recording of the Seventh Symphony, Arnshtam recalls: 'We put the record player on the floor, sat down on the blanket, and heard the record twice. Shostakovich was not happy, no' (Sofiya Khentova, *D. Shostakovich v gody Velikoy Otechestvennoy voiny* (*D. Shostakovich in the Years of the Great Patriotic War*), Muzyka, Leningrad, 1979, pp. 165–66). In the same publication, Khentova contrasts this private response with Shostakovich's public politeness:

> The interpretation of A. Toscanini was far from the interpretation achieved by Ye. Mravinsky with his objective, emotional restraint. On 23 April in VOKS [the All-Union Society for Cultural Ties Abroad] there was a public hearing – a sort of 'record premiere'. Here Shostakovich did not consider it proper just to talk about the errors; since there was a sign of friendship, Shostakovich immediately, in VOKS, wrote in pencil a telegram with warm words to the old maestro: 'Please accept my warm gratitude for the pleasure I received from this hearing. I send you my best wishes. Dmitry Shostakovich'.
>
> From the autograph in the Museum of Musical Culture, GTsMMK, f. 32, No. 155.

[234] Harvey Sachs, *Toscanini*, J. B. Lippincott, New York, 1978, p. 280.

> I asked myself, did I conduct that? Did I spend two weeks memorizing that symphony? Impossible. I was stupid![235]

> Did I really learn and conduct such junk?[236]

When thrown together, Shostakovich and Toscanini were more likely to knock heads than to embrace. Toscanini would not conduct Shostakovich's Fifth Symphony because 'he could not accept the indicated tempi, but at the same time considered them to be authoritative, and did not dare deviate from them'.[237] A similar situation arose with the Eighth Symphony:

> Toscanini was extremely interested in the Eighth Symphony. However, a projected performance by him did not take place because of Shostakovich's categorical refusal to sanction a change of tempo in one of the episodes of the first movement. An intensive exchange of telegrams between Toscanini and Shostakovich took place through the musical section of VOKS. Neither wanted to back down. Shostakovich insisted on the necessity of observing the tempo indicated by the metronome marking. In his last telegram Toscanini advised that, with the marked tempo of the given passage, he would not be able to perform the symphony. The composer's answer followed with an expression of polite regret.[238]

8. Maxim Shostakovich: Now

Maxim's statements after his defection in April 1981 reveal a gradual movement away from total rejection of *Testimony* to endorsement. Boris Schwarz reports of his conversation with Maxim in June 1981:

> When I questioned Maxim more closely about *Testimony*, he

[235] Howard Taubman, *The Maestro: The Life of Toscanini*, Simon and Schuster, New York, 1951, p. 289.

[236] George R. Marek, *Toscanini*, Atheneum, New York/Vision Press, London, 1975, p. 234 (hereafter Marek, *Toscanini*).

[237] Mravinsky, quoted by Wilson, p. 140.

[238] Grigory Schneerson (Shneyerson), 'At the Birth of Dmitri Shostakovich's Eighth Symphony', transl. Laurel E. Fay in *Russian and Soviet Music: Essays for Boris Schwarz*, ed. Malcolm H. Brown, UMI Research Press, Ann Arbor, 1984, p. 255 (hereafter *Essays for Boris Schwarz*).

> said that many statements ascribed to his father had possibly been made over a cup of tea, in the course of a casual conversation, and should not be taken as absolute truths.[239] Yet, he said, 'if the book accomplished one good thing, it is that it revealed for the first time the tragedy of the mask of loyalty that my father had to wear all his life'. He underlined these words with a sweeping gesture from face to waist. 'And all those official pronouncements', he continued with a frown, 'I never saw my father write down any speeches or statements. They were brought to him all prepared from the Composers' Union, and he just signed them or delivered the speech as written for him.'[240]

A few months later, in August 1981, Maxim repeated this assessment:

> the attitude of Shostakovich toward the regime is correct. [. . .] My father hated the tyranny. If this book changed in any way the attitude of the public toward Shostakovich as a court musician of the Soviet government, it's very good. If it proved that Shostakovich wasn't a servant of the Communist party, then thank God.[241]

Maxim's recent statements and actions are still more revealing. On 27 September 1986, in a television interview (on BBC2) with the composer Michael Berkeley, he admitted: 'It's true. It's accurate. Sometimes, for me, there is too much rumour in the book, but nothing major. The basis of the book is correct'.[242] This was followed by:

(1) his collaboration with Volkov on 'On "Late" Shostakovich – A Conversation', which Maxim included as programme notes to his performance of Shostakovich's

[239] One of Maxim's few doubts about *Testimony* concerns the relationship between his father and Prokofiev. In a conversation with Volkov, Maxim said 'Dmitry Dmitriyevich criticised Prokofiev during breakfast, but praised him during dinner'. Volkov responded, 'my meetings with Dmitry Dmitriyevich were usually during breakfast time'. The latter is consistent with Volkov's statement in *Testimony*, p. xiii/xvii, that he and Shostakovich would work 'usually early in the morning'. For Shostakovich's similarly conflicting comments about Tchaikovsky, *cf*. p. 181.

[240] Schwarz, p. 645.

[241] Edward Rothstein, 'Musical Freedom and Why Dictators Fear It', *The New York Times*, 23 August 1981, Section 2, p. 1.

[242] Ian MacDonald, *The New Shostakovich*, p. 7.

Fourteenth Symphony with the New York Chamber Symphony (17 January 1988, 92nd St. Y);[243]

(2) his statement to Seppo Heikinheimo, printed in the Finnish edition of *Testimony* (1989), that:

> Everything that the book says about the persecution of my father and politics in general is certainly true. *The language is for the most part such that I can recognise it to be my father's language*, but some places make an odd impression on me. (He was hinting at the criticism of Glière and Prokofiev.)[244]

(3) his endorsement of Ian MacDonald's *Testimony*-centred study, *The New Shostakovich*, in 1990 as 'one of the best books about Dmitri Shostakovich that I have read';[245]

(4) his acknowledgement in the May 1991 issue of *Gramophone* that 'when we take this book [*Testimony*] in our hands we can imagine what this composer's life was like in this particular political situation – how difficult, how awful it was under the Soviet regime';[246]

[243] Will Crutchfield, 'Music: Shostakovich 14th', *The New York Times*, 19 January 1988, p. C17. For the text of this conversation, *cf. DSCH*, No. xiii, August 1989, pp. 35–38. Significantly, this was not an isolated incident. Three years earlier, Volkov's article 'Dmitri Shostakovich's "Jewish Motif": A Creative Enigma' was similarly included with the programme for the USA premiere of *From Jewish Folk Poetry*, Op. 79a, conducted by Maxim in New York on 23 and 24 November 1985. According to one observer, Volkov and Maxim also 'greeted each other warmly after the concert' (Derek C. Hulme, *Shostakovich: A Catalogue, Bibliography and Discography*, 2nd ed., Oxford University Press, Oxford, 1991, p. 365; hereafter Hulme, *Catalogue*).

[244] Seppo Heikinheimo, 'A Decade of Struggle About Authenticity', manuscript (in English), p. 3 (emphasis added), provided courtesy of the author; also included (in Finnish) in the Finnish edition of *Testimony*, 1989, p. 353 (hereafter Heikinheimo, 'Decade of Struggle'). Maxim's questions about the criticism of Prokofiev have been addressed previously; his concern over the statements about Glière is misplaced and seems to stem from *Literaturnaya Gazeta's* editorial 'The Bedbug' (*cf.* pp. 62 and 66, note 70).

[245] From the dust jacket of the Northeastern University edition. *Cf.* p. 242, note 1.

[246] David Fanning, 'Always a Great Composer, Not a Papa', *Gramophone*, Vol. 68, No. 816, May 1991, p. 1992. According to Fanning, Maxim's remarks gave a 'general endorsement both of Volkov and of Ian MacDonald's *The New Shostakovich*'. Maxim also made clear what he thought

(5) his participation with Volkov in a Shostakovich symposium at Russell Sage College (25 January 1992, New York), at which he stated, publicly:

> Mr. Volkov wrote a book which is a very important book, and which revealed a whole aspect of the composer and his life in his homeland that was really unknown before. Of course, from the very beginning his book evoked very sharp criticism from the ruling Communist Party in the Soviet Union because it did exactly show the truth of Shostakovich's political views and political feelings. In my opinion, that's the most important achievement of this book. [. . .] In Russia, I would say, a successful work on Shostakovich really has not yet appeared and I think that's because there's a weight of political baggage that still prevents people from describing everything the way it really was[247]

(6) his interview with Volkov on Radio Liberty (23 November 1992), during which he said:

> We, Solomon, unfortunately, meet rarely in life and in front of the microphone, but, now that we are here, I would like to take this opportunity and thank you for your book about my father – for your description of the political atmosphere of suffering of this giant artist. I think this is the most important point in this book. And if someone in Russia has not read it yet, I strongly recommend reading it, because here, in the West, only after Volkov's book were people's eyes opened regarding the conditions surrounding this musical genius[248]

(7) his vouching for the authenticity of a generous selection of excerpts from *Testimony* included in *Composers on Music* (1997), edited by Josiah Fisk.[249]

---

of Sofiya Khentova's 1200-page study of Shostakovich: 'I hate, I *khhhate* her book and I told her so, because all the explanations come from the wrong political angle. The facts are okay, but she makes him look like a genuine son of the Communist Party [expletive deleted]'.

[247] Robinson, p. 374–75.

[248] Tape on file with the authors.

[249] Northeastern University Press, Boston, pp. 354–62. On p. xvi, Fisk notes: 'I enlisted the help of Maxim Shostakovich, who vouched for the authenticity of the passages included here from Solomon Volkov's controversial book'. Significantly, these sixteen excerpts from *Testimony* (pp. 150/196, 181/234, 123/162, 97/129, 30/42, 44/60, 28/40, 23–24/33, 152/198, 25/35, 26/36, 102/134–35, 140/183, 117–18/154–56, 168/218 and

Maxim's endorsement of *Testimony* and praise of Volkov became significantly stronger after August 1991, when the Soviet regime fell. Moreover, after reading a draft of this essay in Spring 1997 (and examining the original Russian text of *Testimony*), Maxim confirmed that his father told him about 'meeting a young man from Leningrad [Volkov] who knows his music extremely well'[250] and that 'Volkov did meet with Shostakovich to work on his reminiscences', even if he [Maxim] does not know how often, since by that time he was no longer living with his father. He agreed that his sister Galina 'got it right' in her statement[251] in which she admits recognising their father's voice but finds 'too much "kitchen talk" and anecdotes' in *Testimony*. Maxim added that, as the composer's son, he understandably disagrees with some 'minor details' in the book; at the same time, however, he acknowledged that his 'father loved telling anecdotes and that it's possible he said all these things and Volkov wrote it down'. Finally, Maxim described *Testimony* as 'a great book, showing the life of the artist under the totalitarian regime', and confirmed that he 'maintains good relations with Volkov'. He emphasised several times that, contrary to what some people may think, 'I am a supporter both of *Testimony* and of Volkov'.[252]

177/229, respectively) reveal Shostakovich's admiration for Glazunov, Mahler and Berg; mixed assessment of Wagner; changing views of Prokofiev; love for Stravinsky's music but dislike of the man; criticism of Skryabin's symphonic poems and knowledge of orchestration; inspirations for and true meanings of his Fifth and Seventh Symphonies; and work habits (composing away from the piano). (Shostakovich's political views, previously authenticated by Maxim, are not included because of the focus of Fisk's book, which is composers writing about music – letter from Fisk to the authors, 2 June 1997.)

[250] *Cf*. Flora Litvinova's comments, p. 251.

[251] *Cf*. pp. 83–84.

[252] On-the-record conversation between Maxim Shostakovich and the authors, 19 April 1997.

B. Fools: Holy and Regular, *or* An Essay on the Dangers of Casting Stones in Glass Houses

A major revelation for Western readers of *Testimony* was its portrait of Shostakovich not as a good Communist but as a closet dissident, whose protest was in the time-honoured tradition of the *yurodivy*, or 'holy fool'. As Volkov explains in his Introduction,

> Whether consciously or not, Shostakovich became the second (Musorgsky being the first) great *yurodivy* composer. [. . .] The *yurodivy* has the gift to see and hear what others know nothing about. But he tells the world about insights in an intentionally paradoxical way, in code. He plays the fool, while actually being a persistent exposer of evil and injustice. [. . .]
>
> The origins of *yurodstvo* go back to the fifteenth century and even earlier [. . .]. During all that time, the *yurodivye* could expose things and remain in relative safety. The authorities recognized the right of the *yurodivye* to criticize and be eccentric – within limits. [. . .]
>
> Stepping onto the road of *yurodstvo*, Shostakovich relinquished all responsibility for anything he said: nothing meant what it seemed to, not the most exalted and beautiful words. The pronouncement of familiar truths turned out to be mockery; conversely, mockery often contained tragic truth. This also held for his musical works.
>
> [. . .] It is important to note that Shostakovich not only considered himself a *yurodivy*, but he was perceived as such by the people close to him. The word 'yurodivy' was often applied to him in Russian musical circles.[1]

[1] *Testimony*, pp. xxi–xxii/xxv–xxvii. Schönberger adds that 'the yurodivy is a living paradox: he plays the fool who exposes evil and attacks the prevalent code of moral behavior but is strict with himself; within certain limits he is entitled to be critical and eccentric. The yurodivy of old had license to tell the tsar the truth; the modern yurodivy was able to taunt Stalin and subsequently be distinguished by the dictator with the highest accolades of honor' ('Dmitry Shostakovich's Memoirs: Testimony', *Keynotes*, 10/2, 1979, p. 58) (hereafter Schönberger, 'Memoirs'). The most famous example of *yurodstvo* in Russian literature is that in Pushkin's *Boris*

Shostakovich, in the main body of *Testimony*, applies the title *yurodivy* sparingly and with caution. He considers Musorgsky 'probably the most *yurodivy* of the Russian – and not only the Russian – composers'[2] and warns that

> Some people think that the *yurodivye* who dared to tell the whole truth to tsars are a thing of the past. A part of literature, *Boris Godunov* and so on. [. . .] But the *yurodivye* aren't gone, and tyrants fear them as before. There are examples of it in our day.[3]

Although he mentions only one occasion in which he himself was called a 'yurodivy',[4] parallels between Shostakovich and Musorgsky are readily apparent in *Testimony* and this view of Shostakovich as 'holy fool' has gained general acceptance.[5]

The title *yurodivy* also has been applied, more recently and with less caution, by Richard Taruskin in his article 'The Opera and the Dictator'. Praising Laurel Fay for 'meticulously' testing *Testimony's* claims and 'absolutely demolish[ing] its credibility' in 'Shostakovich versus Volkov: Whose *Testimony*?', he pronounces her a *yurodivaya* (or female 'holy fool').[6] Unfortunately, 'holiness', like beauty, is

---

Godunov, when Tsar Boris allows a *yurodivy* to accuse him of murdering the true heir to the throne. Interestingly, the *yurodivy*'s closing words in Musorgsky's like-named opera remain prophetic to the present day, when another Boris (Yeltsin) wrestles with very similar problems: ethnic strife, famished people and political corruption.

2 *Testimony*, p. 182/235.

3 *Ibid*., p. 147/192.

4 *Ibid*., p. 15/22.

5 Wilson, p. 428. In *The New Shostakovich*, Ian MacDonald notes that 'the parallel between the English court jester [and Russian *yurodivy*] is more or less exact and it is significant that the Fool in *King Lear* was, after Hamlet, Shostakovich's favourite Shakespearian creation' (p. 8). He later concludes that Stalin made 'a private decision concerning Shostakovich that [he . . .] was not to be arrested but instead taken aside and whipped like a jester out of favour with the king' (p. 106). Shostakovich himself may have intended to say more about *yurodstvo* in a planned, but unrealised, opera on the folk hero Ivan the Fool (Yevgeny Yevtushenko, *Fatal Half Measures*, ed. and transl. Antonina W. Bouis, Little, Brown and Co., Boston, 1991, p. 297) (hereafter Yevtushenko).

6 Taruskin, 'Dictator', p. 34.

in the eye of the beholder, and one man's holy fool may be another man's fool.

Taruskin's mis-assessment of Fay's research has been echoed by other writers. Teachout reports that Fay 'demonstrated conclusively that parts of *Testimony* had been plagiarized from previously published Russian-language articles signed by Shostakovich' and that her 'article was subsequently accepted by most scholars as a definitive refutation of the authenticity of *Testimony*'.[7] Even Ian MacDonald, a staunch supporter of the 'new' Shostakovich in *Testimony*, concedes that 'within academic circles, Fay's piece was deemed conclusive'. Summarising the position of *Testimony*'s critics, he states that 'Volkov, known to have been preparing a conventional biography of Shostakovich, had clearly gone for the big money by turning his material into a set of bogus "memoirs". The fact that he failed to rebut Fay's charges spoke for itself'.[8]

Although Fay's arguments do seem convincing at first glance, applying the same scrutiny to her text as she applies to *Testimony* reveals a different picture, one which is distorted and lacks perspective. Equally troublesome is the way Fay's own overstated findings have been exaggerated by others upon repetition. For example, Fay identifies eight passages in *Testimony* that she suggests were 'plagiarized' by

[7] Teachout, p. 47.

[8] *The New Shostakovich*, p. 4. As noted previously (*cf.* pp. 41–42), Volkov's silence often has been interpreted (wrongly) as a sign of guilt. In fact, *no* evidence has been found that Volkov was first writing a conventional biography. Quite the contrary, witnesses at *Sovetskaya Muzyka* confirm that Volkov always said he was working with Shostakovich on his memoirs (*cf.* pp. 134–37).

When contacted in August 1995 for his latest views on *Testimony*, MacDonald replied:

> Were I to revise *The New Shostakovich*, I would certainly alter or eliminate those observations on *Testimony* which are excerpted in your essay. Ultimately, though, I concur with Vladimir Ashkenazy and Semyon Bychkov in considering the disputed letter-by-letter authenticity of *Testimony* to be vastly less important than the now firmly established authenticity of its overall style and content. As I proposed in *The New Shostakovich*, the essential truth of *Testimony* is what matters and what will continue to matter to future generations.

Volkov from previously published articles by Shostakovich. This figure then was inflated in *The New York Times* by Donal Henahan, who reported that Fay's 'article marshals evidence to show that *much* [emphasis added] of Mr. Volkov's material [...] actually had appeared previously in virtually the same form in well-known Soviet publications'.[9] But just how 'much'? Fay's 'borrowed' passages account for less than 3% of *Testimony's* 215/276 pages.[10]

1. Handed on a Soviet Platter[11]

Fay begins her article by noting that rumours of an 'authorized' memoir by Shostakovich were in circulation at least two years before *Testimony* was published.[12] She then reports that 'Soviet reaction [...] has been swift and unambiguous', citing as evidence the afore-mentioned letter in *Literaturnaya Gazeta* signed by six former students and friends of Shostakovich, accompanying editorials that 'savagely blast Volkov and trace the Soviets' unsuccessful legal attempts to block the publication of *Testimony*', Khrennikov's speech to the Sixth Congress of Composers 'brand[ing] the work as "that vile falsification, concocted by one of the renegades who have forsaken our country"', and Irina's statement: 'I don't see how he [Volkov] could have gathered enough material from Dmitrich for such a thick book'.[13]

Fay's summary of these views, while accurate, lacks perspective. She accepts without question or qualification all of the statements handed to her on a 'Soviet platter' and does not consider carefully who made the statements, nor when, where and why they might have been made. She does not

[9] Donal Henahan, 'Music View: Myths Just Keep Coming Back', *The New York Times*, 15 February 1981, Section 2, p. 17; *cf.* also pp. 188–89.

[10] I.e., in the British and American editions respectively.

[11] *Cf.* p. 54 for a Central Committee memorandum of 14 December 1978 suggesting use of 'foreign organs of mass media to describe the publication [*Testimony*] as an anti-soviet forgery, discrediting the name of the great composer'.

[12] Fay, p. 484.

[13] *Ibid.*, p. 485.

mention – or does not know – that Karayev signed the letter to avoid being kicked out of the hospital in which he was undergoing treatment for a heart condition,[14] nor does she acknowledge that Khrennikov had ample personal reason to condemn *Testimony*, being the target of some Shostakovich's most vicious attacks.[15] Fay also assigns undue weight to these denunciations by not mentioning that such statements were common in the USSR, that even Shostakovich signed them for fear of reprisal or to rid himself expeditiously of a nuisance, and that those who signed usually had not even read the document.[16] Is Fay's silence on such matters due to the same Western naïveté she attributes to others[17] or, worse, a conscious attempt to deceive?[18] Even Robert Craft, who is not an expert in Soviet cultural affairs, could read between the lines: 'in the letter in the *Gazeta* [. . .] the reasons stated therein for condemning the book prove that the signatories have not even seen it [. . .]'.[19]

2. Inscriptions and Photographs

Fay's lack of perspective is again evident as she challenges the nature of the Volkov-Shostakovich relationship. She states that 'in examining Volkov's evidence [. . .] there are some indications that his own autobiography [as given in the Preface] may be as misleading as the one he ascribes to Shostakovich'.[20] To support her claim, she considers the photographs and inscriptions reproduced in *Testimony* as

[14] *Cf*. p. 64.

[15] *Cf*. p. 69.

[16] *Cf*. pp. 63–67.

[17] Fay, pp. 486 and 493.

[18] Incredibly, this deception continues: in *1996* Malcolm Brown was still citing 'Pitiful Forgery' as evidence against *Testimony*: *cf*. Malcolm Brown, 'Shostakovich: Expropriated and Exploited' (paper, Shostakovich conference, California State University, Long Beach, 17 February 1996; hereafter Brown, paper).

[19] Craft, 'Testaments', p. 77. Also *cf*. p. 66, note 70.

[20] Fay, p. 491.

well as Volkov's statements regarding his 1968 production of Veniamin Fleishman's opera, *Rothschild's Violin.*[21] Fay writes:

> Volkov indicates that in November 1974 Shostakovich inscribed and presented him with this picture [reproduced in the frontispiece] in order to facilitate acceptance of the manuscript in the West. The inscription reads: 'To dear Solomon Moiseyevich Volkov in fond remembrance. D. Shostakovich. 13 XI 1974. A reminder of our conversations about Glazunov, Zoshchenko, Meierkhol'd. D. S.' Nothing about the picture itself or the inscription betrays any special degree of intimacy or conspiracy. The politely posed figures of Irina Shostakovich, Boris Tishchenko, Shostakovich and Volkov, the use of Volkov's full name and the specific wording (in Russian) of the inscription – all betoken a more formal relationship than the one we are expected to believe existed. And why are only three names mentioned? Shostakovich might have inscribed the picture in a manner both more personal and more pointed, 'A reminder of our conversations', which would have implied much more as a document of authentication. The inscription could, in my view, as well be read as a *precise* reference to the limited content of their conversations and not a blanket acknowledgement.[22]

According to Fay, the inscription on the frontispiece photo suggests a 'more formal relationship than the one we are expected to believe existed'.[23] Undoubtedly, she would also question Shostakovich's inscription on the score of his Thirteenth Symphony, presented to Volkov after work on *Testimony* had begun: 'To dear Solomon Moiseyevich Volkov with my very best wishes. D. Shostakovich. 3 V 1972. Repino' (reproduced between pages 142 and 143/182 and 183 of the memoirs). What Fay fails to mention is that the wording in both of these inscriptions ('in fond remembrance' and 'with my very best wishes') is typical of the composer. Krzysztof Meyer notes that Shostakovich had standard dedications that he almost automatically wrote down for everybody, close and distant acquaintances, autograph collectors and friends: 'With fond memories' or 'With best

[21] For a detailed discussion of *Rothschild's Violin, cf.* pp. 128–33.

[22] Fay, p. 492.

[23] *Ibid.*, p. 492.

wishes'.[24] Fay also forgets (or does not know) that Shostakovich was exceptionally polite and formal in his speech, dedications and inscriptions, and usually did use full names, even with children. Finally, as Russian experts should know, the use of the patronymic in Russian does not necessarily imply distance in a relationship, but may also reflect degrees of respect and differences in ages.

The formality of Shostakovich's language was well known to his family, friends and colleagues. Meyer recalls that Shostakovich addressed very few people by their Christian names and that he would refer even to his closest friends in a formal way or by means of their patronymic. Thus to Sollertinsky he would say 'Ivan Ivanovich', to Glikman 'Isaak Davidovich'.[25] Shostakovich's son-in-law, Yevgeny Chukovsky, adds:

> [The chauffeur] Alexander L'vovich Lemonade [actually Limonadov] was a nice fellow, and everybody called him just Sasha; that is everybody except Dmitri Dmitriyevich, who always addressed people, irrespective of who they were, with the formal name and patronymic. Dmitri Dmitriyevich didn't like familiarity, and was constantly bewildered at how, in the cinema studio, for instance, harassed and grey-haired employees who had worked there all their lives continued to call each other by the diminutives 'Petya' and 'Kolya'. He told us that even when he had occasion to teach at a children's music school he had imposingly addressed all the children by their name and patronymic, preparing them for future adult life.[26]

Still more revealing are the dedications on Shostakovich's compositions. From the juvenilia, such as the Scherzo, Op. 1 (1919), to the Viola Sonata (1975), proofs of which he corrected four days before his death, Shostakovich consistently used the dedicatee's full name, even with his fiancée and first wife Nina Varzar, third wife Irina, son Maxim, and long-time friends and colleagues, such as Atovmyan, Glikman, Malko, Mravinsky, Oistrakh, Rostropovich, Shebalin, Sollertinsky and Vishnevskaya. One wonders why Fay should

[24] Meyer, p. 56.

[25] *Ibid.*, p. 2.

[26] Wilson, p. 283.

expect Shostakovich to refer to Volkov in more familiar terms than he does to his first and third wives and, especially, to his then nineteen-year-old son:

Dedications on Shostakovich's Works[27]

Fantasy for Two Pianos (Aleksandr Konstantinovich Glazunov)
Scherzo, Op. 1 (Maksimilian Oseyevich Shteinberg)
Tahiti Trot, Op. 16 (To dear Nikolay Andreyevich Mal'ko, as a token of my best feelings. D. Shostakovich. 1.X.27. Leningrad)
Six Romances on Japanese Poems, Op. 21 (Nina Vasil'yevna Varzar)
Lady Macbeth, Op. 29 (Nina Vasil'yevna Varzar)
Cello Sonata, Op. 40 (Viktor L'vovich Kubatsky)
Piano Sonata No. 2, Op. 61 (To the memory of Leonid Vladimirovich Nikolayev)
Six Romances on Verses by British Poets, Op. 62 (Lev Tadevosovich Atovmyan; Nina Vasil'yevna Shostakovich; Isaak Davidovich Glikman; Yury [Georgy] Vasil'yevich Sviridov; Ivan Ivanovich Sollertinsky; Vissarion Yakovlevich Shebalin)
Symphony No. 8, Op. 65 (Yevgeny Aleksandrovich Mravinsky)
Piano Trio No. 2, Op. 67 (To the memory of Ivan Ivanovich Sollertinsky)
Quartet No. 2, Op. 68 (Vissarion Yakovlevich Shebalin)
Violin Concerto No. 1, Op. 77 (David Fyodorovich Oistrakh)
Piano Concerto No. 2, Op. 102 (Maksim Dmitriyevich Shostakovich)
Cello Concerto No. 1, Op. 107 (Mstislav Leopol'dovich Rostropovich)
Quartet No. 7, Op. 108 (To the memory of Nina Vasil'yevna Shostakovich)

[27] Compiled from Hulme, *Catalogue*, and Volkov, 'Tea for Two', p. 224. Hulme, in a letter to the authors (26 October 1995), confirmed that 'Dmitri Shostakovich did use full names and patronymics for all his dedicatees except on Opus 2 when he gave the initials 'N.K' (I filled in the name Natasha Kuba). The dedications on your list all came from facsimile and printed scores or Sadovnikov's catalogue [1965]'.

Schumann's Cello Concerto [re-orchestration], Op. 125 (Mstislav Leopol'dovich Rostropovich)
Satires, Op. 109 (Galina Pavlovna Vishnevskaya)
Musorgsky's *Songs and Dances of Death* [orchestration] (Galina Pavlovna Vishnevskaya)
Quartet No. 9, Op. 117 (Irina Antonovna Shostakovich)
Quartet No. 10, Op. 118 (Moisey Samuilovich Vainberg)
Cello Concerto No. 2, Op. 126 (Mstislav Leopol'dovich Rostropovich)
Seven Romances on Poems of Aleksandr Blok, Op. 127 (Galina Pavlovna Vishnevskaya)
Violin Concerto No. 2, Op. 129 (David Fyodorovich Oistrakh)
Violin Sonata, Op. 134 (David Fyodorovich Oistrakh)
Suite on Verses of Michelangelo, Op. 145 (Irina Antonovna Shostakovich)
Viola Sonata, Op. 147 (Fyodor Serafimovich Druzhinin)

Fay also questions the second half of Shostakovich's inscription: 'A reminder of our conversations about Glazunov, Zoshchenko, Meierkhol'd. D. S.' 'Why are only three names mentioned?', she asks: Shostakovich could have inscribed the picture in a manner 'both more personal and more pointed'. She then concludes that this 'inscription could, in my view, [. . .] be read as a *precise* reference to the limited content of their conversations and not a blanket acknowledgement'.[28] Fay's argument, again, lacks perspective. She dismisses, without careful consideration, the possibility that Glazunov, Zoshchenko and Meyerhold, three of the main figures in Shostakovich's memoirs, are merely representative and not all-inclusive.[29] Her question, 'Why only three names?', calls to mind Steinberg's complaint, mocked by Shostakovich in *Testimony*, about pairs of names in a speech by Stalin:

This was his [Stalin's] first major speech since the war began

[28] Fay, p. 492.

[29] For example, Glazunov may have been mentioned because he was a central figure in Shostakovich's youth and because Shostakovich's reminiscences of Glazunov had been cut from his preface to *Young Composers of Leningrad*, published just a few years earlier. Meyerhold and Zoshchenko,

> and he spoke, in part, about the great Russian nation – the nation of Pushkin and Tolstoy, Gorky and Chekhov, Repin and Surikov . . . and so on. You know, two of every living creature. And of the composers, Stalin singled out only Glinka and Tchaikovsky for praise. This injustice shook Steinberg to the very foundations of his being.[30]

Just as Shostakovich readily dismissed Steinberg's complaint, he probably gave little thought to the exact number of names in his inscription on *Testimony's* frontispiece photo. For Shostakovich, questions such as 'Why only two names?' or 'Why only three?' were the concerns of 'a musician of limited scope'.[31] Of course, what Fay (like Steinberg) really is questioning is not just the number of names, but the selection. Why didn't Shostakovich write: 'A reminder of my attacks on Stalin, Khrennikov and the Soviet system'? This, after all, would have been 'more pointed' and would have validated the controversial portions of *Testimony*. It also might have got Shostakovich shot.[32] Shostakovich may have been a *yurodivy*, but he was not a fool.

Fay's description of the frontispiece photo itself is accurate: 'Nothing about the picture itself [. . . the politely posed figures of Irina Shostakovich, Boris Tishchenko, Shostako-

---

on the other hand, represented victims – one shot, the other made to lose his mind, one a teacher figure, the other a contemporary. *Cf.* also p. 140, note 90.

[30] *Testimony*, p. 50/67. (Steinberg expected a reference to Rimsky-Korsakov, his father-in-law.)

[31] *Ibid.*, p. 50/67. One wonders if Fay is similarly troubled by trios of names elsewhere in Shostakovich's works. Consider *Rayok*: its preface mentions Yasrustovsky, Srulin, and Srurikov, three officials whose names had been subtly altered to include 'sru', the root of the verb 'to shit', while the score itself spotlights three trios of personalities – Yedinitsyn, Dvoikin, and Troikin on the podium, and Glinka, Tchaikovsky, Rimsky-Korsakov and Glinka, Dzerzhinka, Tishinka in their speeches.

[32] Or at least 'in big trouble'. It is important to remember that Shostakovich's own 'sense of danger', unrealistic as it may have been in the 1970s, was formed in the 1930s and '40s, when people did get shot for such things. Shebalin warned Shostakovich that he could be shot for his anti-Stalinist satire *Rayok* (Wilson, p. 296), and Shostakovich, in forgiving Sollertinsky for condemning *Lady Macbeth* in 1936, stated: 'Ivan Ivanovich, you had to

vich and Volkov] betrays any special degree of intimacy or conspiracy'.[33] But again she errs in expecting Shostakovich to have displayed the closeness of his relationships in posed photographs. Examination of numerous photographs in *Testimony*, Wilson's *Shostakovich: A Life Remembered*, Grigoryev and Platek's *Shostakovich: About Himself and His Times*, N. V. Lukyanova's *Shostakovich: His Life and Times* and Khentova's many studies reveals that Shostakovich usually was not demonstrative before cameras, the most emotional images being those captured spontaneously after a performance of his music. In proper perspective, therefore, Shostakovich's pose with Volkov is no more distant than others with his mother, wives, son and long-time friends, and probably reflects nothing more than the awkwardness he describes in *Testimony*:

> I wonder if the public knows how historic photographs are taken. When two 'celebrities' are seated next to each other and they don't know what to talk about. The traditional method is to say to each other with a smile, 'What do we talk about, when we have nothing to say?' Flash. The other method, which I myself invented, is to say, 'Eighty-eight, eighty-eight'. You don't even have to smile, because the words stretch your lips into a smile and you give the impression of having a lively conversation.[34]

---

denounce me, because your life is still ahead . . . You must stay alive . . . It's not clear what will come of me, they'll probably shoot me' (G. Glikman, 'Shostakovich As I Knew Him', Vol. 38, p. 341). Along similar lines, Shostakovich in *Testimony* acknowledges that 'awaiting execution is a theme that has tormented me all my life' (p. 140/183) and Maxim remembers that 'under Stalin, everyday as Shostakovich left home, he would take a small packet of soap and a toothbrush with him, not knowing if he would return' (Albert, p. 406). Many of Shostakovich's friends recall his familiar refrain: 'I never was arrested, but it's not too late, not too late' (conversation between Volkov and the authors, August 1995; *cf.* *Testimony*, p. 92/122: 'I wasn't sent to the camps, but it's never too late'). In addition, Anaida Sumbatyan reported meeting Shostakovich in an elevator and hearing him say: 'Your phone is still working? Mine is not, mine is not', in apparent reference to his impending arrest (conversation between Anaida Sumbatyan and Dmitry Feofanov, 1974; *cf.* also p. 9).

[33] Fay, p. 492.

[34] *Testimony*, p. 214/275.

Another photograph in *Testimony* that has been attacked unjustly is the one depicting Volkov at Shostakovich's funeral. In 'The Opera and the Dictator', Taruskin writes:

> In the days following Dmitri Shostakovich's burial in August 1975, a story went around Moscow of a bearded stranger [Volkov] who elbowed his way through the crowd of mourners at the bier until he stood right between the composer's widow, Irina, and his daughter, Galina. He stood there for no more than the time it took a woman, who popped up just as mysteriously at the other side of the deceased, to snap a picture, whereupon the two of them disappeared. The picture may be seen facing page 183 in *Testimony: The Memoirs of Dmitri Shostakovich as Related to and Edited by Solomon Volkov*. [. . .] Later that year, together with his wife Marianna, a professional photographer, he joined the great wave of Soviet Jewish emigration that followed in the wake of détente.[35]

The spreading of such libellous and unsubstantiated gossip is unbecoming a self-described 'proper scholar'.[36] Equally unbecoming is Taruskin's insinuation that Marianna Volkov, 'a professional photographer', was the 'mysterious woman' at the funeral. Had Taruskin checked his facts rather than engaging in tabloid musicology, he might have ascertained that the picture opposite p. 143/183 (together with others depicting different moments) actually was taken by a (male) TASS photographer, V. Mastyukov,[37] and only later obtained by Volkov. Furthermore, eyewitnesses (including Maxim and Galina Shostakovich and Rodion Shchedrin)[38] and additional photographs taken at Shostakovich's funeral verify that Volkov was in attendance far longer than 'the time it took [. . .] to snap a picture'. A photograph of Solomon and

[35] Taruskin, 'Dictator', p. 34.

[36] *Cf.* p. 38.

[37] Interview with ITAR-TASS personnel, Moscow, May 1996.

[38] Conversations between Volkov and the authors, August 1995, and Galina Shostakovich and the authors, October 1995. Maxim Shostakovich, Shchedrin and Aram Khachaturian all demonstratively embraced Volkov at the Novodevichy Cemetery, despite the fact that he was *persona non grata* as one who had applied to emigrate.

Marianna Volkov following Shostakovich's coffin while it was still at the Moscow Conservatory, where the memorial service took place (that is, hours before the burial), is included in Khentova's book *Shostakovich. Thirty Years 1945–1975*;[39] three other photographs taken at the Novodevichy Cemetery, each with a different mourner in the foreground and Volkov in the background (thereby documenting his presence longer than the time it takes to snap one picture), are also reproduced in the Appendix to this essay.[40]

This obsession with photographs is, apparently, not limited to Fay and Taruskin. Gavriil Glikman recalls that Khentova, the author of many books and articles on Shostakovich, wanted him to draw a picture of Dmitry Dmitriyevich listening to Khentova reading one of her books:[41]

> The husband of this musicologist once asked me: 'Gavriil Davidovich, I will pay you well (!) – would you please draw a picture in which my wife reads a manuscript to Shostakovich. We were not able to make a photograph during his life – can you imagine what kind of loss it is for us?'[42]

In fact, such a picture was made (though not by Glikman),

[39] Sofiya Khentova, *Shostakovich. Tridtsatiletiye 1945–1975* (*Shostakovich. Thirty Years 1945–1975*), Sovetsky Kompozitor, Leningrad, 1982, after p. 288 (hereafter *Shostakovich. Thirty Years*); *cf*. p. 308. Although this photograph is small and includes many people, Volkov's image is unmistakable (three heads directly behind the left edge of the coffin). Others who were in this procession have confirmed Volkov's position in this photograph.

[40] *Cf*. pp. 308–9.

[41] Khentova has published at least 'fifteen books and hundreds of articles on Shostakovich' (Laurel Fay, paper), including *Shostakovich and Siberia*, *Shostakovich in Petrograd-Leningrad*, *Shostakovich in Moscow*, *Shostakovich in Volgograd* and *Shostakovich in Ukraine*.

[42] G. Glikman, 'Shostakovich As I Knew Him', Vol. 38, p. 330. Khentova's desire for a picture may have been an indirect result of *Testimony* – that is, Volkov got a picture but she did not. It is interesting that Khentova was 'not able to make a photograph [with Shostakovich] during his life'. Shostakovich, apparently, was not a fool to get photographed with just anyone.

and published – three times.[43] It is ironic that real photographs are used to attack the authenticity of *Testimony*, while a fake goes unchallenged.

3. *Rothschild's Violin*

Fay and Taruskin's misinterpretation of inscriptions and photographs in *Testimony* is indicative of larger fallacies in their research. For example, in challenging the closeness of the Volkov-Shostakovich relationship, Fay also questions the significance of Volkov's April 1968 resurrection of *Rothschild's Violin*, an opera begun by Veniamin Fleishman in 1939 and completed by Shostakovich in 1944. She begins by distorting Volkov's words in his Preface: 'Volkov strongly implies that this [1968 production] was the *first* and *only* performance of the work'.[44] She then proceeds to prove him wrong by mentioning a performance at the Moscow Composers' Union on 20 June 1960 and a radio broadcast in February 1962. But Volkov never implies that the 1968 production was the work's first performance. Quite the contrary, he makes clear, four times, that the significance of his production was that it was staged (unlike the concert – unstaged – performances in 1960 and 1962):

> I decided that *Rothschild's Violin* had to be staged. [... In Leningrad, April 1968, a] marvellous opera was born onstage, and with it a new opera theatre – the Experimental Studio of Chamber Opera. [...] Then the official administrators of culture accused all of us of Zionism: poor Chekhov, poor

[43] Painted by Solomon Gershov, it was included in Khentova's *Shostakovich. Thirty Years*, after p. 288, then reappeared in Khentova's *Shostakovich*, Vol. 2, again after page 288. Finally, a new version by the same painter was used as the frontispiece of Khentova's *Amazing Shostakovich*. In his reminiscences (*DSCH Journal*, No. 2, Winter 1994, pp. 3–6, and *DSCH Journal*, No. 3, Summer 1995, pp. 6–11), Solomon Gershov mentions trying to get Shostakovich to sit for a painting (a difficult thing to do given Shostakovich's nervous nature) but does not mention any joint sitting of Shostakovich with Khentova, seemingly corroborating Gavriil Glikman's account of how this one came into existence.

[44] Fay, pp. 491–92.

> Fleishman. Their resolution read: 'The staging of the opera pours water on the enemy's mill' – and it meant an irreversible closing of the production. [... T]he opera was never staged again.[45]

Fay continues her attack by challenging Volkov's statement that 'the only thing available to researchers is the score, written from beginning to end in Shostakovich's characteristic nervous handwriting'.[46] She then points out that 'the piano score had been published, with a foreword by A. Livshits, in 1965'.[47] Again Volkov is nearer the truth, while Fay has feasted off the Soviet platter, without question or qualification. Confusion as to how much of *Rothschild's Violin* was completed by Fleishman and how much by Shostakovich remains to the present day. According to Yakubov:

> Shostakovich made his orchestration not from sketches, but from a piano score which exists in manuscript, partially in Fleishman's hand and partially in that of a copyist. Shostakovich, in the preface to his score, stated that he had merely finished editing and orchestrating the manuscript, and that he marked in his score everywhere that Fleishman's score was 'untouched'. Actually, Shostakovich also completed some portions of the vocal part and the orchestral episode at the end [which is lacking in the piano score]. Undoubtedly, Kirkor

[45] *Testimony*, pp. x–xi/xiii–xiv. Fay's source, G. Golovinsky, 'S lubov'yu k cheloveku' ('With Love towards Men'), *Sovetskaya Muzyka*, 1962, No. 5, p. 34, makes clear that *Rothschild's Violin* had not yet been performed in the theatres; furthermore, A. Livshits' preface in V. I. Fleishman, *Skripka Rotshil'da*, ed. Georgy Kirkor, Muzyka, Moscow, 1965, also mentions only concert (unstaged) performances. In his interview with Drubachevskaya and symposium with Robinson, pp. 317–19 and 391, Volkov again describes the 1968 performance as the first staged production. Khentova concurs:

> After the war [...] the opera was played on the radio. On 20 June 1960, at the Composers' Union, there was a premiere in concert performance. The staged premiere was mounted by the Experimental Studio of Chamber Opera in the Great Hall of the Leningrad Conservatory [i.e., Volkov's group].
>
> Khentova, *Shostakovich*, Vol. 2, p. 76.

[46] *Testimony*, p. x/xiii.

[47] Fay, p. 492.

made his piano reduction (probably on Shostakovich's initiative) with consideration of Shostakovich's score [because it includes the new ending].[48]

Much of the misinformation about *Rothschild's Violin*, printed by Livshits, then regurgitated by Fay, can be traced to Shostakovich himself. In the preface to his orchestration (now in the Central Archives of Literature and Art, Moscow), he gives his favourite pupil more credit than was due:

> Veniamin Fleishman worked on the score of *Rothschild's Violin* from 1939 to the summer of 1941, when the war broke out. By that time the piano score of the opera and the bigger part of the full score were completed ... Fleishman volunteered for service at the very beginning of the war. Since then nothing has been heard of him. He was probably killed early in the war. Before going off to the front he left the manuscript of the opera at the Leningrad Composers' Union. At the end of 1943 the manuscript was delivered to me. All I had to do was to complete the orchestration and copy the author's pencil score. Dmitri Shostakovich. Moscow, February 5, 1944.[49]

Shostakovich also referred to Fleishman's manuscript in a letter of May 1942 to another pupil in Leningrad, Orest Yevlakhov:

> I am sorry not to have taken *Rothschild's Violin* with me. I could have completed its orchestration. Dear friend, if the opera is still at the Leningrad Composers' Union, please take care of it, and still better make a copy of it and if possible send it to me in Kuibyshev when the occasion arises. I like the opera very much and am worried it may get lost ...[50]

Both of these passages make clear that *Rothschild's Violin* was a work close to Shostakovich's heart. What is, perhaps, less evident is that Shostakovich actually orchestrated half of

[48] Interview with Manashir Yakubov, March 1995.

[49] Gennady Rozhdestvensky, liner notes to Melodiya A10–00019 (1983; hereafter Rozhdestvensky, liner notes). Only later did it become known that Fleishman, born 20 July 1913, had been killed on 14 September 1941, in the district of Luga, Krasnoye Village, near Leningrad.

[50] Rozhdestvensky, liner notes. One wonders if the pages in the hand of a copyist, mentioned by Yakubov, originated at this time.

the opera, 'noting[,] with touching tact, the number of bars',[51] and finished several parts (as confirmed by Yakubov).[52] The complete piano score that Shostakovich mentions in his inscription has never been located.[53] In light of this information, Volkov's complete statement makes sense: 'Before he [Fleishman] left for the front, he *allegedly finished the reduction*. But the only thing available to researchers is the score, *written from beginning to end* in Shostakovich's characteristic nervous handwriting'.[54] Volkov actually used Kirkor's piano reduction, cited by Fay, in rehearsals for the 1968 staging; but even at this early date he questioned Fleishman's role in the composition and orchestration of *Rothschild's Violin*.[55]

The importance of *Rothschild's Violin* to Shostakovich is evident on several pages in *Testimony*. In fact, here, in his memoirs, he comes closest to disclosing the true genesis of the work:

> my student Veniamin Fleishman wrote an opera based on Chekhov's 'Rothschild's Violin'. I suggested he do an opera on the subject. [. . .] Fleishman sketched out the opera but then volunteered for the army. He was killed. [. . .] I'm happy that I managed to *complete* Rothschild's Violin *and orchestrate it*. [. . .] I'm sorry that our theatres pass over Fleishman's opera. It's certainly not the fault of the music, as far as I can see.[56]

[51] Rozhdestvensky, liner notes. The following indications appear in the full score: 'From the start to 17, 7th bar, the orchestration is my work. D. Shostakovich'; 'From 18, 1st bar, to 91, I've copied V. L. Fleishman's score. D. Shostakovich'; and 'From 92, 1st bar, to the end, the orchestration is my work. D. Shostakovich' (*cf.* the libretto accompanying Rozhdestvensky's second recording of the work, RCA 68434–2).

[52] Interview with Yakubov, March 1995.

[53] Interview with Yakubov, March 1995.

[54] *Testimony*, p. x/xiii; emphasis added.

[55] Volkov has always questioned the extent of Fleishman's work on the opera, as also in his lecture 'Shostakovich and the Jewish Motif', Jewish Music Society, Toronto, March 1991.

[56] *Testimony*, p. 173–74/225; emphasis added.

Shostakovich also may have been alluding to his own 'hidden' hand in the work when he recalled another opera, Borodin's *Prince Igor*, being completed by Glazunov, his mentor. Supposedly, the Overture and entire third act had been written 'from memory', Glazunov merely recalling what Borodin had composed:

> But when he [Glazunov] was in his cups [i.e., drunk, . . .] he would admit that it wasn't 'from memory' – he simply wrote for Borodin. This says many good things about Glazunov [. . .]. It doesn't happen often that a man composes excellent music for another composer and doesn't advertise it (to talk while drinking doesn't count). It's usually the other way around – a man steals an idea or even a considerable piece of music from another composer and passes it off as his own.[57]

In *Testimony*, Volkov states that 'for Shostakovich *Rothschild's Violin* represented unhealed guilt, pity, pride, and anger: neither Fleishman nor his work was to be resurrected. The defeat brought us closer together'.[58] Recently, he has elaborated on this point:

> Having staged Fleishman's opera, we touched something that was very dear and important to Shostakovich. Two themes came together here: Shostakovich and the Jews, and Shostakovich and the war. It was quite painful for Shostakovich to accept that a very young Jew, his own pupil, had volunteered to go to the front and had been killed. Dmitry Dmitriyevich himself had a terrible guilt complex regarding his 'sitting on the fence' during the war.[59]
>
> [. . .] the staging of Fleishman's opera caused a stir. Even after the very successful premiere we were summoned to appear in front of an extremely important official, who asked us: 'Are you aware that you are playing into the enemy's hands? This is a Zionist opera!' It was absurd to talk about Zionism in this respect, but this official, who had not read Chekhov, naturally

[57] *Ibid.*, pp. 123–24/162. Shostakovich provides several examples of such theft, mentioning Mukhtar Ashrafi as well as a woman in the Composers' Union who had plagiarised from William Schuman (*Testimony*, pp. 132/172–75). *Cf.* p. 268, note 59.

[58] *Testimony*, p. xi/xiv.

[59] *Cf.* p. 318.

> had not looked into the opera very closely. Just because the name 'Rothschild' had been mentioned, it meant Zionism. Shostakovich was aware of all our torments, and this drew us even closer together. It was at that time that I got the idea of writing a book on the young composers of Leningrad and Dmitry Dmitriyevich agreed to write a preface.[60]

Although Fay seems not to perceive the importance of issues raised in such statements,[61] Timothy Jackson and other scholars recognise the true significance of *Rothschild's Violin* in the Volkov-Shostakovich relationship:

> Volkov showed great courage in daring to produce an opera on a Jewish theme at a time [1968, less than a year after the Six-Day War] when anything remotely Jewish was discouraged if not forbidden by the authorities. This opera is intimately connected with the early formation of Shostakovich's Jewish identity and, by staging it, Volkov touched a chord in Shostakovich's innermost being. Thus, he began to earn the trust which later made *Testimony* possible.[62]

4. Biography or Memoirs?

Besides challenging the Volkov-Shostakovich relationship described in *Testimony*, Fay also questions whether 'Volkov misrepresented the nature and contents of the book to Shostakovich just as he may be misrepresenting them to the reader'.[63] She asks 'Was this book originally conceived as biographical?', but provides little evidence to support her suggestion that only later did *Testimony* become 'memoirs'. Fay mentions Irina Shostakovich's surprise that Volkov 'could have gathered enough material from Dmitrich for such

[60] *Cf.* p. 319.

[61] Fay, p. 492.

[62] Timothy L. Jackson, 'Dmitry Shostakovich: The Composer as Jew', pp. 604–5, below (hereafter Jackson). Just a few years earlier, Shostakovich himself had come into conflict with the authorities over the Jewishness of his Thirteenth Symphony (1962).

[63] Fay, p. 491.

a thick book'.[64] Otherwise, her only proof is an 'ironic [...] note accompanying Volkov's article "Artistry as Dissent", *N. Y. Times*, 16 April 1978, p. E19, in which the author was described as "working, at Columbia University, on a biography of Dmitri Shostakovich"'.[65] This citation is typical of Fay's research. She suggests a Freudian slip, an admission by Volkov that *Testimony* was a biography in progress in 1978. What she fails to make clear is that her 'ironic note' comes from a brief biographical blurb added by an anonymous copy editor after the end of Volkov's article. This is hardly the type of 'hard evidence' expected in a scholarly article.

Fay's suspicion that Volkov may first have been working on a traditional biography stems, in part, from the lack of tape recordings of, or witnesses to, the Volkov-Shostakovich conversations. Volkov, in his Preface, explains that 'we discarded the idea of taping for a variety of reasons, chief among them the fact that Shostakovich would stiffen before a microphone like a rabbit caught in a snake's gaze. It was a reflex reaction to his obligatory official radio speeches'.[66] He also states that while a senior editor of *Sovetskaya Muzyka*, which was located in the same building as Shostakovich's apartment, Shostakovich would call him to work on *Testimony* 'usually early in the morning, when the office was still empty'.[67] Fay points out, 'In other words, there were no witnesses'.[68] What she fails to mention, however, is that although the actual Volkov-Shostakovich conversations, for obvious reasons, were kept confidential, witnesses are available to confirm that Volkov and Shostakovich met regularly in the early 1970s to work on the latter's *memoirs*. Volkov has stated repeatedly that he originally intended to have *Testimony* published in the Soviet Union. When asked about this again in 1992, he responded:

[64] *Ibid.*, p. 485. For Volkov's response to Irina's statement, *cf.* pp. 76–80.

[65] *Ibid.*, p. 491, note 21.

[66] *Testimony*, p. xiii/xvi.

[67] *Ibid.*, p. xiii/xvii.

[68] Fay, p. 491.

> Yes, sure, sure. And that's why I never made a secret out of it.[69] And everybody, all of my colleagues in *Sovetskaya Muzyka*, knew about it; also the chief editor [Yury Semyonovich Korev] of the magazine knew and they even encouraged it because eventually they wanted to publish it.[70]

Fay, too, acknowledges Volkov's claim (first stated in *Testimony*), but instead of investigating the matter, is content, again, to twist Volkov's words. Volkov states: 'It was clear to both of us that this final text could not be published in the U.S.S.R.; several attempts I made in that direction ended in failure'.[71] Here, two phrases, both in the past tense, are juxtaposed. A reasonable person would understand that the realisation that *Testimony* could not be published in the USSR resulted from several failed attempts to do so. But Fay

[69] This was confirmed by the late Rostislav Dubinsky, who recalled Volkov telling him and other members of the Borodin Quartet in 1974 about his meetings with Shostakovich, how he would write everything down carefully, and later Shostakovich would check it (*cf.* p. 64, note 59). Had Volkov fabricated this story, he would have been extraordinarily bold in bandying it about to performers as close to Shostakovich as was the Borodin Quartet, while the composer was still alive and able to deny it.

[70] Robinson, p. 393.

[71] *Testimony*, p. xvii–xviii. Censorship was intrinsic to Soviet life: *cf.* A. V. Blyum, *Za kulisami 'ministerstva pravdy': Tainaya istoriya sovetskoy tsenzury, 1917–29* (*Backstage at the 'Ministry of Truth'. Secret History of Soviet Censorship, 1917–29*), Akademichesky Proekt, St Petersburg, 1994; D. L. Banichenko, *Pisateli i tsenzory* (*Writers and Censors*), Rossiya Molodaya, Moscow, 1994; D. L. Banichenko (ed.), *'Literaturny front': Istoriya politicheskoy tsenzury 1932–1946* (*'Literary Front': History of Political Censorship 1932–1946*), Entsiklopediya Rossiyskikh Dereven', Moscow, 1994; and the numerous examples and discussion of Soviet censorship in K. Chukovsky, *Dnevnik, 1901–1929* (*Diary*; Vol. 1), Sovetsky Pisatel', Moscow, 1991, and *Dnevnik, 1930–1969* (*Diary*; Vol. 2), Sovremenny Pisatel', Moscow, 1994. Examples of musical censorship include a speech by Prokofiev in 1944, which was prepared for publication in 1975, but not published until 1991 (Rakhmanova, 'Afterword', p. 103). A particularly egregious example of 'Ministry of Truth scholarship' can be found in Prokofiev and Myaskovsky, *Pis'ma* (*Letters*), p. 181. There, in a letter of 3 January 1924, all cuts are allegedly indicated, but a hidden cut (a disparaging comment about Russia) goes unmentioned. The original excerpt is reproduced on page 73 of Yu. Kremlyov's *Esteticheskiye vzglyady S. S. Prokof'yeva* (*Aesthetic Views of S. S. Prokofiev*), Muzyka, Leningrad, 1966. One wonders how many other such deletions await discovery.

places the cart before the horse, distorting Volkov's explanation. She asks, 'Knowing without a doubt that it could not be published in the Soviet Union, an assumption which subsequent events have decisively corroborated, why then did Volkov bother to make "several attempts [. . .] in that direction"?'[72]

Significantly, several of Volkov's colleagues at *Sovetskaya Muzyka* corroborate his statements, refuting the earlier 'official' claim that 'there is no supporting proof anywhere for Volkov's statements, except his own'.[73] In her interview with Volkov, Drubachevskaya acknowledges:

> I remember how one fine day you came to work at the editorial office of *Sovetskaya Muzyka*. You sat down at your desk and for a long time stared intently out the window. It was a very sunny day and the dirty red-brown wall of the opposite building seemed cheerful. I asked you what you saw out the window, what you were staring at. And you answered: 'I just came back from Shostakovich's. We are working on his memoirs. [. . .] He is so candid. His criticism is so frightening and caustic'. When, later on, you gave me the chapters that had already been reviewed by Shostakovich, I felt that the pages were impregnated with the smell of death not of a man, but of an era, an era with which, before departure, he decided to clear up the most important relations.[74]

In the same interview, Volkov states:

> Having heard about our conversations, he [Yury Korev] invited me to see him and expressed his interest in publishing some excerpts. I began to tell him how the material was taking shape, particularly in the case of Glazunov, Prokofiev and Stalin. And his response to me was that that kind of material could not appear in his magazine no matter whose lips it came from. Naturally I told Dmitry Dmitriyevich everything and he understood that the publication of his memoirs would be possible only in the West.[75]

[72] Fay, p. 493.

[73] Bonosky, p. 12.

[74] Drubachevskaya, pp. 315–16. When contacted in December 1993, Drubachevskaya confirmed the accuracy of this statement as well as her belief in the authenticity of *Testimony*.

[75] *Cf*. p. 320.

Volkov's comments about Korev were published in *Muzykal'naya Akademiya*, when Korev was its chief editor and in a position to object to false or misleading statements, especially about himself. But Korev did not object to publishing this material and, when contacted in March 1995, confirmed that 'Volkov, on numerous occasions, mentioned that he was working on a book of *memoirs* of Shostakovich, and that he [Korev] often asked see the materials, so that he would be "in the know", but somehow this did not work out'.[76]

Volkov also spoke of memoirs rather than a biography immediately after arriving in New York. Even Taruskin, in his letter of recommendation for Volkov (16 July 1976; i.e., two years before Fay's 'ironic' note), states that Volkov will

[76] Interview with Korev, Spring 1995. Korev admitted that he 'did not see a single line of Volkov's opus either in Russian or in English and knows the book only based on the reports of others'. This is consistent with Volkov's statement, before *Testimony* was published, that a preface and a description of the book's contents had been submitted to Soviet publishers, 'but I never showed them the entire book' (Mitgang, 'Shostakovich Memoir', p. C14).

In an interview in October 1996, Irina Shostakovich, alerted to the fact that Korev had corroborated some of Volkov's statements in the present publication, lashed out at the former editor-in-chief of *Sovetskaya Muzyka*:

> As regards Korev's story – the newspaper today has a miniscule circulation and is threatened with closure. And so he is looking for all kinds of ways to draw attention and to find a 'way out' of this situation. I find that it [is] dishonest of him to talk like this – to look to save himself in this way. I think that Korev's moral values are rather low.

'Remembering Shostakovich', *DSCH Journal*, No. 6, Winter 1996, p. 5.

As before (*cf.* pp. 76–84), Irina's comments are suspect. She had not actually read Korev's statements before attempting to discredit him (again 'denounce first, read later'); furthermore, Korev's position is not a recent turn-around precipitated by financial woes or job insecurity, but is on record from the early 1990s and was merely confirmed in early 1995. Significantly, Irina does not mention her own earlier statement (that before the publication of *Testimony*, 'Everyone whom this concerned knew about it. The journal *Sovetskaya Muzyka* knew about it as well'; *cf.* p. 135), nor does she make it clear how Korev will benefit from contradicting the words of Shostakovich's widow and corroborating statements by Volkov, who even today is *persona non grata* in many circles. For the record, Korev's comments reproduced herein were made freely, without any remuneration or even any discussion of remuneration.

be preparing 'Shostakovich's *memoirs* for publication'.[77] Taruskin again confirms Volkov's mention of memoirs in his 1989 article 'The Opera and the Dictator':

> Volkov disclosed to me that he had enjoyed a close, clandestine relationship with Shostakovich, and had elicited extensive memoirs from him during the last years of the composer's life. He was now awaiting their piecemeal arrival from various way stations in Europe, whither they had been smuggled by willing travelers. Their publication, he hinted, would fundamentally revise our image of Shostakovich, and also of a whole era in the history of Russian music, indeed of Russia itself.[78]

While suggesting that Volkov had fraudulently turned a biography into memoirs, Fay neglects clear evidence that Shostakovich himself had contemplated writing his autobiography, at least for the last twenty years of his life. Flora Litvinova, one Shostakovich's neighbours, wrote in her diary entry for 27 October 1956:

> We talked of his songs written to texts of Dolmatovsky [probably Op. 98]. I said that I didn't think much of them (in reality I didn't like them one little bit), and the words were terrible. 'Why did you write music to those texts?' I asked. Shostakovich replied, 'Yes, the songs are bad, very bad. They are simply extremely bad.' And I piped up again, 'But why did you write them?' He answered, 'One day I will write my autobiography, and there I will explain everything, and why I had to compose all this'.[79]

Had Fay 'meticulously tested *Testimony's* claims', as Taruskin averred in proclaiming her a *yurodivaya*,[80] she might have uncovered such information. At the very least, however, Fay should have been aware of Shostakovich's own statements from 1965 and 1973:

> I am now getting on in years, and it has been on my mind that I should start writing my memoirs, that I should write about the people who have been important in my life and for my

[77] *Cf*. pp. 81–83 and Appendix, Exhibit 1, p. 300; emphasis added.

[78] Taruskin, 'Dictator', p. 34.

[79] Wilson, pp. 269–70.

[80] Taruskin, 'Dictator', p. 34.

> music. One of the first of these would be Mikhail Tukhachevsky.[81]
>
> A few days ago I read the memoirs of Marietta Shaginian and Vera Panova and thought – what a pity I have not kept a diary or note-book, or written memoirs. I have met many interesting people and seen many interesting things ... No, I cannot say I live in the past; I live now, and will live longer – for a hundred years! But it is important to remember one's past. However, I have not given up hope of returning to this ...[82]

Shostakovich, actually, did 'return to this' idea of documenting his life. Flora Litvinova recalls the composer telling her, in the last years of his life, that he was now meeting 'constantly' with a young Leningrad musicologist, who writes down 'everything I remember about my works and myself'.[83] Maxim similarly acknowledged in November 1979 that his father 'was himself planning to write his memoirs. He even asked me to buy him an address book type of notebook to facilitate the writing'.[84] Although Maxim claimed that Shostakovich would not have asked for assistance in this project, evidence indicates otherwise. The composer could, and did, sometimes turn to friends and colleagues, such as Glikman and Zhitomirsky, for aid in writing.[85] Moreover, Edison Denisov recalled, 'I once asked him why he did not write his memoirs, and he said, "Edik, I

[81] Grigoryev and Platek, p. 261; originally in *Marshal Tukhachevsky*, Moscow, 1965. Tukhachevsky is, in fact, a prominent figure in *Testimony*.

[82] Grigoryev and Platek, p. 313; originally in *Komsomol'skaya Pravda*, 26 June 1973. Both of Shostakovich's statements also appear in the very first paragraph of the 'Introduction' in Grigoryev and Platek, p. 5.

[83] Litvinova, pp. 168–69. *Cf.* p. 251 below for the complete passage.

[84] *BBC Summary of World Broadcasts*, 26 November 1979, SU/6281/C/2 (available in LEXIS, News Library, Archiv file). Also *cf.* p. 82 for Irina Shostakovich's acknowledgement of her husband's interest in writing his memoirs.

[85] *Cf.* pp. 89–90. Many other articles were written by Composers' Union hacks and merely brought to Shostakovich for signing. In such cases, it is inaccurate to say that he used ghostwriters. On the contrary, ghostwriters used him – or rather the *apparat* foisted articles on him in order to firm up his public image as a loyal son.

am not a writer, I am not a writer". He didn't like writing'.[86] Given Shostakovich's distaste for writing, as well as his crippling hand problems of the 1960s–70s, it is easy to understand how Volkov, a professional journalist skilled in shorthand, became the necessary means to a desired end. In Volkov's words, 'I was a mouthpiece with specific gifts, one that was suitable for the work at hand, but still just a mouthpiece'.[87]

Shostakovich's motivations for working on *Testimony* are clear from the start:

> These are not memoirs about myself. These are memoirs about other people. Others will write about us. And naturally they'll lie through their teeth – but that's their business. [. . .] Looking back, I see nothing but ruins, only mountains of corpses. And I do not wish to build new Potemkin villages on these ruins. Let's try to tell only the truth. It's difficult. I was an eyewitness to many events and they were important events. I knew many outstanding people. I'll try to tell you what I know about them. I'll try not to colour or falsify anything. This will be the testimony of an eyewitness.[88]

Elsewhere, he emphasises the importance of correcting earlier mistakes and half-truths:

> What hurts is that here they lie about their own Russian musicians. Lately I've been thinking about my relationship with Glazunov. This is a special topic that's very important to me. As I see, it's also popular among those who are becoming interested in my humble self. They're writing about our relationship. Quite a bit, and it's all wrong.[89]

He also says that the plaque that reads 'In this house Meyerhold lived' should continue with 'And in this house his wife was brutally murdered',[90] and regrets that so many figures

[86] Wilson, p. 432.

[87] Drubachevskaya, p. 322.

[88] *Testimony*, p. 1/3.

[89] *Ibid*., p. 33/45.

[90] *Ibid*., p. 58/77. Almost immediately after Meyerhold's arrest on 20 June 1939, 'bandits came to [Zinaida] Raikh's house. They killed her. Seventeen knife wounds, and she was stabbed in the eyes' (*Testimony*, p. 59/79). Heikinheimo, who translated the Russian text of *Testimony* into Finnish, follows the phrase 'And in this house his wife was brutally murdered' with 'at the instigation of some official body' [absent in the English version]

important in his own life are virtually forgotten by the younger generation:

> It's so unfair. People suffered, worked, thought. So much wisdom, so much talent. And they're forgotten as soon as they die. We must do everything possible to keep their memories alive, because we will be treated the same way ourselves. How we treat the memory of others is how our memory will be treated. We must remember, no matter how hard it is.[91]

Finally, Shostakovich admits that the truth may hurt:

> I choose the truth. And perhaps it's hopeless and a mistake, because the truth always brings problems and dissatisfactions. Insulted citizens howl that you've hurt their most noble feelings and didn't spare the finest strings of their exalted soul.[92]

In preserving his memories, Shostakovich continued the tradition of many other Russian composers, who felt compelled to sum up their life's achievements in words. Glinka, for example, spent the last years of his life 'assembling his *Memoirs* in 1854, and then going through his own compositions and writing out from memory pieces that had been lost'.[93] Other composers who wrote important autobiographies or reminiscences include Nikolay Cherepnin,[94]

(Seppo Heikinheimo, 'Shostakovich: The Official Version', typescript, p. 4, provided courtesy of the author; a revised version of this article, without this passage, appeared in *Musical America* – *cf.* p. 48, note 9). Obviously, doing justice to Meyerhold's memory was extremely important to Shostakovich, hence the mention of his name on the frontispiece photo.

[91] *Testimony*, p. 22/31.

[92] *Ibid.*, pp. 33–34/46. Shostakovich was right! (*cf.* pp. 36–37, 52–53, 61–62 and 85–86).

[93] David Brown, 'Glinka', *New Grove Dictionary of Music and Musicians*, 6th edn., ed. Stanley Sadie, Macmillan, London, 1980, Vol. 7, p. 440.

[94] *Vospominaniya muzykanta* (*Reminiscences of a Musician*), Muzyka, Leningrad, 1976.

Mikhail Ippolitov-Ivanov,[95] Prokofiev,[96] Rimsky-Korsakov,[97] Anton Rubinstein,[98] Sergey Vasilenko[99] and, with collaborators, Aram Khachaturian,[100] Rachmaninov,[101] Shebalin[102] and Stravinsky.[103] Shostakovich, clearly, was no exception, either in writing memoirs (even in collaboration with another) or in speaking candidly and, at times, caustically about his contemporaries. He even seems to have been influenced by the autobiographies of Stravinsky and Rimsky-Korsakov. Stravinsky died in 1971, at the outset of work on *Testimony*, and Shostakovich refers several times to Stravinsky's memoirs while telling his own story.[104] In addition, Rimsky-Korsakov's *Chronicle of My Musical Life* remained one Shostakovich's favourite books. It was written over a

[95] *50 let russkoy muzyki v moikh vospominaniyakh* (*50 Years of Russian Music in my Reminiscences*), Muzgiz, Moscow, 1934.

[96] *Avtobiografiya*, ed. M. G. Kozlova, Sovetsky Kompozitor, Moscow, 1973; *Prokofiev by Prokofiev*, ed. David H. Appel, transl. Guy Daniels, Doubleday, Garden City, New York, 1979.

[97] *Chronicle of My Musical Life*, St. Petersburg, 1909; transl. J. Joffe, Alfred A. Knopf, New York, 1942.

[98] *Autobiography of Anton Rubinstein, 1829–1889*, Little, Brown, Boston, 1890; and Rubinstein with M. Semevsky, '"Avtobiograficheskiye rasskazy" Antona Rubinshteyna' ('"Autobiographical Stories" of Anton Rubinstein'), *Literaturnoye naslediye v tryokh tomakh* (*Literary Works in Three Volumes*), Muzyka, Moscow, 1983, Vol. 1, pp. 65–104.

[99] *Vospominaniya* (*Reminiscences*), Sovetsky Kompozitor, Moscow, 1979. Consider also the reminiscences by Vernon Duke, Musorgsky, Skryabin, Nicolas Slonimsky, Tchaikovsky (lost) and Dimitri Tiomkin.

[100] *Stranitsy zhizni i tvorchestva. Iz besed s G. M. Shneyersonom* (*Pages of Life and Work. From Conversations with G. M. Shneyerson*), Sovetsky Kompozitor, Moscow, 1982.

[101] *Rachmaninoff's Recollections told to Oskar von Riesemann*, transl. Dolly Rutherford, Macmillan Co., New York, 1934.

[102] Shebalin, 'Reminiscences', pp. 11–85.

[103] Various collaborations with Robert Craft.

[104] *Testimony*, pp. 3/6, 24/34 and 151–52/197–98; *cf*. also p. 262. Shostakovich seems to have long had an interest in biographies. In her diary for May 1943, Shaginyan notes that 'Now (as before) he [Shostakovich] is enthusiastic about other people's biographies, the diaries of Tchaikovsky, Verdi, etc., and he talks about them' (Shaginyan, p. 76).

period of thirty years, yet even Rimsky-Korsakov's closest friends were unaware of its contents; the composer also left specific directions that it be published only after his death.[105] The parallels between Rimsky-Korsakov's *Chronicle* and Shostakovich's *Testimony* are obvious.

5. Factual Discrepancies

Critics often forget that *Testimony* is a set of memoirs, not a Ph.D. dissertation, and that, as such, its text is selective, subjective and filtered through hindsight. Small errors, contradictions and omissions do not necessarily impeach *Testimony's* authenticity, nor do they automatically point the finger of blame at Solomon Volkov.[106] Yevtushenko, on the subject of memoirs, notes:

> when I wrote my *Precocious Autobiography*, I was absolutely convinced that everything in it was absolutely true, but [. . .] my mother found fifty-four mistakes! [. . . What] I can promise you [is] that I'm completely sincere when I say something – it's how I remember it now.[107]

Robert Heinlein also once quipped that 'autobiographies are usually honest, but never truthful'.[108]

[105] Nikolay Rimsky-Korsakov, *Polnoye Sobraniye Sochineny* (*Complete Works*), State Music Publishers, Moscow, 1955, Vol. 1, p. viii (the first complete publication, without any cuts). The composer's request was observed and an edition of his memoirs was first printed, posthumously, in 1909.

[106] Vladimir Ashkenazy has wisely noted that 'if there are any inaccuracies in *Testimony*, and I'm not sure that there are, I am sure that they arise out of the normal problems of recording interviews and conversations – just misunderstandings and misinterpretations. As far as the character and image of Shostakovich are concerned, I'm sure it is true to life' ('Shostakovich Was Not an Enigma', *DSCH*, No. xx, Spring 1992, p. 13) (hereafter Ashkenazy, 'Shostakovich').

[107] Robinson, pp. 379–80.

[108] Robert A. Heinlein, *Friday*, Ballantine Books, New York, 1982, p. 230.

Suspecting a forgery, Laurel Fay, among others, carefully scrutinised *Testimony* for all possible errors. In her 'conclusive' article, she reports that 'many factual discrepancies, both in the text of *Testimony* and in Volkov's annotations, have been uncovered'.[109] Unfortunately, only one of these passages, presumably her most convincing example, is discussed in detail:

> Shostakovich is quoted as saying in connection with his Fourth Symphony (1936):
>
> 'After all, for twenty-five years no one heard it and I had the manuscript. If I had disappeared, the authorities would have given it to someone for his "zeal". I even know who that person would have been and instead of being my Fourth, *it would have been the Second Symphony of a different composer*.' [emphasis added; p. 163/212]
>
> In his annotation to this passage, Volkov identifies the mysterious composer as Tikhon Khrennikov, the long-time head of the Composers' Union and a conspicuous target of Shostakovich's abuse. Unacknowledged either in the text or in the footnote is the well-known fact that Khrennikov's *own* Second Symphony was begun in 1940, first performed in 1943, performed again in revision in 1944, and published by 1950. Obviously, something is not quite right. But in this case, as in many others, it is difficult to tell whether the discrepancy should be attributed to faulty memory, or deliberate maliciousness on Shostakovich's part, or to inept scholarship on Volkov's part.[110]

The truth may, in fact, be closer to home. What 'obviously is not quite right' is Fay's own reading of this passage. Fay

[109] Fay, p. 486.

[110] Fay, p. 486. The passage quoted from *Testimony* follows Shostakovich's remark (p. 163/212) on the interchangeability of Soviet composers:

> The only thing that matters is the inexorable movement of the state mechanism. A mechanism needs only cogs. Stalin used to call all of us cogs. One cog does not differ from another, and cogs can easily replace one another. You can pick one out and say, 'From this day you will be a genius cog', and everyone else will consider it a genius. It doesn't matter whether it is or not. Anyone can become a genius on the orders of the leader. [...] it's impossible to forget that at any moment a new 'Red Shostakovich' can appear and I'll disappear.

applies the phrase 'for twenty-five years' to the second sentence, when it pertains only to the beginning of the first. Shostakovich expresses three ideas in these two sentences: (1) 'for twenty-five years no one heard it'; (2) 'I had the manuscript'; and (3) 'If I had disappeared, the authorities would have given it to someone for his "zeal"'. The phrase 'for twenty-five years' clearly does not apply to the second idea, since, earlier in *Testimony*, Shostakovich recalls:

> It's thanks to Gauk that the manuscripts of my Fourth, Fifth and Sixth Symphonies [were] lost [in 1941, during the siege of Leningrad]. And he replied to my feeble objections with: 'Manuscripts? So what? I lost a suitcase with my new shoes, and you're worried about manuscripts.[111]

If the phrase 'for twenty-five years' does not apply to the second idea, why, then, does Fay assume that it applies to the third, in a new, completely separate sentence? Instead of 'If I had disappeared [after 25 years]', as the text must be read in order to find 'something not quite right', Shostakovich meant simply 'If I had disappeared [after composing the work]'. The latter makes perfect sense. Khrennikov completed his First Symphony in 1935, Shostakovich his Fourth in 1935–36. If Shostakovich had 'disappeared' sometime between 1936 and 1942 – a distinct possibility[112] – before Khrennikov's own Second Symphony was completed, then Shostakovich's Fourth could, indeed, have become Khrennikov's (bogus) Second. Shostakovich had good reason to worry about 'disappearing' at this time (1936–42). In 1936 he had been attacked twice in *Pravda* (in the articles 'Muddle Instead of Music' (28 January 1936) and 'Ballet Falsehood' (6 February 1936)), and the 'Great Terror' of 1937 was about to begin.[113] By 1939, over seven million people had been arrested, including Shostakovich's friends Mikhail Tukhachevsky, who was shot in Summer 1937, and Vsevolod

[111] *Testimony*, p. 28/39; also *cf.* Wilson, pp. 90–91, 347–48, Hulme, *Catalogue*, p. 114, and Kondrashin, p. 509.

[112] *Cf.* p. 146, note 114.

[113] Robert Conquest, *The Great Terror: A Reassessment*, Hutchinson, London, 1990/Oxford University Press, New York, 1991.

Meyerhol'd, who 'disappeared' in Summer 1939 and died in prison six months later.[114]

Other 'troublesome' passages in *Testimony*[115] can be attributed more to differences in interpretation than to discrepancies in fact. For example, Craft's, Karlinsky's and Yakubov's questions about three different passages stem largely from misreadings of the text. Craft, complaining that Volkov 'fails to note discrepancies between Shostakovich's and other people's version of events',[116] takes particular exception to the description of a meeting between Stravinsky and Boris Yarustovsky in Moscow in 1962: 'Stravinsky offered his walking stick instead of his hand to one of these hypocrites [Yarustovsky], who was forced to shake it, proving that he was the real lackey'.[117] According to Craft:

> this is a gross misinterpretation. Stravinsky, extending his cane for help in climbing some stairs, was quite unaware that one of his Soviet biographers was on the other end of the stick. The composer often made this gesture – for example, in getting out of an automobile – but never insultingly.[118]

Craft totally misses the point. This episode is not an attack on Stravinsky's manners, but on Yarustovsky, whom Shostakovich obviously despised, having altered his name in *Rayok* to Yasrustovsky (or, as one writer translated it, something akin

[114] Wilson, pp. 120–21. The list of Shostakovich's friends and family who 'disappeared' around this time is extensive: in 1937 alone famous physicist Vsevolod Konstantinovich Frederiks (his brother-in-law), astronomer Sofiya Mikhailovna Varzar (his mother-in-law), and Maksim Lavrent'yevich Kostrikin (his uncle) all were arrested, and Mariya Shostakovich (his sister) was exiled from Leningrad; those who were executed included N. A. Zhilyayev, whom Shostakovich frequently visited, and Adrian Piotrovsky, who wrote the story for the ballet *The Limpid Stream* (*cf.* Khentova, 'Shostakovich: Legends and the Truth', p. 6). Shostakovich's position was made even more perilous by having relatives abroad: an aunt, the important physicist Nadezhda Vasil'yevna Galli-Shohat, and an uncle, Boris Boleslavovich Shostakovich. In *Out of the Red Shadows*, Gennadi Kostyrchenko provides several examples of how 'connections abroad' (in the form of relatives) often led to accusations of espionage and to repression.

[115] *Cf.* Fay, p. 486, note 11.

[116] Craft, 'Testaments', p. 80.

[117] *Testimony*, p. 24/34.

[118] Craft, 'Testaments', p. 81.

to 'I-shit-sky'[119]). Craft also suggests that Volkov should have verified this story with Vera Stravinsky in summer 1976, when she was asked to read his manuscript.[120] But Volkov's role was not to interpret, censor or validate Shostakovich's impressions, only to notate them accurately, whether or not they agreed with the memories of others.[121]

Karlinsky, in his review of *Testimony*, questions the manner in which Shostakovich attributes the suicide of Anastasia Chebotarevskaya in 1921 'to a trivial spat with her husband and describes [Fyodor] Sologub's despair in the wake of his loss in an insensitive, jeering tone that reduces a tragedy to ridiculous farce'.[122] The passage is as follows:

> The Sologubs lived very well. But one day mystical vapours thickened in their house, or they had a fight. In any case, one not very fine autumn evening Sologub's wife left the house and didn't return. [. . .] *Someone* had seen a woman throw herself into the Neva River from the bridge on that fateful night. [. . .] The poet suffered and emoted. He languished for his wife. *They say* he set a place for her at dinner every night. [. . .] Winter passed and spring arrived. The ice on the Neva broke and right in front of Sologub's house, by the Tuchkov Bridge, a drowned woman surfaced. [. . .] *This story* was much discussed. There was something mysterious about it. Why had the body surfaced right in front of Sologub's house? 'She came to say farewell', *one writer* decided.[123]

Karlinsky, too, misses the point. Shostakovich is not mocking Sologub or his wife, but the many who would turn this tragedy into something more than it is, something mystical. He attributes his 'facts' to others: 'Someone', 'they say', 'this story', 'one writer'. This mystery was also too much for Shostakovich's idol, Zoshchenko, who published a parody,

[119] Lebedinsky, 'Rayok', p. 31, note. *Cf.* pp. 275–76.

[120] Craft, 'Testaments', p. 81.

[121] The divergent views about Stravinsky, Prokofiev, Rachmaninov and others in *Testimony*, *Balanchine's Tchaikovsky* and *From Russia to the West* support Volkov's contention that he has no personal agenda to promote, but merely records his subjects' opinions as accurately as possible.

[122] Simon Karlinsky, 'Our Destinies are Bad', *Nation*, 24 November 1979, p. 535 (hereafter Karlinsky).

[123] *Testimony*, p. 8/12; emphasis added.

'The Lady with the Flowers'. The latter caused a scandal, but, like Shostakovich,

> Zoshchenko hadn't intended to mock Sologub at all. He was laughing at people who wove all sorts of nonsense out of a sad and altogether prosaic event. [. . .] So she drowned? Why turn Sologub and his wife, Chebotarevskaya, into Tristan and Isolde?[124]

Finally, Yakubov, in a recent issue of *Melos*, wonders why Shostakovich would say to Alban Berg, upon the latter's departure from Leningrad, 'So fly off . . . the sooner the better'. Yakubov points out that these words, from Pushkin's tragedy *Mozart and Salieri*, are 'spoken by Salieri at parting after he has put poison in Mozart's wine' and that 'Dmitry Dmitriyevich, who perfectly knew Russian literature, especially Pushkin and Gogol, [and also admired Berg's *Wozzeck*] [. . .] would never have put himself in such a ridiculous position'.[125] Some question remains, however, whether Shostakovich actually uttered Salieri's words to Berg or merely, in retrospect, considered Berg's hasty departure fortuitous. The passage reads: 'Berg, it seemed to me, left Leningrad with relief. "So fly off . . . the sooner the better", as Pushkin wrote'.[126] Between Berg's departure in 1927 and the writing of *Testimony*, Shostakovich had witnessed, repeatedly, the poisoning of talent in the USSR, the killing of creativity even in its greatest composers. 'Yes, get out of here, the sooner the better', Shostakovich says *about* Berg. Similarly, only eleven pages earlier, he notes that Stravinsky, too, left the USSR ahead of schedule in 1962. 'He did the right thing. He didn't make the mistake of Prokofiev, who ended up like a chicken in the soup.'[127]

Other explanations are also plausible. For example, the phrase 'the sooner the better', following the acknowledgement that Berg 'left Leningrad with relief', may reflect nothing more than Shostakovich's concern for Berg's life,

[124] *Ibid*., p. 9/13.

[125] Nikolska, p. 84.

[126] *Testimony*, p. 32/45.

[127] *Ibid*., p. 24/34.

given the bomb scare in Leningrad mentioned two pages earlier:

> Just before the premiere [of *Wozzeck*], he [Berg] received a telegram from his wife begging him not to enter the opera house because she had learned that they would throw a bomb at him. You can imagine his condition. He had to go to the rehearsal and he kept waiting for the bomb.[128]

Finally, Shostakovich may have quoted Pushkin not to imply the full context of *Mozart and Salieri*, but merely because the expression happened to pop into his mind at the time. People often incorporate quotations, out of context, in everyday conversations.[129] Ian MacDonald makes a similar point with regard to Shostakovich quoting the title of Dobrolyubov's essay 'A Ray of Light in the Kingdom of Darkness' in an article on *Lady Macbeth*. Challenging Taruskin's deduction of a 'clear influence' here, MacDonald notes that

[128] *Ibid.*, p. 31/43. *Cf.* the obituary-reminiscences about Berg published by composer and music critic Nikolay Strel'nikov:

> I met him in April of 1927 [. . .]. Berg kept me informed with respect to all of his hesitations – whether to go to that faraway Soviet Union, surrounded by fog and Western-created legends.
>
> Apparently, in Vienna they scared the poor author of *Wozzeck* with all kinds of horrible things that awaited him up North, including the bomb which might be thrown in the theatre staging *Wozzeck*. Even when the lot was cast and he sat among us, on the day of the premiere he received a telegram from his wife, which he, not without embarrassment, gave me. I read in the telegram: 'Congratulations premiere. Take care yourself. Avoid theatre'. In response to this marital warning, I promised Berg to sit with him in the theatre.
>
> 'Pamyati Al'bana Berga' ('In Memory of Alban Berg'), *Rabochy i teatr* (*The Worker and the Theatre*), 1936, No. 2, pp. 22–23.

Strel'nikov, apparently, was notoriously talkative. The rumours of such a telegram spread around Leningrad, and, obviously, reached Shostakovich. In *Testimony*, p. 31/43, Shostakovich states: 'It was known before hand how pleasant a man Berg was because the critic Nikolay Strelnikov told everyone. [. . .] He dragged Berg to a rehearsal of one of his operettas and then told everyone how Berg had praised him'.

Berg's fears of a terrorist attack during his visit to Leningrad were confirmed to Volkov by Helene Berg (conversation between Volkov and the authors, October 1995).

[129] *Cf.* Grigoryev and Platek, pp. 96 and 191, for examples of Shostakovich quoting from *Mozart and Salieri* in 1942 and 1957.

Dobrolyubov's title was [. . .] sufficiently famous in Russia as to be virtually proverbial, and the fact that Shostakovich refers to it [. . .] means next to nothing, since it was perfectly possible to use the phrase without having read Dobrolyubov's original polemic, let alone agree with it.[130]

6. The Seventh Symphony

The meaning of and inspiration for Shostakovich's Seventh Symphony remains hotly contested. According to *Testimony*, the work was planned before the war and inspired, at least in part, by Stalin, contradicting earlier statements by the composer that it depicted Leningrad under siege by the Nazis.[131] Not surprisingly, the gestation of the Seventh Symphony has become one of the central issues in the debate over the authenticity of *Testimony*.

Laurel Fay points to 'contradictions' about the Seventh Symphony in *Testimony* itself. Shostakovich states:

> I wrote my Seventh Symphony, the 'Leningrad', very quickly. I couldn't not write it. War was all around. I had to be with the people, I wanted to create the image of our country at war, capture it in music. From the first days of the war, I sat down at the piano and started work. I worked intensely. I wanted to write about our times, about our contemporaries who spared neither strength nor life in the name of Victory Over the Enemy.[132]

Fay emphasises that '*Less than one page* after he tells us "From the first days of the war . . . " (*cf.* the complete quotation above) we read the following':

[130] Ian MacDonald, 'Glivenko', p. 539, note 18.

[131] In October 1941 Shostakovich explained:

> The exposition in the first movement tells about the happy and peaceful life of people, confident in themselves and in their future. This is the simple and peaceful life led by thousands of Leningrad volunteers, by the entire city, by our entire country . . . In the development, war erupts in the middle of this peaceful life that these people are then engaged in . . .
>
> Zhitomirsky, 'Shostakovich', pp. 450–51; quoting from Sabinina, *Shostakovich: The Symphonist*, p. 165.

[132] *Testimony*, pp. 117/154–55.

> The Seventh Symphony had been planned before the war and consequently it simply cannot be seen as a reaction to Hitler's attack. The 'invasion theme' has nothing to do with the attack. I was thinking of other enemies of humanity when I composed the theme.[133]

'Subsequently', Fay points out, 'Volkov quotes Shostakovich as explicitly equating these "enemies of humanity" with Stalin and his henchmen. Which explanation are we to believe?'[134]

As is so often the case, Fay's contradictions are more imagined than real. When it suits her purpose, she suggests that Shostakovich's words be read precisely: if Shostakovich's inscription mentions only three names (Glazunov, Zoshchenko and Meyerhold), then this is 'a *precise* reference to the limited content of their conversations'.[135] Here, however, as also in her statements about the Fourth Symphony, Fay distorts Shostakovich's meaning, equating 'writing' the Seventh Symphony with 'planning' it. Shostakovich states that he wrote the Seventh Symphony when war was all around, but planned it before the war. This was typical of Shostakovich's composing habits, and is even mentioned, but strategically censored by Fay, between the two passages quoted above:

> I do write quickly, it's true, but I think about my music for a comparatively long time, and until it's complete in my head I don't begin setting it down.[136]

133 *Ibid.*, p. 118/155.

134 Fay, p. 490.

135 *Ibid.*, p. 492.

136 *Testimony*, p. 117/155. Shostakovich's family and friends corroborate this statement. Maxim states: 'Shostakovich was a man to whom the gestation period was far more significant than the day of birth. [. . .] My father always said, "I think long; I write fast"' (Albert, pp. 407 and 411). Lebedinsky adds that 'having composed his entire symphony with all its details in his head, Shostakovich would sit down and score it straight for full orchestra, making no preliminary sketches' (Lebedinsky, 'Code, Quotation, and Collage', p. 480) (hereafter Lebedinsky). Vishnevskaya, too, recalls that 'Dmitri Dmitriyevich never showed the rough drafts of a new composition to anyone. No one knew what he was writing until the work was finished; and he never rewrote anything' (Vishnevskaya, *Galina*, p. 352; also *Rostropovich and Vishnevskaya*, p. 58).

Furthermore, since Shostakovich despised composing at the piano, his reference to 'sitting down at the piano and beginning work' clearly implies a later stage in the compositional process (i.e., notating the work).[137] In *Testimony* he emphasises that

> composing at the piano was always a secondary way for me. That's for the deaf and those who have a poor sense of the orchestra, who need some aural support for their work. [. . .] As a rule, I hear the score and write it down in ink, finished copy – without rough drafts or studies [. . .].[138]

Finally, Shostakovich does not deny that the war influenced his Seventh Symphony, but points out that the work as a

[137] This has been confirmed by Irina Shostakovich. When asked 'Did Dmitry Dmitriyevich write most of his music away from the piano?', she responded: 'Dmitry Dmitriyevich didn't compose his music at the instrument. He would say that a composer should compose in his head, not with his hands. Usually he would start playing *after* he had the image in his mind and in his heart. And he would immediately write the score' (Irina Shostakovich, conference; emphasis added).

[138] *Testimony*, p. 177/228. Rostropovich corroborates that 'Shostakovich in general never made any sketches for his compositions. He held the whole preparatory process in his head. Then he sat down at his desk, and without ever touching the piano, he simply wrote down the complete work from beginning to end' (Wilson, p. 396). Zoya Shostakovich, the composer's sister, concurs, noting that even when Dmitry Dmitriyevich was a child 'I always found it amazing that he never needed to try things out on the piano. He just sat down, wrote whatever he heard in his head and then played it through complete on the piano' (Wilson, p. 9). Chukovsky elaborates:

> He composed in his mind [. . . and] never approached the old upright piano on the ground floor. Once he said, although in jest, that all instruments should be taken away from composers, as they should have no need for them. To observe him writing down what he heard was like a miracle. Placing a large sheet of manuscript paper in front of him, with hardly an interruption and practically no corrections or rough copies, Shostakovich created his new scores. They were created in entirety and instantaneously. It looked as if he wasn't composing, but just copying down sounds heard in his innermost self.
>
> Wilson, p. 288.

Finally, Basner confirms, 'as it was no problem for him [Shostakovich] to hold the whole of a symphony in his head, he just wrote out his music directly in full score. He never bothered with a piano score and usually didn't make any preliminary sketches. As far as he made a skeleton outline

whole 'simply cannot be seen as a reaction to Hitler's attack'.[139]

Taruskin, aping Fay, also distorts this passage, arguing that

> To uphold the view of the Seventh as exclusively anti-Stalinist one has to ignore the imagery of actual battle, as well as that of repulsion [...] and finally of victory [...]. These musical events can hardly be read out of the context of the war and its immediate, overriding urgencies, conditions that could not have been foreseen when Volkov's Shostakovich claimed to have had his first thoughts of the Seventh.[140]

Another example of this 'shoot-from-the-hip' scholarship can be found in Yakubov:

> Solomon Volkov puts in the mouth of Shostakovich the following text (I must note that I cite it from the article by D. Zhitomirsky from *Daugava*, as no Russian edition is in existence[141]): 'I have no objection against calling the Seventh "Leningrad". It does not speak of the Leningrad of the blockade, though. It speaks of the Leningrad that was condemned by Stalin to destruction. (...)' Let us assume that Shostakovich really talked about it. Volkov needed that the symphony be not anti-Hitler, but anti-Stalin, not anti-fascist, but anti-Soviet. Please explain to me how you would discriminate in the *music* the Leningrad of the blockade from the Leningrad 'that Stalin destroyed'. Forgive the pun, but you

---

of a work, it would fit on to one or two lines of manuscript paper' (Wilson, p. 437). Such was the case with the Ninth Symphony. Zhitomirsky recalls:

> I noticed with surprise that he always had in front of him the same few sheets of music paper [... with] only the themes, now and then 'hints' of the development, and in many cases – everything was written on one line. To my knowledge, he wrote no other draft; and based on the abovementioned sketches, Dmitry Dmitriyevich immediately wrote the final score.
>
> Zhitomirsky, 'Shostakovich', p. 458.

139 *Testimony*, p. 118/155.

140 Richard Taruskin, review of the facsimile of Shostakovich's Symphony No. 7, *Notes*, 50/2, December 1993, p. 759 (hereafter Taruskin, review).

141 For Zhitomirsky's article, *cf.* Bibliography, p. 753.

need not be a Solomon to see that your leg is being pulled.[142]

Yakubov's abbreviated quotation from *Testimony* (via *Daugava*) reveals the same selective scholarship practised by Fay and Taruskin. In fact, it is Yakubov, Taruskin and Fay who 'pull our legs'. Shostakovich never says that the Seventh is '*exclusively* anti-Stalinist' or 'anti-Soviet'; to the contrary, he makes clear that Hitler and Stalin were co-evils, as proven by the unexpurgated text:

> Naturally fascism is repugnant to me, but not only German fascism, any form of it is repugnant. Nowadays, people like to recall the prewar period as an idyllic time, saying that everything was fine until Hitler bothered us. Hitler is a criminal, that's clear, but so is Stalin. I feel eternal pain for those who were killed by Hitler, but I feel no less pain for those killed on Stalin's orders. I suffer for everyone who was tortured, shot, or starved to death. There were millions of them in our country before the war with Hitler began.
>
> The war brought much new sorrow and much new destruction, but I haven't forgotten the terrible prewar years. That is what all of my symphonies, beginning with the Fourth, are about, including the Seventh and Eighth.
>
> Actually, I have nothing against calling the Seventh the Leningrad Symphony, but it's not about Leningrad under siege, it's about the Leningrad that Stalin destroyed and that Hitler merely finished off.[143]

That Yakubov should mischaracterise this material in 1992 is difficult to understand. Could it be that he failed to notice that most of the text quoted above is included in Zhitomirsky's *Daugava* article? Could it be that he also missed the articles published a year earlier in *Sovetskaya Muzyka* and *Pravda*, in which Mazel' and Lebedinsky called attention to this very passage? (Mazel', for example, notes, 'A few lines later, though, Hitler and Stalin are allotted equal status as criminals',[144] and Lebedinsky quotes the entire

[142] Manashir Yakubov, 'Istoriya, Sud'by, Mify i Real'nost'' ('History, Fates, Myths and Reality'), *Muzykal'noye obozreniye* (*Musical Review*), 18 October 1992, p. 5 (hereafter Yakubov, 'History').

[143] *Testimony*, pp. 118/155–56.

[144] *Sovetskaya Muzyka*, 1991, No. 5; *cf*. p. 485.

passage from *Testimony*, including Shostakovich's conclusion that the Seventh is 'about the Leningrad that Stalin destroyed and that Hitler merely finished off'.[145]) Finally, could it be that the curator of the Shostakovich family archive and an internationally known authority on the composer still did not know what was stated in *Testimony*, twelve years after *Testimony* was published and after he had denounced it as inaccurate and a forgery? Again, 'denounce first, read later'. Much later.[146]

Fay's imagined contradictions regarding the Seventh Symphony could have been easily resolved had she remembered Shostakovich's composing habits and considered all of his comments about this work in *Testimony*. Yet again, what is sorely lacking in her research is perspective. Shostakovich himself questions the genesis of his compositions:

> Is a musical concept born consciously or unconsciously? It's difficult to explain. The process of writing is long and complicated. Sometimes you start writing and then change your mind. It doesn't always work out the way you thought it would.[147]

He even notes another important influence on his Seventh Symphony:

> I began writing it having been deeply moved by the Psalms of David; the symphony deals with more than that, but the Psalms were the impetus. I began writing. David has some marvellous words on blood, that God takes revenge for blood, He doesn't forget the cries of victims, and so on. [. . .] if the Psalms were read before every performance of the Seventh, there might be fewer stupid things written about it.[148]

This revelation in *Testimony* now has been confirmed by Khentova and Yakubov. Khentova states that initially Shostakovich began composing 'a work for soloist, chorus

[145] 'O Chesti Mastera' ('The Master's Honour'), *Pravda*, 19 March 1991 (hereafter Lebedinsky, 'The Master's Honour').

[146] *Cf*. pp. 64–67, 81–82 and 137, note 76, for other notable examples.

[147] *Testimony*, p. 117/154.

[148] *Ibid*., p. 140/184.

and orchestra based on the text of the Psalms of David'.[149] Yakubov adds:

> It is also known that initially Shostakovich wrote the Seventh (military) Symphony as a choral work based on the Psalms of David. Khentova and Volkov wrote about this. It is confirmed by different writers of memoirs, independently from each other.[150]

Other passages in *Testimony* make clear that the Seventh Symphony was already planned, even if not notated, before the war. Shostakovich states that

> Even before the war, in Leningrad there probably wasn't a single family who hadn't lost someone, a father, a brother, or if not a relative, then a close friend. [. . .] the sorrow oppressed and suffocated us. It suffocated me too. I had to write about it, I felt that it was my responsibility, my duty. I had to write a requiem for all those who died, who had suffered. [. . .] And then the war came [. . .].[151]

On the next page he identifies his Seventh and Eighth Symphonies as 'my requiem'.[152] Still more revealing is the following:

> The Sixth Symphony was finished and I knew for sure what the next one would be about, so I sat down with the complete composer's piano reduction of *Boris* published by Lamm [. . .].[153]

149 Khentova, *Shostakovich*, Vol. 2, p. 18. *Cf.* also *D. Shostakovich v gody velikoy otechestvennoy voiny* (*Shostakovich during the Days of the Great Patriotic War*), Muzyka, Moscow, 1979, p. 30, where Khentova in 1979 (while still constrained by Soviet censorship) makes an oblique reference to a work based on a 'text from ancient literature'.

Shostakovich's interest in the Psalms of David stemmed, in part, from Stravinsky's *Symphony of Psalms* (1930), a work he much admired. Upon evacuation from Leningrad, 'among the few things Shostakovich took with him were his transcription [for piano four-hands] of the *Symphony of Psalms* and the manuscript of his Seventh Symphony' (Volkov, *St Petersburg*, p. 429).

150 Yakubov, 'History', p. 5.

151 *Testimony*, pp. 102/135–36.

152 *Ibid*., p. 103/136.

153 *Ibid*., p. 178/230.

Since Shostakovich completed his Sixth Symphony in 1939 and his new orchestration of *Boris Godunov* in 1940, his Seventh Symphony, 'the next one' mentioned above, must have been planned by 1939.

The true chronology and meaning of the Seventh Symphony, first revealed in *Testimony*, now has been corroborated by documentary evidence and numerous witnesses. Volkov notes that

> [the] Seventh Symphony was included in the programme for the Leningrad Philharmonic's 1941–42 season, that is, before the German invasion [22 June 1941]. That could have been done only with the composer's consent and indicates that Shostakovich had a clear idea of his Seventh Symphony and was sure that he would complete it by the fall season.[154]

Furthermore, Khentova quotes Yuly Vainkop, who kept abreast of the composer's creative plans, as reporting in May 1941: 'In the near future, D. Shostakovich, apparently, will finish his Seventh Symphony (the completion of which was postponed by the composer because of his work on the orchestration of Musorgsky's opera *Boris Godunov*)'.[155] This confirms the statement in *Testimony* that completion of the Seventh was delayed by the orchestration of *Boris* in 1940.[156] Additional support for the account in *Testimony* comes from a sketch of the 'invasion theme' recently reported discovered among the papers of Pavel Lamm, whose edition of *Boris Godunov* Shostakovich had been consulting in 1939–40. According to Aleksandr Sherel', this sketch is dedicated 'In Memory of the Master' (meaning Meyerhold) and dated

[154] Volkov, *St Petersburg*, p. 427.

[155] Khentova, *Shostakovich*, Vol. 1, p. 526. (When contacted in November 1995, Khentova confirmed the accuracy of Vainkop's statement.) Khentova elaborates on the chronology of composition of the Seventh Symphony in *Shostakovich*, Vol. 1, p. 543:

> On 31 May 1941 there was a meeting of the officers of the Leningrad composers' organisation, at which Yu. Ya. Vainkop reported on the subscription concerts of the Philharmonia for the season of 1941/42. The plan included the First [and] Fifth symphonies, Suite from [. . .] Hamlet, First Piano Concerto, and from the new works – the Seventh Symphony of Shostakovich: it was considered to be quite real.

[156] *Cf.* p. 156.

26 June 1939 (six days after Shostakovich witnessed Meyerhold being arrested), indicating that the so-called 'invasion' was not by Nazis but by Stalin's own henchmen.[157] If genuine, this manuscript would further demolish yet another of Fay's 'conclusive' arguments and, again, corroborate *Testimony*: 'The "invasion theme" has nothing to do with the attack', Shostakovich says in *Testimony*. 'I was thinking of other enemies of humanity when I composed this theme.'[158]

Shostakovich's statements in *Testimony* also have been corroborated by his family, friends and colleagues. At a seminar in 1990, Maxim acknowledged:

> Critics felt it [the Seventh Symphony] described the tragedy of the war; but it was *not* just about the war. The times before the war were very difficult; Stalin was schizophrenic, a maniac of greatness and paranoia; it was a time of 'Processes' – a euphemism for the show trials. Accusations were made against different groups at different times: engineers, scientists, artists; all were 'organized plotting enemies against the State and against Stalin'. Everyone was a German spy; the prisons were overcrowded, so there needed to be more and faster trials, outside the norms of human jurisdiction; people were tortured with the purpose of getting them to sign a full confession; the accused were deceived – they were told that if they signed, they'd be released; then they were given 'nine grains of lead in the basement' [executed by firing squad].
>
> My father always said, 'I think long; I write fast' – the time preceding the war was probably the inspiration of Symphony No. 7, the tragedy of a nation. There were negative evil forces – in Germany and in the USSR; the USSR had its own fascism and its own 'Hitler'. The Seventh Symphony is *not* just military.[159]

Dubinsky, too, points out that 'Soviet musicologists conveniently forgot that the first movement of the Seventh Symphony already existed a year before the war, back when Stalin was still Hitler's faithful friend',[160] and Lebedinsky adds:

[157] Interview with Aleksandr Sherel', March 1995.

[158] *Testimony*, p. 118/155.

[159] Albert, pp. 410–11.

[160] Dubinsky, p. 155. Presumably it existed in Shostakovich's mind, even if not on paper, a year earlier.

> The 'Leningrad' Symphony [... was] planned and begun *before* Hitler's attack on Russia in 1941. The tune of the notorious march in the first movement was conceived by Shostakovich as the 'Stalin' theme (all who were close to the composer knew this). After the war had started, Shostakovich declared it to be the 'Hitler' theme. Later, when the work was published, he renamed it the 'Evil' theme – justly, since both Hitler and Stalin met the specification.[161]

Finally, Flora Litvinova, one of Shostakovich's neighbours when the Seventh Symphony was completed, documented (in contemporaneous notes) the composer's thoughts:

> 'Fascism, yes, but music, real music, is never literally bound to one theme. Fascism is not just National Socialism; this music is about terror, slavery, the bondage of spirit'. Later, when Dmitry Dmitryevich got used to me and started to trust me, he told me straight out that *the Seventh (as well as the Fifth) were not just about fascism, but also about our system, about any tyranny and totalitarianism in general.*[162]

Mazel' adds: 'Here, three decades before Shostakovich's talks with Volkov, everything is said'.[163]

7. The Eighth Quartet, Fifth, Tenth and Eleventh Symphonies, and Other Notes in a Bottle

The philosopher Leo Strauss perceptively noted that

> Persecution [...] gives rise to a peculiar technique of writing [...] in which the truth about all crucial things is presented exclusively between the lines. That literature is addressed,

[161] Lebedinsky, pp. 481–82.

[162] Mazel', p. 488 (emphasis added), and Wilson, pp. 158–59. Vladimir Zak concurs: the Seventh Symphony is not only about 'a foreign fascism – German – but also (and this is so very unbearable) of our own native fascism. This is the reason why many listeners seem to hear in the "invasion theme" not only the aggressors drawing near and defacing the Russian land, but also the trampling of the boots of the NKVD [...]' (Zak, p. 500). *Cf.* also pp. 590–96.

[163] Mazel', p. 488.

> not to all readers, but to trustworthy and intelligent readers only. It has all the advantages of private communication without having its greatest disadvantage – that it reaches only the writer's acquaintances. It has all the advantages of public communication without having its greatest disadvantage – capital punishment for the author.[164]

Shostakovich, too, understood the value (and necessity) of writing 'between the lines', of disguising the true meaning of his works for his own survival and that of his music. Unfortunately, many scholars continue to focus only on the literal meaning of the composer's words and music, while ignoring its deeper, hidden, more symbolic aspects.[165] The true meanings of works such as the Eighth Quartet and Fifth, Tenth and Eleventh Symphonies were first revealed to a wide audience in *Testimony*. As with the Seventh Symphony,[166] however, these revelations often contradicted the composer's own earlier statements and, accordingly, were rejected, branded as 'revisionist', and used as additional ammunition by Fay, Taruskin *et al.* to attack the authenticity of the memoirs. Significantly, many of Shostakovich's friends and family (part of the 'trustworthy and intelligent readers' alluded to by Strauss) now have corroborated the once controversial revelations of *Testimony*.

a. The Eighth Quartet

Shostakovich's Eighth Quartet (1960), long thought to be 'In memory of victims of fascism and war' because of its inscription, is now generally acknowledged to be 'in memory' of the composer himself, who planned to commit suicide soon after being forced to join the Communist Party.[167] The autobiographical nature of this work was first admitted publicly by Shostakovich in *Testimony*. There he notes:

[164] Leo Strauss, *Persecution and the Art of Writing*, The Free Press, Glencoe, Illinois, 1952, p. 25.

[165] Crucial differences of interpretation arise when this music is assessed not in isolation, but in the context of the composer's life. *Cf.* pp. 565–84.

[166] *Cf.* pp. 150–59.

[167] *Cf.* Shostakovich's letter to Isaak Glikman, quoted in Dorothea Redepenning, 'And Art Made Tongue-Tied by Authority', *Shostakovich Studies*, pp. 210–11, note 12 (hereafter Redepenning).

> When I wrote the Eighth Quartet, it was also assigned to the department of 'exposing fascism'. You have to be blind and deaf to do that, because everything in the quartet is as clear as a primer. I quote *Lady Macbeth*, the First and Fifth Symphonies. What does fascism have to do with these? The Eighth is an autobiographical quartet, it quotes a song known to all Russians: 'Exhausted by the hardships of prison'.[168]

The true meaning of this Quartet has since been confirmed by documentary evidence and by the composer's friends and family. Shostakovich himself, in a letter to Isaak Glikman (19 July 1960), sarcastically noted that his Quartet is 'ideologically flawed',[169] and explained the motivation for his piece in no uncertain terms:

> When I die, it's hardly likely that someone will write a quartet dedicated to my memory. So I decided to write it myself. One could write on the frontispiece, 'Dedicated to the author of this quartet'.[170]

In addition, Dubinsky recalls that 'when, at the first performance at the Composers' House, the chairman announced the quartet and started talking about the war and the heroism of the Soviet people and the Communist Party, Shostakovich jumped up and shouted, "No, no . . . that is, you see, I, I, myself, personally, so to speak, am protesting against any sort of Fascism"'.[171] The composer also confided to the Borodin Quartet that the Eighth Quartet 'is myself'.[172]

Among the members of Shostakovich's inner circle who have corroborated the statements in *Testimony* are Lebedinsky and Maxim. According to Lebedinsky:

> The composer dedicated the Quartet to the victims of fascism to disguise his intentions, although, as he considered himself a victim of a fascist regime, the dedication was apt. In fact he intended it to be a summation of everything he had written before. It was his farewell to life. He associated joining the Party with a moral, as well as physical death. On the day of his

168 *Testimony*, p. 118/156.

169 I. Glikman, *Letters to a Friend*, p. 159.

170 Wilson, p. 340.

171 Dubinsky, p. 282.

172 *Ibid.*, p. 283.

return from a trip to Dresden, where he had completed the Quartet and purchased a large number of sleeping pills, he played the Quartet to me on the piano and told me with tears in his eyes that it was his last work. He hinted at his intention to commit suicide. Perhaps subconsciously he hoped that I would save him. I managed to remove the pills from his jacket pocket and gave them to his son Maxim, explaining to him the true meaning of the Quartet.[173]

Maxim, speaking at a symposium in 1992, also confirmed the special, personal significance of this work to his father:

My father cried twice in his life: when his mother died and when he came to say they've made him join the Party. [. . . T]his was sobbing, not just tears, but sobbing. It was in the 1960s that they made him join the Party. There was simply no other way for him at that time. [. . .] The powers-that-be put a lot of pressure on Shostakovich to give some kind of title to the Eighth Quartet in order to explain its pessimism. Something about Dresden, or the destruction of Dresden at the end of World War II. And, of course, only a stupid person could not understand the combination in that quartet of his musical signature ('DSCH'), along with the tune of a well-known Russian prison song ('Tortured by grievous bondage'). And the knocks on the door by the KGB, you can also hear them there.[174]

Volkov, sharing the panel, pointed out: 'You said quite correctly that only stupid people couldn't understand that. But there are still a lot of these stupid people around'.[175]

[173] Wilson, p. 340. The abbreviated references to the 'Dies irae' at the end of the third and fifth movements, sometimes juxtaposed to DSCH, may also allude to the composer's anticipated death.

[174] Robinson, pp. 397–8 and 390.

[175] *Ibid.*, p. 390. Those who maintained the old interpretation of the work even after *Testimony* was published include Robert Stradling, who states that the Eighth Quartet 'shows the composer now able to feel for the sufferings of the German enemy – or rather, perhaps, the German civilian-comrade. [. . . It does not seem] susceptible of an interpretation connecting [it] with a wider dissatisfaction or profounder disease [. . .] ('Shostakovich and the Soviet System', Norris, pp. 211 and 204). Norris, in the same collection, also finds in the Eighth Quartet a 'literal evocation of the Dresden bombing' ('Shostakovich: Politics and War', p. 179), and Khentova, inexplicably, concludes that a 'major mood predominates' in this

Even Taruskin now accepts this explanation, but wrongly concludes that the Eighth Quartet is 'the one composition of

---

work (*Amazing Shostakovich*, p. 161). In contrast, Ian MacDonald, p. 583, observes, for example, that the three-note pounding in the fourth movement represents not gunfire or bombs dropping, but 'a fist pounding peremptorily on a door in the middle of the night'.

The 'revisionist' interpretation of the Eighth Quartet should not have come as a surprise to the 'experts'. In 1956, a few years before the Eighth Quartet, Shostakovich described his own 'torture by grievous bondage' while berating Picasso:

> 'Don't tell me anything about him, he is a bastard! He is a bastard: he salutes the Soviet regime and our communism while his followers, the painters, are being persecuted in the Soviet Union, they cannot work, they are hunted . . . ' I interjected, 'Your followers are also being persecuted'. 'Yes, I am a bastard too, coward, etc., but I am in jail. You understand that I am in jail, I am afraid for my children and myself, but he is in freedom, he does not have to kick us! I am being invited to all countries, but I do not go, and won't go till the time when I can tell the truth, to answer the question of how I like the Decree of the Central Committee on music, about my works. And he? Who pulls his tongue? All of them – Hewlett Johnson, Joliet-Curie, Picasso – all bastards. They live in societies where life is not easy, but you can tell the truth and you can work, do what you have to do. And he – Dove of Peace! I hate it, that Dove! I hate the slavery of thought no less than physical slavery'.
>
> Litvinova, pp. 174–75; Wilson, p. 271.

Imprisonment was a constant concern of Shostakovich. When his suggested Soviet anthem was selected a finalist in a competition instituted by Stalin in 1943 (the finals took place in July, at the Bolshoi Theatre, the eventual winner being Aleksandr Aleksandrov's *Bolshevik Party Anthem*), Shostakovich remarked: 'Would be nice if my anthem won. Would guarantee they won't send me to jail' (Litvinova, p. 171). In addition, when Gavriil Glikman showed Shostakovich a picture of two prisoners in uniforms, one of whom looked like the composer, Shostakovich responded: 'This is the genuine, the most true likeness of me' (G. Glikman, 'Shostakovich as I Knew Him', Vol. 37, p. 381). The latter has been confirmed by Vadim Prokhorov:

> [Shostakovich] always kept in his desk a photograph of Gavriil Glikman's painting, portraying Shostakovich and Prokofiev in prisoners [*sic*] clothes, carrying out a bucket used as a toilet. Though never being imprisoned, Dmitri Dmitrievich believed that it was the one true representation of how he felt living in the Soviet Union.
>
> Vadim Prokhorov, 'A Personal View of Shostakovich: Son Reflects on Shostakovich before Friends of Music Concert', *Fairfield Minuteman*, 4 April 1996, pp. B16 and 19, and 'A Conversation with Maxim Shostakovich', *American Record Guide*, 60/2, March/April 1997, p. 27.

his that does ask expressly to be read as autobiography – the one time Shostakovich did put an explicit note in a bottle'.[176] Actually, Shostakovich left many such notes in a bottle, not to mention a whole book, *Testimony*. It is extraordinary that Taruskin, having rather belatedly discovered Shostakovich's 'note' in the Eighth Quartet, should now so confidently proclaim the non-existence of other such 'explicit notes' in the composer's *œuvre*.[177]

b. The Fifth Symphony

In view of the enormous popularity of the Fifth Symphony (1937), it is not surprising that the revelations about this work in *Testimony* also have been quoted and debated repeatedly. Before the publication of the memoirs, Shostakovich's Fifth had routinely been viewed as the composer's 'creative reply to a just criticism' – his return to the fold of socialist realism following two highly critical articles, 'Muddle Instead of Music' (attacking *Lady Macbeth*)[178] and 'Ballet Falsehood' (attacking *Limpid Stream*).[179] In 1940, Shostakovich himself announced:

> I can still remember the joy I felt when my newly finished Fifth Symphony was heard by an audience of Party activists from the Leningrad branch. I should like to express my wish that the previewing of new works of music by a Party audience be practised more often. Our Party devotes great care and attention to the development of our country's musical life. I have felt this concern all through my career. [. . .] The central idea of the work is man and all his sufferings, and the finale of the symphony resolves the tragic, tense elements of the first movements on a joyous, optimistic level.[180]

[176] Taruskin, 'Who', p. 71.

[177] In explicit self-contradiction, Taruskin belatedly devotes forty pages to pondering the hidden message of another work, 'a richly coded utterance', in his article on Shostakovich's Fifth Symphony (*cf*. Taruskin, 'Lies', pp. 17–56).

[178] *Pravda*, 28 January, 1936.

[179] *Pravda*, 6 February 1936.

[180] Grigoryev and Platek, p. 83. For rule-of-thumb methods for deciphering such babble, *cf*. pp. 173–75.

This description again contrasts strikingly with that in *Testimony*. Speaking particularly of the joy and optimism in the finale, Shostakovich states:

> The rejoicing is forced, created under threat, as in *Boris Godunov*. It's as if someone were beating you with a stick and saying, 'Your business is rejoicing, your business is rejoicing', and you rise, shaky, and go marching off, muttering, 'Our business is rejoicing, our business is rejoicing'.[181]

The true meaning of the Fifth Symphony was not a mystery for the work's first listeners. Volkov notes:

> The Fifth Symphony from the very beginning was interpreted by Leningraders as a work about the Great Terror [. . . even if, at the premiere, it] was wrapped by the author and his friends in 'protective' words to blunt its impact. [. . .] One of [the first Soviet listeners] noted that the start of the last movement is 'the iron tread of a monstrous power trampling man'. Upon first hearing the symphony, Alexander Fadeyev wrote in his diary, 'The end does not sound like an outcome (and ever less like a triumph or victory), but like a punishment or revenge of someone'.[182]

[181] *Testimony*, p. 140/183.

[182] Volkov, *St Petersburg*, pp. 423–25. Rostropovich adds:

> The applause went on for an entire hour. People were in uproar, and ran up and down through the streets of Leningrad till the small hours, embracing and congratulating each other on having been there. They had understood the message that forms the 'lower bottom', the outer hull, of the Fifth Symphony: the message of sorrow, suffering and isolation; stretched on the rack of the Inquisition, the victim still tries to smile in his pain. The shrill repetitions of the A at the end of the symphony are to me like a spear-point jabbing in the wounds of a person on the rack. The hearers of the first performance could identify with that person. Anybody who thinks the finale is glorification is an idiot [. . .].
>
> Juliane Ribke, 'From a Conversation with Mstislav Rostropovich', notes accompanying Deutsche Grammophon 410 509–2.

Georgy Khubov similarly perceived hidden, darker meanings in the work (Taruskin, 'Lies', pp. 34–38 and 52), and even Nicolas Nabokov, who admitted he couldn't tell one Shostakovich symphony from another, clearly understood the forced rejoicing in Shostakovich's music:

> To a Russian there would not be anything particularly surprising in the optimism of Shostakovich. But his kind of optimism takes a redundant, blatant, and unconvincing form. One always feels a kind of compelling force behind it, a force of an extramusical order. It appears to be based on the official syllogistic formula: before the

Even the composer's much publicised 'official' statements were understood for what they were: 'foam in the mouth of a man who has been forced to eat soap'.[183] Vishnevskaya explains:

> Before the Fifth Symphony was allowed to be performed, it was heard by the Party *aktiv* in Leningrad. A few dozen nincompoops together to judge a genius: to make objections, to lecture him, and in general to teach him how to write music. He had to save his newborn from their talons. But how? He tried to deceive them in the most rudimentary way, and succeeded! All he had to do was use other words to describe the huge complex of human passions and suffering that is so apparent in his music – he described his music to the Party as joyous and optimistic – and the entire pack dashed off, satisfied.[184]

Unfortunately, the words put into Shostakovich's mouth[185] continue to be parroted by those 'without ears to listen'. Eric Roseberry, for example, in 1993 again questioned the 'forced rejoicing' in the finale: 'After all', he says, 'Shostakovich's original pronouncements on this symphony at the time of its premiere made no mention of such a hidden agenda'.[186] Roseberry's observation is startlingly naïve. Only someone utterly unaware of the Soviet historical background

---

revolution life was desperate, therefore art was gloomy; now the revolution is victorious, therefore art must be optimistic. It is obvious that this *must* rings [*sic*] like a command of the gods rather than a logical conclusion of a syllogism.

Old Friends and New Music, Little, Brown, Boston, 1951, pp. 173 and 268.

[183] Martin Cooper, quoted in Lebedinsky, p. 479.

[184] Vishnevskaya, *Galina*, p. 212. Inna Barsova agrees, noting that Shostakovich would 'defend the truth of the music with untruthful words about it' ('Between Social Demands and the Music of Grand Passions (The years 1934–37 in the life of Dmitry Shostakovich)', paper, University of Michigan, 28 January 1994; typescript, transl. Karen Rosenflanz, provided courtesy of the author; hereafter Barsova, paper).

[185] Including the phrase 'a creative artist's reply to a just criticism', once attributed to Shostakovich, but now known to have been coined by a Soviet journalist (*cf.* p. 44).

[186] Eric Roseberry, 'Some Thoughts After a Re-reading of *Testimony*', *Melos*, 1/4–5, Summer 1993, p. 24.

could imagine that Shostakovich had the option of 'mentioning' the hidden agenda of the Fifth Symphony during 1937–38 (or, indeed, at any time before the Thaw) without paying for such a disclosure with his life: as Isaak Babel' noted, 'Now a man talks frankly only with his wife, at night, with the blanket over his head'.[187] In fact, Shostakovich's response to misinterpretations of his Seventh and Eighth Symphonies provides a ready answer to Roseberry: 'I'm astounded sometimes by how lazy people are when it comes to thinking. Everything that was written [. . .] in the first few days is repeated without any changes to this very day, even though there has been time to do some thinking'.[188]

c. The Tenth and Eleventh Symphonies

The revelations in *Testimony* about the Tenth and Eleventh Symphonies also contradicted Shostakovich's earlier words, and, consequently, in the minds of Volkov's critics, cast an even larger shadow of doubt on the memoirs. Again, however, as in the cases of the Eighth Quartet and Fifth and Seventh Symphonies, newly discovered evidence both corroborates *Testimony* and vindicates Volkov. In 1954, when

[187] Volkov, *St Petersburg*, p. 423.

[188] *Testimony*, p. 117/155. For an insightful discussion of the finale of the Fifth, *cf*. Barsova, paper, pp. 3–4. Others who have 'done some thinking' include Gerard McBurney, Ian MacDonald and Elizabeth Wilson, all of whom call attention to Shostakovich's hidden reference to the first of his *Pushkin Romances*, 'Rebirth', in the finale of the Symphony. This 'note in a bottle', intended for future generations who, not having suffered under the Great Terror, might otherwise misinterpret his intent, is explained by Wilson:

> The four notes that set the first three words of that poem ['A barbarian painter with his somnolent brush / Blackens the genius's painting, / Slapping over it senselessly / His own lawless picture'] form the kernel of the initial march theme, while a whole later section makes reference to the lilting accompaniment to the poem's final quatrain, 'Thus delusions fall off / My tormented soul / And it reveals to me visions / Of my former pure days' [p. 127].

Here the 'barbarian painter' is, of course, Stalin, who repeatedly defaced the works of Shostakovich and his colleagues, forcing them to conform to the dictates of socialist realism. Shostakovich also predicts (correctly) that these old delusions will eventually fall off, revealing the original work and its true meaning.

asked about his Tenth Symphony (1953), Shostakovich responded with a lengthy comment most remarkable for how little it says. Typical of this 'double-speak' (or 'no-speak') are his words on the Scherzo: 'The second movement, in my opinion, answers my purpose in the main, and occupies its intended place in the cycle. It is perhaps too short, however, especially since the other movements are rather long'.[189] Shostakovich was much more forthcoming in his memoirs:

> I did depict Stalin in music in my next symphony, the Tenth. I wrote it right after Stalin's death, and no one has yet guessed what the symphony is about. It's about Stalin and the Stalin years. The second part, the scherzo, is a musical portrait of Stalin, roughly speaking. Of course, there are many other things in it, but that's the basis.[190]

Although these statements appear unrelated at first glance, when viewed in perspective the account in *Testimony* again rings true. First, the admission that the Tenth Symphony is 'about Stalin and the Stalin years' and that the scherzo, in particular, is a 'musical portrait' of the Great Terror himself is consistent with the statement in 1954 that this movement 'answers my purpose *in the main*'. Second, the acknowledgement in *Testimony* that 'no one has yet guessed what the symphony is about' relates to another comment by the composer documented by Rabinovich in 1959: 'When Shostakovich was asked whether the Tenth Symphony had a "programme", he answered with a smile, "No, let them listen and guess for themselves"'.[191] Finally, the disclosure that 'there are many other things in it' recently has been corroborated by Nelly Kravetz: in a paper delivered in January 1994, Kravetz revealed the work's passing quotation from the second *Pushkin Monologue* ('What is in my name for you?') as well as a hidden reference to the name 'Elmira' (Nazirova), a female pupil with whom Shostakovich had corresponded intensely in the summer of 1953.[192]

[189] *Sovetskaya Muzyka*, 1954, No. 6, p. 120; transl. in SCR *Music Bulletin*, August 1954, pp. 12–13, and reproduced in Schwarz, p. 279.

[190] *Testimony*, p. 107/141.

[191] Schwarz, p. 279; quoting from D. Rabinovich, *D. Shostakovich*, Foreign Languages Publishing House, Moscow, 1959, p. 132.

[192] Wilson, p. 263; also *cf*. pp. 183–84.

Testimony's revelations about the Eleventh Symphony have now, similarly, been confirmed by others. Shostakovich states:

> I was born after that [the Revolution of 1905], but the stories deeply affected my imagination. When I was older, I read much about how it all happened. I think that it was a turning point – the people stopped believing in the tsar. The Russian people are always like that – they believe and they believe and then suddenly it comes to an end. And the ones the people no longer believe in come to a bad end.
>
> But a lot of blood must be shed for that. [. . .] I think that many things repeat themselves in Russian history [. . . and] I wanted to show this recurrence in the Eleventh Symphony. I wrote it in 1957 and it deals with contemporary themes even though it's called '1905'. It's about the people, who have stopped believing because the cup of evil has run over.[193]

Igor Belsky also recalls the composer saying, 'Don't forget that I wrote that symphony [the Eleventh] in the aftermath of the Hungarian Uprising',[194] and Lebedinsky explains:

> What we heard in this music was not the police firing on the crowd in front of the Winter Palace in 1905, but the Soviet tanks roaring in the streets of Budapest. This was so clear to those 'who had ears to listen', that his son, with whom he wasn't in the habit of sharing his deepest thoughts, whispered to Dmitri Dmitriyevich during the dress rehearsal, 'Papa, what if they hang you for this?'[195]

[193] *Testimony*, p. 4/8.

[194] Wilson, p. 320. Shostakovich maintained a keen interest in contemporary events. In 1956, he said to Flora Litvinova: 'Have you heard anything on the BBC? What about Budapest? What about Poland? The Empire falls apart, on its seams. It is always like that. You have to keep the fist tight, if you let go just a little, the Empire falls apart. Only He knew how to do it' (Litvinova, pp. 173–74).

[195] Wilson, p. 317, and Volkov, *St Petersburg*, pp. 461–62. Shostakovich links the tragedies of the past and present by quoting the music of several revolutionary songs, which, in turn, call to mind texts apropos for 1956–57. The first movement quotes the prison song 'Listen', the original text of which reads: 'The autumn night is as black as treason, black as the tyrant's conscience. Blacker than that night a terrible vision rises from the fog – prison'. The finale quotes a famous revolutionary song with the words: 'Rage, you tyrants – Mock us, threaten us with prison and chains. We are strong in spirit, if weak in body. Shame, shame on you tyrants!'

d. Other Works

Shostakovich's practice of 'writing between the lines' and placing 'notes in a bottle' has long been understood by those 'with ears to listen'.[196] For example, about the finale of the Ninth Symphony, Mravinsky perceptively told his orchestra, 'You have the wrong sound. I need the sound of the trampling of steel-shod boots'.[197] Violinist Yakov Milkis adds, 'We knew he wasn't referring to ordinary soldiers, but to KGB forces'.[198] Zak also notes that when asked by a reporter if it was 'a toy store' that was represented in the first part of the Fifteenth Symphony, 'Shostakovich immediately parodied by saying: "Yes, yes, yes, of course, of course, it is a 'toy store'. A store. Toys! How can it be otherwise! It can't be! It can't be!"'[199] Maxim, however, stresses:

> Don't you believe those who say that the beginning of the Fifteenth Symphony is meant to be a 'toy store'. My father, who constantly had to overcome inconceivable difficulties

[196] Kurt Sanderling confirms

> that for us contemporaries who knew and worked with Shostakovich, it has never been difficult to interpret his works along with their double meanings. For us, it was all very clear. Shostakovich would have loved to be the 'Soviet Mussorgsky'. And so he has shown himself as a teller of history in, for example, the Eleventh and Twelfth Symphonies. Also, in the Fifth Symphony, with the so called 'Triumph' at the end – we understood what he was saying. And it was not the 'Triumph' of the mighty, those in power. There was no need for further explanation.
>
> Sanderling, p. 12.

[197] Wilson, p. 315.

[198] *Ibid.*, p. 315.

[199] Zak, p. 499. As an example of the multi-layered meanings in Shostakovich's works, Jackson notes that the quotation from Wagner's *Tristan und Isolde* in this Symphony may come via Debussy's parody in 'Golliwogg's Cakewalk', which, in turn, does have some small connection with a toy store (Jackson, p. 634). Furthermore, given the quotation from Beethoven's Quartet, Op. 135, pointed out by Maxim (Albert, p. 416), Shostakovich's response, 'How can it be otherwise! It can't be! It can't be!' may be a paraphrase of Beethoven's enigmatic inscription: 'Must it be? It must be! It must be!', a reasonable question to be posed in Shostakovich's last symphony.

> with the verbal 'decoding' of his instrumental works (which communist propaganda demanded be crammed into the official ideology's Procrustean bed), jumped at the harmless idea of a 'toy store', in order to protect his new symphony in some way against that spurious ideology.[200]

Shostakovich's inner circle not only was aware of his hidden messages but sometimes assisted the composer in deceiving the censors. For example, Vishnevskaya suggested that the song cycle *Satires* be called 'Pictures of the Past', because otherwise the authorities would never approve verses such as 'Our Posterity', which, though written in 1910, was also 'an indictment of the current Soviet regime and its insane ideology'. 'Throw them that bone and they might sanction it. Yesterday is part of the past, too; the public will see it that way.' Shostakovich responded: 'Beautifully thought out, Galya! Beautifully thought out. Under "Satires" we'll put "Pictures of the Past" in parentheses, like a kind of fig leaf. We'll cover up the embarrassing parts for them'.[201] Subterfuge also was used to save the song cycle *From Jewish Folk Poetry*. Natalya Vovsi-Mikhoels recalls that at its premiere the 'presenter' gave an explanation of each song, declaring about 'Lullaby' that 'it all took place in Tsarist Russia'. 'There was animation in the hall and people barely restrained themselves from laughing. For a long time after that Dmitri Dmitriyevich loved to repeat, "It all took place in Tsarist Russia, it all took place in Tsarist Russia"'.[202]

8. 'Soviet Russia's Most Loyal Musical Son'?

'Experts', such as Taruskin, still cling to the notion that Shostakovich was a good communist, or, at the very least, a 'fellow traveller'. Such an assertion has always been difficult

[200] Zak, p. 499. One should also recall that the USSR's central toy store was right across from the Lubyanka, the USSR's central prison.

[201] Vishnevskaya, *Galina*, pp. 268–29.

[202] Wilson, p. 230.

to fathom. As a perceptive Western commentator recently observed:

> In retrospect, it seems astonishing that anyone in the West, listening to the terrifying parodies of military bombast, the mordant irony and sarcasm, the hollow laughter and the despairing lamentation of his late symphonies and quartets [and not only late –EDS.], could take Shostakovich as a propagandist mouthpiece for the Soviet regime.[203]

Besides his symphonies and quartets, a wealth of other information is now available to refute the myth that Shostakovich was ever 'Soviet Russia's most loyal musical son'[204] and to corroborate the 'new' Shostakovich first revealed in *Testimony*.[205] Among this data are the testimonies of the composer's confidants, both émigré and non-émigré, as well as documentary evidence in his letters and manuscripts, including, especially, the recently discovered anti-Stalinist satire *Rayok*.[206]

[203] Canning.

[204] Taruskin, 'Dictator', p. 40. Incredibly, Taruskin was still clinging to this notion over three years after the fall of the Soviet regime. *Cf.* Richard Taruskin, 'A Martyred Opera Reflects Its Abominable Time', *The New York Times*, 6 November 1994, Section 2, p. 35 (hereafter Taruskin, 'Abominable').

Actually, Shostakovich *was* loyal – not to the Communist Party, but to the great Russian musical tradition, a distinction apparently lost on Richard Taruskin.

[205] *Testimony*'s seminal role in correcting Shostakovich's political image is indisputable. John Rockwell notes that *Testimony* 'single-handedly purges Shostakovich of his reputation as a Stalinist hack' ('Shostakovich Finds Many Advocates, No Great Champion', *The New York Times*, 19 April 1992, Section 2, p. 28, while Donal Henahan observes that 'in the space of a few years, Shostakovich went from being treated as a musical and political hack to enshrinement as a hero' ('How Time Alters Our Views of Music', *The New York Times*, 1 August 1982, Section 2, p. 17). Wilson, p. xi, agrees:

> there was a drastic re-evaluation of the composer's personality after the publication of *Testimony: The Memoirs of Dmitri Shostakovich as Related to and Edited by Solomon Volkov* in 1979. Hitherto, the official Soviet point of view had represented Shostakovich as an obedient socialist-realist and model Soviet citizen; he emerges from Volkov's book as a passionate anti-communist and embittered, life-weary individual.

[206] *Cf.* pp. 271–86.

a. A Primer for Musicologists

According to Vladimir Zak,[207] Daniil Zhitomirsky[208] and Inna Barsova,[209] among others, Shostakovich often spoke 'in code', out of fear for his family and himself. His own speech was highly individual and when the composer strayed from his familiar patter, friends knew that he intended either to convey the meaning directly opposite the literal text or to make a sarcastic commentary on the subject being discussed. Consider the following:

> Comrade Smirnov has read me the libretto for a ballet, *The New Machine*. Its theme is extremely relevant. There once was a machine. Then it broke down (problem of material decay). Then it was mended (problem of amortization). Then everybody dances around the new machine. Apotheosis. This all takes up three acts.[210]

This utterance provides simple clues for deciphering Shostakovich's 'Aesopian language'. Stilted phrases, *Pravda* clichés, deliberate exaggerations or excessive repetitions – all indicate that the words are not to be taken in their literal sense. Accordingly, when Shostakovich says that the ballet's theme is 'extremely relevant', what he means is that its theme is completely moronic. Additionally, it is clear that Shostakovich does not care much for the communist hack, Comrade Smirnov, who believed that such idiocy could last for three acts.

Several classic examples of Shostakovich's Aesopian language are found in Wilson's *Shostakovich: A Life Remembered*. After Khrushchev's dismissal, Shostakovich greeted fellow composer Sergei Slonimsky with 'Well, Sergei Mikhailovich, now we will most certainly enjoy an even better life?'[211] Here deliberate exaggeration is evident in the phrase 'an even *better* life?' while further subtext is provided

[207] Zak, pp. 495–506.

[208] Zhitomirsky, 'Public and Private'.

[209] Barsova, paper, pp. 1–2.

[210] Wilson, p. 90; from a letter to Sollertinsky (February 1930).

[211] Wilson, p. 381.

by 'a barely discernible ironic smile'[212] and a not-so-well-disguised reference to Stalin's famous description of 'victorious socialism', familiar to any Soviet.[213] A *Pravda* cliché may be found in Shostakovich's description of his father-in-law: one who had suffered from 'infringement of revolutionary law'.[214] 'Infringement of revolutionary law', of course, was a Sovietism that came to refer to the millions of people shot or sent to concentration camps for no reason at all. Among them was Irina's father.

Awareness of Shostakovich's Aesopian language also makes the following easy to decipher:

> 1944 is around the corner. A year of happiness, joy, and victory. This year will bring us much joy. The freedom-loving Peoples will at long last throw off the yoke of Hitlerism, and peace will reign throughout the world under the sunny rays of Stalin's Constitution. I am convinced of this, and therefore experience the greatest joy. Now we are apart; how I miss you; would that together we could rejoice at the victories of the Red Army led by its Great Commander, comrade Stalin.[215]

Here Shostakovich uses the device of excessive repetition.[216] As pointed out by Zak, when the composer repeated a phrase

[212] *Ibid.*, p. 381.

[213] 'Life became better, life became merrier', Stalin asserted in the midst of the Great Purges.

[214] Wilson, p. 351, quoting from I. Glikman, *Letters to a Friend*, p. 176.

[215] Wilson, p. 175, quoting from I. Glikman, *Letters to a Friend*, p. 62.

[216] *Cf.* the literary uses of *vranyo* (ludicrous exaggeration) discussed in Ian MacDonald, *The New Shostakovich*, pp. 109–10, as well as the following little masterpiece of Shostakovich's Aesopian language (letter of 29 December 1957, Odessa; I. Glikman, *Letters to a Friend*, p. 135):

> Dear Isaak Davydovich!
>
> I arrived in Odessa on the day of the all-people's celebration of the 40th anniversary of Soviet Ukraine. This morning I went out into the street. You, of course, yourself understand that one cannot stay indoors on such a day. Despite rainy and foggy weather, the whole of Odessa was out of doors. Everywhere were portraits of Marx, Engels, Lenin, Stalin, and also of comrades A. I. Belyaev, L. I. Brezhnev, N. A. Bulganin, K. E. Voroshilov, N. G. Ignatov, A. P. Kirilenko, F. R. Kozlov, O. V. Kuusinen, A. I. Mikoyan, N. A. Mukhitdinov, M. A. Suslov, E. A. Furtseva, N. S. Khrushchev, N. M. Shvernik, A. A. Aristov, P. A. Pospelov, Ya. E. Kalnberzin,

or word several times, it was for the purpose of bringing it to the listener's attention in its opposite meaning.[217] Accordingly, although the words 'joy' or 'rejoice'[218] are repeated four times within five sentences, it is clear that Shostakovich himself does not expect much joy after the end of the War. This passage also is stuffed with Soviet clichés: 'A year of happiness, joy, and victory', 'freedom-loving Peoples', 'yoke of Hitlerism', 'peace will reign', 'sunny rays of Stalin's Constitution', 'rejoice at the victories of the Red Army', 'Great Commander, comrade Stalin' – seven clichés in five sentences. Wilson is correct in noting the passage's 'unmistakable irony'.[219]

A. I. Kirichenko, A. N. Kosygin, K. T. Mazurov, V. P. Mzhavanadze, M. G. Pervukhin, N. T. Kalchenko.

Everywhere are flags, slogans, banners. All around are happy, beaming Russian, Ukrainian, Jewish faces. Here and there one hears eulogies in honour of the great banner of Marx, Engels, Lenin, Stalin, and also in honour of comrades A. I. Belyaev, L. I. Brezhnev, N. A. Bulganin, K. E. Voroshilov, N. G. Ignatov, A. P. Kirilenko, F. R. Kozlov, O. V. Kuusinen, A. I. Mikoyan, N. A. Mukhitdinov, M. A. Suslov, E. A. Furtseva, N. S. Khrushchev, N. M. Shvernik, A. A. Aristov, P. A. Pospelov, Ya. E. Kalnberzin, A. I. Kirichenko, A. N. Kosygin, K. T. Mazurov, V. P. Mzhavanadze, M. G. Pervukhin, N. T. Kalchenko, D. S. Korotchenko. Everywhere one hears Russian and Ukrainian speech. Sometimes one hears the foreign speech of the representatives of progressive humanity, who have come to Odessa to congratulate its residents on the occasion of their glorious holiday. I too wandered around and, unable to restrain my joy, returned to my hotel where I resolved to describe, so far as I can, the all-people's celebration in Odessa.

Do not judge me harshly.
All the best,
D. Shostakovich.

This letter is discussed on the website 'Music under Soviet Rule': Ian MacDonald and Dmitry Feofanov, '"Do Not Judge Me Harshly": Anti-Communism in Shostakovich's Letters to Isaak Glikman' (http://www.siue.edu/~aho/musov/doubletalk.html); *cf.* also *DSCH Journal*, No. 8, Winter 1997, pp. 11–14.

[217] Zak, p. 497.

[218] *Cf.* p. 164. The use of the word 'rejoice' calls to mind Shostakovich's oft-quoted phrase 'Our business is to rejoice', uttered to Zhitomirsky after the bombing of Hiroshima in 1945 and repeated in *Testimony* to describe the forced optimism in the finale of the Fifth Symphony.

[219] Wilson, p. 175.

b. Internal Dissidence

Although Shostakovich's criticisms were, by necessity, encoded in public, they were also expressed openly and regularly to his confidants. His student Denisov recalled:

> Once I said something nice about Voroshilov; for some reason I felt particular sympathy for him. Dmitri Dmitriyevich said to me, 'Edik, if Budyonny is up to his knees in blood, then Voroshilov is up to his balls in blood'. 'And Kaganovich?' 'Kaganovich is up to his neck in blood.' I remember his exact words.[220]

Budyonny, Voroshilov and Kaganovich were Stalin's henchmen. The crescendo of blood (knees, balls, neck) leaves no doubt about Shostakovich's opinion of the Great Friend of Composers himself. Shostakovich's ongoing loathing of officials is confirmed by his long-time friend, Flora Litvinova, who, after Stalin died, expressed her hope that the head of the secret police, Lavrenty Beriya, would establish justice and release the prisoners from the camps. Shostakovich 'pounced' on her:

> How can you believe such deliberate lies, lies that have been put into circulation by *that* department! *Beriya*, who personally cut up corpses and flushed them down the toilet, now wants people to believe that he has grown wings. And you are inclined to believe it![221]

Litvinova also recalls that in 1970 Shostakovich characterised the situation as 'a bit easier', but still denounced the authorities for 'contort[ing] us, [. . .] warp[ing] our lives!' Without 'Party guidance', Shostakovich said, he would have been 'stronger and sharper' in his work and could have 'revealed his ideas openly instead of having to resort to camouflage [. . .]'.[222] Unfortunately for the composer, those

[220] *Ibid.*, p. 303.

[221] *Ibid.*, p. 261; emphasis in the original.

[222] *Ibid.*, p. 426. Shostakovich, however, knew that such 'easier' times would not last: 'We have to use the short period of the thaw. The novel [by Il'ya Ehrenburg] is bad, and the word is found – "the thaw". Have to use it. Experience teaches there will be frosts, and big ones' (Litvinova, p. 174).

without ears to hear or eyes to see continue to mistake the camouflage for the man.[223]

Finally, Shostakovich's internal dissidence is corroborated by yet another student, Veniamin Basner, who recalled the composer engaging in an act familiar to anyone living in the USSR during the 'stagnation' period:

> We also used to listen to the BBC Russian Service. These programmes were transmitted on the radio at 1.45 p.m. Dmitri Dmitriyevich only let it be known to his most intimate circle of friends that he listened to the BBC. I was always struck by a detail, typical of his punctiliousness: after listening, he was always careful to tune the radio back to the bandwave of Radio Moscow – just in case anybody bothered to check![224]

Since Soviet authorities certainly did not think 'loyal sons' had anything to gain from listening to foreign broadcasts (and, in fact, spent considerable sums jamming the most pernicious 'voices'), why then would Shostakovich tune-in to the BBC? Clearly, Shostakovich knew that the whole truth was not on Radio Moscow.

9. Other Contradictions

Other 'contradictions' in *Testimony* can be readily resolved by putting the passages into proper perspective. For example, did Shostakovich witness Lenin's arrival at the Finland Station in Petrograd on 3 April 1917? Two versions of this story in Wilson's study deviate in details from that in

[223] *Cf.* Zhitomirsky, 'Public and Private):

> Most of the objections to Volkov's memoirs were based on the complete failure of its Western accusers to distinguish the real Shostakovich from the prestigious official figure.

[224] Wilson, p. 436. Confirmed by Galina Shostakovich in a conversation with the authors, 15 October 1995.

Shostakovich's 'fear of being discovered' was obviously formed in the 1930s, when listening to foreign broadcasts could be hazardous to one's health. After the Thaw, and especially in the 1970s, the authorities more or less gave up hope of maintaining total control over information. 'Once bitten, twice shy', nonetheless, and Shostakovich was bitten more than once.

Testimony. The composer's sister, Zoya Shostakovich, remembered that

> when the Revolution started and Lenin arrived at the Finland Station, a whole group of boys rushed off there. Mitya came back home in raptures, saying he had seen Lenin. Well, he was only a young boy of ten.[225]

Lebedinsky also recalled discussing this event with the composer: ' "What did you go to the Finland Station for?" I asked Shostakovich [many years later]. "I wanted to hear Lenin's speech", he said. "I knew a dictator was arriving" '.[226] The second account, obviously, is filtered through hindsight, while that in *Testimony*, again, seems closest to the truth. Shostakovich begins his memoirs stating, one 'must speak the truth [. . .] only the truth [. . . and] not colour or falsify anything'.[227] Of Lenin's arrival he acknowledges:

> They say that the major event in my life was the march down to the Finland Station in April 1917, when Lenin arrived in Petrograd. The incident did take place. [. . .] But I don't remember a thing. If I had been told ahead of time just what a luminary was arriving, I would have paid more attention, but as it is, I don't remember much.[228]

The version in *Testimony* has been corroborated by Galina Shostakovich and Yevgeny Chukovsky, both of whom 'had no memory of the composer ever giving them an account of this event [witnessing Lenin's arrival]'.[229] In addition, Boris Lossky attributes this story to 'sheer invention by the guardians of this Soviet composer's "ideological purity" '.[230]

[225] Wilson, p. 6.

[226] *Ibid.*, p. 335.

[227] *Testimony*, p. 1/3.

[228] *Ibid.*, p. 4/7. This admission is not inconsistent with Shostakovich's exceptional memory. Like Aitken (*cf.* p. 199, note 325), Shostakovich did not have 'total recall' of everything that happened in his life, but remembered things of importance or interest to him.

[229] Wilson, p. 19.

[230] *Ibid.*, p. 20.

Shostakovich's comments about people and works also may seem contradictory at first glance: he both praises and criticises Stravinsky, Prokofiev, Glazunov, Mravinsky and many others. Yet, a closer reading of *Testimony* makes these assessments perfectly understandable. Shostakovich says 'Glière wasn't a bad fellow, but he was a mediocre composer'.[231] On the other hand, he adored Stravinsky's music but often despised the man.[232] Shostakovich further admits that his tastes for various works and composers have changed over the years, as have his opinions of performers such as Mravinsky, who fell out of favour when he withdrew from the premiere of the Thirteenth Symphony. In *Testimony*, he explains:

> I spoke of these people, my acquaintances, in various ways throughout my life. Occasionally I contradicted myself – and I'm not ashamed of that. I changed my mind about these people and there's nothing shameful in that. There would have been, had I done so because of external pressures or to make my life better. But that was not the case. These people simply changed and so did I. I listened to new music and grew to know the old better. I read, I was told many things, I suffered from insomnia, and I spent many nights ruminating. All this affected me. And that's why today I don't think about people the way I did thirty, forty or fifty years ago.[233]

On another page, he acknowledges that 'I'm often asked why I do this and that and say this and that, or why I sign such-

[231] *Testimony*, p. 30/42.

[232] This is evident on many pages of *Testimony*. Furthermore, in a letter to Isaak Glikman (9 September 1971), Shostakovich states: 'Stravinsky the composer, I worship. Stravinsky the thinker, I despise' (Wilson, p. 377; quoting from I. Glikman, *Letters to a Friend*, p. 279). Glikman elaborates: 'Shostakovich had expressed more than once his admiration for Stravinsky's music. He even had Stravinsky's portrait on his desk in Moscow. But he couldn't stomach Stravinsky's egotism and his disregard for artists who had been persecuted while Stalin was in power' (Fisk, *Composers on Music*, p. 357).

[233] *Testimony*, p. 57/75. Flora Litvinova confirms that Shostakovich's opinions about many composers, especially contemporary ones, 'changed with time. I remember, once he praised *Wozzeck*, but at another time characterized it as a superficial and not profound work' (Litvinova, p. 176). *Cf.* also pp. 97–98 and 148–49.

and-such articles. I answer different people differently, because different people deserve different answers.'[234]

Family, friends and colleagues confirm that contradictions were characteristic of Shostakovich, from youth to old age. Zoshchenko, in a letter to Shaginyan (4 January 1941), noted that the composer was extremely contradictory: 'In him, one quality obliterates the other. It is a conflict in the highest degree. It is almost a disaster'.[235] Many years later, Meyer similarly described Shostakovich as a man of contradictions,[236] and Denisov, too, acknowledged that 'Shostakovich was full of paradox'.[237]

Changes in Shostakovich's opinions were sometimes baffling. For example, in his youth, one could find him participating in a conversation about 'kike domination in the arts',[238] but later he became so closely associated with Jewish

[234] *Testimony*, p. 141/185. Shostakovich also attributes his fascination with Jewish folk music to its multifacetedness: 'It can appear to be happy while it is tragic. It's almost always laughter through tears' (*ibid.*, p. 118/156).

[235] Shaginyan, p. 73.

[236] Meyer, p. 52.

[237] Wilson, p. 301.

[238] Volkov was surprised to read among Valerian Bogdanov-Berezovsky's papers, which included some 100 letters from Shostakovich, that at the age of sixteen 'Mitya came and for three hours we talked about kike domination [*zasil'ye zhidov*] in the arts'. According to Volkov:

> Nowadays this seems unbelievable and not only with regard to Shostakovich: how could Mitya have talked about such a topic with anyone; especially, how could he have talked with Bogdanov-Berezovsky about it. B.-B. had been my patron in Leningrad, it was thanks to his interceding on my behalf that the book about young composers was published. I also knew V. M. [Valerian Mikhailovich] as a true gentleman .... For me, this is the most striking evidence that a person does change, and changes a lot and assuredly not always for the better, but in various directions. A man acts differently at different times of his life, during the various days and hours of his existence. But we say: 'this man is a genius, we love this genius, we recognize his art, therefore he must be a saint'.
>
> Drubachevskaya, p. 337.

Shostakovich, too, acknowledges such discussions in *Testimony*, p. 119/157: 'In my youth I came across anti-Semitism in my peers, who thought that Jews were getting preferential treatment'.

causes that many thought (mistakenly) he was himself a Jew. Maxim also recalls that his father would say 'at breakfast that he detested Tchaikovsky's developments, then assert something else at lunch and conclude at dinner that there was nothing more beautiful than the *Queen of Spades*'.[239] Lebedinsky, too, remembers that

> Over the years, he [Shostakovich] assumed a mask, and played the role of an obedient Party member. Nevertheless, he often lost his orientation in the complex labyrinths of political behaviour. His writings often contradicted what he said, and, even worse, his actions contradicted what he had written. The most tragic example of his neurotic behaviour was his joining the Communist Party in 1960, which he hated and despised.[240]

In proper perspective, Volkov's acknowledgement that Shostakovich 'often contradicted himself [and] then the true meaning of his words had to be guessed, extracted from a box with three false bottoms',[241] rings true. Even Wilson recognises 'contradictions and differences of opinion' in her study, but concludes that the 'overall picture of Dmitri Shostakovich built up from this mosaic of many pieces is a consistent one'.[242] In some ways, contradictions actually support, rather than impeach, the authenticity of *Testimony*, revealing a three-dimensional, changing image of the composer that belies Soviet and some Western charges that the 'new' Shostakovich is one-sided.

[239] Interview with Patrick Szersnovicz and Grégory Thomas, 'Prénom Maxime', *Le Monde de la Musique*, No. 118, January 1989, supplement, p. xv; transl. Malcolm H. Brown in his review of Ian MacDonald's *The New Shostakovich, Notes*, 49/3, March 1993, p. 958 (hereafter Brown, review). Maxim elaborated on this during a lecture at the University of Houston, 7 June 1990: 'I remember him sitting at the breakfast table and listening to the Tchaikovsky Fourth. He made a face, groaning that Tchaikovsky's developments are always so four-square. Later that day, we heard *The Queen of Spades*. His only words for it were "sublime genius"' (Albert, p. 402).

[240] Wilson, p. 336.

[241] *Testimony*, p. xiv/xvii.

[242] Wilson, p. xvi.

10. Omissions

The authenticity of *Testimony* has been challenged from all angles. The image of the 'new' Shostakovich, for example, has been criticised as one-sided, even while the much more one-sided 'old' Shostakovich was accepted without question and anything remotely contradictory (that is, more than one-sided) was quickly condemned. *Testimony* also has been judged not only on what it contains but on what it omits. Veniamin Basner recalls a story Shostakovich told him about being interrogated, one Saturday in Spring 1937, by an NKVD investigator named Zanchevsky. The latter wanted to know what Shostakovich knew about Marshal Tukhachevsky and the plot to assassinate Stalin. Shostakovich eventually was told to go home and return the following Monday, but was saved when Zanchevsky himself was arrested over the weekend. In December 1988, Basner stated:

> I think Dmitri Dmitriyevich only ever told this story to me, and that was many years after the event. This fact contributes to various reasons why I am forced to believe that the memoirs attributed to Shostakovich in Solomon Volkov's *Testimony* are in fact a falsified account, as this story does not appear there. [. . .] Surely Dmitri Dmitriyevich would have included this story if he was writing his candid memoirs.[243]

It is ironic that Basner, who, as one of 'Les Six Soviétiques', originally proclaimed *Testimony* a forgery because it was anti-Communist,[244] now proclaims *Testimony* a forgery because it is not anti-Communist enough. Like Fay, Basner wants to have his cake and eat it, too. Although Basner's logic is clearly flawed,[245] Volkov confirms that Shostakovich did tell him about this interrogation, three times. But each time Shostakovich could not recall the exact name of the interrogator – Zanchevsky, Zakrevsky or Zakovsky – and Volkov,

[243] *Ibid.*, p. 125.

[244] *Cf.* pp. 60–61.

[245] Why does Basner expect Shostakovich to make public in *Testimony* a story he withheld from everyone else? In addition, memoirs are never complete, and these were to be about other people (*Testimony*, pp. 1/3 and 87/116).

thus, decided to omit this episode.[246] This was a case in which a guess was impossible 'from the box with three false bottoms'. Indeed, critics would have had a field day had Volkov guessed, and guessed wrong.

Volkov also admits that Shostakovich told him about a hidden reference to an Azerbaijani girl in his Tenth Symphony, but did not mention her by name. Nelly Kravetz, in 1994, identified this woman as Elmira Nazirova, and demonstrated that the third movement, which incorporates the composer's own DSCH (D-E flat-C-B) motive, also includes a motive derived from the name 'Elmira' (E-L(a)-Mi-R(e)-A: E-A-E-D-A; Horn I, figure 114). Kravetz was the first to elaborate on the significance of these motives: Shostakovich had carried on 'an intense (and probably largely one-sided) correspondence' with Nazirova, his former pupil at the Moscow Conservatory, during the summer of 1953, and the 'Elmira' motive may also relate to the passing quotation from his second *Pushkin Monologue*, 'What is in my name for you?'[247] According to Volkov, the information about Nazirova was not included in *Testimony* because it was considered

[246] Conversation between Volkov and the authors, Spring 1995. Volkov believes that Shostakovich made up this story. (Also *cf.* Ian MacDonald, 'You Must Remember!: Shostakovich's Alleged Interrogation by the NKVD in 1937', *DSCH Journal*, No. 6, Winter 1996, pp. 25–27.)

Volkov's statement that Shostakovich mentioned different names (Zanchevsky, Zakrevsky, Zakovsky) in retelling this incident has been unwittingly corroborated by Basner himself. In Wilson's book he identifies the interrogator as 'Zanchevsky', but in the second part of *Soviet Echoes*, Channel 4's 1995 documentary series on Soviet music, Basner, supposedly recalling 'word for word' the composer's account of the interrogation, gives the name as 'Zakovsky' (*cf.* Ian MacDonald, 'You Must Remember!', pp. 25–27). Krzysztof Meyer, in his biography of the composer, also recalls hearing about this incident (*Dimitri Chostakovich* (Fayard: Paris, 1994), p. 211). This time, however, Shostakovich identified the interrogator as 'Zakrevsky', the third name cited by Volkov.

[247] Wilson, p. 263; based on Nelly Kravetz's paper, 'A New Insight Into the Tenth Symphony of Dmitri Shostakovich', University of Michigan, 28 January 1994.

The period of most frequent communication between Shostakovich and Nazirova was in August and September 1953, i.e., exactly during the composition of the Tenth Symphony. In August, Shostakovich wrote to Nazirova up to one letter per day, and in September up to two letters per day. In a letter of 29 August, he demonstrated how he had transformed her

too personal. Volkov had good reason to be leery of including the story. Flora Litvinova recalls Shostakovich guarding his privacy and saying 'Can you imagine what Chekhov's reaction would have been had he known his wife would expose him in front of honest people [by publishing their correspondence]? She should be ashamed of herself, publishing all the intimate details of their life together'.[248] Shostakovich revisited the issue, but with more ambivalence, in *Testimony*: 'I'm quite sorry that the correspondence between Anton Pavlovich and his wife was ever published; it's so intimate that most of it should not be seen in print. [. . .] On the other hand, when you read Chekhov's letters you gain a better understanding of his fiction [. . .]'.[249]

Volkov's critics will be quick to assert that he is merely taking credit for information gained after the fact. However, Volkov has not claimed knowing about even more significant revelations. At a Shostakovich symposium in 1992, Maxim stated that his father 'thought about [emigrating] [. . .]. Especially in the '50s and '60s [. . .]. I know when there were difficult times in his life there were instances when he thought about it. [. . .] he didn't ever think about exactly where he would go, Germany or America or France or whatever, but just sort of generally'.[250] Volkov's immediate

---

name into the notes of the horn theme of the third movement, and on 17 September mentioned still another parallel between this theme and Mahler's *Das Lied von der Erde* ('Revelations – the 10th Symphony', *DSCH Journal*, No. 1, Summer 1994, pp. 24–25, summarising Nelly Kravetz's paper) (hereafter 'Revelations – the 10th Symphony').

[248] Wilson, p. 165.

[249] *Testimony*, p. 136/178.

[250] Robinson, p. 397. Actually, Shostakovich may have considered emigrating as early as Autumn 1928. In an interview on 4 May 1980, Mrs Joseph Schillinger recalled: 'The last telephone call he [her husband] received before quitting Leningrad had been from the mother of his close friend Dmitri Shostakovich, who had pleaded with Schillinger to do what he could to arrange for her son's emigration to America as well' (S. Frederick Starr, *Red and Hot: The Fate of Jazz in the Soviet Union 1917–1980*, Oxford University Press, New York, 1983, p. 76). Schillinger's early friendship with and lasting respect for Shostakovich also are mentioned briefly in Frances Schillinger's *Joseph Schillinger: A Memoir*, 1949; reprinted by Da Capo Press, New York, 1976, pp. 163 and 211.

Serge Tcherepnin also recalls his father, Alexander Tcherepnin, receiv-

response was that Shostakovich 'never expressed any such thoughts to me. [. . .] I never even suspected that he would think about emigration. That's absolutely a revelation'.[251]

Volkov also claims no knowledge of Shostakovich's earlier plans to write his memoirs,[252] of the Eighth Quartet being dedicated 'in memory of Shostakovich himself' and relating to the latter's planned suicide,[253] or of the Tenth Symphony being written in 1951 instead of 1953.[254] In Wilson's study, Tat'yana Nikolayeva states:

> One day I came to the house (in the early months of 1951), and saw a large score on the piano. He [Shostakovich] said to

---

ing a letter from Shostakovich in the 1950s or '60s (it may have been brought by Igor Oistrakh or his accompanist on their first visit to Chicago in 1955), asking for his help in emigrating (conversation between Serge Tcherepnin and Martin Anderson, 18 April 1998).

[251] Robinson, p. 397. Maxim previously had skirted this issue, even in his conversation with Schwarz in 1981 (Schwarz, p. 645). Shostakovich, of course, never acted on these thoughts of emigration, probably for the reason expressed in Dubinsky's parable (p. 257):

> Two worms crawl out of the ground, father and son, and the little one asks, 'Papa, what's that long and green thing there?'
> 'That, son, is a blade of grass.'
> 'Pretty! And that big yellow-and-green thing?'
> 'That's a tree.'
> 'How pretty! And there, all around, the blue?'
> 'The sky.'
> 'It's so pretty! And that bright red one?'
> 'The sun.'
> 'Oh, what beauty! And why, Papa, if everything is so beautiful, do we live down there in the dark and muck?'
> 'Because, son, that's our motherland. Let's go home!'

Lebedinsky, by the way, recalled a sociologist saying to Shostakovich ' "I know you are a well-known composer, but who are you in comparison with our great Leader". Thinking of Dargomyzhsky's famous romance with its text, "I am a worm in comparison to His Excellency", he [Shostakovich] immediately interjected, "I am a worm". "Yes, that's just it, you are indeed a worm", this idiot said, "and it's a good thing you possess a healthy sense of self-criticism"' (Wilson, p. 273).

[252] Conversation between Volkov and the authors, 15 November 1995. *Cf.* pp. 138–39.

[253] Conversation between Volkov and the authors, August 1995.

[254] Conversations between Volkov and the authors, July and August 1995.

> me, 'Today I will play you something different'. It was the exposition of the first movement of his Tenth Symphony. He started writing this wonderful work simultaneously with the composition of the Preludes and Fugues. [...] Soon Dmitri Dmitriyevich went on to play me the other movements of the Tenth Symphony as it was being composed. I can't remember the exact date when he completed it; but it was during 1951, and not in 1953, the date always given in programme notes and textbooks.[255]

Although the Tenth Symphony may have been begun in 1951, then substantially revised in 1953, evidence is lacking to confirm the earlier date. On the other hand, Shostakovich's letters from June to October 1953 chronicle the creation of each movement and, in effect, corroborate the date in *Testimony*.[256] The 'Elmira' motive in the third movement also seems to point to Summer 1953, when Shostakovich was engaged in 'intense correspondence' with Nazirova.[257]

Two other 'omissions' may be examined in brief. First, Robert Craft, in his review of *Testimony*, complains:

> Volkov should also have tried to explain some of the text's many mysterious absences. At one place, Shostakovich alludes to Mme Furtseva (the Minister of Culture), or so Volkov identifies the reference. But since she played a role of major importance in the composer's life, he must have had some feelings, as well as inside information, about her fall from power and Roman-style wrist-slashing death –

[255] Wilson, pp. 256–57.

[256] 'I wrote it right after Stalin's death [1953]' (*Testimony*, p. 107/141).

[257] Wilson, p. 262, states that 'it would seem far-fetched for him [Shostakovich] consciously to wish to create the fiction of writing a work two years after its actual completion'. She acknowledges, however, that a movement of an unfinished violin sonata (1946) has a first theme resembling that in the Symphony and second themes that are identical, suggesting 'that Shostakovich had been mulling over this musical material for many years before it eventually got written down in finished form as the Tenth Symphony'. Hulme, who is currently revising his catalogue of Shostakovich's works, also is unaware of any evidence supporting Nikolayeva's contention (letter to the authors, 5 December 1995). Ironically, some of the same scholars who reject an earlier date for the Seventh Symphony, despite the evidence (*cf*. pp. 150–59), willingly accept an earlier date for the Tenth, based solely on Nikolayeva's word.

> announced in *Pravda*, with no details, on the same day as the obituary for David Oistrakh.[258]

Actually, there is no such allusion to Furtseva in *Testimony*,[259] nor anything mysterious about its absence. Furtseva died on 24 October 1974, and Volkov states in his Preface:

> [On 13] November 1974, Shostakovich invited me to his home. We talked for a while and then he asked me where the manuscript was. 'In the West', I replied.[260]

Clearly, *Testimony* was already complete by late October and Shostakovich had no time to comment on Furtseva's 'Roman-style wrist-slashing death'.

Finally, Dr Dajue Wang, a neurologist from Beijing, reports in *The Musical Times* that

> in the 1950s he worked with a leading Soviet neurosurgeon, who told him about a patient he once treated who had been hit by German shrapnel during the siege of Leningrad in World War II. [...] The Soviet doctor told him that the patient, Shostakovich, was X-rayed and discovered to have a metal fragment lodged in his brain, evidently in 'the temporal horn of the left ventricle (a hollow cavity within the brain filled with cerebrospinal fluid), the very part of the brain, of course, that is concerned with hearing'. Shostakovich, however, was reluctant to have the metal removed and no wonder: 'Since the fragment had been there, he said, each time he leaned his head to one side he could hear music. His head was filled with melodies – different each time – which he then made use of when composing. Moving his head back level immediately stopped the music.' [...] the Soviet doctor consulted with his superior [...] who examined Shostakovich and agreed that the fragment should be left where it was, because 'a German shell will have done some good if it helps produce more music'.[261]

[258] Craft, 'Testaments', p. 81.

[259] Furtseva is mentioned only in the caption of a photograph reproduced between pp. 142–43/182–83 of *Testimony*. The authors have sought clarification from Craft, but without success.

[260] *Ibid.*, p. xiv/xviii.

[261] Dajue Wang, 'Shostakovich: Music on the Brain?', *The Musical Times*, 124, June 1983, pp. 347–48, as summarised in Donal Henahan, 'Did Shostakovich Have a Secret?', *The New York Times*, 10 July 1983, Section 2, p. 21 (hereafter Henahan).

Donal Henahan asks facetiously: 'Why is a war injury not mentioned in any Shostakovich biography and not even in *Testimony*, which purports to be the composer's memoirs as dictated to Solomon Volkov?'[262] Curiously, while Laurel Fay has difficulty understanding that the Seventh Symphony could have been inspired by both Stalin and the Nazis ('Which are we to believe?'), she finds Wang's theory of 'Music on the Brain' (that German shrapnel helped Shostakovich compose) credible enough to include in her updated bibliography to Schwarz's 'Shostakovich' article.[263]

11. Plagiarism or Self-Quotation?

Fay's most 'conclusive'[264] evidence that *Testimony* is a dishonest presentation are eight passages that she claims were 'plagiarized' by Volkov from earlier articles by Shostakovich:

Testimony	*Earlier Articles*
23/32–33	[D. Shostakovich] in B. M. Iarustovskii, ed., *I. F. Stravinskii: stat'i i materialy* (Sovetskii kompozitor, Moscow, 1973), pp. 7–8.
[36–37/50–51	'Stranitsy vospominanii', *Leningradskaia konservatoriia v vospominaniiakh* (Muzgiz, Leningrad, 1962), pp. 125–26.]
58/77–78	'Iz vospominanii', *Sovetskaya Muzyka*, 1974, No. 3, p. 54.
80/106–7	'Tragediia-satira', *Sovetskoe Iskusstvo*, 16 October 1932; reprinted in L. Danilevich (ed.), *Dmitrii Shostakovich* (Sovetskii kompozitor, Moscow, 1967): 13.
117/154–55	'Kak rozhdaetsia muzyka', *Literaturnaya Gazeta*, 21 December 1965; reprinted in Danilevich, *Dmitrii Shostakovich*, p. 36.
136/178–79	'Samyi blizkii', *Literaturnaya Gazeta*,

[262] Henahan, p. 21.

[263] Schwarz and Fay, p. 218.

[264] *Cf*. pp. 117–18.

	28 January 1960; reprinted in Danilevich, *Dmitrii Shostakovich*, pp. 34–35.
175/226–27	'Partitura opery', *Izvestiia*, 1 May 1941; reprinted in Danilevich, *Dmitrii Shostakovich*, pp. 14–16.
190/245–46	'O vospominanii o Maiakovskom', in *V. Maiakovskii v vospominaniiakh sovremennikov* (Khudozhestvennaia literatura, Moscow, 1963), p. 315.[265]

In noting the dates of these articles, which span from 1932 to 1974, Fay suggests that some of these passages were written so long ago that it is unlikely that Shostakovich could have repeated them in his conversations with Volkov. What she does not demonstrate, however, is that Shostakovich had never reviewed these materials in the interim. She also does not make clear that all of these sources were printed or reprinted between 1962 and 1974, and that two are exactly contemporaneous with the Volkov-Shostakovich meetings. In *Testimony*, Shostakovich says about books about himself 'I do read them rather carefully, I think'.[266] He even alludes to Danilevich ('my biographer, you might say, a Shostakovich specialist'[267]), the editor of the collection published in 1967, just four years before work on *Testimony* began, that reprints half of Fay's eight sources. Fay concludes that 'the sheer length of the identified quotations as well as their formalized language make it utterly inconceivable that the composer had memorized his previously published statements and then repeated them exactly in his conversations with Volkov'.[268] Here, apparently, she assumes that the Volkov-Shostakovich meetings consisted solely of informal chitchat and off-the-cuff comments. If, however, Shostakovich intended to document his memoirs, to speak about

[265] Fay, p. 488. Fay incorrectly cites the title of the last article, which should be '*Iz* vospominanii o Maiakovskom'. She credits Simon Karlinsky with previously identifying the first and last examples, and Malcolm Brown with identifying the second (added above in square brackets from Fay's note 17).

[266] *Testimony*, p. 31/42.

[267] *Ibid.*, p. 92/122.

[268] Fay, p. 490.

things and finally get it right,[269] it is entirely conceivable that he might sometimes work with the same type of precision with which he composed music, committing his thoughts to paper in finished form.[270] (Even Volkov found some of Shostakovich's responses 'highly stylized', as if they had 'been polished over many years'.[271]) Significantly, Fay provides absolutely no proof that Shostakovich would not or could not repeat himself in much the same words, while neglecting pertinent information to the contrary. In particular, Fay does not mention Shostakovich's phenomenal memory, which often made the seemingly impossible possible.

Shostakovich's feats of memory were well known to his family, friends and colleagues, and are sufficiently important in Wilson's study to warrant an entry in the index. The composer, too, modestly mentions his own memory in *Testimony*, while praising that of his friends and idols, such as Glazunov,[272] Sollertinsky[273] and Musorgsky:

> I turned out to have absolute pitch and a good memory. I learned notes quickly, and I memorized easily, without repetition – it came on its own.[274]

> I can't complain about [my musical memory] and Mussorgsky memorized Wagner's operas on first hearing. He could play Wotan's scene by heart after only one hearing of *Siegfried*.[275]

On other pages, Shostakovich admits orchestrating *Boris Godunov* 'from memory, act by act',[276] and notes: 'I love

269 In contrast to much of what had been written earlier, which he says is wrong (*Testimony*, pp. 1/3, 33/45, 117/155).

270 *Cf.* pp. 151–53, notes 136–38.

271 *Testimony*, p. xiv/xvii.

272 *Ibid.*, pp. 51–52/68.

273 *Ibid.*, pp. 27–28/38 and 29/41.

274 *Ibid.*, p. 2/5. This statement repeats, nearly verbatim, Shostakovich's assessment in his 'Autobiography', *Sovetskaya Muzyka*, 1966, No. 9, p. 24: 'It turned out that I had perfect pitch and a good memory. I learnt music very quickly, I memorized without repetitious learning – the notes just stayed in my memory by themselves' (Wilson, p. 10).

275 *Testimony*, p. 184/238.

276 *Ibid.*, p. 175/227.

Gogol. I'm not bragging, but I know pages and pages by heart'.[277]

The scope of Shostakovich's memory, however, is best revealed in the testimony of others. Kondrashin stated that Shostakovich 'had a photographic memory',[278] Yury Tyulin stated that Shostakovich possessed 'an incredible memory [. . . and] remembered everything he heard',[279] and Valerian Bogdanov-Berezovsky noted that Shostakovich's 'memory created the impression of an apparatus which made a photographic record of everything he heard'.[280] Shostakovich's incredible musical memory was evident from the start. Nadezhda Galli-Shohat recalled how Mitya, in 1911, 'sat breathless through the performance [of Rimsky-Korsakov's *Tale of the Tsar Saltan*], and the next day surprised the family with his unusual memory and ear. He recited and sang correctly most of the opera'.[281] In later years, his memory continued to impress his colleagues: Arnold Ferkelman noticed that when playing chamber music Shostakovich 'knew all the music from memory';[282] Rostropovich 'never ceased to be amazed by Dmitri Dmitriyevich's memory and his capacity for total recall when it came to details of scoring and orchestration';[283] Berlinsky remembered that Shostakovich, at his first meeting with the Borodin Quartet in 1945, forgot the score of his First Quartet (1938) and, thus, played it 'from memory, beginning to end, to demonstrate the tempo';[284] and Meyer, too, recognised Shostakovich's 'phenomenal ear and phenomenal memory'. One incident

[277] *Ibid.*, p. 157/205.

[278] *Cf.* p. 508.

[279] Wilson, p. 34.

[280] *Ibid.*, p. 25.

[281] Wilson, p. 10. Shostakovich himself gave the date of this performance as Spring 1915 (*Autobiography*, 1927; Lukyanova, p. 16). By age 15, he could also play from memory all 48 preludes and fugues from Bach's *Well-tempered Clavier* (p. 611, note 25).

[282] *Ibid.*, p. 104.

[283] *Ibid.*, p. 187.

[284] Nikolska, p. 73.

that especially impressed him was Shostakovich's performance of Beethoven's *Grosse Fuge*, on the spur of the moment, when their discussion turned to Beethoven:

> I remember one day he suggested, 'Let's play Beethoven's Grosse Fuge,' and handed me the score. In his study there were two pianos which were always out of tune.
>
> 'You play the first violin and viola parts on that piano, and I'll play the second violin and cello parts on the other one.'
>
> As we only had one copy of the score, I asked, 'How are we going to divide the music?'
>
> Shostakovich waved his hand. 'It's all right, I'll play it from memory,' and then proceeded to play the whole quartet with me without a single mistake.[285]

This scarcely believable feat was no exception. According to Il'ya Slonim, when Shostakovich spoke about music 'he would rush to the piano to illustrate his point [. . .]. I remember him playing nearly all of *Boris Godunov* when the conversation touched on Musorgsky, and nearly all of *Petrushka* when we talked about Stravinsky'.[286] Flora Litvinova adds:

> Shostakovich's amazing memory is much talked about. He knew all of classical music by heart, and much contemporary music. It was enough for him to look at a score or to listen to a work once for him to remember it. [. . .] His musical memory was a delight to us all, but on the other hand it didn't surprise me, because it seemed like a natural extension of his genius.[287]

Maxim also confirms that his father 'knew everything that was written before him from memory'. He further states, 'I know of no other composer who could sit down at the piano and play and sing the entire *Ring Cycle* from beginning to end from memory'.[288]

Significantly, Shostakovich's prodigious memory was not confined to music. Slonim notes that 'when talking about

[285] Wilson, pp. 464–65; also Meyer, p. 9.

[286] Wilson, p. 171.

[287] Wilson, p. 166; Litvinova, p. 163.

[288] Albert, p. 402.

books, he [Shostakovich] would quote whole passages verbatim',[289] and Grigory Kozintsev remembers that Shostakovich 'often, to his own delight [. . .] would recall from memory whole chunks of Chekhov or Gogol'.[290] Flora and Tat'yana Litvinova describe other feats:

> I was flabbergasted by the way he knew and remembered literature. Once I was lamenting the fact that I didn't bring Gogol's *Dead Souls* with me; Dmitri Dmitriyevich immediately started quoting long extracts from it, about the carriage, the speculation as to whether the wheel would arrive in Moscow. Laughing he recited the piece about Chichikov dressing for the evening party.[291]

> Once, during a sitting, he [Shostakovich] noticed that I was reading Dostoevsky's *A Raw Youth*. He began to recite the book from memory, paragraph by paragraph. [. . .] He could also recite from memory whole pages of Zoshchenko.[292]

Other witnesses to Shostakovich's incredible memory include Yevtushenko and Vishnevskaya, who note that 'he always remembered [. . .] birthdays, and never failed to send a telegram of congratulations'.[293] Glikman, too, observed that Shostakovich 'never preserved any letters. But amazing as it may seem, his phenomenal memory, undimmed by the passage of time, allowed him to recall their content many years later'.[294] Finally, Meyer remembered that at their last meeting Shostakovich kept returning to the past; he even played on the piano the subject of the counterpoint exam set by Glazunov: 'He referred to Shebalin, to his old students. [. . .] it was clear that he lived mainly on his memories'.[295]

Fay also does not mention that Shostakovich frequently incorporated quotations and self-quotations in his music,

[289] Wilson, p. 171.

[290] *Ibid.*, p. 75.

[291] *Ibid.*, p. 166.

[292] *Ibid.*, pp. 169–70.

[293] Wilson, pp. 279; Robinson, p. 384.

[294] Wilson, p. 112.

[295] Meyer, p. 64. The Glazunov fugue subject obviously was the one mentioned in *Testimony*, pp. 37/50–51.

told and retold favourite stories, and repeated himself literally, whether consciously or not. The autobiographical Eighth Quartet, for example, includes quotations from his First, Fifth, Eighth and Tenth Symphonies (such as the DSCH motive), *Lady Macbeth*, Second Piano Trio, First Cello Concerto, *Young Guards*, the political prisoners' song 'Zamuchen tyazhyoloy nevoley' ('Tormented by grievous bondage'), the funeral march from Wagner's *Götterdämmerung* and a theme from Tchaikovsky's 'Pathétique' Symphony.[296] Similarly, Stalin's favorite song, 'Suliko', is quoted in *Rayok* and the First Cello Concerto;[297] the Odessa street song 'Bubliki, Kupitye Bubliki' ('Bread rolls, buy our bread rolls') appears in the Second Cello Concerto;[298] 'Rebirth', the first *Pushkin Romance*, is introduced in the Fifth Symphony;[299] Beethoven's 'Moonlight' Sonata is alluded to in the Viola Sonata; material from *Rayok* and *Bolt* is re-used in *Moscow-Cheryomushki*;[300] the second *Pushkin Monologue* is hinted at in the Tenth Symphony;[301] several revolutionary songs ('The Prisoner', 'Listen, Comrade!'

[296] *Testimony*, p. 118/156, and Vishnevskaya, *Galina*, p. 229. Shostakovich called attention to most of these quotations in a letter to Glikman (19 July 1960):

> The main theme is the monogram D, Es, C, H, that is – my initials. The quartet makes use of themes from my works and the revolutionary song 'Tormented by Grievous Bondage'. My own themes are the following: from the First Symphony, the Eighth Symphony, the Piano Trio, the Cello Concerto and *Lady Macbeth*. Wagner's Funeral March from *Götterdämmerung* and the second theme from the first movement of Tchaikovsky's Sixth Symphony are also hinted at. And I forgot – there's also a theme from my Tenth Symphony. Quite something – this little miscellany!

Wilson, p. 340, quoting from I. Glikman, *Letters to a Friend*, p. 159.

[297] Wilson, pp. 323 and 477–79.

[298] *Ibid*., p. 394.

[299] *Ibid*., p. 127.

[300] According to Gerard McBurney, 'the incredibly stupid dance of the two baddies [in *Moscow-Cheryomushki*], Drebyednyetsov and Barabashkin, is made out of the 'Dance of the Bureaucrats' from the ballet *Bolt* and the awful fanfares that greeted the arrival of Stalin and his henchmen in *Rayok*' (*BBC Music Magazine*, April 1995, p. 10). The *Rayok* fanfare itself is a quotation of the well-known Russian greeting-music, 'Tush'.

[301] Wilson, p. 247.

'The Warsaw March', 'Rage, Tyrants!' and 'March in Step, Friends!') are borrowed in the Eleventh Symphony;[302] and the Seventh Symphony, Bach's *Art of the Fugue* (B-A-C-H motive), Beethoven's 'Pastoral' Symphony and Quartet Op. 135,[303] Glinka's romance 'Doubt', Rossini's *William Tell*, and Wagner's *Die Walküre* and *Tristan und Isolde* are quoted in the Fifteenth Symphony.[304]

Shostakovich also made prominent use of quotation and repetition in his speech, incorporating passages from literature, aphorisms and favorite stories. In doing so, he may have been influenced by his close friend, Sollertinsky, who introduced him to Mikhail Bakhtin's ideas on 'reported speech'.[305] Denisov recalled Shostakovich repeating several times the same critique of Georgy (Yury) Sviridov: 'Yura has passed through the trials of fire and water, but the brass trumpets have destroyed him'.[306] Nikolayeva similarly notes that for 25 years Shostakovich's response to the question 'Which preludes and fugues should she play?' was always the same: 'Choose whichever you please, but, come to think of it, play this one, that one and that one. . .'.[307] Meyer, too, remembers Shostakovich's repetition of phrases. After Meyer had played his Piano Sonata at their first meeting, Shostakovich commented: 'Your Sonata is, I would say, an interesting, good music and I would say I like it'. Shostakovich then examined Meyer's String Quartet, but repeated his earlier sentence as if he had not seen the other work: 'Your Sonata is an interesting, good music. I liked it, I would say, very much. It is good that you play it by yourself because every composer should play the piano.' At the end of their meeting, Shostakovich's final words were: 'That Sonata of

[302] Lukyanova, p. 126.

[303] Albert, p. 416.

[304] Grigoryev and Platek, p. 316 and Jackson, pp. 632–38. For many other examples of quotation and, especially, self-quotation, *cf*. Redepenning, pp. 205–28.

[305] *Cf*. Katerina Clark and Michael Holquist, *Mikhail Bakhtin*, Harvard University Press, Cambridge, 1984, pp. 233–36.

[306] Wilson, p. 302.

[307] *Ibid*., p. 258.

yours is an interesting, good music. I liked it, I would say, a lot. It is good that you play it by yourself because every composer should play the piano'. Meyer notes that Shostakovich repeated the last sentence at *each* of their subsequent meetings.[308]

Several of Shostakovich's stories also were repeated in much the same words. Vishnevskaya and Dubinsky, in their respective memoirs, recall the composer telling them about trying to get a ticket to the film *The Young Guards*, for which he had written the score:

> The other day I went to the movies to hear my music in *Young Guards*. There were, of course, no tickets. I was standing in the street like everyone else, hopelessly asking, 'Have you a spare ticket by any chance?' Somebody told me to go to . . . No, not to hell, but to the manager, you know . . . I'm led to a little window. Such a small, low one . . . I bend down one way, another . . . Can't quite adjust to it, it's so low, seems especially done to humiliate people . . . Finally somebody's head appears in the window.
>
> 'What d'you want?'
>
> 'Well, a ticket. Just one for myself.'
>
> 'Who are you?'
>
> 'I am Shostakovich, forgive me . . . '
>
> 'Shostakovich? So what? You're Shostakovich, I'm Rabinovich. Why do I, Rabinovich, have to give a ticket to you, Shostakovich?'
>
> 'I don't know.'
>
> 'Neither do I', he said, and slammed the window shut.[309]

'Shostakovich liked to tell this story, adding with a laugh: "And he was right. So what that I'm Shostakovich? He was Rabinovich!"'[310] Another oft-repeated tale was the following:

[308] Meyer, p. 56.

[309] Dubinsky, *Stormy Applause*, pp. 280–81. *Cf.* Vishnevskaya, *Galina*, p. 233, where the character is called Smirnov.

[310] Rostislav Dubinsky, 'The Interior Shostakovich', statement read at a conference organised by Bucknell University, New York, 1980, typescript, pp. 3–4 (hereafter Dubinsky, 'Interior Shostakovich'). The story is referred to yet again in a letter to Tishchenko (8 January 1965; Tishchenko, *Letters*, p. 44).

> I was an eye-witness, you know, an eye-witness to this event. After the siege of Leningrad I saw a funeral procession in the streets ... The coffin was being loaded onto an open lorry. Just imagine, an open coffin on the back of the lorry, which is bumping and shaking, together with a band of musicians playing Chopin's *Funeral March*. All of a sudden the corpse gets up from his coffin, and all the relatives and friends fall into a faint. Can you imagine, it wasn't a corpse they were going to bury, but somebody who was in a state of lethargic sleep. Only the musicians kept their wits about them, and seeing that the man was all right they stopped halfway through a bar of the *Funeral March* and started playing the 'Internationale'. Yes, I saw this with my very own eyes ....[311]

Shostakovich told this story to Rostropovich 'regularly, maybe twice a year', even if the latter gave it little credence.[312]

Apparently, once a phrase or story became formulated in Shostakovich's mind, it could (and often would) reappear in later conversations, verbatim or near-verbatim.[313] It is not surprising, therefore, that his opinions about major figures in his life, such as Musorgsky, Stravinsky, Chekhov and Mayakovsky, first expressed in separate articles, would be repeated in his conversations with Volkov and, subsequently, reappear in *Testimony*.[314] In much the same way, Shostakovich rarely

[311] Wilson, p. 188. This may be another example of Shostakovich's Aesopian language (Zak, pp. 495–506), through which he is actually mocking the absurd things other eyewitnesses have claimed to see. In *Testimony* he notes, 'Of course, we do have the saying "He lies like an eyewitness"' (p. 13). The story also appears to be one of Shostakovich's homegrown political jokes (the corpse being Communism, or the belief in it).

[312] Wilson, p. 188.

[313] Even Taruskin agrees, conceding that Shostakovich 'repeated [...] all his life' the satire 'The Man Who Spoke About the Omelette' (Richard Taruskin, *Text and Act*, Oxford University Press, Oxford, 1995, p. 64; *cf.* also p. 298).

[314] A similar observation was made by Anatoly Nayman in his book *Remembering Anna Akhmatova*:

> 'Gramophone records' was the name she gave to a particular genre of oral narrative, polished by many performances, which had its details, turning points and barbed passages definitively adjusted, but which still disclosed its improvised origin in its intonation and its responsiveness to the circumstances of the moment. 'Haven't I

altered his music once it was set in his mind, despite suggestions from performers and other parties.[315] Basner states that 'only in very rare cases would he [Shostakovich] change anything. Usually he said, "I'll change it in my next work"'.[316] This has been corroborated independently by Valentin Berlinsky, Yakov Milkis and Rudolf Barshai.[317]

Fay asserts that 'careful comparison of the original passages with their counterparts in *Testimony* indicate that some significant alterations have been made. In several instances, sentences which would date the reminiscences have been altered or removed from the variants in the book'.[318] In the context of her argument, the second sentence suggests that Volkov, not Shostakovich, had altered passages to disguise his 'plagiarism'. However, no proof is provided, and Shostakovich himself could have made these changes. Fay discusses only one 'representative' example of the similarity between a

---

played you the record about Balmont? ... about Dostoyevsky? ... about the sparks from the steam engines?' and then would follow a brilliant short etude, a lively anecdote in the manner of Pushkin's table talk, with aphorisms applicable, and subsequently applied, to similar or reversed situations. Once she had written them down – and the majority she did write down – they became more imposing and immutable, but, I think, lost their spontaneity.

Anatoly Nayman, *Remembering Anna Akhmatova*, transl. Wendy Roslyn, Peter Halban, London, 1989, p. 18.

[315] Among the few exceptions is *Lady Macbeth*, which was revamped as *Katerina Izmailova* at the urging of the Central Committee's Department of Agitation and Propaganda. Shostakovich also heeded David Oistrakh's plea to let 'the orchestra take over the first eight bars in the Finale [of the First Violin Concerto] so as to give me a break [... to] wipe the sweat off my brow' (Wilson, p. 207) and accepted a mistake in entrance by Barshai, which resulted in a passage in imitation between cello and viola in the finale of his Piano Quintet. Berlinsky notes that this imitation was not in the original score, but Shostakovich 'approved it and it was included in later editions' (Wilson, pp. 244–45).

[316] Wilson, p. 397.

[317] *Ibid.*, pp. 207, 245, 312 and 414. In addition, Otto Klemperer once asked Shostakovich to reduce the number of flutes in his Fourth Symphony because it was difficult to find six first-rate flautists on tour. Shostakovich remained adamant, quoting a proverb on the tip of every Russian tongue: 'What is written with the pen cannot be scratched out with the axe' (*ibid.*, p. 118).

[318] Fay, p. 488.

'borrowed' passage in *Testimony*[319] and an earlier source.[320] Close examination of all eight of her passages, however, reveals varying degrees of similarity. For example, the passage about Stravinsky[321] is almost identical to that in Yarustovsky's collection,[322] not only in word choice and sentence construction but also punctuation.[323] In contrast, the passage about Musorgsky[324] is similar in ideas, but substantially different in structure: whole blocks of text are rearranged and sentences are added or deleted. Comparison may be facilitated by assigning letters to the main ideas, as demonstrated on the following pages: the 1941/67 text has the form ABCDEFGHIJK, whereas *Testimony* has B'A'C' D'E'H'J'K'I'F'G'; (-) indicates passages without a parallel.[325]

Since plagiarists usually do not change their *modus operandi* in mid-text (i.e., cleverly rearrange, paraphrase, add and delete sentences to avoid detection in, say, the 'Musorgsky' material, and then reproduce the 'Stravinsky' section verbatim and in a most conspicuous spot, i.e., the first page of a

[319] *Testimony*, pp. 117/154–55.

[320] 'Kak rozhdayetsya muzyka' ('How Music is Born'), *Literaturnaya Gazeta*, 21 December 1965; reprinted in L. Danilevich (ed.), *Dmitry Shostakovich*, Sovetsky Kompozitor, Moscow, 1967, p. 36.

[321] *Testimony*, pp. 23/32–33.

[322] 'D. Shostakovich', in B. M. Yarustovsky (ed.), *I. F. Stravinsky: Stat'i i materialy* (*I. F. Stravinsky: Articles and Materials*), Sovetsky Kompozitor, Moscow, 1973, pp. 7–8.

[323] Duplicating the exact punctuation is not as difficult as Western minds might think, given the strict rules for the use of commas, etc., in Russian.

[324] *Testimony*, pp. 175/226–27.

[325] The translation of Shostakovich's article in *Izvestia/Danilevich* was done without referring to *Testimony*, hence the similar, but not identical, word choice in many passages. For another translation, *cf.* Grigoryev and Platek, pp. 88–89. The reshuffling of material in this example is similar to that documented in Ian Hunter's study of Alexander Aitken (I. M. Hunter, 'An Exceptional Memory', *British Journal of Psychology*, No. 68, 1977, pp. 155–64). Hunter notes (pp. 160–62) that Aitken, when recalling information from thirty years earlier, reproduced the material correctly but not always in proper sequence. Apparently, like Shostakovich, Aitken remembered information not as one sequence, from beginning to end, but in blocks of relevant, important ideas. *Cf.* also p. 178.

chapter),[326] the more pronounced similarity between the 'Stravinsky' passages may be due to their closer proximity in time. The Stravinsky article was published in 1973, at exactly the same time that Volkov and Shostakovich were working on *Testimony*, whereas the Musorgsky article dates from thirty years earlier (1941). In view of the larger gap in time between the Musorgsky texts, it is understandable that some of Shostakovich's views would change. For example, in Section D, the second half of the statement 'I wanted to edit the opera [*Boris Godunov*] [. . . to] make it reflect, as much as possible, the Soviet era' has been cut[327] while Section F has been much expanded. In the earlier article, Shostakovich states merely that 'some musicologists assert that these scenes do not sound badly' whereas in *Testimony* he adds a lengthy indictment of Boris Asafiev, specifically. Shostakovich's mockery of Asafiev makes sense in proper perspective. When the original article was written in 1941, Asafiev had not yet participated in the 1948 Conference of Musicians, presided over by Zhdanov.[328] According to Yury Levitin,

> It was the academician Boris Asafiev who played a perfidious role in preparing the initial measures for the Central Committee's Decree that followed. Although he himself did not take an active part in the ensuing persecutions, he lent his protection to his willing and trusty assistants. The chief targets were, of course, Shostakovich and Prokofiev [. . .].[329]

Wilson also notes that 'Shostakovich never forgave Boris Asafiev's treachery'[330] and Denisov confirms that one 'of Shostakovich's bugbears was Boris Asafiev. When I was a student I read Asafiev's books, and every time I mentioned

[326] A conclusion based on the authors' many years of college teaching.

[327] This passage in Danilevich is also missing in the translation in Grigoryev and Platek, p. 88.

[328] In notes written during her conversation with Shostakovich on 20 December [1940], Shaginyan reports: 'Asafyev advised him to read Leskov's *Lady Macbeth of Mtsensk Uyezd*, he did so, was impressed, and wrote the opera forthwith' (Shaginyan, p. 72). Apparently, the relationship between Shostakovich and Asafiev was significantly better in 1941, when the earlier version of the 'Musorgsky' text was written.

[329] Wilson, p. 209.

[330] *Ibid.*, p. 112.

Asafiev's name Dmitri Dmitriyevich bristled. He would repeat: "I have met many good people and many bad people in my life, but never anybody more rotten than Asafiev"'.[331]

Shostakovich on Musorgsky: Similarities and Differences

	Testimony (1971–74)		*Izvestia/Danilevich* (1941/67)
(-)	Mussorgsky and I have a 'special relationship'. He was an entire academy for me – of human relations, politics and art. I didn't study him with only my eyes and ears, for that's not enough for a composer or any professional. (That holds for other arts as well. Think how many great painters spend years slaving over copies without seeing anything shameful in it.)	A	Almost immediately with the creation of the quintet I was making a new edition of Musorgsky's opera *Boris Godunov*. I had to revise the score, smooth out the harmony, unsuccessful and strained orchestration, and some harmonic progressions. A few instruments not used by either Musorgsky or N. Rimsky-Korsakov, who edited *Boris Godunov*, were included in the score.
B'	I revere Mussorgsky, I consider him one of the greatest Russian composers.	B	I adore Musorgsky, considering him the greatest Russian composer.
A'	Almost simultaneously with the creation of my piano quintet, I was busy on a new edition of his opera *Boris Godunov*. I had to look through the score, smooth out a few wrinkles in the harmonization and some unfortunate and pretentious bits of orchestration, and change a few discrete progressions. A number of the instruments had been added to orchestration that had never been used by either Mussorgsky or Rimsky-Korsakov, who edited *Boris*.	(-)	My task was to penetrate deeply into the initial artistic idea of this genius-composer, to carry it to the listeners.

[331] *Ibid*., p. 303. *Cf*. also *Shostakovich Studies*, ed. David Fanning, Cambridge University Press, Cambridge, 1995, p. 2 (hereafter Fanning, *Shostakovich Studies*).

C'	Mussorgsky had made many changes and corrections on the advice of Stasov, Rimsky-Korsakov and others, and then Korsakov made quite a few changes on his own.	C	Musorgsky made many changes and reworked a lot under the influence of V. Stasov, N. Rimsky-Korsakov, and others. N. Rimsky-Korsakov himself changed a lot in the opera in the process of editing.
D'	Korsakov's edition of *Boris Godunov* reflects the ideology, ideas and artistry of the last century. You can't help respecting the enormous amount of work done by him. But I wanted to edit the opera in a different way, I wanted a greater symphonic development, I wanted the orchestra to do more than simply accompany the singers.	D	The N. Rimsky-Korsakov edition reflects the ideology, thoughts, and mastery of the last century. One cannot consider the tremendous labour of N. Rimsky-Korsakov with anything but tremendous respect. But I wanted to edit the opera from a different perspective,
		(-)	to make it reflect, as much as possible, features of the Soviet era.
		D cont.	I tried to achieve more symphonic development in the opera, give the orchestra a role more important than just accompanying singers.
E'	Rimsky-Korsakov was despotic and tried to make the score submit to his own style, rewriting a lot and adding his own music. I changed only a few bars and rewrote very little.	E	Rimsky-Korsakov was despotic, tried to fit Musorgsky's score into his own artistic manner, recomposed a lot, added some. I only changed a few separate bars, and recomposed only a little.
(-)	But certain things did have to be changed.	F	In Musorgsky's score the bell ringing, the coronation scene (at the beginning of the opera), and the polonaise – in the Polish act, sounded very badly. Nevertheless, they should be the scenes of tremendous symphonic tension. Some musicologists assert that these scenes do not
H'	The scene in the forest outside Kromy had to be given a worthy spot. Mussorgsky had orchestrated it like a student afraid of failing an exam. Falteringly and badly. I did it over.		

	sound badly, but quite well. Supposedly, the composer, to show the lowly nature of knighthood, to show that the people were not happy with the coronation of Boris Godunov, deliberately wrote these scenes this way.		
J'	This is how I worked. I placed Mussorgsky's piano arrangement in front of me and then two scores – Mussorgsky's and Rimsky-Korsakov's. I didn't look at the scores, and rarely looked at the piano arrangement either. I orchestrated from memory, act by act. Then I compared my orchestration with those by Mussorgsky and Rimsky-Korsakov. If I saw that either had done it better, then I stayed with that.	G	This is easy to refute. The late Glazunov remembered that Musorgsky played for him on the piano the bell ringing scenes. They were magnificent, as well as the coronation scene. Glazunov recalled that Musorgsky himself with particular pleasure played to his friends the most successful excerpts.
(-)	I didn't reinvent bicycles.	F cont.	The bell ringing scene in the opera *Boris Godunov* sounds like a miserable parody.
K'	I worked honestly, with ferocity, I might say.		
I'	Mussorgsky has marvellously orchestrated moments, but I see no sin in my work. I didn't touch the successful parts,	G cont.	On the other hand, from the transcription made by Musorgsky for performance on piano four-hands, we can see how rich these pages were made by the composer.
(-)	but there are many unsuccessful parts because he lacked mastery of the craft, which comes only through time spent on your backside, no other way.	H	The folk scene 'Kromy' in the new edition took a more important place than before. It is one of the most important scenes. In the score it is orchestrated very badly, timidly. I had to rework it.

F'	For instance, the polonaise in the Polish act is abominable, yet it's an important moment. The same holds for Boris's coronation. And the bell – now, what kind of bell is it? It's just a pathetic parody. These are very important scenes and can't be tossed away.	I	My principle was not to change every note no matter what. Let's take, for example, the scene in the monastery – its beginning is orchestrated brilliantly. Obviously, it should not be changed.
(-)	Of course, there was one notable character, Boris Asafiev, who proposed that there was a theoretical basis for Mussorgsky's incompetence. This Boris was known for his ability to invent a theoretical basis for almost anything. He spun like a top.	(-)	It would be ridiculous to change violas in this scene to cellos, or clarinets, or bassoons. I did not touch this scene. Quite mistaken are those who think I left no stone unturned in this orchestration.
F cont.	Anyway, Asafiev maintained that all the scenes I just mentioned were orchestrated wonderfully by Mussorgsky, that it was part of his plan. He intended the coronation scene to be lacklustre to show that the people were against Boris's coronation. This was the people's form of protest – clumsy orchestration.	J	I worked on a new edition in the following manner. I had the scores of Musorgsky and Rimsky-Korsakov laying in front of me, but I did not look at them. I occasionally looked only at the piano arrangement of Musorgsky, and orchestrated whole acts. Then I compared what I wrote with the scores of the two composers. And if I found that one or another spot was made better and I had it worse, then I immediately restored the better.
(-)	And in the Polish act, Asafiev would have you believe, Mussorgsky was exposing the decadent gentry, and therefore let the Poles dance to poor instrumentation. That was his way of punishing them.	K	I worked with tremendous agitation on the editing of *Boris Godunov* ....

G' Only it's all nonsense. Glazunov told me that Mussorgsky himself played all these scenes for him on the piano – the bells and the coronation. And Glazunov said they were brilliant and powerful – that was the way Mussorgsky wanted them to be,

(-) for he was a dramatist of great genius from whom I learn and learn. I am not speaking of orchestration now. I'm talking about something else.

Finally, again contrary to Fay, it is not unusual for writers to repeat their own words, verbatim or near-verbatim. Consider, for example, Taruskin's article 'Who Was Shostakovich?' in *Atlantic Monthly*. On page 6, this material is said to have been 'adapted from a keynote address given at an international Shostakovich conference', but nowhere does the author acknowledge that three of his ten pages, from the last paragraph of page 66 to the second-to-last paragraph of page 68, have been recycled, nearly verbatim, from Taruskin's review of the facsimile of Shostakovich's Seventh Symphony.[332] In fact, this one example of Taruskin's unacknowledged self-quotation constitutes almost as many words as all of the passages Fay suggests Volkov 'plagiarized' in *Testimony*. Taruskin has made a few changes in his text: some passages have been paraphrased, others expanded or abbreviated, citations have been omitted, and tenses, punctuation and paragraph structure altered slightly. Significantly, these are the same types of modifications found in the occasional 'borrowed' passages of *Testimony*.[333] Do people sometimes re-use their own words to restate their own opinions? Yes. Do they sometimes modify their original statements to update them or incorporate new ideas? Yes. Do

[332] Taruskin, review, pp. 756–58.

[333] *Cf*. the Musorgsky text above.

they sometimes engage in self-quotation without acknowledging it? Yes. Is it plagiarism? No.[334]

Fay's suggestion that Volkov 'plagiarized' from previously published sources is intended to explain how 300 pages of memoirs could have been produced from the three or four two-hour meetings acknowledged by Irina Shostakovich. If, however, Volkov and Shostakovich met 'constantly', as the composer told Flora Litvinova, and if, as Shostakovich also said, he examined what was written down from these sessions,[335] 'plagiarism' makes no sense. Furthermore, given Shostakovich's phenomenal memory, which allowed him to remember other composers' music, other writers' words and even other people's birthdays; his fondness for quotation, self-quotation and repetition; and the common practice of writers (Taruskin included) to recycle text, it is entirely conceivable that Shostakovich would remember his own opinions and restate them in his own words to Volkov.

Again, Fay's points are based on supposition, not substance. Her claim that Shostakovich, in his sessions with Volkov, could not have repeated passages from his earlier published texts – passages of deep importance to him – has not only never been substantiated but is seriously questioned or entirely rejected by several leading research psychologists. When consulted about the eight recycled passages identified by Fay, these authorities agreed that, given the other feats of memory attributed to Shostakovich, his ability to produce such verbatim or near-verbatim repetition is, on the basis of established experimental precedents, certainly possible. Some went further: Professor Elizabeth Valentine (Royal Holloway College, University of London), co-author of the study *Superior Memory* (1997),[336] noted that it is plausible that someone with Shostakovich's 'superior' memory would

[334] *Cf.* the Chicago-Kent College of Law *Ethics Guidelines For Legal Writing Classes*, in which plagiarism is defined as (1) quoting the words of *another* without attribution, (2) paraphrasing the words of *another* without attribution, or (3) using the ideas of *another* without attribution (emphasis added).

[335] Litvinova, pp. 168–69. *Cf.* p. 251 for the complete passage.

[336] John Wilding and Elizabeth Valentine, *Superior Memory*, Psychology Press, Hove, 1997.

engage in this type of verbatim recycling more than someone with a 'normal' memory;[337] Professors Elizabeth Loftus (University of Washington; president of the American Psychological Society), Roddy Roediger (Washington University), and Andreas Lehmann (Florida State University) found the aforegoing arguments against the charge of plagiarism 'good', 'persuasive' and 'compelling';[338] and others called attention to feats of memory similar to and even exceeding Shostakovich's, including lengthy verbatim recall over extended periods of time. Several such case studies are reproduced in Ulric Neisser's *Memory Observed*, including Ian Hunter's classic, thoroughly documented report on Professor Alexander Craig Aitken (1895–1967), a subject whose feats of natural memory (i.e., without conscious effort or resort to mnemonic devices), studied over thirty years, closely resemble those of Shostakovich.[339] When consulted about precedents for Shostakovich repeating his own

[337] Elizabeth Valentine, letter to the authors, 19 October 1997.

[338] Elizabeth Loftus, letter to the authors, 3 November 1997; Roddy Roediger, letter to the authors, 17 October 1997; and Andreas Lehmann, letter to the authors, 21 October 1997.

[339] Ulric Neisser, *Memory Observed: Remembering in Natural Contexts*, W. H. Freeman and Co., San Francisco, 1982, pp. 418–24 (hereafter Neisser). 'Aitken could produce a host of recondite facts about numbers, calculative methods, mathematics and mathematicians; play, on the violin, many pieces by heart; recall many musical compositions; securely identify many snatches of music heard or seen in written notation; quote extensively from English literature; and recite tracts of Latin and English verse. He could recall details of many events he had witnessed, so much so that committees often consulted him as an unofficial minute book. In daily affairs, he was conspicuously, but not officiously, precise about names, dates, locations' (Hunter, in Neisser, p. 419).

Shostakovich's parallels with Aitken, acknowledged by Professors Hunter, Neisser and Valentine, are striking, not only in his ability to accurately recall reams of literature and music, but in his precision with names and dates (*cf.* pp. 121–24 and 193 concerning Shostakovich's formality with names and recall of everyone's birthdays, and Wilson, pp. 122, 170, 236–37, 243 and 310, on his absolute punctuality). It is also worth noting that neither Shostakovich nor Aitken had 'total recall': that is, 'the mythical ability to recall absolutely anything [they] had ever experienced' (Hunter, in Neisser, p. 420). Their memory for uninteresting, irrelevant material was no better than average; on the other hand, their accurate, verbatim recall of material of meaning or importance to them was exceptional, even after many years. This accounts for how Shostakovich could

printed texts, verbatim or near verbatim, in his sessions with Volkov, Professor Hunter (University of Keele) responded as follows:

> There are certainly people with superior memory powers. Aitken was one and I was fortunate to be able to study him at first hand and while he was still known to many people as a man with 'a gift' for memory. An exceptional memorist of another sort was Thomas Macaulay about whom there is a lot of documentation. In the field of music, there was Toscanini[340] – and no doubt many others because music lends itself to the acquisition of high expertise. There is no doubt about the reality of superior memory.[341]

Asked specifically about the possibility of Shostakovich repeating, verbatim or near-verbatim, the 'autobiographical narratives' contained in *Testimony*, Professor Hunter replied:

> Volkov's claims do not strike me as outlandish under the circumstances. Assume that Shostakovich was deeply interested in his own biographical development and that he pieced

---

repeat, verbatim or near-verbatim, eight passages *of prime importance* to him in his meetings with Volkov, while, at the same time, admitting that he does not remember certain details (such as Lenin's arrival by train at the Finland Station, an event which, at the time, held little significance for the young Mitya; *cf.* p. 178).

[340] *Cf.* Marek, *Toscanini*, p. 192: 'It has been estimated that [Toscanini] knew by heart every note of every instrument of about 250 symphonic works and the words and music of about 100 operas, besides a quantity of chamber music, piano music, cello and violin pieces, and songs'.
Sir Adrian Boult recalled a report of

> the bass clarinet player who came to [Toscanini's] room in great trepidation just before an opera performance: a key was broken on his instrument and could not be repaired in time for the show. A few minutes' deep thought (of course, without reference to the score) and the Maestro was telling him how the loss would in most cases be covered by other instruments, but then carefully detailed a few passages where he must arrange for the cello or bassoon to supply the missing notes. [. . .] I myself have heard him correct a player who began a long *diminuendo* one note before it was marked.

Boult on Music, ed. Martin Anderson, Toccata Press, London, 1983, pp. 86 and 93.

[341] Ian Hunter, letter to the authors, 29 October 1997.

> together a coherent account of that development with appropriate structure and wording; given his interest and intellectual abilities, it is not at all unlikely that he would produce much the same narrative, even years apart. The argument of 'beyond belief' doesn't cut much ice in itself when dealing with very superior minds.[342]

In *Memory Observed*, Professor Neisser (Cornell University) concurs with Professor Hunter that 'literal, verbatim memory does exist', that the documented 'accomplishments [of these memorists] are real', and that 'the abilities described in Selections 38–44 [various case studies] may not be as unusual as generally believed [. . .] may not even be very rare.'[343] When asked specifically about the eight recycled passages in *Testimony*, he responded:

> I see no reason to doubt that Shostakovich produced all that text verbatim. It is something that Aitken could also have done. Verbatim memory is not all that hard if one has the motivation and opportunity to rehearse, as Shostakovich evidently did. And I'm impressed by the record of his other memory feats, some of which seem far more impressive than remembering some passages from one's own autobiography.[344]

12. 'Chital [Read]. D. Shostakovich'

Besides accusing Volkov of at least eight counts of 'plagiarism', Fay also suggests an even worse deception. 'Is it possible', she asks, 'that Volkov misrepresented the nature and contents of the book to Shostakovich just as he may be misrepresenting them to the reader?' This question follows her 'most disturbing' discovery that seven of her eight 'borrowed' passages 'occur at the beginning of chapters [. . . on] pages on which Shostakovich's inscription "Read. D. Shostakovich" is alleged to appear [. . .]'.[345]

[342] *Ibid.*

[343] Neisser, pp. 242, 379–80.

[344] Ulric Neisser, letter to the authors, 4 November 1997.

[345] Fay, pp. 490–91.

Fay's distrust of much of *Testimony* stems, in part, from Shostakovich's decision to sign only the first page of each chapter. Admittedly, had Shostakovich signed every page of the 404-page manuscript, fewer questions would have been asked. But it does not follow that the absence of Shostakovich's signature on the remaining pages of chapters implies that he did not read or did not approve this material. As the composer's daughter, Galina, caustically observes: 'Shostakovich did sign some stupid articles about inconsequential subjects without reading them, but he would not have signed something this big and important without reading it'.[346] Again, the evidence must be viewed in proper perspective. Writers seldom sign every page of their book manuscripts and Shostakovich was never in the habit of signing every page of his articles, letters or scores. As such, one wonders why Fay would expect Shostakovich to have written 'Read. D. Shostakovich' on all 404 pages, especially late in life, when he was plagued by hand problems. In *Testimony*, Shostakovich refers to his ailment several times: 'It's hard for me to play the piano and write with my right hand', 'I'm training my left hand to write, in case I lose ability in my right', and, again, 'I'm teaching myself to write with my left hand in case my right one gives out completely'.[347] Meyer,[348] Druzhinin,[349] Kondrashin[350] and Rozhdestvensky confirm that in his last years Shostakovich was 'very ill, and his arms and hands hardly functioned'.[351]

The appearance of 'borrowed' passages at the beginnings of chapters is neither suspicious nor coincidental. Each of *Testimony*'s chapters begins with a clear topic: (1) the importance of remembering others who have been forgotten and of telling the whole truth; (2) Stravinsky; (3) Meyerhold; (4) the writing of *Lady Macbeth*; (5) the writing of his Seventh Symphony; (6) Chekhov; (7) Musorgsky; and (8) Mayakovsky.

346 *Cf*. p. 83.

347 *Testimony*, pp. 115/152, 177/228 and 214/275, respectively.

348 Wilson, p. 468.

349 *Ibid*, p. 470.

350 Kondrashin, pp. 511 and 518.

351 Wilson, p. 450. Also *cf*. p. 88, note 154.

Given the importance of these topics to Shostakovich, it is not surprising that he would have expressed some of his opinions in earlier articles. Furthermore, given his phenomenal memory, it is not surprising that, in speaking about these matters again to Volkov, he would first recall his earlier statements. Where does one expect to find 'Stravinsky is one of the greatest composers of our time and I love many of his works. My earliest and most vivid impression of Stravinsky's music is related to the ballet *Petrouchka* [. . .]' except at the beginning of a chapter on Stravinsky? Where does one expect to find 'I met Meyerhold in Leningrad in 1928 [. . .]' except at the beginning of a chapter on Meyerhold? Where does one expect to find 'I really love Chekhov, he's one of my favourite writers [. . .]' except at the beginning of a chapter on Chekhov? Where does one expect to find 'I revere Mussorgsky, I consider him one of the greatest Russian composers [. . .]' except at the beginning of the chapter on Musorgsky? And where does one expect to find 'I became fascinated by Mayakovsky's poetry at an early age [. . .]' except at the beginning of a chapter on Mayakovsky?

In focusing her attention on these 'borrowed reminiscences', 'none [. . . of which] could be considered controversial or inflammatory',[352] Fay fails to mention that the controversial 'new' Shostakovich *is* evident on the first *signed* page of chapter 1: 'Others will write about us. And naturally they'll lie through their teeth – but that's their business. [. . .] Looking back, I see nothing but ruins, only mountains of corpses. And I do not want to build new Potemkin villages on these ruins'.[353] The 'new' Shostakovich also appears on the first signed page of chapter 3, where he notes that the plaque that reads 'In this house lived Meyerhold' should also say 'And in this house his wife was brutally murdered'.[354]

Together, these two flagrantly 'inflammatory', yet signed, pages completely demolish still another of Fay's 'conclusive' arguments.

[352] Fay, p. 490.

[353] *Testimony*, p. 1/3. 'Potemkin villages' refers to the sham villages constructed by Count Potemkin to impress Empress Catherine II on her visit to the region under his charge.

[354] *Ibid.*, p. 58/77; *cf.* also p. 140, note 90.

As for the dearth of what Fay calls 'borrowed' passages in the more controversial sections of *Testimony*, this is clearly accounted for by Shostakovich's inability to tell the whole truth in Soviet publications. Significantly, Shostakovich's family, friends and colleagues now confirm that he voiced many of these same opinions in private. Lebedinsky, for example, estimates that 'though they were preserved in the minds of many musicians, [a]bout 90 per cent of his [Shostakovich's] real opinions never got into print; they are certainly not be found among the articles signed with his name'.[355]

Critics of *Testimony*, such as Malcolm Brown, continue to harp on Volkov's statement in his Preface that 'Gradually, I shaped this great array of reminiscence into arbitrary parts and had them typed'.[356] They wonder, if the organisation of *Testimony* was 'arbitrary', how did recycled passages just happen to appear at the beginning of seven of the eight chapters? First, recycled passages do not appear only at the beginnings of chapters, they are just more visible there. One of Laurel Fay's own recycled passages appears on an interior page of a chapter; so does a passage from Shostakovich's 'Autobiography' (*Sovetskaya Muzyka*, 1966, No. 9), as well as several phrases used by Shostakovich in print and in conversations, and other material remembered by his family and friends.[357] Second, while Volkov, in 1979, thought the organisation of *Testimony* arbitrary (as did several reviewers[358]), this assumption does not preclude an organisation on Shostakovich's part about which even Volkov was unaware. To this day, Volkov maintains that everything in *Testimony* came from Shostakovich's mouth, that no secondary sources were used, and that he was not even aware of the recycled passages until they were identified by Fay and others.

355 Lebedinsky, p. 480; *cf.* also pp. 239–40.

356 *Testimony*, p. xiv/xvii; cited by Brown in a handout distributed at the 1997 Midwest Chapter meeting of the American Musicological Society (Chicago, 4 October 1997).

357 *Cf.* pp. 83–84; 94, note 172; 99, note 193; 113, note 249; 190, note 274; 239–40; 258–59.

358 *Cf.* p. 257–58.

Given Shostakovich's usual manner of composing (like Mozart, he usually formulated an entire work in his head before writing it down on paper), it is entirely conceivable that he had mapped out his memoirs in his mind even before Volkov, merely the conduit for and recorder of these reminiscences, became involved. Evidence suggests that Shostakovich thought as carefully about his memoirs as he did about his musical works, that he did not merely ramble and leave the organisation of his own very important life-story to Volkov or to chance. (As he says in *Testimony*, he wanted to write about his relationships with others and, finally, *get it right*.) Significantly, Shostakovich (1) contemplated writing his autobiography for twenty years ('I think long, I write fast'); (2) read other peoples' memoirs as models for his own; (3) considered selecting an appropriate motto; (4) asked for a notebook in which to write the names of people he wanted to mention; (5) kept abreast of what others had written about him and his music (much of which he considered 'all wrong'); and (6) always decided when he would meet with Volkov, calling him on the phone whenever he, Shostakovich, was ready to work.[359] The last point is especially important because Shostakovich would then have had ample opportunity to think about or actually review his earlier writings on topics he wished to relate to Volkov. His superior memory would then have taken care of the rest.

Besides thinking about and preparing to work on his memoirs, Shostakovich, during the same time period, may well have begun formulating what he wished to say about his life, first as a series of articles on people and events of deep importance to him. Significantly, six of Fay's eight recycled passages date from no earlier than eleven years before he began dictating *Testimony* and two are exactly contemporaneous with the Volkov-Shostakovich meetings.[360] Upon selecting Volkov as a suitable assistant, Shostakovich may

[359] *Cf.* pp. 138–39; 139, 142, note 104; 82; 85; 140–41, 316; and 80, respectively.

[360] Since Volkov submitted chapters to Shostakovich for approval throughout their meetings (1971–74), it is also possible that the passages about Stravinsky and Meyerhold, published elsewhere in 1973 and 1974, had actually been recycled from *Testimony* rather than the other way around. This would further account for their verbatim nature.

then have decided to assemble and expand upon these already formulated parts (adding the remaining two from 1932 and 1941 when they came to his attention as a result of being reprinted in 1967), and, as was his wont, left unchanged whatever, in his own mind, did not require change.[361] Since Shostakovich had little experience writing books ('I am not a writer, I am not a writer', he told his student Denisov), it is hardly surprising that the seams in such a compilation might continue to show in *Testimony* – the passages from earlier articles appearing at the beginnings of chapters because of their importance to the composer (dictating a prominent position) or merely because they provided convenient starting points for further ruminations.[362] It is also far from 'utterly inconceivable' that in writing his 'autobiography in words' (*Testimony*) Shostakovich might incorporate the same abundance of exact self-quotation to be found in his 'autobiography in sound' (the Eighth Quartet).[363] Indeed, based on what we know of Shostakovich's habits of mind, the likelihood is strong. Moreover, the feasibility of such an accomplishment is well established both in theory and in the specialist literature on 'superior' memory.[364]

With regard to the authorisation 'Chital. D. Shostakovich' itself, Fay, in subsequent publications, fails to mention that

[361] *Cf.* pp. 195–98.

[362] It is even possible that Shostakovich had a musical form, rather than a standard literary design, in mind: an introductory chapter followed by original themes (the recycled passages, arising from key characters and events in his life) and variations, or 'expositions and developments' (this being the title of Stravinsky's 1962 volume of memoirs, about which Shostakovich was no doubt familiar). Lest this be considered fanciful speculation, it is worth remembering that Shostakovich himself called attention to such musical structures in literary works. He shared his ideas on the subject with a literary critic, who published a 'scholarly article' on it, and also observed that one of his favourite writers, Chekhov, 'constructed his works the way musical ones are constructed. Naturally, this wasn't conscious, it's just that musical construction reflects more general laws. I am certain that Chekhov constructed *The Black Monk* in sonata form, that there is an introduction, an exposition with main and secondary themes, development, and so on' (*Testimony*, p. 172/223).

[363] *Cf.* pp. 160–64.

[364] *Cf.* pp. 205–9.

Shostakovich's signature has been authenticated not only by a handwriting expert hired by Harper and Row,[365] but by the composer's inner circle, including Shchedrin,[366] Maxim[367] and Galina.[368] Fay also seems unaware that both the German and Finnish editions of *Testimony* reproduce all eight of Shostakovich's signatures (each slightly different, and hence not a duplication of one original) that appear at the beginning of each chapter of the manuscript, and that one of these has been available since 1979, a year before her 'conclusive' article was published.[369]

Volkov, too, has recently commented on Shostakovich's authorisation. In an interview in 1992, he stated:

> I was not asking for nor was I expecting his signature, since I was aware that the situation was too serious and he, naturally, was wary of possible complications. But the chapters kept coming back with: 'Read. Shostakovich'. It was only later, here [in New York], when I had the time to think about various incidents, that I understood the following: Dmitry Dmitriyevich's signature was an intuitively infallible reaction. He had invented a formula that authenticated the text, but at the same time created a certain distance in the event the book were nonetheless published during his lifetime or the KGB began to apply strong pressure on both of us. It is obvious that a person would not write about his own text 'I have read it'. Dmitry Dmitriyevich could have signed: 'I am in agreement. Shostakovich', or simply 'Shostakovich'. 'Read. Shostakovich' signaled that he had examined the content. There were practically no corrections. This was his style too: to work quickly and cleanly.[370]

Liana Genina, another of Volkov's colleagues and a deputy editor of *Sovetskaya Muzyka*, has confirmed that 'Chital. D.

[365] Fay, p. 487.

[366] Letter from Shchedrin to the authors, 27 October 1992.

[367] Heikinheimo, 'Decade of Struggle', p. 3.

[368] Conversation with the authors, 15 October 1995.

[369] Schönberger, 'Memoirs', p. 58.

[370] Drubachevskaya, pp. 320–21.

Shostakovich' was an authentic formula used by the composer.[371]

13. The Original Russian Text

Although *Testimony* has appeared in some twenty different languages, it has not yet been published in its original Russian text. Some critics, in an attempt to add weight to their charges that Volkov is a liar and thief, have suggested that Volkov himself has withheld the manuscript to prevent scholars from scrutinising the 'borrowed' passages and assessing the accuracy of the English translation by Antonina W. Bouis.[372] Volkov maintains that he has always wanted to have the Russian text published, but that his publisher decides in which languages the book is printed[373] and that recent delays have been due to economic problems in the former Soviet Union.[374] The latter has been confirmed by Yury Korev, who acknowledges that the complete text of

[371] 'Razbeg pered propast'yu' ('Running start to an abyss'), *Muzykal'naya Akademiya*, 1992, No. 3, p. 13.

[372] Karlinsky, p. 535, questions the accuracy of the translation, which he describes as 'crude and occasionally semiliterate [. . . with] a profusion of anachronistic American slang which cannot possibly correspond to anything in Shostakovich's Russian'. For Yakubov's criticisms, *cf*. p. 72.

[373] Malcolm Brown, in his paper at California State University, Long Beach (1996), made a defamatory assertion that Volkov personally prevents the publication of *Testimony* in Russian for fear of exposure of the book's 'fraudulent' nature. In fact, while the copyright to the book belongs to Volkov, the world rights to this material (including those to the Russian text) were sold to his publisher (conversation between Volkov and the authors, February 1996). In his interview with Drubachevskaya, Volkov also notes:

> I am no longer told where a translation is published nor do I receive complimentary copies. Thus, one learns that the book has been published in Yugoslavia only by the fact that it has been paid for.
>
> Drubachevskaya, p. 345.

Volkov openly admits receiving many requests to publish the Russian text (*cf*. Drubachevskaya, p. 348, and Lili Pann, 'Muzyka prosvechivayet vsego cheloveka naskvoz'' ('Music Shines through the Man'), *Literaturnaya Gazeta*, Vol. 27, No. 5659, 2 July 1997, p.14), but these have never been formal offers (i.e., contracts) extended to his publisher from another.

[374] Conversation between Volkov and the authors, Spring 1995.

Testimony had been considered for publication in a projected supplement to *Muzykal'naya Akademiya* (the successor to *Sovetskaya Muzyka*). But 'the country went the market route and money for culture dissipated'. He adds that plans remained only preliminary and that no contract was ever drawn between the journal and Volkov or his publisher.[375]

Laurel Fay notes in 1980 that her request to view the original manuscript was refused by the publisher.[376] Curiously, however, neither in this article nor in later writings does she mention that since 1979 the complete original Russian text has been examined by numerous parties, including translators such as Seppo Heikinheimo, and numerous Soviet and émigré artists,[377] such as the violinist Mark Lubotsky, the composer Rodion Shchedrin, conductor-cellist Mstislav Rostropovich, conductor-violist Rudolf Barshai, and theatre director Yury Lyubimov, all of whom believe it to be authentic.[378] Lubotsky's assessment of *Testimony*, following his examination of the original Russian text, appeared in *Vrij Nederland* on 15 December 1979 (i.e., almost a year before Fay's 'conclusive' article) in an interview titled 'There is nothing which makes me doubt at all the authenticity of the book – Mark Lubotsky about Dmitri Shostakovich's memoirs'. Here he also states that he 'knew about the existence of such a document already in 1976, when he was still living in the Soviet Union. In musicians' circles it was generally known that Volkov had had conversations with Shostakovich and that on their basis he was writing a book'.[379] Heikinheimo's access to the original Russian text was acknowledged as early as 1981 when *Musical America* noted that he had translated *Testimony* into Finnish not from

[375] Interview with Korev, June 1995. The right to reproduce the Russian text also has been complicated by recent negotiations between Volkov and several libraries to purchase his archives, including the manuscript of *Testimony*.

[376] Fay, p. 491.

[377] Heikinheimo, 'Decade of Struggle', p. 2.

[378] Others who have examined pages of the manuscript signed by Shostakovich include the authors, Maxim and Galina Shostakovich (*cf.* p. 83), and Tony Palmer (*cf.* '*Testimony* – A Film: Based on a Conversation with the Producer', *DSCH*, No. iii, September–October 1987, p. 19).

[379] Schönberger, 'Lubotsky', p. 21.

the English edition, but from the Russian text.[380] Heikinheimo also states, in the 1989 Finnish edition, that Rostropovich, Barshai and Lyubimov, among some fifty others, were allowed to examine the copy of the manuscript loaned to him for translation, that Rostropovich 'said he heard exactly the voice of Shostakovich in the memoirs', and that Barshai 'also regarded the book as authentic, as did Lyubimov'.[381] Finally, Shchedrin, in a letter to the authors (27 October 1992), similarly confirmed examining the original Russian text, 'with signatures, without any doubt, in the hand of D. D. Shostakovich'.

Although the testimony of these knowledgeable witnesses may have escaped the notice of most scholars, Shostakovich 'experts' who had 'meticulously tested *Testimony's* claims'[382] should have known better. It is ironic that Fay openly acknowledges the denunciations of 'Les Six Soviétiques', who clearly had not read the printed memoirs carefully, if at all,[383] but remains silent on the many figures who actually examined the signed Russian text and believe it to be authentic. Indeed, one wonders if failure to mention this information is due to 'inept scholarship', to borrow Fay's own criticism of Volkov.[384]

[380] Heikinheimo, 'Memoirs', p. 20; confirmed in Seppo Heikinheimo, *Mätämunan muistelmat*, Otava, Helsinki, 1997, p. 392 (hereafter Heikinheimo, *Mätämunan*).

[381] Heikinheimo, 'Decade of Struggle', p. 2. Heikinheimo goes on to note that Gidon Kremer now [in 1989] 'thinks the book is 100 per cent genuine', that Emil Gilels 'said before his death that the book is "of course authentic"', and that Sviatoslav Richter, according to his student Andrei Gavrilov, was 'known to support the idea of authenticity'. Add to these Il'ya Musin, the second conductor of Shostakovich's Seventh Symphony, who in a recent conversation with Mark Wigglesworth not only stated that 'Everything in *Testimony* is true, everything', but 'brought out [a copy of] the manuscript, in type on A4 sheets' (David Nice, 'The Welsh Shostakovich', *Gramophone*, Vol. 75, No. 891, August 1997, p. 22). This is only one of several copies of the Russian typescript known to be in circulation. *Cf.* Heikinheimo, *Mätämunan*, pp. 285 and 329.

[382] Taruskin, 'Dictator', p. 34, in praise of Fay.

[383] *Cf.* p. 66, note 71.

[384] Fay, p. 486; also *cf.* p. 144. Contrary to rumours spread by anti-*Testimony* forces who have never seen the complete Russian text, those who have examined the manuscript find nothing at all suspicious about it. Antonina W. Bouis states: 'I did not notice any differences in type face

14. Bravery in the Artist

A nagging question in the minds of many critics is why Shostakovich, in committing his memoirs to print, would jeopardise that which he loved most, his family. Fay asks, 'Why would Shostakovich, while insisting that the manuscript be published only after his own death, callously disregard the ominous ramifications of its publication for his wife and family?'[385] Phillip Ramey similarly acknowledges the threat that *Testimony* would pose to the well-being of the Shostakovich family and wonders if the composer, 'in his last days, dogged by illness and the fear of death, [. . .] was – to put it politely – not quite himself?'[386]

By focussing on Shostakovich's fears for his family, Fay, Ramey and others fail to perceive the entire man. Shostakovich was, without doubt, a dedicated and devoted father, who loved his children 'with a kind of abnormal, morbid love',[387] 'lived in constant fear that some misfortune would befall them',[388] and often kept his mouth shut for their safety.[389] At the same time, however, he was a man of principle and enormous courage, willing to take calculated risks in his

---

or font [between signed and unsigned pages] or any other "monkey business". [. . .] I am certain that Solomon Volkov is an honest, reliable, and brilliant scholar, I am proud to have translated the book, and I believe it to be just what it is – the memoirs of Dmitri Shostakovich' (letter to the authors, 11 June 1997).

385 Fay, p. 493.

386 Ramey, p. 24.

387 Vishnevskaya, quoted in Wilson, p. 278.

388 Vishnevskaya, quoted in *ibid*, p. 278.

389 Rostropovich, quoted in Curt Suplee, 'The Anatomy of a Defection: Maxim Shostakovich's Lifelong Quest for the Music of Freedom', *Washington Post*, 24 April 1981, p. F1; *cf.* also p. 58; 90, note 161; 162, note 175; 236, note 440. Shostakovich himself seems to acknowledge these fears in his Thirteenth Symphony:

A fellow scientist of Galileo's age
Was no less wise than Galileo.
He knew the earth revolved,
But – he had a family.

(Transl. Valeria Vlazinskaya, notes to the recording conducted by Kurt Masur on Teldec 90848).

struggles with the regime. Viewed in proper perspective, therefore, *Testimony* is not an anomaly attributable to callous disregard for others, illness or old age, but the last of a lifetime of courageous, one could even say suicidal, acts. As Andrey Bitov notes:

> Bravery in the artist does not mean fearlessness in the man. After all, the artist will have a richer imagination than the hangman; he himself knows better how he has transgressed, and how far. [. . .] The man's human fear engendered greater and greater bravery in the artist. His passion to be heard always exceeded his fear of exposure.[390]

Shostakovich's 'bravery in the artist' was already apparent in his music for the 1932 'comic, anti-sentimental' staging of *Hamlet* at the Vakhtangov Theatre, directed by Nikolay Akimov. Yury Yelagin recalls:

> in the famous scene with the flute, Shostakovich angrily mocked both the Soviet authorities and a group of proletarian composers who at that time were at the height of their power and caused much harm to Russian music and musicians. In this scene, Hamlet held the flute to the lower part of his torso, and the piccolo in the orchestra, accompanied by double bass and a drum, piercingly and out of tune played the famous Soviet song 'They Wanted to Beat Us, to Beat Us' written by the composer Alexander Davidenko, the leader of the proletarian musicians. The song had been written on the occasion of the victory of Soviet troops over the Chinese in 1929 [and remained popular right up to World War II].[391]

This vivid portrayal of blowing 'official' Soviet music out of one's backside is not mentioned in *Testimony*, but Shostakovich does spare a few choice words for the tune:

> Once the Association came to control music, it seemed that Davidenko's 'They wanted to beat us, to beat us' was going to replace all available music. This worthless song was performed by soloists and choirs, violinists and pianists, even string quartets did it. It didn't get as far as a symphony

[390] Andrey Bitov, pp. 523 and 528 below (hereafter Bitov).

[391] Wilson, p. 82, and *Testimony*, pp. 84 and 222/112; *cf.* also Ian MacDonald, *The New Shostakovich*, p. 82.

orchestra, but only because some of the instruments were suspect – the trombone, for instance.[392]

Shostakovich's courage also was evident in defending his opera *Lady Macbeth* from unjust criticisms. In *Izvestia* (3 April 1935), the composer wrote:

> In the past, I have been subjected to powerful attacks from critics, mainly for Formalism. I did not accept those reproaches then, nor do I accept them now. I have never been a Formalist, and I shall never be one. To defame any work as Formalist on the grounds that the idiom of that composition is complex and sometimes not immediately understandable, is to be unconscionably frivolous.[393]

As Vishnevskaya noted, 'he not only snapped back at his critics but brought charges against them; in those days that demanded a great deal of courage'.[394] The issue became even more heated the following year with the publication of 'Muddle Instead of Music' in *Pravda* on 28 January:

> From the first minute of the opera, the listener is dumbfounded by a deliberately dissonant, confused flow of sounds. Fragments of melody, the beginnings of a musical phrase, sink down, break loose, and again vanish in the din, grinding, and screeching. To follow this 'music' is hard, and to remember it is impossible. [. . .] And all of it is crude, primitive, vulgar . . . The music quacks, moans, pants and chokes in order to render the love scenes as naturally as possible.

[392] *Testimony*, p. 84/112. This low opinion of Davidenko is confirmed in several unpublished letters to Shebalin. On 28 and 29 September 1931, Shostakovich admitted that his own ballet '*Bolt* is shit, but compared to Davidenko it is Beethoven'. He also expressed surprise and anger that 'Ronya' [Shebalin] had sold out and was now defending Davidenko's music. This 'defending of Davidenko' is mentioned again in *Testimony*, p. 84/112: 'One after another, with bowed heads, they joined the ranks of RAPM. For instance, my friend Ronya Shebalin suddenly began singing the praises of Davidenko'. Shostakovich normally did not use the familiar forms of names (*cf.* pp. 121–24), but in both *Testimony* and his letters made a rare exception, referring to his close friend Vissarion Shebalin as Ronya.

[393] Vishnevskaya, *Galina*, p. 208.

[394] *Ibid.*, p. 208.

> And 'love' is smeared all over the opera in the most vulgar form . . . .[395]

Shostakovich again rejected the criticism, but this time by refusing to respond for nearly two years, when his Fifth Symphony was premiered in Leningrad (21 November 1937) and said to be his 'reply to a just criticism'. To Vishnevskaya, this was 'a heroic silence, a symbol of disloyalty and resistance to the regime'.[396]

Other examples of Shostakovich's 'bravery in the artist' are easy to find. His strong opposition to anti-Semitism, for instance, often manifested itself at the most perilous of times. On 12 January 1948, Solomon Mikhoels was murdered, and soon thereafter the Jewish Theatre was closed, the only Yiddish newspaper *Der Emes* (*Truth*) was banned, Mendelssohn's portrait was removed from the Moscow Conservatory's Bolshoi Hall, campaigns were launched against 'cosmopolitans' and 'bourgeois nationalists' (i.e., Jews), Jews were fired from teaching and administrative jobs, and people were encouraged by newspapers to insult Jews with impunity;[397] at the same time, Shostakovich composed his song cycle *From Jewish Folk Poetry*. Writing this work in 1948 was even more courageous than publishing *Testimony*, because the songs symbolised Shostakovich's 'unrepentance' in the wake of the Zhdanov Decree and were a sign of open support for beleaguered Jews.[398] Natalya Vovsi-Mikhoels, the daughter of Solomon Mikhoels, recalls:

> The impact of the poems of those simple Jewish songs [. . .] at

[395] *Ibid.*, p. 211.

[396] *Ibid.*, p. 212. *Cf.* Ian MacDonald: 'Seen in context, his Fifth Symphony is by far the most courageous gesture made by a Russian artist under Stalin' (*cf.* p. 581).

[397] Dubinsky, p. 5.

[398] Shostakovich also assisted behind the scenes, in 1948 hiding Moshe Beregovsky, compiler of *Yiddische Volks-Lieder* (1938), at his apartment until he could help rescind his arrest order (Wilson, p. 234), and, in February 1953, writing a letter to support Vainberg (Weinberg). The latter's wife recalls 'how dangerous it was for Shostakovich to vouch for an enemy of the people, a Jew, and furthermore, Mikhoels's son-in-law [. . .]' (Wilson, p. 231). Khentova also notes that Shostakovich requested the release from incarceration of composer Iogann Admoni, protested the arrest of Iosif Brodsky, helped Anatoly Efros, housed Zoshchenko in

> that particular time was simply shattering for me and my husband Moisei Weinberg. After all, not a day passed without those 'rootless cosmopolitans' (who all bore Jewish surnames) being slandered and abused in the press. This cycle voiced what we dared not ever express in conversations. It was an open protest by Shostakovich against the hounding of the Jews in this last five-year plan of Stalin's.[399]

Shostakovich first showed *From Jewish Folk Poetry* at the Moscow Composers' Union in early 1953, just after the press had denounced the 'Doctors' Plot'.[400] The latter linked 'assassins in white coats' (Jewish physicians) with a terrorist group that admitted murdering Zhdanov in 1949 and supposedly had tried to poison even the Great Friend of Physicians. The song cycle eventually was premiered in Leningrad on 15 January 1955, seven years after its composition. According to Zhitomirsky, early listeners exchanged frightened looks on hearing, in Shostakovich's final song, the line 'Doctors, doctors are what our sons have become!'[401]

Recently, Laurel Fay has attempted to downplay the significance of *From Jewish Folk Poetry*, and, in her article 'The Composer Was Courageous, But Not as Much as in Myth',[402] again displays her 'naïveté or worse'. She states that 'something does not add up here': why would Shostakovich compose a 'setting of Jewish folk texts at the time [immediately after the Zhdanov Decree (1948)] when his own survival stood in manifest jeopardy'?[403] Typifying of her lack of perspective, Fay nowhere mentions that Shostakovich had begun an even more suicidal work, *Rayok*, in the wake of the same Decree.[404]

Moscow during the latter's prosecution, and said to Anatoly Mariengof, a friend of Yesenin, who was blacklisted in 1946: 'Let's go to Moscow. I have money' (Khentova, 'Shostakovich: Legends and the Truth', p. 6).

399 Wilson, p. 229.

400 *Ibid.*, p. 238. The 'Doctor's Plot' was intended to provide Stalin with the pretext for a wholesale extension of his anti-Semitic campaign.

401 Zhitomirsky, 'Public and Private'.

402 *The New York Times*, 14 April 1996, Section 2, pp. 27 and 32 (hereafter Fay, 'Myth').

403 Fay, 'Myth', p. 27.

404 *Cf.* pp. 271–86.

Ironically, what does 'add up' is Fay's own errors and distortions. Finding it utterly inconceivable that the composer could display such 'selfless courage', such 'principled solidarity with persecuted Jews', Fay questions the very extent to which Jews were being persecuted in 1948: 'By the autumn of 1948, they [Shostakovich and the vast majority of his compatriots] could have received few hints [of Stalin's scheme for the eventual containment or eradication of Soviet Jewry]'.[405] As 'evidence', she points out (1) that in May 1948, Stalin had 'publicly upstage[d] Truman by making the Soviet Union the first country to grant de jure, not merely de facto recognition to the nascent State of Israel'; (2) that 'a front-page editorial published at the time in *Pravda* touted equality and mutual respect for the ethnic cultures of all of the Soviet Union's constituent nationalities, great and small, as the country's special and unique strength'; and (3) that when 'Golda Meir arrived in Moscow to become Israel's first ambassador to the U.S.S.R.[, a]n estimated 50,000 Soviet Jews turned out to greet her [. . .]'.[406] Incredibly, Fay accepts, without question, the 'truths' in *Pravda* as well as Stalin's other official, public denials of anti-Semitism. She totally misconstrues Stalin's rush to recognise Israel, attributing it to his love (or at least 'mutual respect') for Jews, rather than to a cold, calculated plan to gain a Soviet foothold in the Middle East.[407] She ignores a wealth of documentary evidence that Jews had been singled-out for persecution at least from 1942,[408] and that Shostakovich was aware of, and had

[405] Fay, 'Myth', pp. 26 and 32.

[406] *Ibid*., p. 32.

[407] Kostyrchenko, pp. 101 and 104.

[408] For example, Agitprop functionaries, in a report of 17 August 1942 preserved in the Russian Centre for the Preservation and Study of Documents of Modern History (henceforth RTsKhIDNI; formerly the Central Party Archives), claimed a 'Jewish conspiracy' in the arts. Lists were drawn (*cf*. Kostyrchenko, pp. 16–17; RTsKhIDNI f.17, op.125, d.123, l.22) demonstrating that the Bolshoi Theatre, Moscow Conservatory and literature and art departments of *Pravda*, *Izvestia*, *Vechernyaya Moskva*, *Literatura i iskusstvo* and *Muzgiz* were dominated by Jews, thereby justifying the ousting of such non-Russians in favour of 'real' Russians. That Jews were immediately and acutely aware of this new discrimination is evident from Yakov Grinberg's letter to Stalin dated 13 May 1943:

protested against, this anti-Semitism by 1943.[409] Finally, she dismisses, outright, the testimonies of Jews and non-Jews who actually lived through the terrible '40s and '50s: 'Memory is fickle',[410] according to Fay; thus Maxim Shostakovich, Edison Denisov, Nina Dorliak, Abraam Gozenpud, Kirill Kondrashin, Natalya Vovsi-Mikhoels and Daniil Zhi-

---

> Dear leader and teacher I. V. Stalin.
>
> How can one explain that at such a grim time for the Soviet country a muddy wave of disgusting anti-Semitism has risen again and penetrated some Soviet institutions and even Party organizations? What is this? Is it a criminal stupidity of excessively zealous people who unintentionally assist fascist agents, or is it something else?
>
> ... There are rumors and conjectures that a directive might have been given from above to develop Russian national culture, perhaps even to promote national regulations for personnel. In bodies that manage art organizations this is mentioned with a secretive look and a whisper in one's ear. This resulted in hostile attitudes toward Jews who are engaged in this field. In practice, the personnel department of the Art Affairs Committee and of other bodies dependent upon it select only Russian employees or officers even for [a position as insignificant as] a manager of a traveling theater. Today Jews of any qualification cannot count on getting an independent job, even of a modest rank .... some Communists (Russians) and even secretaries of local Party organizations [...], in a perfectly official way raise the question about [official] bodies being 'choked up' apparently with Jews, [and] bring accusations of 'pushing Jews through'. At the Directorate of Art Affairs they have had to count to determine whether the Jewish quota was violated, i.e., 4 Jews per 30 staff members.

Kostyrchenko, pp. 19–20; RTsKhIDNI, f.17, op.125, d.136, l.123–124.

For other examples of official persecution of Jews, *cf.* Kostyrchenko, pp. 18–23, and Yehoshua A. Gilboa, *The Black Years of Soviet Jewry, 1939–1953*, transl. Yosef Shachter and Dov Ben-Abba, Little, Brown, Boston, 1971.

[409] Kostyrchenko, p. 18, reports:

> The scale of the purge at the Moscow Conservatory would undoubtedly have been much greater had not the country's musical elite – among them the greatest Russian musicians and composers – supported the persecuted. For example, in September 1943, when a professor at the conservatory, Ye. M. Guzikov, was threatened with dismissal because of his nationality, N. Ya. Myaskovskii', D. D. Shostakovich, Yu. A. Shaporin, and others signed a petition in his support.

Preserved in RTsKhIDNI, f.17, op.119, d.12, l.126–133.

[410] Fay, 'Myth', p. 27.

tomirsky, all of whom acknowledge Shostakovich's courage in composing and premiering *From Jewish Folk Poetry*, are not to be believed.[411]

Fay goes on to suggest that composing a work with Jewish elements in 1948 was neither unusual nor risky. After all, when another composer, Moisei Vainberg (Weinberg), submitted 'his new Sinfonietta, audibly saturated with Jewish themes, to the scrutiny of his peers at the Composers Union [, t]he reception was gratifying'.[412] Actually, while it is not surprising that Vainberg, a Jew, would draw upon his heritage, or that the Composers' Union would accept such a fig leaf from a Jew, it is admirable that a non-Jew, Shostakovich, would publicly ally himself with this traditionally persecuted group. Contrary to Fay, there was no mad rush, no long line of non-Jewish composers champing at the bit to write Jewish-flavoured works.[413]

[411] *Cf.* Wilson, pp. 229, 236, 238 and 357, and p. 227 below. When contacted in Israel, Natalya Vovsi-Mikhoels stated that Fay's allegation that anti-Semitism was little known in the USSR prior to the writing of *From Jewish Folk Poetry* is 'incorrect', as is her suggestion that Shostakovich 'just happened to pick the wrong "folk" as his inspiration'. 'That choice was not accidental. This subject was important to him' (conversation with the authors, 1 March 1997). Boris Tishchenko also characterises *From Jewish Folk Poetry* as having been 'written with the courage of a kamikaze during the time of the "Doctor's Plot"' (Tishchenko, *Letters*, p. 44).

For a point-by-point rebuttal of Fay's incredible assertion that Jews were not persecuted in Soviet Russia until 1948, *cf.* Ian MacDonald, pp. 684–718 (marshalling numerous historical sources that indicate that persecution of Jews continued, almost non-stop, since the revolution of 1917).

[412] Fay, 'Myth', p. 32. Typical of her 'selective scholarship', Fay does not mention that Vainberg was arrested in 1953 for planning 'to create a Jewish conservatory in the Crimea, [. . .] composing two cycles of Jewish songs employing lyrics by Isaac Leib Peretz and Samuil Galkin, [. . . and] giving Yu. A. Shaporin the idea of writing *Vokaliz*, based on a Jewish melody' (Kostyrchenko, p. 196, note 67). Shostakovich, in what Vainberg's wife considers another act of unusual courage ('to vouch for an enemy of the people, a Jew, and furthermore, Mikhoels' son-in-law'), wrote a letter to Beriya asking to rescind Vainberg's arrest (Wilson, p. 236).

[413] A search through the present authors' *Biographical Dictionary of Russian/Soviet Composers*, Greenwood Press, Westport, 1989, reveals only one work with the word 'Jewish' in its title written in the USSR in 1948: Shostakovich's song cycle.

Fay further points out that singers did not balk at performing *From Jewish Folk Poetry*, as some did when the Thirteenth Symphony was to be premiered in 1962. How dangerous could it have been to perform this song cycle in 1948, she wonders. What she fails to understand, however, is that the performances of *From Jewish Folk Poetry* to which she refers were private affairs, for family and trusted friends, and therefore substantially different from the very public premiere of the Symphony. She also overlooks that a performance of the songs scheduled for 20 December 1948 at the Composers' Union *was* cancelled, causing Zhitomirsky to note in his diary that this was 'very good', because he 'feared that new attacks would take place. Anti-semitism was already gaining ground higher up [. . .]'.[414] Nina Dorliak, the soprano in the first (private) performance, also recalls worrying that her 'colleagues might balk at the idea of singing [this] "unacceptable" music', because 'at the time of its composition there could be no possibility of a public performance of the cycle'.[415] Therefore – again contrary to Fay – Zhitomirsky and Dorliak clearly, and in 1948, recognised the risk in performing *From Jewish Folk Poetry*, even in private.

Fay concludes that Shostakovich chose his text for *From Jewish Folk Poetry* not out of courage (in solidarity with persecuted Jews), but out of sheer stupidity. She writes:

> Kowtowing to the Composers' Congress back in April, Shostakovich had enumerated the steps he planned to take to rehabilitate himself. He pledged above all to place melody at the heart of his work, melody steeped in the bountiful heritage of national cultures. [. . .] When Shostakovich chose to compose songs on Jewish folk texts for his first major work in the aftermath of Zhdanov's purge, he was making a good-faith effort to redeem his well-publicized pledges. [. . .] He

[414] Zhitomirsky, 'Shostakovich', p. 471. In another article, Zhitomirsky gives the date of this diary entry as 18 October 1948 and the planned premiere as 'in two days' time' (i.e., 20 October). He goes on to note: 'But it was not to be. First came casual warnings, followed by unexplained delays – then, finally, explicit prohibition decreed from "above". In the end, the premiere actually took place seven years later (in Leningrad on 15 January 1955) – that is, when the Chief Director of Ideological Threats was no longer alive' (Zhitomirsky, 'Shostakovich: Public and Private').

[415] Wilson, p. 236.

> did what was required of him. It was his rotten luck that of all the available nationalities, great and small, he just happened to pick the wrong 'folk' as his inspiration.[416]

Fay here rejects the image of Shostakovich as a 'holy fool' (*yurodivy*), and portrays him as a real fool, incredibly naïve and totally unaware of the significant differences between 'available nationalities', great and small, Jewish and non-Jewish. One may reasonably conclude that her statement in fact reveals more about its author than about Shostakovich; one may also reasonably inquire whether it 'just happened' to be written, or was the result of an agenda to fulfil.[417] At the very least, one should question Fay's familiarity with the documentary evidence from the relevant period.[418]

[416] Fay, 'Myth', p. 32.

[417] For example, *cf.* Adam Hochschild, 'Cleaning Up Stalin's Act', *The New York Times*, 8 May 1996, p. 23. Hochschild asserts that '[c]areers are built, institutes are founded and tenure is granted' on the basis of modern academic revisionism [or, in the case of Shostakovich, *anti*-revisionism]. He notes that such

> claims invariably offer few human voices or faces. Instead, they have only the dry, cold feeling of studies based largely on official documents. This is sometimes a legitimate way to write history, but it's an oddly limited method for a period from which there are millions of living survivors. And where the Soviet Union is concerned, official documents can easily lead into a dream world.

For more on Fay's 'oddly limited method', *cf.* p. 246, note 17.

[418] In contrast, *cf.* Ian MacDonald's thoroughly documented rebuttal of Fay's position, pp. 686–720, below. Even Joachim Braun, whom Fay herself describes as 'the leading authority on the "Jewish" facet in Shostakovich's music', rejects her conclusions and criticises her selective scholarship.

When contacted by the authors in September 1997, he provided the following statement for publication:

> The conditions of Soviet artistic life were much more complex than some Western musicologists may imagine (I say this both as a scholar of this culture and its witness). No greater harm can be done to and no greater danger exists for scholarship than vulgar simplification. Dr. Fay has used in her *New York Times* article a journalistic style of quoting selectively out of context, without referring to sources and to the authors of the material she used. My position on Shostakovich's Op. 79 is clear enough from the title of the mentioned MQ [*Musical Quarterly*] article: 'The Double Meaning of Jewish Elements in Dmitri Shostakovich's Music'.
>
> In December '47 to January '48 there was hardly anyone among the Soviet intellectuals who had illusions about the anti-Semitic

Shostakovich again challenged the Soviet Union's anti-Semitism with his Thirteenth Symphony, commemorating the enormous Jewish sacrifice at 'Babi Yar'. Its controversial text by Yevtushenko caused the original bass soloist Boris Gmyrya and conductor Mravinsky to withdraw from the premiere:[419]

---

tendencies in Soviet politics. To claim that the case of Weinberg, who was complimented by Khrennikov, was a sign of tolerance is equivalent to proclaiming that the slogan over the gates of Theresienstadt 'Arbeit macht frei' ['In work there is freedom'] was a true reflection of life in Nazi concentration camps (*cf.* my 'Jews in Soviet Music' in J. Miller, ed., *Jews in Soviet Culture*, London, 1984, p. 91). The falsehood of public and personal life in the Soviet Union usually made straightforward, unequivocal behaviour impossible, especially for intellectuals. As a great artist, Shostakovich – consciously or unconsciously – reflected dissidence in nearly every one of his works. To bring this meaning to the surface, certain conditions of perception were needed. I must quote another passage from my Boris-Schwarz-Fs. [Festschrift] article: 'Conceived and composed as an expression of human desperation, *From Jewish Folk Poetry* had been turned overnight into an ideological protest of potentially nation-wide political significance – a remarkable case of sudden change in value and meaning of an artistic work due to circumstances independent of its creator' (pp. 263–64). The meaning of Shostakovich's music is disclosed to the 'aware listener' (Braun). It is his 'rotten luck' (Fay) that among the unaware are also some musicologists.

Shostakovich's dissidence is manifested by his music, and his music only. I have to add, in this regard, that this fact cannot be confirmed nor disproved by the authenticity or unauthenticity of the Volkov/Shostakovich *Testimony*, a collection of lobby gossip, in my opinion a clever (both in terms of legality and content) piece of falsification. It is regretful that the author who wrote a convincing review on this, to use an expression of Richard Taruskin, 'shameful' publication, falls in the trap of a style she condemned. [Note: Professor Braun had not yet examined the detailed rebuttal of Fay's review nor the other evidence corroborating *Testimony* in *Shostakovich Reconsidered*. He admitted not having followed the *Testimony* debate over the past eight years. –EDS]

[419] Johnson, p. 31, notes:

this same composer was capable of astonishing acts of defiance. [. . . T]here is the fascinating, grimly compelling compound narrative of the events leading up to the premiere of the Thirteenth Symphony – the seemingly shy, apologetic, painfully nervous composer inwardly determined that Khrushchev's Russia should hear that monumentally challenging work, while apparently stronger men cave in around him.

Now I seem to be a Jew.
Here I plod through ancient Egypt.
Here I perish crucified, on the cross.
And to this day I bear the scars of nails.
I seem to be Dreyfus,
The Philistine is both informer and judge.
I am behind bars. Beset on every side.
Hounded, spat on, slandered . . .[420]

Gmyrya was shown the score in late July 1962; by mid-August, 'under pressure from the local Party Committee, [he] wrote to Shostakovich to say that, in view of the dubious text, he refused to perform the work' (Wilson, p. 355). Vishnyevskaya, at Shostakovich's request, then approached Aleksandr Vedernikov to sing the premiere, but he too declined, for similar reasons (Vishnyevskaya, pp. 275–77). Next, Kondrashin suggested that Viktor Nechipaylo be the soloist. Nechipaylo, however, withdrew at the last moment (*cf.* p. 519), leaving the premiere to his understudy, Vitaly Gromadsky.

[420] Vishnevskaya, *Galina*, pp. 274–75.

Even Yevtushenko, after the first two performances (18 and 20 December 1962), revised several lines of the text so that the Symphony would not be banned. However, contrary to the statements by Kondrashin (Kondrashin, p. 516; Wilson, p. 361) and Vishnevskaya (Vishnevskaya, *Galina*, p. 279), a much altered and expanded second version was never prepared by Yevtushenko nor published in *Literaturnaya Gazeta*. Yevtushenko, in fact, tells quite a different story, even denying that Kondrashin and Shostakovich were surprised by his changes:

> Kondrashin [after meeting with 'higher-ups'] asked me to save the Symphony. I understood what he was saying. Shostakovich never asked me about this personally. He was too subtle for that. But Kondrashin came to see me immediately after visiting Shostakovich. And so I wrote additional lines [i.e., substitutions]. Kondrashin and I brought the lines to Shostakovich. He sighed and wrote them into his piano score.
>
> Albert Todd, 'The Many Literary Worlds of Babi Yar', paper, Brown Symposium XVII, Southwestern University, 25 February 1995; tape on file with the authors.

Also *cf. Yevgeny Yevtushenko: The Collected Poems, 1952–1990*, ed. Albert C. Todd, with Yevtushenko and James Ragan, Henry Holt and Co., New York, 1991, pp. xix–xx; hereafter Yevtushenko, Todd and Ragan).

Todd, a long-time friend of Yevtushenko, confirms that a second version of 'Babi Yar' was never published in *Literaturnaya Gazeta* or in any other possible Soviet journal. Furthermore, Yevtushenko himself acknowledges only a few changes in his text, which he justifies as follows:

> On the eve [of the next performance] Kondrashin was called 'upstairs' somewhere and told that they would not allow the performance if there was no mention of Russian and Ukrainian victims in the text. Those victims did exist and no one was forcing me to lie.

Significantly, this support for Jews was only one important manifestation of the composer's artistic independence and courage. For example, rejecting the dictates of socialist realism espoused in the Zhdanov Decree, he also composed the potentially suicidal satire *Rayok*, which viciously parodies the officially sanctioned music as well as the officials themselves (Stalin, Zhdanov, Shepilov and others). Shebalin advised Shostakovich to destroy all trace of *Rayok*: 'you could be shot for such things';[421] however, again the composer risked life and family, and even called attention in *Testimony* to this unknown work that 'says it all'.[422]

Shostakovich also displayed uncommon bravery in initially refusing Stalin's request that he attend the Cultural and Scientific Conference for World Peace in New York (25–28 March 1949). As first revealed in *Testimony*,[423] and now corroborated by Yury Levitin[424] and recollections of the event by Nina Vasil'yevna, the composer's first wife,[425] he eventually agreed to go to America, but only on the condition that Stalin lift the ban on his own and other composers' works imposed by the State Commission for Repertoire.

[. . .] What could I do? I wrote these four lines: 'I stand here, as if by a well, giving faith in our brotherhood. Here Russians lie and Ukrainians lie with Jews in the same earth.'

[. . .] I showed these four lines to Shostakovich and with his permission they were included in the symphony. Was I right then in making this compromise? I think so. Otherwise the world would not have heard Shostakovich's work of genius for another twenty-five years – until today's glasnost. Don't forget that this was the first poem against anti-Semitism printed in the Soviet press after so many anti-Semitic campaigns of the Stalinist times. The Thirteenth Symphony was the first infant cries of glasnost from its cradle. Glasnost was almost smothered in its cradle, but the infant lived and cries to this day.

Yevtushenko, pp. 296–97.

421 Wilson, p. 296.

422 *Testimony*, p. 111/147; *cf*. also pp. 271–86.

423 *Testimony*, pp. 111–12/147–48.

424 Wilson, pp. 212–13.

425 Zhitomirsky, 'Shostakovich', p. 434; Zhitomirsky, 'Public and Private'.

Shostakovich's rejection of Stalin's authority culminated with his Ninth Symphony. Schönberger notes:

> the last drop in the bucket for Stalin [. . .] and the one which made the Great Gardener boil with rage, was the composer's omission to hail the Great Railroad Engineer with 'quadruple winds, choir and soloists' in his Ninth Symphony. It did not depict the mighty upsurge of the spirit of millions of people in the days of the great triumph. We were offered a symphony-scherzo, a joke, almost, one might say, a sinfonietta![426]

After Stalin's death, bravery in the artist continued to overcome fear in the man:

> [At] the open meeting of the Composers' Union, convened [on 14 September 1960] for the admission of Shostakovich into the Party [. . .] Shostakovich mumbled his prepared text without lifting his eyes from the paper, except for one moment when he suddenly raised his voice dramatically: 'For everything good in me I am indebted to . . .' The audience expected the standard and obligatory 'the Communist Party and the Soviet government', but Shostakovich cried out, '. . . to my parents!'[427]

Still another affront to authority occurred several years later:

> Shostakovich was to read the Introduction for the opening of the Fifth Congress of Composers. The text had been cooked-up in the depths of the Communist Party and contained a flattering passage directed at L. I. Brezhnev. And Leonid Il'yich himself was all set to listen. But what on earth was taking place? . . .
>
> Shostakovich comes to the podium, picks up the typed sheets of paper, and ostentatiously (as if in a slow-motion movie scene) gives them a 180-degree turn. Then, he looks at them for a long time and reverses them again. Silence. Seconds seem to be years. In the Presidium, everyone is perplexed: 'Why is Shostakovich "fooling around"?'

[426] Schönberger, 'Memoirs', pp. 56–57. Mravinsky, however, reading the Aesopian language of the symphony, correctly perceived it as a paranoid commentary on Soviet reality (*cf.* p. 170).

[427] *Testimony*, p. xxxii/xxxix; confirmed in Zhitomirsky, 'Shostakovich', p. 467, and Zak, p. 496.

> But he is in no hurry. Once again, 'with a flourish', he turns the pages upside down. Once again!![428]

Given these many examples of open defiance and incredible courage, it is not surprising that Shostakovich would have his say, even after death, in *Testimony*. Indeed, any of the above incidents could have jeopardised his life and family much more than publishing his memoirs. Shostakovich understood the regime that imprisoned him much better than most critics allow. As such, he could, and did, take calculated risks. His survival and that of his family prove that he correctly anticipated the reactions of Soviet officials. But what Shostakovich could not fathom was the ignorance of Western academics, who would not accept his memoirs without him signing every page 'Approved. D. Shostakovich', inscribing the frontispiece photo 'in remembrance of my attacks on Stalin, Khrennikov, *et al.*', and documenting every conversation with a tape recorder – that is, without *absolutely* jeopardising his life and family. Thirty years after his horrendous experience in New York, Shostakovich still was faced with 'the typical Western journalist [. . .] uneducated, obnoxious, and profoundly cynical [. . . who asks that I] risk my life [. . .] to satisfy the shallow curiosity of a man who doesn't give a damn about me'.[429]

15. Testimony of Guilt

In proper perspective, *Testimony* is no surprise. For at least twenty years, Shostakovich had contemplated working on his memoirs; furthermore, *Testimony* represents the culmination of his 'bravery in the artist' as well as another manifestation

[428] Zak, p. 496.

[429] *Testimony*, p. 151/196. In addition, Shostakovich's criticism of Western humanists – people who closed their eyes to the real situation in the USSR, to the abasement and oppression to which the Soviet creative elite and Soviet people in general were subjected – has been corroborated by Flora Litvinova (*cf. Testimony*, pp. 153–54/200, and Wilson, pp. 271–72). Other notable 'Soviet' memoirists who vented similar fury against Western 'humanists' include Nadezhda Mandelstam (re. Louis Aragon) and Alexander Solzhenitsyn (re. Jean-Paul Sartre) (Ian MacDonald, *The New Shostakovich*, p. 254).

of his deep-seated guilt for, in his own words, being a 'coward all my life' and simply having survived. Volkov confirms that Shostakovich wanted his memoirs to be called *Testimony of Guilt*; only later was this shortened to *Testimony* at the suggestion of the publisher.[430]

Shostakovich's title is particularly apt since the theme of guilt (both the composer's own and that of others) resonates throughout these memoirs, which are akin to a deathbed confession: a last chance to tell the truth, to document what one has experienced and endured, to put one's life into perspective.[431] Gavriil Glikman noted: 'On his deathbed he [Shostakovich] wrote and left us his confession (I call it "A Cry from the Grave").'[432] Kondrashin concurred:

> This book changes everything. Dmitri Dmitriyevich to a large extent is attempting to rehabilitate himself, and I can understand why it is such an angry book. This is revenge from the grave – in one of the reviews it was written that 'from the grave we could hear the powerful voice'.[433]

Shostakovich, understandably, wished to tie-up loose ends and to define his own historical image before death. After all, death, in the composer's mind, was the end. Dubinsky recalls Shostakovich saying about his Fourteenth Symphony: 'I was advised to make the finale of this symphony comforting, to say that death was only the beginning. But it is not a beginning, it is the real end; there will be nothing afterward, nothing'.[434] Lubotsky also remembers the composer's words before the 'closed' premiere of the work in the Small Hall of

[430] Conversation between Volkov and the authors, Spring 1995. *Testimony of Guilt* has previously been acknowledged as the original title in Evans, 'Moscow'; Whitney, p. C7; and Schwarz, p. 575.

[431] Compare with Federal Rule of Evidence 804(b)(2): statements made in anticipation of imminent death, and concerning the cause or circumstances of this death, are admitted into evidence as an exception to the hearsay rule.

[432] G. Glikman, 'Shostakovich As I Knew Him', Vol. 37, p. 373.

[433] Interview between Kondrashin and Volkov, 22 February 1980. Tape on file with the authors. The review referred to by Kondrashin is 'A Cry from the Tomb', *The Economist*, 273, 27 October–2 November 1979, p. 120.

[434] Dubinsky, p. 278.

the Moscow Conservatory (June 1969): 'Death is terrifying, there is nothing beyond it. I don't believe in life beyond the grave'. Shostakovich then quoted from Nikolay Ostrovsky's novel, *How the Steel Was Tempered*. 'The essence of the passage was that one should die with a clear conscience, "so that one need not be ashamed of oneself".'[435] According to Yevtushenko, Shostakovich also 'suggested we create a new symphony on the theme Pangs of Conscience. All that came out of it, unfortunately, is my poem, dedicated to him'.[436]

Throughout his life, Shostakovich often confessed his own guilt, in private, to friends and colleagues. About his speech before the 1948 Composers' Union Congress, Shostakovich told Sabinina in March 1956:

> I got up on the tribune, and started to read out aloud this idiotic, disgusting nonsense concocted by some nobody. Yes, I humiliated myself, I read out what was taken to be 'my own' speech. I read like the most paltry wretch, a parasite, a puppet, a cut-out paper doll on a string!![437]

Denisov also recalls that after a Composers' Union meeting in Sverdlovsk (October 1957), Shostakovich, feeling ill, asked that he stay with him. All night long Shostakovich

> recalled his past and kept returning to the same phrase: 'When I think about my life, I realize that I have been a coward. Unfortunately I have been a coward'. He then added that if I had seen the things that he had, then I too would have been a coward. For instance, he told how during the period of the purges he would go visit a friend, only to discover that that friend had disappeared without a trace [. . .] and strangers were occupying his flat.[438]

Lebedinsky remembers similar confessions. After Shostakovich had been forced to join the Party in 1960, he stated:

> I am scared to death of them. You don't know the whole truth. From my childhood I have been doing things that I

[435] Wilson, pp. 417–18. Ostrovsky's novel is also mentioned in *Testimony*, p. 62/83.

[436] Yevtushenko, p. 297. This poem is included in Yevtushenko, Todd and Ragan, pp. 210–12.

[437] Wilson, pp. 294–95.

[438] *Ibid*., p. 304.

> wanted *not* to do. I'm a wretched alcoholic. I've been a whore, I am and always will be a whore.[439]

Lebedinsky adds that the composer, after signing the official letter condemning Sakharov and Solzhenitsyn, 'cursed himself, saying that he'd never forgive himself for having done it'.[440]

Shostakovich's guilt in *Testimony* (*of Guilt*) is largely that of a survivor: he says at the beginning, 'looking back, I see nothing but ruins, only mountains of corpses', and, at the end, 'I was remembering my friends and all I saw was corpses, mountains of corpses'.[441] This survivor's guilt also is evident in 'Hamlet's Dialogue with his Conscience' from the *Six Poems of Marina Tsvetayeva*, a work composed in 1973 and, thus, exactly contemporaneous with *Testimony*. Robinson points out:

> Hamlet's guilty conscience resonated deeply in Soviet intellectuals and artists, who felt great remorse over even having survived when so many others had perished. It was this feeling that Boris Pasternak expressed when he remarked upon the suicide of Marina Tsvetayeva [. . .], noting that he and his colleagues had failed to save her. [. . . 'Dialog Gamleta'] addresses very directly the issue of the Soviet artist's guilt for simply having survived, while witnessing so much slaughter and torture.[442]

16. Summary

As has been demonstrated repeatedly, critics of *Testimony*, such as Laurel Fay, are guilty of the very same sins of which

[439] *Ibid*., p. 337.

[440] *Ibid*., p. 338. With regard to joining the Party, making many 'ill-fated "correct Party-line" speeches', and signing the letter against Sakharov, Flora Litvinova recalls: 'Shostakovich was quite simply afraid. He feared for his children, his family, himself and his neighbour' (Wilson, p. 308).

[441] *Testimony*, pp. 1/3 and 215/276; *cf*. also p. 132.

[442] Harlow Robinson, 'And Art Made Tongue-Tied By Authority: The Dialogue Between Shostakovich and Shakespeare', paper, Brown Symposium XVII, Southwestern University, 23 February 1995, typescript, pp. 8, 9 and 11, provided courtesy of the author.

they falsely accuse Volkov. Fay charges Volkov with misrepresenting the truth: passing off a traditional biography as memoirs, plagiarising from Shostakovich's articles, lying about his relationship with the composer, and the like. But her arguments lack both substance and perspective, and often wildly distort the facts.

Frequently, Fay argues on both sides of an issue: she criticises *Testimony* for its one-sidedness, while accepting, without question, the even more one-sided 'official' image of the composer. She accuses others of 'inept scholarship', while accepting, without qualification, Soviet propaganda. She asks, 'Which explanation are we to believe?', finding it incomprehensible that the Seventh Symphony could have been inspired by both Stalin and the Nazis, while complaining that in 'much of the new material and revisionist writing about Shostakovich [. . .] questions are framed using Cold-War binary logic: either/or, yes or no'.[443]

Fay asks several important and legitimate questions but, perhaps as a result of 'faulty memory, maliciousness, or inept scholarship', to borrow her own criticisms of Shostakovich and Volkov, provides few answers. Her 'conclusive' article, 'Shostakovich versus Volkov: Whose *Testimony*?', makes clear why people who live in glass houses should cast no stones.[444]

[443] Fay, paper.

[444] Indeed, having been so pre-occupied casting stones at others, Fay remains oblivious to fallacies in her own 1980 article. On 3 November 1995, she described Ian MacDonald's *The New Shostakovich* as a 'moronic tract' and claimed that Sofiya Khentova's publications display 'a level of error that is not merely sloppy, but irresponsible' (Fay, paper). Taruskin, Norris and Brown, similarly, have been more concerned with 'mud instead of music', wherever *Testimony* is involved. However, before passing judgement on others for 'errors of omission', 'misrepresenting information', and failing to put things into 'proper historical context', Fay and company would do well to correct their own mistakes (*cf*. pp. 116–237, 242–55, 287–95, 643–723).

III. The Case for the Defence: Corroborating *Testimony*

Evidence that *Testimony* was the authentic memoirs of Dmitry Shostakovich began to emerge immediately after its publication, despite the arduous efforts of Soviet officials and some Western scholars to mute the truth. Robert Evans reported on 7 November 1979, one week after the release of the book, that simultaneous with the official Soviet denunciation of *Testimony*, 'other cultural figures who knew Shostakovich well felt the language ascribed to him in the book, of which they had learned through Western radio broadcasts, rang true. The sources said many of the incidents recounted in the book were identical in both form and content to those the composer had related in private to his friends over many years'.[1] Harlow Robinson, who was in Moscow in 1979 when *Testimony* began circulating clandestinely, also recalls that 'while Soviet musicologists and musicians (including those who knew him well) expressed reservations about Mr. Volkov's motives and methods, they agreed almost unanimously that this was the Shostakovich they knew'.[2] Other scholars confirmed the 'ring of truth' of the book, even if they had to protect their sources with anonymity. John Warrack begins his review of *Testimony* as follows:

> 'I wish they were not true; but I am afraid they are.' Thus a very distinguished Soviet musician, privately; and other Soviet musicians and acquaintances have confided more or less the same thing.[3]

[1] Evans, 'Moscow'.

[2] Harlow Robinson, 'His Music Never Lied', *The New York Times*, 25 November 1990, Section 7, p. 16.

[3] John Warrack, review of *Testimony*, *Opera*, 31, March 1980, p. 245 (hereafter Warrack).

Gerald Abraham also was convinced of the authenticity of the book after consulting a 'reliable source',[4] and Detlef Gojowy acknowledges:

> the book by Solomon Volkov was already considered an authentic document without any reservation during the last years of the Soviet system. The legend that circulated earlier, insinuating that the book was a falsification, was completely disposed of and is at the most still disturbing some Western minds.[5]

After the fall of the Soviet regime in August 1991, corroboration of *Testimony* no longer had to be whispered anonymously but could be shouted openly, even in former Soviet publications. Endorsements of *Testimony* came from Shostakovich's inner circle, and appeared in many post-Soviet publications, including *Muzykal'naya Akademiya*, *Novy Mir* and even *Pravda*. Maxim's praise of *Testimony* has been mentioned previously.[6] Similar sentiments have been voiced by Kurt Sanderling, Kondrashin, Lebedinsky, Zhitomirsky, Ashkenazy, Barshai, Dubinsky, Gilels, Lyubimov, Richter, Rostropovich and Yevtushenko.[7] Sanderling, Mravinsky's assistant for twenty years with the Leningrad Philharmonic, asserted that 'everything Shostakovich related from his own experience in the disputed Solomon Volkov memoir is essentially accurate'.[8] Kondrashin, who premiered

[4] Abraham, 'Citizen Composer', p. 609.

[5] Vahid Salehieh, interview with Detlef Gojowy, *Melos*, 1/4–5, Summer 1993, pp. 50–51.

[6] *Cf.* pp. 111–15.

[7] *Cf.* Heikinheimo, 'Decade of Struggle'.

[8] *Classical Music*, 18 May 1991, p. 15, as reported by Norman Lebrecht. In a more recent interview in Lyon, France (October 1996), Sanderling was again asked about his 'thoughts on the book *Testimony*', to which he responded:

> I have no doubt that it's true. Shostakovich himself told me a significant number of things that appear in the book. If I had any doubts, they would be with reference not to the events he lived out himself, but rather to the stories told to him by others. It might be, that in these cases, there were things he wanted to believe. For example, he tells, in a very explicit way, that his private enemy, Khrennikov, pissed in his pants from fear during an audience with Stalin. I can well imagine that someone else told him this story

several of Shostakovich's works, also acknowledged: 'It was with the greatest agitation that I read Shostakovich's memoirs, prepared by Solomon Volkov. Much of what comes as a surprise to the Western reader was not a surprise for me. I knew many of the things and guessed many others'.[9]

Even stronger, more detailed endorsements have come from Shostakovich's long-time friends and colleagues Lev Lebedinsky and Daniil Zhitomirsky. Lebedinsky states:

> I regard *Testimony* as one of the most important publications devoted to the composer, and its authenticity does not raise any questions. There is no doubt about it. I am ready to put my signature under every word of it. This is the truth about Shostakovich. Many of our talks found its place in Volkov's book, which came as a big surprise to me since Shostakovich's works were commonly evaluated in a different way.[10]

This opinion was seconded by Zhitomirsky:

> I read the book with excitement, unable to put it down. I reread it, reflected on it, compared it with my own materials (diaries, letters and clippings). I checked it with statements made by Shostakovich's friends and, finally, with my own memories. From every angle, I found myself contemplating the same picture – exactly what I had seen happening around him, even inside him, at the beginning of the '60s. I wrote such details down whenever I had the chance of meeting or contacting Dmitri Dmitriyevich. I got to know the workings of his mind: its sensitivity, its power. I was familiar with his tricks of speech: short sentences; apt, pithy replies; well-aimed witticisms; entire scenes of parody enacted for his closest friends (whenever he was in 'good form'). [. . .] I'm convinced that no serious scholar of Shostakovich's work – and, in particular, of his life and times – should disregard this source.[11]

Ivan Martynov, another colleague, adds:

---

and – even if it was not true – he found it so wonderful he wanted to believe it.

Sanderling, p. 14.

[9] Ian MacDonald, 'Reply', p. 44.

[10] Nikolska, p. 78.

[11] Zhitomirsky, 'Public and Private'; Ian MacDonald, 'Reply', p. 44.

> My perception of Shostakovich's music corresponds to the image created by Solomon Volkov. I have no doubts in the authenticity of these confessions, but I do not have any arguments except my own feeling and Shostakovich's music. But it is beyond any doubt that the image of the composer is one-sided in Volkov's book. There are a lot of different testimonies that Shostakovich was soft, lenient and benevolent. But I cannot see any contradiction in it. Both portraits are authentic. But the one shown by Volkov is more surprising. The gloomy and stern Shostakovich as presented by S. Volkov did not reveal himself to everybody.[12]

Finally, Boris Pokrovsky notes:

> Those people who surrounded Shostakovich in his later years, who visited him in his home and today publish memoirs claiming the closeness of their relationship, these are the enemies of Shostakovich, not Stalin and Zhdanov. When it comes to understanding Shostakovich's music, a sixteen-year-old boy with talent understands it more than any of the 'friends'. You need a gift to understand Shostakovich, just as you do to understand Mozart, Bach or Beethoven.[13]

Pokrovsky's comment was intended as a criticism of Volkov,[14] but, ironically, turns out to be an endorsement. Volkov is not one of the 'friends' who publish their own memoirs and claim a close relationship with Shostakovich; in fact, Volkov has never claimed to be a friend of the composer, just a collaborator in his projects.[15] On the other hand, the 'sixteen-year-old boy with talent [who] understands [...] more than any of the "friends"' was indeed the young Volkov, who at the age of sixteen published a review of Shostakovich's Eighth Quartet that much impressed the composer and began their professional relationship.[16]

[12] Nikolska, p. 81.

[13] Wilson, p. 387.

[14] Interview with Boris Pokrovsky, October 1995.

[15] *Cf.* p. 322.

[16] Volkov, 'Novy kvartet D. Shostakovicha' ('New Quartet of D. Shostakovich'), *Smena* (*Change*), 7 October 1960; *cf.* p. 79.

A. Selective Scholarship

In spite of the abundance of pro-*Testimony*, pro-Volkov statements such as these, some writers persistently continue to cite only the earlier, adverse comments about the Shostakovich memoirs. Typical of such 'selective scholarship' is Malcolm Brown's 1993 review of Ian MacDonald's *The New Shostakovich*, in which Brown quotes liberally from Maxim's rejection of *Testimony* but includes none of his more recent pro-*Testimony* views, nor mentions the respect with which the composer's son now holds Volkov. In an attempt to explain why Maxim 'highly recommends' the *Testimony*-centred *New Shostakovich* as 'one of the best books about Dmitri Shostakovich that I have read', Brown suggests that Maxim has 'allowed his family name to be co-opted for commerce' (i.e., sold out) or, as a devoted son, hopes to salvage 'the memory of a beleaguered father'.[1] Or is he suggesting that Maxim failed to read the book carefully or read only the first page of each chapter?[2] Like father, like son!

[1] Brown, review, pp. 958–59. Brown provides no evidence that Maxim 'allowed his name to be co-opted for commerce' and, apparently, is merely parroting Khrennikov's assessment of Soviet émigrés: 'Every emigré has to say bad things about his homeland – it brings in the bucks' (Seppo Heikinheimo, 'Tikhon Khrennikov in Interview', *Tempo*, No. 173, June 1990, p. 19). When contacted by the authors, MacDonald explained that 'this endorsement', which first appeared on the dust jacket of the Northeastern University edition, 'came about when my American editor sent Maxim an advance copy of the book. He responded quite freely and there was no formal arrangement' (letter of 17 July 1995).

Ironically, despite its selective scholarship, defamatory allegations, and inaccuracies, Brown's review was awarded the Eva Judd O'Meara Award (given for the best review published in *Notes*) because it supposedly 'sort[ed] out historical and aesthetic issues with equal skill' ('Notes for *Notes*', *Notes*, 51/4, June 1995, p. 1277).

[2] Fay and others have similarly suggested that if Shostakovich did, indeed, sign the first page of each chapter of *Testimony*, he did not read or approve of the 'controversial' material in the following pages, which they attribute to Volkov. *Cf.* pp. 209–16.

In a response in *Notes*, MacDonald points out the error of Brown's ways, noting the strong support of *Testimony* by Maxim and many others, especially since the fall of the Soviet regime in 1991.[3] Brown's reply, however, displays a startling close-mindedness and desire to win an argument by any means, including character assassination and libel. Rather than addressing the issue with facts, Brown dismisses it, stating: 'it makes ordinary commonsense not to trust someone you know to be a liar, and that's what we know Solomon Volkov to be. It doesn't really matter how many ex-Soviets believe that *Testimony* is "essentially accurate"'.[4]

Taruskin's academic probity has been questioned previously.[5] In addition, his close-mindedness is evident in his statement that 'even if the authenticity of *Testimony* could be vindicated, the equally troublesome question of its veracity would remain':[6] that is, even if the words did come from Shostakovich's mouth and were read and approved by the composer, Shostakovich himself may have been lying.[7] This, of course, could be said about any set of memoirs, but, as

[3] Ian MacDonald, 'Communications', *Notes*, 50/3, March 1994, pp. 1207–10.

[4] Malcolm H. Brown, 'Communications', *Notes*, 50/3, March 1994, p. 1210. Brown, a few years ago, wrote to Antonina W. Bouis (the translator of *Testimony* and three of Volkov's later books), asking her whether she considered Volkov an 'honest man'. She replied 'yes'. He ignored it (conversation between Antonina Bouis and the authors, December 1995). This type of 'Ministry of Truth' scholarship is akin to Shneyerson's investigation of Volkov. *Cf.* p. 55.

[5] *Cf.* pp. 126–28.

[6] Taruskin, 'Dictator', p. 35.

[7] Taruskin states this more explicitly in 'Public Lies and Unspeakable Truth' (p. 47):

> It is also understandable, should it ever turn out that Shostakovich was in fact the author of *Testimony*, that he, who though mercilessly threatened never suffered a dissident's trials but ended his career a multiple Hero of Socialist Labour, should have wished, late in life, to portray himself in another light.

For still another example of post-Soviet waffling contrasting stikingly with his earlier braggadoccio ('as any proper scholar could plainly see, the book was a fraud'), *cf.* Taruskin, review, p. 760 ('even if the authenticity of *Testimony* as the composer's retrospective recollections could be confirmed [. . .]'). *Cf.* also p. 292.

noted previously, no major, compromising error has yet been found in *Testimony*.[8] Taruskin's criticism stems from Fay and reminds one of the classic 'alternative plea', taken to the idiotic extreme in the apocryphal common-law 'case of the kettle':

> In a suit in which the plaintiff sought damages for his broken kettle, which he alleged the defendant had borrowed and returned in a cracked condition, the defendant responded: 'I never borrowed your kettle, and if I did, it was never broken, and if it was broken, it was that way when I borrowed it'.[9]

In other words, 'Shostakovich never met with Volkov, and if he did, he never dictated his memoirs, and if he did dictate his memoirs, he was lying through his teeth'.

'Selective scholarship' also is manifested in how *Testimony* itself is mentioned (or not mentioned) by some writers. Fay, in her revision of Schwarz's *New Grove* article on Shostakovich, merely repeats, with slight alteration, Schwarz's one-sentence comment about Shostakovich's 'controversial "memoirs"'[10] and keeps *Testimony* in the bibliography. Furthermore, she includes none of Volkov's other writings on the composer (while adding three of her own), portraying

[8] Ian MacDonald, *The New Shostakovich*, p. 2. Other writers agree. Calum MacDonald notes in his article on the discovery of *Rayok*, 'in this matter, as others, Volkov proves to have been accurate' (Calum MacDonald, 'The Anti-Formalist "Rayok" – Learners Start Here', *Tempo*, No. 173, June 1990, p. 23) (hereafter Calum MacDonald). Also *cf.* p. 143, note 106.

[9] Richard L. Marcus, Martin H. Redish, Edward F. Sherman, *Civil Procedure – A Modern Approach*, West Publishing Co., St. Paul, 1995, pp. 133–34.

[10] Schwarz's original statement reads: 'His controversial "memoirs", published in the USA after his death (and disputed by Soviet authorities), would seem to bear out his discontent with Soviet officialdom' ('Shostakovich', *New Grove Dictionary of Music and Musicians*, Macmillan, London, 1980, Vol. 17, p. 272). The revised version, presumably by Fay (*cf.* p. 245, note 12), subtly changes the focus: 'His controversial "memoirs", published in the USA after his death, would seem to bear out his discontent with Soviet officialdom, but their authenticity is disputed by both Soviet and Western authorities' (Schwarz and Fay, p. 204). Of note is Fay's reference to 'Western authorities' (i.e., herself).

him falsely as one lacking a track record as a scholar.[11] Schwarz's original text (printed in 1980), understandably, does not discuss *Testimony* at length, because most of it was written before the memoirs were published in late 1979.[12] However, one would have expected an update of this material in 1986 at least to summarise the controversy surrounding the Shostakovich memoirs, especially since Schwarz had expressed a desire to do so.[13] Two things are clear: first, that additions to the main text could have been made, since new mention is made of a recording and subsequent revivals of *Katerina Izmailova*; second, that Schwarz would have included some discussion of *Testimony* had he lived to revise his own article. This assumption is based on the eight references to *Testimony* in Schwarz's *Music and Musical Life in Soviet Russia, 1917–1981*, revised shortly before his death in 1983. In Schwarz's book, Volkov is referred to as an 'expert', several passages from *Testimony* are quoted, and the initial

[11] This continues the silence in Fay's 'conclusive' article (p. 491), in which she questions Volkov's credentials and notes that he was 'virtually unknown in the West when he emigrated to the United States in 1976'. Although musicologists, in general, may have been unfamiliar with Volkov's name before *Testimony*, Shostakovich scholars were not. Even Fay herself, in a letter to Volkov (17 April 1978), states: 'And, of course, I am acquainted with your writings on Shostakovich, and young Leningrad composers'. Inexplicably, however, Fay does not mention Volkov's *Young Composers of Leningrad* either in her 1980 article or 1986 update of Schwarz's article. Since this well-received book includes a preface by Shostakovich, it provides evidence of their professional relationship. Nor does Fay mention articles such as 'Dmitry Shostakovitch and "Tea for Two"', pp. 223–28, a revision of a more thoroughly documented article in *Slavica Hierosolymitana*, Vol. 3, The Magnes Press, The Hebrew University, Jerusalem, 1978, pp. 264–71, which includes the first publication of a letter from Shostakovich to Nikolay Malko; and 'On the Inevitable Meeting: Shostakovich and Dostoyevsky', *Rossiya/Russia, Studi e ricerche a cura di Vittoria Strada No. 4*, Giulio Einaudi, Torino, 1980, pp. 199–222, which Krzysztof Meyer considers 'among the best Shostakovich studies ever' (letter from Ian MacDonald to the authors, 19 July 1994).

[12] In a letter to the authors (15 February 1996), Stanley Sadie confirmed that '*Testimony* was published after the article for *The New Grove* was written, too late to permit more than a brief reference [top of the second column, page 272]'.

[13] Conversation between Volkov and the authors, August 1995.

Soviet response to, Fay's questions about, and Maxim's partial endorsement of the memoirs all are acknowledged.[14] Schwarz concludes that '*Testimony* contains some revealing statements about Shostakovich's music' and that even if every word attributed to Shostakovich in *Testimony* cannot be verified as actually having been said by him, 'the overall impression is very persuasive'.[15] Unfortunately, none of these comments is included in Fay's update of Schwarz's article (a true disservice to this fine scholar),[16] just as mention of *Testimony* is scarce in Fay's other articles.[17]

[14] *Cf.* Schwarz, pp. 538; 532–33, 537, 573 and 576; 541 and 575–76; 576–77; and 645–46, respectively.

[15] Schwarz, p. 576.

[16] In his letter of 15 September 1996, Sadie states:

> for the 1986 reprint [*Russian Masters 2*], it would not have been appropriate, in the Editor's view, to add any considerable discussion of a controversial book within a text written by an author who was no longer living.

Given the importance of *Testimony*, however, the authors believe that even if 'considerable discussion [. . .] within' Schwarz's text was deemed inappropriate, more than a *one*-sentence reference to the composer's 'controversial memoirs' should have been included by Fay as an editorial note *after* the main text, summarising Schwarz's own views (c. 1981–83) as well as other pertinent, up-to-date information.

[17] For example, 'Musorgsky and Shostakovich', *Musorgsky: In Memoriam 1881–1981*, ed. by Malcolm H. Brown, UMI Research Press, Ann Arbor, 1982, pp. 215–26 (one reference to *Testimony*, p. 224, note 1), and 'The Punch in Shostakovich's *Nose*', *Essays for Boris Schwarz*, pp. 229–43 (one reference to *Testimony*, p. 240, note 7); 'From *Lady Macbeth* to *Katerina*: Shostakovich's Versions and Revisions', *Shostakovich Studies*, pp. 160–88 (no reference to *Testimony*).

Apparently, Fay hoped that scant mention of *Testimony* in her articles would help make it disappear. On 3 November 1995, however, she conceded: 'It has been clear to me for some time now that nothing I or anyone else can do is going to make *Testimony* go away' (Fay, paper).

Fay seems poised to practise additional 'selective scholarship' in her forthcoming book on Shostakovich. After her paper on 3 November 1995, she admitted dismissing the testimonies of the composer's friends and family, including Maxim. These data she considers, as a whole, unreliable; furthermore, she stated that she 'didn't want to become compromised by having them tell me their stories and then being obliged somehow to retell them' (including statements that might disagree with her own views?) (tape on file with the authors). Ironically, Fay now questions what Maxim knows about his father, since he was born only in 1938. Yet, in her 'conclusive' article, she accepted without hesitation Irina's comments

Additional examples of Fay's selective scholarship[18] involve Shostakovich's photographs and inscriptions, the history of the Volkov-Shostakovich relationship, the true nature of *Testimony*, the origin and meaning of works such as the Fourth and Seventh Symphonies, Volkov's supposed 'plagiarism', and the composer's authorisation, 'Read. D. Shostakovich'. Unfortunately, Fay is not alone in distorting evidence through selective editing and/or misleading paraphrase. For example, Christopher Norris, in his symposium *Shostakovich: The Man and His Music* (1982), casts numerous aspersions on *Testimony* and Volkov.[19] Only a few most egregious examples warrant discussion.

The most appalling example of Norris's selective scholarship involves a totally unwarranted (and libellous) accusation that Volkov misrepresented the true nature of the Twelfth Symphony. Norris writes:

---

about *Testimony*, even though Irina knew Shostakovich for only thirteen years.

Since Fay has assumed the role of a public prosecutor of *Testimony* and Volkov, she would do well to remember the admonition of the American Bar Association Model Rules of Professional Conduct, Rule 3.8(d):

> The prosecutor in a criminal case shall [. . .] make timely disclosure to the defense of all evidence or information known to the prosecutor that tends to negate the guilt of the accused [. . .].

Cf. also Rule 3.3(a)(3):

> A lawyer shall not knowingly [. . .] fail to disclose to the tribunal legal authority in the controlling jurisdiction known to the lawyer to be directly adverse to the position of the client [. . .].

[18] *Cf.* pp. 118–26, 128–40, 143–46, 150–59, 188–228 and 684–721.

[19] For example, *cf.* the following gems (p. 9):

> What is suspect about the *Memoirs* is the way in which every [. . .] suggestive ambiguity is worked up into a more or less conscious gesture of private defiance. It is hard to credit Volkov's claim that these expertly barbed and slanted anecdotes were the product of a series of rambling monologues conducted (on Shostakovich's part) in a state of extreme nervous depression.
>
> In other words, the *Memoirs* are just too good to be true from an anti-Soviet propaganda viewpoint. The overall effect is of a cunning narrative tactician at work, creating an impression of vague, roundabout talk but in fact homing in on every loaded point with relish and impeccable timing. One certainly wouldn't guess at such qualities of mind from anything that Shostakovich published – or was quoted as saying – during his lifetime.

> The Twelfth [Symphony] is explained as a failed attempt – 'the material put up resistance' – to celebrate Stalin's heroic virtues. (Since by all accounts the intended subject was Lenin, not Stalin, one can only assume a momentary lapse either in Shostakovich's memory or in Volkov's otherwise well-oiled machinery of slanted reconstruction.)[20]

One wonders, where is this 'explained'? The passage in *Testimony* is as follows:

> [In the Twelfth Symphony] I began with one creative goal and ended with a completely different scheme.* [* signifies Volkov's editorial note.] I wasn't able to realize my ideas, the material put up resistance. You see how hard it is to draw the image of leaders and teachers with music. But I did give Stalin his due, the shoe fits, as they say. I can't be reproached for avoiding that ugly phenomenon of our reality.[21]

In paraphrasing this text, Norris completely ignores Volkov's editorial note (indicated with an asterisk) and links Shostakovich's Stalin reference with the wrong work. Norris asserts that Shostakovich (or, worse, the stumbling 'cunning narrative tactician',[22] Volkov) 'explained' the Twelfth as a 'failed attempt to celebrate Stalin's heroic virtues', yet Volkov states clearly in his editorial note: 'According to Shostakovich's plan, the Twelfth Symphony (1961) was supposed to contain a musical portrait of Lenin'.[23] Obviously,

[20] Norris, p. 170.

[21] *Testimony*, p. 107/141.

[22] *Cf*. p. 247, note 19.

[23] *Testimony*, p. 223/141, note. In 1988–89, Lebedinsky corroborated *Testimony*'s account and elaborated on Shostakovich's initial plan:

> In 1961 Shostakovich made another attempt to express his true attitude to what was going on in his country. He decided that his Twelfth Symphony was to be a satire of Lenin. When he told me this I tried to talk him out of it. It was too dangerous and nobody would understand anyway. He brushed off my advice with, 'He who has ears will hear' (a favourite Shostakovich expression). [. . . Shostakovich later] explained: 'I wrote the symphony, and then I realized that you had been right. They'd crucify me for it because my conception was an obvious caricature of Lenin. Therefore I sat down and wrote another one in three or four days. And it's terrible!'
>
> Wilson, p. 346.

Shostakovich also instructed Lebedinsky to keep quiet about the full history of the Twelfth Symphony, which the latter agreed to do at the time

Shostakovich's reference to Stalin pertains not to the Twelfth Symphony, but to the Tenth, mentioned only two paragraphs earlier (and conveniently ignored by Norris): 'But I did depict Stalin in music in my next symphony, the Tenth [...]. It's about Stalin and the Stalin years. The second part, the scherzo, is a musical portrait of Stalin [...]'.[24] In proper context, therefore, it is Norris, not Shostakovich or Volkov, who has suffered a 'lapse'.

Another example of Norris's distortion of evidence concerns Shostakovich's signatures in *Testimony*. Norris writes:

> It is claimed that Shostakovich signed every page of the Volkov transcript as a witness of its authenticity. The book would certainly have carried more weight and silenced much dispute if the publishers had troubled to reproduce at least a few of those pages.[25]

Again, 'claimed' by whom? Volkov states in *Testimony*, 'Gradually, I shaped this great array of reminiscence into arbitrary parts and had them typed. Shostakovich read and signed each part'.[26] Norris, a professor of literature, seems to have mistaken 'part' for 'page'. Furthermore, Volkov has made abundantly clear in interviews from 1979 on that Shostakovich signed the first page of each chapter, not 'every

---

(Wilson, p. 347). According to Khentova, sketches of the earlier version of the Twelfth, satirising Lenin, exist in the Shostakovich family archive and include 'a parodying waltz based on material from the fourth song, "Misunderstanding", of the vocal cycle *Satires*. The waltz motif coincides with the song's text, "he did not understand the new poetry"' (Wilson, p. 344; citing Khentova, *Shostakovich*, Vol. 2, p. 363), and appears to be still another note-in-a-bottle (*cf.* p. 167, note 188, regarding the similar self-quotation in the Fifth Symphony from the song 'Rebirth').

Nor was the suppressed programme of the Twelfth Symphony entirely undetectable to sympathetic listeners before Lebedinsky published his revelations in 1990. Discussing the work in 1989, Ian MacDonald posited just such a reality (*The New Shostakovich*, pp. 224–27). Indeed, MacDonald also anticipated Lebedinsky's disclosures about the political background and conceptual motivations of the Eighth Quartet (*ibid.*, pp. 221–24).

[24] *Testimony*, p. 107/141.

[25] Norris, pp. 9–10.

[26] *Testimony*, p. xiv/xvii.

page'.[27] Even Laurel Fay acknowledges this in her article published in 1980, two years before the publication of Norris's book.[28]

In spite of clear misreadings of these and additional passages by Norris and others,[29] the chief critics of *Testimony*, practising the now-familiar selective scholarship, have called no attention to such glaring mistakes, apparently being loathe to set the record straight. Paraphrasing Pushkin, 'The "experts" are silent'.[30]

A subtler form of 'selective scholarship' is apparent in Elizabeth Wilson's otherwise admirable *Shostakovich: A Life Remembered* (1994). Wilson's index includes fourteen references to *Testimony*.[31] Curiously, all of these pertain either to material drawn from *Testimony* or to statements made by contributors that disagree with the memoirs.[32] Although, as has been demonstrated repeatedly, much of Wilson's text actually corroborates *Testimony*,[33] Wilson does not call attention to statements that agree with it, nor does she acknowledge (even in footnotes) the pro-*Testimony* views expressed in MacDonald's *The New Shostakovich*, published

[27] Even before *Testimony* was published, Mitgang ('Shostakovich Memoir', p. C14) quoted Volkov as saying that each chapter had been signed by Shostakovich. *Cf.* also pp. 209–15, 'Chital [Read]. D. Shostakovich'.

[28] Fay, p. 487. Facsimiles of all eight of Shostakovich's signatures are now included in the German and Finnish editions of *Testimony*. *Cf.* p. 214.

[29] *Cf.* pp. 146–50 and 153–55.

[30] *Cf.* the last line of Pushkin's *Boris Godunov*.

[31] Several other passages also seem to stem from *Testimony*, but go unacknowledged, such as that concerning Stravinsky offering his walking stick to Yarustovsky (Wilson, p. 134, note 40) and that about Dzhambul Dzhabayev (Wilson, p. 484).

[32] For the latter, *cf.* Wilson, pp. 19–20, 125, 180–81, 187–88.

[33] Reviewers of Wilson's study agree: Johnson, p. 32, notes that 'in the midst of purely musical observations come sudden echoes of *Testimony*, particularly its wicked sense of humour', and Patrick J. Smith adds, *Testimony* 'has come in for severe criticism as fraudulent in part or whole, but its central thesis that the composer lived a "subtext" existence in both his music and his life [. . .] has never been successfully challenged, and it is reinforced by Elizabeth Wilson's new volume [. . .]' (*Opera News*, 59/6, 10 December 1994, p. 67).

four years earlier (and in its account of historical events virtually identical to hers).[34]

Another unfortunate omission in Wilson's text is that of Flora Litvinova's unequivocal corroboration of both the genesis and authenticity of *Testimony*. In the unexcerpted, unexpurgated version of her reminiscences of Shostakovich published in December 1996 in *Znamya* (*The Banner*), Litvinova states:

> I read Solomon Volkov's book. Unfortunately, a long time ago and in English. I must admit that most of the stories retold by Volkov we also heard from Shostakovich. Dmitry Dmitriyevich liked, especially when somewhat inebriated, to shoot the breeze, hyperbolising them, sharpening them, and, of course, making some of them up.
>
> One more thing – in the last years of his life we met rarely, and not for long, or accidentally. And once, at such a meeting, Dmitry Dmitriyevich said: 'You know, Flora, I met a wonderful young man – a Leningrad musicologist (he did not tell me his name – F. L.). This young man knows my music better than I do. Somewhere, he dug everything up, even my juvenilia'. I saw that this thorough study of his music pleased Shostakovich immensely. 'We now meet constantly, and I tell him everything I remember about my works and myself. He writes it down, and at a subsequent meeting I look it over.'[35]

Since Litvinova provided this passage to Wilson,[36] its absence in *Shostakovich: A Life Remembered* is most peculiar. Was this powerful testimony in corroboration of *Testimony* among the 'many pages' of Litvinova's text cut by Wilson

[34] Wilson, apparently, accepts Laurel Fay's debunking of *Testimony* and thus wastes little time with opposing views. In her acknowledgements (p. xx), she expresses her gratitude to Fay for 'stimulating discussions, arguments and speculation' and for keeping her 'up to date with new publications'. Fay, after her paper of 3 November 1995, reciprocated, referring to Wilson as her 'close friend' (tape on file with the authors).

[35] Litvinova, pp. 168–69. Litvinova and Wilson agree that the unnamed musicologist was Solomon Volkov. No other young male Leningrad musicologist has ever claimed to have worked with Shostakovich on his memoirs.

[36] Conversation between Litvinova and the authors, 19 April 1997.

supposedly 'for reasons of space'?[37] When asked about this specific omission in 1997, Wilson responded:

> Thank you for your letter of March 26. Excuse my delay in answering, but for a variety of reasons I have had little time available. I also wanted to think carefully about my reply.
>
> On one level your question can be answered very simply. Originally it was at my request that Litvinova wrote her reminiscences of Shostakovich. The original was over 70 pages long, and I had to be quite selective about what I used – partly because of space problems, and also because from my point of view some things were repetitive.
>
> The passage in question about Volkov was indeed there in Litvinova's original. I have not seen the version published recently in Russia, but I expect it is the same full version of what Litvinova gave me.
>
> You ask why I omitted this passage. It may have been a mistaken decision on my part, but I did not want to get too involved in the whole vexed question about the authenticity of Volkov's *Testimony*, so I tended to omit references[,] as it seem[ed] to me material that was irrelevant to my main subject.[38]

Selective scholarship also is apparent in Wilson's section reproducing Aram Khachaturian's account of writing a new national anthem with Shostakovich.[39] Although most of Khachaturian's version agrees with Shostakovich's in *Testimony*, Wilson, in her footnotes, points only to the few discrepancies, while ignoring significant parallels, such as the following:

[37] Wilson, p. 511.

[38] Elizabeth Wilson, letter to the authors, 14 May 1997.

[39] From Sofiya Khentova, 'Shostakovich i Khachaturyan: Ikh sblizil 1948-y god' ('Shostakovich and Khachaturian: They Were Drawn Together by the Year 1948'), *Muzykal'naya Zhizn'*, 1988, No. 24, p. 11. It should be emphasised that Khachaturian died in 1978, before *Testimony* was published, so it is unlikely that he was paraphrasing the account in Shostakovich's memoirs.

The competition took place in July 1943 at the Bolshoi Theatre. Some 500 anthems were submitted, with several composers submitting multiple entries. The eventual winner was Aleksandr Aleksandrov's 'Bolshevik Party Anthem'.

Shostakovich: 'During the war it was decided that the "Internationale" was not fit to be the Soviet anthem.' (*Testimony*, p. 198/256)
Khachaturian: 'It was during the war that the decision was made to create a new national anthem of the USSR.' (Wilson, p. 179)

Shostakovich: [After being taken to 'a small antechamber' in Stalin's box] 'First Stalin made a profound statement on what the national anthem should be like.' (*Testimony*, p. 202/261)
Khachaturian: [After being taken to the 'green room'] 'Stalin outlined the characteristics of a national anthem and defined how to make it "Soviet".' (Wilson, p. 180)

Shostakovich: 'Stalin [. . .] commanded that Khachaturian and I write an anthem together.' (*Testimony*, p. 199/256)
Khachaturian: 'Voroshilov [one of Stalin's appointees] suggested that Shostakovich and I write an anthem together.' (Wilson, p. 180)

Shostakovich: 'So we got together. [Day 1] We ate and drank, discussed the latest news. We didn't write a single note, we didn't even bring up the subject of work. [. . .] We set another date. [Day 2] [. . .] We got together, and it turned out that Khachaturian [. . .] was saddened by something. He didn't want to write [. . .]. [W]e had to drink a bit. Next thing we knew, it was evening, time to go. And we still hadn't written a single note of our joint anthem. We had to do something, so we made a decision worthy of Solomon. Each would write his own anthem, then we would get together and see who had done the better job. [. . .] Each wrote his own sketch at home, then [Day 3] we met, compared [. . .]. It went quickly, even though there were some difficulties.' (*Testimony*, pp. 200/257–58)
Khachaturian: 'For two days we didn't get anywhere with it. We composed separately, then corrected together. By the third day, something started taking shape.' (Wilson, p. 180)

Shostakovich: [To determine who would do the orchestration] '[. . .] I asked Khachaturian to guess which hand held a matchstick. Khachaturian guessed [correctly] [. . .]. (*Testimony*, p. 201/259)
Khachaturian: [To determine who would do the orchestration] 'Shostakovich said, "Let's break a match [. . .]". The "head" fell to me [. . .].' (Wilson, p. 180)

Shostakovich: 'Several dozen anthems [including Aleksandrov's] had been orchestrated by one very experienced hand.' (*Testimony*, p. 203/261)

> *Khachaturian*: 'Many of the anthems (including Alexandrov's) had been orchestrated by Victor Knushevitsky.' (Wilson, p. 180)
>
> *Shostakovich*: [When asked if another had orchestrated their joint anthem] 'I expressed my deep conviction that a composer cannot entrust the orchestration of his works to anyone else.' (*Testimony*, p. 204/262)
> *Khachaturian*: [When asked if another had orchestrated their joint anthem] 'Shostakovich answered: "A composer should be able to orchestrate himself", and then repeated this phrase convulsively.' (Wilson, p. 180)
>
> *Shostakovich*: '[. . .] it became apparent that the greatest judge and expert of all time on anthems [Stalin] considered the one by Khachaturian and me the best.' (*Testimony*, p. 204/263)
> *Khachaturian*: 'Stalin rejoined, "And I like their joint effort better than their separate anthems".' (Wilson, p. 180)

Even when a discrepancy is noted, little attempt is made to fathom the truth. Wilson points out that in *Testimony*, p. 201/259, Shostakovich takes credit for orchestrating the joint anthem, whereas Khachaturian claims he did it. She also notes that in *Testimony*, p. 204/263, Shostakovich's response to Stalin's question 'Will three months be enough time for you [to revise the refrain]?' is given as 'Five hours will do', whereas Khachaturian reports Shostakovich as saying 'Five days will do'.[40]

In fact, Shostakovich's statements in *Testimony* are closer to the truth. As noted previously, Shostakovich always stressed that 'a composer cannot entrust the orchestration of his works to anyone else'[41] and that writing a work and orchestrating it 'are one and the same as far as I'm concerned'.[42] It would have been uncharacteristic of him to give this task to another, even to such a skilled (although somewhat lazy), colleague as Khachaturian. Still more importantly, an orchestration of Khachaturian and Shostakovich's joint 'Anthem of the Soviet Union', written in Shostakovich's hand, is preserved in the Glinka Museum in

40 Wilson, pp. 180–81, notes 33–34.

41 *Testimony*, p. 204/262.

42 *Ibid*., p. 171/221.

Moscow.[43] This autograph, the first page of which is reproduced in the Appendix,[44] irrefutably supports the account in *Testimony*, but goes unmentioned in Wilson's book.

Finally, given the speed with which Shostakovich worked, 'Five hours will do' has the louder ring of truth than 'five days will do'. Shostakovich orchestrated Youman's 'Tea for Two' in 45 minutes and supposedly *composed* the famous *Festive Overture* in a matter of hours.[45] Anyone could have fixed the refrain in five days. Shostakovich, of course, was not just anyone.[46]

[43] This joint anthem ($\frac{4}{4}$, F major, text by Mikhalkov and El-Registan) exists in two versions: voice and piano, and voice and orchestra, both in Shostakovich's hand. Three other anthems, by Shostakovich alone, also are in the Glinka Museum: the first is in two versions (E flat and D major), the second is in D major, and the third is again in two versions (both in E flat major).

[44] Appendix, Exhibit 14, p. 311. The authors wish to express their gratitude to the Glinka Museum for the kind permission to reproduce the first page of the Anthem score.

[45] *Testimony*, pp. 51–52/69; Volkov, 'Tea for Two'; and Wilson, pp. 62 and 264.

[46] Similar observations may be made about the selective scholarship in David Fanning's *Shostakovich Studies*, which includes predominantly negative references to *Testimony*. Fanning himself acknowledges, in footnotes, the existence of pro-Volkov articles but, in his main text, continues to question the authenticity of *Testimony*, recalling Volkov's alleged 'dishonesty about the provenance of the book' and describing the latter as 'a curious mixture of rumour, fact, and slanted reminiscence' (*Shostakovich Studies*, pp. 4–5).

Actually, what *really* is curious is that both Fanning (*Shostakovich Studies*, p. 4) and Taruskin (review, p. 759) cite Volkov's interview with Drubachevskaya in *Muzykal'naya Akademiya*, but remain silent on her *first-hand*, *first-paragraph* corroboration of the genesis of *Testimony* (*cf.* p. 136). For a detailed rebuttal of Fanning's and others' allegations, *cf.* pp. 46–298 and 643–723.

B. The Ring of Truth

Many of Shostakovich's friends and colleagues, as well as musicologists and other writers, have acknowledged that *Testimony* has the 'ring of truth'. What exactly rings true, however, is different for different readers. Shostakovich seldom revealed himself completely to anyone; accordingly, various acquaintances hold select memories of the composer and often one detail in *Testimony* will ring a bell, while others make no sound at all. Only gradually will the true portrait of Shostakovich be assembled, piece by piece, like a mosaic. Only gradually will the memories of individuals corroborate the image of the composer in *Testimony*.

The ring of truth in *Testimony* has been attributed to both its style and substance. Torsten Ekbom states, 'It is interesting to compare the main text with Volkov's prologue in the English edition. [. . .] In the main text a totally different voice speaks'.[1] This difference has been perceived by many others, including Craft:

> The genuineness of Volkov's overall impression will ultimately be shown by the inimitable character of his hero, whose voice, in *Testimony*, is that of a natural writer. [. . . Volkov's] preface, introduction, and notes are the work of a different person [. . .].[2]

Bitov agrees:

> I read it [*Testimony*] without putting it down and was convinced [. . .] the book was authentic from first letter to last [. . .]. Volkov's individuality finds expression in his footnotes, at least; the footnotes sometimes express him even more than he might wish. But the book – from beginning to end – is in Shostakovich's words, his alone. Volkov wouldn't have said it that way.[3]

[1] Vahid Salehieh, interview with Torsten Ekbom, *Melos*, 1/4–5, Summer 1993, p. 26.

[2] Craft, 'Testaments', p. 79.

[3] Bitov, p. 526.

Finally, Shafarevich adds:

> [*Testimony*] is a document of tremendous power. We can discuss whether it is worthy of the pen of, say, Dostoyevsky, but one can have no doubt that it could not have been written by Solomon Volkov.[4]

The difference in writing styles is still more apparent in comparing *Testimony* with Volkov's later books with George Balanchine, Nathan Milstein and Joseph Brodsky. Shostakovich's short sentences, filled with quotations from Ilf and Petrov[5] to Chekhov and Gogol, aphorisms, sports analogies, vivid imagery, contradictions, profanity, wit and satire are unique to these memoirs, and contrast with the much more polished, sober styles in *Balanchine's Tchaikovsky* and *From Russia to the West*, and with the sophisticated, confrontational style in the books with Brodsky.[6]

The 'rambling, repetitive, almost in stream-of-consciousness style'[7] of *Testimony*, while criticised by some, has been accepted as further evidence of its authenticity by others. Irving Kolodin notes:

> There are repetitious references to Stalin and to Prokofiev, also to Alexander Glazunov [. . .]. All these, and the many other references to things of absorbing interest, could easily

[4] Shafarevich, Vol. 2, p. 456. Edwin Safford also notes: 'The mixture of sardonic humor, despair and stubborn fortitude easily can be, as it has been, compared with Dostoyevsky. As spasmodic relief here and there you might consider scenes to be out of Gogol' ('Shostakovich: Rise and Fall' (a review of *Testimony*), *Providence Sunday Journal*, 3 February 1980, p. H16.

[5] 'Ilf and Petrov' were Il'ya Arnoldovich Fainsilberg (1897–1937) and Yevgeny Petrovich Katayev (1903–42), a duo of humorist writers active in the 1930s. Their characters and quips, particularly from the books *The Twelve Chairs* and *The Golden Calf*, became extremely popular in the USSR, achieving the status of folklore. Shostakovich enjoyed their humour and, in 1938, even considered writing an operetta on *The Twelve Chairs* (Grigoryev and Platek, p. 72).

[6] Volkov's own, quite different, writing style can best be seen in *St Petersburg: A Cultural History*, a book written in his voice alone, without collaborators. *Cf.* the same conclusion by Heikinheimo (*Mätämunan*, p. 397), who translated both *Testimony* and *St Petersburg* into Finnish.

[7] Harold C. Schonberg, 'Words and Music Under Stalin', *The New York Times Book Review*, 21 October 1979, Section 7, p. 3.

> have been copy edited for easier reading. That they remain as they are suggests that *Testimony* is exactly what it professes to be – a book difficult to read but even harder to forget.[8]

Hugh Macdonald adds:

> The text is disorderly in sequence and often self-repeating: all the sentences are short and paragraphing is haphazard. The prose has no sense of style, and this seems to be a faithful translation of what Shostakovich (who had no claims to literary ability) said, pained and weary from a life of struggle and bitterness.[9]

Members of Shostakovich's inner circle also have found much in *Testimony* that reminds them of the composer. 'I write in short sentences, for the poor',[10] Shostakovich's close friend Mikhail Zoshchenko admitted, and the same could be said of the composer's prose, in speech, letters and memoirs. Dubinsky notes:

> When I read *Testimony* I saw Shostakovich himself. I saw him behind every sentence, heard the characteristic manner of his nervous, jagged conversation, always carrying a subtext.[11]

Even Maxim now admits, 'The language is for the most part such that I can recognize it to be my father's language [. . .]',[12] while Galina is completely certain: 'Definitely the style of speech is Shostakovich's – not only the choice of words, but also the way they are put together'.[13] Zhitomirsky elaborates:

> In private, D[mitry] D[mitriyevich] spoke in an amazingly lively and expressive manner. He had his own style of speech: short sentences, that almost always sounded like aphorisms, in which all the unnecessary terms had been deleted; and his

[8] Irving Kolodin, 'Music to My Ears: Open Door to a Closed Society', *Saturday Review*, 10 November 1979, p. 50.

[9] Hugh Macdonald, review of *Testimony*, *Books and Bookmen*, April 1980, p. 55.

[10] Volkov, 'Tea for Two', p. 224.

[11] Dubinsky, 'Interior Shostakovich', p. 3.

[12] Heikinheimo, 'Decade of Struggle', p. 3.

[13] Conversation with the authors, 15 October 1995. *Cf.* p. 83.

sentences always hit the mark, as does a sniper; his enunciation was extremely precise, each word and even individual sounds (including consonants) were endowed with a meaningful significance. The specific expressiveness of his speech lay in the humour and sarcasm that emanated from an unruffled seriousness. This was brilliant artistry.[14]

Zhitomirsky also recognised in *Testimony* a phrase heard many years earlier, directly from Shostakovich. In describing the finale of his Fifth Symphony, Shostakovich notes that its optimism is 'forced, created under threat [. . .] as if someone were beating you with a stick and saying, "Your business is rejoicing, your business is rejoicing", and you rise, shaky, and go marching off, muttering, "Our business is rejoicing, our business is rejoicing" '.[15] Shostakovich used the same phrase back in August 1945, after he had learned about the immense destruction caused by the atomic bomb. Zhitomirsky recalls: 'Lost in contemplation of the horror of Hiroshima, I suddenly found myself babbling compulsively about our hopeless future. Cutting me short, Shostakovich gazed loftily into the sky and said: "Our business is to rejoice" '.[16]

Other aspects of *Testimony* also support its authenticity. In several passages, Shostakovich openly admits being unsure of details. For example, about witnessing Lenin's arrival at the Finland Station (April 1917), he says 'I don't remember a thing'. Had the text been forged, such an episode probably would have been left out rather than highlighted. Furthermore, Shostakovich's opinions in *Testimony* are often highly

[14] Zhitomirsky, 'Shostakovich', p. 432. Lukyanova, p. 148, also notes:

Shostakovich disliked panegyrics and bombastic speeches, the idle talk of windbags. He spoke and wrote simply, without the floweriness of subordinate clauses. A short phrase. Period. Another phrase. Period. He tried to avoid magnificent epithets and superlative statements. It can be seen from his articles, autobiographical notes and remarks that he very often used the simplest verbs in common usage, such as *wrote*, *came*, *finished*, 'this is good and this is bad for such and such reason'.

[15] *Testimony*, p. 140/183. Also *cf.* p. 164.

[16] Wilson, p. 177; Zhitomirsky, 'Shostakovich', p. 427. Several other phrases in *Testimony* also were characteristic of the composer: the mention of 'new shores' with regard to Musorgsky, and of 'Bach to Offenbach' in describing his unusually wide musical tastes (*cf.* pp. 99 and 94).

complex and multi-dimensional. Although some critics would prefer to believe that Shostakovich either loved or hated individuals or works, and that once his opinion was formed it was cast in stone, what emerges from *Testimony* are realistic assessments that even the composer admits changed over the years and may differ from the views of others. Smith concludes:

> It would take a literary talent of a very high order to have fabricated this record. [...] (I cannot imagine how these opinions could have been wholly fabricated by Volkov; they ring too true as a composer's opinions.)[17]

Schwarz agrees:

> Certain sections have a particular ring of authenticity – Shostakovich's discussions of Glazunov, Meyerhold, and Zoshchenko; or his chilling descriptions of the mental anguish during the Stalin terror. [...] His unflattering remarks about Prokofiev have raised objections, but, in fact, the dislike was mutual.[18]

Craft also finds the portrait of Glazunov (a 'wonderful musician' who wrote 'boring symphonies') especially believable, 'a character study that goes directly to the man's unique and interesting qualities without overlooking or minimizing his weaknesses'.[19]

As noted previously, 'experts' have pointed to many perceived contradictions in *Testimony* without realising that contradictions were an integral part of Shostakovich's character and behaviour. Similarly, the content and focus of *Testimony* often seems peculiar at first glance,[20] but with further research and reflection rings true. Some readers, for

[17] Patrick J. Smith, review of *Testimony*, *Musical America*, March 1980, pp. 12–13. Also *cf.* Shafarevich's comments, pp. 34–35.

[18] Schwarz, p. 576. Unlike Fay (*cf.* pp. 124–25), Schwarz shows a willingness to accept as authentic material beyond that mentioned on the frontispiece photo.

[19] Craft, 'Testaments', p. 82.

[20] Especially to those, such as Norris and Schaeffer, who view these memoirs as 'Cold War propaganda' by Volkov. If the latter, why no specific denunciation of Communism or detailed description of The Terror, and why, instead, so many personal (non-political) digressions, anecdotes, and even anti-Western sentiments?

instance, may be surprised by Shostakovich's sports references in *Testimony*,[21] such as the admission that his

> profoundly lowbrow devotion to soccer knows no bounds. And how can televised soccer compare with the fantastic impact of watching a match at the stadium. It's like distilled water and export Stolichnaya.[22]

Although the bespectacled composer seems far from the athletic type, those close to him confirm that he was, indeed, an avid soccer fan. Zhitomirsky, for example, acknowledges the composer's 'interest in active sports, especially soccer';[23] Sabinina notes that Shostakovich 'liked watching sports events; he even attended football matches';[24] Khentova devotes an entire section of her book *Amazing Shostakovich* to Dmitry Dmitriyevich's love for the game; and Mikhail Meyerovich recalls the younger Shostakovich participating in billiards and football in August and September 1944:

> He [Shostakovich] insisted we join him in a game of football; he played with passion, throwing himself wholeheartedly into the game. Once I inadvertently knocked his glasses off his nose. I was embarrassed, but he said, 'That's all right. That's what the game is about.'
>
> It was a mystery to me how he managed to compose so much music at the same time. [. . .] I was intrigued and began to observe him closely. He would play football and fool around with friends; then he would suddenly disappear. After forty minutes or so he would turn up again. 'How are you doing? Let me kick the ball.'[25]

The topic of sport also appears in Shaginyan's notes from her talk with Shostakovich (20 December 1940: 'I love games: tennis, volleyball, football'[26]) and in an unpublished letter to Shebalin (28 May 1938): 'And one more request: on the 24th

[21] *Testimony*, pp. 14–15/21–22, 85/113, 157/204 and 183/237.

[22] *Ibid*., p. 183/237.

[23] Zhitomirsky, 'Shostakovich', p. 459. Shostakovich even wrote a ballet, *The Golden Age*, about a Soviet soccer team named 'Dynamo'.

[24] Nikolska, p. 66.

[25] Wilson, p. 197.

[26] Shaginyan, p. 72.

there is going to be a soccer game between the Leningrad Dynamos and Moscow Storm Petrels. Would you buy me two tickets. Forgive the trouble. Thank you in advance. D. Shostakovich.'[27]

Critics also have been surprised by the lack of detailed discussion of music in *Testimony*. John Warrack writes:

> It is frustrating that more is not said about music, in particular Shostakovich's own music. But [even though] he is insistent that he is not trying to explain his art [. . .] the closing pages are as bleak as anything in his late music.[28]

Although one might expect a composer to explain his music in his memoirs, Shostakovich despised 'talking shop'. In *Testimony* he states: 'I wouldn't want to spend too much time on all possible interpretations [of *Lady Macbeth*]; after all, I'm not talking about myself in these pages and certainly not about my music'.[29] Later, he expresses his belief that his music will speak for itself:

> I write music, it's performed. It can be heard, and whoever wants to hear it will. After all, my music says it all. It doesn't need historical and hysterical commentaries. In the long run, any words about music are less important than the music. Anyone who thinks otherwise is not worth talking to.
>
> [. . .] There's no point in talking to the deaf, and I'm addressing only those who can hear and it's only with them that I plan to converse, only with those people for whom music is more important than words.
>
> [. . .] let people judge me by my music. I have no intention of providing commentaries on it and I have no intention of telling how, where, and under what circumstances I was drenched by the 'sweaty wave of inspiration'.
>
> [. . .] And I have no intention of doing a measure-by-measure analysis of my scores either. That's certainly not very interesting in Stravinsky's memoirs. So what if I inform you that in my Eighth Symphony, in the fourth movement, in the fourth variation, in measures four through six, the theme

[27] RGALI, fond 2012, op. 1, ed. khr. 188.

[28] Warrack, p. 246.

[29] *Testimony*, p. 81/107.

> is harmonized with seven descending minor triads? Who cares?[30]

This attitude has been confirmed, repeatedly, by members of Shostakovich's inner circle. Maxim states:

> [Shostakovich] didn't talk very much about his music. He tried to find people who thought like he did, meaning people who would understand what he was saying in his music without having to be told. Once he said to Rostropovich, 'come, let's go to my place and sit and be silent'. [. . .] And if somebody didn't understand him, then there was just no hope. If he encountered people who didn't understand him, he just didn't have anything to do with them.[31]

Zhitomirsky also acknowledges that

> Dmitry Dmitriyevich disliked very much talking about himself or his works. At various preliminary performances, he limited himself to the stingiest of comments, mainly about form and keys. I think that the more substantial comments that appeared in the press were, as a rule, either secretly pumped out of him, or were written for him.[32]

The composer remained tight-lipped even with favourite performers. He states in *Testimony*:

> Awaiting execution is a theme that has tormented me all my life. Many pages of my music are devoted to it. Sometimes I wanted to explain that fact to performers, I thought that they would have a greater understanding of the work's meaning. But then I thought better of it. You can't explain anything to a bad performer and a talented person should sense it himself.[33]

[30] *Ibid.*, pp. 151–52/196–97.

[31] Robinson, p. 389. Rostropovich confirms that he 'was urgently called to Shostakovich's house [on several occasions]. On arrival he would sit in silence with the composer for half an hour or so before being sent home' (Wilson, p. 320). In *Testimony*, Shostakovich describes a similar meeting with Akhmatova: 'We sat in silence. I was silent and Akhmatova was silent. We said nothing for a while then parted' (p. 214/274). Akhmatova later said, 'We sat in silence for twenty minutes. It was wonderful' (Wilson, p. 321).

[32] Zhitomirsky, 'Shostakovich', p. 466.

[33] *Testimony*, p. 140/183.

Exactly the same sentiment has been recalled by Kondrashin, Meyer, Sanderling, Vishnevskaya and Karen Khachaturian.[34] Vishnevskaya states:

> Shostakovich did not like to talk about his compositions, and never explained the significance of given musical phrases to the performers of his works. It was as if he were afraid of words – afraid that words might destroy his inner musical vision. He always granted artists the right to interpret his works and so put the responsibility squarely on their shoulders.[35]

Khachaturian adds:

> Shostakovich hated being asked questions about his music and whether this or that theme represented something or had any particular meaning. When asked, 'What did you want to say in this work?' he would answer, 'I've said what I've said'. Either you had it in you to understand, or, if not, then it would be fruitless to try and explain anyway.[36]

Shostakovich's letters also contain 'little about his music beyond [. . .] "statistics" – number of movements, timing, keys'.[37]

Another aspect of *Testimony* that has been questioned is its emphasis on the 'Jewish element'. According to Steiner, among the 'very troubling points about the book as we have it [. . . is] the emphasis on the Jewish question and Shostakovich's purported involvement in this question. It is very difficult to escape the impression that Volkov has colored or arranged the conversations he set down – has added bile from

[34] 'He himself did not like to discuss the subtext of his music and usually said nothing [. . .]' (Kondrashin, p. 520); 'I became aware that he did not have the slightest wish to discuss his music' (Meyer, p. 56). 'Most of the time he limited himself to "acoustic advice". He asked that one could hear this or that a little bit more – but, as a matter of fact, in public as well as in private, he spoke rather seldom about the content of his works. In his opinion, although he may have written the music, it was not his role to give a verbal interpretation' (Sanderling, p. 12).

[35] Vishnevskaya, *Galina*, p. 350.

[36] Wilson, p. 376.

[37] Taruskin, 'Who', p. 66.

his own incensed spirit'.[38] Another writer echoes this opinion: 'It is possible to doubt that Shostakovich was so emphatic about anti-Semitism (I do not doubt that he loathed it but rather too much of it is made here for credence) and perhaps the fact that his interlocutor was Jewish has coloured this as well as other matters'.[39] Such disturbing comments display a total unfamiliarity with Shostakovich and his music. As noted previously, Shostakovich's interest in Jewish music and opposition to anti-Semitism permeated his life, especially from the late 1930s forward. He taught and much admired Jewish composers such as Fleishman (whose opera *Rothschild's Violin* he completed),[40] wrote letters on behalf of Vainberg and many others persecuted during the campaigns against 'rootless cosmopolitans',[41] composed a song cycle *From Jewish Folk Poetry* in 1948 and had it premiered shortly after the so-called 'Doctors' Plot',[42] and commemorated the Jewish sacrifice at Babi Yar in his Thirteenth Symphony (1962) at a time of renewed anti-Semitism.[43] (The last affront elicited a complaint from the district Party secretary: 'This is outrageous, we let Shostakovich join the Party, and then he goes and presents us with a symphony about Jews'.[44])

Shostakovich's intense hatred of anti-Semitism in *Testimony* was no surprise for his friends and colleagues. 'Anti-Semitism is a struggle with culture and reason', he told Flora Litvinova. 'It is an admission that we are worse, more

[38] Steiner, p. 132.

[39] Review of *Testimony*, *Music and Musicians*, 28, March 1980, p. 23.

[40] *Cf.* pp. 130–32.

[41] *Cf.* p. 222, note 398.

[42] *Cf.* pp. 222–23.

[43] *Cf.* pp. 229–30. Sabinina, too, confirms that Shostakovich had 'a predilection' for Jewish culture:

> at the time when [his Second Piano] Trio was written [1944], hundreds of thousands of Jews were murdered in gas chambers and burnt at concentration camps. As an artist, Shostakovich could not remain silent, unresponsive to those atrocities.
>
> Nikolska, p. 70.

[44] Wilson, p. 359.

stupid, less cultured than Jews.'[45] Berlinsky, too, recalls that 'Shostakovich's attitude towards anti-Semitism was very negative'[46] and Volkov, confronted with notion that the composer could not have been so outspoken in his defence of Jews, responded:

> This is ridiculous. Kirill Kondrashin, who premiered Symphony No. 13 (about the Jewish victims of the autumn 1941 Nazi massacre at Babi Yar, a ravine in Kiev), told me about the Russian soloist [Vitaly Gromadsky] at [the] rehearsal who said to Shostakovich 'why are you writing about anti-Semitism when there isn't any?' Shostakovich went off like a bomb. The rehearsal was ruined. He wouldn't calm down. There isn't another non-Jewish major figure in 20th century art who became so involved in his creative life with using Jewish themes and motifs. Perhaps he identified with their (the Jews') struggle for freedom.[47]

Kondrashin confirms that Shostakovich, almost shouting, told Gromadsky, 'No there is, there is anti-semitism in the Soviet Union. It is an outrageous thing, and we must fight it. We must shout about it from the roof-tops'.[48] He also notes:

> Although officially unacknowledged, anti-semitism had existed in Russia since the war. Shostakovich was much preoccupied by this problem. He was not a Jew, but he sympathized with the Jewish people, as is testified firstly by the many Jewish themes to be found in his music, and secondly, by the fact that he twice raised the Jewish theme specifically in his works.[49]

Given Shostakovich's track record, is it really a surprise that he would again praise Jewish music and criticise anti-Semitism in *Testimony*?

> I think, if we speak of musical impressions, that Jewish folk music has made a most powerful impression on me. I never

[45] Litvinova, p. 171.

[46] Nikolska, p. 75.

[47] Littler, p. D4; confirmed in Kondrashin, pp. 513–17.

[48] Wilson, pp. 358–59.

[49] Wilson, p. 357. For more on the Jewish element in Shostakovich, *cf.* Jackson, pp. 597–639.

tire of delighting in it, it's multifaceted, it can appear happy while it is tragic. It's almost always laughter through tears.

This quality of Jewish folk music is close to my ideas of what music should be. There should always be two layers in music. Jews were tormented for so long they learned to hide their despair. They express despair in dance music. [...] Many of my works reflect my impressions of Jewish music.

[...] I often test a person by his attitude towards Jews. In our day and age, any person with pretensions of decency cannot be anti-Semitic. [...] My parents considered anti-Semitism a shameful superstition, and in that sense I was given a singular upbringing. In my youth I came across anti-Semitism among my peers, who thought that Jews were getting preferential treatment. They didn't remember the pogroms, the ghettos, or the quotas.

[...] I never condoned an anti-Semitic tone, even then, and I didn't repeat anti-Semitic jokes that were popular then. But I was much gentler about this unworthy trait than I am now. I broke with even good friends if I saw that they had any anti-Semitic tendencies.

[...] Jews became a symbol for me. All of man's defencelessness was concentrated in them. After the war, I tried to convey that feeling in my music. It was a bad time for Jews then. In fact, it's always a bad time for them.[50]

Last, but certainly not least, of the factors contributing to *Testimony*'s ring of truth is its inclusion of information not available elsewhere at the time of publication. The many revelations in *Testimony* include details about (1) Shostakovich's fears of 'disappearing';[51] (2) his anti-Stalinist feelings;[52] (3) his conversations with Stalin about attending

[50] *Testimony*, p. 119/156–57. Shostakovich bristled when confronted with anti-Semitism. Dubinsky recalls how a Ukrainian, who asked to join Shostakovich in a drink, imitated a Jewish accent and began in an unpleasant voice, 'Abram! What front did you fight on? The Tashkent line? And how much did your medals cost? And how much did you sell them for?' Shostakovich muttered 'What filth!' and was visibly shaken by these obnoxious comments (Dubinsky, p. 119). A similar account is given in *Testimony*, p. 119/157: 'all I heard people saying was "The kikes went to Tashkent to fight". And if they saw a Jew with military decorations, they called after him, "Kike, where did you buy your medals?" '

[51] *Testimony*, pp. 92/122, 141/183, 163/212–13. Also *cf.* p. 124, note 32.

[52] *Ibid.*, pp. 75/99, 86/114–15, 104/138, 106–8/140–44, 118/155–56, 145/190, 147/192–93 and 180/232; also *cf.* pp. 231–32, above, and 271–86.

the World Peace Conference and writing a new national anthem;[53] (4) his criticism of Prokofiev's orchestration and both composers' mutual dislike;[54] (5) his dislike of Stravinsky the man;[55] (6) his criticism of Toscanini as an interpreter;[56] (7) his bitterness towards Mravinsky;[57] (8) his disdain for Western journalists and 'humanists';[58] (9) his involvement in the investigation of plagiarism by Ashrafi;[59] and (10) his exposure of the Dzhambul Dzhabayev hoax.[60] The fact that all of these points were, and in some cases continue to be, hotly contested indicates that they were, indeed, revelatory in 1979; furthermore, as has been demonstrated previously, even the most controversial passages in *Testimony* now have been corroborated by a wealth of documentary evidence and statements from the composer's inner circle.

Among the most striking of *Testimony*'s 'revelations that have come to pass' are those concerning the Seventh Symphony, *Rothschild's Violin* and *Rayok*. The discovery, in 1994, of a sketch of the Seventh Symphony's 'invasion theme', dated 26 June 1939 and dedicated to the recently

[53] *Ibid.*, pp. 112/147–48, 203/254, 205–6/256–64; also *cf.* pp. 231 and 253, above.

[54] *Ibid.*, pp. 26/28, 27/34–38; also *cf.* pp. 91–105, above.

[55] *Ibid.*, p. 152/198; also *cf.* p. 179, note 232, above.

[56] *Ibid.*, pp. 17/24–25; also *cf.* pp. 108–10, above.

[57] *Ibid.*, p. 141/183; also *cf.* pp. 105–7, above.

[58] *Ibid.*, pp. 153–54/196–201.

[59] *Ibid.*, p. 134/175. Khentova also acknowledges:

> Shostakovich was the first to uncover the Uzbek musical mafia. When it became known that composer Mukhtar Ashrafi made others write 'his' music, and signed it himself, oppressed many talented people, tormented them, being supported by Rashidov [the former Communist Party boss of Uzbekistan], Shostakovich, still in Brezhnev times, went to Tashkent and exposed Ashrafi at risk to his own life: they attempted to poison him. Ashrafi was expelled from the Composers' Union.
>
> Khentova, 'Shostakovich: Legends and the Truth', p. 6.

[60] *Testimony*, pp. 161/209–11, 171/222. With respect to Dzhambul, the only other source acknowledging the spuriousness of this alleged folk 'composer and poet' appears to be Andrey Olkhovsky's clear-sighted *Music Under the Soviets: The Agony of an Art*, 1955, reprinted by Greenwood Press, Westport, 1975, p. 87.

arrested Meyerhold, confirms that this material, as stated first in the memoirs, was written before the siege of Leningrad and depicts Stalin and his henchmen.[61] Other evidence, including the testimony of Shostakovich's friends and family, Vainkop's mention of the Seventh Symphony as a work in progress before 1940, and the inclusion of this work, by May 1941, on the schedule of programmes for the Leningrad Philharmonic's 1941–42 season, all corroborate the account in *Testimony* that the Seventh Symphony was 'planned' before the Nazi invasion.[62]

Shostakovich's admission that he orchestrated and completed Fleishman's *Rothschild's Violin* also contradicted the facts at hand when *Testimony* was published, but now seems closest to the truth. Previously, as mentioned in Livshits' preface to the piano score (1965) and both Shostakovich's letter to Yevlakhov (1942) and his inscription on the full score (1944), it was believed that Fleishman had completed his piano score and most of the orchestration, and that Shostakovich merely had finished the latter. Shostakovich's larger role in the genesis of this work, acknowledged first in *Testimony*, now has been confirmed by Yakubov and Rozhdestvensky.[63]

A third revelation that has come to pass is a musical work alluded to several times in *Testimony*. Shostakovich notes that 'there are compositions yet to be performed, and no one knows when they will be heard'.[64] On another page, he mentions an unknown work about the battle between formalism and realism that 'says it all'.[65] The latter is described in

[61] *Cf.* p. 157

[62] *Cf.* pp. 156–59.

[63] *Cf.* pp. 131–32.

[64] *Testimony*, p. 120/158.

[65] *Ibid.*, p. 111/147. Writing 'for the desk' was common under the Soviet regime. Yevtushenko recalls discussing his poem 'Babi Yar' with Mikhail Sholokhov:

> 'It's a wonderful poem, and it's wonderful that you wrote it, but why did you publish it?' I didn't understand him. [... 'I]f you write a good poem it must be published'. But he said, 'You gave your enemies a weapon against you. You are defenceless now, you just helped your enemies. [... I]nside my writing desk, there are so many wonderful pages of prose, but I am not foolish. I will not publish

more detail by Volkov. In the Introduction he states that 'one work, which mocked Stalin and his henchmen for organizing the "antiformalist" campaign of 1948, has yet to be performed or published'.[66] He further identifies it as a 'satiric vocal work' in his note on page 223/147. All of these comments refer to Shostakovich's *Struggle between Formalism and Realism in Music*, now usually referred to as *Rayok*. Following its premiere on 12 January 1989 (Kennedy Center, Washington, DC), nine years after it was first described in *Testimony*, corroboration came from Shostakovich's family and close friend Lebedinsky. The latter noted:

> Dmitri Dmitriyevich played it [*Rayok*] only for his family and chosen friends. He then gave me the manuscript for safekeeping. After his marriage, his wife Irina Antonovna asked me for it back. I returned it to Dmitri Dmitriyevich [in 1965], but naturally I kept my own copy. Before he left the Soviet Union, Solomon Volkov came to see me to try and get hold of my copy.[67]

Volkov admits that he was unsuccessful in examining this material, which Lebedinsky held in secret for another twelve years. He also confirms that Shostakovich directed him to Lebedinsky for the libretto and Atovmyan for the score.[68] The fact that Shostakovich described *Rayok* to Volkov in some detail and revealed its location indicates his trust of the latter. After all, as Shebalin warned, Shostakovich could have been shot for such a work.[69]

---

them. I will not give my enemies the chance to use these pages against me'.

Robinson, p. 383.

[66] *Testimony*, p. xxx/xxxvii.

[67] Wilson, p. 299.

[68] Conversation between Volkov and the authors, Spring 1995.

[69] Wilson, p. 296.

C. *Rayok*

By far the most vivid corroboration of *Testimony* comes from Shostakovich's anti-Stalinist musical satire *Rayok*. *Testimony* and *Rayok* are, in a sense, twins in mind and spirit: both were to be made public only after the composer's death; both reveal an uncommon candour and courage. Curiously, the authenticity of *Rayok* has never been challenged, even by those who in 1979 rejected *Testimony* because of its bitterness, sarcasm and profanity. Maxim 'confirmed that he heard his father play the score at the family home'[1] and Irina not only defended the work in an article in *Sovetskaya Kul'tura* (20 January 1989), but produced a page of the manuscript to show that the work was not titled *Rayok*, but *The Struggle between Realism and Formalism in Music*, with a superscript 'for the guidance of students'. She also stated that, according to Isaak Glikman, Shostakovich wrote both the text and music and that the piece had already existed, with the exception of Troikin's last speech, in summer of 1948.[2] Wilson confirms that Irina produced the manuscripts of *Rayok*, all of which are undated, but 'written in the characteristic purple ink Shostakovich used until the early 1960s'.[3]

Others who have accepted the authenticity of *Rayok* without question include Tishchenko, Pokrovsky and Rostropovich. Tishchenko has orchestrated the original piano-vocal score and Pokrovsky has performed it as a completion of Shostakovich's opera *The Gamblers*:[4] 'at the point where Shostakovich abandoned his opera, officials confiscate the

[1] Hugh Davies, 'Shostakovich Score Inspired by Stalin Era', *The Daily Telegraph*, 12 January 1989, International Section, p. 10 (hereafter Davies); Calum MacDonald, p. 24.

[2] Andrey Aleksandrov, 'Juvenilian Lash', *Music in the USSR*, January–March 1990, p. 43; originally in *Sovetskaya Kul'tura*, 20 January 1989.

[3] Wilson, p. 296.

[4] For example, with the Moscow Chamber Opera (Anatoly Levin, conductor) at the Brighton Festival's Roedean Theatre, 23–24 May 1993.

score, accusing it of being formalistic, [and] replace it with the music of *Rayok*'.[5] In addition, Rostropovich attests:

> I knew that such a piece had been written by Shostakovich. He would sing the melodies for me quite often, and would smile slyly. Of course, during that time, it was impossible – or very dangerous to publish this. [. . .] The role of the chorus was to applaud the speakers and laugh at their jokes, evidently as average citizens in the Stalin era.[6]

Elsewhere, he describes *Rayok* as '1000% original' and states that 'in the Soviet Union today, musicologists still write books saying what a good Communist Shostakovich was. This score proves how he really thought'.[7]

[5] Letter from Derek C. Hulme to the authors, 29 September 1993.

[6] Davies, p. 10.

[7] John Rockwell, 'Rostropovich to Conduct Premiere of Unpublished Shostakovich Work', *The New York Times*, 11 January 1989, p. C17. All sources agree that the Preface to *Rayok* is pure Shostakovich. However, some question remains as to when the work was composed, who wrote the libretto, and whether the newly found ending actually belongs to this score or another. According to Yakubov, *Rayok* was begun in 1948, shortly after the Zhdanov Decree; expanded after the Second Composers' Union Conference in 1957; and completed around 1965–68, after Shostakovich's dispute with authorities over his Thirteenth Symphony (Manashir Yakubov, 'Musorgsky's Rayok, Shostakovich's Anti-Formalist Rayok, and the Traditions of Russian Musical Satire from Alexander II to Stalin and Brezhnev', paper, transl. Elizabeth Wilson, 28 January 1994, University of Michigan, typescript, pp. 1 and 3, provided courtesy of the author; hereafter Yakubov, paper). Yakubov also acknowledges that most of the new ending was found in May 1989 and, subsequently, linked to *Rayok* by Basner, who recalled Shostakovich playing the work around 1967 (Wilson, p. 296). Lebedinsky, in contrast, claimed that he wrote the libretto for *Rayok* and cited Maxim and Galina Shostakovich, Yevgeny Chukovsky and M. A. Meyerovich as witnesses of his collaboration on the work in 1957 (Lebedinsky, 'Rayok', pp. 31–32; Lebedinsky, 'The Master's Honour'). He also believed that Yakubov's new ending was inconsistent with the rest of the work, whose 'unfinished nature was in fact an essential aspect of Shostakovich's conception' as mentioned by 'Opostylov' in the Preface: 'Comrade Troikin's speech is unfortunately left unfinished' (Calum MacDonald, p. 30). The Preface itself probably dates from after 1948, since it mocks Apostolov, who at that time was still a post-graduate student specialising in military-march music. Apostolov came to prominence only in the 1950s and was first mentioned by Shostakovich in a letter to Denisov (22 July 1957; *cf.* p. 274, note 14; Khentova, 'Shostakovich: Legends and the Truth', p. 7).

Parallels between *Testimony* and *Rayok* are numerous. Both works reveal Shostakovich's low opinion of musicologists, contempt for political leaders and official policies, admiration for Musorgsky, fondness for quotations and hidden meanings, use of profane language, and general wit and satire. One of Shostakovich's main complaints about musicologists was their misinterpretation of his music. In *Testimony*, he laments that his Seventh Symphony and Eighth Quartet still are misunderstood, even if 'everything is clear' in the Symphony and 'everything in the quartet is as clear as a primer'.[8] Shostakovich again tried to express himself, in no uncertain terms, in *Rayok*, which actually is a primer, a 'learner's manual' according to the title page, complete with fourteen review questions.[9]

In *Testimony*, Shostakovich criticises musicologists for their lack of perspective[10] and laziness,[11] for writing about his relationships with others (such as Glazunov) and getting it 'all wrong',[12] and for misinterpreting his own works and those of others. Several figures are named or alluded to, including Asafiev, Apostolov and Yarustovsky. Shostakovich's low opinion of Asafiev has been noted previously.[13] Of Apostolov he writes:

> Words are some protection against absolute idiocy, any fool will understand when there are words. [. . .] This was confirmed at the final rehearsal of the Fourteenth. Even the fool

[8] *Testimony*, pp. 103/136 and 118/156.

[9] This is yet another allusion, this time to the (in)famous *Concise History of the Communist Party*, probably written, at least in part, by Stalin, and familiar to anyone who lived through the 1930s–50s. The study of the *Concise History* became a (coerced) national pastime; people were tested on their knowledge of the text, and were given credit for being able to recite, near-verbatim, the wooden language of the book.

[10] *Testimony*, p. 153/199.

[11] *Ibid.*, p. 31/42: 'It's amazing how lazy some musicologists can be. They write books that could cause a cockroach infestation of their readers' brains. At least, I've never had the occasion to read a good book about myself, and I do read them rather carefully, I think' [transl. slightly modified in the Hamish Hamilton edition].

[12] *Testimony*, p. 33/45.

[13] *Cf.* pp. 200–1.

> Pavel Ivanovich Apostolov understood what the symphony was about. During the war, Comrade Apostolov commanded a division, and after the war he commanded us, the composers. Everyone knew that you couldn't get through to that blockhead with anything, but Apollinaire was stronger. And Comrade Apostolov, right there at the rehearsal, dropped dead. I feel very guilty, I had no intention of killing him off, even though he was certainly not a harmless man.[14]

Shostakovich goes on to say that 'Comrade Apostolov (what a name!) had in his youth taken vocal courses named after Stravinsky. Poor Stravinsky'.[15] The meaning of his aside, 'what a name!', is revealed in the Preface to *Rayok*, in which Apostolov's name is quietly altered to Opostylov to remind Russian listeners of the word 'postyly' (detestable).

Shostakovich's Preface is a brilliant parody of the pseudo-scientific style of Soviet musicologists. Here 'Opostylov' details how he located a manuscript in a drawer[16] containing excrement and how further research (i.e., carefully removing said excrement) revealed a work 'of a vocal kind'.[17] Oposty-

[14] *Testimony*, p. 141/184. The Fourteenth Symphony, with its warning that death is the end and that one should die with a clear conscience, apparently was too gloomy for Apostolov, a Party organiser, who died of a heart attack on 21 June 1969. As Yuli Turovsky put it, this was a case not of Salieri killing Mozart, but of Mozart killing Salieri (William Zagorsky, 'From Moscow to Montréal in Pursuit of Music: An Afternoon with Yuli Turovsky', *Fanfare*, 14/2, November–December 1990, pp. 526–27). Shostakovich's disdain for Apostolov is confirmed in a letter to Denisov (22 July 1957), written soon after the Second Composers' Union Conference that also provided inspiration for *Rayok*: 'From the village of Stepanichkov[,] Foma Fomich Opiskin [meaning 'Scribbler' or 'Pisser'] has come to settle in Moscow under the pseudonym P. A. [. . . In] his latest newspaper article [. . .] he throws himself into the struggle for music to be melodic and graceful' (Wilson, p. 297).

[15] *Testimony*, p. 141/184.

[16] It should be remembered that *Rayok* was, in fact, one of Shostakovich's works written 'for the drawer'.

[17] A note 'From the Publishers' reads: 'P. I. Opostylov goes on to describe in detail how he removed the excrement from the manuscript. However, as this description is of no immediate scientific interest, the Publishers are omitting it'. Actually, fiction followed reality. Shostakovich's first wife, Nina Vasil'yevna, told Zhitomirsky that the manuscript of the Seventh Symphony, wrapped in a quilt, had accidentally been thrown into the toilet of the over-crowded train during evacuation from Moscow to Kuibyshev

lov's discovery, *Rayok*, is a model of socialist realism and certainly as fine as anything ever written by Professor Mukhtar Ashrafi, the recipient of two Stalin Prizes and the Order of Lenin. In *Testimony*, Shostakovich recalls a similar experience. Sent to Uzbekistan to sift through Ashrafi's manuscripts, he notes: 'We dug around in shit, "analysing" his music [. . .]. It was exhausting work'.[18]

According to a note 'From the Publishers' (actually by Shostakovich), 'Opostylov's' commentary is incomplete:

> Some time ago Comrade Opostylov, struggling to the left and to the right in accordance with the inspiring Party directives lost his balance and fell into the drawer with excrement. His comrades in arms who were with him at the time, the member of the Collegium of the Ministry of Ideological Purity B. S. Srurikov, and also the employees of the Department of Musical Security of the MIP, B. M. Yasrustovsky and P. I. Srulin, immediately called from a telephone booth (which happened to be in the same part of town) the district Sewage Disposal Unit, who arrived without delay at the venue of the described accident. Armed with the latest technology, the best of the capital's sewage-disposal experts extracted from the drawer of excrement a mere seven pieces of faeces none of which, however, could be identified as P. I. Opostylov. In a talk with one of our colleagues, a doctor – sewage-disposal expert Ubiitsev – said that such cases were known to happen and if a person such as Opostylov were to be put into a drawer of excrement, then he, so to speak, would dissolve in the excrement, making it impossible to distinguish between the excrement and P. I. Opostylov.[19]

Here musicologist Yarustovsky, described as a hypocrite and lackey in *Testimony*,[20] makes his debut in *Rayok*. Shostakovich has subtly altered his name, as well as those of his comrades-in-arms, to include 'sru', the root of the verb 'to

---

in 1941. 'You can easily imagine what we saw when, out of necessity, we managed to get there. It was horrifying to touch the blanket which was in the middle of a puddle. I will spare you the details . . .' (Zhitomirsky, 'Shostakovich', p. 461).

[18] *Testimony*, p. 134/175. For more on Ashrafi, *cf*. p. 268, note 59, below.

[19] Translation from the Boosey & Hawkes score.

[20] *Testimony*, p. 24/34.

shit': Yarustovsky, Rurikov and Rumin thus become Yasrustovsky, Srurikov and Srulin.[21]

The image of authorities full of shit or, in the case of Opostylov, immersed in it, is paralleled in *Testimony* in a story about Khrennikov soiling his pants after being given 'the eye' by Stalin.[22] This contempt for Khrennikov is underscored at the end of Troikin's speech in *Rayok*. The libretto reads 'Hey! Glinka, Dzerzhinka, Tishinka, my pets, / What a shitty lot of poems, quartets and fughettes . . .'. Given Shostakovich's preferred use of formal names out of respect for his family, friends, and colleagues, the appearance here of diminutives for Ivan Dzerzhinsky [Dzerzhinka], composer of the 'model' Soviet opera *Quiet Flows the Don*, and Tikhon [Tishinka] Khrennikov indicates his profound disrespect for these individuals.[23]

In *Testimony*, Shostakovich admits that it's hard 'to draw the image of leaders and teachers with music'. He says the

[21] Wilson relates Srulin both to Rumin (p. 497) and to Party official V. N. Surin who, with Yarustovsky, was sent to Leningrad in 1937 to investigate the success of Shostakovich's Fifth Symphony (p. 134; also *cf*. Ian MacDonald, p. 676, note 83, regarding their 'telephone call'). Sewage-disposal expert Ubiitsev's name, on the other hand, is derived from 'ubit', meaning 'to murder'. Shostakovich loved such plays on words and names. His nickname for Maximilian Steinberg was Oatsovich, a play on the latter's patronymic (Wilson, p. 36), and he referred to Aleksandr Gauk as 'Papa Gauk', because it sounded like 'popugaï' (parrot) (*Testimony*, p. 28/39). Glivenko also remembered Shostakovich wanting to combine a waltz with another piece so as to call it 'Dance of Shit', a play on the usual title 'Dance of Death' resulting from the change of one letter ('Tanets Smerti' becoming 'Tanets Smerdi'; Wilson, p. 57). According to Lydia Zhukova, the composer himself acquired a nickname at the Leningrad Conservatory: 'Shtozhtakovich', meaning roughly 'What's-the-matter-ovich' (Wilson, p. 63).

[22] *Cf*. p. 69.

[23] Khrennikov *earned* Shostakovich's disrespect. Vishnevskaya states:

> The [1948] campaign had been planned by Khrennikov. [. . .] He had sold his soul to the devil, had paid dearly for it with his own creative sterility, and had exhausted himself in impotent rage and professional jealousy. Figuring that after the government's reprisals against writers in 1946 the time had come to strike at the composers whom he could not best with his own paltry works, Khrennikov gathered together kindred spirits from the Central Committee and

scherzo of his Tenth Symphony is a musical portrait of Stalin, though no one has guessed this, and that the Twelfth, which originally was to include a portrait of Lenin, 'put up resistance [. . .] and ended with a completely different scheme'.[24] The composer's problem with portraits became easier with words. He acknowledges:

> In recent years I've become convinced that the word is more effective than music. Unfortunately, it's so. When I combine music with words, it becomes harder to misinterpret my intent.[25]

Shostakovich's combination of words and music in *Rayok* yields his most vivid portraits of Iosif Stalin, Andrey Zhdanov and Dmitry Shepilov. In this parody of a Central Committee meeting, these political leaders appear under the pseudonyms I. V. Yedinitsyn, A. A. Dvoikin and D. T. Troikin, respectively, but can be readily identified by their initials, quotations from their speeches and other mannerisms.[26] The pseudonyms themselves refer to No. 1 ('odin'), No. 2 ('dva') and No. 3 ('tri'), their hierarchy on the podium (and elsewhere), and to school grades – F ('yedinitsa'), D ('dvoika') and C ('troika'), respectively (the three poorest grades). Shostakovich's grading of these speakers

---

> placed at their head that 'great authority on music and literature', Politburo member Andrei Zhdanov.
>
> Vishnevskaya, *Galina*, p. 219.

Dzerzhinsky, on the other hand, was mainly incompetent. 'While writing his *Quiet Flows the Don* [. . . this] composer of limited talents had received generous assistance from Shostakovich, who had orchestrated large chunks of the opera on his behalf' (Wilson, p. 109).

[24] *Testimony*, p. 107/141.

[25] *Testimony*, pp. 140/183–84.

[26] Parodying the authorities (in secret) was not uncommon for Shostakovich. Sabinina recalled that on a wintry evening in 1949/50 (i.e., while *Rayok* was in progress) 'a meeting of the Academic Council had just finished and the teachers and professors were dispersing. Dmitri Dmitriyevich started to imitate their smug, obsequious and fawning behaviour, their pompous manners of speech. Miming certain of the professors, he played out whole scenes, displaying a brilliant gift for comedy in his simultaneous impersonations of several characters' (Wilson, p. 225).

relates to the inscription on the title page, 'for the guidance of students'.[27]

The parody in *Rayok* is two-fold, involving both the content of the speeches and the musical language. The work 'begins with a C major phrase of mindless placidity in bare octaves, which recurs many times in the course of the work as a kind of Leitmotif of banality'.[28] The thinly disguised Stalin (Yedinitsyn) then mounts the platform, with a circular, question-begging utterance about realistic and formalistic music. 'Why do people's composers write realistic music?', Yedinitsyn asks. 'Because being people's composers they cannot help but write realistic music.' He then concludes that 'anti-people composers, being formalists, cannot help but write formalistic music'. This example of the Great Leader's profundity is set to the melody of 'Suliko', Stalin's favourite song. Coupled with improper accentuation (Stalin stresses the wrong syllable of 'kompozitory'), the image created is one of utter stupidity.[29]

[27] The number of semantic levels in *Rayok* is often remarkable. According to Yakubov, the names of the principal characters also may come from literature:

> In the 1930s, [...] Shostakovich was friendly with Mikhail Bulgakov, and was evidently acquainted with early drafts of the novel *The Master and Margarita*. One of the earliest titles of that novel – 'The Adviser with the Cloven Foot' – endows Yedinitsyn's title with an extremely lofty status – he is not just the leader of all peoples, but Satan himself! It is also well known that Shostakovich greatly admired Mayakovsky – he wrote the music for Meyerhold's production of his play *The Bedbug*. In Mayakovsky's play *The Bathhouse*, we [also] meet characters called Comrade Dvoikin and Comrade Troikin. Shostakovich found these characters extremely funny and loved to mention them in his conversations during those years.
>
> Yakubov, paper, p. 4.

[28] Calum MacDonald, p. 25.

[29] *Cf.* Vishnevskaya, *Galina*, pp. 95–96, recalling how the conductor Samuil Samosud had been summoned to Stalin's box during an intermission. The 'little father of the people' stated:

> 'Comrade Samosud, your production tonight is ... somehow ... lacking flats.' Samosud went numb and was totally confused. Could it be a joke? But the members of the Politburo and all the others were nodding seriously and adding, 'Yes, do pay attention to the flats', although among them were the likes of Molotov who surely under-

Zhdanov (Dvoikin) fares no better. Having taken a few voice lessons and being able to pluck-out a tune on the piano with one finger, he considered himself well qualified to teach Shostakovich about composition.[30] Actually, as Vishnevskaya put it, he was a 'nincompoop judging a genius'.[31] Zhdanov's lecture begins with superfluous vocalisation (a warm-up recalled from his voice lessons), then incorporates quotations from actual speeches. As was his wont, he demands that music be beautiful and elegant, and Shostakovich accommodates with a suitably melodious and idiotic waltz as a background. Zhdanov then compares dissonance to 'a piercing road drill or a musical gas chamber', and the composer responds with mocking minor-seconds. Zhdanov's analogy originates from an actual speech given in 1948:

> Without mincing words, I have to say that a whole series of works by contemporary composers are infiltrated and overloaded to such a degree by naturalistic sounds that one is reminded – forgive the inelegant expression – of a piercing road drill, or a musical gas-chamber.[32]

Zhdanov ends his lecture by insisting that Georgian operas must have a 'legitimate lezghinka'. Here the music is appropriately 'popular, plain and folksy', but the regular misaccentuation of the text raises questions about Zhdanov's 'truly amazingly penetrating mind'.[33]

Word painting also is important in Shepilov's (Troikin's) portrait. His call for composers to imitate the 'classics' includes quotations from Glinka's *Kamarinskaya* and the

---

> stood that they were making idiots of themselves. Samosud collected himself and replied soberly, 'Good, Comrade Stalin. Thank you for your comment. We will not fail to pay attention to that.'

Samosud's response echoes the choir's sycophantic 'We thank you, we thank you, we thank you for your historic words' following Yedinitsyn's (Stalin's) speech in *Rayok*, which was itself a parody of real-life cheers (*cf*. Alexander Werth, *Musical Uproar in Moscow*, Turnstile Press, London, 1949).

[30] Rostropovich, quoted by Davies, p. 10.

[31] Vishnevskaya, *Galina*, p. 212.

[32] Wilson, p. 209.

[33] Translation of the text accompanying Erato ECD 75571.

popular song 'Kalinka'. In addition, his blatant mispronunciation of 'Rimsky-Korsakov' in the phrase 'Glinka, Tchaikovsky, Rimsky-KorSAkov', originating from a speech in 1957,[34] suggests a stupidity comparable to Stalin's and Zhdanov's.

Many phrases and ideas in *Rayok* are echoed in *Testimony*. There Shostakovich recalls the obviously tone-deaf Zoshchenko confusing Tchaikovsky's *Romeo and Juliet* with Shostakovich's own Fifth Symphony: 'I just knew that you weren't capable of writing anti-people music', Zoshchenko said,[35] reminding one of Stalin's (Yedinitsyn's) speech. Shostakovich also mentions ' "Suliko", the leader and teacher's favorite song' and confirms Stalin's musical stupidity: 'As for music, he [Stalin] naturally didn't understand a damn thing [. . .]'.[36] On other pages, Shostakovich refers, sarcastically, to Zhdanov (Dvoikin) as 'a great specialist in the musical arts' and notes that he 'stood fast for beautiful and graceful music', mentions Shepilov's (Troikin's) troika ('Glinka, Tchaikovsky, Rimsky-Korsakov'), describes Muradeli's music in typical socialist realist terms ('melodious and harmonious'), admits that 'from now unto forever, music had to be refined, harmonious, and melodious', and explains the call for legitimate lezghinkas.[37] About Muradeli's opera *The Great Friendship*, Shostakovich notes:

> The main problem was the *lezghinka*. The opera was based on life in the Caucasus, so Muradeli crammed it full of native songs and dances. Stalin expected to hear his native songs, but instead he heard Muradeli's own *lezghinka*, which he had composed in a fit of forgetfulness. And it was that *lezghinka*

[34] Calum MacDonald, p. 31; Wilson, p. 298.

[35] *Testimony*, p. 207/266. In Wilson, p. 138, Mikhail Chulaki confirms hearing about this from Shostakovich, but identifies Tchaikovsky's work as *Francesca da Rimini*.

[36] *Testimony*, pp. 166/216 and 145/190, respectively.

[37] *Ibid.*, pp. 121/159, 50/67, 109/144, 110–11/146–47 and 108/143, respectively. Vishnevskaya also recalls that in celebrating the Central Committee's great historical decree 'On Abrogating the Great Historical [Zhdanov] Decree' (26 May 1958), 'Shostakovich began to croon to the tune of a lezghinka: "There must be refined music, There must be beautiful music"' (Vishnevskaya, *Galina*, p. 244).

> that angered Stalin the most [and led to the Zhdanov Decree of 1948].[38]

Even the newly found ending to *Rayok* has a parallel in *Testimony*. Shostakovich's libretto calls for 'vigilance, vigilance [. . . towards] bourgeois ideology', while his memoirs acknowledge that in the 'new socialist national art [. . .] there always had to be a traitor; that was necessary, it called for increased vigilance'.[39]

Given the vicious but true portraits of Stalin, Zhdanov, Shepilov and others in *Rayok*, it is clear that Shostakovich was not the loyal Communist portrayed in the Soviet literature but an 'internal' dissident. His words in *Testimony* take on new meaning:

> I have never tried to flatter the authorities with my music. And I never had an 'affair' with them. I was never a favourite, though I know that some accuse me of it. They say I stood too close to power. An optical illusion. What was not, was not.[40]

Rayok also reveals the same 'bravery in the artist' that allowed *Testimony* to be written. In the latter, Shostakovich notes that 'Stalin liked to put a man face to face with death and then make him dance to his own tune'.[41] In *Rayok*, the composer's response is similar to Figaro's: 'Se vuol ballare'. That is, if Stalin, Zhdanov and Shepilov want to dance (or sing), Shostakovich will call the tunes. Such behaviour, he acknowledges, is risky:

> I'm particularly touched by Hamlet's conversation with Rosenkrantz and Guildenstern, when Hamlet says that he's not a pipe and he won't let people play him. A marvellous passage. It's easy for him, he's a prince, after all. If he weren't, they'd play him so hard he wouldn't know what hit him.[42]

Equally evident in *Rayok* is the composer's deep admiration for Musorgsky, who is mentioned on numerous pages in

[38] *Testimony*, p. 108/143.

[39] *Ibid*., p. 167/216. *Cf*. p. 272, note 7.

[40] *Ibid*., p. 71/94.

[41] *Ibid*., p. 111/147.

[42] *Ibid*., p. 63/84.

Testimony. On page 177/229, Shostakovich notes that Musorgsky 'wrote a marvellous musical lampoon, *The Classic*, directed against critics; the subtitle reads "A propos the Musical Scribblings of Famintsyn"'. This reference is significant since Shostakovich's *Rayok* is modelled on both 'The Classic' and Musorgsky's own 'Rayok'. Shostakovich mentions many other connections with his predecessor. He orchestrated Musorgsky's *Boris Godunov*, *Khovanshchina* and *Songs and Dances of Death*, and notes that Musorgsky's *Sunless* song cycle 'has much in common with the opera I'm determined to write, *The Black Monk*'. He also states:

> Work on *Boris* contributed greatly to my Seventh and Eighth Symphonies, and then was recalled in the Eleventh. (There was a time I considered the Eleventh my most 'Mussorgskian' composition). Something from *Khovanshchina* was transferred to the Thirteenth Symphony and to *The Execution of Stepan Razin*, and I even wrote about the connection between *Songs and Dances of Death* and my Fourteenth Symphony.
>
> Naturally, this is not an exhaustive list of possible parallels. With time, willing lovers of parallels can expand it greatly. Of course, in order to do that they would have to seriously dig around in my works – both those that have been given voice and those that are still hidden from the eyes of 'musicological officials'. But for a true musicologist, with a musical education and musical goals, this could be fruitful, albeit hard, work. That's all right, let them sweat a little.[43]

The second paragraph, obviously, is another allusion to *Rayok*, which remained hidden from musicological scrutiny until 1989 and displays additional parallels with Musorgsky's like-named work. Both *Rayoks* have texts written by their composers, and both mix sarcasm and wit with quotations from their protagonists. Just as Musorgsky used excerpts from 'Zaremba's lectures, Rostislav's feuilletons and Serov's articles'[44] against them, Shostakovich used Stalin's, Zhdanov's and Shepilov's words to mock his subjects.

Immediately after its publication, critics questioned the authenticity of *Testimony* because its style was considered

[43] *Ibid*., p. 186/240.

[44] Yakubov, paper, p. 3.

atypical of the composer. Craft wrote, 'Volkov's Shostakovich has an appealing wit [. . .] and this was not even suspected from his music, in which the playful passages are often the most painful';[45] Maxim added, 'the language [i.e., profanity and contemptuous remarks] in the book attributed to his father [. . .] led him to doubt the book's authenticity';[46] and Fay concluded that it was 'utterly inconceivable' that the 'borrowed reminiscences' (i.e., quotations) came from Shostakovich and questioned the existence of hidden meanings in works such as the Seventh Symphony.[47]

Rayok convincingly refutes these statements. Contrary to Craft, wit and humour abound in this anti-Stalinist satire; furthermore, Maxim's and Fay's doubts are silenced by the work's earthy, tell-all language and wealth of quotations and hidden meanings.[48] 'Shit' appears throughout *Rayok*: on the manuscript found by Opostylov, as Opostylov himself, and in the names Yasrustovsky, Srurikov and Srulin. The same is true of *Testimony*. Shostakovich describes Ashrafi's music as 'shit' and notes:

> Digging around in shit is also vile.

45 Craft, 'Testaments', p. 78.

46 'Shostakovich's Son Says Moves Against Artists Led to Defection', *The New York Times*, 14 May 1981, p. A18. Contrast this with Galina's and Maxim's more recent statements (pp. 83–84 and 111–14).

47 Fay, p. 490.

48 Shostakovich's profanity in this work also is in keeping with the genre. According to Yakubov:

> [the traditional rayok] was the most popular form of entertainment at fairs in Russia in the eighteenth and nineteenth centuries. The word 'rayok' means a 'theatre of pictures', and used to be a large box with round holes to peep through. Inside the box there was a revolving drum to which were attached pictures, making up a ribbon. The role of the 'cinema-operator' in this ancient version of the cartoon was carried out by the rayoshnik, someone who turned the drum with the paper ribbon, and commented loudly on what was being shown, amusing the public and usually never being too careful about his language.

Paper, p. 2.

Significantly, Shostakovich may have seen and heard some of the last rayoshniks in Petrograd in the 1920s. He wrote to a friend in 1925: 'I've been looking at the history of the rayoshnik recently and therefore sometimes express myself as if I was one myself' (Yakubov, paper, p. 4).

> So remember, yesterday you were the best, the most talented, and today you're no one. Zero. Shit.
>
> The poet made sweets from shit, as we say – forgive my vulgarity.[49]

The composer also admits: 'When I was younger, I often used swear words in conversations with friends. With the years I came to use them less and less'.[50] This is confirmed in some of Shostakovich's letters[51] and by episodes such as those recalled by Flora Litvinova and Anaida Sumbatyan. According to Litvinova, Shostakovich left a note for his first wife, Nina Vasil'yevna, listing chores for her to do in his absence. 'Tell the librettist to f— off', he wrote, hoping to rid himself of a famous playwright who wanted to collaborate on an operetta.[52] On another occasion, Anaida Sumbatyan, a childhood teacher of one of the authors, was sitting next to Shostakovich at a concert, where a piece by Kabalevsky was performed. As the music commenced, Shostakovich whispered into her ear: 'And this is the great Russian river Volga'. As the music proceeded to some major/minor harmonies typical of Kabalevsky, Shostakovich whispered again: 'And this is the shit floating in the great Russian river Volga'.[53]

[49] *Testimony*, pp. 33/46, 163/212 and 168/217, respectively.

[50] *Testimony*, p. 57/76. Shostakovich also seems to have watched his language around his children.

[51] *Cf*. p. 221, note 392, and Volkov, 'Universal', p. 16. Volkov recalls, 'I read Dmitry Dmitriyevich's correspondence with Shebalin. [. . .] In one of the letters, with the foulest language, Shostakovich writes about Zhelobinsky, saying that he is a scoundrel, that he shot his wife in the . . . [*sic*]'. Unfortunately, many such letters were later destroyed, Shostakovich explaining that 'he had used too much crude language' (Drubachevskaya, pp. 336–37).

[52] Wilson, p. 162 (abbreviation in original); Litvinova, p. 161. Litvinova also recalls Shostakovich calling Picasso a 'bastard' because the latter 'hails Soviet power and our communist system at a time when his followers here are persecuted, hounded, and not allowed to work' (Wilson, p. 271; Litvinova, pp. 174–75).

[53] Shostakovich's low opinion of Kabalevsky's music was probably coloured by the latter's successful attempt to have his name replaced with Gavriil Popov's on Zhdanov's blacklist in 1948 (*cf. Testimony*, p. 223, note 25/pp. 145–46 note).

The quotations and allusions in *Rayok* also call to mind the numerous borrowings in *Testimony* from the composer himself, Ilf and Petrov,[54] Chekhov, Gogol and others, as well as his discussion of hidden meanings in works such as the Eighth Quartet and Fifth, Seventh, Tenth and Eleventh Symphonies. Several examples of these traits have been mentioned previously: the quotation of well-known tunes ('Suliko', 'Kamarinskaya' and 'Kalinka') and phrases from actual speeches, as well as the use of thinly veiled pseudonyms for musicologists, rival composers and government officials. But these are only the tip of the iceberg. For example, the call to fight bourgeois ideology and send dissidents to the labour camps is 'sung to the unnaturally slow tune of Serpoletta's song from [Robert] Planquette's operetta *Les cloches de Corneville*, which sounds in this combination particularly mocking'.[55] Also, Troikin's speech uses material from 'various party functionaries, from Zhdanov to Khrushchev',[56] and his 'Glinka, Tchaikovsky, Rimsky-KorSAkov' song 'begins with an exact quotation from a song composed by Khrennikov for the propaganda film "Faithful Friends"'.[57] Troikin's closing speech also has been interpreted in various ways. According to Yakubov:

> Troikin advises composers to write suites, poems, sonatas and even symphonies to the [. . .] hackneyed tune of Kalinka (one of Stalin's favourite melodies), and then (this is figure 33, bars 17–22 [in the Boosey and Hawkes score]), he says, getting carried away, 'Ech, Glinka, Dzerzhinka, Tishinka my pets'. Glinka is a composer, Dzerzhinka and Tishinka are the nicknames of Moscow streets and squares: Dzerzhinka is what is now called the Lyubyanka [formerly Dzerzhinsky Square], where the citadel of State Security [the KGB] is situated, and Tishinka might be understood as the name of another square, although it is more natural to hear here the everyday name for the 'Matrosskaya tishina' – a famous prison with close links to the Lyubyanka. Why do these toponyms appear so suddenly and inopportunely after the name of a famous composer? The

[54] *Cf.* p. 257, note 5.

[55] Yakubov, paper, p. 4.

[56] *Ibid.*, p. 4.

[57] Calum MacDonald, p. 29.

> row of puns, thought up by Shostakovich, has two semantic layers linked to names. After Glinka, another's name ought to follow (remember, Glinka, Tchaikovsky, Rimsky-KorsAkov in figure 29) but we have 'not-Glinka'. He turns out to be the Leningrad composer Ivan Dzerzhinsky – an old and active enemy of Shostakovich. After him comes Tikhon Khrennikov, hiding in the words '. . . Tishinka my pets, What a shitty [rasKHRENovaya] . . . ' (Tishinka is similar to Tisha and Tishenka, the diminutive, affectionate nicknames for 'Tikhon'). We can thus decipher the phrase: Dzerzhinka is Tisha's old fogey 'khren'.[58] The following anecdote shows that it is Khrennikov himself appearing in the role of not-Glinka: Stalin is asked which street could be named after Khrennikov, and he answers that there already is a Neglinka ('not-Glinka') street (Neglinka is the old name for Neglinnaya street in Moscow).[59]

This intricate web of wit and satire, quotation and allusion, is also the fabric of *Testimony*.

[58] 'Khren', in Russian, means literally 'horseradish' but is also a euphemism for penis.

[59] Yakubov, paper, p. 5.

IV. Closing Argument: A Rush to Judgement

The phrase 'rush to judgement', used previously in several celebrated cases,[1] applies equally well to the assessment of *Testimony* by some Western scholars. As has been demonstrated above, the supposedly 'conclusive' findings of Laurel Fay are based not on objective evidence but on subjective and selective editing of the facts. In many ways, Fay is guilty of the same inept scholarship of which she accuses Solomon Volkov and of the very same Western naïveté she attributes to supporters of *Testimony*. Rather than 'digging' for and 'sweating' to find answers – as Shostakovich doubted most musicologists would do[2] – Fay has been content to regurgitate material handed to her on a Soviet platter, while looking to like-minded senior scholars for confirmation.[3] In 'Shostakovich versus Volkov: Whose *Testimony*?', Fay repeatedly asks, 'Must it be [a forgery]?' 'It must be!' replies Richard Taruskin; 'It must be!' replies Malcolm Brown.[4]

[1] *Cf.* Mark Lane, *Rush to Judgment* (a critique of the Warren Commission's inquiry into the murders of President John F. Kennedy, Officer J. D. Tippit and Lee Harvey Oswald), Holt, Rinehart and Winston, New York, 1966; ABC News, *Rush to Judgment*? (*Anita Hill* vs. *Clarence Thomas: The Untold Story*; originally telecast on the programme 'Turning Point'), Films for the Humanities, 1994; and numerous statements by the defence team in the Simpson *vs.* State of California 'trial of the century' in 1995.

[2] *Testimony*, p. 186/240.

[3] Ironically, what Fay 'wish[es] for right now is an approach to Soviet music scholarship no more revisionist than a healthy dose of the old musicology: painstaking basic research and fact finding guided by open minds and common sense, rather than by polemical agendas, shopworn clichés, and double standards' (Fay, paper). One wonders why, in her 'conclusive' article, she does not practise what she preaches.

[4] *Cf.* Beethoven's Sixteenth Quartet, Op. 135 ('Muss es sein? Es muss sein! Es muss sein!), and p. 170, note 199. This quartet was a work Shostakovich knew well; he quoted it in the Fifteenth Symphony.

Indeed, the uncritical, mutual praise sung by these scholars recalls Krylov's 'Cock and Cuckoo', a fable well known to all Russians:

> 'Dear Cock, how proud your noble chant, your voice – how strong!'
> – 'Dear Cuckoo, how you can sustain
> Those long-drawn tones,
> So sweet and smooth, it's music fit to move the stones;
> No bird lives in the forest who can match your song!
> Your beauteous melodies should never ever end . . .'
> – 'Your silence makes me die
> Until you start once more;
> Whence did you get this voice, those tunes that swell and soar?
> The nightingale must envy you, my dearest friend!'
> – 'I thank you much, and as for you, I do declare,
> The birds in Eden, they could not compete;
> In all this life, your singing is the greatest treat!
> Ask whom you will, they must agree if they are fair.'
> Just then a sparrow who had heard the whole ado
> Told both of them: 'Your so-called songs are one bad joke;
> Go on and praise each other till you're hoarse and croak,
> But no one who knows music will be fooled by you.'
> Why did the Cuckoo praise the Cock,
> Do tell!
> The Cock had praised the Cuckoo's song so well.[5]

Fay's arguments are severely deficient both in general perspective and in specific historical knowledge.[6] She suggests that the inscription and photograph reproduced as *Testimony*'s frontispiece indicate a more distant relationship

[5] Translation by Dr Frederic Kirchberger (used by permission). Written in 1834, 'The Cock and the Cuckoo' originally was a satire of reactionary journalists Faddey V. Bulgarin and Nikolay I. Grech, who shamelessly sang each other's praises in their articles and were despised by progressive intellectuals (Nikolay Stepanov, *Ivan Krylov*, Twayne Publishers, Inc., New York, 1973, p. 92). Shostakovich, too, appreciated Krylov's fables and set a pair of them, 'The Dragon and the Ant' and 'The Ass and the Nightingale', in his Op. 4 (1922). In *Testimony*, p. 192/247, he also quotes from Krylov's 'The Wolf and the Lamb', saying, 'in condemnation and mockingly', 'For the strong, it's always the weak who are wrong'.

[6] For an examination of the extent of Laurel Fay's historical ignorance, *cf.* Ian MacDonald, pp. 686–721.

between Shostakovich and Volkov than that described in the preface. What she does not mention – or does not know – is that Shostakovich consistently used a very formal language in speech, inscriptions and dedications, and rarely displayed the closeness of his relationships in posed photographs. She also suggests that Volkov 'plagiarized' eight passages from earlier published articles by Shostakovich, finding it 'utterly inconceivable' that the latter could restate his own opinions in his own words, verbatim or near-verbatim. What she does not mention – or does not know about – is Shostakovich's phenomenal, 'superior', memory; his ability to recite pages of literature (i.e., other people's words) verbatim; his frequent repetition of phrases and stories during conversations; and his fondness for quotation and, especially, self-quotation.[7] Fay's incessant pecking at Volkov and at every perceived factual discrepancy misses the larger picture. Shostakovich himself warned about such musicological myopia: 'No, it's much easier to believe what you see. And you always see what you want to see. The mentality of the chicken – when a chicken pecks, it sees only the one grain and nothing else. And so it pecks, grain by grain, until the farmer breaks its neck'.[8]

Elsewhere, Fay asks that Shostakovich's words be read precisely – that if his inscription says 'a reminder of our conversations about Glazunov, Zoshchenko and Meyerhold', this may be considered 'a *precise* reference to the limited content of their conversations'. On the other hand, she blatantly distorts Shostakovich's words on his Seventh Symphony, finding his statement that he was writing the work from the first days of the war contradicted a page later by his acknowledgement that the work had been planned before the Nazi invasion. Such distortions abound in Fay's article. She states that Volkov 'strongly implies that the performance of *Rothschild's Violin* in 1968 was its premiere', then proceeds to mention concert and radio performances to prove him wrong, even though Volkov never implied that

[7] Nor has she substantiated her charge that such verbatim or near-verbatim self-quotation is impossible; indeed, six leading authorities on memory specifically contradict her on this question (*cf.* pp. 206–9).

[8] *Testimony*, p. 153/199.

this was the work's first concert (i.e., unstaged) performance. In fact, he emphasises, four times, that the significance of the 1968 performance was that it was staged. Fay also suggests that Volkov first may have been working on a biography of Shostakovich, rather than memoirs, and cites an 'ironic' note to this effect accompanying one of Volkov's articles. The implication is that Volkov, in a Freudian slip, had there acknowledged the true nature of *Testimony*. In fact, her source is nothing more than a biographical blurb added by an anonymous copy editor after the end of Volkov's article – far from convincing support for a scholarly article, but the only 'hard' evidence offered. At the same time, she ignores ample documentation that Shostakovich had intended to write his memoirs at least for the last twenty years of his life.

In many instances, Fay argues on both sides of an issue. She casts stones at others for 'inept and irresponsible scholarship', 'errors of omission', 'misrepresenting information', and failing to put things into 'proper historical context',[9] but remains oblivious to the same deficiencies in her own research. She asks, 'Is the Seventh Symphony about Stalin or the Nazis?' (even though *Testimony* makes clear that both provided inspiration), then complains about the 'Cold-War binary logic: either/or, yes or no' in much of the 'revisionist' writings on Shostakovich.[10] She challenges some passages of *Testimony* because they are inconsistent with her image of the 'old' Shostakovich, then challenges others because they are too consistent (i.e., 'plagiarized').[11] She questions the veracity of *Testimony*, echoing Soviet complaints that *Testimony* is one-sided, then considers anything remotely contradictory as further evidence of *Testimony*'s spuriousness.[12] Such conflicting behaviour suggests that Laurel Fay is unaware of how cultural history was written in the USSR: 'everyone embraces everyone else, everybody blesses everyone else. They write sweet notes on laurel

[9] *Cf.* p. 237, note 444.

[10] *Cf.* pp. 151 and 236.

[11] *Cf.* pp. 188–209.

[12] *Cf.* pp. 118–19, 128–29, 144–46, 150–59 and 217–28.

wreaths'. As Shostakovich put it, 'they can take their laurel wreaths with sweet messages and shove them'.[13]

Richard Taruskin concluded in 1989 that 'as any proper scholar could plainly see, the book was a fraud. Yet even those who could did not want to see'.[14] Since then, neither he, nor Fay, nor Brown have retracted any of their condemnation of *Testimony*. Fay, on 3 November 1995, at the national meeting of the American Musicological Society, stated: '***For the record***, I have not found any evidence to change my opinions about the authenticity of those memoirs. The questions I raised then have never been answered, the proof I demanded has never been [given]'. In apparent contradiction, she then dismissed *Testimony* as 'the deathbed memoirs of a sick and embittered old man [. . . which] actually poses only a very slight impediment [to my own ongoing research on Shostakovich], really nothing more than a nuisance'.[15] Taruskin and Brown, sharing the podium, gave at least tacit approval to Fay's remarks. Brown, at a Shostakovich conference at California State University, Long Beach (17 February 1996), also attacked *Testimony* explicitly and at length.[16] But, significantly, he could do nothing more than trot out the same old canards and defamatory allegations levelled at Volkov and *Testimony* by their detractors – from 'Les Six Soviétiques' to Laurel Fay, all of which have been dealt with and discredited above.[17]

[13] *Testimony*, pp. 33–34/46–47; Shostakovich's recommendation has been toned down in the Hamish Hamilton edition.

[14] *Cf.* p. 38.

[15] Fay, paper.

[16] Brown, paper.

[17] *Cf.* pp. 60–128, 134–43, 150–71 and 187–218. Indeed, Brown's only new 'evidence' that Volkov 'was guilty of nothing less than expropriation once removed, as well as blatant exploitation of the composer's name for the purpose of lining his own pockets' and that *Testimony* was 'a fraudulent mix of previously published material, second-hand scuttlebutt, and [. . .] whatever candid information Volkov actually did obtain in face-to-face conversations with the composer' was his supposed memory of a conversation with Volkov in August 1977 at a meeting of the International Musicological Society, Berkeley, California: 'Volkov told me he was writing a biography of Shostakovich, in connection with which he had been fortunate to interview the composer. [. . .] He never mentioned

As it happens, Taruskin has recently moved to cover himself with an admission that *Testimony* might, after all, be genuine:

> It is [. . .] understandable, should it ever turn out that Shostakovich was in fact the author of *Testimony*, that he, who though mercilessly threatened never suffered a dissident's trials but ended his days as a multiple Hero of Socialist Labour, should have wished, late in life, to portray himself in another light.[18]

It is extraordinary that Taruskin should make this statement without withdrawing the insults he has persistently directed against *Testimony* and Volkov. (Does he or does he not still believe *Testimony* to be bogus? If he does, why the sudden reservation? If he does not, why no admission of the obvious: that he has been wrong about it for the past seventeen years?) What is worth observing is that Taruskin is prepared to make this admission only on the basis that, regardless of whether every word in it is authentic, *Testimony* is nonetheless false inasmuch as Shostakovich, during his final years, supposedly wished to misrepresent his life. In other words, Taruskin refuses to countenance the revisionist view of the composer not because *Testimony* is bogus but simply because he, Taruskin, refuses to accept that Shostakovich was a clear-sighted, decent human being and a secret opponent of Stalin's regime.

In the best Ministry of Truth tradition, Fay, Taruskin and Brown have distorted facts and withheld information that might corroborate *Testimony*. Fay's sins of omission have been noted above. Taruskin has added his own insinuations in the style of the tabloid press: 'Solomon Volkov, – speaking

---

anything at all about memoirs [. . .,] never made reference to memoirs passed along from Shostakovich through him'. Brown does not mention that Taruskin in 1976 and again in 1989 confirmed that Volkov had told *him* about Shostakovich's *memoirs* (*cf*. Appendix, Exhibit 1, pp. 38 and 138). Brown also does not mention that Galina Drubachevskaya, Yury Korev, Rostislav Dubinsky and other contemporaries of Volkov and Shostakovich recall Volkov speaking of memoirs repeatedly before his emigration in 1976, even while the composer was still alive (*cf*. pp. 134–37), and that Drubachevskaya read chapters of the manuscript as they were returned signed by Shostakovich.

[18] Fanning, *Shostakovich Studies*, p. 47.

through his little puppet Mitya [Shostakovich]'.[19] Brown, too, is guilty of tabloid musicology and sloppy, selective scholarship: his defamatory charge that Volkov is a 'liar'[20] remains unproven; his questions about Prokofiev's orchestration habits demonstrate that this Prokofiev expert is not acquainted with the relevant literature;[21] and his failure to acknowledge Maxim's recent pro-*Testimony* statements, both in his 1993 review of Ian MacDonald's *The New Shostakovich* and in his 1996 paper,[22] indicates a willingness to distort evidence to make his case.[23]

Functioning as 'spin doctors' rather than scholars in search of the truth, Fay, Taruskin and Brown have attacked the messenger (Volkov) to kill the message. Taruskin is willing to accept as 'probably authentic' the portions of *Testimony* 'about Glazunov, Zoshchenko, and Meyerhold' that do not ruffle feathers, that 'do not set everyone agog'.[24] But he continues to question the harsh assessment of government officials and of Shostakovich's colleagues in *Testimony*, preferring to view the composer as 'perhaps Soviet Russia's most loyal musical son'.[25] After the premiere of *Rayok* in January 1989 and the publication of Elizabeth Wilson's *Shostakovich: A Life Remembered* in 1994, Taruskin's continuing denial of Shostakovich's deep-rooted dissent, acid criticism and anti-Stalinist sentiments is especially difficult to fathom. Indeed, numerous statements from Shostakovich's friends and family as well as important revelations in

[19] Taruskin, 'Lies', p. 31. Taruskin's rewriting of history is thus complete: instead of Shostakovich – a man with a computer-sharp mind till his last day – there is a senile old man; instead of Volkov – a faithful Eckermann – there is a Magician-manipulator. Orwell would have appreciated. For more on Volkov's puppets, *cf.* p. 302.

[20] *Cf.* p. 243.

[21] *Cf.* pp. 100–5.

[22] Brown, paper.

[23] *Cf.* also the authors' 'Shostakovich and the *Testimony* Affair', *DSCH Journal*, No. 8, Winter 1997, for additional, still more recent examples of Brown's selective scholarship.

[24] Taruskin, 'Dictator', p. 35.

[25] Taruskin, 'Abominable', p. 35; Taruskin, 'Dictator', p. 40.

his manuscripts and letters now corroborate *Testimony* and vindicate Volkov.[26]

In spite of the ill-founded attacks it has suffered, *Testimony* remains one of the most important and influential books in the history of music. Its insights into the life of an artist under Stalin as well as the creative mind of Shostakovich were revelatory in 1979, providing new information on the composer's fears of arrest, personal relationship with Stalin, caustic evaluations of Prokofiev, Stravinsky, Mravinsky and Toscanini, disdain for Western 'humanists', discovery of musical forgeries in the provinces, and inspiration for, and meanings of, several landmark works. More importantly, almost twenty years later, these insights have proven to be not only revelatory but accurate. No alternative view of Shostakovich has been proposed that accounts for the composer's numerous quirks and ostensible contradictions as successfully as that of the real Shostakovich of *Testimony*. Furthermore, the 'experts' have entirely failed to explain

[26] Even Irina Shostakovich endorses a view of the composer which, for all intents and purposes, is identical to that in the memoirs:

> A Russian composer, whose music is known and played throughout the world, Dmitri Shostakovich continues to acquire new and ever-fervent admirers. He epitomises the most noble traditions and values of our society.
>
> The personality of Shostakovich has proved a powerful moral influence on his contemporaries. During the hard and cruel era of Stalinism, the composer had the courage to express in his music the misery of his people by means of an extraordinary dramatic feeling and to denounce the hidden forces that were then eliminating millions of human lives.
>
> His music became a mortal [*recte*: moral] support for all who were pursued. Belief in the final victory of justice, brought about through his works, transformed his music into a powerful weapon which stimulated the spirit of resistance and freedom.
>
> The internal power of his music has always been of great vividness. It has enriched the thousands of new listeners who hear it with eagerness and pleasure. Thus, Dmitri Shostakovich, even after his death, continues to lead towards light and reason. His work, of universal value, is recognised by everyone.

This founding declaration of the 'Shostakovich Academy/Foundation' (now Centre Chostakovitch), which Irina established and sponsors, is one page of a sixteen-page prospectus disseminated in 1991 by Dominique Barre, to whom Mme Shostakovich had 'handed over responsibility for the project'.

how, if *Testimony* is not Shostakovich's authentic memoirs, Volkov could have guessed about so many hidden facts, personal confessions and unknown manuscripts, and guessed so well.

Assessing the importance of *Testimony* in 1995, Ian MacDonald wrote:

> I believe the book to be a brilliant work straddling the genres of the traditional Russian memoir and the modern Russian satire. Far from 'rambling' and 'styleless', as some musical commentators have claimed, *Testimony*, at its best (for example, the final section) is a tour de force. The finest of today's comic authors would be hard pressed to write as well as Shostakovich talks. Those who imagine that it is easy to counterfeit this downbeat style – and that Solomon Volkov could have faked it – display a naivety which would make most professional writers laugh. Though apparently artless, the literary effects employed in *Testimony* are extremely sophisticated. The eminent English novelist Julian Barnes holds a high opinion of *Testimony* for precisely this reason. (I should add that he admires the intellectual content as well as the style of the book.)[27] As such, and because of its historical role (shared with Solzhenitsyn's *The Gulag Archipelago*) in revealing to the wider world the truth about Soviet Russia, I would further suggest that *Testimony* is one of the half-dozen most significant books to have appeared in any language and in any genre since 1950. As this fact becomes more widely recognised, as I believe it will, Solomon Volkov's heroic role as a conveyor of this material to the West, together with his skills as an interviewer and editor, will eventually become as appreciated and respected as they have, so far and for the most part, been unjustly and ineptly vilified.[28]

[27] The leading contemporary Russian writer Andrey Bitov has an equally high regard for the 'prose style' of *Testimony*, in which he detects the influence of the master of understated irony Mikhail Zoshchenko:

> This book is gruesome, beautiful, fascinating, and unbearable [...] authentic from first letter to last [...] I'm enough of a professional, certainly, to make that inference. Volkov's individuality finds expression in his footnotes, at least; the footnotes sometimes express him even more than he might wish. But the book – from beginning to end – is in Shostakovich's words, his alone. Volkov wouldn't have said it that way (Bitov, p. 526)

[28] Letter from Ian MacDonald to the authors, 12 August 1995. On comparisons with Solzhenitsyn's *Gulag*, *cf*. pp. 34.

Norman Lebrecht, who has written extensively on Soviet music and interviewed many ex-Soviet artists, shares this enthusiasm:

> *Testimony* was, and remains, a revelation. For those of us trying in the late Brezhnev era to write about artists living under communist and fascist tyrannies, it pierced the clouds of lies and diplomacy with a voice that was transparently honest and direct. Unlike any other Russian source, resident or exiled, it spoke an objective, unadorned truth.
>
> A broader perspective has been obtainable since the collapse of communism, but *Testimony* stands above all subsequent confessions and self-exculpations in both sincerity and depth. Shostakovich, the recording angel of Soviet Russia, amplified in these recollections what he had already encoded in his symphonies. Volkov, a perceptive observer in his own distinguished right, acted merely as the receptacle, Eckermann to the composer's Goethe. He could have made a bigger splash by following up with a biography of his own, but has conscientiously refrained from muddying the purity of the testament he received. Beset by Kremlin-serving and self-serving detractors, Solomon Volkov deserves better than the mealy-mouthed quibbles of tenured academics. He deserves a place in history.[29]

Gratitude also has come from native Russians and émigrés, who recognise in *Testimony* the real Shostakovich. Lev Lebedinsky is emphatic:

> I regard this book as one of the most important publications devoted to the composer, and its authenticity doesn't raise any questions or doubts in me. I am ready to put my signature under every word of it. This is the truth about Shostakovich.[30]

Additional endorsements of *Testimony* have come from Vladimir Ashkenazy ('As far as the character and image of Shostakovich are concerned, I'm sure it is true to life'[31]), Rudolf Barshai ('It's all true'[32]), Il'ya Musin ('Everything in

[29] Letter from Norman Lebrecht to the authors, 24 December 1995.

[30] Nikolska, p. 78.

[31] Ashkenazy, 'Shostakovich', p. 13.

[32] Interview with Michael Oliver, BBC Radio 3 (1983).

Testimony is true, everything'[33]), Mstislav Rostropovich ('basically everything that is stated there is true'),[34] Daniil Zhitomirsky ('I'm convinced that no serious scholar of Shostakovich's work – and, in particular, of his life and times – should disregard this source'[35]), Galina Shostakovich ('I am an admirer of Volkov. There is nothing false there'[36]), Maxim Shostakovich ('It's true. It's accurate. [. . .] The basis of the book is correct'[37]), and, most recently, Flora Litvinova, whose reminiscences of Shostakovich, published complete in December 1996, reveal what the composer himself said about his memoirs, completely exonerating Solomon Volkov from the indefensible charges of his detractors.[38]

Other Russians have found in *Testimony* and Shostakovich a link with their past. Yevgeny Yevtushenko, in an inscription to Volkov, writes: 'My dear Solomon – You saved for children of our children [the] real portrait of Shostakovich. Thank you, Yevtushenko 1991 N.Y.'[39] Similarly, the composer Alfred Schnittke states:

> I had a conversation with Solomon Volkov, who proved (at that time I regarded Shostakovich rather critically) that through Shostakovich we experience a contact with people who have already left us and their world, which continues to exist in him. This, of course, is so.[40]

Even unsympathetic readers seem to owe a debt to *Testimony*. The genre of memoirs 'related to and edited by' another was mocked in *Literaturnaya Gazeta* in 1979.[41] But

[33] Nice, p. 22.

[34] Wilson, p. 188.

[35] Zhitomirsky, 'Public and Private'.

[36] *Cf.* p. 83.

[37] Ian MacDonald, *The New Shostakovich*, p. 7. Also *cf.* pp. 111–14. In an interview in October 1996, Kurt Sanderling, a long-time colleague of Shostakovich and resident of the USSR, agreed: 'I have no doubt that [*Testimony* is] true' (Sanderling, p. 14).

[38] Litvinova, pp. 168–69. *Cf.* p. 251, above.

[39] *Cf.* p. 310.

[40] A. V. Ivashkin, compiler, *Besedy s Al'fredom Shnitke* (*Conversations with Alfred Schnittke*), RIK Kul'tura, Moscow, 1994, p. 82.

[41] 'The "Bed Bug"', p. 9.

what does one find among recent publications? *Tikhon Khrennikov: About the Time and Himself*, 'as related to and edited by' V. Rubtsova!

In evaluating the authenticity, accuracy and importance of *Testimony*, every effort has been made to accept Shostakovich's challenge that musicologists (and others) view things in perspective (unlike a chicken),[42] 'seriously dig around' in his works and actually 'sweat a little',[43] use the ensuing years 'to do some thinking'[44] and, when writing about him, finally, get it right.[45] Of course, were Shostakovich himself to defend his memoirs, his own reply would have been much different. If sufficiently provoked, he might have written a satire about 'The Man Who Spoke About the Omelette', with the names of his detractors subtly altered, as in *Rayok*. Shostakovich remembered this lesson from his early piano studies with Leonid Nikolayev, whose nephew had prepared an omelette for the starving Dmitry Dmitriyevich:

> Just think, Misha cooked the omelette, you are eating it, but a third person passes by who neither knows how to cook an omelette nor wants to eat one, but he comes just in order to talk about the omelette. That person is the musicologist, whose sole aim is to hold a discourse about the essence of an omelette. Who needs him? Do you, the hungry person eating it, or Misha who prepared it? No, absolutely nobody needs him.[46]

On the other hand, Shostakovich might have resisted satirising those with eggs on their faces and retreated into stoic silence. Shostakovich often left his critics in silence, frustrated. The deaf cannot hear, he says in *Testimony*, and the dumb cannot read the handwriting on the wall.

[42] *Testimony*, p. 153/199.

[43] *Ibid*.,, p. 186/240.

[44] *Ibid*., p. 117/155.

[45] *Ibid*., pp. 1/3, 33/45, 117/155.

[46] Marina Sabinina, quoted in Wilson, p. 226.

APPENDIX

July 16, 1976

Prof. William Harkins
Russian Institute
School of International Affairs

Dear Professor Harkins:

Although my acquaintance with Solomon Volkov and his work is at present limited to one morning's conversation and the perusal of a small body of articles and essays, I can confidently state that he is unquestionably the most impressive and accomplished among the Soviet emigré musicians and musicologists whom I have had occasion to meet in the last few years.

Mr. Volkov had already made a mark in the musical life of the USSR at the time of his emigration. He had organised a chamber opera company in Leningrad, and at the time of his leaving he was a senior staff editor of Sovetskaia muzyka, the official organ of the USSR Composers Union. As a critic, he was a recognized authority on the young composers of Leningrad, and a respected and trusted intimate of many of them. He had also served one of them, Valery Arzumanov, as librettist. Mr. Volkov's articles, however, were not mere echoes of an official line. Often sharply polemical, they were at times the focal point of controversy, and of official disapproval.

As musicologist, Mr. Volkov has done most of his work in two areas--the psychology of musical perception and Russian musical life and thought at the turn of the century. His writings display a lively intelligence and a broad acquaintance with the relevant literature, both Russian and to an extent Western. His competence and training far surpasses that of any musicologist of his generation whom I have met.

Mr. Volkov indicated to me in conversation that one of his major areas of interest is the composer Modest Musorgsky, particularly Musorgsky's relations with the počvenniki and the Slavophiles, and also the history of the reception and evaluation of Musorgsky's work. It can easily be seen that both of these topics are potentially "political" in Soviet eyes, and Mr. Volkov implied that carrying on such research was difficult in the ideological conditions that prevail in the USSR. He seemed eager to turn his attention to these questions once again. The work could yield important results in my opinion, and ought to be encouraged.

Finally, you are probably aware that Mr. Volkov is acting in the capacity of literary executor for the late Dmitri Shostakovich. When it will be time for the preparation of Shostakovich's memoirs for publication, Mr. Volkov will need library access and other advantages of university affiliation. The sponsorship of such work would reflect credity,I believe, upon the Russian Institute and upon Columbia University generally.

For all these reasons I am happy to endorse most heartily Mr. Volkov's request and application for a research fellowship in the Russian Institute. I would be happy to discuss the matter further with you if you should desire it, and in general to assist in any way I can.

Very truly yours,

Richard F. Taruskin
Assistant Professor of Music.

Exhibit 1. Richard Taruskin's letter of recommendation for Solomon Volkov (16 July 1976). *Cf.* pp. 37–38.

(212) 362-7100
201 West 79th Street
New York, N.Y. 10024
December 18, 1979

Mr. Harvey Shapiro
The New York Times Book Review
229 West 43rd Street
New York, N.Y. 10036

To the Editor:

In his letter of December 9th regarding Testimony: The Memoirs of Dmitri Shostakovich, Professor Malcolm Brown defends Sergei Prokofiev's method of producing the orchestra scores of his music. Since the opinions expressed in the book on this subject are Shostakovich's, not mine, I am not going to discuss them here. I do, however, want to correct two points in Professor Brown's letter.

Contrary to Professor Brown's assertion, only three of Prokofiev's letters to Pavel Lamm have been published, not "many" (all three were written between June and November, 1942). Prokofiev's published correspondence is heavily censored and his archives in the Soviet Union are closed to outsiders.

Furthermore, nowhere is it asserted in Testimony that Boris Pogrebov (a member of the Bolshoi Orchestra) is listed in the program booklet of "Romeo and Juliet." Nevertheless, I would like to direct the attention of Professor Brown (and that of other interested scholars) to a letter published by Maestro Gennady Rozhdestvensky in the official Soviet journal, Sovetskaya Muzyka in December 1973 (pp. 56-58). In this letter (which remains unchallenged by any Soviet musician) the conductor states explicitly that not only did Pogrebov participate in the orchestration of the Bolshoi's production of "Romeo and Juliet," but that the scores used in the stage productions of two other Prokofiev ballets, "The Stone Flower" and "Cinderella," are not the composer's own.

Cordially,

Solomon Volkov

Solomon Volkov
Research Associate, Russian Institute,
Columbia University

Exhibit 2. Solomon Volkov's response (18 December 1979) to unjust criticisms in Malcolm H. Brown's 'Letters: Shostakovich', *The New York Times Book Review*, 9 December 1979, Section 7, p. 37. *Cf.* pp. 100–3.

March 3, 1995

Mr. WILLIAM WHITWORTH
Editor
The Atlantic Monthly
745 Boylston St.
Boston, MA 02116

RE: Richard Taruskin's "Who Was Shostakovich?"
The Atlantic Monthly, February 1995

Dear Mr. Whitworth:

With some fascination I observe Richard Taruskin's obvious obsession with me and with the book I've collaborated on: Testimony: The Memoirs of Dmitri Shostakovich. For more than a dozen years now he attacks it and tries to undermine its credibility in every publication and at every forum that will allow it.

For me this obsession could be explained only in psychoanalitical terms. Many years ago, as a young emigre musicologist from Russia, I happened to influence decisively Richard Taruskin's thinking on Mussorgsky and Stravinsky, the main figures of his future field of expertise. First profoundly grateful, later on he tried, apparently unsuccesfully, to come to terms with this interaction. So Taruskin's struggle with me continues, not unlike the struggle of Stravinsky's hapless Petroushka against his Magician.

Sincerely yours, Solomon Volkov
Solomon Volkov

Exhibit 3. Solomon Volkov's response (3 March 1995) to unjust criticisms in Richard F. Taruskin's 'Who Was Shostakovich?', *Atlantic Monthly*, 275/2, February 1995, p. 63. *Cf.* pp. 37–38 and 292.

Exhibit 4. Dmitry Shostakovich and Solomon Volkov, Moscow, 1974. *Cf.* p. 50.

Exhibit 5. Boris Tishchenko and a 'certain Solomon Volkov' in Tishchenko's apartment (1976). *Cf.* p. 72.

Мон!
Я на море
у старой
лодки
Б.

Exhibit 6. Boris Tishchenko's note to Solomon Volkov (1971): 'Mon! I am at the sea by the old boat'. *Cf.* p. 72.

Милый
Мончик!
Спасибо тебе
за твою
работу —
за книгу
уже вы-
шедшую, а
особенно за
те, что еще
не вышли,
над которыми
ты сейчас ра-
ботаешь и я
счастлив при
этом присут-
ствовать.
Нам будет
много о чем
вспомнить.
Твой Б.
9 V 72 г.
С днем
победы!

Б. ТИЩЕНКО

КОНЦЕРТ

для виолончели, семнадцати духовых, ударных и фисгармонии

ПАРТИТУРА

B. TISCHENKO

CONCERTO

for cello, seventeen wind instruments, percussion and harmonium

SCORE

ИЗДАТЕЛЬСТВО „МУЗЫКА". ЛЕНИНГРАД 1968

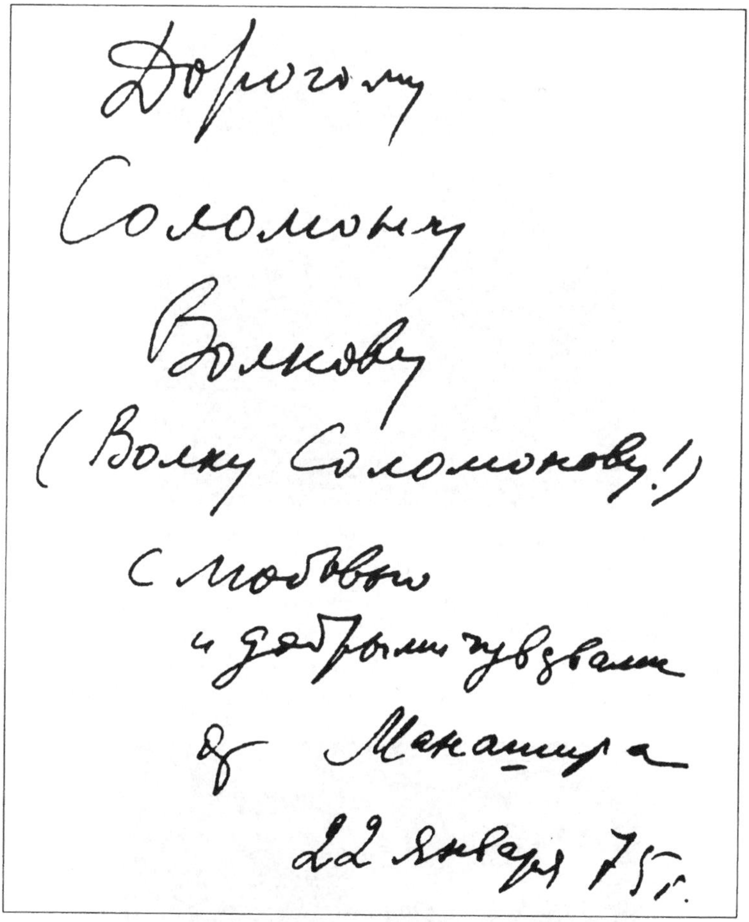

Дорогому
Соломону
Волкову
(Волку Соломонову!)
с любовью
и добрыми чувствами
от Манашира
22 января 75 г.

Exhibit 8. Manashir Yakubov's inscription to Solomon Volkov (22 January 1975): 'To dear Solomon Volkov (Solomon's Wolf!) with love and good feelings from Manashir'. *Cf*. p. 73, note 96.

Exhibit 7. Boris Tishchenko's inscription to Solomon Volkov (9 April 1972): 'Dear Monchik! Thank you for your work – for the book already published, and especially for those that have not yet appeared, on which you are working presently, and I am happy to be present at this moment. We will have a lot to reminisce about. Yours B. 9 IV 72. Happy Victory Day!' *Cf*. p. 72.

Exhibit 9. Solomon and Marianna Volkov following Dmitry Shostakovich's coffin (three heads behind the left edge) down the steps of the Moscow Conservatory (14 August 1975). This and the following three exhibits refute Taruskin's charge that Volkov was at the funeral only long enough to have one picture taken. *Cf.* pp. 126–28.

Exhibit 10. The Novodevichy Cemetery (14 August 1975), with Galina Shostakovich in the foreground and Solomon Volkov (centre-right) in the background.

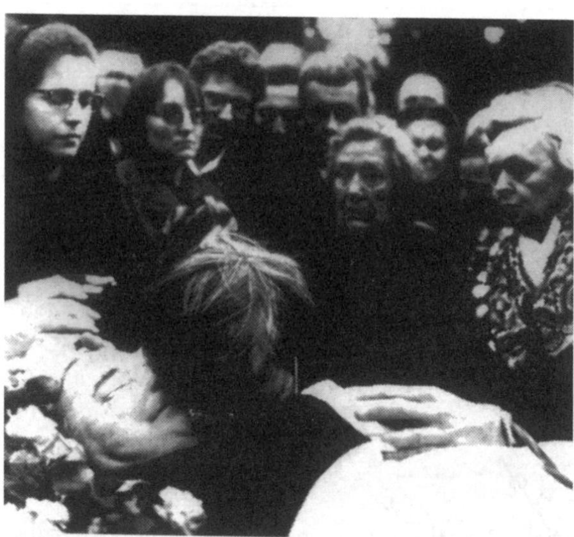

Exhibit 11. The Novodevichy Cemetery (14 August 1975), with Maxim Shostakovich in the foreground and Solomon Volkov (centre) in the background.

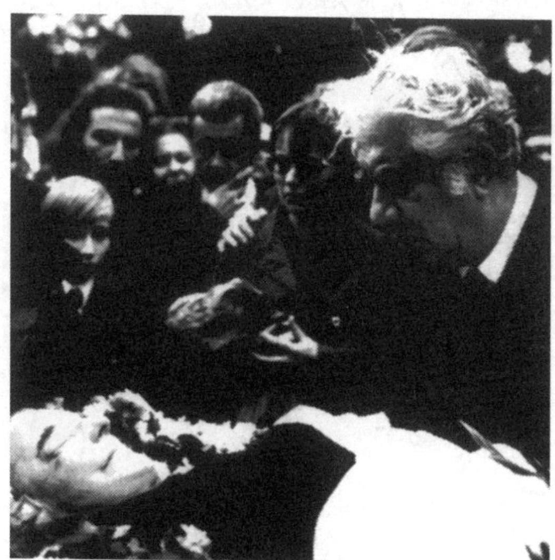

Exhibit 12. The Novodevichy Cemetery (14 August 1975), with Aram Khachaturian in the foreground and Solomon Volkov (left) in the background.

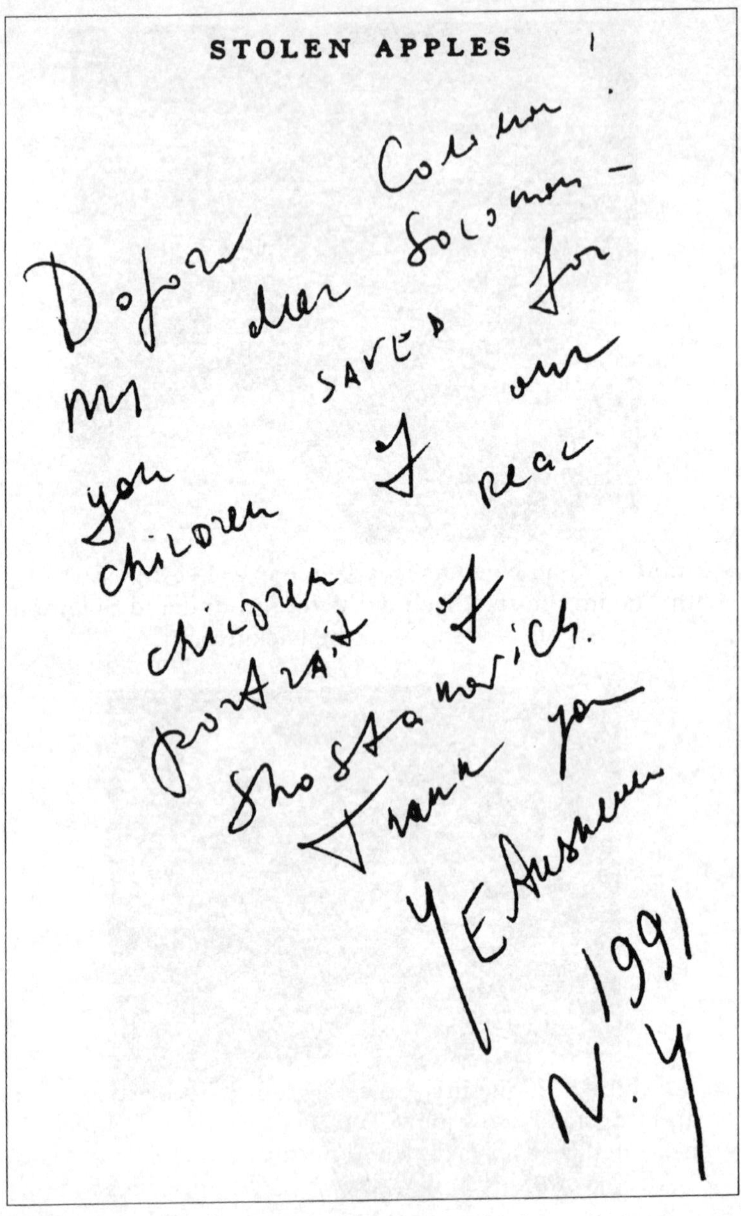

Exhibit 13. Yevgeny Yevtushenko's inscription to Solomon Volkov (1991): 'My dear Solomon – You saved for children of our children [the] real portrait of Shostakovich. Thank you, Yevtushenko 1991 N.Y.' *Cf.* p. 297.

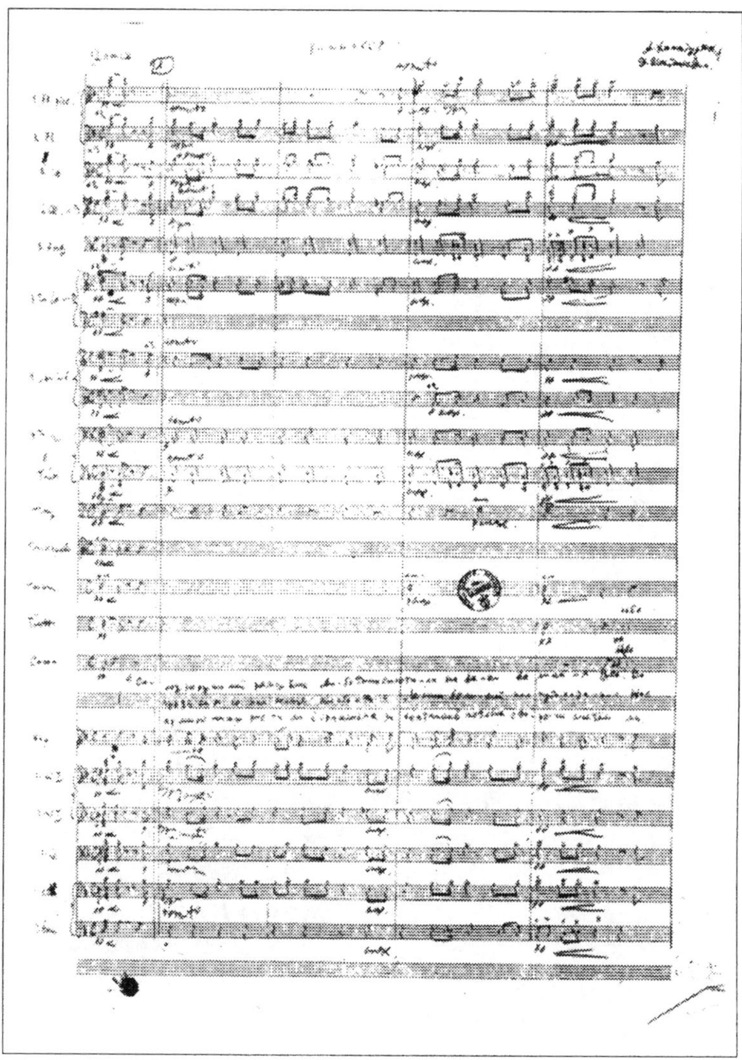

Exhibit 14. The first page of Aram Khachaturian and Shostakovich's joint *Anthem of the Soviet Union*, orchestrated by Shostakovich. This autograph corroborates the account given in *Testimony*. *Cf*. pp. 252–55.

VARIATIONS ON A THEME

Variation I

'A MAN HAS BURNED-UP HERE'[1]

Galina Drubachevskaya

The young violinist and musicologist, Solomon Volkov, began working for the editorial staff of our journal in the early 1970s. His social and artistic standing in Leningrad was good and respected musicians interceded on his behalf. It took a lot of effort, but eventually we succeeded in 'transferring' him from Leningrad to Moscow. Several years later S. Volkov left the Soviet Union and settled in the United States. A short time thereafter he achieved fame in the music world as the person who had recorded Dmitry Shostakovich's memoirs and successfully brought them to the West. Our correspondent Galina Drubachevskaya discussed this remarkable – even for those times – feat in the artistic history of our fatherland and the issues it has raised, as well as the more general social problems it has generated.

Well, here we are, in New York, fifteen years later. Let's talk about what, in essence, was the reason for your departure. Let's talk about how Dmitry Dmitriyevich Shostakovich's famous memoirs came to light. Surely, at the time, you didn't know yet that you would call them Testimony. *As for me, I can begin with a testimony of my own. I remember how one fine day you came to work at the editorial office of* Sovetskaya Muzyka *[*Soviet Music*]. You sat down at your desk and for a long time*

[1] Originally in *Muzykal'naya Akademiya* (Moscow), 1992, No. 3, pp. 3–14. English version by Véronique Zaytzeff and Frederick Morrison.

stared intently out the window. It was a very sunny day and the dirty red-brown wall of the opposite building seemed cheerful. I asked you what you saw out the window, what you were staring at. And you answered: 'I just came back from Shostakovich's. We are working on his memoirs'.

'Well, how is it going?'

'He feels that he is going to die soon.'

'Why do you think that?'

'He is so candid. His criticism is so frightening and caustic!'

When, later on, you gave me the chapters that had already been reviewed by Shostakovich, I felt that the pages were impregnated with the smell of death not only of a man, but of an era, an era with which, before departure, he decided to clear up the most important relations. Do you remember that day?

I do. At the time I could never have foreseen what was going to happen next. I was completely 'seized' by this man, by his truthfulness and his bitterness. Later on, I was amused to read in the Soviet press: 'how could Shostakovich have opened up to some drop-out violinist, some insignificant little reporter, when he had not even confided in his best friends!' It was amusing for many reasons, but most of all because of the fact that before beginning this work, Shostakovich had known me for many years.

We had first met when I was sixteen years old. He had read – later I learned that he carefully read every article about his music – my review, one of my very first ones, of his Eighth Quartet (it is included in all of the Soviet bibliographies about Shostakovich).[2] That happened in Leningrad. I was still a school-boy; we were just introduced and he immediately told me that he had read my review in the Leningrad *Smena* [*Change*]. That was the beginning and he remembered me. His memory was excellent. The years went by and there were several stages to our relationship. The first one was the Leningrad Conservatory festival dedicated entirely to Shostakovich's music. I had played a very active role in the

[2] 'Novy kvartet D. Shostakovicha' ('New Quartet of D. Shostakovich'), *Smena* (*Change*), 7 October, 1960; also *cf.* Ye. Sadovnikov (ed.), *D. Shostakovich. Notografichesky i bibliografichesky spravochnik* (*D. Shostakovich. Musical and bibliographical dictionary*), Muzyka, Moscow, 1965, p. 256. –EDS.

organisation of the festival. My ensemble was playing his recently composed Ninth Quartet – one of its first performances – from the collotype edition. So we again met. During another encounter I asked him about his creative plans. I remember him making a wry face when he said that he was composing the score for a movie on Karl Marx. That grimace of his surprised me then, but later I would see it on many occasions.

At that time, when you were still a teenager, did you ever imagine, even as a remote possibility, what *would bind you to this man*?

Yes, I really did! From the very moment I saw him, because I already knew *his music* and I knew it well. I would like to point out: you can spend twenty years with somebody, virtually side by side, and never be on the same psychological wavelength. But from the first notes I heard of his music, I knew that it was for me and about me. Many people felt the same way as I did, which is why Shostakovich has such a vast audience. Really, it is only when you feel art belongs to you personally that you understand it as a phenomenon of contemporary culture.[3]

Going back to my association with Shostakovich, the most important juncture in that relationship turned out to be when I organised, with some friends in Leningrad, the Experimental Ensemble of Chamber Opera, which gave the first staged performance of *Rothschild's Violin* by Veniamin Fleishman, a student of Dmitry Dmitriyevich (previously the opera had been heard only on the radio). This work turned out to be very important for Shostakovich, even if it did not deal with his own music. In general, others were important to him. By the way, our working on his memoirs began with the agreement that he would not talk about himself, but about others. And the idea itself took shape during one of our conversations, when I began speaking about Misha Sokolovsky – the founder of TRAM [Theatre of Young Workers] in Leningrad. Dmitry Dmitriyevich was astonished that I knew about him: 'For forty years no one has

[3] The following paragraph, a small digression about the Brodsky Quartet, has been omitted. –EDS.

talked to me about him', he said. He was genuinely surprised to see that there was a young man who had dug out some old books in the library about people and events already forgotten.

Having staged Fleishman's opera we touched upon something that was very dear and important to Shostakovich. Two themes came together here: Shostakovich and the Jews, and Shostakovich and the war. It was quite painful for Shostakovich to accept that a very young Jew, his own pupil, had volunteered to go to the battle and been killed. Dmitry Dmitriyevich himself had a terrible guilt complex regarding the impression that he had 'sat on the fence' during the war. Today, of course, we know that the famous photographs showing Shostakovich on a roof during the siege of Leningrad were merely staged. Later I did see still another photograph: on that same roof, next to Shostakovich, Sofronitsky[4] with some other professors from the Leningrad Conservatory. All of them together. Now, what if a bomb had struck just then? Today, it is common knowledge that all these famous people – Akhmatova,[5] Zoshchenko[6] and Shostakovich – on Stalin's personal order, had been practically

[4] Vladimir Sofronitsky (1901–61), a much-admired Soviet pianist and pedagogue closely associated with the music of Skryabin and Chopin. –EDS.

[5] The pseudonym of Anna Andreyevna Gorenko (1889–1966), whose works Shostakovich much admired, especially *Requiem*, which immortalises a mother's anguish over the imprisonment of a son (her own) and can be viewed as symbolic of other tragedies under Stalin. In August 1946, she was denounced by Andrey Zhdanov for her 'eroticism, mysticism and political indifference' and for writing poems 'alien to the Soviet people'. After Stalin's death, her work became better-known and more fully appreciated, leading to her recognition as the outstanding woman poet in Russian literature. –EDS.

[6] Mikhail Mikhailovich Zoshchenko (1895–1958), satirist and playwright who penned some of the best comic literature of the Soviet era and influenced Shostakovich's own manner of expressing himself. In the 1920s–30s, he was among the most popular of living writers, appreciated especially for his humorous short stories based on 'the many incongruities of everyday Soviet life', which 'proved a refreshing antidote to Communist bombast' (Victor Terras, *Handbook of Russian Literature*, Yale University Press, New Haven, 1985, p. 534). This changed in 1946 when he, with Akhmatova, was made a sacrificial victim by Zhdanov and expelled from the Union of Soviet Writers. –EDS.

forcibly evacuated from Leningrad. Was it possible that during the bombings such people would be on duty on the roofs? This was a cunning propaganda move, and even now it works remarkably well. When you talk about it, people get indignant: how can the legend be destroyed, even though it is clearly understood that Stalin's era was an era of myths, of hundreds and thousands of frauds. Yet this one is somehow particularly dear. Nonetheless, Shostakovich himself knew it was a myth and because of it he felt extremely uneasy.

So, then, the staging of Fleishman's opera provoked resistance. Even after the very successful premiere we were summoned to appear in front of an extremely important official, who asked us: 'Are you aware that you are playing into the enemy's hands? This is a Zionist opera!' It was absurd to talk about Zionism in this respect, but this official, who had not read Chekhov, naturally had not looked into the opera very closely. Just because the name 'Rothschild' had been mentioned, it meant Zionism. Shostakovich was aware of all our torments, and this drew us even closer together. It was at that time that I got the idea of writing a book on the young composers of Leningrad and Dmitry Dmitriyevich agreed to write a preface.[7]

Strictly speaking, this was the very first time we worked together. We had several long talks, after which I put the material together and sent it back to him for his approval. Shostakovich was satisfied with both the text and the published book, which he, being supportive of young composers, considered helpful.

However, the very first snag took place here – the forerunner of many to come. The problem was that Shostakovich had told me a lot more in our conversations than what was eventually included in his preface, and the tenor of his statements to me was much more candid. But when I showed the editors the first version, they rolled their eyes, particularly at the passage regarding Glazunov, which they found excessively 'naturalistic', and immediately struck out this section from the text. Now something that had never crossed our minds became very clear to us: we could only expect

[7] Volkov here refers to his book *Molodyye Kompozitory Leningrada*, Sovetsky Kompozitor, Leningrad, 1971. –EDS.

enormous difficulties if Dmitry Dmitriyevich continued to present his recollections in the same fashion.

Incidentally, the very first one to see this so clearly was Yury Semyonovich Korev.[8] Having heard about our conversations, he invited me to see him and expressed his interest in publishing some excerpts. I began to tell him how the material was taking shape, particularly in the case of Glazunov, Prokofiev and Stalin. And his response to me was that that kind of material could not appear in his magazine no matter whose lips it came from.

Naturally, I told Dmitry Dmitriyevich everything and he understood that publication of his memoirs would be possible only in the West. For him, intimidated and hunted down for so long, such publication could occur only posthumously. He talked to me about this often in his characteristic 'recurring speech' pattern: 'Only after my death, only after my death'. From the instant I heard his request, I took it as an order and carried it out. Prior to my leaving for the West, I sent him, by trusted hands,[9] a letter in which I confirmed the following: while he was alive, the book would not be published . . . . Incidentally, when I gave him the material I had assembled to read, and this was done, if you recall . . .

Yes, I do. It was done in a very rapid fashion.

. . . I was not asking for nor was I expecting his signature, since I was aware that the situation was too serious and he, naturally, was wary of possible complications. But the chapters kept coming back with: 'Read. Shostakovich'. It was only later, here [in New York], when I had the time to think about the whole story, that I understood the following: Dmitry Dmitriyevich's signature was an intuitively infallible reaction. He had invented a formula that authenticated the text, but at the same time created a certain distance in the event the book were nonetheless published during his lifetime or the KGB began to apply strong pressure on both of

[8] Then the chief editor of *Sovetskaya Muzyka*. –EDS.

[9] Through Boris Tishchenko. –Solomon Volkov (SV), 1997.

us. It is obvious that a person would not write about his own text 'I have read it'. Dmitry Dmitriyevich could have signed: 'I am in agreement. Shostakovich' or simply 'Shostakovich'. 'Read. Shostakovich' signaled that he had examined the content. There were practically no corrections. This was his style too: to work quickly and cleanly.

And where is the manuscript now?

In a bank, in Switzerland. I had to put it there because there was a real hunt for it all these years. At first, when we were living at a hotel [in New York City], there were several rather crude moves to snatch it. And even on my way to the States, my suitcases had been ripped open and all the manuscripts (others) crumpled and twisted, and the photographs torn in two.

Even those with Anna Andreyevna Akhmatova?

All of them, nothing was spared. Naturally, they didn't find anything: the [Shostakovich] book had been sent well ahead of my departure and followed a different route from mine. When I was interrogated in Moscow as to its whereabouts, I could honestly answer that it was not in the country. Indeed, the only manuscript – I did not make copies! – had been sent to the West in instalments. It also arrived here [in New York] piecemeal. I was taking a great risk: people, unknown to me, would give me a call or just show up, hand me the latest part, and then disappear.[10] I never questioned anybody about anything.... Knowing the ways of the KGB, I had every right to expect that they would try to wring the location of the manuscript out of me or out of my wife: 'where's the manuscript?' So, when in New York, I saw to it, I created a

[10] Seppo Heikinheimo, in his posthumous memoirs *Mätämunan muistelmat* (p. 395), erroneously states that Luigi Nono smuggled the manuscript to the West. Although Nono helped to get Volkov out of the USSR, he was not involved in bringing *Testimony* to the West. –EDS.

situation, that whatever the pressure, I could give only one answer: I don't have the faintest idea.

Then, when *Testimony* was supposed to see the light of the day, every kind of pressure imaginable was exerted on the publishers not to let it happen. One of the arguments they stuck to was that they kept reminding me of my alleged promise to Irina Antonovna [Shostakovich's widow] to show her the book (after she told me: 'the KGB instructed me to ask you for the manuscript'). Living in the USSR, I had never learned that a legal principle exists in the West that promises made under threat are not binding and are worthless. However, even though I was unaware of it, I had said to Irina Antonovna that as long as I was a hostage, I would show her nothing, but if we could meet outside the USSR, then I would show her the manuscript. Now that we are on equal footing, she never came, and never asked me to see anything. . . . Now why did Shostakovich choose me to work with him on his memoirs? I can only repeat: over the years we had grown close. But even more to the point, in this instance he used me as his mouthpiece. I was a mouthpiece with specific gifts, one that was suitable for the work at hand, but still just a mouthpiece. A time had come when he felt the need to express his opinion on a host of problems deeply troubling to him. In the first place, he saw that the misunderstanding of his work was growing deeper among the young people and the dissidents in the Soviet Union. Having arrived in the United States, I now fully appreciate the degree to which the misunderstanding was strong here, primarily due to the unanswered question: what was Shostakovich's relation to Stalin. People continually read that despite all his previous persecutions Shostakovich, from time to time, would still receive a State Prize, or that he was the heralded Soviet classical composer, the Soviet representative abroad, while an internal opposition was growing in the country. As for Shostakovich – it must be admitted, straightforwardly and unequivocally, that he never joined the human-rights dissident movement. There is no doubt that A. D. Sakharov became a dissident because of his having taken part in the creation of the Soviet hydrogen bomb. We know that Shostakovich bore some kind of silent grudge against Sakharov because of that connection with the bomb. It was a very complex psychological state, his grudges against Solzhenitsyn and Sakharov. I don't want to delve into the case. I merely affirm that it existed. Right now we are talking about something else. While it is true that Sakharov was a scientist of genius, I ask you to name those creative geniuses in the arts who, having sacrificed their work, became dissidents.

I guess that there aren't any. We know that Nabokov said he wanted to cross the border into the USSR and end up in one of our labour camps to see everything with his own eyes. At the time, he was writing Podvig [Glory]*, in which the hero, Martin, does disappear in the USSR. But Nabokov himself did no such thing since he understood that, had he done so, his creative career would have come to an abrupt end.*

Shostakovich knew that he was a genius and he fulfilled the task for which he was destined. However, that resolute devotion to his work created a real abyss between him and the best of the country's intelligentsia. Many were to ask: 'isn't he, after all and basically, Stalin's creature?' People forgot what 1948 had meant to Shostakovich. Only recently have I come to understand how much the government's 'sentiments' to the effect that Shostakovich's music was beyond the comprehension of the people were shared not only by the broad masses but also by the masses of the scientific and technocratic intelligentsia. The majority of academicians could pleasantly relax at *Swan Lake* or, at best, listening to Beethoven or Bach. Now, suddenly the man of genius found himself listed as another one of Stalin's 'hobby-horses'. Shostakovich suffered bitterly. I think that almost everyone had underrated the composer's own doubts regarding his political position. In fact, he had very definite ideas only about his own music and in this field he did not welcome criticism. But, when it came to political and social questions, he had many doubts and hesitations.

Close to the time we began working together, Dmitry Dmitriyevich felt the need to express his own opinion about his politics and, most of all, about Stalin. The question was frequently asked: 'why hasn't he talked about David Oistrakh or another one of his friends?' The reason is that these were unusual memoirs: the book has turned out to be an elucidation of his political stand, but began as a simple conversation about those who, at the time, were no longer among us –

Misha Sokolovsky,[11] Meyerhold[12] and Zoshchenko. He had considered it important to give their memory its due. As for Oistrakh, Rostropovich and the others dear to his heart, he had already written enough about them in the press. He now had a different purpose in mind. And it was at that moment that I was to begin the role of his 'mouthpiece'. Looking back now after almost twenty years, I feel that I have fulfilled my role and I have a perfectly clean conscience about any debt to Dmitry Dmitriyevich Shostakovich. I have accomplished everything we agreed to. As for the effect produced by my book, it is possible that he, a genius, had foreseen it, but as for me, I could never even have imagined it.

We absolutely must talk about this. To begin, tell me: for you personally, didn't your experiences with this book become a living ordeal, the catalyst for serious decisions? I understood that issue, both at the time you were writing it and at the time you were making preparations to leave the country. But while all this was going on – you wrote it down, and he read it – they wouldn't let you out of the country, and then they raised every imaginable obstacle to letting the book out – did all these circumstances influence your attitude toward your hero and his music?

Mstislav Rostropovich once told me that three composers and Solzhenitsyn had had a radical influence on his life. The composers were Prokofiev, Shostakovich and Britten.[13] Furthermore, Rostropovich told me that after having met Shostakovich – despite his profound admiration for Dmitry Dmitriyevich – he had nonetheless felt that something had burnt out in him; to be specific, Rostropovich was incapable of playing romantic music anymore. I shuddered because I

[11] Mikhail Sokolovsky (1901–41), the founder and director of the avant-garde Leningrad Theatre of Young Workers (TRAM), for which Shostakovich wrote incidental music in the late 1920s to early 1930s. –EDS.

[12] Vsevolod Yemilyevich Meyerhold (1874–1940), theatre, opera and film director, best-known for his experiments in non-realistic theatre. His pupils included Sergey Eisenstein. –EDS.

[13] *Cf.* Solomon Volkov, 'Tradition Returns: Rostropovich's Symbolism', pp. 359–72, below. –EDS.

had had the same feeling. This is why I do not trust people who called themselves his friends, but who would say with a saccharine lisp what a good man Dmitry Dmitriyevich was, what a gentle man he was: they are either lying or are incapable of understanding him, or never had any serious relations with him. Because Shostakovich was 'burning' everything around him and burning himself as well. One can apply Fet's words to him: 'A man has burned-up here'. Really, there are many things that we truly do not know about Shostakovich. We may know a bit more about some of those who were his kindred spirits, such as Zoshchenko and the members of the OBERIUTY Circle [Young Leningrad Dadaists] – Kharms, Oleynikov and Zabolotsky.[14] And judging by the fact that their lives had been burnt to a crisp and utterly mutilated . . .

. . . and how Zabolotsky – after his stay in the camps – wrote a poem addressed to the poets, his friends who had been dispatched to the other world: 'Are you at peace, my dear comrades, is it easy for you, and have you forgotten everything?'

But that is just the point. The dead could forget, but the living could not. Yes, Zabolotsky and his fate was the most appropriate tuning fork for me to use to check many aspects of Shostakovich's life and to detect the distant peals in his soul. These two people had lived in the same city, they had undergone common ordeals, they had similar dispositions, and an identical world view. As for personal contacts with Shostakovich, he exerted the most spiritual, psychological, and disturbing (call it whatever you wish) influence on you, one you could not escape. I keep feeling it even now, it

[14] The participants in Oberiu (Ob'yedineniye real'nogo iskusstva [Association for Real Art]), an avant-garde literary and artistic group active in Leningrad from 1927–30. Its members included the poets and writers Daniil Ivanovich Kharms (the pseudonym of Yuvachev, 1905–42), who, in late 1931, was arrested for 'distracting people from the tasks of industrial construction with "transsense" poetry' and, in summer 1941, was returned to prison, where he died of starvation; Nikolay Oleynikov (1898–1942), a favorite writer of Shostakovich, who was arrested in 1937 and also died in prison; and Nikolay Zabolotsky (1903–58), who was arrested in 1938, sentenced to heavy physical labour until 1946, then exiled from Moscow and Leningrad. –EDS.

changed my entire attitude, and to a great extent, since that time, I look at everything and everyone through Shostakovich's eyes.

Whether it was fortunate or not, I don't know, but fate kept sending me people – no matter how diverse – who had also gone through the same type of schooling. For instance, Balanchine, with whom I wrote the book *Balanchine's Tchaikovsky*,[15] was born in the same Petersburg, studied at the same conservatory, also suffered in the same revolution and later on with NEP [the New Economic Policy], and left Russia, as a grown man, on the eve of renaming the city 'Leningrad'. Whichever way we look at it, Balanchine is an utterly different person from Shostakovich, but, at the same time, is unbelievably like him. And the same can be said of Joseph Brodsky.

Yes, this 'à la Shostakovich' *bitterness that flows from his poetry, or at times seems to flow, even against his own wishes, in clots. You almost physically feel it.*

And you cannot escape from this bitterness either, once you get to know him. And if Balanchine was to a certain extent different from those two, it is only because he was a believer, a practising Christian who went to church and received communion, and for whom a burial service was read. As for the other two, whatever their thoughts about God and religion, they were not practising believers and their relationship with God was extremely complex.

Now I can say that, by comparison, my relations with Anna Akhmatova were the easiest ones. And here I foolishly guess that the reason was that she . . .

. . . was a woman. No doubt about it. And, incidentally, she was also a true Christian. Furthermore, any little boy – whether she realised it or not, and I assume she realised everything – became her little boy. And she went through so much for the sake of her *little boy . . . . Her third husband, N. Punin, during lean times,*

[15] Translated by Antonina W. Bouis, Simon and Schuster, New York, 1985. –EDS.

would insist that the butter that was in the house be given to his daughter, and not to her son. Later her son spent eighteen years in the camps. When you read in her Requiem: '*And the mother stood silently, no one even daring to glance in her direction*', *– she herself was afraid to look at her life, but she did – through her poetry. And so you were her little boy.*

And although I was uncomfortable, timid and quivering, still with Akhmatova I felt utterly different. Not that I would get relaxed – in her presence, that was out of the question – but certain undercurrents were absent. While talking with those three gentlemen – Shostakovich, Balanchine and Brodsky – I always expected a blow in the solar plexus, figuratively speaking. When Shostakovich spoke with you, behind his every word shone triple meanings and you were to guess which was the correct one. It was an ongoing exam that you were continuously taking. I must say that I enjoyed a 'preferential treatment'. Obviously, all three of them took me for a professional who was doing his job.

It was the same with Brodsky. We had many conversations. My book[16] seems like it is ready and it is weighing down on me; nonetheless, I constantly feel that something is missing in it – perhaps his forthcoming trip to Petersburg and the impression it would make on him. At any rate, the book keeps on growing. Furthermore, I have recorded more than 25 hours of conversations with Vladimir Horowitz, a record amount of time. But, when these several books are finished, I intend to completely renounce the genre of conversations or memoirs, because it is a completely exhausting activity. Even in my relations with such a congenial person as Nathan Milstein, who isn't given to psychological flogging, against my own will I have completely entered his universe and begun to 'live through' him everything all over again. To relive with a person his entire life is the greatest trial in the writing of memoirs. As for the individuals being interviewed, they, the great ones, are wonderful psychological membranes: they know immediately when your attention

[16] *Conversations with Joseph Brodsky: A Poet's Journey through the Twentieth Century*, The Free Press, New York, 1998. –EDS.

wanders, and if they do not hold your sympathy, they close up immediately. And this is catastrophic in an interview. This is why I am amused when it is said that this person and that person was a friend of Shostakovich. And B. Tishchenko, who even now keeps on saying God knows what about me, claims that I pose as a friend of Shostakovich. I have never once said such a thing! This is absolute nonsense! I never claimed I was a friend of Balanchine nor a friend of Milstein. I was a collaborator in their projects. They had faith in me. My task was not to let them down.

To some extent, any conversation about friendship is, by its nature, strange. Yu. Levitin loves to go on and on about it.[17] As for Shostakovich, he would say nothing at all. He was surrounded by all kinds of people. They sat at the same table with him, drank, played cards and told anecdotes. Someone would go with him to a soccer game – it was everyday life. But when Boris Tishchenko appeared on the horizon, Dmitry Dmitriyevich saw him as the sunlight in a window: here was a man of a totally different calibre, whose cultural level was, to begin with, on a different plane of regard (I don't know how it is now), so unlike the usual milieu . . . .

Tell me now: has your attitude changed with respect to Shostakovich's music?

No. It really was my attitude toward his music that compelled me to do the book. So many things have to be said here. . . . Let me set the record straight and even name names. There was [the violinist] Oleg Kagan: we have known each other for many years. We went to school together in Riga. I always regarded his talent highly. Once we met in Moscow. I asked him what he was doing. And he said: 'well, we are just coming home from Shostakovich's, we played his violin sonata for him'.

'Well?'

'The music is crap.'

'Then why do you play it?'

[17] Yury Levitin (1912–95), composer, student of Shostakovich at the Leningrad Conservatory (1937–40).

'The old man promised to keep me out of the army.'

Ye gods, I recognise that line! Did they really believe that Shostakovich wouldn't notice their attitude in their performance?

Not so long ago I was telling this to a composer, and he said: 'it's impossible, what?!' It means that people forget. Today, they won't believe what the real attitude toward Shostakovich's music was at that time.

Even Edison Denisov – he is still so cautious – admits that he did not like many things in Dmitry Dmitriyevich's behaviour and music. But it wasn't just many things – he didn't like anything and he wasn't the only one. And Shostakovich was keenly aware of all this. We have already talked about the fact that Shostakovich's music was 'incomprehensible for the broad masses' as well as for the scientific and technocratic intelligentsia that, in our country, has always been an important part of the art-consuming public. I will add a third element: twenty years ago the elitist avant-garde musicians held Shostakovich of no account. I heard so many contemptuous, disparaging words from young composers about Dmitry Dmitriyevich the moment I arrived in Leningrad, having moved there from Riga – from the young composers who criticised him left and right, but later wrote quartets and symphonies to Shostakovich's memory! The only exception was B. Tishchenko, who, if my memory serves me right, always worshipped his music.

And so, from the first note of Shostakovich that I heard, my attitude toward his music has not changed. I always intuitively felt in his music a protest against the regime. This is what I had tried to express, as much as was possible, in that Leningrad newspaper, in my review of the Eighth Quartet when I was sixteen. He knew that and was grateful to me because he already sensed that young people were changing their attitude toward his music. He was also thrilled to realise that there were some young people who still understood his music and comprehended the real meaning of the dedication: 'To the Victims of War and Fascism'. I've spent so many years trying to prove that this quartet did not deal with some abstract fascism, but that its music was autobiographical! Finally, thank goodness, Galina Dmitriyevna Shostakovich testified: 'Dad said – this quartet was dedicated to myself personally'. Then even M. Yakubov wrote the very same thing.

Generally speaking, what is so important is to realise to what extent people hear *Shostakovich's music. In conversations about his memoirs more than once I heard: 'Well, how could that be? Dmitry Dmitriyevich was such a tactful and benevolent man. Even if he had said such a thing, he would never have signed it'. That was the reasoning of a man who had known Dmitry Dmitriyevich for many years. I want to ask them: Have you really listened to his music? Its bitterness, its bite, its tragedy, and its sarcasm? This is where we hear how he saw reality and see what it cost him! Why wouldn't he, on the eve of his demise, say the same things in words that he had said in music?*

You have to immerse yourself in his music your entire life – and that is hard to do. So, even if, in principle, your attitude toward the music does not change, fresh nuances appear and there's a natural enrichment. I once asked Rostropovich whether the fact that he knew Prokofiev personally had changed his perception of the music itself. He answered: 'You would never believe how much that changes it. You remember how he reacted to particular instruments, colours, and some specifics, such as tempi'. Knowing Shostakovich's psychology helps in amazing ways: you understand why some of his metronome markings can be deliberately incorrect. At times he would feel uneasy about playing his own composition and wanted to 'do away with it', so he would indicate quicker tempi on the metronome. This is why many of his performances of his own works don't satisfy me.

Let me repeat, my attitude toward Shostakovich's music didn't change – from the very first moment I heard the Eleventh Symphony in a concert by the Leningrad Philharmonic conducted by Yevgeny Mravinsky, and figured out that it was about the shooting of innocent people – remember what Yesenin wrote: '... he did not shoot the guiltless ones in dungeons'? I understood that this music was for me, about me, and about my time.

In arguments I would be told: 'well, it is quite understandable that Dmitry Dmitriyevich could have said that about real life but for him to say "such a thing" about Prokofiev or Mravinsky, that can't be true'. Even though it is known that, during his lifetime, at the 1943 Plenum of the Soviet Composers, when Prokofiev criticised him for his lack of melodiousness, he said to him, said to his face, so to speak: 'melodiousness is a gift from God, as for orchestration, one can take lessons in that'.[18]

Now let's talk about something else. He worried about how people would respond to his music and to his political stance. Nonetheless, he must have been aware that in his professional circle he was regarded as some kind of Santa Claus, who had signed letters containing thousands of requests, written petitions about apartments, helped people get out of military service, signed articles, etc.

People who took the time to think about Shostakovich's music understood a long time ago what kind of person he was. Once again I refer to Yu. Korev, who told me one day regarding Shostakovich: 'a man who loves everybody so much loves nobody'. I remember how struck I was by the insight in this remark. There is a letter to Marietta Shaginyan,[19] published in *Novy Mir* [*New World*], in which Mikhail Zoshchenko gave an extremely keen depiction of Shostakovich's harshness and affectation. Shostakovich – kind? Shostakovich – artless? Until recently no one could talk about his secret, internal affectation – he was always so harmonious, always so 'kind and guileless'.

Now, going from the specific to the general: the fact is that in Russian as well as Soviet society a fundamental hypocrisy has always existed, and still appears in many guises as regards the appreciation of great people. In Russia, there are basically two ways to look at a great man or at men in general. Either the man is dragged through the dirt: he is a villain and

[18] Alluding to the fact that Prokofiev used help in orchestrating many of his late works. *Cf.* pp. 98–105. –EDS.

[19] Marietta Sergeyevna Shaginyan (1888–1982), poet, novelist, journalist and investigative reporter. Her friendship with Shostakovich from 1936 until his death is documented in a collection of fifty letters from the composer published in 1984 (*cf.* Bibliography, p. 748). –EDS.

a miscreant (for example, Grishka Otrepyev[20] and Grishka Rasputin[21]). Or he is made into an icon (as was the case with Dmitry Dmitriyevich): he could never have a mistress, he could never be an alcoholic, which Shostakovich definitely was at a certain period in his life, etc. Nikolay Andreyevich Malko (his widow and I became friends here) knew a lot about Shostakovich: Malko conducted his earlier compositions and had social ties with him. He left some remarkably interesting reminiscences about the young Shostakovich – I don't know whether they have been published in Russian. These reminiscences paint a picture of the young Shostakovich that, to tell the truth, do not fit into any usual portrait. For example, they went on a tour to Kharkov and there, on Shostakovich's initiative, argued about who would have the greatest number of flies stuck to the fly-paper in the morning. During the night Malko woke up and saw Mitya sticking flies on his fly-paper so that he could win at all costs ....

But, as a matter of fact, how about this: a huge, well detailed and documented two-volume biography of Nabokov has recently been published here in English.[22] In Russia there isn't even such a big, real biography of Pushkin. Again, here, in America, a multi-volume biography of Dostoyevsky has been published,[23] and in Russia they haven't done anything like that. We have no substantial, comprehensive and well-documented biographies that take into account

[20] Grigory Bogdanovich Otrep'yev, best known as the monk Grigory who challenged Boris Godunov's right to the throne and in 1601–2 claimed he was the son of Ivan the Terrible, Dmitry Ivanovich, who had died in 1591. He is immortalised in history, literature and opera as 'The False Dmitry'. –EDS.

[21] Grigory Yefimovich Novykh (?1872–1916), he earned the surname 'Rasputin' ('debauched one') from his loose lifestyle. Often portrayed as a 'mad monk' and mystic, he exerted a tremendous influence on the imperial family after seeming to improve the health of Aleksey Nikolayevich, the hemophiliac son of Nikolay II and heir to the Russian throne. –EDS.

[22] Brian Boyd, *Vladimir Nabokov*, Chatto & Windus, London, 1990. –EDS.

[23] Frank Joseph, *Dostoevsky: The Seeds of Revolt, 1821–1849, Dostoevsky: The Years of Ordeal, 1850–1869, Dostoevsky: The Stir of Liberation, 1860–1865* and *Dostoevsky: The Miraculous Years, 1865–1871*, Princeton University Press, 1976, 1983, 1986 and 1989/Robson, London, 1977, 1983 and 1987. –EDS.

reminiscences by contemporaries; biographies that provide a picture of the whole person, with his sweat and tears, and contradictions. What we have in Russia are highly discreet booklets in which facts are made to support basic theses. Why? Because of our hypocrisy. Because if we were to write the whole truth, the idol would cease to be an idol. The authorisation to criticise geniuses was granted only from higher up. Then it was possible to spit upon them to your heart's content.

And how we spat on them! Akhmatova was depicted as half-nun, half-slut, and Zoshchenko as some sort of degenerate. It was said that Sakharov, having degraded himself as a scientist, went into politics so that he could keep himself in the limelight, and so forth.

Quite true. Even today, they are unable to write a truthful biography of Musorgsky. Recently I bought a book of memoirs about him, memoirs that were not published for decades because they depicted a frightening picture of alcoholism. And once again, these memoirs contain deletions; once again, in the foreword, the author even attempts to prove the unprovable: that the man was not a victim of his alcoholism. Today, the question of Tchaikovsky's homosexuality still has not been treated openly in a scholarly discussion; instead, they keep whispering about it in each other's ear.

When Akhmatova wrote: 'If you only knew from what kind of refuse poetry grows and knows no shame', I think that she had in mind not only life refuse but also the refuse of human nature. Recently I read a shattering document on this very theme – Sergey Efron's letter of 1924 to Maksimilian Voloshin, in which he writes, specifically, about the nature of his wife Marina Tsvetayeva's creativity. He wrote: 'M. is a person full of passions: much more than it used to be before – prior to my departure. To surrender herself wholly to her own hurricane has become for her a necessity, the very breath of life. Who, at the present moment, is the source of this hurricane is of no importance. Almost always (now as before), more exactly, always, everything is built on self-delusion. The person is invented and the hurricane begins. If she soon discovers that the stimulus of the hurricane is worthless and narrow-minded, then Marina abandons herself to the hurricane of despair. Her condition will improve with the appearance of a new stimulus. What it is has no importance; what is important is how: not the essence, not the source, but the rhythm, the frenzied rhythm. Today is despair, tomorrow bliss, love, and total abandon, the day after tomorrow, despair again. And she goes through this kind of turmoil despite the fact that she is endowed with a sharp, cold (perhaps, cynical à la *Voltaire) intelligence. Yesterday's thrillers are scoffed at today in a witty and spiteful manner (almost always justly). Every bit is recorded in the book. Everything is calmly and mathematically cast in a formula. A huge furnace whose stoking necessitates wood, wood, and more wood'. In this letter the character of Tsvetayeva's art is disclosed with more clarity, relief and spontaneity than in dozens of pages of excellent research.*

I lost my respect for Ol'ga Tchaikovskaya[24] when she wrote an article about Pyotr Ilyich Tchaikovsky in *Novy Mir*: 'how dare those scoundrels, these dregs of humanity, rummage in great people's lives and tell whom they slept with, ate with, and drank with'. Yes, we dare, it's our business! This element of hypocrisy was born from unending deprivations of political freedom. Here, in the West, it is very clearly understood that if you are a private, ordinary person, no one will scrutinise your personal life and you have a right to your privacy. However, if you become a person of some stature and lay a claim to the attention of society, then you can count on total scrutiny.

A famous person here does not have the right to sue reporters, even for slander. This fact is not understood in Russia and by some of the Russians who came here. It was amusing to read how Voynovich[25] told-off some generals who had slandered him: had they been living in the West, he said, he would have brought them to trial. I don't know how things

[24] A contemporary Russian journalist. –EDS.

[25] Vladimir Nikolayevich Voynovich (b. 1932), Soviet writer best-known for his satires *The Life and Extraordinary Adventures of Private Ivan Chonkin* (1963–70), which circulated widely in *samizdat*, but had to be published abroad, and *The Ivankiad, or, The Tale of the Writer Voynovich's Installation in His New Apartment* (published in the USA in 1976). He was expelled from the Union of Soviet Writers in 1974 and emigrated to West Germany in December 1980. –EDS.

are in Europe, but in the US it would have come to naught. Because if you decide to have a career in the public eye, then this public has the right to know everything about you and has the right to evaluate you by knowing all the facts.[26]

Such a concept has not been accepted in Russia. How could it be? At first you would be interested in the personal life of, say, Smoktunovsky, then Tolstikov, then Stalin, Brezhnev, and so forth. But such a system is in place that, starting from the very top and going down to the last functionary, you could learn nothing. Years of lies are wound around this hypocrisy.

And they base it all on Pushkin's famous sentence, 'the pettiness of great people is different . . . '. A large enough section of our society is outraged by Andrey Sinyavsky's Progulki s Pushkinym [Strolls with Pushkin]*.*[27] *I am not talking about the lack of understanding of the genre or the trend of this book, but, after all, it contains facts, only facts.*

It was with greatest pleasure that Pushkin himself wrote down anecdotes about everyone and everything, his letters are full of gossip in the spirit of his time. But, naturally, he defended his right to stand out in that respect from the crowd. Ask any actor, writer or political figure and he will tell you: 'it is a disgrace, it must be stopped'. That's right, each one of them refuses to live under glass; he wants to be given the privilege of being adored by the crowd, but not judged by it. This is the reason why, in Russia, we still have no true biography of our first national poet – Pushkin – or of any other prominent figure in the arts. Instead of authentic biographies we are only able to write some kind of ideological leaflets, some fictional histories of art that enable us to hide the real facts of its development.

[26] Volkov is not entirely correct here. Even a public figure can succeed in a defamation suit if the defamatory statement was made with 'malice' – knowledge of falsity, or reckless disregard of the truth. *Cf.* Gertz vs. Robert Welch, Inc., 418 U.S. 323 (1974). –EDS.

[27] Abram Terts (Andrey Sinyavsky), *Progulki s Pushkinym*, Overseas, London/Paris, 1975. –EDS.

And to present it almost exclusively as a continuum, asserting, consequently, the essentiality of the traditional development, while ignoring the fact that there is a great deal, to put it mildly, of rejection and conflict.

All research should be based only on facts. For example, the fact that Musorgsky hated Tchaikovsky and that, in his letters, he called him derisively Sadyk-Pasha, was painted over. As for Tchaikovsky, the nice, mild-mannered, and polite Pyotr Ilyich, who loved everyone, wrote his brother: 'with all my heart I send Musorgsky's music to hell, since it is a foul caricature of music'. It is so convenient to forget the simple fact, and it has been forgotten, that creative people permit themselves to attack one another brutally.

Rimsky-Korsakov really was not particularly grieved by Tchaikovsky's death . . .

. . . and after this the former's creative block came to an end. He began composing opera after opera, and pointed out to Prokofiev: 'right here, Pyotr Ilyich bungled his score'. But what is important is that all of this is normal. And when the multi-volume biographies are published, that will become obvious to everyone.

If the problem, as stated above, is of such paramount importance with regard to historical figures, just imagine the extent of the problem in writing about our own contemporaries! Moreover, defending Shostakovich's kindness is not so selfless after all. Someone reading one of his attacks might easily think: 'and what if he also said something about me! And this Volkov put it in writing. Let's hush up everything and it will be more peaceful for everyone'. For example, I read Dmitry Dmitriyevich's correspondence with Shebalin. And what if this correspondence were to be published in its entirety? In one of the letters, with the foulest language, Shostakovich writes about Zhelobinsky, saying that he is a scoundrel, that he shot his wife in the . . . .[28] And this was written by a Shostakovich who was certainly no longer wet behind the ears.

[28] The ellipsis in Drubachevskaya's article stands for the word 'cunt' in the original letter. –EDS.

The story that unfolded in front of me . . . As a man dealing with Shostakovich's works, it only makes me want to weep. Valerian Bogdanov-Berezovsky[29] received one hundred letters written by the young Shostakovich, who, at the time, still did not conceal his feelings. After Valerian Mikhailovich's death, a committee was created to sort out his archives. I was also invited to look at the papers. In one of his diaries, I read a statement whose shattering effect I still feel today: Mitya came (according to the diary, he must have been sixteen years old), and for three hours they talked about the kike domination [*zasil'ye zhidov*] in the arts. Nowadays this seems unbelievable and not only with regard to Shostakovich: how could Mitya have talked about such a topic with anyone; especially, how could he have talked with Bogdanov-Berezovsky about it. B.-B. had been my patron in Leningrad, it was thanks to his intercession on my behalf that the book about the young composers was published. I also knew V. M. as a true gentleman . . . . For me, this is the most striking evidence that a person does change, and changes a lot and assuredly not always for the better, but in various directions. A man acts differently at different times of his life, during the various days and hours of his existence. But we say: 'this man is a genius, we love this genius, we recognise his art, therefore he must be a saint'.

This is an utterly false premise. Who can say that Shostakovich died an anti-Semite? No one. But here it comes to light that there was a time when he was able to talk about such a topic with his friend without interrupting him with a 'have you gone mad?!'

And what happened to the letters?

These members of the committee in a zealous, sycophantic impulse asked Dmitry Dmitriyevich what they should do with them, and he answered: 'bring them to me'. And he destroyed them. Only a short excerpt was preserved, because Bogdanov-Berezovsky published it earlier. This single excerpt is a priceless testimony of Dmitry Dmitriyevich's

[29] Valerian Mikhailovich Bogdanov-Berezovsky (1903–71), music critic and composer. He was a close friend of Shostakovich during the early 1920s. –EDS.

philosophy at the time, and imagine, there had been one hundred of them! When I asked Shostakovich why he did such a thing, he said that he had used too much crude language. Thus, Chopin could swear in his letters and name by name the female organs, but Shostakovich was not permitted to do the same. I truly hope that his letter to Shebalin won't be destroyed. If it is, people will then tell me: 'you are out of your mind, it is not possible, Shostakovich would never write such a thing!'

Yes, and Mozart was permitted to say and write almost everything he felt like saying, and, at the same time, he was the genius among geniuses of harmony and beauty.

They have finally caught up with Mozart. In the West, they recently published his complete 'pornography' containing not only the letters in which he discusses, in whatever terms he chooses, all his sexual problems, but also his music with its obscene lyrics, lyrics which, it turns out, Mozart himself had composed.

And this did not hamper his writing the Requiem and Magic Flute.

When 'pornographic' texts by Pushkin or Lermontov are published by a state publishing house, and not by a black-market outfit, this will be one of the signs that this process of writing real biographies is accelerating. Then, perhaps, the politically pure will decide that Shostakovich, too, had the right to express himself as he wished.

Berta Aleksandrovna Malko told me how Prokofiev was made indignant by Shostakovich's 'obscene music' in *Lady Macbeth of the Mtsensk District*: 'The waves of lust keep on coming and coming'. And what about Stravinsky's statements about Shostakovich's music! I found it amusing when, in one of his interviews, Rostropovich declared: 'One of these days I am going to write a book and tell what Shostakovich said to me about Stravinsky and vice versa'. Incidentally, some things have already been published in English, but that is a totally different matter. What Stravinsky did with respect to Shostakovich cannot be called anything less than political denunciation. He exerted every effort to prevent Shostakovich from coming to the US, considering him his rival, and treated him ruthlessly as a competitor. When, in 1949, Shostakovich came to the US for the first time, Stravinsky, having branded him as an envoy of communist ideology, succeeded in having Shostakovich's invitation to Yale cancelled. And Dmitry Dmitriyevich knew it. At the time, at a press conference, Nicolas Nabokov, Stravinsky's man, completely under his control, stood up and, at the great master's instigation, said: 'Dmitry Dmitriyevich, here, in this article in *Pravda*, Stravinsky and Hindemith are condemned. Do you side with this condemnation or do you consider that *Pravda* is incorrect?' You can guess that none of the American correspondents would have asked such a question. They couldn't have cared less! After all, they had Shostakovich himself in front of them! The next day, *The New York Times* appeared with the headline: 'Shostakovich denounces his colleagues'. This was because the trembling and pale Shostakovich was incapable of saying anything at the press conference. This was a war fought without rules.

In our conversations, Shostakovich did talk about his grudges against Prokofiev, including the one that Prokofiev did not understand his music – Prokofiev did not like something about the tremolos of the Fifth Symphony – and this was included in the memoirs. Several years later, after I was already in the States, I read letters from Prokofiev to Shostakovich that had been published in the Soviet Union. And what did I see in one of those letters? That very same criticism of tremolos. Personally, I can understand a person hiding his life-long resentment regarding this silly question of tremolos. I kept being told: 'see, Shostakovich did say good things about Prokofiev at that time and in that place'. In other words, people wanted to believe that if he had once said something about someone, it was an opinion written in stone. But things do change. The year 1948 was one thing. That was when they were both in the same boat. The year 1954 was another: then it was necessary to rehabilitate Prokofiev, and Shostakovich did everything in his power to see that he was awarded the Lenin Prize posthumously. It was still another thing when Prokofiev became a universally recognised composer and it was possible to remember offences inflicted in youth or at a later, mature period of one's life. In his youth, Dmitry Dmitriyevich could adore Prokofiev and be under his influence. However, later on, and this is quite obvious, they both found themselves laying a claim to a position of certain importance. At present, it seems that we somehow forget the following fact: Shostakovich was the first of them to receive the Stalin Prize in music, while Prokofiev was granted the same prize two or three years later. A biographer's task is to establish what the atmosphere was in 1943 or 1944, why things happened the way they did, and restore the true context of events.

Up until now – I am again going back to the theme of the biography – Shostakovich's complete correspondence has not been published, and this is the main source for any future biography. What has been published are some selected texts, which in *Sovetskaya Muzyka* we used to call 'abdrashki' [official materials].[30] It is in the letters, no matter how much they are weighed, thought over, and polished that we can find first-hand information on a life. Only when these letters are published will it be possible to recreate the authentic – year by year – lifetime of Shostakovich.

In Shostakovich's life there are many obscure and intriguing pages. For example, even now I still do not clearly understand Shostakovich's position regarding RAPM [Russian Association of Proletarian Musicians], but that connection clarifies many a thing in his subsequent choice of friends. Read Shostakovich's address at the anniversary of RAPM's dispersal in Leningrad. He so clearly did not share his colleagues' enthusiasm regarding this matter. My feeling for the man, my ability to understand him, my knowledge of his psychology and the way he expressed himself, compels me to think that he was speaking sincerely: when Dmitry Dmitriyevich begins paraphrasing Saltykov-Shchedrin,[31] for me this is the first sign that he is using his own words. He recalls how all of them went around like the citizens of Glupov [Fool-City], embracing one another. This is authentic Shostakovich. An additional fact: he chose his friends

[30] Since then, Isaak Glikman's book has appeared: *Pis'ma k drugu: Dmitry Shostakovich Isaaku Glikmanu* (*Letters to a Friend*), DSCH, Moscow/ Kompozitor, St. Petersburg, 1993. –EDS.

[31] Mikhail Saltykov (1826–89), who wrote under the pseudonym N. Shchedrin, was one of the greatest Russian satirists. He is famous for his portrayals of the 'tragic truth of Russian life' and mockery of the highest Russian officials, often via Aesopian language. –EDS.

from among RAPM's leading figures. What did that mean? One of the possible answers is that RAPM felt a deep hostility toward Prokofiev and considered him an alien and a foreigner, while it was Shostakovich who received their commissions. The Second and Third Symphonies went through RAPM.

The reality of a situation is much more complex than all our contrived schemes! ... They say: 'oh! Shostakovich suffered so much during the times of RAPM that he must have hated it'. Yu. Levitin, too, tried to hit L. Lebedinsky with the fact that, since he had been a member of RAPM, he could not therefore also have been a friend of Shostakovich.[32] However, nothing is as straightforward as some would like it to be. Those who found themselves closer to Shostakovich after the war were the members of RAPM who, around 1948, were no longer in the main orbit (Lebedinsky, at the time, had been sent to Bashkirya). The 'newcomers', such as M. Koval' or V. Zakharov, were now the main attackers of Shostakovich.

Thus, the objections raised to Dmitry Dmitriyevich's memoirs are based either on ignorance of the facts (and a reluctance to find them), or on hypocrisy, whether conscious or subconscious. Shostakovich's true image is besmirched under layers and layers of falsehood and ignorance. They are heaped up not only on Shostakovich, but on any important figure in the world of arts – be it Eisenstein,[33] Mayakovsky[34]

[32] Yury Levitin, 'Fal'shivaya nota, ili Grustnyye mysli o delakh muzykal'niykh' ('A False Note: Some Sad Reflections on Musical Matters'), *Pravda*, 11 November 1990, p. 3 (hereafter Levitin, 'A False Note'). *Cf.* p. 493. –EDS.

[33] Sergey Mikhailovich Eisenstein (1898–1948), film director, teacher and theorist best-known for his use of montage (arbitrarily chosen images, independent of the action, arranged for maximum psychological impact) and for the film classics *Potemkin* (1925), *Alexander Nevsky* (1938), and *Ivan the Terrible* (Part I, 1944; Part II, 1946, but released only in 1958, after Stalin's death, because it was thought to allude to Stalin's terror). –EDS.

[34] Vladimir Vladimirovich Mayakovsky (1893–1930), a leading futurist poet, whose style is often coarse and intended to shock. He is also known for the plays *The Bedbug* and *The Bathhouse*, satires of Soviet philistinism and of bureaucratic stupidity and opportunism under Stalin. –EDS.

or Bulgakov,[35] although much more has been elucidated about the latter than the others. When I read in N. Roslavets's biography – the shortest one in existence[36] – that he worked several years as a Soviet censor, I immediately saw him in a new light. You ask: 'but what was he doing as a censor, even if it was only in the first years immediately following the revolution?'

You have a perfect example of this schematic way of thinking developed by our whole era. Some classification schemes forbid us to cross their boundaries. We have numerous shelves, where the phenomena are spread out: periods, trends and types – some sort of musicological jargon. The a priori *concept that a single individuality does not confine itself to any scheme, nor comply with any specific trends – characteristics which make it, in the first place, unique and allow it to enter the realm of art – this concept, even today in every aspect you look at it, is left behind the door. This pulling the ears in order to make the model fit has become so imbedded in our flesh and blood that no one can see how much time will be needed to 'hammer it out'.*

As for me, it seems that all the developments in this field are now taking place at an unbelievable speed. When *glasnost* was announced, I was surprised by quite a different issue – that so little had been written by the cultural historians 'for the drawer'. A significant part of what is published is based on fashion. I fully understand that twenty or even ten years ago it would have been impossible to publish an objective biography of Pushkin, Lomonosov, Derzhavin or anyone else. But nowadays, when it is possible, we discover that no one

[35] Mikhail Afanasyevich Bulgakov (1891–1940), playwright, novelist and writer of short stories, appreciated especially for his humour, wit, satire and bitter irony. Known principally as a playwright during his lifetime, he received posthumous recognition as a novelist with the publication in the 1960s, mostly in the West, of many of his satirical works, especially his masterpiece, the Gogolesque fantasy *The Master and Margarita*. –EDS.

[36] An entry in B. Bernandt, I. M. Yampol'sky and T. Ye. Kiselyova, *Kto pisal o muzyke, Bio-bibliografichesky slovar' muzykal'nykh kritikov i lits, pisavshikh o muzyke v dorevolyutsionnoy Rossii i SSSR* (*Who Wrote About Music, A Bio-Bibliographical Dictionary of Music Critics and People Who Wrote about Music in Pre-Revolutionary Russia and the USSR*), Sovetsky Kompozitor, Moscow, 1989. –EDS.

has written such a biography of Derzhavin, but rather found it necessary to reprint Khodasevich's.[37] No one in Russia wrote an extensive biography of Dostoyevsky, and so the only solution is to translate an American author.

There may be something, but our publishing houses are so slow. It takes years to get a book published. And now, generally speaking, no one knows what will happen: the publishing houses have one foot in the grave.

Our prominent researchers are perfectly able to deal with such things. Nonetheless, our humanistic elite evidently did not devote itself to the 'imperishable'; instead everyone trilled away like nightingales – which is the norm for those who are novelists, poets, painters or composers. But the field of biography requires selfless devotion to digging for facts, marshalling this material and digesting its significance. But, for the time being, this field is still a desert. I try to keep abreast with your recent publications: that mass of reprinted editions, exact copies of earlier works – hastily put together and quickly reissued. The publishers have no time, nor do they even consider it necessary, to write a new preface or even a commentary. They simply grab editions that go back to the times of Suvorin,[38] and there you are. At the moment I am interested in everything linked with Petersburg. Well, what happened? There was a popular book by Pylyayev;[39] they also reprinted Antsiferov[40] and Stolpyansky's *Muzyka i muzitsyrovanye v starom Peterburge* [*Music and Music-making in the Old Petersburg*].[41] But that was it. Wherever you look, it's the

[37] Vladislav Felitsianovich Khodasevich, *Derzhavin*, Sovremennyiye zapiski/Annales contemporaines, Paris, 1931; reprinted Kniga, Moscow, 1988. –EDS.

[38] Aleksey Sergeyevich Suvorin (1834–1912) a Russian journalist, publisher and owner of many bookstores. –EDS.

[39] Mikhail Ivanovich Pylyayev, *Stary Peterburg* (*Old Petersburg*), 2nd edn., A. S. Suvorin, St Petersburg, 1889. –EDS.

[40] Nikolay Pavlovich Antsiferov, *Dusha Peterburga* (*The Soul of Petersburg*), Brokgauz-Efron, Petersburg, 1922; reprinted Kniga, Moscow, 1991. –EDS.

[41] Mysl, Leningrad, 1925; reprinted Muzyka, Leningrad, 1989.

same thing. You cannot blame the authors: they have to earn their money somehow to survive. But a fact is a fact: the work has just begun and it will be a long process. We still lack the meticulous, objective and unbiased habit of gathering facts. For the time being there are amusing tidbits: in a biography of Musorgsky it is acceptable to kick Tchaikovsky and, in a biography of Tchaikovsky, to kick Musorgsky. However, to criticise Rimsky-Korsakov himself when writing a biography about him is utterly inadmissible.

We sit on a heap of materials and are incapable of rising above them because no objective criteria exist: they have been taken away by the upheaval of our era. The establishment of the new criteria is going to take a long time. Almost everyone is a member of something. But whereas before there used to be one sole 'Party principle', now there are multiple principles.

Yes, and a further obstacle is the lack of objectivity. The subjective identification with one's hero is definitely unacceptable in a researcher and writer.

Let's go back to Shostakovich. How did the attitude toward his music change, here, in the West?

I am not very comfortable talking about that subject. What is important, though, is the music itself and the efforts by the performing artists: first and foremost, by such artists as Mstislav Rostropovich, Vladimir Ashkenazy, Rudolf Barshai and Neeme Järvi. I want to talk, in particular, about Maxim Shostakovich. The reviews of his concerts are often exceptionally telling: people write that his interpretations opened their eyes. Maxim conducts the New Orleans Symphony Orchestra and he is recording the complete cycle of Dmitry Dmitriyevich's symphonies with the London Symphony. This will be something like the fifteenth complete cycle in the process of being recorded in recent years in the West. Nowadays, Shostakovich runs even with Mahler and, at times, ahead of him; and he has joined the ranks of symphonists of Beethoven's stature.

Some fifteen years ago, the attitude toward his music was quite different. For years I have been gathering press clippings – comments on Shostakovich's music. And based only on the materials gathered from New York's newspapers, especially *The New York Times*, I possess a unique, from a sociological point of view, collection which bears witness to the dramatic increase in his popularity. I remember how, after my coming here, I kept trying to convince people that Shostakovich was the Dostoyevsky of music. Everyone made a wry face and smiled. This was due to the fact that here Dostoyevsky is very widely read and honoured, while Shostakovich was still considered Stalin's lackey. They wrote that Shostakovich was the author of second-rate music for second-rate movies. The 'preferred word' for describing his music (his symphonies!) was: 'bombastic'.

How many times in the '60s and early '70s did we read such pronouncements in the journal Melos, *for instance*!

The first histories of twentieth-century music began appearing when the century was only over fifty-years old. These did not give much space to Shostakovich's art – it was thought that he belonged to the nineteenth century. The avant-garde saw him as some sort of dried-out academician. But everything changed before my eyes. When a composer is accepted but his music sounds not quite right, American critics often blame the performers. And vice versa. For example, about Tchaikovsky, it is often written that the artists mightily played his long, watery and boring Trio. Till this day! The same things are said about Rachmaninov and, to an extent, Skryabin. But Shostakovich, before my very eyes, changed from an author accused of all kinds of sin to one who can have no sin. He is correct always. Only the performer can be incorrect. The comparison with Dostoyevsky is also accepted. The memoirs had a role, and this is not just my personal opinion but that of the authors of numerous articles. The book has been translated into twenty languages. I am no longer told where a translation is published nor do I receive complimentary copies. Thus, one learns that the book has been published in Yugoslavia only by the fact that it has been paid for. I have neither the Spanish nor the Polish edition, which, at the time, was published underground by the printing house of Solidarity. The only thing I saw was its review. The total printing of *Testimony* amounts to half a million of copies, which is unheard of for the memoirs of a complex, contemporary composer. This is not the Beatles or Gershwin. I do not think that there is a performer of Shostakovich's music in the West who has not read this book. I am recognised and approached by people in the most unexpected places. Last year I was vacationing, as usual, in Tanglewood, and on one fine day I was listening to Mariss Jansons conducting Shostakovich. Yo Yo Ma approached and told me of the significance *Testimony* had had for him – it completely transformed his understanding of the composer's art. Naturally, I was touched. Or here, in New York, where people are not such avid readers as in Moscow and Leningrad, I was elated to see my book in the hands of a man sitting in front of me in the subway, or in the hands of a young man reading these memoirs aloud to his girl, in a restaurant. What could be more pleasant and moving!

Another additional point: in England and America a book *The New Shostakovich*[42] was published, whose entire concept – acknowledged by the author himself – was completely based on the memoirs.[43]

How did your life turn out here?

While working on the book I had no notion of what the Western cultural *realia* were and, generally, I did not think

[42] By Ian MacDonald, Fourth Estate, London/Northeastern University Press, Boston, 1990. –EDS.

[43] On this point, MacDonald differs with Volkov. He states:

> This claim is not quite accurate. My view of Shostakovich's music altered as a result of reading Solzhenitsyn's *The Gulag Archipelago* in 1978. I wasn't aware of *Testimony* until 1980, by which time my conception of Shostakovich had already extensively changed through a mixture of close relistening and research. Apart from the many new facts it conveyed, what chiefly struck me about *Testimony* was its bleak wit, which caused a further shake-up of my ideas. I was also electrified to find many confirmations of my intuitions about certain characteristic passages in the composer's works (e.g., 'Awaiting execution is a theme that has tormented me all my life. Many pages of my music are devoted to it'). However, my initial revelation of what Shostakovich's music was about came from *The Gulag Archipelago*, a book I found shattering and which obsessed me for several years afterwards.
>
> Ian MacDonald, letter to the editors, 8 June 1996.

On comparisons between *Testimony* and *Gulag*, *cf.* p. 34. –EDS.

about it. I was thinking about the mission entrusted me. However, when my wife and I arrived here, I was faced with the problem of survival, of how to make a living. Naturally, the idea of changing professions was utterly unthinkable. Should I become a computer programmer as so many others did? Or, for example, do you remember Dima Frishman, who edited a collection about Sviridov?[44]

Of course, he had worked with us for a short time.

Well, when I saw him last, he was behind the wheel of a taxi. Where he is now, I don't know. And how about Genrikh Orlov? He is also working outside of his field. He has his own interests, but he doesn't write; life certainly dealt him a blow. Another musicologist from Leningrad became an accountant – he has to support his family. Actually, to take root here is unbelievably difficult and during my first years the fact that *Testimony* was a resounding success helped me very much. However, to survive only on the royalties in a city as expensive as New York was impossible. We bought an apartment that cost an enormous amount of money. And I found a topic, which I considered an honour to write about and which turned out to be, from a commercial point of view, a success. To make the story short, on Broadway, not far from our house, I happened to see Balanchine. I went up to him – on my wife Marianna's instigation and urgent request: I would not have dared to do it myself and she simply pushed me toward him. So, I approached him and we began talking about Tchaikovsky's music. It turned out later that his music has always been extremely dear to Balanchine, even painfully dear and close to him (when we were working on the book, one of our tasks was – we simply agreed on that – to increase the stature of Tchaikovsky's music). This was sheer luck and coincidence.

Balanchine very seldom spoke with journalists. In the list of articles written about him during the years he has lived in America, there are only three or four pieces of his own. This means that he absolutely did not allow his inner self to be revealed. But at the same time, his theatre became a magnet

[44] Dmitry Vladimirovich Frishman, *Georgy Sviridov*, Muzyka, Moscow, 1971.

for the elite of New York. I remember how, at one time, people in Moscow would flock to the premieres of the Taganka Theatre – that is how people here flocked to Balanchine's premieres. In the concert hall one could see philosophers, painters, poets, everyone you would wish, except for, incidentally, musicians. The usual story! This is why, when Balanchine died, the most diverse American newspapers, which never would have agreed on Reagan's or Bush's or anyone else's rating, in this particular case concurred in their appraisal of Balanchine, unanimously calling him one of the three greatest geniuses of the twentieth century – the equal of Stravinsky and Picasso. Not such a bad result for Russia: two out of three. And Nathan Milstein – he is another one from Russia, also a graduate of the Petersburg Conservatory, which I, a humble man, had the privilege of graduating from, too. As it turned out, this particular fact had an important meaning for both Balanchine and Milstein in their choosing me and agreeing to talk with me. The result of this work became Balanchine's and Milstein's memoirs,[45] which were translated into many languages.

Presently I am working on a book about the arts in Petersburg, and there is a publisher who is willing to pay me for this work and is patiently waiting for me to complete this huge volume.[46] But there are things that poison my satisfaction with what I have done. I was under the impression that I was not only earning my living, not only opening the eyes of Americans to certain Russian cultural values, but preserving something that could have been utterly lost to the Russian cultural world. How bitterly disappointing it was to learn, then, when it finally became possible to talk with people arriving from Russia, that, in fact, no one has any use for it. There is an interest in Shostakovich's book, but this interest is political. The many requests from Russian magazines and editors that I receive to give them permission to publish *Testimony* come from people who have never heard one

[45] *Balanchine's Tchaikovsky*; Nathan Milstein and Solomon Volkov, *From Russia to the West*, transl. Antonina W. Bouis, Barrie & Jenkins, London/ Henry Holt and Co., New York, 1990. –EDS.

[46] Solomon Volkov, *St Petersburg: A Cultural History*, transl. Antonina W. Bouis, The Free Press, New York, 1995. –EDS.

single note of Shostakovich, at least not by their own volition. They have no interest in who said all of that. At first, in the States, there was also a great political interest, but it seemed to me that in Russia the interest should have been primarily linked to the fact that Shostakovich's music is heard all over the country. But that is not the case. The situation is tragic because even the best performers who come from Russia are incapable of fathoming the true essence and the sublimity of this art.

The Borodin Quartet came here. They played Shostakovich very smoothly, without fully revealing the tragic and sarcastic aspects of the music. I made this clear to Valentin Berlinsky, who was astonished and insulted by my comment: he believed that they were doing their best to express these aspects. What a tragedy! It looks like the smoothing-out and dressing-up of Shostakovich has become so imbedded .... Let me share something terrible: I am not even satisfied with Yevgeny Mravinsky's recordings. He is a remarkable artist, but at the time, in order to render Shostakovich's symphonies more 'passable', he instinctively smoothed out their sharp corners. In a live performance, the conductor was capable of breaking through his own barriers: I remember how astounded I had been with his conducting of the Eleventh and the Eighth Symphonies. But in his recordings, Shostakovich has all the rat-tails combed out.

In your opinion, whose recordings adequately reflect the music?

Those of Rostropovich are amazing. These are authentic documents. Then there is Mariss Jansons with his Oslo orchestra. He interprets the symphonies in a manner that is very interesting, original, unlike anything else. Among the Western conductors, the late Karajan's and Bernstein's interpretations are unparallelled, and among those living today, those of Haitink. G. Rozhdestvensky is doing very interesting things, but he should have a Russian orchestra of a different calibre . . . although he has been working for a long time with the Stockholm orchestra. When Bernstein appeared with as wonderfully polished a 'machine' – thanks to Solti – as the Chicago Symphony, and performed the Seventh with them, for a whole month the earth burned under my feet when I thought of it. But if you have a mediocre orchestra, despite your best efforts, nothing will come out of it. Generally speaking, among the 'big five' American symphony orchestras, the one which appeals to me most is the Cleveland Orchestra, with all its qualities balanced: the soul and the technique are in harmony. In the Chicago Symphony, the technique overcomes the soul. But for Bernstein it was a case when, given technique, nothing else was necessary: he himself would add the rest. He, indeed, forced them to reveal themselves emotionally, overcoming their magnificent, lubricated machinery, whose every moving part functions brilliantly.

Yes, when they came to Moscow, that was exactly the case.

Rostropovich made a currently unsurpassed recording of *Lady Macbeth* in its original version and he gave many unforgettable live performances. Maxim Shostakovich – I have already mentioned him – more than once allowed one to feel the living nerve of this music. And these artists are giving direction to the students in the West. I am afraid that Russian young people have no model to follow and in those visiting Russians with whom I had the occasion to speak here in the US, I do not see any keen interest in Shostakovich.

But I am even more astonished by everything that is going on now in Russia regarding the ballet. Even when the newspaper *Pravda* deigned to write about the centenary of V. Nijinsky, they misspelled his name and called him Nejinsky. Nobody is moved by S. Diaghilev's name . . . .

. . . and this at a time when the Diaghilevs are needed more than anything else. In the publishing house Muzyka for many years there has been a book about him written by I. Nest'yev – and mum's the word. We don't know what else is buried in the publishing houses. And now, works are being returned to their authors, in the form of ready-to-be-printed manuscripts, set up and even in galley proofs.

So what would be the use of talking about Balanchine! In the US, he was worshipped as the creator of the national classical ballet. However, the national renown is not even that important. Recently I read a volume of lectures given by a respected, now deceased, professor from California.[47] More than once he mentions Balanchine's art, calling him *the greatest creative figure of the twentieth century*. Is it possible to imagine that in Russia some well-respected professor, scholar or philosopher (whether it be S. Averintsev, or D. Likhachev, or V. V. Ivanov[48]) would come out in his lectures (not about music, theatre or ballet) with such a statement? It would be ludicrous and it shows how much ballet is falling out of the common cultural scene in Russia.

In my naïveté, I was under the impression that if the Iron Curtain were to fall (although few of us émigrés had great hopes of that), Balanchine would be performed on all the ballet stages in Russia. Alas, I see that even 'Balanchine's train' has left. Under Stalin and after, when our ballet was an original exotic tradition, more for export, had Balanchine's ballets appeared on Russian stages, they could have struck root. Then it would have been possible to recreate *Agon* or the *Theme and Variations* in Balanchine's spirit, using his discoveries – after all, he is the one who had revolutionised the choreographic understanding of Tchaikovsky's music! All this could have formed, if you wish, a splendid nucleus, from which could have sprung the new Russian choreography. But this did not happen at the time, and now I can't imagine a public filling enormous auditoriums and watching Balanchine's complicated plastic movements that recreate the musical development to perfection.

Tell me, in more detail, about the 'revolution' in Tchaikovsky's ballets. Did Balanchine feel the philosophical side of this music, its worlds, and the 'in the looking-glass quality', particularly in The Nutcracker?

[47] Lance Kaplan (ed.), *Mudrik Transcribed: Classes & Talks by Marvin Mudrik*, University of California Press, Santa Barbara, 1989.

[48] Sergey Sergeyevich Averintsev (b. 1937), a specialist in Biblical and Byzantine studies; Dmitry Sergeyevich Likhachev (b. 1906), an authority on old Russian literature, whose many articles and books include *The Development of Russian Literature from the 10th to the 17th Century: Epochs and Styles* (1973) and *The History of Russian Literature from the 10th to the 17th Century* (1980); and Vyacheslav Vsevolodovich Ivanov (b. 1929), a Russian linguist and translator. –EDS.

Of course. He both felt it and embodied it. In *The Nutcracker*, in particular, although this ballet, with its story-line, is the most accessible one. Over here, this ballet has turned into some sort of a cult event. During Christmas, in Balanchine's Theatre, it is performed every day for a whole month. You never can get tickets. It's like a ritual: next to me, in the box, for example, are a grandfather, his children and their children. The grandfather himself, as a child, had already attended performances of *The Nutcracker*.

The paradox lies in the fact that for America – not for the musical critics, but for the people – Tchaikovsky has become a national composer who has no rival. I assume he is such, to a bigger extent here than in Russia, because in the States he has not been imposed on the public, as was done with classic composers in Stalin's times. They imposed a composer on the people and the people were turned off. Furthermore, Russia is a logocentric country and it does not want to clasp composers to its heart, as it does poets and writers. After all, the people were not turned away from Pushkin, Dostoyevsky or Tolstoy.

I think that in Tolstoy's case, they were somewhat turned away, illicitly, by contrasting him to Dostoyevsky, who was portrayed as the seer of the present era. They don't see anything prophetic in Tolstoy, although it does exist, but on another plane. In my opinion, we are on the verge of a time when people are going to carefully reread Anna Karenina *and understand what was really written in it.*

Be that as it may, a person as serious as Joseph Brodsky made a wry face when I began talking with him about Tchaikovsky, and he said something to the effect that his music was coming out of every loudspeaker.

That's correct. In Bulgakov's The Master and Margarita, *it drifted out of every window.*

But Pushkin's *Onegin* also drifted out from everywhere and, moreover, it was studied in school and never ceased to please. No, in Russia, literature traditionally occupies the first place. For music or ballet to be really important, they must both enjoy equal rights in the cultural process, and they require an audience that is, on the one hand, a mass audience, and on the other, a spiritually elite audience. As for the real elite, they kept destroying it. The audience that was left did not have enough cultural depth to begin loving Tchaikovsky.

And what is more important, they kept destroying not only those who were in the auditorium but also those who were on the stage, in order to fit the public. Which is a harmony of sorts.

In the US, the public's most popular composer is Tchaikovsky. They truly love him. They respect, know and study Dostoyevsky, Chekhov and Tolstoy, but as for Tchaikovsky they simply love him. For the Fourth of July national celebration, you hear his *1812 Overture* all over America, and cannons thundering everywhere. Everyone knows the music. I have already mentioned *The Nutcracker*. At Christmas, walking down the streets, you can hear the music coming out of every supermarket. Last Christmas I counted the number of CDs dumped on the market with *The Nutcracker*. I counted seventeen different renditions of this piece from throughout the world. Seventeen! Beginning with Toscanini's. Because they know that during Christmas it's going to be bought, they provide you with every possible choice. When such a thing happens in Russia, it will mean that Russia needs Tchaikovsky . . . .

The same type of symbiosis achieved by Petipa and Tchaikovsky in their time was achieved here by the collaboration of Balanchine with Stravinsky. Generally speaking, we have a new theme – people of Russian extraction who come to America. Stravinsky, after all, did not leave a Bolshevik Russia, but a tsarist Russia. One feels a strong Chekhovian current in his talent. The same current that moved Skabichevsky[49] to stigmatise Chekhov: a cold-hearted writer scribbles on, and a cold-hearted reader reads him from time to time – prophesying that Chekhov will, thus, die in poverty, because nothing good could come from such writing.

[49] Aleksandr Mikhailovich Skabichevsky (1838–1910), publicist and leading literary critic, who from 1868–84 was on the staff of *Otechestvennye Zapiski*. –EDS.

Mikhaylovsky[50] also defamed Chekhov in the same way. That is to say, that Chekhov was ill-suited to the Russia of his time, because what was required was an engaged art which demanded that he rip the shirt off his own back.

In many respects his dramatic work is still not understood. It is perfectly obvious now: Chekhov was the source of the theatre of the abstract. All that mutual inaudibility, all those seemingly eccentric characters (sometimes the actors who take the parts make them look comical, but nothing could be farther from Chekhov's purpose). It looks like the 'realistic manner of playing' interfered too much here.

Even though America is a country with no great interest in theatre, it is unheard of not to have a performance of one of Chekhov's plays going on somewhere. When they are staged by a good company, it is a true event. And I am not even talking about England or France, where Chekhov is constantly performed on the stage. Recently, in the United States, writers received a questionnaire: which writer has influenced you most? Every second or third form returned named Chekhov. Every fifth added Nabokov.

For me, Stravinsky, Nabokov and Balanchine form a Petersburg group that, maybe, in Russia – a tsarist or even democratic Russia – would not have been able to fulfill itself as it did here. Something in their talents 'clicked' here with the needs not of a mass audience, but of an elite one. In Russia, quite possibly, it would not have 'clicked': these artists would have been silenced like some Sluchevsky.[51] That Nabokovian streak that Balanchine also shows in his work will be a perpetual obstacle to his being accepted and understood in Russia. The interest in Nabokov's books that currently exists in Russia is again related to the privileged

[50] Nikolay Konstantinovich Mikhaylovsky (1842–1904), a leading literary critic and editor of *Otechestvennye Zapiski* from 1868–84, and later chief editor of *Russkoye Bogatstvo* (1892–1904). –EDS.

[51] Konstantin Sluchevsky (1837–1904), hailed by some as Russia's first decadent and expressionist writer. He was silenced, in a sense, by his critics: his early poems were given such a poor critical reception that he abandoned writing, making a career in government, and returned to writing only after his retirement. –EDS.

status of literature in public opinion. It is also political to a certain extent. We'll see whether Russian art will assimilate Nabokov's line or accept it as its own. It is possible that after that happens Balanchine's turn will come, and the spectator will then begin to receive his pleasure not from the plots and 'passions' (I am speaking here only about the choreographic process), but from the exquisite synergy of the choreography and the music.

This is the source of all my sorrow, my pain, this is what forces me to somehow shut myself into my own shell. When I read Voynovich's declaration that 99 per cent of his readers are in Russia, I come to the realisation that my readers, real and potential, are, for the time being, in the West.

Recently a friend from Russia visited me who is a noted specialist on the Russian culture of the beginning of the century. We had long talks in which he, in particular, told me that the last extensive discussion about Musorgsky – of a general, cultural nature – took place, it seems, in 1910: so and so wrote something in the newspaper *Rech'* [*Discourse*], while another wrote something else. I listened on and on and asked him: 'You know all this and talk about it so remarkably well. Tell me, my friend, when was the last time you actually heard a Musorgsky opera?' He thought a little bit and answered: 'But I have never heard one'. In other words, it is still the same thing: he knows everything about Musorgsky, but his knowledge is mainly a literary, bookish knowledge: he does not listen to the music itself. Music and ballet have no role in the general cultural process in Russia. They will start playing a role only when a tiny elite minority comes into being. Then high-browed essayists will appear, who will be read widely, not just by musicologists and rare amateurs. In the US there is such an essayist, Susan Sontag. When she writes something about Balanchine, you can be sure that she will be read by the entire educated public. Her taste and thoughts are taken on trust. S. Averintsev could have written about Stravinsky, but no, he wrote about Mandelstam, and he wrote beautifully.[52] And when did a noted literary figure say

[52] Sergey Averintsev, preface to Osip Mandelstam, *Sochineniya v dvukh tomakh* (*Works in Two Volumes*), Khudozhestvennaya Literatura, Moscow, 1990, pp. 5–64. –EDS.

anything about Tchaikovsky? Everything that is written about music, a lot of it very interesting, stays inside the musical community.

Right now, for instance, a lot of things are coming from this community regarding Musorgsky, perhaps even more about him than anyone else. But this does not become an important cultural item.

Yes, this is only the beginning of a very long journey, a very painful process. Furthermore, I am afraid that a substantial class of rich people is also necessary. I say this based on real-life observations. Who are my neighbours at the New York Philharmonic or at the theatre? First of all, they are rich people. These are people who can afford to pay 50 or 100 dollars for a ticket, a considerable amount of money, even for the US. It is true that there is an element of prestige in it; one should not ignore this fact. As well as the fact that the vast majority of these institutions are supported to a considerable extent by private donations and their entire operation is in the hands of the elite.

It is known that the Boston Symphony is supported by private funds, and in its programmes you can read the substantial list of its donors. Just the same, five years ago, there was no decent ballet in Boston. Now they have built a grandiose building that cost millions and all the necessary conditions were provided to have a first-class ballet company. Who did it and why did they do it? The reason was that a new generation of millionaires had appeared in town and it was held at bay when it came to donating money to support such a prestigious institution as the Boston Symphony. To fulfill their ambitions, these millionaires offered a ballet theatre to the city as a gift. It is the same story with the Philadelphia Orchestra: the right to pay for the orchestra is passed on from generation to generation. This is similar to what used to happen at the Mariinsky Theatre: one had to wait for generations to obtain a season box at the Mariinsky – someone had to die before you would have an opportunity to be granted this honorary place. Here in the US, from time to time it is suggested that the audience should be enlarged, that the milieu should become more democratic. But nothing ever comes of it. If young people come to the philharmonic concerts, they are well-to-do young people. It is very rare to see black people in the audience. Most likely you will see them in the orchestra. This is a simple and indisputable socio-cultural fact. All efforts at popularisation will be useless.

They were indeed useless. The audience of our concert halls and opera houses bear witness to this fact. I am not talking about some super-concerts such as when Horowitz came or when Richter appears on the stage; then, the concert hall bursts with concert-goers. In general, we know that for the performances of superb musicians the Great Hall of the Conservatory in Moscow is frequently half empty or even two-thirds empty. And this is when there is a paucity of performances and theatrical productions. As for the price of the tickets, even nowadays there is no possible comparison with the price you pay in the US. I remember how people were horrified when La Scala came on a tour to Moscow. The price of a ticket, for example, for Karajan's brilliant La bohème *was seven rubles and fifty kopecks. It seemed to be an unthinkable amount of money. A ticket for an evening of David Oistrakh at the Great Hall of the Conservatory was three or four rubles, and that was considered expensive. What's the result? All over the country there were thousands of concerts performed by very good musicians, who earned practically nothing. All this enlightenment strove to make art a necessity for the people and, by the same token, to make it 'understood by the people'. This was not the first time – and not only in Russia – that this ideological tandem came into being. Needless to say, it was an appealing idea. The people had it drilled into them that a man who listens to music becomes morally better. That does happen, but not necessarily so. Remember how they loved their classical music on the fascist Olympus in Germany! . . .*

The results are incredibly sad. The 'immovable rock of values' has been destroyed. What was the most priceless, the most expensive 'commodity', became in our country the cheapest one for the consumer, and the government kept this 'industry' going according to the residual principle. Today it is a catastrophe!

The government does not pay, and the public, for whom it is not essential, does not pay either. What is left for musicians to do in a country where not only have they simply nothing to eat, but mainly nothing to do?

The question, you see, is a very complex one. Numerous different processes have become intertwined simultaneously. I am not going to talk about those which are well known, but about the 'particular' aspect of the situation. A time came when a certain generation of city dwellers dwindled out. For this generation, listening to classical music was not only a matter of prestige (this type of considerations also 'worked' in our society), but it was a generation that, under the harshest conditions (of which there is no need to talk here), lived through art, breathed art, and saved itself through art.

What is to be done? I think that each of us should do what he can. You said that at first, in America, the book sparked a political interest, and as a result – the music was heard. Let Testimony *finally be 'heard' here. People are waiting for it.*

Yes, I have read articles that expressed similar ideas: a simply pioneering one by D. Zhitomirsky in *Daugava*, another by L. Lebedinsky in *Novy Mir*, and one by L. Mazel' in *Sovetskaya Muzyka.*[53]

Pay attention to this tiny detail: these articles were written by people who were contemporaries of Shostakovich, who had lived through 'his' life. Grandchildren and great-grandchildren already don't know about so many things. When and how will they find out? What will be the result? At the minimum, truth – as the genius understood it – will be told. And after that? Remember what Galich wrote: 'Fear only the one who says: I know how it should be!'[54]

[53] For all of these, *cf*. Bibliography, p. 753; pp. 472–82 and 483–94, below, respectively. –EDS.

[54] Aleksandr Galich (1919–77), an actor, dramatist, scriptwriter for films, composer, poet and singer of underground songs. –EDS.

TRADITION RETURNS: ROSTROPOVICH'S SYMBOLISM[1]

Solomon Volkov

Nowadays, the interest of Russian educated society is centred on literature. This is particularly obvious to an outside observer. Naturally, in Moscow, Leningrad (and, perhaps, a dozen of the other larger cities) it is impossible to get tickets for the performance of important musicians. But when we consider the intelligentsia, they are scattered throughout the country, from sea to sea, and they purchase books everywhere. The situation is different regarding music. Now, when a return to tradition is so readily called for, so-called serious music has been almost entirely excluded from discussion, even though that tradition, shielded fortunately by the fence of music notation, has never really ceased to exist in the Soviet Union.

The cellist, conductor and composer Mstislav Rostropovich is the personification of a living tradition. In a specific sense, in spite of all his exclusivity, he is a typical representative of the Russian intelligentsia. His entire career – from the young boy who climbed up on the stage holding a state-owned cello bearing its inventory number painted in water-proof blue paint, to being one of the leaders in the modern artistic world – has been representative, when we use the word in its sociological sense.

Rostropovich is, of course, exceptionally gifted. However, that single trait does not place a musician within a tradition. Additional ethical components are also required: an incredible intuition, persistence, and devotion to one's teachers.

Rostropovich was very fortunate when it came to teachers – probably precisely because he needed them so and was truly seeking their support and advice. In my opinion, Rostropovich

[1] Originally in *Znamya* (*The Banner*) (Moscow), 1, January 1990, pp. 220–26; introductory and closing comments revised by Solomon Volkov in 1997. English version by Vèronique Zaytzeff and Frederick Morrison.

had four mentors – in the elevated and vital meaning of the word: Prokofiev, Shostakovich, Britten and Solzhenitsyn. All of the composers valued the great musician in Rostropovich and wrote works especially for him. Solzhenitsyn promised to write a book about Rostropovich. Perhaps he eventually will write it?

The sequence and connections between these four men, as I see it, is not accidental. Rostropovich closely collaborated with the composers, and they, particularly the great English composer Benjamin Britten, enriched and broadened his musical philosophy. These composers also shaped his civic attitude in many ways.

Solzhenitsyn was the one who most obviously gave the decisive push to Rostropovich's sense of civic duty. It is really through this friendship with the writer that much of what would have remained for him purely musical and guild-like (as happened with some of Rostropovich's gifted colleagues) was transformed into views and deeds that converted the musician into a symbolic figure on a national scale.

Rostropovich prefers not to discuss his relationship with Solzhenitsyn; it is an ongoing process and, therefore, private. To make up for it, on a fine New York day, Rostropovich and I sat down to chat about those of his teachers who are no longer with us – Prokofiev, Shostakovich and Britten.

You were the godfather of Sergey Sergeyevich Prokofiev's compositions for cello. Then you conducted his opera War and Peace *and his symphonies. Did the fact that you were a friend of Prokofiev help you?*

I know his method of working and composing. How he wrote and what he thought at the time. I know the importance he gave to instruments in an orchestra. He was really endowed with humour. Sometimes, he simply made fun of instruments. I will never forget what Prokofiev told me about the second trumpet which in his *Symphony-Concerto* plays one low, droning note. I was trying to show Prokofiev my erudition: 'Isn't it too low for a quick tempo?' He answered: 'What do you mean? You don't understand anything! Just imagine how some trumpet player would sit and play, all red in the face! How he would swell out!'

You did help Prokofiev with his work, after all?

Yes. I deciphered some scores for him. Let me tell you about an amusing case. Prokofiev wanted to force me to write some passages for the cello in his *Symphony-Concerto*. For several days I was extremely busy working on that. Prokofiev was outraged and said in anger: 'Young man, you don't even have Brahms' talent! Brahms at least produced a mass of note-books with exercises for the piano. But you, you are incapable of giving me some sixteen measures.' I was rather shocked and thought to myself: how can I go on, if I don't even have Brahms' talent. This was Prokofiev's way of hurting one's feelings. On another occasion, he forced me to erase something from his manuscript. The sheets were on his piano and I sat at the piano, working with an eraser. I finished and said that everything was in order, and left. Suddenly, Prokofiev called me at home: 'I can't play the piano! With the shavings of your eraser, you have completely clogged the keyboard!'

When the Bolshoi Theatre choreographer, Leonid Lavrovsky, had to extract from Prokofiev a gypsy passage for The Tale of the Stone Flower, *he brought a pianist with him to the composer's dacha. The pianist proceeded to play all sorts of gypsy tunes. Sergey Sergeyevich was horrified: 'Close the windows! I won't allow such sounds coming from Prokofiev's dacha!' He was very critical of such tunes. As for Dmitry Dmitriyevich Shostakovich, to the contrary, he was quite tolerant in this regard. He had a particular interest in thieves' songs and others of that vein.*

Yes, yes. On one occasion, he spent a great deal of time on one piece, Braga's *Serenata*, which was famous in its time. Having reworked it for two voices, he was unable to calm down and kept on repeating, sarcastically: 'Here, I have finally done Braga's *Serenata*!'[2]

How about you? Do you like gypsy romances?

What's a better gift than an umbrella on a rainy day? When you are very sad, you have a small glass of vodka and listen to

[2] *Cf. Testimony*, p. 174/224. This tune was supposed to 'play an important part' in *The Black Monk*, an opera planned just before Shostakovich's death. *Cf.* also Shostakovich's letter of 22 November 1972 (Tishchenko, *Letters*, p. 41). –EDS.

a gypsy romance – what could be better? Nothing. There are different types of music. You cannot force everyone to listen to the same thing. You know, I had already been thinking about that in 1948, at the time when the decree about the struggle against formalism was pronounced. At the time I thought – well, who drafted this decree? It was written, after all, by people, maybe ten people, or maybe five. Or by Stalin himself. Well, he did not like either Prokofiev's music, or Shostakovich's. How nice it would have been if Stalin had said: 'Please, compose something that I also would like personally'.

Were Prokofiev and Shostakovich different as men as well as as musicians?

The cellist Berezovsky performed Prokofiev's Concerto for the first time with Melik-Pashayev as the conductor. It was a total flop. When Prokofiev came into the green room, Melik-Pashayev asked: 'Well, what did you think, Sergey Sergeyevich?' Prokofiev smiled and answered: 'Nothing could have been worse!' But his smile was full of optimism.

And what was Shostakovich's behaviour in a similar situation?

He always praised everything: 'Brilliantly done, brilliantly!' It was only when he believed that the person was a great musician that he allowed himself to express criticism. Shostakovich always kept telling me: 'Why, but why criticise someone when he can't do any better?' At times this astounded me. The performance or the composition was thoroughly bad, but Shostakovich stands up and says: 'Brilliantly done, brilliantly!' If Shostakovich were on friendly terms with a person and liked him, then he was capable of flabbergasting the person with utterly unexpected judgments that reflected his innermost thoughts. Nevertheless, as a rule, he was very secretive and very careful.

In your opinion, as far as character goes, who was more national, Prokofiev or Shostakovich?

Let me tell you the following story. Once I was driving Shostakovich to Gorky. We had driven 400 kilometres from

Moscow. It was raining very hard. I looked and saw that the petrol needle was on empty. However, I knew that there were canisters filled with petrol in the trunk. I put on the brakes and almost simultaneously fainted from horror, for I quickly discovered that in Moscow, at my chauffeur's, I had forgotten to get the key to the petrol tank (my petrol tank had a key lock). I lost my head so much that I said: 'Catastrophe, Dmitry Dmitriyevich, catastrophe!' Shostakovich, an extremely nervous person, simply jerked up in the car: 'What? What?' I told him: 'Dmitry Dmitriyevich, this is the situation: the petrol gauge is on empty, the petrol tank is locked, and the key to it is at my chauffeur's in Moscow'.

Shostakovich said: 'Slava, Slava, what are we going to do?' He jumped out of the car, all nervous, and began running around it. It was raining cats and dogs! I looked at the car and saw that the petrol tank had a protruding cap, so pretty, nickel-plated, made in Germany. I looked around and saw a huge metal rod in the ditch. I grabbed it and began furiously pounding on the German cap. Naturally, I would hit it once, while three or four times I would strike the car itself. As for Shostakovich, he kept running around repeating: 'Good for you, Slava, good for you! Everything that was made by a German will be destroyed by a Russian! Everything that was made by a German will be destroyed by a Russian!' That gave me a great rush of strength! I whacked away with an unexpected vigour! Finally the cap flew a long way off ... I poured the petrol into the tank, and we made it to Gorky.

How about the national aspect in their music?

I consider both of them to be very national composers, very Russian. Although in Shostakovich's music there are more Western influences than in Prokofiev's. For example, the influence of the symphonies by Gustav Mahler, whom Shostakovich adored. Prokofiev did not understand this music at all and he himself told me so ... But the tragic element in Shostakovich's symphonies ... When I see how people listen to Shostakovich's symphonies with tears in their eyes, then I understand that, perhaps, Shostakovich was the most Russian composer of the Soviet period. I do not think that Prokofiev's music is particularly characteristic of the Soviet period, it is not about that. Prokofiev came from a different world, from Diaghilev's world . . . From the world of play . . .

You have conducted both Prokofiev's opera War and Peace *and Shostakovich's opera* Lady Macbeth of the Mtsensk District. *These two compositions exist in different versions by the author and in different variants. Which one should be considered the final version?*

During Prokofiev's last years I lived in his house on Nikolina Gora. Prokofiev often said to me: 'I have only one single wish in my life. I don't want to die before hearing the definitive version of *War and Peace*! But he died and that never happened. That means that the last word on *War and Peace* was not given by the author.

Furthermore, Prokofiev very often made many changes in his compositions. When Sviatoslav Richter and I performed his *Symphony-Concerto*, for example, Prokofiev himself was willing to make changes. After Prokofiev's death, when I conducted *War and Peace* at the Bolshoi Theatre, I noticed that certain improvements should be made. For example, at the end, in the victory scene, before the choral epilogue. The stage director Boris Pokrovsky and I made some small cuts there. It was necessary to pave the way somehow for the festive character of the epilogue. We decided to move a short passage of the music up from the orchestral pit onto the stage, so that it could be played by the stage brass band. At the same time a bright light was directed on the stage, and the result was as if there was some kind of a transition. I asked Shostakovich to re-orchestrate this small part of *War and Peace*. I could not have made such a request of a less gifted composer.

Shostakovich was not very prone to make changes in his compositions.

In my lifetime I have never seen a composer who didn't make some changes after a rehearsal. Never. Everyone makes changes.

Even Shostakovich?

Of course he made changes. Without fail. He would change the dynamics, and sometimes he would slightly change the orchestration. That happened even with him. But Shostakovich was, naturally, the most precise composer.

The fact is: it is important for a composer not only to write, but also to hear what he has written. You remember that in 1963 *Lady Macbeth* was revived at the Stanislavsky and Nemirovich-Danchenko Theatre, under the title of *Katerina Izmailova*. (Incidentally, this was the only time in my life that I played in an opera orchestra.) The opera was staged in the disguise of a new version: the author had understood the criticisms, reworked some passages, and so forth. You understand, something had to be done, otherwise the opera would have had no chance whatsoever to be revived.

I was very much distressed that both the new version and the revival were by no means masterpieces. I was convinced that a third version ought to come out of it. Pokrovsky and I talked about the matter at length. Together we went to see Comrade Polikarpov, at the Central Committee of the Party, and asked: give us the opportunity to make some sort of a third version based on the first one and that which had been revised (not so much revised as simplified). Give us the opportunity to stage it at the Bolshoi Theatre! I talked about this matter at the Ministry of Culture with both Furtseva and her deputies. I told them: 'Shostakovich is a sick man. What will happen if we lose him? Give us the opportunity to stage his opera once, at the Bolshoi Theatre, with the best resources available. Furthermore, the author must be present.' Shostakovich, by the way, had accepted, with great pleasure, that we write the final version together . . . But that never happened.

What were your views regarding this third version of Lady Macbeth, *this version that never came to be?*

It is too late to talk about that now. However, Pokrovsky had had a very serious dilemma. Who was Katerina Izmailova, the opera's heroine? Was she a bitch, excuse the term, or wasn't she? Of course she was a bitch. She killed one man, and then a second one. Really there is no room to feel sorry for her. As for Shostakovich, he constantly sympathised with her. She killed and she is sent to hard labour, but the chorus sings: 'Heartless gendarmes'.

What does that mean –'heartless gendarmes'? In our time

gendarmes sent dissidents off to Siberia, to the back of beyond, simply because they didn't agree with something! They hadn't killed anyone. But nobody sang as a chorus – 'heartless soldiers' or 'heartless Soviet police'. Nonetheless, Shostakovich urges us to have pity on the murderess, the branded criminal.

That was exactly what Pokrovsky wanted to make clear – did Shostakovich really hate the social system so much that he acquitted an assassin? Was Katerina really forced into such a situation? Or do human monstrosities endowed with great temperament and external beauty really exist? In my view, Shostakovich showed us a human anomaly. Still, one can't argue with him now: what is done is done. And Shostakovich is no longer with us.

Are you a religious man?

Yes, I am.

Do you sometimes think about death?

You know, I never think about it. Literally never. I know it will come. And just like any normal person, I don't want to be ill for a long time. However, I never think of death. I consider it unavoidable, but certainly not terrifying. I am so unafraid of it, that simply . . .

Does faith help you in your work? When you are working on music?

You know, faith is like breathing. You don't think about it: you must simply inhale and exhale.

In your opinion, how did Shostakovich feel about religion?

For me music is primarily the expression of the soul. It seems to me that any true musician feels the same way. For a great musician the very approach to art is spiritual.

Wasn't Shostakovich a staunch materialist?

Nobody knows whether he was. No one. I can say that with absolute certainty.

How about Prokofiev?

He never gave it a thought. However, his music is notable for its purity, isn't it? Prokofiev's music can be felicitous, or less felicitous, or simply brilliant, but it is always very pure. And purity, after all, is precisely the ideal of true religion.

I can say the same thing about another late friend of mine – Benjamin Britten. He had such a radiant, strong personality. He glowed from inside as if he were a saint, literally like a saint. I believe that Britten came into my life at a very propitious moment.

In what sense?

You know that Prokofiev died a long time ago. As for my friendship with Shostakovich . . . Remember his sarcasm, his deeply tragic sarcasm toward the many romantic trends in music . . . My friendship, my association with Shostakovich, and my adoration could have, no, I am not going to use such a word as impoverish, but all that could have steered me in one direction, to one side.

It is well known that Shostakovich did not like Tchaikovsky at all.[3] So it was very fortunate that Britten came along with his great love for Tchaikovsky. Britten played his music so wonderfully! One day at the piano he played the duet from *Romeo and Juliet* with his constant companion, the tenor Peter Pears, and Galya.[4] Galya even now can't forget that performance.

Britten bestowed on you – I am saying this exactly in this manner – human friendship and tenderness. Shostakovich was the antithesis of that. Naturally, Shostakovich had a lot of tenderness. However, it existed as an indispensable contrast with his unbelievably snarling strength.

How about Prokofiev's tenderness?

It was of a different sort. There were times when Prokofiev reminded me of a dog.

[3] Also *cf.* Maxim Shostakovich's comments, p. 402. –EDS.

[4] Galina Vishnevskaya, Rostropovich's wife. –EDS.

What type of dog?

A very gentle one. A wonderful dog. Sometimes he would do the following: if he wanted to express his love for me, he didn't speak, but he would raise his hand (and it was huge and very long) and hit me on the shoulder. It rather hurt. He underrated his strength. But this was his highest sign of friendship, you might say.

You have talked about your tender and very close friendship with Prokofiev, Shostakovich, and later Britten. Do you feel that you will ever be able to find or meet a composer equal in strength and gracefulness to these three men?

Well, we always wait for miracles. However, the probability is already fading away. I adored Prokofiev and Shostakovich from my youth. I was their pupil forever. As for now, if I were to meet a great composer... I am no longer a youth. The beginning would be different. As they say in chess, 'it's a different opening', and in line with this, the entire game itself is going to be different, up to the end-game.

You asked me about death. For some people, death seems to be black, but for me it's not black at all. It does not frighten me, because for me Prokofiev, Shostakovich and Britten continue to exist. Even though they have died. They continue to exist in a certain form that is different and unfathomable for me. I feel their influence.

When I was given the opportunity to conduct *War and Peace* at the Bolshoi Theatre, they wanted me to fail. I was allowed only three rehearsals and I was bound to fail. Gennady Rozhdestvensky kept saying to me: 'Don't tackle it. You can't imagine what a difficult thing *War and Peace* is! I am quite simply afraid for you!' The day of the performance I went to Prokofiev's grave. I hugged the gravestone. And asked Prokofiev to help me. He did help me. I am convinced that it was he who helped me. I relate to Prokofiev, Shostakovich and Britten as if they were alive; this is the feeling I have. I associate with them at their present level. At the level of a new, different life. There I have a greater balance than I do in this life, over there, outside this limit. This is the reason why I am not afraid of death.

***

When Rostropovich last came to see Prokofiev, the composer was having difficulty breathing: Rostropovich witnessed the decline of a Titan. What had been the most important aspect of their relationship was that the young artist, for the first time, fully and on equal grounds, had taken part in a creative endeavour that had recently been splendiferously defamed as 'anti-national', and was existing off the beaten path, with no hope for immediate success and recognition. This had been Prokofiev's lesson, the necessity of which is difficult to overestimate in Rostropovich's subsequent career.

One can also call Rostropovich literally the pupil of another giant: for a two-year period he took lessons in orchestration from Shostakovich. The dismissal of Shostakovich from the teaching faculty of the conservatory in 1948 was a deep personal catastrophe for Rostropovich; the young musician realised that public events could have deeply personal consequences.

It seems at times that Rostropovich should have absorbed the whole world's bitterness because of his contacts with a man whose genius and fate, for almost fifty years, condemned him to play the role of the exposed nerve of a huge country. Perhaps it will sound strange, but Rostropovich was fortunate. It is as if he lived through and experienced Shostakovich's fate and lot without being Shostakovich. The bitter wisdom which had poisoned the late years of the composer's life did not eat away at Rostropovich's soul; it only marked it.

Prokofiev's newness was for Rostropovich the newness of the past, of the Russian cultural tradition, as if it had once again been unearthed like the ruins of Pompeii. That was the general impression in the first post-War years. Rostropovich, together with its most prominent victims, lived the catastrophe that followed Zhdanov's decrees. The years passed by and Shostakovich became for the artist his own authentic present, a present he would not repudiate. As for Benjamin Britten, he came to Rostropovich from the future.

As usual, Rostropovich was a pioneer. His friendship with Britten, his appearing on the world stage symbolised the yearning of the Russian intelligentsia, which regained its strength in order to tear itself away from the chains of isolationism, to break through the barriers it had grown to hate, and to overcome the artificially imposed provincialism, one of the worst aspects of the defilement of the artistic personality. (Shostakovich liked to repeat the composer Shcherbachyov's words: 'If Beethoven had been exiled to the Niam-Niam Island, he would have composed nothing there'.[5]*)*

Rostropovich, on behalf of Prokofiev and Shostakovich, had to fight ferociously to demonstrate to the apparatchiks the eminence of these composers' works. The same happened with Britten's 'decadent' works, which were further complicated by Britten being a foreigner, a 'stranger'.

Britten, following Shostakovich's example, also composed music for both Rostropovich and his wife, the soprano Galina Vishnevskaya. However, when in 1962 Britten invited Vishnevskaya to participate in the premiere of his monumental War Requiem *in the restored Coventry Cathedral, an incident destined to 'grace' the pages of twentieth-century music took place. The bureaucrats of our fatherland would not allow the singer to leave for England: 'We oppose the fact that the cathedral has been restored by the Germans. It would have been better if it had been left in ruins'. Shostakovich called* War Requiem *the best composition of our times . . .*

We all see how impetuously the craving for both 'glasnost' and openness is growing in Russia, and how the criteria for 'what is allowed' and 'not allowed' are more and more blurred. At the same time, the line between conformism and yearning toward artistic autonomy is becoming sharper and sharper. Here again, Rostropovich was among those who hewed the road, demonstrating once again his spontaneity, his, if it is possible to say this, 'representativeness'. His ardent participation in the 'Solzhenitsyn affair' is but a single example of the musician's civic involvement, although possibly the best known.

Solzhenitsyn became Rostropovich's fourth mentor at a time when the artist felt cramped and confined within solely and exclusively musical limits, when the sudden need to present a united front of intellectuals against Soviet authorities resulted in loud public and symbolic confrontation with a now aging and decrepit oligarchy.

It began with something that seemed rather innocuous: in 1969 the Rostropoviches provided shelter for the author in their

[5] Vladimir Shcherbachyov (1889–1952); 'Niam-Niam Island' is some fictional, unheard-of place, remote from civilisation. –EDS.

dacha near Moscow. Solzhenitsyn spent four years there and during that period the government's pressure on the Rostropoviches kept increasing. When Solzhenitsyn was awarded the Nobel Prize and a campaign was launched against him in the Soviet press, it was Rostropovich who was the first to respond with an open letter in which he defended the writer and recalled how Prokofiev's and Shostakovich's unfair persecution had ended up shaming the country.

In retaliation, Rostropovich's and Vishnevskaya's tours and recordings were either foiled or forbidden. In 1974 Solzhenitsyn was expelled from the Soviet Union and it became obvious that living in the country was becoming impossible for the couple. It was then that I met them. The timing for the meeting seemed most inappropriate: Rostropovich and his family were leaving for the West, and it was clear to everyone that it would be for a long time. His farewell concert in Moscow (Rostropovich conducted Tchaikovsky's Sixth Symphony) astounded me with its dramatic effect; I wrote my review and took it to the editor-in-chief of the journal Sovetskaya Muzyka, *where I worked at the time. The editor looked at me as if I were insane and hid the article in his desk. Nevertheless, my review reached Rostropovich through the samizdat and he liked it. Soon after I was invited to stop by the Rostropoviches' apartment.*

At the time, I remember how stricken I was by his helplessness and vulnerability. In public, Rostropovich is effusive and often appears to be aggressive: you wouldn't step on his corns. However, in reality it is unbelievably easy to hurt his feelings. He is constantly seeking moral support and the approval of the people he loves and respects. At the same time, he has the integrity of a fast-flowing river. Instinctively he trusts nothing that is already ossified. He strives to recreate everything, to do everything anew, and to constantly begin life 'all over again'.

The Romantics considered that music, like sleep, interrupted the ordinary course of our lives. Rostropovich's aesthetics and their inseparable ethics are opposite of the romantic view: he believes that music is beneficial because it brings you back to life itself, and that it is neither interruption nor 'peace and freedom', but instead movement and free-will.

'Where there is no freedom, there is no creativity' was formulated by Rostropovich long, very long ago. This belief, like all born out of torment rather than received from 'above', is dear to Rostropovich. He wants it to become the property of as many

people as possible – both in the East as well as in the West – and therefore he misses no opportunity to remind us of it and, as always, does that loudly and publicly, à la *Rostropovich.*

Today Rostropovich is a truly international phenomenon. He is at the head of the National Symphony Orchestra in Washington, D.C.,[6] *but appears and records all over the world, continuing to popularise the works of his teachers.*

For a time in Russia, a musician-performer (the expression is awkward, but there is no other) could be a symbol: recall Chaliapin. He did not humour the audience, and they respected Chaliapin for the breadth of his nature, his elemental force and his love of freedom. It is worth noticing that Chaliapin's national cult was preserved even after his departure for the West and after he was stripped by the Soviets of the title 'People's Artist'. Rachmaninov, the émigré, always aroused the same kind of enthusiasm and worship in Russia.

With regard to classical music, I perceive a definite maturing of Russian society, a kind of yearning for harmony, if you wish. When Rostropovich and Vishnevskaya were forced to leave the country, it was far from a 'stagnation' act. To the contrary, the government took active measures to confront and break independent and restless talents. Rostropovich, who once again performs in Moscow, can become one of the symbols of a new and mature Russia. He represents the tradition of an elevated art that never ceased to exist in Russia, a tradition of yearning for freedom for oneself and others, both for the artist and his public.

[6] Rostropovich has now stepped down from this position and been succeeded by Leonard Slatkin. –EDS

SHOSTAKOVICH SYMPOSIUM[1]

Maxim Shostakovich, Yevgeny Yevtushenko, Solomon Volkov and Kenneth Kiesler, participants; Harlow Robinson, moderator

Edited by Harlow Robinson

This symposium was held on Saturday afternoon, 25 January 1992, in the Bush Pavilion at Russell Sage College (Troy, New York). It was the first time that Maxim Shostakovich, Solomon Volkov and Yevgeny Yevtushenko, all of whom knew the composer very well in different ways, had ever gathered together to speak about his music, career and influence.

Robinson. I would like each of our participants today to give short introductory remarks about their relationship with Shostakovich and his music. I will translate for Maxim Shostakovich and Yevgeny Yevtushenko.

[1] This symposium was held as one of the events in the international music festival 'Salute to Shostakovich' held in Troy, New York, 20–25 January 1992. The organisers of the festival were Anne-Marie Barker, who was formerly the Co-Artistic Director of the St Cecilia Orchestra of Albany, New York; and Professor Harlow Robinson, then of the Department of Germanic and Slavic Languages and Literatures, University at Albany, State University of New York. Participants included the St Cecilia Orchestra; the Manhattan String Quartet; the Kalichstein-Laredo-Robinson Trio; pianist Pavlina Dokovska; and trumpeter Barbara Butler. In addition to several concerts and this symposium, the festival included a poetry reading by Yevgeny Yevtushenko and the screening of the Soviet films *Hamlet* and *King Lear*, directed by Grigory Kozintsev, with music by Shostakovich. The festival was sponsored by the St Cecilia Orchestra (Kenneth Kiesler, Music Director), Emma Willard School, Troy Friends of Chamber Music, Rensselaer Polytechnic Institute, Troy Savings Bank Music Hall, New York State Writers' Institute, Hudson Valley Community College, Russell Sage College, Downtown Business Council of Troy, and Troy City Hall.

Maxim. I'd like to speak in Russian because, after all, this is a serious matter we're talking about today. About simple matters I'd be willing to speak in English, but not this [audience laughter]. I'm very happy to be here today and received the invitation to attend with great pleasure. This festival provides eloquent testimony to the fact that the interest in Shostakovich and in his music just continues to grow from year to year. And, of course, interest in his political significance as well. And, of course, it's an honour to be here with Yevgeny Aleksandrovich Yevtushenko, because Yevtushenko's name is connected with a whole layer in the work of Shostakovich. They collaborated, of course, on the Thirteenth Symphony (as we call it, the 'Babi Yar') as well as the *Execution of Stepan Razin.*[2] And it's interesting that the composer, my father, always insisted that this piece should not be called Sten'ka Razin, but *Stepan* Razin, as a mark of respect to its hero, Razin. It's very possible that if not for Yevgeny Aleksandrovich Yevtushenko, there would not be the expression of 'the word' as we have it in Shostakovich's music.

And, of course, Solomon Volkov. Mr Volkov wrote a book which is a very important book, and which revealed a whole aspect of the composer and his life in his homeland that was really unknown before. Of course, from the very beginning his book evoked very sharp criticism from the ruling Communist Party in the Soviet Union because it did exactly show the truth of Shostakovich's political views and political feelings. In my opinion, that's the most important achievement of this book.

We have also seen, in recent years, a great interest in Shostakovich among film makers and among dramatists. You probably know that a play was written about Shostakovich

[2] Shostakovich's Symphony No. 13, Op. 113, composed in 1962, is set to the texts of five poems by Yevtushenko, including 'Babi Yar', which deals with the mass execution of Jews by the Nazis in Kiev in 1941, as well as the Russian legacy of anti-Semitism. It is scored for bass soloist, male chorus and orchestra. *Kazn' Stepana Razina* (*The Execution of Stepan Razin*), composed in 1964, is a vocal-symphonic poem set to a poem by Yevtushenko about the execution of Stepan Razin, a Cossack commander who led a popular uprising against the Tsarist Government in 1670–71. It is scored for bass soloist, chorus and orchestra.

(David Pownall's *Master Class*), and that a film starring Ben Kingsley as the composer was made about Shostakovich's life (*Testimony*). Of course, I'm not always happy about everything that I hear written and said about Shostakovich. But, of course, as his son, the slightest details would disturb me. For example, I know that a lot of work went into making this film *Testimony* with Ben Kingsley about my father. It may bear the same name as Mr Volkov's book, but the two works don't have so much in common. For example, I didn't recognise some of the details about the domestic setting of Shostakovich, how he lived. In this film, for example, there are candelabra all over the place, as if we always had candles burning. And according to the film, the Seventh Symphony was written in a cottage at Ivanovo – the composers' retreat at Ivanovo – when, in fact, it was the Eighth Symphony that was written there, not the Seventh. So these little kinds of flaws and errors crop up all over.

But at the same time, all these films and plays, and all the other attempts to portray my father, they do attempt to show Shostakovich in all the depth of his significance, and that's important. So I'm willing to forgive these little mistakes. I'm sure there's going to be much, much more written and said about Shostakovich. A lot of interesting books have been appearing just recently. In Russia, I would say, a successful work on Shostakovich really has not yet appeared and I think that's because there's a weight of political baggage that still prevents people from describing everything the way it really was. Of course, authors and writers who write about Shostakovich are now attempting to correct themselves. With the arrival of *glasnost* this has been happening. But the fact is that we have to tell even more truth now, that in the future we'll have to reach for even greater truth than we have so far. This is true for authors in Russia as well. And, once again, I just want to thank you all for coming here today. I'm just looking forward to hearing what my colleagues have to say and what you have to say as well. So let's listen. And I'm looking forward to hearing your questions after we have had our say. And we'll all be happy to answer those questions.

Robinson. We'll now turn to Kenneth Kiesler. He's going to talk a little bit about the American response to Shostakovich's music.

Kiesler. I'm the only one here who doesn't speak Russian. And I'm going to ask Harlow that if anytime he thinks I need to be translated he should jump right in [audience laughter]. The people up here on the podium have all had intimate associations with Shostakovich, and one, at least, both musically as well as intimately, in terms of blood. My association with Shostakovich is only through the music, which is, in a way, perhaps, the most intimate way. I'd like to just briefly describe my initial contact with these people here because these days I'm conducting a lot of Shostakovich and it originated with some of these people, the fact that I do that. And I'd like to thank them for the role they've played in my life and in the life of American and worldwide musical audiences.

When I was a student in the small town of Nanuet, New York, in elementary school, one morning, seven or eight years old, the music teacher came into the room. On all the other days all we did was sing folk songs out of a book, No. 32, No. 35. . . . But on this day the teacher seemed to be different in the morning, she seemed to be moved somehow. And she came in and she said, 'Last night I read a poem called "Babi Yar" and I want to share it with all of you'. I think that she told us, I remember fairly well that she told us, she heard the Thirteenth Symphony, so I can't be exactly sure when this happened. She read us the poetry and, in fact, she asked us to memorise some of it. And I went home and spoke to my parents about it. My father had lost several of his relatives in concentration camps, cousins primarily, uncles, or aunts, rather, and we talked about it at length that evening. And I'll never forget that day, I have never forgotten the words 'Babi Yar' since then, or the effect of that introduction.

Several years later when I had the position of Assistant Conductor of the Indianapolis Symphony Orchestra and had, at that time, never conducted a note of Shostakovich, only listened to a good deal of it, Maxim Shostakovich came as guest conductor and I was assigned to be his assistant. I was really assigned to sit in the audience and be of help, take notes or whatever, but, primarily, if he were to come down with some sort of an illness, then I would be able to take over and conduct the performance. And to this day, I remember those rehearsals and those performances and have in my score various notes that say 'M. S. says this about this spot' and various notes about when to do what, which I might say were very helpful when I made my Chicago Symphony debut conducting the Shostakovich Fifth Symphony. And whenever there was a question I'd just say 'But Maxim says . . . ' [audience laughter].

I have also recently conducted several performances of the Fourteenth Symphony, and was particularly moved by the text setting. Those texts are not by Yevtushenko and actually were not originally in Russian, but were translated from the works of García Lorca and others. But I was moved last night to think less musically about the music of Shostakovich, but more about the influence of the language on the rhythms and the colours, as well as the depth of the meaning, but just simply the language on the surface as well as what it means. And then the book *Testimony*, which shed an enormous amount of light, obviously, on the music and the creative/political pressures, on the creative environment in which the composer worked. This book helps to explain to those people who don't already feel in the music what was there – because it's certainly evident: the oppression, the struggle, the constant struggle, the darkness, the depth of the feeling, the depth of emotion.

I'm sometimes asked why an American audience responds the way it does. And I don't presume to talk about a relationship with Shostakovich in the same manner as the three gentlemen on my left, and I agreed to be here today somewhat hesitantly for that reason. But why is it that American performers can perform Shostakovich to the extent we do and get the reactions that we do? And I'd like to comment on this because occasionally someone will say to me (the first violinist of the Manhattan String Quartet, Eric Lewis, also confided that someone had said or implied this to him) that because we are Americans we have less of a right to perform this music or will not identify with it or have contact with it in a way which will be real. You know, to me it's a bit like performing, like what an actor does. We are conduits for the music, whether it's Beethoven string quartets or Brahms piano concertos or a Beethoven symphony or Shostakovich symphony. And we, as performers, need to be available, open to let those things resonate in us and respond. American performers and American audiences are particularly responsive, I think, for several reasons. One is we value – our country is built on – a respect for the individual. We go so far as to protect the individual's right to differ from the government, to differ from the majority in any way. And so we're particularly moved when that right – that fundamental right as we see it – is challenged or taken away. In this time when Americans live such an easy and comfortable life – with five-minute lunches and instant breakfasts – I think that Americans somehow long for profound experience, which reminds us of our own struggle to be independent, of our own faith, of our own belief in the value of the individual.

I remember one performance of Shostakovich's Fourteenth Symphony in Houston: in the time between the last note and the first sound of applause, I heard sobbing and someone walking down the aisle behind me. And this was a chamber orchestra and we were in a church. The piece only requires a chamber orchestra, the Fourteenth Symphony. And I could hear the footsteps because of the acoustics and I turned around and the woman was sobbing as she came to the podium and embraced me. And she said she'd never heard a note of Shostakovich before and how moved she was by the experience. And after the performance we talked a little bit about it. She had no idea about political oppression, she had no idea about *Testimony*, she had only heard the music and she sensed the struggle in the music. We Americans live a life which is not devoid of profound experience by any means, but when we have one we revel in it a little bit.

Someone asked me last week, don't you get depressed conducting all this Shostakovich? No, in fact, just the opposite. I think we are all uplifted by the fact that we find a place in ourselves where we are touched by it and we are grateful for having that experience. I conducted the Fifth Symphony also in Japan with the Osaka Philharmonic and various places in Japan. And invariably someone would come backstage afterwards – well, in Japan they're autograph seekers, as you may know, and they all line up with scores, and so there were Fifth Symphony scores signed by dozens of conductors: Bernstein, Slatkin and Previn, and everybody had done Shostakovich in Japan. Why the reaction there? I found that the sound of Japanese orchestras takes on the darkness of the piece in a way that American orchestras don't. And, in fact, I think someone told me there, it was in the magazine the next day, in the review, that the Fifth Symphony of Shostakovich was the most-often performed work in Japan. And it was way ahead of the second or third most-often performed work. So that I think it has some significance. To conclude, I think that in these days when freedoms are threatened all around the world, and maybe even at home, when there are insidious attacks on freedom all around us, when the times are changing in what was the Soviet Union, that it is incumbent upon us to keep playing the music, to keep passing on the story of how it originated, what the soil was which grew this music.

In the same way, the Jews have a Seder every year to tell the story about freedom from slavery, even though they are no longer enslaved. In the same way, we play Shostakovich in a time of greater freedom, to keep reminding ourselves and to re-experience over and over again the struggle of this one man against terrible odds and the tyranny of the government. So, I'd also look forward to answering some questions later, although I suspect that if there's any kind of crossfire that, perhaps, I'll duck. I want to say that it's a great pleasure to be here with these gentlemen and I'm really a little bit in awe to be up here with them. Thank you.

Robinson. Next we'll hear from Mr Yevtushenko.

Yevtushenko.[3] I have never been a specialist in music, and all my thoughts about music could look probably barbarian in your understanding. But I would like to tell the story of 'Babi Yar' and how important was the event which we call the Thirteenth Symphony of Shostakovich. Because it was not just a symphony, but really a social, political (although that word somehow is humiliating to what really happened) and historic event.

I would like to warn you that when I wrote my *Precocious Autobiography*[4] I was absolutely convinced that everything in it was absolutely true, but I was pretty young at this time, and my mother found 54 mistakes. So remember, no matter what someone says about what he remembers, all of us make a lot

[3] Yevtushenko began speaking in English, which I have edited to conform to standard usage. Later he switched to Russian and I translated for him.

[4] E. P. Dutton, New York/Collins & Harvill, London, 1963.

of mistakes. And so when I use dates or something like that, you should be very careful, and do not believe everything that I am saying to you. But I can promise you that I'm completely sincere when I say something – it's how I remember it now. And remember also not to believe the others when they criticise me [audience laughter].

So, it seems to me, you know, in 1958 or 1957, I went to the construction site of a big new hydroelectric power station. And I was sitting together with two nationalistic Ukrainian writers endlessly drinking their vodka, the kind with red pepper inside – they call it *horilka*. You know, then I was a very young poet, 23 years old, probably even younger, and what surprised me about them was their constant anti-Semitism, because they were playing cards, drinking vodka, reading their poetry, and at the same time openly making some very anti-Semitic statements. I was just surprised. You know, at the beginning I thought they were just joking, they're playing at being anti-Semites, like bad actors, but afterwards I learned that they believed what they were saying. They *were* anti-Semites, real ones. And I met one writer there, Anatoly Kuznetsov; I already liked very much one of his short stories.[5] But these Ukrainian writers said they suspected that he was a Jew. They thought there was something suspicious about him. And they asked the editor of the local newspaper to show them material on his background. And the editor was terribly frightened and he opened his safe and he showed them Kuznetsov's autobiography, written in his hand. It was not a formal autobiography, written very romantically, even a little bit stupidly romantically. But he described his childhood and how he was a witness to the tragic slaughter of Jews at Babi Yar. And so these Ukrainian writers said, oh, of course, he is a hidden Jew, because he is describing what happened in Babi Yar, and with such sympathy.

When I heard the Babi Yar story for the first time in my life, it was a hidden story. Some old people probably, some

[5] Anatoly Kuznetsov (1929–79) was born in Kiev. In 1966, he published the controversial novel *Babi Yar*. In 1969, he defected to the West, where he published a new version of the novel that included passages previously cut by Soviet censors.

people in Kiev, they knew it but it was not very widely promoted. There was even one very good poem before mine, by Lev Ozerov – a very good poem, I like it very much. Wonderful poem, wonderful. Not worse than mine, believe me. But just by some coincidence of circumstances, my poem became famous. But this short poem about Babi Yar was written by Lev Ozerov. And afterwards I asked Anatoly Kuznetsov to tell me something about Babi Yar, and he spent the whole night telling me this story of Babi Yar. And he promised when I come to Kiev he'll show me Babi Yar. So he fulfilled his promise and I warned him about these Ukrainian nationalists and how they were digging around in his background. And so, he brought me to Babi Yar. He showed me this ravine, I was so impressed at that time, and that night wrote my poem 'Babi Yar'.

And I was scheduled to give a performance, to read my poems, in the center of Kiev. (We Russian poets always read each other our new poems immediately by telephone. I hope this tradition never dies.) So I recited it to some people, so that even before this open reading my poem was known in Kiev. The Ukrainian authorities were terribly afraid when they found out, but it was too late to cancel my performance. Why were they afraid? For one thing, they couldn't accuse me of being anti-Ukrainian, because I have Ukrainian blood in me, I admire Ukrainian poetry, Ukrainian culture. But it's a fact that some Ukrainians participated in the shooting of Jews at Babi Yar. The Germans ordered them to do it so they wouldn't have to dirty their own hands, they ordered them, and many Ukrainians agreed, they shot and killed the Jews. And they tried to hide this fact later, knowing that it was not good for their reputation.

And that's why it was a special situation, and the atmosphere in the hall was very tense when I read – they had ripped down all the posters announcing my reading beforehand. When I recited 'Babi Yar' publicly for the first time in Kiev, I didn't know underneath the big October Hall where I was reading that there was a special cellar belonging to the KGB, where they would torture many people. So it turned out I was reading such a tragical poem about such a bloody event, and standing over the blood and bones of other victims. It was a kind of mystery. And the response from the audience was incredible – and the audience was not only

Jewish, but Ukrainian and Russian. After I read the poem there was complete silence. Abject silence. And I thought probably there was a kind of catastrophe. But it's just that people were, you know, shocked by this poem. And afterwards they began to embrace me, to jump on the stage, one old woman even kissed my hand and I was absolutely overcome, and, you know, I blushed. The same thing happened in Moscow when I read for the first time this poem in the Polytechnic Institute. Even our famous stage director, Galina Volchek, she was pregnant during this reading and her contractions began during the reading [audience laughter].

And so the poem began to be dispersed rather quickly, in spite of everything. And you know, in Russian poetry, this theme of anti-Semitism had not been touched; it seems that Mayakovsky wrote one poem against anti-Semites in the early '20s. And so our authorities pretended that anti-Semitism didn't exist in the Soviet Union. And my poem was published in *Literaturnaya Gazeta* mysteriously quickly, because the editor made his own decision – a very courageous decision for that time – to publish it. Before approving my poem for publication, he called his wife, and they took the decision together. And they knew that he could be fired for that. And he was fired, because I was terribly attacked, attacked immediately by Party officials. They fired him. And one Russian poet, Aleksey Markov, immediately wrote an answer to me. And they even tried to use other writers' names against me. For example, they tried to use the name of the writer Ilya Ehrenburg against me. But I must express my gratitude to him. He was in Italy at that time, and although he never loved my poetry, he sent a telegram which was published in *Literaturnaya Gazeta* in which he absolutely denied any kind of attempt to criticise my poem 'Babi Yar' with the help of quotations from him.

But they also criticised me with the help of Mr Sholokhov's quotations.[6] And I called up Mr Sholokhov and I asked him if he would receive me at his village home. And he

[6] Mikhail Sholokhov (1905–84), author of the four-volume epic novel *Quiet Flows the Don*, was a very official Soviet writer who received the Nobel Prize in 1965.

invited me, he exclaimed, 'Oh most favourite poet, of course, my doors are always open to you'. And I came to him, I just asked him to help defend me. Actually I didn't want him to protect me. I hoped he would protect my poem, protect it from anti-Semitic chauvinists who were using his name not only to attack this poem, but to attack Jewish people. And he said, 'Ah, you know...'. And he asked me very strange questions. He promised to help me. He deceived me. And I was so surprised when I encountered near his gate a kiosk with a policeman inside. It's not good for writers. And then he dropped one very suspicious phrase. 'Even, *even*', he said, 'I have some friends who are Jews. But let me ask you, why did you publish this poem? It's a wonderful poem, and it's wonderful that you wrote it, but why did you publish it?' I didn't understand him. I said, I asked him, 'What do you mean? If you write a good poem it must be published'. But he said, 'You gave your enemies a weapon against you. You are defenceless now, you just helped your enemies'. He knocked on his table and he said, 'You know in this writing desk, inside my writing desk, there are so many wonderful pages of prose, but I am not foolish, I will not publish them, I will not give my enemies the chance to use these pages against me'. It was something very paranoic, it was something very foreign to me. And so he promised to help, but he didn't help.

At this moment I got a call from Dmitry Dmitriyevich. I didn't know him personally at the time. He called me where I lived, in our old wooden building, with its communal corridor, communal kitchen, and bathroom for four families. (Actually it didn't even have a bath, just a water closet – one water closet for four families.) A typical Moscow dwelling for the time. And Dmitry Dmitriyevich asked for Yevgeny Aleksandrovich. But nobody called me Yevgeny Aleksandrovich.[7] My mother even hung up after saying, 'There is no such person here'. But then he called again, and this time we talked, and he invited me to come see him. You know, the way he spoke, his language, he was very polite – in the old St

[7] Yevgeny Aleksandrovich is a formal term of address in Russian, using the full first name and patronymic. Most often, Yevtushenko was called Zhenya by his friends and family. Shostakovich's use of this formal style of address also indicates his old-fashioned Petersburg courtesy, a quality his friends and colleagues often remarked upon. (*Cf.* also pp. 121–23. –EDS.)

Petersburgian style. For instance, you know he would always remember everyone's birthday. He was always congratulating people on their birthday – not only me, but my mother, my sister – he was an incredibly polite and wonderful soft man.

And so he asked my kind permission to compose music for my poems, and I, of course, said it's a great honour and why do you even ask. And he said okay, so I went to see him and I heard the first performance of the Thirteenth Symphony as performed by him, with him singing the solo part and the chorus, and playing the orchestra part on the piano. It was beautiful. You know, I was incredibly touched. You know, I am barbarian in music. I was never brought up with music. But, you know, if I could be a composer, then I would write absolutely the same music. He was a great reader of literature, he understood many nuances of each word. Because other composers also set my poems to music later, and sometimes I was shocked, shocked absolutely. From one of my most beloved poems, 'Sleep My Beloved', one composer made hard rock music. I was so ashamed, you know. It was a kind, lullaby song, but they made it into shit [audience laughter]. Sorry. My English isn't good enough [audience laughter]. The only thing I didn't understand at the time was the ending. Because, you know, I was probably too politically minded at that time, we were so-called young fighters for freedom. Our style was loud, like an oratorio, you know. And I didn't understand this very graceful ending with the harmony softly slushing around so many dead bodies. Because there's a peace there. It's a kind of lullaby for the future, you know, after so many victims suffering and spilling blood. I didn't understand it, so I carelessly mentioned to him that 'I don't know, probably you don't need it'. In my opinion it didn't sound like the end. It seemed to me that everything was falling down, too soft for the ending.

Because we poets of our generation, we were pushing *all* the pedals of that time, playing the whole keyboard of Russian poetry, you know [audience laughter]. And these little sounds trembling like butterfly's wings, it was something strange for me. Not strong enough, I thought. And I was stupid, young, I didn't understand. Because there is a power in softness. There is a strength in fragility. So afterwards I understood it. After all this suffering, the Russian woman who lines up for a piece of something, after this Babi Yar, these Jewish victims killed. And you need, now I understand how we need a little sip of harmony. A little sip of something which is not connected with Stalin's policies, something without Stalin's suffering. Something which is about us. I would call it a sense of eternity. I understand it now, I think we dearly need such a kind of harmony in our lives, even in absolutely destroyed Russia or even in McDonaldised America. We need these little sips of eternity, of softness, of peace. It is a kind of blessing, you know. So I came to understand the greatness of Shostakovich's ending for his symphony. And my poetry didn't even deserve such a great ending, my poetry was lower than this. That's why I didn't understand at that time.

So, of course, it was a really historical event. And what happened afterwards? Dmitry Dmitriyevich wanted Yevgeny Mravinsky, who was the brilliant conductor of the Leningrad Philharmonic, to conduct the premiere of the Thirteenth Symphony. He suggested it to Mravinsky, but Mr Mravinsky politely refused as the result of some pressure applied on him as I heard, or I could suppose. And there was a great Ukrainian singer, Boris Gmyrya, with a really great voice, a shining voice. And Mr Gmyrya, he promised that he would perform the solo part in the Thirteenth Symphony, but afterwards he refused because some Ukrainians exerted pressure on him, and threatened to dig up some stories from his past. Because his past was a little bit dubious, because Mr Gmyrya had sung for the Germans when they occupied Ukraine during the War. And Shostakovich even knew about it. And I asked him, 'What do you think about having someone who was singing for German occupants perform in "Babi Yar"?' And Shostakovich said, 'But he's a great singer'. And that was absolutely your father's style: We could, we *must* give everybody a chance for repentance. But Gmyrya refused, he was afraid, he was deadly afraid of the Ukrainian nationalists and some Party officials.

And so, at the last moment, as you remember, a really young singer named Vitaly Gromadsky was found. He learned the music very quickly, probably in just a few days. He was originally the 'cover', and hadn't expected to perform. And there were many dark clouds around the first performance of the Thirteenth Symphony. But it was a really great event. I never heard of a symphony when people were at the same time crying and laughing too. Because in the final movement ('Career') there are these lines:

A fellow scientist of Galileo's age
Was no less wise than Galileo.
He knew that the earth revolved,
But – he had a family.[8]

People were laughing. You know, for me it was a black hole. Shostakovich was a great man, he was a wonderful man to drink with. That's true. He was so confessional. It was not, you know, stupid drinking. He always was confessing something. He had a bleeding heart. But he had the courage to be honest with friends, telling them how he was tortured by life. He was an incredibly sincere man. Remember that I was younger than him, but he spoke to me as an adult with another adult. And it was a great lesson for me. It also was a great lesson for me how he united so many different themes. For instance, in the poem 'Babi Yar' he treated the theme of anti-Semitism, and tragedy; in the poem 'In a Shop', Russian women lining up for food; but 'Humour' is a jolly poem, a bit more open. And 'Career', a very jolly, very challenging poem. Absolutely different poems. And how did he connect them together, why? With his magic touch he glued these different poems together. So it was a great lesson of composition for me. Because I understood that you could connect everything with everything if you understand the secret possibilities of combinations. It's like the time when an old woman made me a bouquet from her garden, and wrapped goldenrod in lilac leaves. Just like that. It was a great, a wonderful combination, the combination of things that would seem like they could not be combined.

As I wrote in my article about Shostakovich,[9] it's true that

[8] Translated by Valeria Vlazinskaya for the Teldec recording of the Thirteenth Symphony, with Kurt Masur and the New York Philharmonic.

[9] Yevgeny Yevtushenko, 'Genius is Beyond Genre: Dmitrii Shostakovich', *Fatal Half-Measures: The Culture of Democracy in the Soviet Union*, ed. and transl. Antonina W. Bouis, Little, Brown, Boston, 1991, pp. 292–99.

Shostakovich did sign a lot of public letters, denunciations of a kind, and he was ashamed of that and, at the same time, didn't attach much significance to this. And we argued about that. And he would say, 'Yes, I have signed letters that I didn't believe, but I've never written a single note of music that I didn't believe'. And now, when critics like to attack figures like Shostakovich and others of his generation for doing that sort of thing, they themselves commit a moral crime, because how do they know how they would behave if they had ended up in such horrible circumstances. Maupassant has a story called 'The Mother of Cripples'.[10] This is about a woman who gave birth to cripples by order, upon commission, so that they would be used by circuses or sold to various kings, members of royalty. So that while she was pregnant she would do things to herself to make the child be crippled, or when they were born she would put them in some sort of brace to make them grow crippled. And the period of Stalinist dictatorship, the totalitarian dictatorship that we lived through, was very similar to this mother making her children crippled. She made them adopt these horrible, grotesque forms. All Sovietologists say, 'Yes, Pasternak was a wonderful poet and he was a victim of Communism', but they forget about the fact that Pasternak dedicated poems to Stalin. And everybody knows that Osip Mandelstam in 1932 wrote a poem criticising Stalin, but they forget about the fact, or neglect to mention the fact, that in 1936, just before he died, he also wrote a poem praising Stalin – because that doesn't somehow fit into the stereotype, the model of how the person was.

I think if Shostakovich did do anything immoral, then he more than repented by writing the music he did and doing all the other good things he did for people. When we remember or point out that he signed these denunciatory letters, we forget another thing – we forget how many other letters he wrote trying to save people all through his life. For example, he wrote a letter defending the poet Joseph Brodsky. He helped an enormous number of people. And when I was in

[10] The original title of the story by Guy de Maupassant is 'La Mère aux monstres', first published in 1883. It is included in the collection of stories entitled *Le Horla et autres contes cruels et fantastiques*.

difficult circumstances, believe me, he helped me and I was only one of many that he helped. And he had an unusual quality in that he loved other composers and helped them. And he loved music, not just his own music, but all music. For example, three times when I was at Shostakovich's apartment he made me listen to Britten's *War Requiem*, and sat and cried as he listened to it. He thought it was such a wonderful piece of music. I remember he called me once and he said 'Sam Barber is coming, and I don't feel so good. Don't you think you could spend some time with him? I don't want him to feel lonely in Moscow'. So when people focus too much on the political aspects of some of his activity, they forget other things like this, his humane behaviour.

During times, very difficult times of totalitarianism, he saved the great meaning of art as art. I'll tell you something else and I don't say it because I'm a Russian, and not because I worked with Shostakovich, but as a man who's lived nearly two-thirds of the century. There have been a lot of talented composers in this century, but I think that Shostakovich is composer number one of this century, without any question. And he paid for that right through his suffering. He was a man who every day was crucified by life. But notwithstanding the fact that he had nails hammered into his hands, he still played the piano every day. [Maxim Shostakovich broke in here: 'And he said once if they cut off my hands, then I'll start writing with my teeth'.]

So, in conclusion, let me say this. You just said, Ken, how some people have asked you, 'Isn't it too depressing to play all this Shostakovich all the time?' You know for me it's the opposite – when I hear silly, empty music, that's when I get depressed [audience applause]. Great tragic art, even that with the most tragic ending, the very most pessimistic art, such art reminds us that there are such people in the world who understand humanity, the suffering of humanity. And as long as there are such people around then there's still hope left for mankind. Thank you.

Robinson. And now we'll hear from Solomon Volkov, author of *Testimony*.

Volkov. It would be very unwise for me to speak after Yevgeny Yevtushenko. It would be like trying to sing after

Pavarotti. So I will not do it. Let's proceed. He really said everything.

Robinson. Perhaps we could go back to you, Maxim. Since you were also a musician from your earliest years, can you tell us, perhaps, a little bit about how your father talked to you about his music. How did he try to explain his music, and what was he like as a teacher in that sense?

Maxim. It's hard to say because he didn't talk very much about his music. He tried to find people who thought like he did, meaning people that would understand what he was saying in his music without having to be told. Like once he said to Rostropovich, 'Come, let's go to my place and sit and be silent' [audience laughter]. I remember, for example, with the Fifteenth Symphony, I was entrusted with the first performance of that. And he took the score and started like that: 'This is the beginning . . . you get it?' [audience laughter]. 'So I think you see what's going on here, right?' So that's what it was like. And if somebody didn't understand him, then there was just no hope. If he encountered people who didn't understand him, he just didn't have anything to do with them. So when he would encounter people who thought the same way he did, his soul-mates, then the kind of observations he would make during rehearsals were just totally of a professional character.

I said to him once, 'Papa, why do you say so little to me about your music?' He said, 'Well, we don't talk much now but, after all, I've been teaching you for twenty years. I have brought you up, raised you for twenty years'. He really thought you only needed four words when you were giving criticisms about music: 'faster, slower, louder, softer' [audience laughter]. And that's the difference between a performance of genius and one that doesn't have any genius – 'louder, softer, faster, slower'. So that's how he would go through things with me – 'here it changes, and here it comes back' [audience laughter]. And I'm very proud of the fact that he trusted me, believed in me.

Robinson. Solomon, perhaps you could tell us, though, about your meetings with Shostakovich? If you could just describe your meetings with Shostakovich and what kind of a man he was in your dealings with him.

Volkov. Well, I don't know. It is a rather long story. First I was introduced to him when I was sixteen and he was 54. And I had just published a review of the first performance of his Eighth Quartet. And that was a very important piece for him, really autobiographical – his autobiography in sound. And he read everything really that was written about him, at least every review, I know that for sure. Although I know that maybe he didn't read all the books about him. In this he resembles the great Russian theatre director Yury Petrovich Lyubimov. Once an acquaintance of mine wrote a book about Lyubimov.[11] And he left his book with Lyubimov thinking that Lyubimov will read this book about him, about Lyubimov. And that he might even say a few words or whatever. So my friend returned once, and the book hasn't been opened. A week later, the book hasn't been opened. And so he asked Yury Petrovich, 'Did you read the book I wrote about you?' And Lyubimov said, 'Well, it's about my life, yes? I know all about it! Why should I read it?' [audience laughter].

Maxim. Let me add something about the Eighth Quartet. The powers-that-be put a lot of pressure on Shostakovich to give some kind of title to the Eighth Quartet, in order to explain its pessimism. Something about Dresden, or the destruction of Dresden at the end of World War II. And, of course, only a stupid person could not understand the combination in that quartet of his musical signature ('DSCH'), along with the tune of a well-known Russian prison song ('Tortured by grievous bondage'). And the knocks on the door by the KGB, you can also hear them there. So all these functionaries were running around like cockroaches on a frying pan, trying to get him to come up with some kind of appropriate title, because just to leave the number eight somehow seemed to them some sort of mistake, some sort of omission in censorship.

Volkov. I only want to add one thing. You said quite correctly that only stupid people couldn't understand that, but there are still a lot of these stupid people around. And they *still*

[11] Aleksandr Gershkovich, *Teatr na Taganke, 1964–1984* (*Taganka: The Rebellious Soviet Theater, 1964–1984*), Chalidze Publications, Benson (Vermont), 1986.

don't admit that this is an autobiographical quartet. They still say . . . 'Oh here Shostakovich' . . . because the subtitle is 'to the victims of fascism'. So, of course, it was dedicated to the victims of fascism, and to the victims also of Soviet fascism, and the most important victim of all was Shostakovich himself. So he dedicated this work to himself. He felt that he was a victim, and he expressed this very clearly.

Maxim. I remember in our family when he wrote that quartet. He came out and he said, 'Well, I finished the quartet and it's in my honour, dedicated to me'.

Volkov. Well, so I had written a review of the Eighth Quartet, and I could see how important this composition was to Shostakovich and how eagerly he read everything that was published about it. And mine was among the first reviews. Then someone introduced me to him and he said to me, 'Well, I read your piece, I liked it', and that was the first step. I remember still this meeting. And from that moment on some kind of relationship started and then I organised the first staged performance of an opera that was started by his beloved pupil Veniamin Fleishman, who then went to fight the Germans in World War II and was killed, and he didn't finish the opera, and Shostakovich finished it for him.[12] This was really a continuation of a very important tradition in Russian music. You know that Musorgsky left his operas unfinished; *Khovanshchina* was finished by Rimsky-Korsakov and others. And Borodin didn't finish his *Prince Igor'*, which was also finished by his friends and colleagues. This is something unprecedented in the music of other countries – this obligation to finish the work, to preserve it for posterity. And Shostakovich finished this small opera, and nobody wanted to perform it because it was written by a Jew on a Jewish subject, 'Rothschild's Fiddle', from the story by Anton Chekhov. And I organised this performance and, by the way, we invited Shostakovich himself. He couldn't come, but Maxim came, I remember, to Leningrad. And that was very important for Shostakovich because, well, he saw that

[12] This was the opera *Rothschild's Violin*, based on a short story of the same name by Anton Chekhov. Shostakovich completed and orchestrated it in 1944. *Cf.* pp. 128–33.

here some young man was doing something important for music.

Then, a mutual friend suggested to Shostakovich that maybe I was a person who could write down his memories and reminiscences or whatever. And Shostakovich agreed – very hesitantly, but he agreed. And it was a very tortured process, very tortured, very difficult and complicated for me, understandably, but also, I should say, for him. Each time we would meet together in his apartment. I worked in the magazine *Sovetskaya Muzyka* in the same building, so it was very easy, very convenient. Whenever he wanted to see me he would just call me and in two minutes I would be upstairs with him. And he would start off very hesitantly. . . . He would always offer me, by the way, a shot of vodka, 'Don't you want to drink something?' And I would always refuse. It wasn't very appropriate. Now that would be different, I believe [audience laughter]. Oh well, I was working.

And he would start very slowly, his face was always very pale. But then, gradually, it would become pink, almost pink with excitement, because he would remember all his friends that are dead now: one who was banished in the gulag, another who was executed, a third who just stopped working and nothing came out of him, and so on and so on. And, you see, from the beginning I used a kind of device. I wouldn't say to him 'Let's speak about you', because then he would just stop. He wasn't accustomed to speak about himself. I did want him to speak about himself, of course, but I suggested to him that we speak about others that he knew – 'Let's remember them'. And that was very important, to remember other people: that he was willing to do. And, of course, when you start to speak about somebody else you return to yourself inevitably. And that's, by the way, the device, because I continued to work with different people in the same way. I did a book with George Balanchine,[13] I did a book with Nathan Milstein,[14] I did a book with Joseph Brodsky.[15] And with everybody it works, this device. So, if somebody wants to do a book with a star, that would be my advice, to tell him

[13] *Cf.* p. 40, notes 30 and 31.

[14] *Cf.* p. 40, note 31.

[15] *Cf.* p. 41, note 33.

to start remembering about his friends. Then inevitably he will tell something about himself as well. And that's how it evolved, step by step, with great difficulty. And still when I remember all this, it's painful, painful for me. That was my first book of this kind and most painful, yes, and most important, I think.

Robinson. Did you originally intend for the book to be published in the Soviet Union?

Volkov. Yes, sure, sure. And that's why I never made a secret out of it. And everybody, all of my colleagues in *Sovetskaya Muzyka*, knew about it; also the chief editor of the magazine knew. And they even encouraged it because eventually they wanted to publish it. But then, one day, the chief editor invited me in and asked, 'Okay, so tell me, what's this about?' And I told him and he said 'No, no, no, no, no, no. I will not touch it.' And also from VAAP, the agency that would try to publish the book abroad, I received a call with the same message. So then I told Shostakovich that it would be impossible to publish this book in the Soviet Union. That was kind of shock to him, really. And then he decided it should be published after his death and he repeated often, repeatedly, 'after my death, after my death' . . . in the West. And that's how it came to be published in the West, first here in America and then eventually in twenty other languages.

Robinson. Your book reveals him as someone who is profoundly alienated from the Soviet establishment, from the ideals of communism, although, of course, on the one hand, internationally particularly, he appeared as the embodiment of Soviet music. When he would come to America he would make loyal speeches in praise of the Soviet Union – for example, when he came to the Waldorf Astoria Conference in 1949. Was it a revelation to you the depth of his alienation?

Volkov. No, it wasn't a surprise for me. It wasn't a surprise for anybody who knew Shostakovich in the Soviet Union. It was a surprise for me when I came *here* and the book was published. The reaction *here* in the West was really surprising, because I never realised how deep the misunderstanding about Shostakovich was, still is, in many quarters. Let me speak about this incident at the Waldorf

Astoria Conference in 1949, because this is a very good example of how this myth developed of Shostakovich as a Stalinist. At first he refused to go to America because it was right after the infamous 1948 Party resolution about Soviet composers, which denounced all the composers, not only Shostakovich – Shostakovich first, but also Prokofiev, Khachaturian, Myaskovsky, every composer of importance in Soviet Union was denounced in this resolution. So they stopped immediately in the Soviet Union performing most of the work of these composers. It was a natural, you know, Soviet reaction.

So one day Shostakovich received a call ordering him to go to this so-called peace conference in New York that was being held at the Waldorf Astoria. And he refused, saying, 'I can't go. Everybody will ask me questions about this '48 resolution. I can't answer them'. And then a call came from Stalin himself to Shostakovich. And Shostakovich said an incredibly courageous thing to Stalin. And Stalin asked him 'Why don't you want to go?' And Shostakovich answered: 'I feel like I'm going to throw up'. To say such a thing to Stalin's face at the time was an incredibly courageous act. And Stalin pretended not to understand Dmitry Dmitriyevich. 'Oh', he said, 'so you are sick. I will send a doctor to you.' And then Shostakovich said: 'No, I will not go because they are not performing the works of my friends'. And Stalin said 'And who ordered this?' And Shostakovich said: 'You did, you did'. And Stalin said: 'No, that's a mistake. Nobody ordered their works to be banned'. And the next day these works were restored to the repertoire. As I said, he was incredibly courageous. Nobody would stand up to Stalin like that.

And he went to New York partly because Stalin did – at the time – what Shostakovich wanted him to do. That is, to restore all this music to programmes so that people would be able to hear it. And then, when Shostakovich went to New York, American composers were greeting him and they were collecting signatures of all the important composers in the United States to greet Shostakovich. And only one important, great composer refused to sign. It was Igor Stravinsky. That was the only person who didn't want Shostakovich to be in America, to be in New York, to be present, to have influence, to be greeted. He just hated Shostakovich. And he expressed it often. Now we have all the published letters where he expresses himself quite clearly.[16] So, when Shostakovich came and there was a press conference, Stravinsky asked his good friend, Nicolas Nabokov, also a Russian émigré composer, to ask Shostakovich if he agreed with the denunciation of Stravinsky, Hindemith, other important Western composers that appeared a few days before in *Pravda*, the official Party newspaper. In my view it was a provocation. Stravinsky knew very well that Shostakovich couldn't say that he didn't agree with the official Party line openly because that would be an end to him, he would be shot when he returned. And that would be an end to him and to his family as well. And he knew extremely well that he was putting Shostakovich on the spot. And he deliberately did it.

And Nabokov rose at the press conference and asked Shostakovich this insulting and stupid and provocative question. And Shostakovich was pressed to reply, he was

[16] *Igor Stravinsky, Selected Correspondence*, three vols., Alfred A. Knopf, New York, 1982, 1984 and 1985. *Cf.* the following letter to Ernest Ansermet (4 April 1935: Vol. I, p. 224):

> I heard *Lady Macbeth* by Shostakovich conducted by Rodzinski with his Cleveland Orchestra. A well-organized advertising campaign bore its fruit, exciting all the N. Y. snobs. The work is lamentably provincial, the music plays a miserable role as illustrator, in a very embarrassing realistic style. It is in recitative form with interludes between the acts – marches brutally hammering in the manner of Prokofiev, and monotonous – and each time the curtains were lowered, the conductor was acclaimed by an audience more than happy to be brutalized by the arrogance of the numerous communist brass instruments. This premiere (and I hope *dernière*) reminds me of the performances of Kurt Weill two years ago in Paris and all the premiere-goers and the snobs of my dear new country. Happily, this was the only event on this trip in the United States that did not make a very good impression on me. [. . .]
>
> I regret being so hard on Shostakovich, but he has deeply disappointed me, intellectually and musically. I regret it more because his Symphony [No. 1] favorably impressed me two years ago, and I expected something very different from a man of twenty-seven. *Lady Macbeth* [italics] is not the work of a musician, but it is surely the product of a total indifference toward music in the country of the Soviets. How good that I am not going there!

Cf. also Vera Stravinsky and Robert Craft, *Stravinsky in Pictures and Documents*, Simon & Schuster, New York, 1978. –EDS.

absolutely pale and he felt dreadful, of course, but he said 'Yes, I agree with everything that *Pravda* said'. He couldn't answer otherwise. The next day *The New York Times* had a headline: 'Shostakovich Denounces Friends and Colleagues'. And that was what Stravinsky wanted to see in *The New York Times*. And that's how this myth about Shostakovich's support of Stalin developed.

Yevtushenko. I wouldn't entirely agree with the use of the word 'provocation' here, although I certainly appreciate what your book has done for Shostakovich's reputation. I think it's a question of the different psychology of two different people. The difference was that Stravinsky was sitting under a spinning fan in Los Angeles, under a softly murmuring fan in Los Angeles, while Shostakovich was sitting in Moscow under an axe about to fall. I remember this time very well . . . '48, '49. It was a cartoonish and terrible time. For example, there was a lecture at the Polytechnic Museum around this time, that I went to with some of my friends, that was called 'Russia, Motherland of Elephants'. And someone was there, when we got there, who called himself a professor and who claimed that because there was such a large number of bones and fossils of mammoths found in Yakutia in Siberia, that this meant that Russia was really the homeland of elephants. And there were placards, posters all over the place, for example, saying 'Russia, Homeland of the Radio'. These were related to the absurd claim that Marconi was simply a pathetic imitator of Popov, a Russian who really invented the telegraph. And this was a time when people were being thrown out of the Writers' Union, thrown out of the Composers' Union, deprived of their works, thrown in prison.

What Stravinsky didn't understand was that Shostakovich was a hostage at the Waldorf Astoria and when he made that answer to that question posed by Stravinsky – the provocation – he was thinking about his family and those close to him. We come back here to the image of the mother intentionally crippling her own children. This is a good example of what the system did to people, even the most talented people like Shostakovich. But I do agree that the condescension that was shown by Stravinsky to Shostakovich, there was something criminal about it. Because who should understand the suffering of another human being better than an artist? I, of course, have great respect for Stravinsky. I think he's a great artist, a great maestro. He belongs to the so-called wonderful, very great craftsmen. He was a great craftsman. His music was very startling and shining, but perhaps not great art. I don't insult such art. It has a right to exist. And it would be boring not have such art. But really great art was, is, and will be based on human suffering. Such art creates the possibility of great understanding for the sufferings of others, in my opinion.

Maxim. It's also interesting that, notwithstanding what Solomon has just told us (all the sad stories), at the same time Shostakovich always remained a great admirer of Stravinsky's music.

Robinson. You know, I wanted to ask all of you if... did Shostakovich ever seriously consider emigration?

Maxim. Yes. He thought about it [audience laughter]. He thought about it, that's all. Especially in the '50s and '60s he thought about it the most.

Volkov. That's a sensation, by the way. That's incredible.

Robinson. He talked about it? How do you mean?

Volkov. He never expressed any such thoughts to me. And the critics said that my book shows him as a great anti-communist. But I never even suspected that he would think about emigration. That's absolutely a revelation.

Maxim. I know when there were difficult times in his life there were instances when he thought about it. But then he never returned to that question. He didn't ever think about exactly where he would go, Germany or America or France or whatever, but just sort of generally.[17]

Robinson. He was a Communist Party member, of course. Later he joined the Party, eventually, right?

[17] *Cf.* also p. 184, note 250.

Maxim. My father cried twice in his life: when his mother died, and when he came home to say 'They've made me join the Party'. And now Yevgeny Aleksandrovich says that he remembered him crying when he listened to the *War Requiem.* But this was sobbing, not just tears, but sobbing. It was in the 1960s that he was forced to join the Party. There was simply no other way for him at that time.[18]

Yevtushenko. Remember, at that time Shostakovich was First Secretary of the Union of Composers of the Russian Republic and was helping a lot of people in that capacity. But it simply wasn't possible in the Soviet Union then for someone in a position of that official responsibility to not be a member of the Party. All editors, for example, were members of the Party.

Maxim. That's right. When I was the director of the Radio and Television Orchestra, I was subjected to criticism for a period of ten years in the press that I really should join the Party, because the conductor of such a prestigious orchestra should be a Party member. But I never did join the Party.

Robinson. Why do you think that Stalin spared Shostakovich, when so many of his close colleagues and friends were executed or imprisoned?

Maxim. It's difficult to answer the question why Stalin allowed him to live. Why he tortured him I can say, I can answer. Stalin understood that when a person really descends into the world of Shostakovich's music, is surrounded by it, at that moment he becomes free. And that he couldn't take, Stalin.

Yevtushenko. I have some idea about this, why Stalin let him live. During the Civil War, ungrammatical, coarse people were robbing the estates of rich people. These people who didn't understand anything about music, they would drag out Bechsteins and beautiful pianos and put them in the cowshed. And that's what Stalin wanted, he wanted to have a

[18] Shostakovich became a full member of the Communist Party in October 1961.

grand piano in his cowshed [audience laughter]. Stalin wanted to have artists and composers that he could manage, that he could control. It gave him pleasure. You cannot forget that Stalin was a poet who didn't succeed, like many dictators. Don't forget that Hitler was a painter who didn't succeed. And such people have a special kind of love-hate relationship with the arts. They understood, instinctively, the importance of art – or probably even exaggerated it by attacking the kind of art which they didn't like too much. But they always appreciated art in their own crippled way, because they were also children of the 'Mother of Cripples'.

Maxim. And, you know, if Stalin was successful in forcing an artist or composer like Shostakovich to sign something or say something, he wanted to enslave Shostakovich or any artist in that situation as an artist, as a musician. Remember that the attack on Shostakovich, the campaign against Shostakovich and others in 1948, for example, was no coincidence. He couldn't forgive Shostakovich for the fact that after the War, after the Seventh Symphony, he didn't write some kind of great work praising Stalin, who had seen the country through the War. Instead, he produced the Ninth Symphony, which is rather light; he wrote that instead of something praising Stalin. So Stalin wanted to control and to strangle him, to manipulate him as an artist. But he didn't succeed.

Yevtushenko. Because you couldn't completely enslave genius. It's hopeless for all dictators, it's like trying to enslave the horizon. But I think dictators try to domesticate great artists, or to rape them, because they know that the artists never loved them. And these dictators have very strange, abnormal pleasures. I could never understand what kind of pleasure a rapist would get out of raping. But it's pathological pleasure, pathological pleasure, and they receive it in exerting force over a thing of beauty. That's the pathology of the relationship between great art and power.

SIX LECTURES ON THE SHOSTAKOVICH SYMPHONIES

Maxim Shostakovich

Transcribed and edited by John-Michael Albert

In the summer of 1990, while he was in Houston to rehearse and perform his father's Fifth Symphony with the Houston Symphony Orchestra, the University of Houston gave a Cullen Professorship to Maxim Shostakovich. In exchange he taught a week-long, intensive course in his father's symphonies which was primarily designed for undergraduate seniors. These are my notes for that course, generally taken in his voice. When there seem to be fewer notes on one day than on others, it usually indicates that we were listening to recordings. Questions and comments from the class appear in italics.

Thursday, 7 June 1990 (Introduction, Symphony No. 1)

People say my father composed very quickly. He would respond that that was not true, 'I just write it down quickly'. It is popular to make film biographies of composers in which they plunge into the turmoil of a storm or a great human tragedy, music paper in hand, agonising and scribbling, scribbling and agonising. Composition does not happen that way. When my father composed, he sat down and wrote. I lived all my life with a great composer and never saw him jump up in the middle of the night and write something. When he was writing and would be called to dinner, he would put his pen down – in the middle of an unresolved dominant seventh – and go. He respected the work of others.

Shostakovich knew that revolution and war were the head-on collision of unreasoned chaos. They sweep individuals up in huge unthinking masses that do astonishing damage. In the midst of this maelstrom, the individual is nothing. The individual is exterminated without a thought.

Don't the Second and Third Symphonies reflect an idealistic Leninist period in your father's life?

This is becoming a popular scholarly posture. Leninism, in a nutshell, is the imperative of the good to destroy everything in its path. He believed in the sanctity of human life. Shostakovich did not think much of his Second and Third Symphonies. Once when I wanted to conduct the Third he looked at me and said, 'Couldn't you conduct something else?'

Which of your father's symphonies did he like the most?

My father said 'I like all my symphonies as I would like all my children. Maybe those more who suffered more'.

'If they were to cut off my hands, I would take the pen into my mouth.'

From a letter from Shostakovich to Balanchine's brother [Andrey Balanchivadze], who was a Georgian composer: 'In our life, we don't only have to be able to create; we have to defend our creations as well'. Once Balanchine's brother visited America. Balanchine gave him a meat grinder as a going-away present. When he got back to Georgia, the customs official berated him, saying, 'Shame on you. Such a famous Georgian composer. You go to America and instead of returning with piles of the latest musical scores, you return with a meat grinder'. To which he replied: 'You're right. What do I need with a meat grinder when there's no meat?' He gave the meat grinder to the customs official.

Shostakovich spoke through his music. For me, every note is a word. From childhood, we have been taught as musicians to understand what composers are trying to tell us. Music influences us immediately without using words.

What composers influenced the genesis of Shostakovich's symphonies?

The history of the symphony is a chain of consequential links. Haydn – Mozart – Beethoven – Brahms – Bruckner – Mahler. There can be no single influence.

Did Shostakovich's contemporaries recognise him for his genius?

There is a Russian proverb, 'A fisherman always knows another fisherman from afar'.

What did Shostakovich think of his contemporaries?

It is said that Shostakovich hated Tchaikovsky. I remember him sitting at the breakfast table and listening to the Tchaikovsky Fourth. He made a face, groaning that Tchaikovsky's developments are always so four-square. Later that day, we heard *The Queen of Spades.* His only words for it were 'sublime genius'.

It is also said that Shostakovich hated Prokofiev. Again, I heard my father complaining once about his orchestration, using tuba with viola in such-and-such a composition. One evening, however, the family had made plans to see *War and Peace.* I wanted to get out of it and go to a party. My father was very stern: 'There will be no party. You will hear *War and Peace.* It is a masterpiece of true genius'.

The bad critics are always around when a composer has something bad to say about another composer and never around when he has something good to say. When writing about great people, you should either say everything or say nothing.

He knew music very well. He knew everything that was written before him from memory. I know of no other composer who could sit down at the piano and play and sing the entire *Ring* Cycle from beginning to end from memory.

My father was a great pianist, but he wanted to devote himself to composition. He told me, 'To be a great conductor, you must be a great pianist'.

In the early days, he was a student of Glazunov, who was unaware that music had entered a new century. Glazunov took my father's First Symphony and re-orchestrated two pages of it. Then he told him: 'There. Now if you continue like that, you will have a good symphony'. The results were something between Rimsky-Korsakov and Kalinnikov.

What did he think of Western music?

I asked him once to make a tape of some dance music for a party. There were no recordings of popular Western music in the Soviet Union and certainly no sheet music for these pieces. He got the necessary tape for the reel-to-reel tape recorder and sat at the piano and recorded forty minutes of the popular dance songs he had heard on the radio – including 'Tea for Two'. Later, when Stalin died, he told me to record some of the many speeches that were being made to commemorate him. On his instructions, I recorded them over the dance tape.

A new artist in a new world must be very brave to break through the wall of tradition.

My father didn't separate music into Western/Eastern, popular/classical. He believed that there is simply good music and bad music. He also believed that there are no bad orchestras, only bad conductors.

What would your father have written if he had not been the object of so much personal persecution and subjected to wars, revolutions and famines?

It is, of course, an absurd question. Perhaps if my father had not lived through so much raw emotions, he would have consigned himself to writing polkas and dance music. That was not the case.

Who are the great links in the symphonic chain today in the Germanic tradition?

Only time will tell. Britten. Others.

The Second and Third Symphonies belong to the New Economic Policy (NEP) period. Lenin allowed some elements of capitalism to enter the Soviet Union. Restrictions on art and music were relaxed. In his Piano Sonata No. 1, 'October', Shostakovich showed that he was aware that the good wouldn't last. Later, when things changed, he removed 'October' from the title page.

He generally gave subtitles to his work under pressure. There were changes in the cycle *From Jewish Folk Poetry* and the set *Satires* on poems by Sasha Chyorny, subtitled *Pictures from the Past*. Each had got a phone call from 'The Way It Should Be' [one of the many Russian euphemisms Maxim Shostakovich used for phone calls from Stalin himself]. In the original of the Twelfth Symphony, there was no dedication to Lenin. Shostakovich added it to the proofs from the publisher, in red.

Symphony No. 1 harkens to the period during which he supported himself and his family by playing music for silent movies. He also wrote scores for films such as *Hamlet* and *King Lear*. He loved Shakespeare. He didn't like to see the movies for which he wrote music.

Symphony No. 1 was a success with the audiences and the conductors. The critics were negative. They called it 'totally giftless' and said that 'it will probably never be performed again'. Of course, they said the same thing about Tchaikovsky's Violin Concerto.

You must conduct it two ways. In the first movement, the happy, young Shostakovich is running down the Nevsky Prospect on a Sunday. In the second movement, it is a rainy, grey, cold day. Both are quixotic adventures. The opening should be compared to *The Nose*. Wake. Yawn. Stretch. The trumpet is the opening yawn. Others may have a different interpretation. No one knows. That's what musical life is about.

A painter friend of mine said that computers are getting so good that soon musicians would not be needed at all. Chess players, too. However, our art is alive because the composer understands himself. And different interpretations are necessary. The horizon is what the composer wants. He can get near it, but he cannot touch it. If he were to touch the horizon, music would die. We do not understand Beethoven the man. But we understand his music.

Did Shostakovich ever conduct?

He tried twice as a student. Once with the first movement of Beethoven's First Symphony. The second time, in Gorky. With me. 'Interludes from *Lady Macbeth*.' The second movement of Symphony No. 10. He also conducted the First Cello Concerto with Rostropovich.[1]

Bernstein's recording of Shostakovich's Symphony No. 1 is deep, excellent and high class. The dynamic range is limited by the old recording.

The first movement is a march, the beginning of a journey. The second movement: on the road; music from an old fairy tale (pianist seems quite nervous); back on the road; the fairy-tale music returns very grand. The third movement is one long phrase.

Critics have always felt there were problems with the last movement. They have claimed that it is weak. Not as good as the others.

The last movement is my favourite. There is no room for cuts or for changes. I like it very much. It works like a film. The fast material means a lot of time is passing quickly. With the sound of the timpani, you're back to real time. Critics felt that the final movement of Symphony No. 1 was a mistake. It was too light.

They also felt that a youth couldn't have written this work, that he couldn't be that deep.

[1] In Gorky, on 12 November 1962, Shostakovich shared a concert with Rostropovich. In one half, Rostropovich conducted Musorgsky's *Songs and Dances of Death* in the Shostakovich orchestration; in the other, Shostakovich conducted his *Festive Overture* and First Cello Concerto, with Rostropovich as soloist (Wilson, p. 378; and *Mstislav Rostropovich and Galina Vishnevskaya: Russia, Music, and Liberty*, conversations with Claude Samuel, transl. E. Thomas Glasow, Amadeus Press, Portland, 1995, pp. 127–28). –EDS.

In Symphony No. 1, he used trumpets in F, which is not very common. The tempo markings are his. Shostakovich knew instruments well. He marked his intentions clearly. String players often praise the bowing. He was merciful to winds by judicious placement of rests for breaths.

Friday, 8 June 1990 (Symphony No. 4)

He was disappointed by movies. He thought that the technical quality was rather low. Also, they showed little creativity. Ready-made scenarios. They were not a waste, however. There were experimental moments.

The scenarios of Shostakovich's ballets imperfectly reflect the early economic experiments of the USSR. Their slogan was: 'We'll destroy the old world completely and build something new!' The musical equivalent was 'Out with Tchaikovsky and Beethoven!'

Each revolution is followed by a search for the new. Eisenstein. Meyerhold. Kandinsky. Mayakovsky. The big talents that can really create something new are rare.

Lady Macbeth was considered very unusual then and now. It was isolated from the experiments, yet radically different. It is now performed 100 times per season in Moscow and Leningrad. Stalin imagined that he was one of the characters in the police scene. He was jealous of someone else's success and played games by condemning the popular. Then, *Pravda* printed the article 'Muddle Instead of Music'.

Stalin moved his focus from subject to subject. Under Stalin, every day as Shostakovich left home, he would take a small packet of soap and a tooth brush with him, not knowing if he would return.

Lady Macbeth (1933); Symphony No. 4 (1934).[2] He thought it would be his end. It is absolutely devoid of happy resolution – which has no relation to pessimism. There is the

[2] The date usually given is 1935–36. –EDS.

prescience of war in Symphony No. 4, much like the bombers in Symphony No. 5. The finale is dark. He attended the rehearsal. The orchestra was nervous because of the difficulty. He decided to withdraw it. It was not performed for thirty years.[3] With the appearance of the Fifth Symphony, critics claimed that he was a 'corrected' composer. That was not true. But the Fifth is less pessimistic than the Fourth. In the Fourth, there is no exit.

Music is abstract. It has no words. Therefore, composers are in a little easier position under totalitarian governments. When you listen to the Fourth, you feel the breath of his time.

Did his fame protect him?

Perhaps.

He never changed anything, not one note, except in *Lady Macbeth* and the Fourth Symphony. When the Fourth was finally unveiled in the '60s, the critics felt they had been justified, 'Shostakovich was not satisfied with the work himself so he made revisions'. During the rehearsal, he wore dark glasses. About halfway through, he was completely constricted, holding his breath. He spoke in low tones. He was spent. Shostakovich was a man to whom the gestation period was far more significant than the day of birth. I have so much faith in my father's musicianship and genius that I feel that the revisions in *Lady Macbeth* and Symphony No. 4 must be improvements. Therefore, those versions are preferable.[4]

[3] Until 30 December 1961. –EDS.

[4] Although Shostakovich had refused Kondrashin's suggestions for cuts in the Fourth Symphony before its premiere in 1961, the composer later 'tinkered with some of its dynamics and tempi to produce a "definitive version", authenticated by Boris Tishchenko and published posthumously in 1984' (MacDonald, *The New Shostakovich*, p. 108, note 2). In addition, manuscript material of the Fourth, unrelated to the published score, is included in his *Collected Works*, and was recorded and discussed by Gennady Rozhdestvensky in 1986 on Melodiya A10 00319 000 ('My Work on Symphony No. 4'; English translation available from Alan Mercer of *DSCH Journal* – e-mail: opus147@dtr.fr; fax: +33 4 7460 1244). –EDS.

Monday, 11 June 1990 (Symphony No. 5)

[Review of the criticism of all that preceded Symphony No. 5, especially *Lady Macbeth*. Then the withdrawal of Symphony No. 4 because of potential repercussions.]

With Symphony No. 5, the critics felt he was 'corrected, improved, and clarified'. On the contrary, he chose clearer language to insure clear communication. The Fifth Symphony is his 'Heroic Symphony'. Fadeyev once said that he was scolding someone in the finale.[5] My father replied: it was not just scolding. The hero is saying: "I am right. I will follow the way I choose" '.

My father told me never to explain.

Stormy introduction. Intense. Not fast. 'Listen to me! I am going to speak now!' *Rehearsal 1*, deep melody, not song. He is thinking about the time he is living in. *Reh. 9*, more intimate musical language. All develops very slowly. The theme requires much time to show the atmosphere of that time. *Reh. 17*, stormy *allegro* intrudes. Attack of evil. Music preceding is human, warm, kind. It asks 'Why aren't we kind to each other?' With the intrusion of the stormy *allegro*, the attack of negative forces begins and grows. Not as much as *Reh. 27*. It climaxes at *Reh. 36*, the hero being torn apart. After *Reh. 39*, everything is a requiem for that man who would have lived a different life if he did not attack the evil.

The critics call the second movement a Mahlerian waltz. I strongly disagree. Mahler was in his tradition, but this is not a waltz. It is the aggression of a soulless negative force. A machine of destruction. *Reh. 57*, violin solo, is a child's voice from beneath a soldier's boot. It is not a waltz. The flute repeats the solo, a defiant fist still raised. *Reh. 61*, the force begins again, and the movement finishes with the victory of evil.

[5] *Cf.* Aleksandr Fadeyev's diary, *Za tridtsat' let* (*During Thirty Years*), Sovetsky pisatel', Moscow, 1957, p. 891. –EDS.

The third movement is the highest achievement of lyricism in all of Shostakovich's work. It compares well with a Mahler *adagio*. Very intimate. Shostakovich divides the violins into three parts to increase the number of voices. It is the last night at home of a man sentenced to the gulag; but the problem is eternal! It could be a man before his execution! Reminds me of Andreyev's *Seven Who Were Hanged*.[6] I see a man who spends his last night before execution with his family. He hears his children breathe. He feels the warmth of his wife. But HE DOES NOT CRY! *Reh. 89*, the regret of a strong man: 'Why! Why me!' Compare it with the *Sonnets of Michelangelo* – 'When, oh Lord?' – but there are no tears! It is the question of a strong man. Shostakovich was not sentimental. He was masculine. Strong. His range of feelings was tremendous. *Reh. 90*, the cello solo breaks your heart. *Reh. 92*, climax. The story of the hero's feelings subsides. He is still, and his family is sleeping next to him.

The finale. An intruding storm. Different associations. A struggle in which the hero wins. This movement is built on forward accelerating motion. It cuts off at *Reh. 112*. The intrusion of a lyrical episode comparable to the third movement. It's not really quiet. There is the premonition of something.

Many great artists have the gift of premonition: Pushkin, Byron, Mandelstam, Khlebnikov each wrote poems with precise descriptions of how they would die – a miracle. The gift of prediction is part of a great artist.

Reh. 121, prediction of war. Drums and low horns are low-flying bombers. Conclusion: if it is not military, then it is something evil threatening Shostakovich personally. *Reh. 128* to the end. It says again and again: 'No. You will not be able to do anything to me'. It is not happiness. It is not victory. It is the determination of a strong man to BE.

[6] A story by the symbolist writer and portrait painter Leonid Andreyev (1871–1919); an English translation of *Seven Who Were Hanged* (1909) was published in 1941 (Avon, New York/Lindsay Drummond, London, 1947). –EDS.

At *Reh. 131* the eighth-note equals 184; not quarter-note equals 184, as in most scores. It is very useful to look at it, think about it, and guess why 'quarter = 184' is not right. Once Shostakovich was taking an exam in counterpoint from Glazunov. He had a lot of trouble with one of the fugue subjects. When he turned in his paper, he told Glazunov that it would have been a lot easier if one note were changed. Glazunov said he had obviously made a mistake when he wrote the exam, but since Shostakovich didn't correct it, he got a lower grade. 'You should have figured it out and corrected it.'

Once when I was studying music in Leningrad, I asked my father to write a fugue for me to hand in for a class assignment. I got a B-minus.

Now, I conduct the Fifth Symphony with a very slow beginning. The second movement should be all down-bows. Twenty years ago, I conducted it twice as fast.

Tuesday, 12 June 1990 (Symphony No. 8)

[The lecture began with a caricature of musicologists: some, for example, spend time on great questions like the history of the F sharp in the early music of Buxtehude.]

Symphony No. 7, 'Military': written at the beginning of the war; photocopies sent to the US; first conducted by Toscanini. Critics felt it described the tragedy of the war; but it was not just about the war. The times before the war were very difficult. Stalin was schizophrenic, a maniac of greatness and paranoia. It was the time of the 'Processes' – a euphemism for the open trials. Accusations were made against different groups at different times: engineers, scientists, artists; all were 'organised, plotting enemies against the State and against Stalin'. Everyone was considered a German spy. The prisons were overcrowded, so there needed to be more and faster trials, outside the norms of human jurisprudence. People were tortured with the purpose of getting them to sign a full confession. The accused were deceived – they were told that if they signed, they'd be released. Then they were given 'nine grains of lead in the basement' [executed by firing squad].

My father always said, 'I think long; I write fast' – the time preceding the war was probably the inspiration of Symphony No. 7, depicting the tragedy of the nation. There were negative evil forces – in Germany and in the USSR. The USSR had its own fascism and its own 'Hitler'. The Seventh Symphony is not just military.

If the Seventh is about cataclysm, struggle, and destruction, the Eighth is a philosophical requiem, a reaction to the content of the Seventh Symphony. The Eighth is a painting of an empty world: no truth, no life, nothing.

First movement: English horn solo is like the last human voice on an empty earth; long, centrally located, the voice of an author.

Looking at the symphonies from a different perspective: Nos. 5, 6, 7 and 8 form a single symphony, a cycle of philosophical problems.

Fourth and fifth movements of Symphony No. 8: the fourth movement is a requiem for the victims of the past, present and future. The fifth movement is the necessary dawn of hope and light that must follow it. The composer does not lose faith in humanity in spite of all the horrors of humanity. There is kindness, a kind future; the human soul is depicted reaching for God. The fourth movement ends in C minor, hopeless; the fifth ends in C major. The bassoon solo has something Shakespearean in it. It reminds me of the grave digger's music in *Hamlet*. There is true peace of the soul, hope, light, faith in humanity; 'it will not always be that bad'.

Previn's recording is very fast, probably because of EMI's insistence that the whole work be on a single LP. The second scherzo, especially, is too fast; it should be played in two, not in one. In it a person is escaping from somewhere with dogs snapping at his legs. Shostakovich hated the word 'scherzo'; his 'jokes' were very serious. Previn's performance: not enough power, the rhythm is too light; Kirill Kondrashin is better, because he always asked Shostakovich's advice. Mravinsky is good, correct. Mravinsky consulted with the composer before making any of his recordings.

Critics always discuss whether Stravinsky conducted well or not; is it a question of good or bad, correct or incorrect?

The later symphonies, after No. 8, are unpredictable. Shostakovich was making major changes in his musical language. I have just recorded the Tenth with the London Symphony Orchestra. The master tape has been shipped to me. I would like to play it for the class to sense your reaction. I want you to pay special attention through the development section. A conductor is used to feeling the audience's response through his back.

Next, we'll discuss Symphony No. 13. In Symphony No. 13, Shostakovich projected an entire nation through music. The poem 'Babi Yar' is about the Jews, but it is also about the destiny of Russia, the destiny of a man in Russia, the destiny of a man who is an artist in Russia. Symphony No. 14 was dedicated to the treatment of all kinds of death in poetry: soldier, suicide, fight in a pub, natural. Symphony No. 15 is an autobiography, his life from birth to death.

Wednesday, 13 June 1990 (Symphony No. 13)

In 1953, Stalin died. There was an ensuing political struggle, with Khrushchev ending up on top. Khrushchev brought a *perestroika* thaw. This was received with great joy; there was new freedom, social relaxation; greater freedom in the arts; artists whose throats were completely throttled could speak with more truth. Today there is complete literary freedom in publishing, except of course state secrets.

Yevtushenko's 'Babi Yar' was published in *Soviet Culture*,[7] a political publication of the government. Shostakovich

[7] Actually *Literaturnaya Gazeta* rather than *Sovetskaya Kul'tura*. *Cf*. p. 382. –EDS.

noticed that the poem touched an extremely important subject. Before the Revolution, anti-Semitism was there. The Bolsheviks brought hope to the Jews; but to their great disappointment, anti-Semitism grew. So 'Babi Yar' speaks of the war and of the execution of the Jews, an event that can be generalised in history with the Dreyfus Affair in France, or Anne Frank. Shostakovich was extremely impressed; especially with the last four lines of the poem.

The first movement is a symphonic poem. Shostakovich was isolated in the hospital when he wrote this. He had had a heart attack. He had broken his leg on the way home from my wedding. While in the hospital, he read more poems by Yevtushenko. Shostakovich felt that this Symphony was a work of tremendous civil importance to the Russians. In it he describes the suffering of the Soviet people, all the horrors after World War II, the economic disasters, the empty stores, starvation.

Second movement, 'Humour': Shostakovich laughs at the power that devastated the USSR – 'No one can forbid one to laugh'.

There was total infiltration of society by informers. Shostakovich was afraid to speak to friends, to his wife, to himself. So, in this Symphony, it is as if he were explaining.

The fifth movement is a call to people to build their careers honestly, like Pasteur, the cosmonauts, Lev [Count Leo] Tolstoy. This provides a humorous moment in the work. There was a much-hailed Soviet writer named Aleksey Tolstoy, whose reputation overshadowed, in the Soviet mind, that of the author of *War and Peace* and *Anna Karenina*.[8] So when the bass solo sings the list of people who made honest careers for themselves and comes to Lev Tolstoy, the men's

[8] A distant relative of the author of *War and Peace*, Count Aleksey Tolstoy (1882–1945) fought for the Whites but went over to the Communists on returning to Russia from exile in 1923. He then enjoyed a career as a propagandist writer of novels and plays, winning several Stalin prizes. –EDS.

chorus barks back in disbelief, 'Lev?' And the bass reiterates emphatically, 'Lev!'

When Shostakovich was in the hospital, I went to visit him. He said that the Symphony was finished. A friend was visiting. My father sent me out to buy some vodka to celebrate, which I did. I brought three little glasses with me. 'Well, I've finished the Thirteenth Symphony. Let's drink.' There was a knock on the door. It was time for an injection. We hid the bottle of vodka in a magazine and attempted to stuff it into a large padded leather chair that had been brought in for him; but we couldn't – there were already five bottles hidden in it. So, after the injection, we had to offer the nurse a drink as well in exchange for her silence.

Then the trouble started. Shostakovich got a phone call 'From Where It Should Come': 'Where did you find this poem?' 'In the newspaper.' One after another, all the conductors used different excuses to get out of conducting the work. And the bass soloists all had excuses. The censors, through the Union of Composers, knew it was practically impossible to stop Shostakovich himself. No one knew what would happen at the end of the Khrushchev thaw and, therefore, everyone was afraid. Except Kondrashin. One day before the premiere, the bass soloist refused to sing because he had been 'Called the Way He Should Have Been Called'. His brave double sang with great success.

The Thirteenth Symphony has always had problems in the USSR. When I left in 1981 (it was the White Nights Festival, near 1 May) – among many other reasons, in search of freedom – I was ashamed to remain in a country where the Leningrad Shostakovich Society refused to perform the Thirteenth Symphony on my request. There were all sorts of excuses: the chorus is too busy, why should we sing about the Jews? In Moscow it is being performed now.

It begins and ends with a bell, as if to say everything is to be repeated. The final line: careers and careerists compromise their principles, betray their friends, betray themselves, betray their collaborators. Party membership was a condition of success. The first performance was as written. Immediately afterward, pressure was applied to revise it. Yevtushenko changed the phrase and Shostakovich was unhappy.[9]

Thursday, 14 June 1990 (Symphony No. 15)

Definition of terms – Socialist Realism: political control of the arts to fool someone; a complex of tools; optimistic. Formalism: pejorative, pessimistic. Socialist Realism originated with Maxim Gorky. Gorky was a talented man, a good writer. Then he met Lenin and gained a lot of influence. During the Stalin terrorism, Gorky was unhappy and used his influence to protect himself and others. Gorky had his own opinion and realised that everything wasn't good under Socialist Realism. Stalin could not touch him. So he died by a Stalinist trick: Gorky was poisoned by his own personal physician, who was later also liquidated. So Maxim Gorky was an instrument in a political game called 'Socialist Realism'.

After completing the Thirteenth Symphony, Shostakovich's health was failing. His right hand was almost paralysed. The right half of his body had nearly completely ceased to function. He thought about death more and more. The Fourteenth Symphony describes different kinds of death; but you must realise that, as he develops the subject of death, he glorifies life. The more horrifying death is, the more beautiful life is. Akhmatova and Tsvetayeva were friends and poets of death. With the completion of the Thirteenth and Fourteenth Symphonies, both of which are song cycles, he thought of another symphony, a symphony that would sum up all of his previous work and turn to a new page in his style.

The Fifteenth Symphony is a chamber symphony; personal, intimate. It describes human life from beginning to end through the prism of his experience. There are many unexpected moments in this symphony. It starts light-hearted and child-like. It includes a quotation from the *William Tell*

[9] *Cf.* p. 230, note 420. –EDS.

Overture. The first movement is nicknamed the 'Toy Store'. The drama intensifies as the Symphony moves from the first to the second movement with a quotation from Wagner's *Götterdämmerung.*[10] There is a big solo for trombone: heroic, prison song; heroic conflict in life. The music rises to a climax; a heart-breaking chord: grief, regret, everything that humans were not created for. It describes the moment when the soul leaves the body and rises to eternity – it was already planned in the *Michelangelo Sonnets*, and in 'The Poet's Death' in the Fourteenth Symphony. From that moment, with the composer, we look at the world from above; calm, dissolve. Then there is the sound of the bell as at the beginning.

I am not a poet or a writer; the rest I have to do by conducting.

Shostakovich did not go to church, but the word 'God' is there very often in the songs and symphonies.

When working on a symphony, my father would give me a score. He truly disliked speaking about his music; he would probably say now: 'What have you been doing for the last seven days?'!

Shostakovich would come to the first rehearsal and make short comments: 'the clarinet should be louder' or 'the strings should be softer'; but he would never explain.

There is a musical language which we have been taught since childhood; if we need verbal explanations, then we're bad musicians.

First movement: the trombone is a proud, strutting fireman. At the first rehearsal, Shostakovich said on the first run-through: 'Don't tell the musicians there will be a quotation from *William Tell*. I want to see their faces when they come to it'. Second movement: no longer a child; long cello solo; trombone sings a prison song. In the fourth movement there are also quotations from Beethoven's Sixteenth String Quartet ('Muss es sein?') and from the opening motive of

[10] The Wagner quotation is in the fourth movement. –EDS.

Tristan (almost). The passacaglia puts us above the earth; violins in overtones [harmonics]; seventh-chord at the end of the climax. This was absolutely new for Shostakovich, the beginning of a new age.

Concluding Comments

It was an enormous joy to live with a musician that great. I have had many teachers and worked under many conductors; but my most important teacher was my father: what he said at home about music, the concerts he heard, advice to musicians and students, comments. He taught before the war and at the end of his life. In the middle of his life he was accused of being a formalist and was fired. Therefore, the atmosphere at our home was unique.

When I was three or four, the family was evacuated to Kuibyshev because the Soviet Army was losing. My father took me to the premiere of the Seventh Symphony. Shostakovich wanted to fight in the war himself, but he was nearsighted -9, -12. My only other memory of Kuibyshev is there was good candy for sale!

In 1946, at the rehearsals for the premiere of the Eighth Symphony, I decided to be a conductor. But father said, 'First learn the piano well'; and so I entered the conservatory as a pianist, studying piano, piano pieces. I entered the school of music in 1946. It was a horrible time: starvation, poverty, the country was ruined. I remember, the students were rationed one bagel and a paper packet containing one teaspoon of sugar per day for food. We lived in the country during the summer. Captured Nazi soldiers were used to build the roads, then. Once a poor, pale German soldier came and asked for cigarettes and bread. My sister and I were very scared because of all the newspaper caricatures of German soldiers in uniform. My father told us not to be afraid of him: he was not guilty of anything; he did not want to kill anyone; he was forced to. In a few words, Shostakovich defined the war from a human, individual point of view. My father gave me the Second Piano Concerto on my birthday, 10 May 1957.

I studied with Yakov Flier (pianist), Igor' Markevich (conductor), Nikolay Rabinovich and Gennady Rozhdestvensky. I was the assistant conductor in many orchestras. Travelled and conducted a lot. Then I became the music director of the State Radio and TV Orchestra for ten years. I had very negative feelings toward what was happening. It seemed that we were in a swamp; and the swamp was growing. People were afraid. The authorities did whatever they wanted. Pessimism spread.

Father was asked, 'Why did you write the cycle on Jewish poetry?' (he often used Jewish melodies). There are many symbols in Shostakovich's music; he used the Jewish people as a symbol of human suffering. Once father was walking along the street after the war. He saw a Jewish man, covered in many medals, a hero of the war. Someone shouted at him: 'Hey, you! Where did you steal those medals?' But that's not the only reason. He had used many Jewish melodies before.

Everything around me told me that I had to leave the USSR. The regime had broken the life and health of my father. It had tortured him. So, once when I was in Germany with my son, we asked for asylum in the US embassy. We have lived in the US since 1981 as US citizens. When there is freedom for everyone, I will return. My wife and I had divorced three years before I left. We are still good friends, though. I work and travel in the US and Europe, and I'm currently the music director at the New Orleans Symphony Orchestra.

After the last class, there were pictures taken of the class and Maxim autographed scores, notes and whatnot. I asked him to autograph my recording of the Violin Concerto No. 1, with David Oistrakh as soloist and him conducting the New Philharmonia Orchestra. It has photographs of Dmitry and Maxim Shostakovich and David Oistrakh on the front and on the back. I remember Maxim looking at the recording for a long time in silence, before turning it over and autographing it. I had the strong feeling that there was a very interesting story in it, but that that was not the time to tell it.

Variation II

SHOSTAKOVICH[1]

Daniil Zhitomirsky

Following a rather extensive break, I am trying again to come closer to what was the source of my strongest impressions and emotional turmoil. A turmoil much more significant and of much more vital importance than the usual interpretation of art, even the highest form of art. For in this particular case, we become aware of our time, of our undistorted reality, around whose 'circles', just like Virgil, he led us, his contemporaries. By some sort of miracle, this was possible even during the '30s and '40s; it was possible only in music and only because there happened to be a Shostakovich.

I know of no other Russian artist who would have been able to accomplish a similar feat in those decades. If there had been one, his voice, as a rule, would not have reached us. We read Solzhenitsyn much later, but that also was a miracle.

Today, we already know many important facts about Shostakovich. Many of them are half-hidden, camouflaged, or simply distorted (mainly by the composer himself – in his own commentaries about his works, as well as in other instances). Apparently, the time has not yet come to tell the *whole truth* publicly. Be that as it may, in my 'Materials' I have given myself an extremely narrow task, since I have no time left nor do I have the strength to write everything I'd like to say.[2]

[1] Originally in *Muzykal'naya Akademiya*, 1993, No. 3, pp. 15–30. English version by Véronique Zaytzeff and Frederick Morrison.

[2] Zhitomirsky died in 1992. – EDS.

'A faithful son . . .'

With regard to the treatment of Shostakovich by the ruling governmental organs, two contradictory tendencies were exhibited. The first was irritation with an elusive form of spiritual independence, with something beyond their complete control, with a powerful deviant influence which created its own milieu – a milieu robustly different from the '*joie de vivre* of the millions'.

The second concerned Shostakovich's usefulness for international relations, for the prestige of Soviet culture, for various types of denunciations and anti-propaganda declarations (very quickly it became apparent that Shostakovich was doing that quite meticulously). In the years following 1948 this is precisely the stimulus that prevailed. Gone was the necessity to avoid taking sides, gone were the abuse and recognition with their various reservations. The highest epithets were immediately mobilised for recognition and glorification. Machiavelli's wisest advice was followed very closely: the prince must not bind himself by any kind of promise, any kind of decision or opinion; the force and the perspective of power rests, to a great extent, on the fact that people forget with incredible ease what was said yesterday and very quickly adapt to what is said today.

Who is Shostakovich? 'A faithful son of the Communist Party, a prominent social and state figure, and an artist-citizen', he 'dedicated his entire life to the development of Soviet music, to the assertion of the ideals of Socialist humanism, and to the international battle for peace and friendship between nations'. This is taken from the obituary which was signed by the leaders of the Party and the government.[3]

The location of this paragraph in the text of the obituary and the order in which Shostakovich's roles were listed quite definitely point to the fundamental accents of the official recognition. What is Shostakovich's place in the history of music? It turns out that together with Prokofiev 'they defined

[3] Quotation from the collection edited by Grigory Shneyerson, *D. Shostakovich. Stat'i i materialy* (*D. Shostakovich. Articles and Materials*), Sovetsky Kompozitor, Moscow, 1976, p. 6.

the main paths of modern musical art'. This is taken from T. Khrennikov's grave-side oration. In 1975 this was the same falsehood that that same Khrennikov and other advocates of the official version had maintained in previous years. At present 'the main paths' are occupied by a new avant-garde (a totally Western one).

Shostakovich's official recognition is characterised by splendid words, solemnity and categorically asserted simplicity, combined with a total indifference toward the complex and tragic essence of the artist and the man. In this case, incidentally, indifference does not mean lack of concern at all. In this recognition and glorification, it was necessary to fence oneself off solidly from the essence, and willfully forget it. It was necessary to pack up the extraordinary phenomenon in the Procrustean box of official virtue. (Isn't that the reason why here, in Russia, Shostakovich's memoirs, published in the west by S. Volkov, were so fiercely criticised? They had refuted to a considerable extent our official conception of the 'faithful son'.)

However, under the superficial layer of official recognition, something else was taking shape in our musical milieu. I had distinctly felt this, in the first half of the '60s, while Shostakovich was still living. Particularly during the preparation of the collection for his sixtieth birthday (I was one of the editors and authors of the collection). For example, in conversations and discussions with E. Denisov, I felt and understood that his position was far from just a matter of personal opinion. This was the position (at first, perhaps, only some moods or motives that gradually became a conscious realisation) of a generation of composers who stepped in precisely in that same decade. For some time, Shostakovich still commanded their respect for being *persecuted*: after all, they, too, were taking the path of *persecuted innovators*. Nevertheless, the purpose for which one would let oneself be proudly persecuted had already become completely different: they could have rejoiced that Shostakovich had finally been recognised, but to them the author of the Eighth himself already seemed utterly *passé*; on their horizon new gods had appeared – from the recent past they had the members of the New Viennese School and, from the present, Stockhausen and Boulez.

Extremely diverse people joined the new movement or

gravitated toward it. They were people with different levels of talent, with diverse motives (business-like, career-like, spiritual, or dependent on fashion, personal relations, or a group membership, etc.). But they all had one thing in common: the opposition to norms, precisely as was happening in the West at the time. But in our country, they were opposed to the norms that had merged with bureaucratic ideological clichés. There was a yearning to set oneself apart from the 'herd', to create a new elite as some sort of self-affirmation of heterodoxy. Yet heterodoxy easily turned into selfish opposition.

They had another common trait – a 'spiritual deficit', although, at times, one was tempted to perceive a lofty concept hidden within extravagant formal solutions. This could also have been a contrivance to comply with the constant request: 'there must be an idea'. The Western avant-garde clearly didn't give a damn about such demands; they were inventing structures!

The reappraisal of Shostakovich himself through his best works was linked to the desire specifically to interpret his evolution. After all, Shostakovich was capable, if he wanted to, of switching from the antagonist to the staunch ally, of becoming some kind of citadel and banner of conquering innovations. How could we do that? Let's look at it closely; had he, too, moved in the direction taken by Schoenberg and Webern? They looked at it closely and – oh joy! – they discovered the number twelve. Yes, twelve-tone themes had appeared! In the Thirteenth Quartet, in the Fourteenth Symphony, and also in other places. They discovered and interpreted it as something highly significant. Twelve, they said, is something that, in essence, is different from, for example, eleven or ten! The composer had finally seen the light!

I remember M. Tarakanov's[4] report at the Congress of Soviet Composers on the excellent Thirteenth Quartet. The speaker's enthusiasm was mainly focused on the number twelve, although the expressive and richly tonal theme of this composition had nothing in common with the musical struct-

[4] An important musicologist of the Soviet era (b. 1928; recently deceased), who wrote about Western music. –EDS.

ures of Schoenberg's series. I remember dear Viktor Bobrovsky,[5] so extremely sensitive to the meaning of music – so sensitive, but also so easily impressed. How persistently, toward the end of his life, he tried to bring Shostakovich closer to the New Viennese School so utterly alien to him! I argued with that position both orally and in writing.[6]

Naturally, all these contrivances were of interest only to a very narrow layer of the composers' and musicologists' milieu. The wide mass of people (even those who formally belonged to the intelligentsia, read newspapers and listened to the radio), people not too educated, but willing to express themselves, willing to judge and try everything and anything, inwardly were not partial either to Shostakovich's music or his fate. In this estrangement, often manifested by an open hostility, at least two reasons reverberated. The first one, the most common, was the lack of receptivity to such a class of music, to such a degree of spiritual complexity as was created by the classical composers – particularly the heightened complexity characteristic of twentieth-century art.

. . . I remember Shostakovich's tour to Baku in February–March 1952. On the programme of two recitals – the First Quartet, the Quintet, the Trio, and piano fugues to be performed by the author. In the local newspaper's review, signed by Sultan Gadzhibekov, it was written: 'The recitals performed by the composer, D. Shostakovich, represent a great and joyful event in the artistic life of our republic. The warm reception given to Shostakovich by the people of Baku once again demonstrates how highly the Soviet people value the creative works of artists', and so on. But what happened in reality was totally different. On the eve of the first concert, only a small handful of tickets had been sold. K. Karayev sent a note, in which he asked me to give an introductory speech ('I think that it must be done, at any cost'). Both Karayev and the philharmonia were trying to save the situation somehow.

[5] Viktor Petrovich Bobrovsky (1906–79), an important Shostakovich scholar, who wrote a book on the composer's instrumental chamber music (*Kamernyye instrumental'nyye ansambli D. Shostakovicha: issledovaniye*, Sovetsky Kompozitor, Moscow, 1961). –EDS.

[6] *Cf.* 'Iz razmyshleniy o stile Shostakovicha' ('Reflections on Shostakovich's Style'), *Sovetskaya Muzyka*, 1976, No. 9 [pp. 55–62.–EDS.]

Some high official took drastic measures in order to avoid shaming the tour by having it perform to an empty concert hall. Specifically, almost an entire military platoon was dispatched to the concert. Now, I no longer remember exactly what I said before the beginning of the concert, but I remember that I suffered, afraid of dragging the speech out, since I saw in front of me a multitude of uniforms and shiny boots. However, this was nothing in comparison with the torture endured by the performer, who, at the end of the first part of the concert, was going to play the fugues (G sharp minor, F sharp major, B major, E minor). On 29 February, I wrote my wife in Moscow about this concert:

> I hasten to report that everything went quite smoothly. In one respect I know that the public liked me – my speech was extremely short: it took me eighteen minutes to give my testimonial of the artist, to talk about his 'creative path', and explain the things he was about to perform. However, I was not even thinking about that, for my soul was aching and crying bitter tears for Dmitry Dmitriyevich. A handful of more or less suitable listeners had disappeared in an utterly alien mass of people, who had been brought here for fear of an empty concert hall. A constant and muffled noise was heard continuously, the squeaks of dried-up seats, which did not bother so much as 'sound', but as an open opposition and rejection. Just imagine what Shostakovich felt, while playing the fugues! He was paralysed and he did not look around. One could feel only a hysterical wish – finish playing as quickly as possible and – get out of here!! It was in this state that he ran backstage, all covered in a cold sweat: 'Let's get on with the intermission, let's get on with the Quintet, and let's finish'. (To this, I can add that he played badly and in a fidgety manner.)

I have never seen him so worn out and old. Leading me to a corner, he whispered almost with desperation: 'This is beyond my power, I can't bear it . . . '.

Later I wrote to Ol'ga:

> At D. D.'s second recital there was no noise, since the concert hall was empty. In the first half he played six preludes and fugues (C minor, A major, D major, B major, F major, and D minor), in the second half the Quartet and the Trio were performed. The introductory word was no longer necessary. All evening long I did my best to convince Shostakovich not to go to the 'reception' scheduled for the morning with

students and professors. The atmosphere in the lobby was ugly (for example, during the intermission of the second concert, a mean note had been forwarded, asking the composer to clarify what the fugues 'express', and the director in earnest asked D. D. or me to talk on this topic with the public), and thus the 'reception' would have brought only mean tricks and grief. Karayev understood me and adopted a position of diplomatically refined neutrality. Shostakovich wavered a little bit. He åttempted to argue with me: disappointment, he said, is generally necessary, it is a 'given', and it's not the first time, he said, and so forth. I prevailed nevertheless: the 'reception' took place, but only with the quartet (I peeked in and seeing that he 'himself' was not present, I went home). (3 February 1952).

. . . At Zhdanov's 'historic' conference in January 1948, A. Gol'denveizer,[7] who, as a senile old man, was not completely informed about what was to be discussed and the manner in which to discuss it, said, by the way, the following: 'If one were to play a Tchaikovsky symphony or the simplest Beethoven sonata to a person who had never heard a symphony orchestra or a complicated piece of music for piano, it is beyond doubt that that person would be deaf to them . . . A Beethoven or Tchaikovsky symphony could very likely seem as incomprehensible to an unprepared listener as the most formalistic work'.[8]

Let me repeat: this is a common problem that concerns our century as well as past centuries, even though, in our times, people have many more opportunities to come into contact with classical music. How much demagogical thunder and lightning befell us all in the name of the truth that 'Art belongs to the people' – a truth that is shamelessly simplified. In this stupidly simplified form it is offered to the people, the people *in general*, the people understood as an abstract entity.

[7] Aleksandr Borisovich Gol'denveizer (1875–1961), pianist, pedagogue, composer and writer. He was an important figure in Russian music education and established the first great Soviet piano school during his 57 years of teaching at the Moscow Philharmonic School and Moscow Conservatory. –EDS.

[8] *Cf. Materialy soveshchaniya. Stenografichesky otchyot* (*Materials of the Conference. Stenographic Account*), 1948, p. 53.

. . . In Chekhov's short story *Svirel'* [*The Reed-pipe*], on a cloudy autumn morning two old men meet in a field – a steward of a farmstead and a shepherd with his herd, 'scraggly, in a torn and coarse cloak, and hatless'. The shepherd was playing on his reed-pipe. They struck up a conversation about serious and sorrowful things: everything is getting worse in nature, 'and the animals, too, and the livestock, and the bees, and the fish', and the rivers are drying up. 'We ourselves are getting worse from one year to the next.' Both had spent their lives in poverty and, it seems, in an utterly pointless way. The music of the shepherd's reed-pipe crystallises and comments on this whole pitiful review. Certain sounds ('no more than five or six notes') 'give the impression of weeping inconsolably, as if the reed-pipe were sick and frightened, while the lowest notes, for some reason made one think of fog, of sad trees, and gray skies'. This was also 'art that belonged to the people'. However, not to 'the people' in general, but precisely to such old men as these. An art that is organically tied to their lives, within the frame and norms of their perception. An utterly serious art, nevertheless not a symphony, but only 'five or six notes'!

Another reason for this alienation that easily turned into hostility toward Shostakovich was often said to be the 'incomprehensibility' of his music: everything in it went 'somewhere, where it was not supposed to', not the way it is in usual music. This interpretation was, in many cases, a self-deception, possibly not even fully understood. The 'incomprehensible' seemed to be so not only because of the unusual melodies and harmonies, but because of the content they conveyed – too strained, dramatic, and intense for the average perception. This content was rejected because of the state of mind that keeps us completely in thrall to the affairs of everyday reality.

The popularity of Shostakovich's name was on the rise and was constantly increasing primarily due to the uniqueness of his brilliant talent. This popularity was constantly fanned with some kind of sensation. This is understandable: in a social structure that reminded one so much of the scene painted in *The Great Inquisitor* – the dictator and the herd, to which everything is permitted in strictly measured doses – genius itself was a sensation. A hard nut for the 'leadership' and a perpetually annoying factor for the 'herd'. The popularity was stimulated by factors which had nothing in common with the true calling of an artist. This popularity was increased by the suspiciousness, envy and 'irritability' of the censors. It was insulted and immediately and magniloquently praised by the highest organs. They tried to use Shostakovich's fame for the most diverse purposes. Nonetheless, there was, naturally, a real recognition! It existed in a circle that was not wide, but which had succeeded in preserving a relative independence. In a circle which was capable of appraising the force and richness of spiritual life, of hearing that toll of the bell of moral alarm that flowed from Shostakovich's works.

'Our business is to rejoice!'

In my entire life, I will not forget either this aphorism, or the moment I first heard it. The year 1945. 'Ivanovo'. Summer. On 8 August, along with Nina Vasil'yevna, who had gone to Moscow for a few days, Dmitry Dmitriyevich arrived. I came to meet the whole family, including his children Galya and Maxim. In the car, on our ride back from the train station, D. D. told me, for the first time, about the 'uranium bomb' that had been dropped on Hiroshima. He was talking about it in short, quick phrases, without any further comments (the one who commented on 'what atomic fission is' was Nina Vasil'yevna, who was a trained physicist). Shostakovich's agitation could be heard in the hoarse, constrained quality of his voice and seen in his vacant look and pallor. Later, we walked in silence from the car to the destitute little dacha, where he was composing the Ninth Symphony at the time. My mind was reeling under the spell of the news and I said something very pessimistic. D. D., staring at a point in space, quickly and automatically cut me off: 'Our business is to rejoice!'

He led a double life: one was official and public and the other was internal and private. Only the second one was true, innate, it was a protest against those forces to which the first one was subjected. Can one be surprised at this and blame him for it? Many of us lived the same strange life, but we bore it and before the court of our conscience, came to terms with it in several different ways. The first life (we are not talking about those who were making a career) was led according to the principle: 'What is necessary and sufficient'. One limited oneself to minimal signs of loyalty, and resisted being drawn into deals and bargains that were *unnecessary* in order *to survive*; in essence, this life became an empty ritual that gave a certain independence to the inner life. But it was something altogether different with Shostakovich. He gave the impression that he purposely let himself be torn to pieces, that he was ready not for the minimum but for the maximum. This is why, in my opinion, his version of the double life was a tragedy – a part of that same unembellished tragic reality that is reflected in his symphonies.

Why did he choose precisely that variant? Was it unavoidable? Many people were painfully perplexed. Those who wished him well were shocked at his efforts on behalf of the 'first' life. Others were ready to interpret it as servility to his career. I often pondered the issues, but my conclusions even now remain a hypothesis. They are as follows: he did not divorce himself from what was on the outside. He consciously took upon himself the same torments and the same despair that he had poured in his music. The poignancy of the torments that he willingly inflicted on himself corresponded with the dramatic nature of his compositions. This was his wholeness: the double life became, from this specific point of view, a single one.

Oksana Leont'yeva's[9] remark in her diary for 1958 speaks to this point. After having listened to the Eighth Symphony, she wrote:

> Shostakovich is an artist and a realist who is absolutely contemporary, not squeamish, without any pettiness, and who does not avoid performing even drudge work (movies, operettas). There is an absence of aestheticism, a human simplicity, an 'acceptance' of reality. Shostakovich did not fence himself off from all the diversity of colors and bad taste in our life, except with the 'safeguard' of his talent. . . . As a musician, he was able to say aloud to his contemporaries everything that, by necessity, would have kept a writer silent. Even now, sounds are still uncontrolled and difficult to catch on earth. It is frightening to create a novel of 800 pages for

[9] Musicologist and prominent specialist in modern music. –EDS.

> oneself and two friends. In Shostakovich's music, there is this novel. . . .
>
> Russia is immersed in hard drinking and indifference toward everything, and mainly toward itself. One hears the gnashing of teeth and the rustle everywhere. And anguish, the anguish of inanimate objects: fields, roads, telephone poles in the rain, night lights, and the darkest night. And an anguish without words, frightening from the first cry of the infant to the last wheeze . . . It is possible that Shostakovich never in his life saw these poles, these nights, and roads. But his intuition felt them and recreated everything, to the very depths.

Here are two lists. I am choosing only the most typical items in them.

First list
1930–1956. *Lady Macbeth – Katerina Izmailova*
1934. Symphony No. 4
1937. Symphony No. 5
1941. Symphony No. 7
1943. Symphony No. 8
1944. Piano Trio
1945. Symphony No. 9
1949. *From Jewish Folk Poetry*
1953. Symphony No. 10
1960. Quartet No. 8
1962. Symphony No. 13
1964. *The Execution of Stepan Razin*
1969. Symphony No. 14

Second List
1935. *Limpid Stream* ballet
1947. *Poem on the Motherland*
1949. *Song of the Forests*
1952. *The Sun Shines Over Our Motherland*
1956. *Festive Overture*
1961. Symphony No. 12 – 'The Year 1917'
1967. *October*, Symphonic Poem

A creative split personality? But in the works from the second list, the situation is more complicated than it appears at first glance. Naturally, the artificiality, the external nature of the creative process does leave a trace: in way too many cases, one can feel in the music the 'commissioned work'. Nonetheless, in whatever Shostakovich's hand touched, one feels his creative talent, his taste and his craftsmanship everywhere; the music often rises to the level of the composer's best works (for example, in the cantata *The Sun Shines Over Our Motherland* there is the naïve and poetic chorus of the little boys). Everything just stated also applies to the cinema music. However, it is impossible to interpret all these works and judge them without taking into account their titles, literary texts and topics. Most importantly – without taking into account the situation in which they were written. The nobility of musical images does not save the situation. When the bare deception, demagogy and 'Potemkin's villages'[10] are endowed with traits of elevated poetry, this nobility results in falsehood. Falsehood, because talent and the dream of perfection surrender to the power of immorality!

Shostakovich's articles often appeared in the press. He gave interviews and speeches. But more often than not, all of this had been 'prepared' by professional journalists, especially the purely political articles and speeches. Naturally, autobiographical texts and even reviews of his new works could not have been written without his participation. The fact that he was able to write without any assistance and in quite an interesting manner at that, both to the point and artistically, can be judged by what he, without any doubt, wrote himself. I have in mind his reminiscences of Sollertinsky and his long review of the movie about Rimsky–Korsakov. However, it is obvious that he was not willing to write just any kind of *texts*. Moreover, he tried, whenever it was possible, *not to have to participate in their composition.*

I became convinced of this fact primarily from my personal experience. On four separate occasions, I was to 'collaborate' with Shostakovich. The first was writing a speech in commemoration of the bicentennial of Bach's death (Leipzig, 1950). The second was the same type of work in

[10] Originally a reference to the sham villages constructed by Grigory Aleksandrovich Potemkin (1739–91) to impress Catherine II upon her visit to the region under his charge, this term 'came to denote any pretentious facade designed to cover up a shabby or undesirable condition' ('Grigory Aleksandrovich Potemkin', *Britannica Online*). –EDS.

conjunction with the celebrations in Beethoven's memory (Berlin, 1952). The third was an article 'About certain vital questions in musical creativity. A composer's remarks',[11] and the fourth was a speech for the Second Congress of Composers.[12] I never heard a single suggestion or thought from D. D., before or after working on the texts.

Regarding the above-mentioned article, it is true that D. D. came to my place on Ogaryov Street to listen to how it turned out. He only interrupted my reading in one place. I had written: 'Musical dogmatists are highly suspicious of every attempt, even the slightest one, at such development and enrichment. Any slightly unusual poetic stroke provokes great waves of doubt and suspicion in them...'. I wrote further: '... Such a stroke irritates them like a nail in a chair'. D. D. tactfully interrupted me, saying: 'Daniil Vladimirovich, please strike out those words about the nail'. That was all! I have kept the drafts and variants of the article. I see that it was an attempt at expressing something essential, that corresponded to the level and criteria of an artist such as D. D. But he said not a word about it.

Funny things happened. In one of the articles, signed by Shostakovich, but not written by him, the famous German musicologist and critic H. H. Stuckenschmidt had been called an avant-garde composer. Stuckenschmidt was quite surprised (it was true that in his youth he had composed some 'avant-garde' music) and asked for explanations, after which he addressed his refutations to the Soviet Embassy. He received no answer. The case was 'settled' only many years later, when an article was published in *Sovetskaya Muzyka* [*Soviet Music*] about the book of Stuckenschmidt's memoirs. Here it became very clear that, in the Soviet Union, he was no longer to be called an 'avant-garde composer' ranking with Stockhausen.

I also remember, as another example, how Shostakovich's speech on Beethoven was prepared. I arrived at his place with the typed text. On my heels high-ranking characters from the Committee on Arts appeared. I read 'Shostakovich's

[11] *Pravda*, 17 June 1956, and also in the collection edited by Lev Danilevich, *Dmitry Shostakovich*, Sovetsky Kompozitor, Moscow, 1967.

[12] *Pravda*, 27 March 1957.

Speech', and then, looking very wise, they discussed it. As it turned out, many things were missing in this speech. Not about Beethoven himself, but about the attitude in the USSR regarding Beethoven and successive ties, and, of course, about the theme 'Beethoven and revolution'. I kept on taking notes. D. D. sat in the remotest and darkest corner and kept silent. His speech 'was being created by the government'! This incident took place in the evening, and early the next morning he was supposed to take a plane to the GDR. To interfere would have made no sense! Later on, I sat at the typewriter (a terrible one that was never used). I made various haphazard additions from memory until three o'clock in the morning. I then dozed for three or four hours on the sofa that Nina Vasil'yevna had thoughtfully prepared for me. I woke up when D. D., already dressed, came in. Out of politeness, he looked at my typed sheets, amusingly scratched the back of his head, and then took his leave: 'Thank you, thank you, it's excellent!' That was the whole 'collaboration'.

Shostakovich, naturally, had both ideas and words, and was generous with his time and efforts. He could indeed collaborate in newspapers and magazines, and appear as a publicist. In the fact that he clearly shunned any real inner responsibility for what was published in his name, I detect a very serious motive: he regarded the entire official press production very sadly and sceptically, and preferred to 'stay on the side': 'let them think what they want. I, for one, know its worth'. However, he did not spare his name and he did not protect it. . . .

In private, D. D. spoke in an amazingly lively and expressive manner. He had his own style of speech: short sentences, that almost always sounded like aphorisms, in which all the unnecessary terms had been deleted; and his sentences always hit the mark, as does a sniper; his enunciation was extremely precise, each word and even individual sounds (including consonants) were endowed with a meaningful significance. The specific expressiveness of his speech lay in the humour and sarcasm that emanated from an unruffled seriousness. This was brilliant artistry.

From official rostrums, D. D. spoke quite differently. Here is one quote from my diary during the '50s: 'Listened to his address with a growing irritation, but also with sympathy.

How alien and artificial to him was the text he was reading: trite newspaper stock-phrases, verbosity and textbook-like quotes. And how he read all this! Patter, total absence of punctuation, no caesuras, total absence of meaningful intonation ... Like an almost illiterate schoolboy answering a question by reading from his crib-sheet something that was way beyond his understanding. But there was also something that was pure artistic parody. As if he were denouncing both himself in his role of official orator and, from a general point of view, the entire practice of propagandistic speeches "from a piece of paper"'.

Now, thirty years later, I understand even better the inner psychological meaning of these oratorical, theatrical performances by D. D. I don't know whether they were 100 per cent premeditated, or born out of an inevitable instant reaction to a moronic and compulsory situation. Indeed, why did he have to read inept texts and present them as if they were his own? Probably, his entire being bristled at this coercion, and he did everything in his power to *divorce himself* from what he was reading, simultaneously hinting at his being not privy to this newspaper banality. He succeeded in doing this in an extremely expressive manner!

Shostakovich lived many years of his life against a background in which the evaluation of his work was undergoing feverish changes. Here is an example of the curve of these appraisals during the '30s and '40s: the first half of the '30s – the huge success of the performances of *Lady Macbeth* in Leningrad and Moscow, a stream of laudatory reviews. On 28 January 1936 – the famous article 'Muddle Instead of Music' in *Pravda*. A new stream of devastating articles and discussions that not only re-evaluated the opera, but all of Shostakovich's works. 1937: the Fifth Symphony – again a huge success and a wave of social recognition. 1941: the Seventh Symphony – an even bigger recognition, but this time also an international one. 1943: the Eighth Symphony – contradictory comments in the press before and after the premiere, and an unofficial recommendation 'from higher up' to abstain from subsequent performances. 1945: the Ninth Symphony – doubts predominate: 'not the type of symphony we were expecting after the victory'. 1948: Central Committee resolution 'Shostakovich the Formalist'. 1949: Iosif Vissarionovich Stalin gives a call to Shostakovich, offering him an opportunity to go to the US to the Cultural and Scientific Conference for World Peace.

According to Nina Vasil'yevna's recollections, the conversation was approximately as follows:

'Hello, Dmitry Dmitriyevich. This is Stalin speaking.'

'Hello, I am listening.'

'First of all, one would like to inquire, how are you, how is your health?'

'Thank you, thank you. I feel fine.'

'We have a favour to ask of you.'

'I will be glad to help, if it is not beyond my power.'

'Of course it won't be beyond your power. We are talking about a trip to America to the cultural and scientific conference. Do you foresee any difficulties?'

'I must confess that there is one. Without any doubt, I will be asked about the Eighth Symphony, about why it is criticised at home and why it is not performed. What answer can I give?'

'Well, the fact that it is not performed, I think it is a misunderstanding. And I think it can be rectified. I think the comrades will heed my opinion.'

'Thank you, thank you, Iosif Vissarionovich. Probably, it can be really set right.'

'I wish you good luck and good health! If any difficulties arise, let me know.'[13]

March of the same year – D. D. made a speech at the Conference and it was published by the entire Soviet governmental press.

All the critical attacks against Shostakovich, since they came 'from higher up', accumulated in various periodicals, in programmes of music education and appreciation. They would be quickly assimilated and would become that element of the directive that 'one cannot help but mention'. This created a huge mess. After all, even in the Central Committee's 'corrected' resolution of 26 May 1958, a total approval of the previous resolution had been formulated twice. As to what the difference was between 'incorrect tendencies in individual works' of the previously condemned Soviet composers and the once again condemned 'formalism' – one

[13] Also *cf. Testimony*, p. 112/148. –EDS.

could only guess. Quite often the contradictions and the confusion put Shostakovich himself in a complicated, at times tragi-comic, situation. Oksana Leont'yeva recalls her state examination for graduation from the conservatory in 1959: 'The chairman of the state commission was D. D. My topic for the examination was: "The 1948 resolution and its amendment in 1958". Looking straight at D. D., I had to tell how he had been insulted, badgered, and later on "forgiven"....'.

Before the Fifth Symphony

The very first time I heard Shostakovich's music was in 1926. It was the First Symphony, performed in Kharkov under the baton of N. Malko. I understood and appreciated the Scherzo best of all. Probably because there were direct links in it with Prokofiev, whose music I already knew a bit. I also liked the first movement a great deal: the intriguing prelude, the first and particularly the second theme. I found the second theme totally understandable and it was highly original in its combination of lyricism with 'transsensual' chilliness. The third and fourth movements, despite their obvious association with familiar and very good music (from Wagner to Skryabin), left me respectfully indifferent.

A year or two later, I saw the young Shostakovich for the first time in N. S. Zhilyayev's[14] cramped little room in Chistyye Prudy. I was working on a problem in the 'strict style'. Somewhere at the opposite end of the big communal apartment 'four short rings' sounded, and Nikolay Sergeyevich shuffled toward the front door in his slippers. The Leningrad guest appeared – a mere boy, but the gaze behind the glasses in their thick black frames was more than mature. He wasn't very loquacious. Very quickly, at Nikolay Sergeyevich's request, he sat at the piano to demonstrate his First Sonata. I understood almost nothing, but I experienced

[14] Nikolay Sergeyevich Zhilyayev (1881–1942), music theorist, pedagogue, composer, and mentor of Shostakovich. He was executed after the Tukhachevsky affair, a victim of the purges in the late 1930s (*cf. Testimony*, p. 91/121). –EDS.

a very strong impression from everything I saw. The sonata's author was unusually severe and utterly concentrated. Authoritative in his artistry and artistic conviction, he seemed to hypnotise us with his seriousness. He did not simply play, but gave the impression that he was practising witchcraft, impressing on his listeners his creative will. Nikolay Sergeyevich stood behind his back, shifting from one foot to the other in his agitation, and his face expressed a complex mixture of curiosity, astonishment and joy.

For decades I have kept in memory that first impression of total incomprehensibility experienced in Zhilyayev's room. I never had the opportunity to listen to the sonata in later years. Now, not trusting those early impressions, I found on a shelf of mine, miraculously preserved, an old copy of the 1927 edition. I managed to play through it. It turned out that there was no incomprehensibility! It had its own, utterly defined logic and an amazing assurance for a beginning composer. However, what is it in essence? A violent energy striking through a solid and prickly medium. Unremitting dynamics. Everything is driven and seething, except for the episode of the *Lento* (before the conclusion). By analogy with études on a given type of movement (for example, Chopin's double-thirds or sixths), the sonata could have been called 'étude on dissonance'. Nonetheless, it was not the Shostakovich that made me follow him starting with his First Symphony. The energy of this sonata is hyperbolically hard and soulless. I understand: this was the way that radical anti-romanticism was interpreted in the '20s. In it Shostakovich had made a 'dash' to tear himself ruthlessly away from the old romanticism, including that of Skryabin: he was taking the path of a new, more rigid style without any softening 'beauties'. The style of the First Sonata is tendentious. It reflects the characteristic accent of the concepts of that time, which not only narrowed those concepts, but constricted the inner world of the composer himself, as well as distanced him from what had already appeared in the First Symphony, in the *Fantastic Dances*, and what would be expressed so clearly in his piano preludes and *Lady Macbeth* some five years later.

The Second Symphony ('To October', 1927) alienated me and even irritated me. For exactly what specific reason, I did not clearly understand: it was the same type of aversion I had felt for the First Sonata. For many years, I did not specifically think about this symphony. It was only recently that I really listened to a recording, looked at the score, and read about it in some new books. Alas, even now it is still utterly alien to me. It repels me from a purely musical standpoint – almost everywhere, i.e., up to the entrance of the chorus – an unnatural combination of strict constructiveness and musical senselessness. The symphony was created not from reality, but from a *scheme*. This scheme was successfully formulated by M. Sabinina: 'A dark chaos, symbolising the cheerless past of workers, the development of revolutionary conscience and, finally, the glorification of October'.[15]

The idea, similar to that of the posters and pieces of propaganda from the '20s, is understood today not as representative of the victory of conscience, but, to the contrary, as the triumph of demagogy that begot blindness. A. Bezymensky's poem, on which the final chorus was based, is correctly assessed by M. Sabinina as being 'full of slogans and bombastic Party rhetoric'. The words about the 'national sorrow', about the 'silence, the suffering, and the oppression' are crammed into verses full of pathetic smugness. The social conflict emerges as a triumph and a rejoicing. The poet flies into a rage of flattering and magnificent verbosity, he is a powerful tribune, everything is clear for him, he proclaims and brings fame! The composer tries to be stern and ascetic. The gloomy and resolute phrases of the basses (at the beginning of the chorus) somehow remind us of the oratorical 'posters' by A. Davidenko. Nonetheless, the symphony decidedly lacks real dramatic human nature, as well as real human spontaneity, qualities that played a paramount role in the events of the past. Nowadays I better understand the purely musical weakness of the symphony: its dynamics, official constructivism, and total lack of spirituality in the intonational content are inseparable from the radical 'leftist' ideas of that time: the energy and the dynamism were then understood as the antithesis of the truly human, in which there is too much unreliability, too much reflection, and too many characteristics of a Hamlet. It was precisely from this

[15] M. Sabinina, *Shostakovich – simfonist* (*Shostakovich the Symphonist*), Muzyka, Moscow, 1976, p. 59.

concept that a greater confidence for the human *mechanism* emerged, rather than from *its organism and its psychology*. This was the source of Meyerhold's idea of bio-mechanics. In the pages of the magazine *Zrelishcha* [*Spectacles*] it had been explained in the following manner: 'Modern man, who lives under conditions of mechanisation, is incapable of not mechanizing the moving elements of his organism ... The modern actor must be shown on the stage as a perfect aircraft engine'.[16]

In spite of Meyerhold's stubborn and cocky polemical attitude, it is well known that his own huge talent forced him to 'apply the brakes to' and depart gradually from these principles. Exactly the same phenomenon took place in music, and, in particular, in Shostakovich's evolution. M. Sabinina claims that 'we should not approach the appraisal of the imagistic style of the Second Symphony from today's aesthetical position'.[17] I find it difficult to agree with this view. *To understand* the composer's intention is one thing. In order to do this, one must, naturally, take the ideological and aesthetic positions of that time into consideration. To evaluate the intention itself is quite another thing. In this case, the historic distance and the point of view of a different era are not only natural, but essential. Sabinina, according to the critical elements in her analysis, proceeds from the new, modern attitude toward the aesthetics of the '20s. Neither artists nor anyone else can fathom all the facets of their time. They are rarely capable of always distinguishing what seems to be from what is real.

My perception of Shostakovich's opera *Nos* [*The Nose*] is seen in my 1929 article, which I imprudently published before I had seen a performance.[18] The article is tendentious, unfair, and contains many errors. I had been simply unable to deal with certain problems. For example, for some reason I

[16] Quoted from K. Rudnitsky's book *Rezhissyor Meierkhol'd* (*Meyerhold the Stage Director*), Iskusstvo, Moscow, 1969, p. 265.

[17] Sabinina, *Shostakovich – simfonist*, p. 68.

[18] 'Nos – Opera Shostakovicha' ('The Nose – Opera by Shostakovich'), *Proletarsky Muzykant* (*Proletarian Musician*), 7–8, Moscow, 1929.

linked the grotesque in art with decadence, not considering, and probably not knowing, where and how the grotesque appeared in works of very different artists and periods. I am particularly ashamed of the passage at the beginning of the article. Gogol's well-known concluding lines ('However, what is even more strange, even less understandable is the fact that authors have the opportunity to choose such topics . . . First of all, they are utterly useless to the fatherland . . .', and so forth). When I read the novel at the time, I understood these lines *literally*, and I was utterly oblivious to the author's irony, an irony that was specifically directed at dolts, such as I was at that time.

How I wish I could 'begin to see clearly' and perceive in the opera *The Nose* what is dearest to me in Shostakovich's work! But, alas, this piece does not appeal to me either. Naturally, I can see his amazing sweep, the originality of his talent and virtuosic technique; I can also see his temperamental sarcasm, the germ of many things that, later on, will be brilliantly expressed in his symphonies. So what is unattractive, what is alienating in it? At the moment, I have still found no convincing answer and I keep on turning it over in my mind. Here is the path I am following.

The satire in Gogol's novel is rooted in the fact that the fantastic and the absurd are accepted by the characters as something scandalous, *nevertheless perfectly possible.* Major Koval'yov did not have one shred of doubt that the 'gentleman in uniform' he saw by chance was his own nose, which had disappeared. In the Cathedral of Kazan, the only thing that perplexed the major was the difficult task of being introduced – how to strike up a conversation with such an important civil servant, and, by the same token, call him to order? As for the councillor, instead of being very surprised by Koval'yov's moronic offer, he was busy putting on airs, suitable to his high rank, and unwilling to allow 'any close relations' with a functionary from a 'different department'. No less absurd was Koval'yov's attempt at filing a complaint, regarding the disappearance of his nose, with the chief of police, and later on, of putting an ad in the newspaper regarding this matter. Thus, the fantastically absurd is included in a series of commonplace nuisances: swindles, frauds, cozenages, intrigues, arbitrary rules of the police, and self-conceit of 'highly placed' people – exactly as in daily life.

The juxtaposition of the weirdness of the situation combined with ordinary reactions is precisely what creates Gogol's sarcasm.

The vocabulary of the novel is extremely close to the vocabulary used in everyday life. As for the vocabulary of the opera, it is almost a total parody. This parody is so radical that it loses any connections with the characteristically primitive standards so accurately caught by Gogol. The effect of the absurd is expressed in the very intonations of the characters; however, they are not Gogol's satirical interpretation of real speech prototypes. More often than not these were musical 'idiotisms' invented by the composer himself, which, in his thinking, were meant to convey, in the best possible way, the absurdity of the characters. However, this considerably changes the satirical tone. The 'strange' intonations in the parts of Koval'yov, the Nose and others are principally *a satire on music*, and they pushed aside the cardinal satire that was present in Gogol's novel. Such a change of emphasis is particularly obvious in the famous octet of the yard-keepers (Scene V). Here again, what was essential in Gogol was the conflict between day-to-day occurrences (a little dog had run away, a coachman and a girl were let go into service, a carriage with a missing spring was sold, and so forth) and then the utterly unusual (the disappearance of the nose). However, the polyphonic character of the octet prevents us from hearing these announcements. Here, as well as in the fugato of the Second Symphony, constructivism was linked with intonational arbitrariness. Perhaps only in two episodes – in the song of the lackey Ivan (Scene VI) and in the fortune-telling scene for Podtochina's daughter (Scene VIII) – did the composer use, as his source, an occurrence characteristic of everyday life and make a parody of it. Later on, Shostakovich (taking into account Stravinsky's experience) took precisely that path. Seeking to express through music stupidity, absurdity and vulgarity, he found *the musical* equivalents of these psychological traits and, without losing the connections with his primary sources, he parodied them. In the opera *The Nose* this essential connection is, more often than not, violated. The fantasy of the musician-satirist has no direct connections and therefore achieves no artistic persuasiveness . . .

Following the loathsome article in *Pravda* ('Muddle

Instead of Music'), no decent individual was capable of – his conscience prevented him from – coming out publicly with any kind of criticism about *Lady Macbeth*. When in the second half of the '50s the official attacks on Shostakovich were coming to an end, and when on 8 January 1963 the premiere of the new *Katerina Izmailova* (its [*Lady Macbeth*'s] second version) took place, the analytical approach to this opera turned out to be, once again, inappropriate and inopportune. What was of utmost importance to our thinking at the time was to fortify the defence of the composer against further outrages and badgering. Shostakovich had already written some of his best, truly greatest symphonies. We wished primarily to vindicate not only the artist's musical authority, but also his moral authority. But, naturally, the first was inseparably linked to the second: it was only with *those words*, with the help of precisely *that* insolent newness of speech, that it had been possible to say what he had said. Said in a *different way*, it would not have been *the same*. But every cloud has its silver lining! A fair respect for Shostakovich and a noble love for him had levelled out, in the conscience of his contemporaries, his complexity, a fact that was also clearly reflected in the appraisals of his earlier works.

The reasons for this change lay in a wider process, which in itself was complex and multifaceted. In answer to the criticism from the right (including the one 'from higher up'), a 'defence activity' from the left was slowly gathering strength, and by the early '60s was already on the offensive. Having started as a righteous defence of authentic innovation, it progressively had turned into an attack against the innovations of the Western avant-garde. In a demagogically clever move it had appropriated the civic authority of the previous offensive by the conservatives. As I have already mentioned, Shostakovich had readily been 'debited', as one of us – the persecuted ones. Those who defended him but did not accept the newest fashion (which in many ways discredited Shostakovich's feat) were branded conservatives. Another side to the conflict was the growing indifference, the nonchalant apathy toward the *essence itself* of what was historically identified with the name of Shostakovich.

During his lifetime people had already begun to cling to him, attracted by the tempting goal, to quote the words from

Katerina Izmailova, 'where we could and how we could profit from troubled waters'. D. D. was surrounded on all sides by 'troubled waters' and he considered this fact the tragic norm of his existence. Once he was dead, 'the troubled waters' overcame the last obstacles. . . .

New articles and new research on Shostakovich bear no comparison with what has been done earlier. Even the most superficial contributions are not devoid of interest, thanks to the abundance of facts and documents. There are even some that are serious and interesting. Nevertheless, as a rule, the complexity of Shostakovich's evolution is oversimplified. At times, the significance of his early radical 'leftist' experiments is tendentiously exaggerated.

With regard to *Katerina*, the simplification remains almost hidden; at any rate, it is nowhere as obvious as, for example, the laudation of *The Nose*. This is helped by the peculiar chronological position of Shostakovich's second opera in his *œuvre*. The opera originated in the years when the composer was just beginning to feel at ease in this world of elevated humanity, whose absolute lord he was to become some five or six years later. He was still being teased and attracted by many things from the recent past, by the extravagance and stunning effects of the 'leftist' front of the '20s. He had not yet freed himself from the schemes and accents of a 'purely revolutionary' art that reigned in the criticism of the time.

. . . I am rereading my collection of newspaper clippings and leaflets relating to *Katerina*. Good heavens, what confusion, stupidity and self-conceited, categorical statements! But at the same time, one does find some flashes of observations reflecting something more substantial. After all, at the time, discussion was still the norm; then, after 1936, a work was *not discussed*, it was only *judged*, and still later, it was only *exalted*.

The requirements and criteria of the late '20s and early '30s were particularly well reflected in the *Katerina* libretto written by A. Preis. However, they were also reflected in the composer's intention: after all, he – at any rate, theoretically – was assiduously following these requirements dictated by every newspaper and journal. In D. D.'s article 'About My Opera', we read: 'My role, as a Soviet composer, was to preserve all the power of Leskov's novel, to approach it critically and provide an explanation, from our Soviet perspective, of the events that take place in it'.[19] What did these words mean at the time? First of all, it was *propagandistic utilitarianism.* It was fierce, scourging and devastating sarcasm directed at the 'old world'. According to the widely accepted canon of the 'Party principle', only a high coefficient of propaganda, in other words, a maximally intense artistic illustration of political slogans, could justify the existence of the artist. Both the librettist and the composer made every conceivable effort; they flogged away with every possible means available to them. And yet, Shostakovich did something more: he began to talk about the tragedy of love, about the dream of love, the suffering, the sacrifice. The vigilant critics immediately 'reproached' him for it.

One of them wrote: 'Leskov's *Katerina Izmailova* could never become the idealised image of the Russian woman. Her tragedy – the tragedy of passionate love – leaves us rather passionless'.[20] 'In Shostakovich's opera amorous interests overshadow all other daily interests. The theme of love forced into the background and crudely pared down the theme of social tragedy.'[21] How characteristic of the period this confrontation of the human with the social! Another critic also thought that Leskov ought to be corrected and brought up to date. However, considering the fact that the composer 'mercilessly mocks and stigmatises' old Russia, he was forced to acknowledge that: 'At times heavy satire may even lead to a hypertrophied, almost farcical caricature, thus depriving the heroes of individuality and bringing them down to generalised and typified "masks of evil".'[22]

The priest at the end of the Fourth Scene, the entire Seventh Scene with its district police officer and policemen,

[19] D. Shostakovich, 'O moyey opere' ('About My Opera') in the collection *Katerina Izmailova*, Leningrad, 1934, p. 11.

[20] M. Sokol'sky, 'Katerina Izmailova', *Sovetskoye Iskusstvo* (*Soviet Art*), 1934, Nos. 4–5.

[21] M. Grinberg, '*Katerina Izmailova.* Opera i spektakl'' ('*Katerina Izmailova.* The Opera and the Production'), *Sovetskoye Iskusstvo*, February 1934.

[22] V. Bogdanov-Berezovsky, '*Ledi Makbet Mtsenskogo Uyezda.* Prem'yera v leningradskom Malom opernom teatre' ('*Lady Macbeth of the Mtsensk District.* Premiere at the Leningrad Maly Opera Theatre'), *Sovetskoye Iskusstvo*, 11 February 1934.

who 'socially' denounce themselves, and the 'local nihilist' (who was added in the second version) – how well all these poster-like preposterous scenes of buffoonery remind me of all my photo journals and 'Blue Blouses'![23] There was no mention of it in Leskov, not even in Saltykov-Shchedrin, who always remained at the height of subtle, psychological portrayal. The 'modernisation' of Leskov's novel was due to the tendencies of the young Soviet theatre, and this fact, even then, in the early '30s, was duly noted by the critics. 'In *Katerina Izmailova* as well as in *The Nose* there are moments of stage craft where the influence of Meyerhold's techniques is very clearly felt.'[24]

Shostakovich seems to have believed that 'Leskov was unable to provide a correct interpretation of the events developing in his novel', and that precisely he, a man of the new era, had to compensate for the imperfection of the literary source and 'rouse sympathy for the heroine of the novel'.[25] This was a characteristic error of the time. For all that is best in the opera – except for his own creative genius and his own sincere responsiveness, the composer is, on the contrary, precisely indebted to Leskov, as well as Ostrovsky, Tolstoy and Chekhov. He is indebted to the whole spirit of Russian classicism, which one must cherish as the apple of one's eye and protect it against any 'modernisation'.

The critic A. Tal'nikov attempted to 'speak on Leskov's behalf' in his article. The novel, he wrote, depicts not a 'murderess'; in reality it is a 'poem about the power of love that sparkles both in blood and mud, and which is brought to the sharpest edge of its dark triumph and its dark tragedy'.[26] Tal'nikov quotes Leskov:

[23] A troupe of Moscow actors formed in 1921 and famous for their enactments of political and ideological themes in sketches, song and dance. The 'Blue Blouses', named for the overalls worn by its members as a basic costume, provided the model for other such groups. The troupe was suppressed by Stalin in 1928, in part because its satire 'inappropriately' extended to post-Revolutionary problems and inequities. –EDS.

[24] E. Braudo, 'Pobeda sovetskoy muzyki' ('The Victory of Soviet Music'), *Literaturnaya Gazeta* (*Literary Gazette*), 30 January 1934.

[25] Shostakovich, 'About My Opera', p. 11.

[26] A. Tal'nikov, 'Katerina Izmailova', *Vechernyaya Moskva* (*Moscow Evening Paper*), 26 January 1934.

'– "Why do I need it?" – says the wretched woman to her lover who entices her to kill the child to gain the inheritance.

"That's right, maybe you are not interested in it, but for my sake" . . . and so forth. An on and on he went, harping on the same theme. . . . And when she would get the capital, then their bliss would know no bounds.'

The author of the article continues: 'In the flames of passion, in the blaze of the agony of love, on her "cross", for Leskov there are no longer categories of murder or evil from the psychological point of view . . . Everything is justifiable in a man: he is himself the powerless victim of this inferno'.[27]

Nevertheless this is not the only aspect in Leskov's novel. What drew Katerina to the pyre of this *sensual, savage* and *blinding passion*? Boredom? Slavery? Locks on the doors? Nothing on which to spend her energies? The Katerina of the opera begins with that passion. The writer, however, addresses himself to the psychological sources; he shows us a Katerina who has not yet been disfigured into rioting flesh and blind vengeance. The dream of love, a dream which nature itself bestows on powerful, whole-hearted beings – this is the true beginning of the inner life of Leskov's heroine. It tells many things, it explains a great deal of what had happened to Katerina behind the gates of the Izmailovs' house. What is really necessary to 'make her better'?

I recall how, in conjunction with one of my articles about Shostakovich's opera that I wrote in the mid-'30s, I thought a good deal about this topic. I reread Leskov's novel, trying to grasp its meaning. I tried to understand what the authors of the opera 'did not quite get' from the book. In one of my old notebooks I have found several quotations that I took from Leskov's novel. Here is one of them:

> Katerina L'vovna raised herself on one elbow and looked at the high grass of the garden: the grass tossed in the moonlight which dotted the flowers and the leaves of the trees. These capricious small spots of light turned the grass into gold, and they trembled as live fire-coloured butterflies, or as though the whole grass under the trees had been caught in a net of moonlight undulating from side to side.

[27] *Ibid.*

> 'Oh! Darling Seryozhechka, how lovely!' exclaimed Katerina L'vovna, turning toward him.

Here it is, the poetic world that had been initially bestowed on Katerina. These lines of Leskov are almost music already. In the opera, they are echoed in the third and fifth scenes in music that is strong and inspired, but whose psychological mood is quite different. In the opera we will not see 'the net of moonlight', nor will we see the sparkling 'fire-coloured butterflies', nor the spots of light. We will not notice this whole weightless loveliness of nature at night; we will not feel her soul, which still believes in this general and unique beauty, and which is still able to express her delight without any sorrow. These lyrical lines of Leskov are the initial point of Katerina's *tragedy*: the illusion that not only she, but also her 'Darling Seryozhechka' understands all of this and that, together with the 'golden night', a true love had begun between the two of them.

No! Leskov should not have been 'modernised'; one should have delved ever more deeply into his poetry. Ever more deeply – in order to realise the height from which Katerina had fallen to end up at the bottom of a merchant's bedroom, to understand her revolt, vengeance, and final failure.

Today, more than half a century later, once again I go over the score, checking myself. I am so afraid of making a mistake! It is even better, even more clearly than then, I see that the opera's spiritual level is multi-layered. The highest layer already belongs to the world of the authentic Shostakovich: the entire final act, particularly the monologue and the chorus of the convicts; Katerina's arioso 'In the depths of the forest, there is a lake'; and certain pages from the third and fifth scenes. Below this level there is craftsmanship applied to problems which are more and more primitive, right up to the obvious vulgarity suggested by the librettist (the clowning priest, the doll-like cretins of policemen). Everything that is lower than the final act, carries in itself the stamp of expressionistic cruelty, of leaden weight and hopelessness. This was the spirit of the time, it enthralled us in Alban Berg's *Wozzeck*, it seemed to be most radical, and this radicalism consisted of an open, screaming show of the abomination that existed in life and in man. Shostakovich was already coming out of this hopeless darkness and the plenitude of tragic feeling was already guiding him toward the world of authentic humaneness. That is, naturally, the cardinal significance of *Katerina Izmailova*.

Three Apexes

In my mind, the Fifth, Seventh and Eighth Symphonies are absolute apexes. Shostakovich's other best scores were only their satellites. Recalling them now, I would have liked to avoid *musicology*. I am not against high-class musicology, but even that class of musicology too often levels off the meaning of various aspects. Here, in this book of mine, I have no need of aspects that are too specific. I choose what has a direct relation to the life that surrounds me and is in me. I choose what had enthralled me in Shostakovich's music, beginning with the Fifth Symphony. What was it? In the most general terms it was 'the tragic art and his place in life' (that was what I wrote in my diary about 'Dialogi o Musorgskom' [Dialogues about Musorgsky] by Asafiev, on 14 March 1947).

'The context of life'. The Fifth Symphony had been written in Leningrad, where it was first performed in 1937. This date in itself speaks volumes. How did I understand and experience this context at the time? With vastly insufficient maturity and inadequate determination. In the foreground, I was experiencing, as were many others, the fears, the painful perplexity and the confusion of the times. I was also trying to make ends meet, trying to accommodate the incompatible, and elaborating various kinds of projects in my mind. All were futile efforts! Even at the time, the shame had already surfaced and was striking to everyone. Even today this fraudulent attempt at trying to accommodate the compatible with the incompatible still can be seen. They say that times were hard but we were making progress. Nonsense! Today, it has all become quite clear to us. Newly erected industrial buildings, gigantic plans designed with the 'toiling field hands' in mind, and the 'March of the Enthusiasts' . . . Many things all in the same vein, and simultaneously – an inexorable, quickening process of degradation. It would be a mistake to think that this type of climate was detrimental only to the soul. No, it was one of the main reasons for the degradation of the 'cause', a degradation that was multifaceted and all encompassing. It was a degradation that touched the technical, scientific, legal, artistic and creative fields; the cultural aspect of work as well as every other aspect of culture. The 'cause', urged on by fears, propaganda and harsh discipline, although it kept progressing, was, by the same token, crumbling. This was carefully concealed then, but in the end it was all exposed.

I regret that, in the '30s and '40s, I did not write down what was most important. There were many reasons for behaving that way. I acted out of fear and because I was not able to understand everything that was taking place. Later on, during the war years, I did not write either, because my main, everyday interests and concerns had shifted. Then again, in the '50s I wrote nothing because of the 'thaw' and illusory hopes. In one of my later entries, I did find one of my attempts to describe, in an abstract way, certain characteristics of the 'climate'.

> The wounds are not allowed to breathe and heal themselves; they are covered up, they are concealed with plaster and varnish; they are always throbbing and suppurating. The living body is attached by thousands of ties to pegs (as Gulliver was, when he fell prisoner to the Lilliputians); and it is unable to get up, look around, and see the horizon. Degenerated or atrophied cells are constantly choking down the live ones; as for the live cells, already infected by dead flesh, they are condemned and what is awaiting them is vacuum and entropy . . . (15 August 1960).

As I recopied these lines, I saw clearly that it was a very feeble attempt to describe the atmosphere of the past decades, the tragic aspect of those years, the abusiveness and brutality, the mendacity, the obtuse and automatised inhumanity, and the perfidious duplicity. Hope has appeared again (is it, perhaps, once more illusory?) that those monstrous years will be reconstructed, based on the documents, and will take shape before the future as a total picture, in comparison with which all the so-called anti-utopias will appear to be innocent pastimes. Incidentally, although nowadays we write openly about all of this, the process of understanding may be curtailed at any time.

The desire to express what is painful knows no limit. Even in solitary cells, even awaiting execution, people have always composed poetry or written memoirs. Why did Shostakovich's Fifth Symphony, and soon after, his Quintet, so powerfully resound in the soul? Faith in the strength of the soul, its rights and possibilities had been quite shattered. From the very beginning any glimpse of hope, any impulse, was shrouded in sceptical bitterness. That was the reason why the attitude toward 'open lyricism', so richly present in the nineteenth century, was undergoing such a change. Simple sincerity of feeling was no longer sufficient to express spiritual and emotional needs. The emotional 'high waters' were felt to be an excess of credulity; in the boundless and lyrical plenitude, the danger of starry-eyed idealism was feared. There were to be no signs of admiration or self-admiration in beauty.

I think that Shostakovich's discovery lies in the fact that, in order to express tragedy and the cruel anguish it begot, he had enclosed it within narrow walls of granite. The spring is tightened in a new way that makes the 'energy of release', coming from the inside, feel stronger and, simultaneously, in close correlation, makes one feel the power of the exterior pressure, something that had forever been caught in the classical Laocoön, but had been so easily forgotten in the arts of the recent past. (Skryabin, one of the last pre-Revolutionary romantics, had reached total freedom from any restraints: he bubbled, exploded, sank in languid bliss and, like a winged elf, freely flew toward the 'distant star'.)

In the tragic pages of the Fifth Symphony, the rhythms are unyielding and inexorably urgent. The melody is gloomy, time and again forcing its way as though through barbed wire; it has that tone of a suppressed soul, permeated with harsh bitterness, but a soul that has not yet been destroyed and which is still resisting. In everything that resists the inexorably tragic, the lyricism is utterly different, without a shred of romantic, sentimental enthusiasm, it is sage and elevated, it 'soars' and, at the same time, it is touchingly simple, child-like, or heavenly. The unforgettable impression in the first movement – the subordinate theme, the coda of the same movement with its soft, somehow magical 'farewell'; and in the Largo – surprising in its emotion, in its combination of simplicity and highest tenderness – the melody in the oboe.

As I write I feel a strange sort of awkwardness. It seems as though I am on the verge of slipping off on a path that carries me away from the inexpressible and burning impressions of those distant years. On a path that is already inert, shadowed by my professional daily occupations.

One can describe a novel, a play, or a movie by relying heavily on the original. One is almost incapable of writing such a work when it comes to a poem. One is even more incapacitated when it comes to describing music. It is true that a good analysis of the structure and the stylistic features does help one to hear the music better. However, one should not humour oneself with vain hopes: all these characteristics of imagery and structural analyses are, for the most part, speculations, 'apropos' thoughts, not the real, co-authoring and co-experiencing. If only for the reason mentioned above: because of the confusion of various aspects. This is utterly impossible and unnecessary if the soul and the conscience are drawn into the process of music itself, and are included musically, but not verbally or out of scientific cognition. Even the most accurate observations, epithets, and associations, born out of the keenest artistic sensitivity, are not very helpful. All these subtle discoveries quickly become popular, they are turned out mechanically in many worthless popularising commentaries: and it is shameful to repeat them.

As is known, the Seventh and Eighth Symphonies are sisters. They both contain the tragedy of war and a tragedy on a larger scale. Because the war had not only legalised, but, as a point of propaganda, had encouraged and made more vivid the theme of 'exposure of evil' (and this evil, 'it goes without saying', was Hitler's fascism), it had become possible to talk about something even greater – the fate of the country and the people. This background for Shostakovich's war symphonies was to many people (perhaps the overwhelming majority) unperceived, and the others were only unconsciously aware of it. After all, there were enough daily first-hand experiences to fill our hearts with the horror, pain and anger. Thus a lock had been opened, and torrents of ire and grief that had accumulated for decades poured out with tremendous force. A fact that could be made clear only in music.

Shostakovich wanted to explain the Seventh Symphony only from a local point of view and in direct connection with events relating to the war, because at the time – and for a long time afterwards – that was the only way to explain it. In October 1941 (before he had finished the finale) the composer explained:

> The exposition in the first movement tells about the happy and peaceful life of people, confident in themselves and in their future. This is the simple and peaceful life led by thousands of Leningrad volunteers, by the entire city, by our entire country. ... In the development, war erupts in the peaceful life that these people are then engaged in. ... The recapitulation is a funeral march, or, more exactly, a requiem for the victims of war. Simple people honour the memory of their heroes. ... After the requiem, an even more tragic episode follows. I don't know how to characterise this music. Perhaps, it is a mother's tears, or even the feeling that the sorrow is so great that no more tears are left.

This passage leads us, in the composer's words, to the conclusion, 'to the apotheosis of life and sun'.[28] In another of the composer's commentaries the conclusion is simply called 'bright and lyrical' (from the annotations for the premiere of the Symphony in Kuibyshev).[29]

There is no doubt the composer wished to avoid certain tendentious overstatements. The finale of the Symphony is characterised by the word 'victory'. In reality its content is much more complex, especially in the middle episode (Sarabande). We have still another statement by Shostakovich regarding a series of works composed during the war years. It stands out because of its greater breadth that allows us to grasp the 'background':

> I wanted to recreate, in artistic form, the picture of the emotional life of man, stunned by the gigantic hammer of war. I wanted to express his anxieties, his fortitude, and his joys ... It seemed to me highly attractive to depict a man who loved life and freedom and who, therefore, courageously rose, to use Shakespeare's words, against a sea of troubles. This man, the hero of my music, moves toward victory through agonising ordeals and catastrophes [...]. It goes without saying that his road is not strewn with roses, he is not accompanied by the sound of merry drummers [...]. The

[28] D. Shostakovich, 'V dni oborony Leningrada' ('During the Days of the Defence of Leningrad'), *Sovetskoye Iskusstvo*, 8 October 1941.

[29] Quoted from Sabinina, *Shostakovich – simfonist*, p. 165.

> optimistic finales of my works [. . .] correspond to the objective logic of events and to my perception of the course of history, which inevitably must lead to the downfall of tyranny and evil and to the victory of freedom and humanity.[30]

In 1981, in Göttingen, I had the opportunity to hold in my hands for one night these very memoirs of Shostakovich which have been so castigated in our country, the memoirs which were posthumously published abroad by S. Volkov. The book was in German. I read, trying to quickly understand and assimilate the content of various chapters, until I was totally exhausted. I was able to make very few notes. Here are the lines corresponding to the symphonies of the war years:

> I have heard so much nonsense about the Seventh and Eighth Symphonies. It's amazing how long-lived these stupidities are. Everything that was written about those symphonies in the first few days is repeated without any changes to this very day, even though there has been time to do some thinking. After all, the war ended a long time ago, almost thirty years.[. . .] The Seventh Symphony had been planned before the war and consequently it simply cannot be seen as a reaction to Hitler's attack. The 'invasion' theme has absolutely nothing to do with the attack. I was thinking of other enemies of humanity when I composed the theme. Naturally, fascism is repugnant to me, but not only German fascism, any form of it is repugnant.
>
> Nowadays, people like to recall the prewar period as an idyllic time [*But I have just quoted the comments of the composer himself. . . . Did he write these lines of his own volition, or was he the one who wrote them? – D. V. Zhitomirsky*] saying that everything was fine until Hitler bothered us. Hitler was a criminal, that's clear, but so was Stalin. I feel eternal pain for those who were killed by Hitler, but I feel no less pain for those killed on Stalin's orders. I suffer for everyone who was tortured, shot, or starved to death. There were millions of them in our country before the war with Hitler began. The war brought much new sorrow and much new destruction,

[30] D. Shostakovich, 'Nasha rabota v gody Otechestvennoy voiny' ('Our Work During the Years of the Patriotic War') in the book *Raboty kompozitorov i muzykovedov Leningrada v gody Velikoy Otechestvennoy voiny* (*Works of Leningrad Composers and Musicologists During the Years of the Great Patriotic War*), 1946.

but I haven't forgotten the terrible pre-war years. That is what all my symphonies, beginning with the Fourth, are about, including the Seventh and the Eighth.

Actually, I have nothing against calling the Seventh the Leningrad Symphony, but it's not about Leningrad under the siege, it's about the Leningrad that Stalin destroyed and that Hitler merely finished off.

The majority of my symphonies are tombstones. Too many of our people died and were buried in places unknown to any one. Where do you put the tombstones for Meyerhold or Tukhachevsky? Only music can do that for them. I am willing to write a composition for each of the victims, but this is impossible, and that's why I dedicate my music to them all.[31]

I received the first news about the Seventh Symphony from D. Rabinovich's letters, sent to me in Sverdlovsk from Moscow. He wrote (apparently at the beginning of March 1942): 'I spent the last two months in Kuibyshev, where, in my presence, Shostakovich's Seventh Symphony was completed. Perhaps you have read about this brilliant composition, in the second issue of *Literatura i iskusstvo* [*Literature* and *Art*], in the article I co-authored with Shlifshtein?' I think that he was talking about the response to some preliminary performance, on the piano, by, perhaps, the composer himself, since the publication ('Seventh Symphony')[32] is dated 13 January, while the premiere of the Symphony took place in Kuibyshev on 5 March 1942.

In another letter (dated 17 March), my friend informed me: 'Samosud arrived here from Kuibyshev. The rehearsals of Shostakovich's Seventh have begun. Samosud is a great procrastinator and he has already postponed the concert from the 22nd to the 29th of March.' On the 29th, in the Hall of Columns, the Moscow premiere of the Symphony took place. I learned only from letters and newspaper reviews

[31] As translated by Antonina W. Bouis in *Testimony*, pp. 118/155–56 (where the paragraph structure differs). –EDS.

[32] The second article by the same authors about the Seventh Symphony – 'Poema o nashikh dnyakh' ('Poem About Our Days'), *Literatura i Iskusstvo* [*Literature and Art*], 4 April 1941 – was undoubtedly a reaction to the Moscow premiere.

about the unbelievably strong impact it had. As for me, I personally heard the Seventh only later, on my return to Moscow.

Thank goodness I was able be present at the first performance of the Eighth Symphony under the baton of Ye. Mravinsky (in Moscow, on 4 November 1943, in the Great Hall of the Conservatory). I sat in on all the rehearsals. The impression grew stronger and stronger. It was equally powerful for everyone else. Friends exchanged glances; all were surprised, moved and excited. This was not simply symphonic music, not simply a rehearsal; it seemed that the music conveyed something that was happening right now, that it was about present stirring discoveries and changes. It was no longer an illusion! The 'Communication', unbelievable in its force and honesty, provoked an identical, if unusual, community of feeling, a solidarity in yearning for the truth, for which we had become so famished at the time.

I made detailed notes during the rehearsals of the Eighth because I was working on a review which was to appear the next morning in *Komsomol'skaya Pravda*, i.e., on 5 November 1943.

I remember I was particularly impressed (right then, during those first auditions) by the third movement – the Toccata. Already its very beginning – the relentlessly regular repetition of the bass ostinato and on this background the cries of the high notes of the wind instruments – like the last, desperate cries for help. Also the middle episode with the trumpet solo. Later on, I thought about it for a long time, pondering its enigma. In no way did it go into the usual antithesis 'good versus evil'. It is frightening, truly terrifying. It is demoniacal – but, at the same time, wonderful and enthralling; it teases and beckons with its sensual splendour. One wishes the theme to be repeated. But no! The composer-dramatist does not meet this natural, but, at the same time, dubious allure. Only once is the theme of the episode heard in its entirety. After that it is taken away, somewhere underneath, into the gloomy depth, into 'the nether world', and it is only hinted at. . . . The mystery of music – is the mystery of life, of human passions and multifaceted motives.

Leaving the Great Hall, I immediately went to the editorial office of *Komsomol'skaya Pravda*. My review was corrected, retyped and sent to typesetting. In the meantime, the editor had made a phone call to some higher-up, and – strangely enough – was waiting for special permission to publish my article. Why was such a permission required? After all, so very recently, after the premiere of the Seventh, approbation of Shostakovich's patriotic glory had reached unprecedented levels. Furthermore, in September, in Soviet government newspapers (*Pravda*, *Izvestia*, *Leningradskaya Pravda*) preliminary information and quite favourable comments regarding the Eighth had already appeared. The clock showed midnight, then one o'clock, then two in the morning, and there was still no answer. I understood by watching the editor's mood that serious obstacles had arisen. Someone higher up began to have doubts, or became indignant. At three o'clock in the morning, I went home. The metro and buses were no longer running; furthermore a curfew was in effect and I had no identification papers on me. The moonlight was very bright, and close to the walls of the buildings there was a very dark shadow. It was in this darkest shadow, at times going into doorways (when I heard footsteps), that I made my way to Bryusovsky Street.

I walked for a long time and, despite my strained looking around and attentive listening – is there a patrol coming? – I kept on thinking. Was it strange and unexplainable? No, in reality, it was not that strange. In military developments, a turn toward victory had already taken place. With every passing day the announcements from the 'Soviet Informbyuro' were becoming mightier and more self-confident; in the newspapers fanfares prevailed, and the evening sky was illuminated by more and more festive fountains of salute salvoes. It was a totally different reality that we heard in the music of the Eighth: another side of reality, with its drama, its excruciating combat with the monster, its sorrow and terror; the Passacaglia compelled profound thought and profound feeling; the main mood of the finale – the communion with the kingdom of eternal beauty, with the harmony between the personal and the general – in no way corresponded to the surrounding rumble of victorious rejoicing. Could not some vigilant eye have noticed this – especially, if there had been someone to have prompted: 'Watch out, this is absolutely *not what it seems*, later on you will be held responsible for everything'....

I kept on carefully making my way along these dark Moscow streets, deep in thought and in the grip of a complex uneasiness. At the time I had no idea that the delay of my review was a symptom of what was to come in 1948. That year at the conference of the leaders of Soviet music of the Central Committee, and later on at the First Congress of Composers, the apprehensions of the 'vigilant eye' had surfaced, although they had been camouflaged in demagogical references to the 'people'. The camouflage was crude and primitive; however, it worked perfectly: its very essence was extremely convenient for some; but others understood clearly that this very essence and its exposure must only be welcome, otherwise – it would be the end of us!

Thanks to the waiving of a baton by the conductor from higher up, it turned out to be a very simple task to look even at the illustrious Seventh in a different light. As it had been 'elucidated' at the Composers' Congress, the symphony revealed that 'Shostakovich's musical thought was more suited to express the sinister images of fascism and the world of subjective reflections than to embody the positive heroic images of our present'. Regarding the Eighth, they were talking about the 'blindness of the artist', about his 'having detached himself from the surrounding reality'. The following words are symptomatic: 'Enough of these symphony-diaries, pseudo-philosophical symphonies which disguise under their external profound thinking an intellectual self-ruminating'.[33]

In one of my essays that was to appear in a popular American magazine, the censor wrote approximately the following: 'The author writes about what he wants to and praises what he likes. That type of essay is not suitable'. Later on, after the war, when I went to Zwickau, my superior-censor (the leader of the delegation) N. Zhiganov gave me a good scolding: 'At the meeting, when you had the floor, you kept on saying "I" ("I thank you", "I am delighted", and so forth). You ought to have said "we". After all, you are not here as a private individual, you are here as a representative

[33] T. Khrennikov, *Pervy vsesoyuzny s'yezd sovetskikh kompozitorov. Stenografichesky otchyot* (*First All-Union Congress of Soviet Composers. Stenographic Account*), 1948, pp. 40 and 43.

of the government!' From now on symphonies, novels and poetry were supposed to be written not in one's name, but 'in the name of the government'. This was the hidden meaning behind the words 'enough of symphony-diaries'.

... The article for *Komsomol'skaya Pravda* was never published.[34] Neither were there any reviews of the premiere of the Eighth in other more important government newspapers. Due to some sort of oversight or a strange stroke of fate, on 5 November I. Martynov's review was printed in *Vechernyaya Moskva* [*Moscow Evening News*] as well as an informational paragraph in the newspaper *Trud* [*Labour*]. Then, on 7 November – two comments in *Literatura i iskusstvo* [*Literature and Art*] by L. Leonov and Jean-Richard Bloch.[35]

From Recollections, Diaries and Letters

What follows is really nothing more than uncoordinated entries. It is possible that many of them are very subjective and that some are nothing more than my recording of the facts. Nonetheless, because they were written immediately after the fact, or had become anchored in my memory, they have acquired the meaning of documents, and it is only because of that that I have decided to include these notes in my book of memoirs.

Summer 1945. The Ninth Symphony. In 'Ivanovo', from July to August of that year I have many impressions and observations. S. Prokofiev, D. Kabalevsky, N. Chemberdzhi, V. Yakovlev, R. Glière, and D. Shostakovich with Nina Vasil'yevna and their children were all staying here at the time. 'Here', – I wrote home – 'there is a mixture of well-being, comfort, and the most elementary disorder. In the manor-house, there are several decently finished rooms, including the common dining room with a grandiose ottoman, luxurious chairs, and so forth. The "seniors" stay here,

[34] At a later date it was printed (more exactly, lithographed) in *Informatsionny sbornik Soyuza kompozitorov* (*Informational Booklet of Soviet Composers*), 1944, Nos. 5–6.

[35] The following section, a digression from Zhitomirsky's reminiscences of Shostakovich, has been omitted. –EDS.

in a room at the manor-house. Others are put in separate, carelessly built and mediocre dachas. One feels a bit sorry for their owners. Shostakovich's "mansion" makes a particularly pitiful impression – from afar it looks like either a lodge or a hen house, and on the inside, is barely better, despite the soft armchairs, excellent beds, and so on. . . . It is surrounded by dirty and neglected, obviously constantly reconditioned and rebuilt barns or storehouses. There are also clumsily put together flower beds with green fences, old, mended small houses for the workers, and a lot of undetermined junk. Naturally, a little bit further, there are fields, a small grove, and further, a real forest. However, the neighbouring ensemble is so chaotic, that it is difficult to make out nature' (25 August). Ration cards were still in use, 'cookery was still based on whatever happened to be at hand', and food was not the smallest attraction of 'Ivanovo'; it was plentiful, tasty, more often than not 'natural', without any ersatz. In the evenings, in the big dining room, the composers' wives played games of mahjongg. I did not even try to join them, since my whole life I have been unable to understand even the simplest of games.

Shostakovich's 'mansion', in addition to everything else, had the silliest location: it was stuck out in open ground, visible from every side, with not even a modest vale of trees. Next to the house, Grisha Shneyerson and I built a table with its legs buried in the ground. It was here that Dmitry Dmitriyevich worked on the Ninth Symphony during the entire month of August. Usually he would work two to three hours in the morning. I noticed with surprise that he always had in front of him the same few sheets of music paper. Later on, I saw that what was written down on these sheets were only the themes, now and then 'hints' of the development, and in many cases – everything was written on one line. To my knowledge, he wrote no other draft; and based on the above-mentioned sketches, Dmitry Dmitriyevich immediately wrote the final score. The intricately polished work was created with amazing ease and speed. The first movement was finished on 5 August (apparently, while still in Moscow); the second on the 12th; the third on the 20th; the fourth on the 21st, and the finale on the 30th. In spite of the intensity with which he was composing this score, the work seemed to progress – at least in the eyes of an outsider – in a casual manner; there were no signs of pre-occupation or profound reflection on the author's part.

At the same time there was no noticeable desire on his part to be sociable. He did not participate in the outings. He showed an obvious antipathy toward any type of passive meditation, and generally any type of unproductive 'neutral' way of spending time. He would decline to participate in those slow strolls along paths in which one gazed at the clouds and the landscape, and struck up idle, totally casual conversations 'about this or that' that are so habitual to the majority of people. One felt that the only indispensable type of existence for Shostakovich was that he had to be engaged in some kind of active process. In my opinion, this is the source of his interest in active sports, like soccer (a trait in him that was utterly alien to me).

In his conversations, he was, as I have mentioned before, extremely laconic; his remarks were pithy, often coloured with ironic implications; outwardly he did not reject the widely condoned habit of standardisation, of using general terms, and of wagging one's tongue, since his rule was to be politely loyal. But if he was forced to participate, then, in his passing remarks, it was possible to catch an element of parody (as in 'If you wish to see a reflection of your own imbecility, then I will show it to you in the guise of a theatrical performance').[36]

Sometimes D. D. felt like playing piano duets. The most impressive ensemble was Shostakovich with Kabalevsky. They played Haydn. D. D. really liked the Symphony in C minor. They often repeated the first movement.[37]

They also played Bruckner's Eighth Symphony. D. D. liked the Scherzo; they played a good part of the first movement and the beginning of the finale.

At times, D. D. kept the Shneyersons and me company, that is to say that quite often he would come by with his family. We would go to the nearest field and sit on bales of hay. But he could not keep still. I recall how once he organised a short-distance race. Little Maxim and Shostakovich

[36] This is a classic *yurodivy* technique. *Cf.* the passage about 'taking the blame' in MacDonald, *The New Shostakovich*, p. 12. – EDS.

[37] Presumably No. 95 (Nos. 52 and 78 are also in C minor.) – EDS.

were the participants: who would be the first one to reach the finish line? These scenes were recorded on photographs, which, alas, have very much faded.

Naturally, I was interested in knowing whether D. D. would be able to make a 'connection' with Prokofiev. Grisha Shneyerson, practically verbatim, told me about their first meeting in 'Ivanovo':

> *Prokofiev*: 'You know that I am working very hard here on my Sixth Symphony. I wrote the first movement (a detailed description of the form followed), now I am writing the second, with three themes, and the third one will probably be in a sonata form. I feel like I need to compensate for the lack of sonata features in the preceding movements.'
>
> *Shostakovich*: 'Is the weather always like this in these parts?'

Later on I never saw any mutual curiosity expressed by either one of them, although as composers they held each other in high esteem. Psychologically they were totally different people. It was perfectly clear that Prokofiev was from another era, from another milieu, and had entirely different character traits. D. D. was acutely sensitive, 'burned' to his last cell by the time. Prokofiev had a lordly independence and was shielded from everyday trivialities, and therefore was probably more simple-hearted. His favourite pastime was to feed the small dog, Zmeyka. Cheerfully, but at the same time with a fatherly resolve, he would take bones and scraps of meat and put them into the crevices of a huge lime tree with a double trunk that stood in front of the terrace. With delight he would watch Zmeyka's bustling efforts to find the dainty morsels. ... On another occasion, Prokofiev spent hours attentively examining the Academy's edition of Pushkin. With cheerful guile he described and quoted drafts of famous poems, in particular, the variants of the beginning of *Eugene Onegin* and Tatyana's letter. He was enthralled by the labyrinth of Pushkin's probing and the technical aspect of his work. I had once written about this topic: 'Generally he [Prokofiev] is simple-hearted and charmingly gay, very practical, without any of the pomposity of a "universally recognised" celebrity, inquisitive, slightly naïve, but brilliantly gifted. "A small boy" with a predilection for precise information and facts'. In another letter (3 August) I wrote:

Prokofiev 'is awfully fond of asking a quiz master's questions (he has a collector's curiosity about them), and I am a little bit afraid of these questions. However, in general, he is extremely sociable . . .'.

As for D. D., he was totally different. He would open up only in those rare and happy moments when the strength of the flow of impressions or the situation overcame his constraint and when he saw himself surrounded by people with whom he felt close. For example, I remember his ironic and brilliant observations in a story about the banquet in the city of Ivanovo, and the local elite headed by the 'governor' of the city.

Nina Vasil'yevna often went to the forest with me to pick mushrooms and strawberries. Or we would take the children and Zhenya Sh. with us. We would sit on the bales of hay and I would read Mérimée and Feuchtwanger aloud, 'almost understanding nothing myself' (an entry in the diary). Because of my feasting my eyes on Nina I was slowly falling in love with her. I realised that this was utterly inappropriate and in bad form, but there was nothing I could do about it. Nina Vasil'yevna was such an intelligent woman and she talked about so many interesting things. Among her stories, incidentally, was a tragi-comic one about the score of the Seventh Symphony, which almost had been destroyed. As is known, Shostakovich took this manuscript with him from Leningrad to Moscow, and then, from Moscow to Kuibyshev, where he finished composing the symphony. Boarding of the Moscow-Kuibyshev train turned out to be extremely arduous. All the passages to the compartments were solidly packed with people who barely had been able to squeeze themselves in, and whose belongings were being passed along from hand to hand. The manuscript of the Seventh was safely wrapped in a quilt, but someone negligently threw this bulky package . . . into the toilet. 'D. D. and I did not think of this quilt for many hours: we were busy making the children comfortable and searching for our suitcases. In the meantime, the place where the ill-fated package was was being visited in earnest. You can easily imagine what we saw when, out of necessity, we managed to get there. It was horrifying to touch the blanket which was in the middle of a puddle. I will spare you the details. . . . It was completely by chance that it had not been thrown out all together. And it was also by chance that we discovered this horror *before* the permeability of the wrapping had had time to damage the sheets of music.'

After the Seventh and the Eighth, everyone was awaiting the triumphal Victory Symphony. We were expecting it, heeding a straightforward, single-minded reading of the situation. Incidentally, it was Shostakovich himself who was guilty of having misled us. In the winter of 1944–45 he had twice begun working on the victoriously solemn symphony. He started it and abandoned it. G. Orlov provides the details in his book,[38] in which, in particular, he quotes the composer's statements from a conversation with D. Rabinovich: 'I wanted to use (in the Ninth) not only the orchestra, but also a chorus as well as soloists'; that he was handicapped by the absence of a suitable text; furthermore, that he feared he would be suspected of wanting to evoke 'certain analogies' (with Beethoven's Ninth). That he interrupted the work he had begun and several months later created a totally new and totally different Ninth – was quite a remarkable fact. This time Shostakovich was totally true to himself – with his masterly ability to catch the complexity, the significance, the whimsical confusion, and the delusiveness of life. He *dared* to do it, clearly going against official dogma, and the pressure of the propaganda which demanded a quick return to the disposition of the 'joyous millions', a disposition that had been lost or, at any rate, badly shaken during the war years.

However, what made the Ninth Symphony powerful and attractive was exactly its paradoxical versatility. Many things were not new in themselves, they already shone brilliantly in previous Shostakovich scores: the natural 'classic' cheerfulness in the spirit of Haydn, the delicate spiritual lyricism, the bustle, the whirlwind gallops, and the rollicking pertness with a touch of sarcasm. But in the condensed scope of the Ninth Symphony, the correlation of all these elements, their indivisibility, is felt very strongly, identical to what we experience in real life. Each element of the complex whole hid within itself its own contradiction. The moronic carelessness, the outrageous vulgarity were suddenly coloured by

[38] *Cf.* Genrikh Orlov, *Simfonii Shostakovicha* (*Shostakovich's Symphonies*), Gosudarstvennoye Muzykal'noye Izdatel'svo, Leningrad, 1961, p. 221.

a dramatic feeling of brute force and despair. A focused grief had as its neighbour a foul, at times caddish, cunningly winking rejoicing; but this caddish 'rejoicing' gave the impression of being embroiled in is own absurdity and its 'aimless' movement. With this lack of direction, this question mark, this unpredictable fate seething with life's forces, everything came to an abrupt end, or, more exactly, was cut off.

'... Certain critical remarks about the Ninth Symphony are related, it seems to me, to the straightforward approach to its content. But the "psychological composition" of this music does not lend itself to such an approach. Many times I have observed how such a straightforward approach is reflected, for instance, in the interpretation of Chaplin's art. In paying attention to what appears only on the surface, many people are convinced that Chaplin is performing pure stunts. But we know very well how psychologically complex and all-encompassing Chaplin's "amusing" situations are, how intimately they are linked with the inner, deeper meaning, and how their expressiveness is linked to the form that the artist so masterfully discovered to embody them. In many instances, these remarks apply also to Shostakovich, for the stylistic kinship of these two artists is beyond question, despite their enormous differences. In the "amusing" little songs of the Ninth Symphony I am constantly aware of several emotional layers. It is not easy to verbally decode this perception.' This was what I had said in my address on the Ninth Symphony on 4 December 1945. Naturally I chose my words with care. The lack of receptivity by the mass of the people to complexity in art is a general problem and is not specific only to this composition. There was something else at issue here as, by the way, is true of many other works of Shostakovich, and this was the rejection of both his tragic and sarcastic aspects, for both tragedy and sarcasm, if one thinks about it, only complicated life and led to more difficult and unsolvable problems. These ideas were shared by those who pondered the deep meaning of the works, but who, above all, valued the well-preserved course of their own lives and perspectives guaranteed by their loyalty.

At first, the debate about the Ninth Symphony took place in an indecisive manner: the enormous success and prestige of the Seventh was still paramount in the minds of commentators. The floodgates for criticism were only opened in mid-1946, following the first of 'Zhdanov's' decrees (14 August, 'About the journals *Zvezda* [*The Star*] and *Leningrad*'). The statements that Zoshchenko was busy 'depicting our reality with malice and hooliganism' no doubt reminded someone about Shostakovich. After the 1948 decree, M. Koval' attacked the Ninth with particular gusto. He wrote: 'Shostakovich showed himself to be such a dwarf in the sublimity of the days of victory. . . . What was Shostakovich counting on when, instead of creating in the Ninth Symphony the image of the victorious man, he created one of a carefree Yankee recklessly whistling a cheerful little tune? Was he counting on the next triumph abroad? On the songs of praise by our critical gawks?'[39] In issues 2, 3 and 4 of *Sovetskaya Muzyka*, the same author (he truly showed his insignificance!) published a huge and rude pamphlet about Shostakovich. Later on, he repeatedly tried to cleanse his conscience of this dirty spot. In his 1951 article he was already calling D. D. 'our remarkable composer', who had finally 'reformed himself' and 'stepped onto the wide road of the art of socialist realism'.[40] I have already written about how Koval' had invited Shostakovich to his house and offered him, as a gift, Glinka's score of *Kamarinskaya* for his own education (D. D., as always, gently endured this humiliating visit; I don't doubt that he was irreproachably polite and 'grateful'). Others expressed themselves less harshly, but displayed an identical tendentiousness (provoked, naturally, by the suspiciousness from higher up about everything that did not fit the simplest scheme). 'The Ninth Symphony leads one to fear that Shostakovich, the profound thinker-humanist, has not yet overcome the ironic sceptic and the stylist that is in him.'[41]

The human heart is a mystery. It is quite possible that the composer subjectively conceived his miniature and, for the most part, bright chamber symphony as a relaxation after

[39] *Sovetskoye Iskusstvo*, 28 February 1948.

[40] *Izvestia*, 8 December 1951.

[41] I. Nest'yev, 'Zametki o tvorchestve Shostakovicha. Neskol'ko mysley, vyzvannykh Devyatoy simfoniyey' ('Notes About Shostakovich's Works. Some Thoughts Provoked by the Ninth Symphony'), *Kul'tura i zhizn'* (*Culture and Life*), 30 September 1946.

such 'difficult', conceptual works as the Seventh and Eighth, or the Trio. However, his personal style was not one of nonchalance, insouciance and 'simple gaiety'.

Tolstoy once wrote about the 'eternal alarm' as a condition that 'no man even dared to think of letting go even for one second'. 'I am amused to remember' – Tolstoy wrote in the same letter (to his aunt A. Tolstaya) – 'how I thought . . . it was possible to build a happy and honest little world, where peace reigns, where no mistakes are made, where there is neither repentance nor confusion, and where one can slowly live one's life . . . It's funny! . . . To live honestly one must desire passionately, get confused, fight, make mistakes, begin and then abandon, and begin once again, and eternally fight and sacrifice. Tranquillity is spiritual cravenness.'[42]

These lines make a nice commentary on the history of the Ninth's creation. After having tried to no avail to create something triumphal and rejoicing ('Our business is to rejoice!'), a 'gaily' symphonic miniature came to light, but in it was the same eternal alarm Tolstoy wrote about, 'entangled' and 'fighting' for a way out.

I heard the first performances of the Ninth in Leningrad (3 November 1945) and in Moscow (20 November of the same year) under the direction of Ye. Mravinsky. It was an outward success. It seemed that everything was intelligible, even easier to understand than in other Shostakovich works; there were many passages in the popular classical style, and many brisk moments. Nevertheless, at the same time there was too much subtlety and indecipherability. This hampered understanding and puzzled people. As for the professionals – more exactly, those who were afraid of taking risks – they looked askance: let's not miss another criminal 'deviation'. However, people belonging to a narrower circle felt an upsurge. Something very necessary and quintessential had resounded. Even D. D. was in the best of moods: he was cheerful, brilliant and inspired.

I remember very well the hours spent in D. D.'s hotel room after the Leningrad premiere. There were few of us: Nina Vasil'yevna, some people from Leningrad, and I.

[42] L. N. Tolstoy, *Sobraniye Sochineniy* (*Collected Works*), Gozlit, Moscow, 1948, Vol. 12, pp. 237–38.

D. D. was, for once, very sociable. This was the occasion when, for the first time, I fully appreciated the brilliance of his speech, so full of original humour and flashes of sarcasm! He suddenly felt the urge to tell a fantastic story. How one musicologist from Moscow – the least talented one – had found that a very intimate item made out of rubber had disappeared from his wife's night-table. And how after having conducted a thorough search he found the missing item in the drawer of his son's desk. And how he gave his son a good scolding for this base deceit and lectured him on the elevated ethics regarding the stolen item, and that his interest for such a thing was extremely reprehensible for a boy of his age and was an indication that the son had chosen the wrong path in life, and that this path would lead him to. . ., and so on, and so forth. But the crux of the matter was not in the topic of the story itself. D. D. had composed extempore a stunningly witty 'scherzo'. And when he finished, everyone asked for an encore. He complied with the request and retold the story from its very beginning, but with virtuosic variations . . . .

D. D. very much disliked talking about himself or his works. At various preliminary performances, he limited himself to the stingiest of comments, mainly about form and keys. I think that the more substantial comments that appeared in the press were, as a rule, either secretly pumped out of him, or were written for him considering the political situation and using all the usual arguments and words. Nevertheless, when he publicly said something about himself, his loyalty and modesty would turn at times into a caricature and a parody on loyalty, as I have already said before. In those cases, even if someone had prepared his theses or even the entire text for him, he often made people aware of the absurdity of what was being said.

Thus, for example, during the First Congress of Soviet Composers in 1948, he declared: 'Speaking about myself, I must say that my working mainly in the sphere of symphonic and chamber-instrumental music had a negative effect on me'.[43] Coming from Shostakovich's lips this was obviously

[43] *First All-Union Congress of Soviet Composers. Stenographic Account*, p. 345.

nonsense and frankly malicious. Naturally, everyone understood that. D. D. himself, on the contrary, was proud of the influence his symphonic craftsmanship had on his vocal cycles; once, he very modestly alluded to this fact during the first performance of the 'Jewish' cycle at his house.

Artificial and imposed situations sometimes roused in him completely unexpected accents and changes that seemed to deviate from what was expected. On the agenda of the open Party meeting of Soviet Composers on 14 September 1960, there was only one item: 'The acceptance of D. D. Shostakovich into the Party'. According to recollections of eyewitnesses, it was rather a travesty. Incidentally, D. D. said: 'For everything that is best in me I am indebted to . . .' Here everyone was expecting: 'the Party', and he said: 'my parents'. This stuck in everyone's memory, as well as his pitiful expression. . . .

As for how he himself understood or felt his own music, despite all his reserve and secretiveness, he would sometimes let out the secret. My notes on the Second Quartet (the premiere took place in the Small Hall of the Conservatory on 14 November 1944) were printed in one of the brochures of the Moscow Philharmonic. I wrote about the third movement, the Waltz: 'Shostakovich's new waltz is the scion of the many, many lyrical and intimate waltzes of the Russian classic composers, but how original it is in its colouring, full of a sort of enticing and exciting mystery; what elevated inspiration and femininity are infused in its form'.[44] In the Great Hall, before the beginning of some other concert, Dmitry Dmitriyevich suddenly said to me: 'this is generally not my habit, everyone is free to write whatever he thinks about my music, but . . . in your lines about the Waltz from the Second Quartet, the epithet *femininity* is far from suitable. More than anything else this is a *valse macabre*. And if it were compared to the classics, it should be compared, for example, to the Waltz from the Third Suite by Tchaikovsky' (diary entry of 14 March 1945).

The Fifth Symphony. 'This is the first performance of the Fifth Symphony after the Party resolution (from

[44] *Moskovskaya gosudarstvennaya filarmoniya, 1944–45* (*Moscow State Philharmonic, 1944–45*), Moscow, 1945, p. 15.

10 February 1948). There were no play-bills, we limited ourselves to a poster at the entrance. The premises for such concerts are not the best, second class. Wagner, the conductor, is unknown and comes from Riga. Naturally, the audience was sparse. Young people, students at the Conservatory, P. Lamm, Nina Vasil'yevna, next to her M. Vainberg, and M. Litvinov; then there are Yu. Litvinov, Lyova Lebedinsky with Ira, B. Maizel', Pava Rybakov (as I write this I am thinking: how many of them have died!). The performance is raw, uncollected, in the expressive passages too correctly rhythmical and combed out; in the lyrical passages it is beautiful, but slightly limp. The hall horribly disperses the sonority and deprives it of all colour. After the second movement (the best in the rendition) there is applause. After the conclusion there is extended applause. There are several individual curtain calls for the composer. On the whole there is a feeling of disappointment (probably because of the general sluggishness and belittlement). After all, the members of the orchestra could have at least risen to the occasion. But they almost did hack work!' (diary, 27 March 1948).

'16 April – a remarkable concert. Mravinsky with Shostakovich's Fifth Symphony (in the first half they played Beethoven's Fourth). Background: (1) Recent campaign against "cosmopolitanism". (2) At the very last moment, D. D.'s trip to America to the congress of cultural leaders. Therefore, on the one hand "from home" and on the other hand "from abroad". Besides, for almost a year nothing by the "real" Shostakovich has been performed. The concert hall is overcrowded. The audience is most select. The rendition is not without flaws (the dynamics and the "approaches" were not up to par, the brasses made some mistakes). But – in good spirits. The mood was coming from the stage, and to a greater extent, from the hall. After each movement there is applause. At the end, there is a storm of applause with cries of rapture. D. D. advances with difficulty through the concert-goers toward the stage. An uninterrupted crescendo. Everyone stands up. After the third curtain call, the entire hall starts clapping rhythmically (at the time this was something new). Fourth, fifth and sixth curtain calls (the lights of the hall had already been dimmed). Many people have a festive appearance and there are many warm handshakes. I did not go to the dressing room. From what I heard, it was very lively there. A lot of artificial friends.' (diary, 17 April 1949).

Encounter at H. Neuhaus.[45] 'About a month ago. Invited to H. G. Neuhaus. Slava (Richter) played his forthcoming Bach programme. In addition to the Neuhauses there were Aleksandr Georgiyevich (Grabichevsky), and Tolya Vedernikov.[46] Later on, D. D. and Nina Dorliak (they had been at Nina's working on the "Jewish songs") came. D. D. looked grey and had an absent look. During the dinner, he tried to be more lively. He talked about how he received the last paycheque from the conservatory. He expressed his surprise at the publication of the score of his Third Quartet. He soon withered. Before everyone else he started to take his leave. We left together. Outside he asked me a few questions about my work. I gave him the standard answer – "things will work out!" (In the diary, at this spot, one line was cut out, precisely *cut out*, and not crossed out. Terrible! Only the end of D. D.'s answer remained "...et worse!" Probably, he was "consoling" me, that we had not yet experienced everything, that "it will get worse"' (diary, 12 December 1948).

'From Jewish Folk Poetry'. 'The day before yesterday there was an unexpected phone call from Nina Dorliak with an invitation to attend a rehearsal of the "Jewish songs". Ol'gusha and I darted out. Two cramped rooms, with a corridor full of rubbish. Nina D., Slava and two partners (T. Yanko and the tenor Belugin from the Stanislavsky Theatre).'

What follows are the initial variants of the names of the entire cycle and individual songs, as well as some of the dates of their composition. Therefore, I will quote everything that was written down in the diary.

'From Jewish Folk Poetry'. Opus 79. For soprano, contralto and tenor (Kellomyaki, August 1948).

[45] Heinrich Gustavovich Neuhaus (1888–1964), pianist and noted pedagogue. His students included Emil Gilels, Sviatoslav Richter, Anatoly Vedernikov and Yakov Zak. –EDS.

[46] Anatoly Vedernikov, pianist and close friend of Sviatoslav Richter at the Moscow Conservatory. He is known for his recordings of modern music. –EDS.

After the horrid musical dregs of this year – everything started to sparkle, because clean. It was real! Subtle, naïve and gentle melodies (much warmer that in the previous 'children' works); at the same time they are fresh in their 'turns', in their unexpected deviations from the expected squareness or repetition. Harmonies and modulations are particularly expressive. These are 'Bay, bay' ['Bye-bye'] and 'Moy synok' ['My Darling Son'], and others.

Tragic recitatives with an amazingly life-like sigh and a desperate gesture, with keenly psychological strokes, with a generally strong mood. These are 'Oy, Abram' ['Oh! Abraham'] and 'Lezhit Sheyndl' ['Sheyndl is in bed']. There is an amazing blending of Musorgsky, Prokofiev (like the tragic scenes in *Semyon Kotko*) and Shostakovich.

There are also certain ones with some kind of sad lining, and at times they are rousing with their hidden tragic undertone. The eleventh song. I remember the particular impression created by this last song of the cycle, when it was performed in the mid-'50s in the Small Hall of the Conservatory (it was probably the Moscow premiere, since the one in Leningrad had taken place on 15 January 1955). The 'Doctors' Plot' was still fresh in our memories – the swan song of Stalin's terror. The exulting conclusion of the song: 'Our sons will become doctors' – words that are musically underscored by means of a totally amazing, unexpected modulation into the basic key at the very end. 'And on the whole it is still the same thing, *the most important thing about the most important thing*, without one single indication of stagnation or compromise medley' (diary, 12 December 1948).

I am going back a little bit. General rehearsal of the 'Jewish Songs' at the house of D. D. (18 December 1948).

Nina Vasil'yevna with the children, Yu. Levitin, K. Karayev, L. Atovmyan, and some unknown young fellow in uniform. Prior to starting the rehearsal, D. D. requests that all the shortcomings of the performance be noted. He discusses, in great detail, where and how the performers are to be. Atovmyan quickly understands and grabs chairs.

The entire cycle is performed twice. The singers are excited and the composer, too – despite all his reserve. The finale sounds beautifully. Especially the jubilation on 'a' and the shift to D major before the end. The first, second, fourth, sixth, eighth and ninth songs turned out wonderfully. One of the most attentive listeners is Maxim. All the fleeting impressions are reflected on his little face that expresses curiosity, surprise and irony. The words: 'You without me, and I without you, is like a door without a door-handle' bring a quick smile. After the rendition there is a general, lively discussion and a collective effort to find new titles for the songs. At D. D.'s suggestion, it is decided to call the fourth song – 'Proshchanye' ['Farewell'], the seventh – 'Pesnya bednyaka' ['Song of the Poor Man'], the eighth – 'Zima' ['Winter'], and the tenth – 'Dudochka' ['The Small Fife']. D. D. shows the collection from which the texts of the songs were taken – *Yevreiskiye narodnyye pesni* [*Jewish Folk Songs*] (published by Ogiz in 1947). The compilers were I. Dobrushin and A. Yuditsky, and the editor was Yu. Sokolov. He praises the texts very highly. 'I literally advise every composer to look into this . . . How good it was that I wrote them one after the other.' After that, we were served a small collation.

'The intended performance of the songs for 20 December 1948 in the Union of Soviet Composers has been cancelled. Therefore, there will be no performance before the plenum of the Union of Soviet Composers (21 to 30 December). That's very good . . .' (diary, 18 December 1948). Why it was 'very good' – I can't remember: perhaps I feared that new attacks would take place. Anti-Semitism was already gaining ground higher up, and it's not an accident that the premiere of the cycle took place only some six years later . . . .

CODE, QUOTATION AND COLLAGE

Some Musical Allusions in the Works of Dmitry Shostakovich[1]

Lev Lebedinsky

In Part Five of *The Gulag Archipelago*,[2] Alexander Solzhenitsyn writes that, on hearing Drozdov perform the old prison song 'How Things Change', he thought: 'What a song! "To each prison its own"! It figures. It figures because that's all our entire convict generation can expect from life'. He adds: 'Why didn't Shostakovich listen more carefully to this song here before writing his Eleventh Symphony? Either he wouldn't have written it or he'd have given it a more contemporary meaning, not an obsolete one'. Having often met the composer around the time the Eleventh Symphony was being written, and consequently being privy to his thoughts, I disagree with Alexander Isayevich and would like to suggest an alternative interpretation of this work.

In the Eleventh Symphony Shostakovich presents his audience with a poetical vision of old revolutionary prison songs. There are no texts in the symphony – yet, though only their melodies are heard, the songs are so well known in Russia that it is as if the words themselves are being sung. In the first movement, the initial verses of the prison song are:

How things change, much like the conscience of tyrants.
Autumn's black night – and in that gloom
There looms from the mist
An awful vision: prison.

[1] Originally in 'Letters', *Novy Mir* (*New World*), 1990, No. 3. A version of this piece appeared in *DSCH*, No. xvii, December 1990, pp. 5–12. English version by Tatjana M. Marovic (Norbury) and Ian MacDonald.

[2] 'Katorga', Chapter 2, Collins Harvill, London, 1974/Harper & Row, New York, 1978, p. 50. –EDS.

As the hours drag by,
In the night's long silence,
Hear, like a sigh, the cry
Echoed slowly, sadly . . . LISTEN!

The solemn exhortation 'LISTEN!' – the song's refrain – exudes the grim atmosphere of prison, the endless sorrow of the convicts' longing for freedom. The same mood attaches to the second song used in the first movement, whose first verse runs:

The night is dark so mark each minute,
Though high walls hide the stars,
And the prison gates are clamped
By iron locks and iron bars.

The 'prison' of the Eleventh Symphony is a universal symbol of captivity. One can sense, brooding over this sombre scene, the presence of the tyrant with his black conscience. This vision opens and closes the movement.

In the last movement, Shostakovich uses the well-known revolutionary song 'Tremble, Tyrants!':

Tremble, tyrants, as you mock us,
Menace us with cells and chains.
Our heads bow but our souls stand tall.
Shame on you, you tyrants! Shame!

At the outset, these melodies are heard in their original form; later, as though representing the main protagonists in a drama, they undergo a symphonic development. Although an analysis of this development is beyond the scope of the present argument, it should be emphasised that, like its preceding exposition, it is a *dramatic* development of extremely concrete vividness – and, moreover, one in which the depicted events are clearly not of the past but very much of the present.

Working on his Eleventh Symphony in 1957, Shostakovich incorporated into it the song 'How Things Change' as it was then sung by prisoners in Soviet labour and concentration camps. Possibly the composer hoped that, by raising it to a symphonic level, the song would be heard not only in the Soviet Union but also in the cities of Europe and America. (A comparable impact, born of the same experience, was made by *The Gulag Archipelago* – published, may I add, a full eighteen years after the Symphony, at the height of Solzhenitsyn's widespread recognition in the West.) Not everyone grasped the contemporary implications of the Eleventh Symphony. In Russia, it is, after all, common practice for artists to resort to the life-saving language of folk-song. However, the allusion to the tyrant's 'night-black' conscience was sufficient to give Shostakovich's quotation an anti-Stalinist inflection, turning the work into a protest against tyranny in general.

In asking 'Why didn't Shostakovich listen to this song here?' (i.e., in prison), Solzhenitsyn implies that anyone who hadn't personally experienced Stalin's death camps – hadn't known that misery and what it meant to long for release from it, hadn't heard the convicts sing – was incapable of giving a revolutionary song a contemporary meaning, only a 'dead' one. This is scarcely fair to Shostakovich.

Though he never knew prison or the camps, the composer was able to recreate the horror and terror of Stalin's Gulag with enormous power, clarity and realism. Aside from his own imaginative genius, this was because of the fact that for a number of years, particularly after the death of his close friend Tukhachevsky, he had himself lived in the daily dread of arrest and punishment. From this experience, his keen intuition was able to deduce the camps' peculiar atmosphere; in his mind, he lived in those places, heard their sad songs, felt their seething resentment against all tyranny and repression.

The true – and highly contemporary – programme of the Eleventh Symphony was deliberately concealed by Shostakovich beneath a kind of 'period costume'. During Stalin's time, such historical allusions, including old revolutionary prison songs, were sanctioned with little concern for their content – a practice mirroring the proverb that 'in a tyrant's home one does not mention the hangman'. In such a context, however, mentioning the hangman, loudly and even in song, is fairly unequivocal.

Did the composer hide the contemporary meaning of his Symphony too carefully to make it generally detectable? Hardly – although there were plenty of sharp-witted people in Moscow and Leningrad who were probably too scared to admit the truth. 'Those weren't rifle shots – those were tanks roaring and people being machine-gunned', remarked an old lady loudly after the premiere of the Symphony in Leningrad. And she was right. In the second movement of the Symphony ('The Ninth of January'), Shostakovich, with immense orchestral mastery, reproduces the roar of engines and clatter of tank-tracks – sounds strongly suggestive of the massacre during the 1956 uprising in Budapest. In answer to Solzhenitsyn's 'What a song!', we who followed the horrible suppression of the Hungarian uprising could exclaim: 'What a symphony, what songs, what a programme – and to what events!'

The Eleventh Symphony can justly be called a product of the anti-totalitarian liberation movement in the USSR. As such, as well as evidencing Shostakovich's talent and mastery, it also testifies to his courage and intelligence. The coolness, even malice, shown towards the Eleventh Symphony by some Soviet musicians (among them several so-called scholars) were, in my opinion, a symptom of their artistic, musical and emotional deafness; they did not realise that, with this work, Shostakovich had inaugurated a completely new genre: socio-political symphonism.

Shostakovich's ability to unite lyrical and humanitarian ideas in music is dramatically expressed in his Eighth Quartet, a work of universal appeal. The quartet begins with the notes D, E flat, C, B – or D, Es, C, H in German notation. These represent the author's musical monogram, Dmitri Schostakowitsch. Numerous quotations from his own works follow, as if the composer wished to describe the main events of his life and call attention to secret and important messages in his music, beginning with the First Symphony, written in 1925–26.[3] But the funeral song 'Tortured By Great Misery' also features not one of Shostakovich's themes but a revolutionary song of folk origin. Note, too, that the composer

[3] The theme first heard on the timpani in the First Symphony (later used in the Eighth Quartet) represents the 'scaffold'. Following the 'Hero's execution', the orchestration is radiant, symbolising immortality. Such was the young composer's reaction to a hero's death. This radiance does not and could not appear in the Eighth Quartet, written as it was as a farewell to life. Death casts its shadow, too, over the entire Fourteenth Symphony, the title of whose final song is 'Death is All-Powerful'. The composer considered it the only true conclusion of anything he had ever written. –LL.

dedicated the quartet to 'the victims of fascism'. Rather obviously the Eighth Quartet is a message in musical code.

What, then, is the meaning of the author's monogram, the initial notes DSCH? Clearly, the composer is telling us that the Quartet is *about himself* – that, to a large extent, it is an account of his life and personality. Thus, the musical themes appearing in the Quartet can be heard as a retrospect, the composer recalling his compositions and, at the same time, his career. Why, though, does he introduce the funeral song into a work otherwise containing only his own themes? This would seem to be a strong hint that the quartet is announcing someone's death – someone connected to the Russian liberation movement. But who? Judging by the presence of the composer's monogram, it can only be the composer himself. In quoting the song 'Tortured By Great Misery', is Shostakovich then describing himself? Yes. His life was full of torture (everybody knew that, it was written on his face). And precisely what was it that tortured him? More than anything else, captivity. A freedom-loving democrat, he was forced to live and work under a totalitarian regime which crushed him in its oppressive machinery.

There is another – extraordinary – reason that the composer introduced a musical retrospect of his works into the Eighth Quartet. It was that he thought it would be *his last work* – hence the self-quotations and the inclusion of a funeral march. In other words: *the Eighth Quartet was conceived as a document explaining to the world the circumstances of its composer's death.* Surely, though, death cannot have seemed imminent to the composer in 1960 when the work was written? Yet, in a very real sense, it did. The Quartet was composed immediately after he had joined the Communist Party – and this, to Shostakovich, was equivalent to death itself.

So why did he join? Could he have been under some kind of pressure? The event was, indeed, widely reported in the world press – chiefly because the much-trumpeted Party plenum, convened to mark the occasion, deteriorated into a farce due to . . . the unexpected absence of the composer! Flimsy excuses were made, along with an announcement that Shostakovich had unexpectedly been taken ill (apparently so suddenly that there had been no time to postpone the meeting!). This ludicrous situation quickly escalated into a major furore. Those present at the meeting left firmly convinced that Shostakovich had been forced to join the Party – and, though the composer's enrollment did eventually take place some months later, the scandal of that first meeting cast a special light on the meaning of the Eighth Quartet, associating it inextricably with that event. A few of the composer's closest friends knew that after finishing the work, Shostakovich had intended to kill himself; luckily, they managed to persuade him not to do it.

There is no doubt that Shostakovich meant his Eighth Quartet to be not only an autobiographical work but also *his final one*.

Up to a point, the Fifteenth and last of Shostakovich's symphonies is also autobiographical. In the first movement, quite unexpectedly – though 'very aptly' – there appears the famous and cheerful march from Rossini's opera *William Tell*. What made the composer choose it? In his youth, this march had been a symbol to him; by his late sixties, his viewpoint had changed: he thought of it as an idealised, indeed romanticised, summons to revolution. Nor was it without irony that the composer called the first movement of his Fifteenth Symphony 'A Music Shop', a remark which made the critics babble naïvely about the 'clatter of children's toys'.

In the fourth movement, we hear, as a repeated question, a famous motif from Wagner's *Twilight of the Gods*. Here, the composer refers to the last period of his life in which he vainly attempted to avoid his obsession with death, diverting himself from the inevitable by turning to lighter, more carefree themes. The obsession, however, proves impossible to ward off and there then follows the final scene: a detailed, realistic foretelling of his death-agony and failing fight for breath.

Death – that is the answer to the question posed by Shostakovich's allusion to Wagner's portentous motif. In the finale of the Fourteenth Symphony, we hear that 'Death is all-powerful'; in the Fifteenth, too, Death has the main role, even though the solution at the end is on a different plane and seen in a different light.

Shostakovich sometimes used quotations from classical and satirical literary works. 'The Kreutzer Sonata', one of his *Five Satires on the Poems of Sasha Chyorny*, opens with the first chords of Beethoven's work of this name. The marriage of high musical pathos with deliberately prosaic observation creates an irresistibly funny satirical effect:

The lodger sits down on his suitcase
And pensively looks at the floor;
There are chairs here, a bed, and a table,
And an upholstered sofa, what's more!

In the second song of the same cycle, the composer quotes from Sergei Rachmaninov's romance 'Spring'. The lyrical phrase 'Spring is coming! Spring is coming!' is set against a darkly grotesque vignette of city-life in St Petersburg:

And my cactus – miraculous thing! –
Fed on tea-leaves and dregs thrown away,
Rises like Lazarus up from the dead
Growing stronger and taller each day.

Irony, one of Shostakovich's main characteristics, often appears in his music in the most unexpected places and forms. The Ninth Symphony is one example of this. Another occurs in the opera *Katerina Izmailova* where a scene in Act Three prompts the composer to an ironic association. Confiding this in truly Pushkinesque style, he introduces a quotation from *Eugene Onegin* – in this case, both music and words. Sergei, in trying to seduce Katerina, piously sings: 'Books provide much nourishment for our minds and hearts'. In thus putting the voice of an elevated artist into the mouth of a pretentious vulgarian, Shostakovich seems to be enjoying the pure incongruity of the situation.

In his First Cello Concerto, Shostakovich set himself an unusual task. As we know, the Georgian motif 'Suliko' is heard in the Concerto – that is, if one wants to hear it. In the development section, the 'Suliko' motif acquires a teasing character: as soon as it appears, it seems to hide, run away; but then it returns and again 'runs away' – as though it were thumbing its nose at someone. Why did Shostakovich use this Georgian melody? Perhaps it reminded him of an amusing story he'd heard from the violinist Galina Barinova, who once played 'Suliko' especially for the Leader. This happened in Crimea, at the time of the Yalta Conference. Following several improvised performances by artists and a festive banquet with mountains of food and drink, this talented violinist – a young and attractive woman – approached

Stalin and told him 'I have prepared something especially for you, Iosif Vissarionovich'. She then began to play 'Suliko'. Barinova told Shostakovich: 'As soon as I'd started, I saw that Stalin was angry. My head swam! How I managed to get to the end, I'll never know.' 'And why', Stalin demanded darkly, 'was this especially for me?' Barinova held her tongue. 'I thought it best not to answer. Later, after some reflection, I worked it out. Stalin liked to think of himself as the Leader of all humanity, not just of one particular nation. And I – in front of everyone, including Churchill and Roosevelt – had thoughtlessly trodden on his corns. No wonder he was furious!' Shostakovich adapted Barinova's wry anecdote to his own satirical purposes. (Those unable to accept that Shostakovich felt this way about Stalin will doubtless attempt to refute my claims by pointing to the composer's declarations in print. All that needs to be said on that score is that the English critic Martin Cooper was absolutely correct in appraising Shostakovich's articles as 'foam in the mouth of a man who has been forced to eat soap'.)

Shostakovich was unique, a man of formidable character. Nearly all his music is alive with socio-political and philosophical thoughts and ideas, conveyed to the listener in a completely distinctive musical language. Whenever planning a large-scale composition, he began from a firmly pre-established conception. ('The main thing in music is to think', he used to say.) Such conceptions were of course governed by his vast knowledge of different musical forms and processes; but they were further modified, multiplied and interrelated by his understanding of the Russian literary tradition. An expert in literature, especially Russian literature, the composer maintained that prose and verse – and *not* cinema, he would stress[4] – were the most important of the arts. (Shostakovich made comparable statements on more than one occasion, particularly during the period[5] when several of his works, including film scores, came under attack. Sadly such pronouncements were rarely published, though they were preserved in the minds of many musicians.

[4] Contradicting Lenin who held that cinema was the 'most important' Soviet art. –IM.

[5] Lebedinsky is presumably referring to the events of 1948. –IM.

About 90 per cent of his real opinions never got into print; they are certainly not to be found among the articles signed with his name.)

It has been said that all of Shostakovich's symphonies have a programme. In a sense, this is indisputably true. However, the 'programmes' in Shostakovich's symphonies do not emulate the schematicism of the traditional 'subject-programme'; it is better to describe them as programmes of dramatically conflicting ideas – ideas which, in Shostakovich's case, were conceived from the outset in their final orchestral colours. This, for many composers, was something impossible and incredible, a fact that sometimes caused amusing misunderstandings.

Once, during the interval in a morning rehearsal at the Great Hall of the Moscow Conservatory, the composer Yury Shaporin sat down next to Shostakovich, handed him some sheets of two-stave paper containing a long phrase from one of his works, and asked: 'What do you think, Mitya. Should I give this theme to the clarinet or to the flute?' 'To the clarinet or the flute', replied Shostakovich. 'But I asked you *which* – the clarinet or to the flute?' '*Either* the clarinet or the flute', confirmed Shostakovich, in whose musical imagination the instruments' timbres were born formed, and to whom Shaporin's question had sounded silly. (Furthermore – another well-known fact – having composed his entire symphony with all its details in his head, Shostakovich would sit down and score it straight for full orchestra, making no preliminary sketches. This accomplishment was a source of envy among other composers, who mostly began by playing their compositions on the piano, then writing a piano arrangement, and only after that scoring it for orchestra.)

Shostakovich's reason for using quotations from folk-songs and other tunes – even entire phrases from pieces by other composers – was that doing so made it easier for him to convey his socio-political messages to a wide public. Such 'parenthetical' allusions were meant to represent an emblem, a musical symbol – sometimes a symbol of a particular era, at other times specific social conditions or emotional-psychological states. As composer-philosopher, supreme dramatist and musical master-architect, Shostakovich knew precisely when and how to employ this 'collage' technique. His enormous individuality as an artist easily subordinated any foreign material, merging it naturally into his own radically original style. (Nor did he make any secret of his musical 'paste-ups'. For instance, in answer to Sergei Prokofiev's sarcastic observation that 'This theme of yours is pure Brahms', Shostakovich, raising his eyebrows, replied 'Any fool can hear that'.[6]) The freedom and ease with which Shostakovich created and manipulated his musical material in accordance with his pre-formed philosophical and literary ideas is clear from a typical passage in the last movement of his choral Thirteenth Symphony. Yevtushenko's verses read:

So three cheers for a career,
At least when it's a career of the likes of
Shakespeare, Pasteur, Newton and Tolstoy.

Shostakovich used a rather striking musical trick in this episode: the last three words '. . . i Tolstogo L'va' ('. . . and Lev Tolstoy') are greatly drawn out. Their timing – in metrical units – is equal to the three preceding lines, with added stress on the last one. Most interesting of all is the way the composer divides the last phrase: it is expanded by allotting the word 'Tolstogo' a fourth syllable, following which the whole word with its extra syllable is repeated. When, however, we are expecting to hear the extra syllable again, it is replaced by a question. 'Lev?' demands the soloist impatiently. 'Lev!' acknowledges the chorus, with *fortissimo* emphasis. In effect, the composer is making us ask: 'Who is this Tolstoy? – Unless, of course, it's Lev Tolstoy, who deserves to be mentioned in the same breath as Shakespeare, Pasteur and Newton. In any case, it can't possibly be Aleksey Tolstoy,[7] who secured himself a cushy career in Stalin's regime'.

There is no room here for a detailed review of Shostakovich's works, whose universal human message was perforce often hidden behind pompous public statements about their supposed programmes. One notable example of this was the

[6] Shostakovich's reply is itself a quotation of Brahms's response to an observation regarding the Beethovenian theme in the finale of his First Symphony. –IM.

[7] *Cf.* p. 413, note 8.

Seventh or 'Leningrad' Symphony, a work planned and begun *before* Hitler's attack on Russia in 1941. The tune of the notorious march in the first movement was conceived by Shostakovich as the 'Stalin' theme (all who were close to the composer knew this). After the war had started, Shostakovich declared it to be the 'Hitler' theme. Later, when the work was published, he renamed it the 'Evil' theme – justly, since both Hitler and Stalin met the specification. In the world's musical circles, however, the second of the three definitions remains the most familiar. In his Eighth and Tenth Symphonies, the composer continued to pursue the same mission of exposing 'evil' – meaning totalitarianism with its cult of war and monstrous cruelty. (A case in point is the scherzo of the Tenth Symphony of 1953.)

In conclusion, I feel I should mention the Twelfth – the so-called 'Lenin' Symphony. Its first-night audience had no inkling of the behind-the-scenes story of this rare failure in Shostakovich's output. The Twelfth had been planned as a criticism of Lenin (I learned this from the composer himself). However, a fortnight before its Leningrad premiere, Shostakovich decided that he had made this criticism dangerously obvious, and so, working around the clock in those two short weeks, he dashed off an almost entirely new if, in the event, rather confusing work. What made it worse were the flattering reviews of unprincipled critics, hailing this failure as a work of genius when its composer was in despair. We can only hope that the original manuscript will someday be recovered.

I should emphasise that the preceding observations refer exclusively to those aspects of Shostakovich's output which embody his little-known struggle with totalitarianism, as seen from the vantage of the environment in which he lived and worked. As for the many differing reactions to his art, their variety is entirely appropriate when considered in the light of his lifelong adherence to the principles of democratic pluralism and freedom of choice – principles consistently present in his music, albeit often in several kinds of necessary disguise.

AN INNER REBELLION
Thoughts on the Current Debate about Shostakovich[1]

Leo Mazel'

As long as human culture lives, the work, life and personality of Dmitry Shostakovich will be minutely examined and discussed. As with Beethoven's life and work, every detail will attract the attention of scholars and of a wide circle of cultured people, just as every trait of Shostakovich's creative and personal life will be studied by future generations – which is why we, the composer's contemporaries, have a moral obligation to make public whatever information, materials and data we have.

This is particularly important now, when the debate on Shostakovich has recommenced with renewed vigour. For years in our country he was mentioned almost secretively; now his name is repeatedly splashed all over newspapers and magazines. Everything connected with Shostakovich is being debated: the meaning of his works and themes, the time they were first conceived and performed, their possible original formats, the changing currents in the composer's life, his statements, who had or had not been close to him, even the authorship of the texts of his vocal works. . . . Naturally I do not propose to consider all these questions in the present article. I merely wish to set forth and comment on several hitherto unpublished testimonies and analytical observations, in an attempt to dispel a few doubts.

First, I want to call the reader's attention to the 'invasion theme' from the Seventh Symphony, composed fifty years ago at the beginning of the war. Although it is important to

[1] Originally in *Sovetskaya Muzyka*, 1991, No. 5. A version of this piece appeared in *DSCH Journal*, No. 3, Summer 1995, pp. 2–5. English version by Tatjana M. Marovic (Norbury) and Ian MacDonald.

recall the work's contemporary circumstances – so often forgotten by the debaters – and to acknowledge that the impressions made by those circumstances prompted the creation of the work, it must also be borne in mind that they are not necessarily related to its contents. The latter are multi-layered and multipartite; as for the overall artistic conception, it is complex, permitting a variety of interpretations, both general and personal. Indeed, one might compare it to an algebraic formula, in which various arithmetical values may be substituted. As with any other medium, different facets of the work will present themselves to each listener. Let us also remember that the act of artistic creation is a miracle and a mystery. It is impossible to 'get to the bottom' of it, and I shall not even try. Usually even the artist himself is uncertain of exactly how it works: the conscious is the servant of the subconscious. For this and other reasons, an artist's statements about his work cannot, in the final analysis, always be taken at face value. Moreover, at different times and in different circumstances, a composer may emphasise different aspects of his work. In other words, the final effect of an artist's work does not always wholly correspond to his initial idea of it.

But let us return to the Seventh. For many years there was no doubt concerning the meaning of the central theme of its first movement: it depicted the invasion of Soviet Russia by German armies. There is, of course, no disagreement about the general intent of the music (an impression of evil, of hostile forces ranged against humankind). Moreover, the concrete fact was that our country had been attacked by the Nazi war machine – which is to say: a specific arithmetical value had been entered in the general algebraic formula. And this made sense, especially during the war years. At that time, the whole country was united in its effort to repel the enemy attack. In spite of the persecutions inflicted on it by Communism, the Orthodox church had no hesitation in exhorting the people to come to the defence of their motherland. Likewise opposed to the regime, Sergei Rachmaninov sent a wagon-load of medical supplies from the United States. Even General Denikin, who in 1919 had ordered the White armies to attack Moscow, supported the Soviet Union in its fight against Hitler's Germany. There can be no doubt whatsoever that Shostakovich, while extinguishing the fires caused by

Nazi incendiaries on the roofs of Leningrad,[2] thought and felt in exactly the same way, harboured the same sentiments as everyone else in the USSR.

I do not consider all of Shostakovich's declarations in Solomon Volkov's book *The Memoirs of Dmitri Shostakovich* [*sic*][3] to be entirely genuine. However, the following words of the composer, quoted in the book, coincide with a statement made by him in an article[4] which undoubtedly reflects his private thoughts:

> I wrote my Seventh very quickly. I felt I simply had to write it. The war was all around us. I was in the midst of the people – I wanted to register in music the image of our country at war. During the first days of the war, I sat down and began working on it. I wrote about my contemporaries, who spared neither their strength nor their lives to achieve victory over our enemy.

This, apart from being an official declaration, is also a thought revealed in confidence. According to the composer, he had been thinking about the Seventh before the war, but had 'sat down and worked on it' only after hostilities broke out – a fact confirmed by the Shostakovich scholar Manashir Yakubov, who has declared that there exists a draft of the first movement of the Symphony dated July 1941. Furthermore, in the above-mentioned *Memoirs* it is said that the 'invasion theme' had been composed earlier and that in writing it Shostakovich had had in mind 'not Hitler, but other enemies of humanity' – most probably Stalin. (A few lines later, though, Hitler and Stalin are allotted equal status as criminals.)

Naturally, until 1941, Shostakovich's notions concerning

[2] Volkov disputes this famed depiction in his interview: *cf*. pp. 318–19. –EDS.

[3] Published in many languages, though so far not in Russian. In this account I refer to the German edition, *Zeugenaussage*, first reviewed in Russia in a very interesting article by Daniil Zhitomirsky: 'Shostakovich: The Public and the Private', *Daugava*, 1990, Nos. 3–4. –LM.

[4] Dmitry Shostakovich, 'Kak rozhdayetsya muzyka' ('How Music is Born'), *Literaturnaya Gazeta*, 21 December 1965. –LM. (*Cf*., though, MacDonald, *The New Shostakovich*, pp. 3–4 and 155–66. –EDS.)

Stalin's criminality were certainly far more complete, concrete and personally experienced than any crimes committed by Hitler. However, by 1941, Hitler had had sufficient time to prove himself and, knowing Shostakovich's feelings about racism and anti-Semitism, it is more than probable that he came to think of the two dictators as 'partners in evil' (even more so after they'd become allies in 1939). If, therefore, the invasion theme had initially been inspired by Stalin, the artist's subconscious can almost certainly be said to have harboured Hitler's image as well.

Bearing all this in mind, let us now examine some of the current arguments. According to Lev Lebedinsky, 'the famous theme from the development of the first movement was conceived by Shostakovich as the "Stalin" theme (all who were close to Dmitry Dmitriyevich knew this). After the war began, Shostakovich himself declared it to be the "Hitler" theme'.[5] In my opinion, there is nothing significant about this: life itself had placed the accent on a common and complex predicament. Hitler, the conqueror of Europe, was at war with Great Britain (and, in fact, with the United States) and had invaded Soviet Russia – it was logical that he should be regarded as enemy number one of the entire human race.

On hearing about Lebedinsky's statement, the composer Yury Levitin said: 'What I know is quite different. I met Shostakovich in Leningrad in August 1941 and he told me: "You know, I've just written some 'defence' music ...". D. D. invited me to his home and played me the newly completed first movement of his Seventh Symphony ...'.[6] Why, though, are these 'quite different' stories? Where is the logical contradiction? Lebedinsky talks about the theme, Levitin of a completed first movement; Lebedinsky about the pre-war period, Levitin about 1941. From a wider historical perspective, the question of which of the two tyrants Shostakovich was concentrating on at different times does not seem terribly important.

Very important, however, is another fact: by as early as the beginning of 1942 Shostakovich was warning some of his

[5] *Cf*. pp. 150–59. –EDS.

[6] Yury Levitin, 'A False Note'.

friends not to form a 'narrowly concrete' opinion of this work. In this connection, I would like to reveal some of Shostakovich's so far unpublished statements (which also have an aesthetic significance) and introduce a new name into the Shostakovich circle. I am speaking of the biologist F. P. Yasinovskaya.

Flora Pavlovna Yasinovskaya-Litvinova was married to the mathematician Mikhail Maksimovich Litvinov, whose father, Maksim Maksimovich Litvinov, was the well-known diplomat and head of the Soviet Foreign Office. Their son, the physicist Pavel Mikhailovich Litvinov, also won fame in August 1968 when, with a small group of comrades, he staged a protest on Red Square against the deployment of Soviet troops in Czechoslovakia. (Arrested and sentenced to five years' internal exile, he was later permitted to leave the country, now works in the United States and was recently honoured by the Czech government.) The Litvinov clan were passionate music-lovers, assiduous concert-goers, and owners of an extensive record library. (I'm giving all these details so that the reader can have an idea of the family, and accept the authenticity of Flora Yasinovskaya's statements.)

As destiny would have it, on being evacuated from Leningrad, Flora Yasinovskaya [Litvinova] went to live in Kuibyshev, in the same block of apartments and on the same floor as the Shostakovich family. They duly became acquainted. For Shostakovich, the greatest attraction was the collection of gramophone records Yasinovskaya had managed to bring with her (his favorite was Mahler's *Das Lied von der Erde*). As a result, he often dropped in on her to listen to them, and the Shostakoviches soon came to regard Flora Yasinovskaya as a member of the family (she became a close friend of the composer's wife, Nina Vasil'yevna). During that year Flora Yasinovskaya began writing her journal. (Her article 'My Recollections of Shostakovich' was printed in the literary magazine *Chronograph*, published by Moskovsky Rabochy). With Flora Pavlovna's kind permission, I herewith quote some excerpts from her notes:

> Dmitry Dmitriyevich finished the piano arrangement of the Seventh [after concluding the orchestral score –LM] and invited Samosud and other friends to listen to it. I, too, was invited. I was so overwhelmed by the music that I can't recall the names of all those present on the occasion, except for Lev

> Oborin, Dulova and Vil'yams. When Dmitry Dmitriyevich finished playing, we all rushed to him. He seemed tired, agitated. We all spoke at once, interrupting one another: about the theme [the 'invasion theme' – LM] and about fascism. Somebody called it a 'rat' theme. We spoke about the war, about resistance, about victory. . . . Samosud predicted an enormous success for the symphony. Later, I dropped in on the Shostakoviches to have a cup of tea. Naturally the talk again turned to the symphony. It was then that Dmitry Dmitriyevich declared thoughtfully: 'Fascism, yes, but music, real music, is never literally bound to one theme. Fascism is not just National Socialism; this music is about terror, slavery, the bondage of spirit'. Later, when Dmitry Dmitriyevich got used to me and started to trust me, he told me straight out that *the Seventh (as well as the Fifth) were not just about fascism, but also about our system, about any tyranny and totalitarianism in general*. [The italics are mine. – LM].

Here, three decades before Shostakovich's talks with Volkov, everything is said. One cannot add anything: the 'invasion episode' possesses an *anti-fascist, anti-totalitarian character in a wider sense . . . .*[7]

Now let us examine the debates on the 'programme' of the Eleventh Symphony ('The Year 1905'), composed in 1957.

Whenever writers, biographers or composers choose their subjects from past history, these usually relate to contemporary events. (I'm not referring to artistic creation in the broader sense.) In approaching this type of subject, authors, while remaining faithful to historical facts, quite often stress more recent ones. Thus, the Eleventh depicts the incidents and atmosphere of 1905 – with masterly realism, beginning with the first movement, 'Palace Square' – when in reality, according to the *Memoirs*, the Symphony was inspired by the crushing of the Hungarian Uprising in 1956.

This is, in fact, how I understood the Symphony from the very start. I did not ask 'was there more 1905 or 1956' in it; the various aspects of an artistic work as a whole do not require quantitative equations. However, Lev Lebedinsky writes that 'the work depicts not so much historical as con-

[7] In his full-length article Mazel' turns to his theory of a link between the 'invasion theme' and the second subject of the finale of Beethoven's Piano Sonata No. 5 in C minor, Op. 10, No. 1. –IM.

temporary events'; that 'the true – highly contemporary – programme was intentionally hidden by the composer behind a historical one'; and, finally, that 'Shostakovich turned the scene of the 1905 massacre into the drama of the 1956 Budapest uprising'.

In the same article we're told of an observation made by a lady at the symphony's premiere: 'Those weren't rifle shots – those were tanks roaring and people being machine-gunned'. In my view, listeners who had lived through two World Wars (and heard Shostakovich's Seventh and Eighth Symphonies) would have been extremely surprised to learn that the savagely realistic portrayal of the 1905 massacre was meant to describe events in foreign lands, however deplorable. In agreeing with the lady listener's remark, Lebedinsky fuses the disparate elements of the work into a single linear conclusion. Thus, workers carrying petitions to the Tsar march to the accompaniment of typically Russian songs (one of them, 'The Ninth of January', composed by Shostakovich long before 1956) – but the people subsequently fired on are . . . the citizens of Budapest! According to Lebedinsky, Shostakovich uses 'Aesopian language' throughout the Symphony (except in the 'massacre scene', where he 'lets the cat out of the bag'). In truth, the Eleventh has no literal contemporary programme nor did the composer 'hide' recent political events behind a historical façade. The programme of the symphony is openly historical; only the style is contemporary. Yet it was, at the same time, inspired by tragic contemporary events – and it is arguably this inspiration which gives the symphony its true meaning and substance.

It must be admitted that Lebedinsky's one-dimensional conclusion gave Yury Levitin (in the article he wrote during the debate which followed the publication of Lebedinsky's) good reason to talk of 'vulgarisation'. Paradoxically, however, Levitin does not even mention the historical programme of the Symphony, associating it *solely* with contemporary events. Thus, he too strips the work of its three-dimensionality.

Similarly, commenting on the Eighth Quartet, Levitin refers only to its dedication to the victims of fascism; he does not (as do Lebedinsky and others) mention its autobiographical aspect, nor the concurrent dramatic events in the composer's life. Without being cognisant of all the facts,

Levitin dismisses the information given by Lebedinsky – and some of it, to be candid, is to be taken 'with a pinch of salt' – as fabrication, conjecture, even slander.[8]

In studying the life and work of Dmitry Shostakovich, one must remember that he, like many other Soviet artists, was frequently forced to evade censorship in its various manifestations. This does not, though, mean that in his music one layer is necessarily true or 'authentic', and the rest a 'mask'. Shostakovich's method was different: by acquiescing in making 'official' statements, he gained the freedom to be authentic in his work – which is why his output is so organically coherent. However eye-catching, the title of Daniil Zhitomirsky's article in *Daugava* does not signify the division of the composer's works into 'official' and 'private' content. Even the occasional pieces (and certain other works Shostakovich was forced to write in obedience to a strict order or decree) show the mark of great talent and mastery. As for the arguments about 'official' and 'private' works, it is true that for many decades conditions leading to such a division were the rule, not the exception, for Soviet artists (and, as such, frequently spelt the termination of their art). In this respect Shostakovich was unique: ostensibly a typical instance of such an artist, he gave all the outward appearances of obeying orders while staging an inner rebellion. We should be eternally grateful that throughout those desperate times he managed to preserve his genius and create works of immense power.

The composer was naturally aided in his rebellion by the fact that serious instrumental music was inaccessible to both

[8] Here I should mention the appearance of a curious pattern: positive, authentic testimonies (what actually happened) are cancelled by negative ones (what did not happen). Surely a witness cannot know everything! For example, Levitin's statement about Shostakovich telling him of his 'defence' music, as well as the declaration of Shostakovich's daughter, Galina, that her father had dedicated the Eighth Quartet to *himself* (from *Dmitrỳ Shostakovich, String Quartets*, by Manashir Yakubov, Moscow Philharmonic Orchestra, 1986, p. 15), are obviously genuine. However, according to Levitin, 'nothing is known' about Shostakovich's dark thoughts in 1960 – and consequently one can only assume that nothing untoward ever happened. He seems to doubt the authenticity of these statements to the point of denying that the events they refer to actually took place. –LM.

cultural censors and political authorities. Even so, many listeners understood very well what Shostakovich was striving to convey (indeed, had this not been so, we would hardly consider him the great artist he is). Luckily these listeners were not obliged to give their impressions in print. It was much more difficult for critics and musicologists, who *had* to express their views on paper.

To disclose the authentic meaning of some of Shostakovich's works would have spelt disaster for both critic and composer. For this reason, critics increasingly turned their attentions to formal issues (such as the different structures and systems the composer used), eventually evolving a conventional style of discourse in which the tragic meaning of Shostakovich's symphonies was justified by comparing it to the time-honoured pathos of Shakespeare's tragedies. In a similar way, officially sanctioned grief for the victims of the War was often usefully invoked; later, critics resorted to subtler allusions. For example, in the introduction to my modest *Guide to Shostakovich's Symphonies*, I used a quotation from his speech on the occasion of the first anniversary of victory, printed in *Soviet Art* (9 May 1946) – another pregnant statement leading to what I regard as the heart of the matter: 'We have to remember the fallen – and, in celebrating the victory of the living, we must not forget the anguish and the agonising pain of *our present* tragedy'. I wrote then that this speech expressed the composer's 'credo' and that it ran through his entire *œuvre*, adding: 'This is crucial to the understanding of his work – understanding, for example, why the last movement of the Seventh Symphony contains a funeral march, and why the dazzlingly brilliant finales of the Seventh and Fifth, both in major keys, are sprinkled with sequences in sharp and minor dissonances'.[9]

Here I refer to the Fifth Symphony, composed before the War. And it appears to me, as the reader will have guessed, that in this symphony both 'the grief for the fallen and the agonising pain' – certainly not caused by the tragedy of war – are quite openly expressed . . . .

Naturally I did not publish my private analysis of the coda

[9] Leo Mazel', *'Sinfonii D. D. Shostakovicha – Putevoditel'* (*D. D. Shostakovich's Symphonies – A Guide*), Moscow, 1960, pp. 8–9.

of the Fifth. Here, the strikingly vivid first subject of the finale is converted into a solemn, albeit standard, *Allegro non troppo* (with *fortissimo* trumpets and trombones), which is repeated, alternating with the sharp pounding of the timpani and accompanied by the continuous, cutting repetition of a single note (in octaves). There follows a simple and ponderous ascending melody, similar to a sequential one, sustained on the lowered sixth. After a sorrowful minor episode (within the harmonic and melodic major key), the tempo accelerates. At the climax of the coda (fig. 133, eight-bar augmented variation for the brass) is a typical Shostakovich sequence, close to the spirit of Musorgsky and one I have often described: the melodic sequence V–VI–V–VII–V in natural minor. Depending on the context of the piece, it can express grief, darkness or pathetic fury; at other times – though less frequently – sadness or tenderness. It is with this sequence, for example, that Katerina Izmailova's aria begins in the opera of the same name ('In the wood': E, F, E, G, E, in A minor); it appears in the pathetic climax of the first movement of the Fifth Symphony (two bars after fig. 38: A, B flat, A, C, A, in D minor); at the beginning of the second of the *Romances on Poems of Marina Tsvetayeva* ('Whence such tenderness?'): C, D flat, C, E flat, C, in F minor); and in the main theme of the finale of the Seventh (G, A flat, G, B flat, G [E flat], in C minor).

In the coda of the Fifth, the augmented sequence (see above: A, B flat, A, B flat, A, C, B flat, A, in D major) does not convey a feeling of exultation – on the contrary, one of darkness – even when frequently invoking a harmonic major. Here, the major context only serves, by contrast, to stress the essentially minor character of the sequence, thereby expressing a feeling of unbearable sorrow. As a whole, this coda conveys the image of an oppressed people, parading and rejoicing under threat.

'Our business is to rejoice', was Shostakovich's reply to Zhitomirsky in August 1945, after hearing the tragic news about the atomic bomb dropped on Hiroshima (a statement used by Zhitomirsky as a subtitle for a section of his article). In the *Memoirs*, we are given an explanation of the finale of the Fifth (i.e., rejoicing under threat); it is also said that Yevgeny Mravinsky didn't understand the finales of the Fifth and the Seventh, thinking the composer's intention had been to express exultation, and that his readings had been incorrect.

In this context, I want to say a few words on the finale of the Seventh. The triumphant return (in the coda) of the lyrical variation of the main theme from the first movement is heard in the upper register, with numerous repetitions of the sequence, wherein lies the link between the fifth and the lowered sixth degree of the scale. After this we hear the finale's main theme, in minor (on double-basses) with the above-mentioned 'Shostakovich sequence'. The motif is then twice pounded out on the timpani, *forte-fortissimo*. Finally, there is the concluding major triad. However, on its fifth there is a trill where the upper auxiliary again uses the lowered sixth. Analysing the aforegoing one could, metaphorically, say: 'Shostakovich is celebrating the coming victory, which he passionately desires – but this victory will not deliver us from our tragedy . . .'.

In conclusion, I would like to make some further points about the articles by Lebedinsky and Levitin. Although I disagree with some of the statements made in the former, it does contain valid observations, previously unpublished information (for example, Shostakovich's use of the song 'Suliko' in the First Cello Concerto), and some interesting ideas. Levitin's article commenting on Lebedinsky's is, on the whole, much less interesting.

In my view, a debate like this is salutary, necessary and healthy. What I lament in both articles, particularly in the latter, is the level of the polemic. Lebedinsky calls Shostakovich's pupils 'so-called students'. Why? Were they not interested in Shostakovich's classes, receiving the highest professional qualifications from a remarkable teacher? Were they not all serious musicians, even if different in character and talent? Regrettably, Levitin's reply to Lebedinsky, as we have seen, is equally ungentlemanly. Is it fair, for instance, to hold Lebedinsky partially responsible for a venomous article written by Marian Koval' on Shostakovich[10] merely because sixty years ago – and sixteen years before the publication of the article in question – Lebedinsky and Koval' were members of the same musical association? In criticising one

[10] *Cf*. pp. 341, 464 and 472. –EDS.

of my colleagues, I am asking him to show 'more moderation, more benevolence'. Yury Levitin recalls the 'kindness and tolerance' of their mutual teacher, Dmitry Shostakovich –'so totally different from what one might expect from a composer'. A little of this tolerance could profitably be absorbed by Mr Levitin himself.

We all remember the courteous and highly intelligent man Shostakovich was. It seems to me that the tone of some of the debates on his personality and his work tarnish the memory of a beloved artist – a composer long and rightly regarded as the conscience of Russian music in the twentieth century.

SHOSTAKOVICH'S IDIOMS[1]

Vladimir Zak

In antiquity Aesop invented a language that allowed him to speak the Truth in a veiled form. This tradition has never died out. For although Mikhail Bulgakov, Andrey Platonov or Yevgeny Shvarts came centuries after Aesop, they too stood up to their oppressors by using 'Aesopian' formulas.

Dmitry Shostakovich has been more 'fortunate'. The abstract language of music allowed him to be outspoken, right to the very end. His great symphonic anthology of the totalitarian regime unreservedly reveals the sufferings of a man condemned 'to play a double game' or, rather, lead a double life.

Americans will understand more easily what 'to lead a double life' means if they remember George Orwell's anti-utopian novel *1984* (a model of 'victorious socialism'). The 'iron regime' not only impelled Shostakovich to use a tragic tone, but also pushed him toward the grotesque, sarcasm and humour that he expressed in his music. But how did he convey his feelings when dealing directly with the people? . . . This is precisely where the 'Aesopian motifs' came into play. Were they correctly understood? Really only those of us who had the opportunity personally to know the Soviet 'delights' could fathom them: we all remember 'the scheme of self-abasement', invented by the ideologues of the Communist Party, and the tactic of 'the double bottom', which at the same time as it abased the individual served to extol the totalitarian system: 'If I was able to do something real, I was indebted to our beloved Communist Party and the Soviet Government'.

[1] A version of this piece appeared in *Yevreysky Mir* (*Jewish World*), 7 May 1993, No. 6 (50), pp. 10–11. Several passages were changed or added by the author in 1994 and appear here for the first time. English version by Véronique Zaytzeff and Frederick Morrison.

At one crowded meeting, Dmitry Shostakovich emphatically declared: 'If I have been able to create something for the people, I owe it to my parents'.[2]

Shostakovich's pronouncement was interpreted as a parody of the generally accepted 'code of conduct' and gave an ineffable pleasure to those of us who heard it, for therein the true value, not the false one, was asserted. It is impossible not to marvel at the persistent uniformity with which Shostakovich managed to speak ironically about the Party. A feat he performed not only with the hidden meaning of his words, but also with the direct 'text' of his behaviour.

I recall the Great Palace of the Kremlin during Brezhnev's time, when Shostakovich was to read the Introduction for the opening of the Fifth Congress of Composers. The text had been cooked-up in the depths of the Communist Party and contained a flattering passage directed at L. I. Brezhnev. And Leonid Ilyich himself was all set to listen. But what on earth was taking place? . . .

Shostakovich comes to podium, picks up the typed sheets of paper, and ostentatiously (as if in a slow-motion movie scene) gives them a 180-degree turn. Then, he looks at them for a long time and reverses them again. Silence. Seconds seem to be years. In the Presidium, everyone is perplexed: 'Why is Shostakovich "fooling around"?'

But he is in no hurry. Once again, 'with a flourish', he turns the pages upside down. Once again!!

This 'silent scene' took place in a deathlike hush, somehow reminding one of the scenes in Gogol's *Revizor* [*Inspector General*]: the functionaries, rooted to the ground, stood motionless . . . .

But anybody who still had a conscience rejoiced and clearly understood: it was to them that Shostakovich was sending 'Aesopian signals', clearly hinting at the fact that he, the composer, had absolutely no relation to what had been written.

And, indeed, this 'preliminary tuning' also determined our interpretation of Shostakovich's speech, for we, the listeners, were now capable of catching the notes of a well-hidden irony in his voice. In essence, Shostakovich had somehow become

[2] *Cf*. p. 232. –EDS.

a real inspector-general – a commentator, who obviously disagreed with the written 'document'.

The humorous style of Shostakovich's pronouncements, 'the secret mold' of his speech structures, remind me of the now distant year of 1948, when, for the first time, I saw Shostakovich on an official rostrum.

According to Stalin's directives, the Party was then inveighing against 'anti-people composers' – the blacklist of formalists began with the name of Shostakovich, then a professor at the Moscow Conservatory. We, students in the musical institute for higher education, were herded like cattle into the 'hall of execution'. At that time the guardians of ideology were criticising the most talented composers of the country. Students betrayed teachers. The teachers 'repented' that they had taught with a hidden agenda in mind, that the education they had dispensed was consciously reprehensible, that they had played the 'westerner' Brahms or the 'formalist' Prokofiev instead of the 'genuinely Russian' Glinka, and finally that they 'they had eaten in vain the people's bread'.

But in this bacchanalia of evil and stupidity, in this monstrous polyphonic chorus of inquisitors and panic-stricken 'heretics', we heard the bewildered voice of Shostakovich: 'Yes, yes, yes', Dmitry Dmitriyevich was quickly repeating. 'We, you understand, stand guilty before the people. We, you understand, are very guilty. We did not think about the people, you understand, about their spiritual needs. As a result, you understand, we stand corrected'.

I had the distinct impression that in Shostakovich's odd patter was a tinge of barely concealed buffoonery.

'Did you pay attention to the "you understand" with every other word?' my professor V. A. Zukkerman asked me. And then he added: 'Don't think that these are "idle" words. Far from it. This persistent repetition is Shostakovich's particular style. If you wish, this is his Aesopian language: where there are more than two "you understands", then one must understand everything the other way round.'

My professor, a very fine analyst, was absolutely right. Time has proven it. Having worked for many long years now in the same organisation with D. Shostakovich, and having observed him in very different situations, in daily activities as well as at work, I have had the fortunate opportunity to see that the richness of his speech consisted of this unexpected switching from the direct meaning of words to a deeply hidden one.

In a totalitarian era all of us learned to read the newspapers 'between the lines'. And we best understood Shostakovich's text when we discovered that his deepest meaning was 'between the words'.

'Why does he speak so strangely?' one woman, a Komsomol activist, asked. And added in irritation: 'After all, he is not in the circus!' As for Shostakovich, he periodically had to give a talk about the Party's 'morality'. It never occurred to the Komsomol activist that Shostakovich put a great deal of irony into his own words. He was openly ironic.

The only factor that saved Shostakovich was that the subtext of his words was not caught by the censors, people who, as a rule, were intellectually limited and sometimes simply obtuse. The 'code' of Shostakovich's patter was deciphered only by those who sympathised with the composer. Clearly it must have been extremely important for him to feel that, when having to speak against his own will, right there he could refute what he said and cleanse himself. He could refute his message and cleanse himself thanks to a secret intonation, the 'code' of which he willingly shared with his well-wishers.

Yes, of course, it was his form of Aesopian speech, a form born in a period of the most frightening persecution of free speech. While here, in America, I have had many contacts with Maxim Shostakovich – the composer's son and famous conductor – he has always paid such close attention to his father's musical and speech patterns. He told me, for example, that Dmitry Dmitriyevich instantly changed his 'tonality' depending on the composition of his audience. The outcome of our numerous discussions firmly convinced me that I was, indeed, right in thinking that Shostakovich was using Aesopian formulas when I knew him in the Soviet Union.

To speak figuratively, Dmitry Shostakovich's 'speech continent' always had two poles: one pole was his outspokenness and the other was his code. With relatives and friends there was one set of words. With the representatives of the bureaucratic apparatus there was another. And if his audience were 'mixed', the 'coded system' would inevitably come into play, giving the impression that the speech he was delivering was dichotomous: the surface meaning was meant for the officials, while the hidden one was meant for everyone else. Who would have dared to talk, in 1973, about the true emotions that permeated the music of Shostakovich's last symphony? The author himself deliberately concealed them. Had this not been the case, not only would the composer have been submitted to an *auto-da-fé*, but all of his scores would have had the same fate. Answering the question of some hapless reporter, 'was it a toy store?' that was represented in the first part of the symphony, D. Shostakovich immediately parodied by saying: 'Yes, yes, yes, of course, of course, it is a "toy store". A store! Toys! How can it be otherwise! It can't be! It can't be!' . . .

The patter 'worked': Shostakovich's friends, understanding his pattern, smiled at him sympathetically; as for the happy reporter, he flew off, as if he had wings, to his editorial office to announce the 'important news'.

Nowadays, thank goodness, it is possible to correct such 'important news'.

'Don't you believe those who say that the beginning of the Fifteenth Symphony is meant to be a "toy store"', Maxim Shostakovich, who is a brilliant interpreter and was the first to perform the score, explained to me. 'My father, who constantly had to overcome inconceivable difficulties with the verbal "decoding" of his instrumental works (which Communist propaganda demanded be crammed into the official ideology's Procrustean bed), latched onto the harmless idea of a "toy store", in order to protect his new symphony in some way from that spurious ideology. In fact, the score of the Fifteenth Symphony is endowed with Shakespearean force. Its "doll-like" character has herein a very serious concealed meaning: what are we to expect after a cloudless childhood? Are we going to have our heads rung off in the same way as happens to "puppets"?'

The talented conductor did not choose these words haphazardly: in a totalitarian regime the people were not even considered to be dolls, but, as we all remember, only 'small cogs' (that was how Stalin christened each one of us).[3]

[3] On 'cogs', *cf. Testimony*, p. 163/212, and Mikhail Heller, *Cogs in the Soviet Wheel: The Formation of Soviet Man*, transl. David Floyd, Collins Harvill, London, 1981 (hereafter Heller, 'Cogs'). –EDS.

The corrections that we, the former Soviets, are making today as we deal with our understanding of 'the Symphonist of Our Age' agree with what the composer felt so deeply, with what he showed so clearly in his scores, but had not dared to convey to us in an 'open manner'.

I beg you to listen once again to the 'Leningrad Symphony'. The highest degree of tragedy expressed therein does not lie in the opposition between Germans and Russians at all, but in the monstrous assault of Fascism on the individual. Not only of a foreign fascism – German – but also (and this is so very unbearable) of our own native fascism. This is the reason why many listeners seem to hear in the 'invasion theme' not only the aggressors drawing near and defacing the Russian land, but also the tramping of the boots of the NKVD, the 'regime's boys', who storm into your house early in the morning, at daybreak, to catch right in their beds 'the people's enemy' – your grandfather, your brother, your husband, or your father . . . .

In the mechanic, cold-hearted 'perpetuum mobile' of the Eighth Symphony's 'Toccata' we have an almost physical sensation of the lashing whip, we hear the moans of our dear ones and relatives. Who are their torturers? Who are the executioners? Hitler? Stalin? How did the composer himself answer this question?

Shostakovich answered it in such a way that you and I can clearly understand everything. He instilled faith in us, talked about the optimistic finale, about 'his own perception of the course of history, which must inevitably bring the downfall of tyranny and evil, and the triumph of freedom and humanity'.

No, the Master did not want to say that evil belongs specifically to the German or Soviet side: evil is always evil, tyranny is still tyranny. Stalin and Hitler are given the same status.

. . . At all times and in all places, whenever it was possible, Shostakovich spoke with us quite openly, but naturally did so by relying on our responsiveness, sensitivity and acumen, or, if you wish, creative inferring.

And if the question was 'the making of man' (Shostakovich's famous definition of the Fifth Symphony), then, indeed, heeding the music in this amazing revelation from the '30s, it was impossible not to infer that the Fifth

Symphony was 'the making of man under repression'.

I recall how Dmitry Dmitriyevich once repeated: 'the making of man!' There was such bitterness in that exclamation! He exclaimed it with such a multitude of layers of semantic meaning! And it was only by looking into the composer's eyes that one saw just exactly what was hidden behind those words that were accompanied by such an eloquent facial expression.

Alas! Many took the composer's words too straightforwardly and immediately fell into accord with the prevailing ideology. The Soviet people had become too accustomed to the monosemantics that had been driven into our consciousness since our school days. And this hammering in did make sense: one single meaning for each spoken word (the singularity being necessary to reinforce totalitarianism). Consequently, we could not recognise the depth of a concealed meaning, a meaning that was quite often the most important point and was revealed through a mass of components, such as the nuances in the timbre of the speaker's voice, or a pregnant pause, or even an eloquent gesture that contradicted the words just spoken. To fully appreciate one of Shostakovich's pronouncements, it would be appropriate to recall S. Mikhoels's words: 'I cannot fathom', remarked the eminent artist, 'why it is that our attention is being focused on the word and on the word only'.

Mikhoels, who worshipped Shostakovich's music, had intuitively underscored this thought in the mid-'30s, a time when every factor that changed the straightforward meaning of a word acquired a huge moral (and political!) meaning – on the stage and, needless to say, most of all, in daily life itself – for in conditions of the most brutal police censorship, Its Highness The Concealed Meaning took the lead.

Nowadays, we underscore in every way possible that not only was what Shostakovich said important, but also the manner in which he said it and the circumstances surrounding the statement. It was only when the listener paid attention to the intonation and observed the behaviour that he could fathom the real meaning of 'Shostakovich's idiom'. All of this makes a very interesting topic that has not yet been investigated. But we can already safely assert that 'Shostakovich's idiom' represents not only the triumph of the Great Artist's Conscience, not only his self-defence against the onslaught of militant, aggressive lies, but also his covert protest against those lies.

What an unusual situation: Shostakovich had never been imprisoned, yet he always felt himself a prisoner. No, this was not a paradox at all, for the Genius who cherished Freedom equated totalitarianism with a concentration camp. And, of course, Shostakovich always disturbed and annoyed the masters with his merciless uprightness, for we always threw away the chains of totalitarianism when listening to his music. This was the reason for the persecutions of Shostakovich and his work. This was the reason that they compelled him (even forced him!) to appear on the podium and follow the liars' scenario. But Shostakovich would give us these alien words that did not belong to him in an inverted manner. He did that quite often using the 'distorting mirror', and the negative became the photo.

For this Aesopian 'I' the artist could have lost his life. One had the impression that the guillotine was longing for him. But Shostakovich was always rescued by his fortitude and his innate sense of humour. As for the rulers, they unsuccessfully tried to break him – not only by intimidation and threats, but also by enticing him with 'sweets' and bestowing on him elevated ranks and titles. And what were Shostakovich's feelings?

On his sixtieth birthday he showed all of us that publicist's novelty –'A Public Letter from the Honoree' – in which, with amazingly subtle self-irony, he chaffed at all his regalia.[4]

This was not an artless stunt by the composer. Far from it. It was the essence of the Genius' morals.

Nowadays when I listen to the sparkling 'Humour' in the Thirteenth Symphony, based on Yevgeny Yevtushenko's verses, I unwittingly exclaim: 'But this is about Shostakovich himself!'

They wanted humour to buy
But humour persistently lingered.
They wanted humour to kill
But humour gave them the finger!

It is precisely here, in the 'Humour' of the Thirteenth

[4] A reference to Shostakovich's *Preface to the Complete Edition of My Works and a Brief Reflection upon this Preface.* –EDS.

Symphony, that Shostakovich really exalted Aesop. Remembering now how Shostakovich spoke in the hall of the Kremlin, where 'tsars, kings, emperors, the sovereigns of the entire Earth' sat side by side, I clearly see that in comparison to Shostakovich they 'looked like beggars'.

The prophets of the 'Bright Future' must have felt much worse when Shostakovich 'began to speak from the grave'. Was this phantasmagoria? No. Even the ever so creative Salvador Dali could not have lighted upon such an effect. Kafka himself would have paled, for it was with incredible ardour that Shostakovich 'spoke from the grave'. If, while alive, the great composer feared more than death itself the thought that the 'guardsmen of Communism' would one 'fine' day separate him from his creative force and deprive him of the physical ability to compose music (recently Mstislav Rostropovich quite correctly underscored this very thought[5]), then, having departed to a better world, the genius no longer had any reason to fear, and his word 'from the next world' acquired a particular weightiness!

Naturally what I am talking about is Solomon Volkov's famous *Testimony*. In a confidential conversation with the musicologist (who bowed to Shostakovich's wish and published *Testimony* only after the composer's death), the composer talked with him, utterly disregarding those who would chastise him. No more subtexts. No more quotations marks. Now Shostakovich's 'idioms' could be clearly revealed to everyone! Total revelation!

Wouldn't this have frightened the 'standard-bearers of Communist morals?' They were perfectly aware, through the agents of the KGB, that the Master's Confession was already being read at secret gatherings of the members of the Moscow art world, that the pages of *Testimony* were reprinted 'clandestinely', and that they were passed along by word of mouth even by the students of the Moscow Conservatory. Even though just to disclose one's agreement with *Testimony* meant courting disaster, the 'secret manuscript' became a sort of Bible for musicians, artists and writers, as well as scholars.

[5] Mstislav Rostropovich, 'Plachu nalog Bogu' ('I pay my due to God'), *Izvestia*, 64, 6 April 1994.

What were the reactions of the keepers of the Regime? *Testimony* for them turned into a kind of a time-bomb, whose detonation shook the very foundations of 'well-developed socialism'.

'What is to be done?' This 'question of Lenin' turned out to be profoundly contemporary for those 'responsible for ideology'. Those in power 'found a solution' – rather primitive, but one typical of totalitarianism. In the silent offices of the Department of Culture of the Central Committee of the Communist Party of the Soviet Union, they concocted a document which said that everything written by Solomon Volkov was a fabrication and a defamation of the USSR. To be sure, they said that this so-called letter addressed to *Sovetskaya kul'tura* [*Soviet Culture*] was written by Shostakovich's students,[6] but the students were forced (that is, really compelled) to sign. Only two of them refused: Georgy Sviridov and Boris Tchaikovsky. They managed....

I personally felt the consequences of the momentum gathered from the '*Testimony* Affair'. I was accused of having written a recommendation for Solomon Volkov to the Union of the Composers, a recommendation in which, in plain terms, I had recommended the musicologist as a man of talent and as an extremely keen student of our country's musical life. Furthermore, I wrote an article for the newspaper *Pravda*, the publication of which was delayed twice 'through my own fault'. The first time, as I found out later, the article was 'pulled out' due to the fact that on the eve of D. Shostakovich's concert, its performer, V. Sukhanov, the Laureate of International Competitions, had asked abroad for political asylum (I had mentioned the pianist in my article). The second time – it was again pulled out, but on this occasion it was due to the fact that the main hero of my review, Maxim Shostakovich, the composer's son and famous conductor, had decided to remain abroad on the eve of its publication in *Pravda*. It turned out that all those having connections with D. Shostakovich were 'deserters' and 'despicable émigrés', and the impression was that I was their 'instigator'! Nothing, but unsolved 'idioms'... No wonder: if Shostakovich's figure was at the heart of the

[6] A reference to 'Pitiful Forgery'; *cf.* pp. 60–67. –EDS.

action, then, for the arms of the Soviet 'law', the 'vicious circle' would surely appear, and sooner or later all of those whom Shostakovich deeply trusted would fall into it.

If Solomon Volkov's inspired work was impregnated with the sincerity of Shostakovich's opinions, then, without any further ado, Volkov was outlawed. If Mstislav Rostropovich, Shostakovich's best friend, fearlessly threw down the gauntlet at the arbitrary inquisitors, then this musician of genius was stripped of his Soviet citizenship. Even the successful and 'silent' Yevgeny Mravinsky, who, at some point, overstepped the permitted norms, 'had to pay for it'. Silent? No. Mravinsky had mastered Shostakovich's 'idiomatic language' and, at a most distressing moment in the composer's life, proclaimed what even to allude to had been categorically forbidden. This took place soon after the Communist Party Decree of 1948, when Shostakovich was 'nailed to the cross'.

There was uproar in the West and, taking into account diplomatic considerations, Soviet authorities gave Mravinsky permission to perform Shostakovich's Fifth Symphony. This concert turned into a real event and this was due to the conductor. Having raised above his head the full score of the symphony, Mravinsky shook it for a long time, as though eloquently underscoring that Russia and all of humanity could be proud of such music. The conductor's 'Aesopian gesture' filled the audience with unusual enthusiasm. But Yevgeny Aleksandrovich had to pay for it: he was severely reprimanded by the 'higher ups' and warned that such escapades were inadmissible. The conductor fell into disgrace, and into the 'closed circle'.

Thank goodness that today this 'closed circle' has definitely been abolished.

. . . In June of 1994, at a wonderful concert dedicated to the memory of Yevgeny Mravinsky, the Russian people listened to Shostakovich's Eighth Symphony and its finale, which carries one into a bright, pastoral world depicting the enchantment of dawn. The victory of light over darkness was a well-loved image for Shostakovich. It was symbolic first that this image triumphed in the new Russia, a Russia that was awakening from a lethargic slumber, and second, that it took place in St Petersburg, Shostakovich's native town, on the concert stage of the Philharmonia named for him, Dmitry

Shostakovich. Maxim Shostakovich stood on the conductor's podium. The performance of the Eighth Symphony was in his interpretation grandiose! In the concert hall, where so often Dmitry Dmitriyevich had appeared himself, the ovation of the grateful listeners went on and on for a long time.

Yes, the triumphal procession of Shostakovich's music, on the threshold of the 21st century, is a *fait accompli*. All those who are devoted to Shostakovich ought to understand his statements and correctly appraise his idioms in the official press and on the radio, during the 'Kremlin speeches'. After all, it was they, those 'Shostakovich idioms', that helped the composer of genius to hold out, to preserve and hand down to us his Great Artistic Œuvre.

Indeed, it is absolutely essential for all of us to take up the study of 'Shostakovich's idioms', for that will explain not only many aspects of the creative heritage of the greatest symphonic composer of our century, but also many aspects of our own history.

TALKING ABOUT SHOSTAKOVICH
Three Documents
Kirill Kondrashin

1: 'The most extraordinary person I ever met'
Interview with Pierre Vidal[1]

In December 1976, a little more than a year after Shostakovich's death, a complete recording of his Symphonies by Kirill Kondrashin and the Moscow Philharmonic was released in France. The conductor, at the time still living in Moscow, came to Paris on a brief visit to conduct the New Philharmonic Orchestra and, during rehearsals, Pierre Vidal was able to conduct the following interview.

Under what circumstances did you meet Shostakovich?

It was in 1937, when I was engaged by Leningrad's Maly Theatre, to which Shostakovich too was connected – though at the time neither his ballets nor his operas were performed there. I watched him from afar, fascinated, not daring to approach him. He was, after all, something of a legend after his First Symphony. I'd performed it that same year on the radio without having met him. But our first real meeting took place during the war, in Moscow, right after his evacuation from Leningrad. He'd lost a lot of weight, was more nervous, but remained extremely courteous and attentive, enquiring

[1] A version of this piece appeared in *DSCH*, No. viii, August 1989, pp. 19–23. English version by Tatjana M. Marovic (Norbury) and Ian MacDonald. Dating from three years *before* the publication of *Testimony*, this piece shows Kondrashin to be extraordinarily open in his comments about the composer and his music. Kondrashin remained one of *Testimony*'s strongest supporters, no doubt because its pages reflected what he already knew about the 'real' Shostakovich. –EDS.

after the health of our mutual friends. He had a photographic memory. Whilst staying at Orenburg, a thousand kilometres away, I'd been invited by the Bolshoi Orchestra to conduct the First Symphony. Knowing the composer was in the audience made me nervous, but I already had my own conception of this idiosyncratic work. Afterwards, I heard a totally different rendition by another conductor, supposedly approved by the composer, but this didn't change my concept. At the end, Shostakovich came on stage and embraced me: 'That was beautiful! I'd kiss you if I didn't have a cold!' That was my first contact with him.

Did he give any advice to the performers of his works?

After hearing this other version of the First Symphony, I realised that he allowed his music to be performed with relative freedom, not wishing to impose his ideas. I rarely heard him express any severe criticism about other conductors. Since his music offered many possibilities, this was fair enough. We can observe such differences in Mravinsky, a conductor of great authority – yet Shostakovich approved of them. However, he'd certainly express disapproval if anyone betrayed his style, as he did, for instance, during the rehearsals of his Eighth Symphony at the Edinburgh Festival. (The conductor had introduced a big *rallentando* into the third movement which made no sense.) After I'd recorded his complete Symphonies, he listened to all of them except the Seventh. In the Soviet Union, if a composer is alive, new recordings are always sent to him for his approval. I visited Shostakovich in the hospital, taking a tape recorder. He listened closely and wrote an enthusiastic report, mentioning soloists and sound engineers.

Did he do anything to get his work performed?

Shostakovich didn't speak about his work; he disliked words. Perhaps he didn't want to impose his own ideas. He never tried to promote his works and never said in advance what he was composing. He was a unique personality – the moral conscience of music in Russia. A very sensitive man, he was always interested in new music, never making any negative comments. If he didn't like something, all you'd get from him was 'That's very nice, very interesting!', followed by a profound silence. When he liked something, he'd talk about it enthusiastically to anyone who'd listen, often repeating the same things. He was a kind man who could become very insistent when defending someone. When the Jewish composer Moisei Vainberg was arrested (his wife was the daughter of Solomon Mikhoels of the Jewish Theatre) Shostakovich inundated Stalin and Beriya with letters pleading for his release. And he got him out! One day, Stalin offered Shostakovich a *dacha*, which didn't exactly delight him. He bought another *dacha* and donated the first one to the state for nothing, saying: 'It came gratis. How can you sell something you never bought?'

One of his most forceful works, the Fourth Symphony – composed in 1936 after the Lady Macbeth *scandal, and withdrawn from circulation while in rehearsal – was premiered by you in Moscow, in 1961. Could you tell us about that?*

The audition of the Symphony had been arranged before the attacks on *Lady Macbeth*. As soon as these appeared, Shostakovich was advised to wait. He withdrew the Symphony after two very short rehearsals. During the War, when everything was burned for heating, the score was thought to have been lost. Fortunately it proved possible to reconstruct it, and I asked Shostakovich whether he had any interest in having it performed. (The task was complicated by the numerous errors the existing score contained; I needed his advice.) Shostakovich took the material and studied it for a couple of days before announcing that he was still pleased with the Symphony and happy to have me perform it. This was our first collaboration. I asked him numerous questions during the rehearsals. Whenever something went wrong, he waited for a pause, and asked the orchestra and the conductor to excuse him, blaming himself for the faults. All his observations were very precise. 'I wrote that *piano*, but it'd sound better *mezzo-forte*' – that sort of thing. All these nuances went into the official edition.

How would you define the line of Shostakovich's evolution over fifty years, from the First to the Fifteenth Symphony?

Shostakovich was a product of the '20s, a period in which techniques in the arts advanced rapidly. The greatest artists were at work: the poet Mayakovsky, the stage director Meyerhold, the painter Dmitriyev, the musicologist Sollertinsky. Shostakovich was attracted to the theatre and cinema by the finest representatives of the intelligentsia, as a result of which his life and inspiration were always socially committed. He was one of those very rare composers whose style is established from the beginning and confirmed again and again in his subsequent work. He never changed – whereas Tchaikovsky's style, for example, altered markedly during the course of his life. At nineteen, Shostakovich was creatively mature, open, and enthusiastic, and he remained like that until his death – so much so that even the illnesses, injustices and persecutions he suffered could be absorbed into his major works. The Tenth Symphony is like that – reflecting those problems, protesting against them, and in the end transcending them. Generally speaking, his development parallelled those of the other great masters of this century, his language becoming increasingly simple and accessible (like Bartók, for instance). In terms of his destiny, Shostakovich remained devotedly attached to his homeland, never for a single moment considering exile.[2] Even so, his music gained a worldwide audience, striking a universal chord with its moving social qualities. Essentially it's about the struggle against fascism – that eternal evil which, though it may change its name,[3] seems indestructible, sustained by the impulses of brutality. And unfortunately it will last for a long time. One can no more ignore this background in the Seventh and Eighth Symphonies than one can overlook the programme of Tchaikovsky's Fourth.

He wrote some very important works during his last ten years. Could you tell us about this period?

In spite of being very ill, Shostakovich wrote many works

[2] But *cf.* the comments of Maxim Shostakovich, Frances Schillinger and Serge Tcherepnin on pp. 184, notes 250 and 251. –EDS.

[3] Kondrashin is here speaking, 'in code', about Communism: *cf.* pp. 158–59. –IM.

during his last ten years. Ten or fifteen years earlier, when he still had his strength, he had become Secretary of the Composers' Union, when he could better have used the time to compose. Towards the end, considering his frail physique, his strength of spirit and willpower were amazing. When he went to the great hall of the Conservatoire, he had to walk down four steps, which was very difficult for him. He used to say: 'If the Symphony's a success, don't be angry if I don't come up on stage'. He hated the idea of anyone pitying him. A close circle of devoted friends surrounded him. His pupils, as well as Khachaturian, used to come and spend the evenings with him. Whenever he finished a work, he liked to play it to his 'entourage'. Beforehand, though, he would mislead people. Pretending to be working on *The Quiet Don*, he'd write something entirely different; the subject held no interest for him.[4] The Fourteenth and Fifteenth Symphonies and the vocal cycles really took up all his attention. I often find myself thinking of these works. For him, those private performances at his home were a testing-ground for what he was writing. Later, a formal audition would be held at the Composers' Union, at which he'd display his new works to those whose opinions he cared less for. I remember the day when he invited us to his *dacha* to let us hear the Fourteenth Symphony. (Shostakovich was a very punctual man who expected the same of his friends. If you were late for a meeting at one o'clock, he'd be on the phone to all the police stations and hospitals in the neighbourhood by five past one.) Well, on that particular day, after tea, Shostakovich seated himself at the piano – finding it difficult to play, as his hands were affected by illness – and sang the two solo parts in such

[4] Shostakovich met Mikhail Sholokhov, author of the Socialist Realist epic *Quiet Flows the Don*, at the Rostov Festival in May 1964, and agreed to write an opera based on the novel. A year later, the composer told reporters that the work had progressed as far as acquiring a libretto. According to bulletins published in 1966, he was still working on it, aiming to finish it in 1967 in time for the fiftieth anniversary of the Revolution. No such opera appeared, however, and nothing more was heard of it. Though Shostakovich reportedly claimed Sholokhov to be one of his favorite authors, this is highly unlikely in that the writer scurrilously attacked all manifestations of dissidence during the '60s. Sholokhov's own position is difficult to interpret. An alcoholic, like so many Russian intellectuals under Communism,

a weak voice that we had to follow the text in the score. But he did it with great tenderness, and this produced a remarkable impression. Having to entrust the manuscript to a copyist cost him a few sleepless nights. Had it been lost, I doubt whether it could have been reconstituted. Really, I could go on talking about him for hours – he was the most extraordinary person I ever met!

What do you think of the texts he chose for his settings?

The verses are brilliant, but their translations are almost always bad; the approach is childish, and the Russian vocabulary poor. We did tell him quite clearly that we disagreed about the way he used those foreign texts. The right method would have been to start with a word-by-word translation into Russian and then get a final version done by a good poet. Shostakovich didn't like hearing the audience turning pages during a concert. He wanted, for concerts performed abroad, translations into each country's own language; that's an attitude I approve of.

What about the Fourteenth Symphony and its powerful message of despair?

Shostakovich always pondered on the problems of life and death. The manner in which one ought to live continually preoccupied him. 'We should live lives we're not ashamed of.' Those were his words. At the dress rehearsal of the Fourteenth, he added that he couldn't accept the idea of death – that it was his hatred of it that had shaped the polemical character of the Symphony as a whole.

---

he is known to have derided officials and top literary functionaries in a casual, insolent style – yet the Party continued to represent him as its leading literary light. As a writer, his reputation is equally fuzzy (some believe he stole his work from the pre-Revolutionary Cossack author Fyodor Kryukov). Whatever the truth, his gargantuan novel – to which there is a sarcastic reference in *Testimony* (p. 45/60) – was scarcely of a kind to have appealed to Shostakovich. –IM.

2: The Thirteenth Symphony and Other Matters[5]

I struck up a fairly close friendship with Shostakovich. Having written a new work, he would invite me to his home to listen to it. In later days, he still played [the piano], although with difficulty, humming at the same time in a plaintive childlike voice.

Once, in 1962, he called me up and said: 'Kirill Petrovich, I've just written a new symphony. Come and listen to it'. I went. Eight or ten people were at his place. Dmitry Dmitriyevich said that he had written an unorthodox five-movement work of a 'non-symphonic cycle' to poems by Yevtushenko, but he regarded it as a symphony because they all were united by a common idea. 'As I will probably play poorly', he added, 'and will also sing, I will first read the texts to you.' And before each movement he read an appropriate poem.

He played the first movement, the second, the third and the last. The latter was a magic finale, even in his imperfect interpretation. The music made us all sit silent. Only Aram Khachaturian, tears in his eyes, rose and said: 'Mitya, this is overwhelming!' Then a practical question arose: who will sing? The rest was clear: in Leningrad the first performance should be conducted by Mravinsky. As we discussed the organisational questions, Dmitry Dmitriyevich remained silent. Within five days he offered the conducting to me, 'if I agreed and liked the symphony'.

Naturally, I was astounded. I said that it was a great honour and refrained from asking him why Mravinsky wouldn't do the conducting. We began to discuss the question of the soloist. I suggested Nechipaylo, a young man who played leading roles in the Bolshoi Theatre. He had a deep baritone and was very musical, also a nice fellow. 'I fully trust your choice', said Dmitry Dmitriyevich. 'I don't know Nechipaylo, so let's talk to him.'

Just in case, I was advised to select an understudy for

[5] Abridged from *Muzykal'naya Zhizn'*; reproduced courtesy of *Sputnik*. A version of this piece appeared in *DSCH*, No. xviii, May 1992, pp. 9–12. For another (slightly different) account by Kondrashin, *cf.* Wilson, pp. 357–62. –EDS.

Nechipaylo from the Philharmonic Society. It had just acquired a young bass singer, Vitaly Gromadsky, a former sailor, a robust man with a none-too-beautiful voice, but a musical fellow and a hard worker. Shostakovich listened to both singing to his accompaniment, and said: 'Very good. I like them both'.

Gromadsky then commented in his deep bass voice: 'Dmitry Dmitriyevich, don't you think that we might get into trouble with the first movement?'

'What sort of trouble do you mean? After all, we *are* talking about things which exist', replied Shostakovich.

Gromadsky: 'But where is the anti-Semitism in our country? There isn't any'.

Shostakovich: 'Yes, there is. And we must put an end to it!'

And he blew up. And I realised that this was a sensitive subject. Jewish melodies occur in many of his works. Personally, there was nothing Jewish about Shostakovich, as regards nationality, culture or terms of upbringing. But I see in his Jewish motifs a manifestation of his subconscious, or perhaps even conscious, protest. His Jewish songs were written at the height of the anti-Jewish campaign in the late '40s. His First Violin Concerto, which also contains vivid Jewish intonations, was written in 1947 and denied publication until 1955.

We got down to orchestral rehearsals amid a mild stir already caused by the Symphony. I learned why I had replaced Mravinsky. Shostakovich had given him the score, asking him, as always, to introduce the work. Under a trifling pretext, Mravinsky returned it – in other words, declined the offer. The stir which got out reached high places. Above all, it was caused by the Jewish problem raised in Yevtushenko's poem 'Babi Yar'. As soon as it became known that Shostakovich had written a new symphony, *Literaturnaya Gazeta* ran a long article criticising Yevtushenko's 'one-sided' interpretation of the Babi Yar tragedy. It was pointed out that not only Jews but also Russians and Ukrainians lay buried in Babi Yar. Furthermore, the key role in defeating fascism had been played by Russia, while the poem made no mention of this fact.

For a while nobody bothered me. The premiere was scheduled for the end of 1962. Shortly before, Khrushchev gave hell to all our intelligentsia at a notorious meeting with personalities in literature and the arts. And, as ill luck would have it, this coincided with the premiere of the Thirteenth Symphony. All troubles seem to come together.

In the morning I received a telephone call from Nechipaylo: 'I've lost my voice and cannot sing'. 'You'll have to sing even if you have to crawl to the concert', I replied. 'But I can't.' He was a terrible coward, but not in the political sense – Nechipaylo was really sick. Another singer taken critically ill may collect himself and still sing, but he knew that the house would be packed and was afraid of giving a poor performance, that was all.[6]

The dress rehearsal was about to commence. Everybody was seated. The Hall was full of bigwigs. But there was no soloist. We began to search for Gromadsky. But nobody knew whether he would come or not and what shape he would be in if he came. Dmitry Dmitriyevich was nervous: 'What shall we do? Will Gromadsky come? Will he sing? If he makes a poor showing at the rehearsal, we will have to cancel the premiere'.

Just then Popov, the Minister of Culture of the Russian Federation called me up.

'Well, how's the symphony?'

'We're rehearsing. Another soloist will sing.'

'But doesn't the first movement give you doubts?'

'Not me.'

'And how are you feeling?'

'I'm feeling fine.'

'And what if you play it without the first movement? Perhaps you could suggest this to the composer?'

The premiere took place in the evening. The Symphony

[6] In *Galina* (p. 278), Galina Vishnevskaya gives a different account:

> Suddenly, early in the morning of the day of the concert, before the dress rehearsal, Nechipailo called me at home in a panic to say that he couldn't sing the Thirteenth Symphony that night because he had been scheduled for a production at the Bolshoi. [. . .]
>
> A singer whose name was on the showbill – *Don Carlo*, I believe – had been ordered to 'get sick' so that Nechipailo, who would not cooperate by refusing to perform in the premiere of the Thirteenth Symphony, would be obliged that evening to fill in at the Bolshoi production.

—EDS.

caused a terrible musical and political stir. A second performance was to take place in another two weeks. Unexpectedly, I was invited by Dmitry Dmitriyevich to visit him. He showed me a new issue of *Literaturnaya Gazeta* with a new variant of 'Babi Yar' – twice as long and written with all critical remarks in view.

'Now, what shall I do? Yevtushenko has done us a bad turn: he has written a new variant without saying as much as a word to me, let alone seeking my advice.'

'Dmitry Dmitriyevich, I have already received a request to sound out what you would say if asked to re-work the first movement.'

'I won't do that. Let's try to save the Symphony. It must be performed.'

On the following day, Shostakovich called me: 'I have found eight lines which I can replace'.

The replacement was none too apt, because the best lines which we had in the first movement –'All buried victims here are Jews, all buried victims here are children' – fell out. Gromadsky re-learned these eight lines, and the work was performed, but it was not recommended for further performance. (In our country, musical works are not banned, they are 'not recommended for performance'.) At Party activist meetings, the Symphony was talked about as if it were not Soviet music, although Shostakovich had recently joined the Party. Participants in those meetings asked: what sort of Party candidate is he, writing such a symphony?[7]

When I was touring the West a year later, I was presented with a pirate record of this Symphony. It had been originally recorded for the powers-that-be; one of the recording engineers had sold the tape to the West. The Thirteenth

[7] Kondrashin's version of events, including seeing a new issue of *Literaturnaya Gazeta* with a substantially revised 'Babi Yar' and being surprised by Yevtushenko's changes, has recently been challenged by Albert Todd in his paper 'The Many Literary Worlds of 'Babi Yar',' Brown Symposium XVII, Southwestern University, Texas, 25 February 1995. Todd, a long-time friend of Yevtushenko, pointed out that the second version supposedly printed in *Literaturnaya Gazeta* does not exist; furthermore, he quoted Yevtushenko saying that Kondrashin himself, after meeting with Shostakovich, requested that he alter the text so that the work would not be banned. *Cf.* p. 230, note 420. –EDS.

Symphony thus spread all over the world, but, if my memory serves me right, it was not published in Russia until the mid-'60s. Then came a sudden command to record it. After the West had been flooded with the unofficial records, it was decided that we must have our own, Soviet, record. Then all hell broke loose, and it was shelved until 1972 . . . .

Some people like to talk about Shostakovich's 'repentances', but these bore a purely ritual character. Externally, he 'democratised' some of his works. For instance, he wrote his *Song of the Forests* to order. He was utterly hard up in those days, so he had to write something to earn a bit of money. Shostakovich also wrote music to some awful texts by Yevgeny Dolmatovsky. During the difficult period after 1948 (when Shostakovich's work came under severe criticism and he was dismissed from the Leningrad Conservatoire), he was asked what he was writing. He said: 'Now I am writing music for a film. It is most unpleasant to have to do this. I wouldn't advise anyone to do it unless you are faced with dire poverty'.

In the West, people were under the impression that criticism had spoiled Shostakovich, that he had begun to write exactly what was demanded of him. I disagree with this view. Of course, such criticism irreparably harmed our culture. It also robbed us of many great operas which the composer failed to realise. But following the first harsh criticism when his music was described as a jumble of sounds, he wrote his great Fifth Symphony. After 1948, he wrote his Tenth Symphony, which was also given a hostile reception. It is an exceedingly complex symphony, but now it is so clear to me.

I must confess that I deified him. But there *was* a period when our relations became clouded. In 1966, I was the chairman of the jury of the second Conductors' Competition. Among the competitors was Shostakovich's son, Maxim – but he had strong rivals. When the question of the third round – which was to include only six participants to be rewarded with six prizes – came up, it became clear to me that Maxim fell far short of getting in among the best and that, consequently, he could not be included among the six. This cost me sleepless nights. I had to decide for myself how to act. Addressing the closing session of the jury, I said what I thought: Maxim did not deserve to progress, being weaker than many others, so far. Someone supported me, others objected. In short, Maxim was chosen as the sixth participant in the third round.

On the following morning I went to see Dmitry Dmitriyevich. He met me in an absolutely proper manner, but was obviously nervous. I could feel that this conversation was a trying experience for him.

'Kirill Petrovich', he said, 'I am grateful to you for coming and saying this to my face. I appreciate this action, but I don't agree with you. Maxim was much stronger than all the other participants.'

It was depressing to see how painful it was for him, and I thought that he would never invite or call me up again. But after our difficult conversation, Dmitry Dmitriyevich began to call me every other day (he usually called me once a month or once in three weeks.) He hated me to think that he had taken offence. Shostakovich appreciated the fact that I had my own view and that I had openly stated it to him.

Later, I went to see him fairly regularly. He complained about his ailments. I remember him saying as we were sitting on the veranda: 'I don't know what to do. My hands don't obey me. I can't help it. I write having to hold my right hand with my left. My pen jumps, and my legs won't walk. But my memory is still all right'.

3: The Interior Shostakovich[8]

There are two types of symphonic music. In one type, programme music, the content lies 'on the surface'. In order to convey the content to the audience, the conductor must somehow add the music to a known plot. As a rule, the performer and the audience have less trouble orienting themselves in such music. Music written by the rules of 'pure' symphonic composition is another matter. It is felt that such music cannot be 'deciphered' verbally, and it elicits individual associations in each listener. Does that mean that in this

[8] Statement read at a symposium organised by Bucknell University, New York, 9 September 1980; English version by Antonina W. Bouis. This piece appeared in *DSCH*, No. xix, Autumn 1991, pp. 34–35, and is reproduced by kind permission of Antonina W. Bouis, © 1980.

case the interpreter must refuse to search for a biographical subtext and merely follow the metamorphoses of pure musical forms?

I am an adherent of connecting musical images with events from life. Not every work can be 'decoded' in detail, of course, but I feel that a conductor can better sense the form and significance of a work if he feels, behind the movements of musical thought, emotions and feelings that can be put into words. Sometimes he even finds a programmed logic that is close to a plot. This also helps him to read more quickly the appropriate emotional state for the concert he is about to conduct.

Naturally, the performer can only speak for himself and cannot pretend to have a literal solution of the composer's intention. But without question, the richer the interpreter's creative intuition, the closer his reading will be to the thoughts and feelings of the composer; similarly, the stronger the interpreter's hypnotic suggestion, the closer the associations of the orchestra and audience will be to his vision – and thereby the emotional effect, born of the spiritual collaboration between performer and audience, will be more powerful.

The work of D. D. Shostakovich is inseparable from the events of his life. That is why, until now, it spoke more to the hearts of audiences in his homeland than outside it. But we may now speak of a renaissance of Shostakovich in the West, since the facts of his life have become known here as well and have forced people to look at his music with new eyes.

I have had the opportunity to conduct all fifteen of Shostakovich's symphonies. Some of them can be called programme music. This includes, first of all, the works that incorporate a chorus or solo singers. In these, Shostakovich's music strives to convey the meaning of the poetry, even though it often conceals poetry that is not very good (or poorly translated) and says much more to the listener than the sung text. Two symphonies, the Eleventh and Twelfth, have titles given by the composer: 'The 1905' and 'The 1917'. (The 'Leningrad' subtitle of the Seventh was not the composer's.) Here, the music describes events well known to the listener – yet even these symphonies are associative as well as illustrative; that is, they throw out a bridge between historical events and the present.

The majority of Shostakovich's symphonies do not have titles and at first glance appear to be plotless. Nevertheless, contemporaries associate each of his symphonies with a specific period in the life of the composer. And this allows the listener to transform the development of musical thought into emotions close to the human heart and into direct plot situations.

I had the good fortune to conduct the premiere of the Fourth and Thirteenth Symphonies, *The Execution of Stepan Razin*, and the Second Violin Concerto (with David Oistrakh). I met Shostakovich many times and we spoke of music and various problems. He was seven years my senior – an enormous gap when you are young, and inconsequential when you are over fifty. I worked in Leningrad when Shostakovich lived there, and then in Moscow, where the composer moved after the War. The historical cataclysms that gave life to Shostakovich's music passed before my eyes as well, and they were part of my life, too.

Several of his symphonies elicited such vivid associations with our reality that I developed them to full programme detail. Dmitry Dmitriyevich knew about my 'decodings'. He himself did not like to discuss the subtext of his music and usually said nothing, although he did not contradict me either. Since he was usually pleased with my performances, I believe he had no objection to such an approach to his music.

It was with the greatest agitation that I read Shostakovich's memoirs, prepared by Solomon Volkov. Much of what comes as a surprise to the Western reader was not a surprise for me. I knew many things and guessed many others; but there were new things in it even for me, things that made me look at some of his works differently.

This will probably lead to a re-evaluation of some of my interpretative concepts, since there is a definite connection between a performing interpretation of music and what we know about the composer's inner motives and reasons. A striking confirmation of this position is the music of the great symphonic composer of the twentieth century, Dmitry Dmitriyevich Shostakovich.

THE GULAG AND SHOSTAKOVICH'S MEMORIAL[1]

Andrey Bitov

No matter how independent or even oppositional we think we've been since they stopped murdering us, no matter how crude we think their methods of ideological pressure, propaganda does its job. Its power lies in the very fact that it's beneath any intellectual level. A slogan works by boring you. No one is summoning you to do anything; the whole end and aim is to fatigue you into apathy. You don't respond with action, but your subconscious is at work. And then the task is even easier: to lower the level, not of your consciousness, which naturally is higher, but of your subconscious; i.e., to demoralise you. Your celebrated critical faculties are fertilised by propaganda and bear an ugly, vigorous fruit – *vulgarity*. You have been *brainwashed*.

Was Akhmatova a loose woman? Why didn't Zoshchenko fight? Does Solzhenitsyn have lots of money in the West? Isn't this interesting? And you've already forgotten to tell yourself that it's none of your damn business.

What was the main thing on my mind (if I could have admitted it to myself) when I met Solomon Volkov in New York, in the spring of 1988? It was this: were Shostakovich's memoirs authentic?

Some years ago, when I first saw the newspaper that pilloried, in statements from 'a soldier' and 'a milkmaid', the despicable insinuator and falsifier who had faked the great composer's memoirs, one glance was enough to tell me that the fake was the newspaper, not the memoirs. Besides, the

[1] This review of *Testimony* (translated here by Susan Brownsberger) was written in 1989 in anticipation of the book's first publication in the USSR. Its appearance, however, has been delayed because of economic problems in the former Soviet Union. *Cf.* pp. 216–18. –EDS.

very fact of their publication filled my soul with triumph and a mysterious pride. And yet . . .

It was 1979. The Shostakovich scandal was a preface to Afghanistan. Overnight I found myself with nothing – no home, no family, no job, and not the slightest prospect of any of these, in either the near or the distant future. But I did have time, enough and to spare. As I lay in someone else's apartment, on someone else's cot, with all the household valuables – including the television – locked up in the next room (the style of home-owners abroad), I stared at the ceiling and thought about Shostakovich. I don't remember how long. Perhaps a week, perhaps even longer. I could have thought for a year – this was a tough case, to use the language of the detective. Not one shred of evidence, not one witness. What would you say of a man who couldn't read but who discussed Pushkin on the basis of a radio programme about 'The Fisherman and the Fish'? But in fact, that's just the kind of relationship most people in our country have with serious music. Z flat, as Aleshkovsky puts it.[2] So, possessing no copy of the notorious memoirs, not even a record player or a single recording of any Shostakovich opus – possessing only distant memories of one symphony and one trio – I sank deeper and deeper in thought. The fruit of this meditation was an essay provisionally titled 'Bravery in the Artist'. The essay was unpublishable and got lost in subsequent moves, but even so, it proved useful. I retold it, in words that were more my own than my prose had been, to Solomon Volkov, thereby both veiling my ignorance and keeping the conversation going. Strangely enough, he nodded and agreed. And it was he who insisted that I tell about the book now, before its first publication in the USSR.

Here is the train of thought I had at that time – the point being that the general reader, when he at last receives the Shostakovich-Volkov book, is in more or less the same position now as I was then.

[2] Yuz Yefimovich Aleshkovsky (b. 1929), a writer well-known in 1960s *samizdat* for his poem 'Tovarishch Stalin, Vy Bolshoi Uchenyi' ('Comrade Stalin, You Are a Great Scientist') and for the short stories *Nikolay Nikolayevich* and *Maskirova*. After his emigration to the USA, he became famous for *The Hand* and *Kangaroo*. –EDS

When Russians think about fame, it most often has two variants, undeserved and posthumous – both of them unjust. There is also 'deserved' fame, but that's already boring, an official title. Actually, a man as great as Shostakovich deals with all three forms while still alive. But apart from regalia, how do we measure fame? By the prominence of the name. Either way, we leave aside the very thing for which the artist is famous – his work – which is merely a necessary condition, of little import.

'Shostakovich' became a word to everyone, rather than a name, a very long time ago – before the war, in the era of the article 'Muddle Instead of Music' (which in 1936 played the same role as would future decrees). It later acquired national and worldwide significance, in the era of the blockade (the Seventh Symphony), but was raised to unattainable heights by Zhdanov in 1948.

Meanwhile, the word 'Shostakovich' has been secured by his music. We may not know or understand Shostakovich, but we can hardly fail to recognise that he expressed the tragedy of our people and country with the greatest directness and depth, and at the time when it was happening, not later. What saved him was partly that music is a different language, it's not words. Mandelstam and Klyuyev forfeited their lives in the same effort.[3] And yet, no matter how well shielded from political accusation music is by its nature, we can hardly overestimate Shostakovich's bravery. In his fullness of expression – not to detract from anyone – he was alone. Bravery in the artist does not mean fearlessness in the man. After all, the artist will have a richer imagination than the hangman; he himself knows better how he has transgressed, and how far. Therefore, when he imagines a punishment appropriate to the extent of his crime, it will paradoxically be appropriate to the imagined extent of his recognition as an artist. He endows even evil with his own talent. Meanwhile life is life, and therein lies our salvation: we are both punished wrongly and recognised wrongly. How surprised Zoshchenko was when he got in trouble for his innocent 'Little Monkey' – he forgot that he was

[3] Nikolay Alekseyevich Klyuyev (1887–1927), a peasant poet who like so many other writers – Babel', Kharms, Mandelstam, Pil'nyak – was a victim of Stalin's purges. –EDS.

Zoshchenko, worthy of the supreme penalty merely because he was a great writer. Recognition finds a mocking echo in the sentence. An echo is a phenomenon reflected and distorted. In this sense, too, words are a mirage. But an execution is not. Stalin is a Lenin 'given to us in sensation'.

Shostakovich was not a lost sheep. He knew. He knew what he was doing and what to expect for it. Shostakovich survived nothing less than execution. For him, the execution lasted at least two decades. His rival and antagonist Prokofiev did not survive the news of a possible stay of execution – he died on 5 March 1953, the same day as Stalin. Shostakovich survived. Or did he?

The Shostakovich of the thaw and stagnation eras no longer struck the average liberal as the same Shostakovich who had been the first to write about victims of repression and had endured the Zhdanov period. I too was puzzled. How could he? Endure all, do all, and surrender after it had all been overcome? Faint just when the threat had passed? Join up, become a deputy at all congresses, allow himself to be decorated like a Christmas tree with Brezhnev-era awards, make official speeches, even sign things of a dubious nature . . . How could he?

But this is how, I thought as I studied my shelterless ceiling: it's perfectly natural for a man to discover the true scope of a danger when it has passed, not while he's overcoming it. The rubble is falling on you, miraculously you race out from under it, and it crumbles to dust behind you. . . . When you look back to see what you escaped, you may die of a heart attack. Anyone who has triumphed over torture suffers terrible sequelae that we cannot appreciate. This is death by diagnosis, not by disease. Death by that same rich imagination.

Nevertheless, I was very unwilling to surrender Shostakovich to them. My conscious mind made some subtle distinction with respect to him, excusing him; besides, one glance at his tragic countenance was enough to still my hand (and tongue). . . . And again, I was taking for granted our right to judge a man who had done this at the time when no one and nothing . . . Why should he go rushing after everyone else through the gap that he himself had breached?

The Politburo signed the obituary. For the first time – a decision also made at the level of the Politburo – the formula 'great' was applied: 'a great composer of modern times has passed away'. So that after this precedent they could apply the formula to Vuchetich and Sholokhov as well.[4] Before, only 'eminent' men had died. The Stalin tradition: he alone was great. But now 'great' men, too, had begun to die. With this final official title, the Shostakovich case was closed.

That is why the scandal of Shostakovich's memoirs, edited and published by Solomon Volkov in America, was so painful for the authorities. Not without reason does our country love only the dead – a dead man can no longer make a statement. As it turned out, we must never relax our vigilance. Shostakovich's voice from beyond the grave laid to rest all doubt as to his personality and fate. Obviously this was the Shostakovich of the Fifth, Sixth, Seventh and Eighth Symphonies, and not merely a coat-hanger for regalia. He made his statement. But we didn't know, until now, what he had said.

Wise Solomon didn't publish it in Russian. The book appeared in all languages except its own – yet another excuse and argument for accusing Volkov of falsification. Thus we couldn't read Shostakovich in a Russian edition printed abroad, as we were occasionally fortunate enough to read Nabokov, Solzhenitsyn and Brodsky in the era of stagnation.

So the original of the book is being published first, not in the West, but in its native land. One more posthumous mark of fate.

Shostakovich's life – not the life in his works, but his real, living life – isn't over yet. When everyone reads this book . . . Oh, his life will go on for quite some time!

It's a fairy-tale triumph. A man feared to reveal his secret to the world (in our day, truth has become a secret), but the secret was too big for him to keep. He dug a hole, then, in a secluded place, and whispered into it. He seemed to feel a bit better. But a slender reed grew up from the hole, a little

[4] Yevgeny Viktorovich Vuchetich (1908–74), a leading sculptor of the Stalin era, responsible for many of the largest Soviet memorials, including the Soviet Army memorial in Berlin, War Memorial in Volgograd, and Feliks Dzerzhinsky statue in front of the Lubyanka in Moscow. For Sholokhov, *cf.* p. 382, note 6. –EDS.

shepherd cut it and made a fife, and that which had been secret was made plain.

In return for that little fairy tale, Solomon Volkov gave me the book. I read it without putting it down and was convinced of the vulgarity of my subconscious – the book was authentic from the first letter to the last, even when read not in the original but in translation. I'm enough of a professional, certainly, to make that inference. Volkov's individuality finds expression in his footnotes, at least; the footnotes sometimes express him even more than he might wish. But the book – from beginning to end – is in Shostakovich's words, his alone. Volkov wouldn't have said it that way. But although the voice in this book belongs invariably to Shostakovich, Volkov's authorial role is highly unusual, and this leads to a thought. Volkov played the part of the hole, the reed, the fife and the shepherd, all at once. Which was most important? The hole, I think. After all, if Shostakovich hadn't meant to speak, he wouldn't have said it to anyone – but he said it to Solomon Volkov. And for some reason Balanchine, too, though he had refused everyone, revealed everything to Volkov before he died . . . .[5] What is his talent for listening?

'I was very unlucky in life' – you can't say this to just anyone.

This book is gruesome, beautiful, fascinating, and unbearable.

It is gentle to people, harsh to non-people, and merciless to self.

This book has no fear of our opinion.

It is Shostakovich's last, and perhaps also his first, freedom as a man. A proud man, shattered but not crushed.

This is how he answered my speculations:

> And it's important to remember that there's work and there's work, and not every job gives a man the right to take on a prosecutor's role . . . things are not healthy in our criteria for nobility and decency. Things are not right in that area. To put it bluntly, it's an insane asylum.
>
> I refuse to speak seriously with lunatics, I refuse to talk to them about myself and others, I refuse to discuss questions about my proper or improper behaviour.
>
> I write music, it's performed. It can be heard, and whoever

[5] *Cf.* Solomon Volkov, *Balanchine's Tchaikovsky*. –EDS.

> wants to hear it will. After all, my music says it all. It doesn't need historical and hysterical commentaries. In the long run, any words about music are less important than the music. Anyone who thinks otherwise is not worth talking to.[6]

> I have the same fears when I look at the famous humanists of our times. They have rotten teeth and I don't need their friendship . . .
>
> I am backed up by the bitter experience of my grey and miserable life . . .
>
> Don't believe humanists, citizens, don't believe prophets, don't believe luminaries – they'll fool you for a penny.[7]

> I don't need brave words on music and I don't think anyone does. We need brave music. I don't mean brave in the sense that there will be charts instead of notes, I mean brave because it is truthful . . .
>
> . . . Why do I have to answer? Who are they? Why do I have to risk my life? And risk it to satisfy the shallow curiosity of a man who doesn't give a damn about me![8]

Indeed, how is a man to explain himself, when all of his compositions are forbidden, and every year, instead of the supreme penalty, he gets the Stalin Prize for a film score?

Like a horse too busy grazing to twitch off the flies . . . This is the book of a man who laboured unstintingly to express his era, who spoke with all the might of a symphony orchestra about things which people dared not speak in a whisper, in private, in a friend's ear . . . .

Shostakovich's *Gulag* was performed in 1937.

> The majority of my symphonies are tombstones. Too many of our people died and were buried in places unknown to anyone, not even their relatives . . . Where do you put the tombstones for Meyerhold or Tukhachevsky? Only music can do that for them. I'm willing to write a composition for each of the victims, but that's impossible, and that's why I dedicate my music to them all.
>
> I think constantly of those people, and in almost every major work I try to remind others of them.[9]

[6] As transl. by Antonina W. Bouis in *Testimony*, pp. 150/195–96. –SB.

[7] As transl. by Bouis in *ibid.*, pp. 154/201, 157/204 and 157/205, respectively. –SB.

[8] As transl. by Bouis in *ibid.*, pp. 150–51/196–97. –SB.

[9] As transl. by Bouis in *ibid.*, p. 118/156. –SB.

This is the memorial! Not the safe monumental postscript to crime that will someday be erected by a vain sculptor for millions of rubles from an impoverished nation.

> Now everyone says, 'We didn't know, we didn't understand. We believed Stalin. We were tricked, ah, how cruelly we were tricked.
>
> I feel anger at such people. Who was it who didn't understand, who was tricked? An illiterate old milkmaid? The deaf-mute who shined shoes on Ligovsky Prospect? No, they seemed to be educated people – writers, composers, actors. The people who applauded the Fifth Symphony [1937. –AB]. I'll never believe that a man who understood nothing could feel the Fifth Symphony. Of course they understood.
>
> And this makes it even harder for me to compose . . . But here everything is back to front, because the larger the audience, the more informers there are.[10]
>
> Awaiting execution is a theme that has tormented me all my life. Many pages of my music are devoted to it. Sometimes I wanted to explain that fact to the performers . . .[11]

The man's human fear engendered greater and greater bravery in the artist. His passion to be heard always exceeded his fear of exposure. I was always somewhat puzzled by Shostakovich's later predilection for vocal cycles. To me, the words interfered with his music. In the book I find this answer to my puzzlement:

> Yet in recent years I've become convinced that the word is more effective than music. Unfortunately, it's so. When I combine music with words, it becomes harder to misinterpret my intent.
>
> I discovered to my astonishment that the man who considers himself its greatest interpreter does not understand my music.[12]

The most important musician, and specifically a great one, never loses the traits of the restaurant dance band, in his seeming cynicism and openhearted, circus-style naïveté. In this sense even Mozart is a dance musician, and so was Shostakovich in Meyerhold's home. Shostakovich's direct speech is as frank as that between members of an orchestra.

[10] As transl. by Bouis in *ibid.*, p. 102/134. –SB.

[11] As transl. by Bouis in *ibid.*, p. 140/183. –SB.

[12] As transl. by Bouis in *ibid.*, p. 140/183. –SB.

That is why I found it perhaps most interesting of all, though I know nothing about orchestration, to read about how different people orchestrated. In a professional, everything characterises not the subject, but the man.

To appreciate the fairness of Shostakovich's confession you must love three men: Musorgsky, Chekhov and Zoshchenko. So that you will not suspect him of other motives – jealousy, or scores to settle. Only a genius can be so candid in his apprenticeship. He copied Musorgsky, seeing in this no indignity for professionalism (why, an artist copies great painters, and no one cares – again, the naïveté of the dance musician, which also shows in his attitude to words). As a man he imitated Chekhov – and perhaps it is Shostakovich who preserved, throughout our age, Chekhov's gruelling standard of behaviour. He took the tone of his life from Zoshchenko – you will find the influence of his style on many pages. Shostakovich understood these three idols of his as well as he did himself. He had scarcely any other friends.

> So let's not talk about correcting mistakes, because it will only make it worse. And more important, I like the word 'rehabilitation'. And I'm even more impressed when I hear about 'posthumous rehabilitation'. But that's nothing new either. A general complained to Nicholas I that some hussar had abducted his daughter. They even got married, but the general was against the marriage. After some thought, the emperor proclaimed: 'I decree the marriage annulled, and she is to be considered a virgin'.
>
> Somehow I still don't feel like a virgin.[13]

A part of history . . . it has a proud sound. But what does it mean to be a part of history? To be a bucket of blood, a bucket of vodka, a bucket of shame. Or nothing.

> The fear hadn't disappeared completely, of course, it never does. The fear was in their blood forever . . .[14]

The man who more than anyone else deserved trial and the death sentence, who expected them at any hour, was so accustomed to the prospect of being arrested and giving testimony that at the end of his life he gave it voluntarily.

The book is called *Testimony*.

[13] As transl. by Bouis in *ibid.*, p. 116/153. –SB.

[14] As transl. by Bouis in *ibid.*, p. 167/217. –SB.

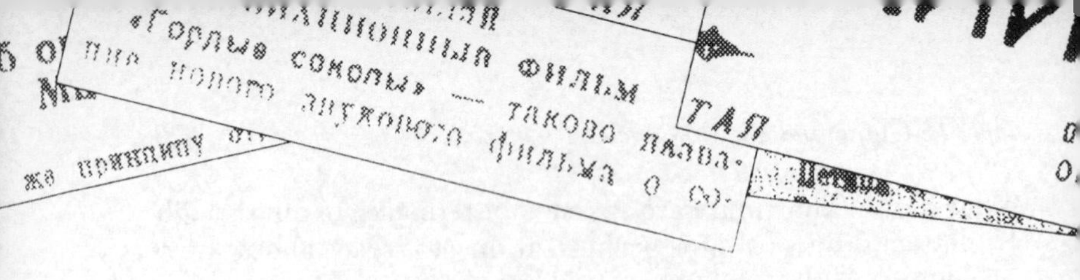

Variation III

HIS MISTY YOUTH
The Glivenko Letters and Life in the '20s[1]

Ian MacDonald

In *Testimony*, Shostakovich says next to nothing about what he calls his 'misty youth', save to imply that he had once believed in 'leaders' and 'luminaries' but been so decisively disillusioned by them that he later regarded any interest in power whatever as a sort of perversion. As to how deeply his former faith was rooted, in whom it was placed, and how long it endured, he tells us nothing – yet answers to these questions are crucial to understanding his work.

Addressing the last of these questions, I suggested in *The New Shostakovich* that the composer's disillusionment with his country's political system (and thus with its leaders and ideologues) may be dated from the opera *Lady Macbeth of Mtsensk*, which he began in October 1930 and completed in August 1932:

> His return to tragedy in this opera, six years after his First Symphony, was clearly the most important creative decision he ever took in the absence of outside pressure – a decision

[1] An earlier version of this piece appeared in *Melos*, 1/4–5, Summer 1993, pp. 14–21. The author – who wishes to thank Holbrook Robinson, Dmitri Babich and Dr John Spiegel for their assistance in expanding some points outlined in that earlier version – has had access to all of the letters from Shostakovich to Glivenko that came up for auction in January 1990, and not only those few passages quoted in the Sotheby catalogue. The Glivenko letters are now in the possession of Maxim Shostakovich.

> which, in context, can only have been made in conscious disregard of political orthodoxy. If he had ever concluded a compact with Communism, Shostakovich broke it in 1931. How long it took for this impulse towards freedom to mature into consistent dissidence is, again, a question answerable only in terms of probability. There seems, however, to be little room for it to have been later than 1935 and the Fourth Symphony [. . .].[2]

Whether Shostakovich's maturation into 'consistent dissidence'[3] can be dated to the Fourth Symphony, or the Fifth, or even to some later work, is nowadays a fine point of dispute. All that really matters is that no one now publicly subscribes to the official billing of the Fifth Symphony as a sacrificial offering to the Soviet state, a shift in opinion which effectively acknowledges that Shostakovich's apostasy was in full swing by, at the latest, early 1937. As to the earliest point at which this change in the composer's outlook could be said to be under way, it can be argued that such a renunciation is implicit in the Cello Sonata of mid-1934, the year in which Stalin was formally deified at the Congress of Victors and the dogma of Socialist Realism became holy writ at the First Congress of the Writers' Union. Indeed, stepping back a further year, it is possible to discern a deep cynicism typical of its time in the Twenty-four Preludes and First Piano Concerto of late 1932-early 1933. Whether this cynicism is sufficiently considered and concerted to be described as dissidence is doubtful. What it can reasonably be called is 'disillusioned' – and, since the origin of Shostakovich's disillusionment is what I am trying to pinpoint, this seems to be a plausible place at which to pick up the trail.

Unfortunately, disagreement on how far the trail leads back from here arises almost immediately in that Shostakovich's main preceding work, *Lady Macbeth of Mtsensk*, has been the subject of some radically different interpretations. Richard Taruskin, for example, argues that the work is less a tale of individual passion in a proto-collectivist society than

[2] *The New Shostakovich*, p. 246.

[3] Strictly speaking, the term 'dissidence' is an anachronism, since it was not coined until the '60s. The state of mind involved is, however, timelessly applicable to anyone harbouring resistance to a totalitarian or authoritarian regime, and it is in that sense that the word is used here.

an apologia for Stalin's genocidal campaign of 1930 against the *kulaks*.[4] In Taruskin's view, *Lady Macbeth* is 'a profoundly inhumane work of art' in which its composer ('Soviet Russia's most loyal musical son') by various means 'dehumanizes' his heroine's persecutors and victims so as to 'perpetrate [the] colossal moral inversion' of legitimising her murders. Shostakovich's opera, claims Taruskin, is a politically motivated travesty which presents all of its cast except Katerina as 'class enemies' to be despised and destroyed: 'Its chilling treatment of the victims amounts to a justification of genocide'.[5] Setting aside the more obvious objections to this theory,[6] there remains a point of interest in Taruskin's con-

[4] *Kulaks* (literally 'fists') were so-called 'rich peasants', meaning those who farmed holdings outside the commune.

[5] Taruskin, 'Dictator'.

[6] Taruskin's conception fails, crucially, to account for the life-long meaning the opera had for its composer. Like Solomon Volkov and Galina Vishnevskaya, I see *Lady Macbeth* as the artistic foundation of Shostakovich's moral individualism – a view which not only does the work no interpretative violence but also explains why he quotes from it at a key moment in his Eighth Quartet. Taruskin's contorted reading not only makes nonsense of the wider context of Shostakovich's life in the early '30s but raises the seemingly unanswerable question of why the composer should quote an alleged apologia for genocide in a quartet dedicated to 'the victims of fascism'. That an artist with so many friends in the 'individualist' literary milieu should, during the rabidly collectivistic Cultural Revolution of 1929–32, have chosen to turn Leskov's apolitical melodrama into a hymn to the expropriation of six million peasants is absurdly unlikely. Even supposing it were true, it would raise further insoluble problems. Why, for example, should Shostakovich have concealed (as he did) the composition of this supposed apologia from the very powers it was designed to please? And why make its alleged endorsement of collectivisation so hard to spot that Stalin banned it? (Had Shostakovich really intended his satirical approach to the opera's subsidiary characters to support Stalin's anti-kulak campaign, he would have included at least one positive peasant to set these villains off. As for 'dehumanization', one has only to read Maxim Gorky's autobiography (*The Autobiography of Maxim Gorky*, transl. Isidor Schneider, Citadel Press, Secaucus, New Jersey, 1949) to see how far Russia's peasants were capable of dehumanising themselves without outside help.)

In any case, Taruskin's indignation over *Lady Macbeth* (a vexed issue, too, for David Fanning, in his notes for Myung-Whun Chung's recording of the opera on Deutsche Grammophon 437 511-2) is surely exaggerated. As a murderess, Katerina naturally arouses a complex response – yet such ambiguous characters are a fixture of nineteenth-century Russian lit-

tention that Shostakovich was influenced in composing the opera by Nikolai Dobrolyubov's famous essay on *The Storm* – a play written in 1856 by Aleksandr Ostrovsky[7]

---

erature (Dostoyevsky, *passim*), as well as of post-war existentialist writing and much modern cinema. As Nicholas Till (*Mozart and the Enlightenment: Truth, Virtue and Beauty in Mozart's Operas*, Faber & Faber, London, 1992, p. 28) observes, even the morally didactic eighteenth century understood the role of protagonists like Katerina: 'For the rebels without cause of *Sturm und Drang* the problem was how the individual could maintain his personal integrity in a society that exerted all its powers to dispossess him of it. In many *Sturm und Drang* works an apparently criminal deed is seen as evidence of the possession of sincere emotion – the sign of a potentially great soul'. Shostakovich's avowed wish to present Katerina as 'a positive personality' is partly accountable in terms of this tradition of alienated anti-heroes. Yet it is also clear that he identified with her passionately and did all he could to justify her, including caricaturing almost every other character in the opera. Why? The answer lies in the context of the opera's creation (1930–32). Though Fanning (in his notes to the Deutsche Grammophon recording) calls this period 'one of the happiest of [Shostakovich's] life', he is contradicted by both *Testimony* and Nataliya Lukyanova (*Shostakovich: His Life and Times*, transl. Yuri Shirokov, Paganiniana Publications, Neptune City, New Jersey, 1984). Moreover, these sources are congruent with our knowledge of the Russian Cultural Revolution (1929–32), a chaotic interlude in which non-Party artists were, as part of a general drive against the bourgeois intelligentsia, violently persecuted. Surrounded as Katerina is by vicious, soul-destroying mediocrities similar to those who beset him and many of his colleagues during the opera's genesis, Shostakovich's identification with his beleaguered heroine is not hard to understand. Clearly he needed to let off some avenging steam; hence anyone who is no friend of hers – meaning everyone else in the opera – gets short shrift. All of this, though, is of secondary importance to the composer's overriding wish to depict passionate sexual love in a collectivistic society which regarded such concentration on the individual and such emphasis on personal feeling as anti-social. The sheer intensity of Katerina's ardour, which must have struck a chord for the young Shostakovich during his fraught courtship of Nina Varzar, was unavoidably subversive – and it was precisely this troublesome 'individualism' which Stalin wanted to extinguish in 1936. (The much-parroted idea that the dictator was puritanically shocked by the opera's sex scene is rather difficult to reconcile with a man who, during 1927, visited the Vakhtangov Theatre no less than eight times to inspect the half-naked prostitutes on display in Bulgakov's 'pornographic' bordello drama *Zoya's Apartment*.)

[7] Not to be confused with Nikolai Ostrovsky, author of *How The Steel Was Tempered* (1934), a 'Five Year Plan' novel described by Shostakovich in *Testimony* as 'horrible'. (Aleksandr Ostrovsky's play formed the basis of the libretto for Janáček's opera *Kát'a Kabanová* (1919–21)).

which in several important respects anticipates Leskov's novella of 1865. During his short life, Dobrolyubov, a colleague of Nikolai Chernyshevsky, won notoriety with the utilitarian reductionism of his literary criticism which, in effect, attacked all literature failing to polemicise on behalf of Russia's serfs. The most celebrated targets of his critical assaults were Tolstoy and Turgenev, the latter getting his own back by turning Dobrolyubov into Bazarov, the unsavory Nihilist hero of his anti-radical novel *Fathers and Sons* (1862). Had Shostakovich found anything to his taste in Dobrolyubov, he would probably have shared the critic's low opinions of Tolstoy and Turgenev. Yet while he is damning towards Turgenev in *Testimony*, his views on Tolstoy expressed in the same book are neutrally respectful. All the more significant, then, that his opinion of Tolstoy is very different in several of the 150 letters written, mostly between 1923 and 1927, to his girlfriend Tanya Glivenko. Addressing Tanya on 29 November 1923, Shostakovich is scathing about Tolstoy, whose 'whole philosophy' offended him. Given this attitude, it is a safe bet that Turgenev would similarly have annoyed him at that age (seventeen) – although, like Gogol, Turgenev goes unmentioned in this source. Here then is exactly the sort of young firebrand who might have taken to the sweepingly dismissive tracts of Nikolai Dobrolyubov (and conceivably to the writings of his friend Chernyshevsky, who was, after all, an historical friend of the family[8]). Were it to be agreed that the Glivenko letters provide a reliable picture of Shostakovich as a young man, Richard Taruskin would be entitled to claim that they provisionally support his contentions about the politico-literary influences on *Lady Macbeth*. In reality, however, any such impression is at best undependable, and at worst thoroughly misleading.[9]

[8] *Cf.* Sofia Khentova, 'Shostakovich and Poetry', *DSCH*, No. xx, Spring 1992, pp. 64–73. As intellectual leader of mid-nineteenth-century Russian radicalism, Chernyshevsky (1828–89) was a major influence on Lenin.

[9] Far from ideologically neutral – let alone supinely conformist in the sense claimed by Taruskin – Shostakovich's choice of Leskov's novella carried high political risk. As an active enemy of nineteenth-century radicalism ('nihilism'), Leskov was regarded with hostility by the Communist regime, which officially classified him as 'a second-rate writer' and banned his books from Soviet schools. Indeed, as a fierce critic of the novel which

The first thing that has to be grasped about the Glivenko letters is that they are the work of a teenager. It goes without saying that Shostakovich was about as exceptional a teenager as it is possible to be; quite apart from his musical genius, the sheer range of his contemporary interests testifies to that. Yet there is also abundant evidence that his teenage self was capable of being silly, arrogant, contemptuous and inconsiderate to the point of cruelty. A case in point is the young composer's attitude to his family, known from other sources to have been fraught, and confirmed as such in the Glivenko letters. Indeed, Shostakovich himself bears extensive witness to his unpleasant characteristics as a young man in the

---

Lenin described as his political primer – Chernyshevsky's *What Is To Be Done?* (1864) – Leskov was as much anathema to Lenin's heirs as he had been to the radicals of the 1860s. ('To stage an opera on the writings of an author who dared to attack Lenin's "life handbook" was a crime in itself by Stalinist standards.' – Russian author and journalist Dmitri Babich, in a letter to me dated 16 February 1996.) As an independent liberal, Leskov wrote critically of the Tsarist government but, like Turgenev, Dostoyevsky and Chekhov, saved his most pungent vitriol for the very 'nihilists' upon whose inflammatory writings Lenin's Bolsheviks based the core of their philosophy (*cf.* Tibor Szamuely, *The Russian Tradition*, Secker and Warburg, London, 1974, pp. 282–434.) Dobrolyubov (1836–61) died too young to feel the lash of Leskov's scorn, but Chernyshevsky came under attack from him in 1861 over the crude illiberality of his support for student rioters in St. Petersburg, for which Leskov charged him with 'the violence of the Montagnards, the brazen ignorance of the Old Believers'. For the *faux pas* of attacking the fashionable Chernyshevsky, Leskov was publicly shunned in progressive circles and threatened with assassination by student radicals. Owing to his arrest and exile to Siberia in 1863, Chernyshevsky was unable to mount any criticism of *Lady Macbeth of Mtsensk District* (1865), although his colleague Dmitri Pisarev, in an article later reprinted as 'Cardboard Heroes', castigated Leskov as 'a cowardly and stupid hater of the future'. (As recently as the reign of Mikhail Gorbachev, Soviet schools and universities deified Dobrolyubov, Chernyshevsky and Pisarev, with the inevitable adverse consequences for Leskov's reputation.) Hailed by Tolstoy in 1890 as a pioneer moralist of Russia's early years of ideological intolerance, Leskov was an ambiguous figure caught between moribund autocracy on the one hand and conscienceless radicalism on the other. As such, he was arguably exactly congruent with Shostakovich's own independent outlook during the composition of *Lady Macbeth*. For these reasons, Leskov (however discreetly modified) is almost the last literary figure upon whose work Shostakovich would plausibly have based anything intended to appeal to Stalin in the way Richard Taruskin suggests.

opening chapter of *Testimony*, to the extent of resuscitating something of that 'harsh and intolerant youth' in the tone and content of his reminiscences about the period fifty years later. In *The New Shostakovich*, I speculated that, at the height of the New Economic Policy (NEP) during the middle '20s, the young composer had succumbed to the then-fashionable identification of rudeness with honesty, a supposition likewise borne out in the Glivenko letters by his confessed sympathy for 'boorishness'.[10] This trait, common among Soviet youth at that time (and encouraged by the agitprop publications of the Komsomol), took the form of a dogmatic disregard for bourgeois manners expressed in a deliberately rough, confrontational style supposedly aped from the Russian proletariat. Just such calculated rudeness is observable in the section of *Testimony* describing the young Shostakovich's dealings with the poet Fyodor Sologub, a passage which simultaneously displays the effects of another unsavory trend among youngsters during the first post-Revolutionary decade: brusque intolerance towards those 'unenlightened' by scientific materialism (meaning the older generation as a whole, and in particular anyone harbouring religious or similarly 'pretentious' spiritual beliefs). In manifesting such traits, Shostakovich's attacks on Tolstoy in the Glivenko letters may betray not so much a personal view as the external influence of an often-romanticised but, in truth, rather shallow and callous epoch in Russian history. It was, for example, during this period that youth became routinely exalted over age, the teenage composer's semi-serious wish to administer 'a thrashing' to the 60-year-old author of *The Kreutzer Sonata*[11] being typical of the world-turned-upside-down reversals then popular among the Soviet young. (The same applies to his paradoxical dismissal of this story – in which Tolstoy urges sexual abstinence – as 'filth'.[12]) Inevitably, attitudes like these proved to be as temporary in Shostakovich's personal development as the relative freedom of NEP in the prisonhouse history of the Soviet Union. Notwithstanding his dismissal of *The Kreutzer Sonata*,

[10] Letter to Tanya Glivenko dated 1 May 1925.

[11] Letter to Tanya Glivenko dated 6 February 1924.

[12] Letter to Tanya Glivenko dated 29 November 1923.

Shostakovich was still interested enough in Tolstoy to progress straight to *Anna Karenina* ('not bad') and to approve the author's criticisms of Wagner.[13] Indeed, by his early thirties he had sufficiently revised his view of Tolstoy to consider an opera on *Resurrection*, a novel dating from the same moralising period in the writer's work as *The Kreutzer Sonata* and *What Is Art*? As for Dobrolyubov's arch-enemy Turgenev, we find the composer confessing 'delight' in reading him only three years after the last of his letters to Tanya Glivenko.[14]

The context of turmoil and change wherein Shostakovich's teenage mind was formed suggests that many of the 'radical' opinions expressed in the Glivenko letters may be little more than conscious posturing – the sort of showing-off most young men of the time were wont to employ with a view to impressing potential female conquests. Shostakovich's loves and hates at that age were probably as volatile as those of any other teenager – that is, prone to diametrical alteration overnight and capable of co-existence in mutual contradiction at high intensity. In view of the likelihood of their giving way under the slightest testing, it would be imprudent to put too much weight on any of the cultural attitudes the young composer strikes in his epistolatory campaign to seduce Tanya Glivenko. Even where these are not demonstrably either the passing thoughts of a developing mind or a parroting of the fads of a highly circumscribed historical interlude, the very discontinuity of a one-sided correspondence is bound to misrepresent the writer's general opinion on any given subject.[15]

A similar caution should be applied in evaluating the more

[13] Letter to Tanya Glivenko dated 6 February 1924.

[14] Letter to Elena Konstantinovskaya dated 17 July 1934.

[15] His rapid switch of opinion over the merits of Horowitz's pianism is one example of this ('The best pianist I've ever heard.' – 2 November 1923; 'His influence is positively harmful.' – 24 October 1924). Another is his attitude to Skryabin. In later life – despite his 'official' pronouncements – he, like Prokofiev, disdained Skryabin as an exotic mystifier (Boris Schwarz, *Music and Musical Life in Russia, 1917–1970*, Barrie & Jenkins, London, 1970, p. 388). His approval during the '20s of Skryabin's late piano compositions – he calls their author a genius (22 June 1926) – is consistent both with the prevailing non-Party musical opinion under NEP

exclusively political attitudes expressed in the same source. For example, while it may be true that certain of the teenage Shostakovich's tastes in reading-matter are ostensibly compatible with an interest in proto-revolutionary literary criticism (and thus with Richard Taruskin's thesis about Dobrolyubov's alleged influence on *Lady Macbeth*), what is equally plain from the Glivenko letters – and completely at odds with Taruskin's thesis – is that the literary figures the composer then admired most of all were Chekhov and Dostoyevsky.[16] Moreover, these allegiances seem to have remained consistent throughout his life, providing a rare seam of intellectual continuity from his boyhood to his old age – a fact of no little significance in view of the 'ideological' outlooks these writers held. Humble in social origin compared to the blue-blooded Tolstoy and gentrified Turgenev, Chekhov nevertheless shared their low opinion of the so-called 'Generation of the Sons' – the 'Nihilists' of whom Dobrolyubov and Chernyshevsky were leading examples. As

---

and with his own temporary idiom in the First Piano Sonata. To judge from a letter to Tanya Glivenko dated 14 October 1924, Shostakovich drew the line at Skryabin's orchestral works, such as the *Poem of Ecstasy* (to which there appears to be a passing parodistic allusion in the Second Symphony).

[16] Shostakovich's early preferences for, among modern writers, Mayakovsky and Ehrenburg clearly represent a passing phase in the development of his literary taste. We know from *Testimony* and other sources that his approval of Mayakovsky failed to survive their collaboration on *The Bedbug*, while, with competition from the likes of Babel and Zoshchenko, Ilya Ehrenburg is unlikely to have lasted long as his favorite contemporary prose-writer. Averse to the Bolsheviks and refusing to take sides in the Civil War, Ehrenburg left Russia in 1919 with a reputation as a 'sceptic' and 'nihilist'. (A friend of Zamyatin, he thought *We* 'magnificent'.) Like Prokofiev, he lived in Europe until returning to the USSR – by cautious stages – in the late '30s. In a letter to Tanya Glivenko dated 12 November 1925, Shostakovich rates Ehrenburg his favorite modern writer, singling out his novel *The Amazing Adventures of Julio Jurenito*, which among other things sent up Soviet institutions. He must also have known *The Grabber*, a scattergun satire on NEP which, despite being pruned of its anti-Soviet jokes before publication in Russia in 1926, was – along with Zamyatin's *We* and Pilnyak's *Mahogany* – pilloried as 'reactionary' by the Russian Assocation of Proletarian Writers (RAPP) in 1929. (RAPP was founded by Leopold Averbakh and Aleksandr Fadeyev in 1925 as the literary equivalent of RAPM – *cf.* note 27 on p. 543.)

for Dostoyevsky, Shostakovich's letters to Tanya Glivenko show that the young composer admired *The Devils* – the definitive attack on nineteenth-century radicalism – from as early as his middle teens (making it the most enduring of his recorded literary enthusiasms).[17] The fact that the teenage Shostakovich was impressed above all by Chekhov and Dostoyevsky renders the possibility that he could ever have endorsed a writer like Dobrolyubov vanishingly slight.[18] Indeed, unless he misunderstood *The Devils* completely, his early approval of it – and hence of an author later denounced as a 'posthumous traitor to the Revolution' – seriously undermines the handful of politically radical opinions on show elsewhere in the Glivenko letters.[19] More caution is necessary here, though – for if Shostakovich's teenage cultural opinions were at times contradictory, the same is almost certain to have been true of his political views (to the extent that the latter can be disentangled from the former).

A superficial reading of the teenage composer's declarations to Tanya Glivenko might lead to the conclusion that, at least until the age of twenty, he revered Lenin, supported Communism, and was enough of a hard-liner to have rejected NEP as a sell-out. Taking any of this at face value would, however, amount to a dangerous oversimplification in that as many inconsistencies lurk in these political statements as in the cultural opinions the Glivenko letters contain. A fair

[17] Letter to Tanya Glivenko dated 24 January 1924.

[18] Shostakovich's essay on *Lady Macbeth* in the programme for the production in the Maly Theatre in Leningrad, premiered on 22 January 1934, quotes the title of Dobrolyubov's essay 'A Ray of Light in the Kingdom of Darkness'. This, and the fact that an element in the libretto of the opera may have been adapted from Ostrovsky, leads Richard Taruskin to deduce a clear influence. Dobrolyubov's title was, however, sufficiently famous in Russia as to be virtually proverbial, and the fact that Shostakovich refers to it (if it *was* Shostakovich who wrote the essay) means next to nothing, since it was perfectly possible to use the phrase without having read Dobrolyubov's original polemic, let alone agree with it.

[19] Described by Lenin as 'loathsome', *The Devils* was banned throughout Stalin's reign and for some years after. To be politically orthodox in the Soviet Union and approve of *The Devils* was logically impossible. (Dostoyevsky's book was a major influence on Zamyatin's anti-utopia *We*.)

example of this is the mismatch between the young Shostakovich's low regard for NEP and his enthusiasm for the enormously increased sexual freedom associated with it (unmistakably a new development for those experiencing it at the time).[20] It is not that a 'revolutionary' outlook was in itself incompatible with approval of the new sexuality; rather, that it would have been clear to most contemporary observers that the New Economic Policy and the new sexual policy (not to mention the equally new and unprecedented slackening of overt censorship) were all manifestations of a single shift in the government line away from absolute dictatorship towards limited freedom. Because of this, those who took a puritanical view of 'Nepovshchina' (the recrudescence of capitalism in the form of private enterprise and urban crime) were usually consistent in holding comparably puritanical opinions on sexuality and the arts. Shostakovich's adoption of liberal views on the one hand and an authoritarian stance on the other is interpretable in only two ways: either he hadn't thought out his position (betokening a less-than-serious political commitment) or he genuinely drew a distinction between economic freedom and freedom in culture and morality (indicating that his politics, whether or not similar to those of mainstream Communism, were nonetheless individualistic enough to be by definition unorthodox). Leaving aside for a moment the complicating factor of external influences, deciding between these two positions depends on the degree to which one believes the teenage composer's unusually deep feelings on some subjects outweighed his more trivial and irresponsible sentiments about others. What is crucial to observe, however, is that in neither case can we

[20] This approval was by no means unqualified. The young Shostakovich's principled agonising over the institution of marriage (*cf.* Sofia Khentova, 'A Russian Love Story', *DSCH*, No. xxi, Summer 1992, pp. 18–21; first published, in Russian, in *Muzykal'naya Zhizn'* (*Musical Life*), No. 3, 1992) shows him out of step with the carefree eroticism then common among Soviet youth. There is also a disapproving reference to 'pornographic' trends in modern ballet in a letter of 14 November 1923. His teenage opinions were, however, nothing if not inconsistent: his paradoxical dismissal of Tolstoy's plea for chastity ('Filth!') followed only a fortnight later (29 November 1923), while by 1926 he is reading 'erotic novellas' (29 June) and casually referring to his 'affairs' (24 March), not all of which involve love, some being mere 'chance encounters'.

accurately classify him as a Communist since, even under the relaxed conditions of NEP, orthodoxy demanded a selfless commitment to the Party line that was irreducibly anti-individual.

Unlike Mayakovsky, who was prepared, although with little real conviction, to 'step on the throat of his song' and divest himself of his own voice in the name of revolutionary collectivism, Shostakovich seems to have found no virtue in relinquishing his individuality. In this, though, he directly affronted his peer group's ideals of 'political correctness',[21] just as he did with his recurring interest in suicide, an act regarded in Communist eyes as a criminal dereliction of duty tantamount to desertion of one's post. (Mayakovsky, who ultimately solved his problems by blowing his own brains out, drily alludes to this harsh fact of Soviet life in his satire *The Bedbug* where one of his characters rushes in crying 'Zoya Beryozhkina's shot herself! They'll give her hell for this at the Party meeting!'[22]) Shostakovich's politically incorrect individualism is further confirmed by his inclination, in the dual guise of audience and colleague, towards the non-Party satirical writers of the '20s (notably Bulgakov, Olesha, Zamyatin and Zoshchenko). How far these leanings were instinctive and how far rational is hard to say – although the very fact that they existed and were firmly established by 1929 would seem to be a fatal blow to Taruskin's thesis that the writings of the extreme anti-individualist Dobrolyubov had any influence on *Lady Macbeth*.[23]

Whichever way one looks at him, the young Shostakovich remains a complex character. 'He is', noted his contemporary Mikhail Zoshchenko, 'extremely contradictory. One thing in

[21] The concept of 'political correctness', currently an issue in American colleges, is Bolshevik in origin, having sprung up among the younger generation in Russia during the '20s.

[22] Mayakovsky had rebuked the poet Yesenin in similar terms for hanging himself five years earlier. Tsvetayeva would in turn rebuke Mayakovsky – only to end up herself emulating Yesenin a decade later.

[23] *Cf.* my 'Shostakovich and Bulgakov: A Significant Affinity', *DSCH*, No. xviii, May 1991, pp. 54–58. This article can be consulted on the website *Music under Soviet Rule*, at http://www.siue.edu/~aho/musov/bulgakov/bulgakov.html.

him cancels another. It is a conflict of the highest degree.'[24] As with almost everything about the composer at this age, gauging the extent of his 'contradictions' is inevitably a speculative activity. Was he, for example, sufficiently inconsistent, illogical or divided in his mind to maintain equally sincere beliefs in collectivism and individualism?[25] If he was, how – and for how long – did this fundamental dichotomy survive the counsels of his individualist friends on the one hand and the pressures of revolutionary conformism on the other? Describing the '20s, Nadezhda Mandelstam has shown how what at first seemed like an efflorescence of personal freedom rapidly turned into a mass voluntary surrender of self to the political machine, a process in which even the most emphatic individualists denied or inverted their own personalities in the name of revolutionary unanimity. Often this involved striking differences between one's public and private personalities. Mayakovsky, for example, fulfilled his public 'quota' by dismissing as 'pointless, pathetic and comic anachronisms' poems by Akhmatova which, privately, he loved. Hypocrisy or revolutionary schizophrenia? And can we find here a rationale for the similarly contradictory behaviour and beliefs of the young Shostakovich?

Shostakovich's creative development in the mid-'20s is bewilderingly inconsistent. The most glaring example of this is his First Piano Sonata, Op. 12, written in 1926 (and unfortunately all but unmentioned in the Glivenko letters[26]). Sharing the acrid intensity of Skryabin's violent Sixth and

[24] Letter to Marietta Shaginyan (4 January 1941), published in Marietta Shaginyan, 'Fifty Letters from Dmitri Shostakovich', *Soviet Literature*, 1984, No. 1, p. 73.

[25] In the Glivenko letters Shostakovich chastises himself for being 'weak-willed' ('except in music') – that is, he lets others put upon him (6 October 1924, 31 December 1924). He complains of being constantly picked on by Leningrad and Moscow musicians; on the other hand, he declares that he will not 'lick boots' to advance his career (8 April 1925).

[26] He refers to it in passing in the context of his newly adopted 'modernism' in a letter dated 10 July 1925 (a letter which also mentions his plans for a 'second symphony', clearly unconnected with the work of this title produced to an official commission two years later). There is a further reference to the sonata – 'My first experience of a big piece for the piano' – in a letter of 2 September 1926.

Seventh sonatas, this work was originally entitled 'October Symphony' – an extraordinary fact in view of its sarcastic tone and aggressively exclusive idiom which could hardly have been further from the unambiguous populism then being demanded by the musical Left. Indeed, the sheer density of some of its passages amounts to a direct challenge to audience comprehension. The issue here is that, in both mood and form, Op. 12 shows Shostakovich to be wildly out of tune with the prevailing social atmosphere of voluntary uniformity and revolutionary pseudo-mysticism – and yet his next but one opus is the ostensibly conformist Second Symphony, while the work in between is *Aphorisms*, which, confusingly, opts for simplicity of method while evincing an ironic distance no less aloof than the thorny scorn of the First Sonata. Was Shostakovich, in this sequence, following his own aesthetic star; trying and failing to synchronise with the demands of the time; or merely being perverse for the sake of it? The likeliest explanation would seem to be that he was then in an alienated state in which satire had become his dominant medium, one of the main objects of his contempt being the coarse pontificating of the Proletkult.[27] In the absence of further biographical data, one can only note these 'contradictions' and the enigmatic twists and turns they presumably indicate in the composer's thoughts and feelings.

As for the equally confusing picture of Shostakovich's political motivations presented in the Glivenko letters, conceivably at least part of the solution lies in their very medium of expression: communication by state mail. It is a fact that anything sent via the Soviet postal system before August

[27] Krzysztof Meyer, in *Dimitri Chostakovitch*, Fayard, Paris, 1994, pp. 83 and 85, contends that Shostakovich's family tradition of socialist allegiance 'certainly' encouraged a sympathy with the leftwing organisations of the late '20s – such as the Russian Association of Proletarian Musicians (RAPM), founded in 1923 as a Left rival to the Association of Contemporary Musicians (ACM) – and led to the composition of the Second Symphony. These convictions, he suggests, were subsequently eroded by the composer's clashes with the authorities. Meyer gives no evidence for his assumptions, and the weight of testimony in Wilson's *Shostakovich: A Life Remembered* suggests that they are entirely false. Almost all of the sources listed in Meyer's bibliography date from earlier than 1986. Only

1991 was liable to be 'inspected' and/or misappropriated – which, in view of the Shostakovich family's bourgeois origins and SR connections,[28] is sufficient reason in itself to read the composer's pro-Communist remarks in his letters to Tanya Glivenko with a tinge of scepticism. That Shostakovich was wholly or partly inventing an enthusiasm for Lenin and Communism for the benefit of the Cheka's surveillance bureau is a possibility it would be unwise to ignore, however fanciful such an idea might at first appear. Indeed, weight has been lent to this possibility by Sofia Khentova's revelations about the mysterious disappearance of the score of the First Piano Trio, Op. 8, and the eventual arrest and execution of its bearer Mikhail Kvadri.[29] Surely this episode must have caused Shostakovich to review his position.[30] Even supposing

---

two or three are later than that, and none of the Russian material published since 1990 is referred to (Lebedinsky is quoted once, from a paper written in 1930; Zhitomirsky not at all).

[28] SR = Socialist(s) Revolutionaries. Founded in 1902 as an offshoot of the Populist movement, this party regarded the peasants as the main revolutionary class, in contrast to the Bolsheviks' bias towards the urban proletariat. As rivals of the Bolsheviks, the SRs manœuvered against them during 1917. Their left wing (the Left SRs) supported the Bolsheviks for a while, but the SRs as a whole went into opposition when Lenin dissolved the Constituent Assembly in January 1918 (*cf.* p. 550, note 45). The SR party was liquidated during the Red Terror of Summer and Autumn 1918. (*Cf.* Richard Pipes, *The Russian Revolution 1899–1919*, Collins Harvill, London, 1990, pp. 143–45, 479–80 and 541–48.)

[29] *Cf.* Khentova, 'A Russian Love Story', p. 19 (English version by Katia Vinogradova and Ian MacDonald):

> The exact date of his First Piano Trio can be gauged from his letters to [Tanya Glivenko]. The work was started in August 1923, in Gaspra, from where he wrote to her: 'It's dedicated to you, if you've no objections'. Keen to present the new work to its dedicatee, Shostakovich sent off the score to Moscow in the care of his friend Mikhail Kvadri – but for some reason it never reached its goal. The autographed score probably lies deep within the vaults of what was then the GPU, since Kvadri was later charged with 'political conspiracy' and shot.

[30] He destroyed most of his letters to his mother shortly after her death in 1955. His sister Zoya recalls him 'coming into the room, a bundle of nerves, and burning them all in the stove' (Wilson, p. 9). Presumably they contained compromising passages.

that this turns out to be yet another oversimplification, it remains necessary to place his ostensibly pro-Communist statements in their context as love-letters – hardly a genre in which to be glum or even faintly reserved, let alone about the ideology of a police state. To ascribe the few pro-Communist statements in the Glivenko letters to romantic high spirits would certainly be to stretch a point. Yet the atmosphere of mid-'20s Russia was such that exaggerated optimism, whether or not youthful or romantic, was wholly characteristic of its uniquely unstable conditions. For this reason alone, Shostakovich's remarks in the Glivenko letters may wildly overstate not merely his early faith in Communism but his general interest in politics per se.[31]

Nikolai Malko, who conducted several Shostakovich premieres and whom the Glivenko letters confirm as having been a close friend, was, like most of the older musical generation in '20s Russia, a discretely sceptical conservative. Committed to paper after he fled the USSR early in the Stalin era, Malko's portrait of Shostakovich corroborates other sources in depicting the young composer as a somewhat sheltered boy prone to silly and even obnoxious behaviour.[32] More revealingly, Malko observes that, in 1923, Shostakovich failed to answer a single question in the political section of his piano finals. If this is true, Malko must have learned of it either from the staff of the Leningrad Conservatoire or from Shostakovich himself, implying so many potential conclusions about the development of his political beliefs that further speculation would be foolish. What should be observed, however, is that Shostakovich's peculiarly clichéd remarks in the Glivenko letters about the suppression of German Communism were set down only six months after he had demonstrated zero interest in Russian Communism in a

[31] The (supposedly Revolutionary) 'youthful optimism' reported by Geoffrey Norris (*The Daily Telegraph*, 11 November 1991) as typical of the Glivenko letters is, in fact, hard to find in them. The most frequent moods are of dissatisfaction and depression (his *Weltschmerz*, for example: 24 November 1923; 29 November 1923; 29 May 1926), with four references to suicide (18 April 1925; 29 May 1926; 28 May 1927; 30 October 1930).

[32] Nikolai Malko, *A Certain Art*, W. Morrow, New York, 1966.

written exam.[33] One can only conclude that his sympathy for the German Communists, if genuine, was nonetheless shallow and quite possibly little more than a pose. Certainly, the secondhand language he employs in expressing his 'distress' strongly suggests that he had hastily mugged up on the subject after being caught out on it earlier in the year. (Perhaps something similar applies in the case of the 'patriotic music' for the tenth anniversary of the Revolution which he commenced in mid-1924.[34] This might explain his apparent shelving of it – though not why he should have 'rushed' to finish it more than three years before it would have been needed, had it been finished.)

As for Shostakovich's avowed sadness about the death of Lenin, this has to be set against Malko's assertion that, as little as two years later, the young genius was in the habit of cracking a remarkably risqué joke about 'Ilyich'.[35] It is possible that the composer's joke was made not in a spirit of anti-Communism but rather out of simple disapproval of the Lenin cult (which he expressed in the same letter in a derisive passage about the renaming of Petrograd).[36] Since such disapproval could have been made from almost anywhere on the political spectrum, it might initially seem fair to infer that Shostakovich's sarcasm about Lenin's New Economic Policy emanated from a Leftist position close to, if not identical with, that of the Proletkult and Komsomol – which, apart from anything else, would place an interpretation on the Second and Third Symphonies very different from the ones I advanced in *The New Shostakovich*. Against this, however, we know from many sources, including Shostakovich's own

[33] Letter to Tanya Glivenko dated 24 November 1923:

> I am very distressed by events in Germany. The only party which now protects the interest of the people, the communist party, is crushed. And now they have fascists there. This means that the top one percent will have privileges, that is princes, dukes, the aristocracy and [illegible]. Once again they will suck the blood of the proletariat, make them their slaves. It's awful.

[34] Letter to Tanya Glivenko dated 13 May 1924.

[35] *Cf. The New Shostakovich*, p. 136, note 1.

[36] Letter to Tanya Glivenko dated 24 January 1924: 'If I become as great a man as Lenin, when I die will the city be renamed Shostakovichgrad?'

testimony in the Glivenko letters,[37] that he deplored Aleksandr Bezymensky's Lenin-lionising verses for the Second Symphony, while Malko, Vishnevskaya and Yelagin alike confirm that he felt only contempt for the Proletkult. As for the Komsomol, the slim chance that for a short period of sheltered innocence Shostakovich shared their strident outlook is rendered even slighter by the fact that he ironically gives his address in two letters written during summer 1924 as 'Saint Leninburg', the irreverence of which is difficult to reconcile with serious Young Communist commitment.[38] (On the face of it, it also clashes with the theory that, in other letters, the composer might have been feigning or exaggerating leftwing sympathies in case his mail was being overseen by the secret police. However there is no necessary incongruity here. This correspondence was, after all, sustained over about seven years – enough time for the young Shostakovich to change his assumptions and alter any precautionary measures he might have adopted. It would, of course, help to know precisely what, in Glivenko's letters, he was responding to in making his remarks about Communism, and whether she herself – like his lover of the mid-'30s, Elena Konstantinovskaya – happened to be a member of the Komsomol.)

Setting aside the testimony of his own music, the most obdurate evidence against Shostakovich's 'pro-Communism' having survived (if it ever existed) much later than the last of the main sequence of the Glivenko letters is, once again, his association with such anti-Communist satirists of the late

[37] Letter to Tanya Glivenko dated 28 May 1927. Also *cf.* Malko, *A Certain Art*, p. 204; Meyer, p. 108; Wilson, pp. 42–44, 61.

[38] Letters to Tanya Glivenko dated 26 April and 3 June 1924. In a letter to Tanya dated 2 March 1924, he quotes Lenin's remark that film is the most useful of the arts, adding, pointedly, that he himself prefers the 'useless' ones: music and ballet. The insinuations in such passages – that Lenin was a man, not a god or a saint – may seem harmless to Westerners, but in the USSR the suggestion that the dictator was anything less than a Red pseudo-Christ was thought shockingly iconoclastic. Already in the mid-'20s the dead Lenin was said, like Jesus, to 'live' – invisibly omnipresent, watching over his people as a kind of benign Communist All-Father. A mystic-sentimental 'Love of Lenin' was an essential prerequisite for orthodoxy and his name became the first word children were taught when learning to speak.

'20s as Bulgakov, Olesha, Zoshchenko and Zamyatin. It has been suggested that the reason that the last of this sequence of letters dates from May 1927 is that in August he met his future wife Nina Varzar. Perhaps more relevant is that, in April, Shostakovich met Ivan Sollertinsky and, through him, entered the masked, ironic world inhabited by the satirists and the more sceptical citizens of a Russia even then growing increasingly tense and embattled under the creeping influence of Iosif Stalin.

Close examination of the Glivenko letters reveals that taking them either too literally or without regard to their chronology can only produce a misleading conception of their teenage author. Addressing a different aspect of the problems this sort of source entails, Michael Scammell has observed that 'working in a subject area affected by Soviet propaganda is like working in a mighty blast of wind. You learn to lean into it in order to stay upright, but there is an ever-present danger that you will lean too far – and, if the wind should stop blowing for a moment, fall flat on your face'.[39] How much of Shostakovich's letters to Tanya Glivenko consists of 'wind' – from whichever compass-point – is something we will know only once further researches in Russia have located other sources relating to the composer's youth (or, failing this, once scholarship has established a more comprehensive picture of life and culture under NEP than is presently available). As for the question of when Shostakovich began his break with Communism – and at the risk of falling flat on my face in pushing these speculations a step too far – it seems fair to deduce from the Glivenko letters that a significant change in the composer's development occurred around the time of his encounter with the forward-thinking theoretician Boleslav Yavorsky in Moscow in April 1925. Before then, Shostakovich repeatedly dwells on his own (artistic) conservatism, the tone of his remarks, both cultural and political, being often rather prim, not to say virginal. In the months after his meeting with Yavorsky, his letters become lighter, more

[39] Michael Scammell, *Solzhenitsyn: A Biography*, W. W. Norton and Co., New York, 1984, pp. 14–15.

scabrous and, on sexual subjects, easier-going.[40] At the same time, he reports himself casting off his conservative traits and 'becoming more of a modernist' (a key composition for him in this respect being the Scherzo from Op. 11).[41] By 1926, the transformation is complete: he is enjoying Ehrenburg's picaresque satires, reading erotic French novellas, and teasing Tanya with tales of his sexual conquests. A letter of 21 March finds him 'amused' by reviews of his First Symphony in 'the red press'. His only subsequent political reference (a week later) is a grumble at the Soviet government for hurting the low-waged with new economising measures.[42] The few other

[40] Yavorsky was homosexual. Shostakovich, of course, was not; nor am I suggesting a sexual liaison between them. What may have happened is that, at approximately the same time, Shostakovich (then eighteen) lost his virginity and, in meeting Yavorsky, encountered a different sexual world which amused him and, over a period, helped relax his attitudes, rendering him less tartly intolerant in general. Shostakovich's interest in Yavorsky is announced in a letter to Tanya dated 26 March 1925 in which he declares that, if he moves to Moscow as planned, he'll study with him. Yavorsky, he tells Tanya on 8 April 1925, is 'the only real musician in Moscow and Petrograd – the only ray of light in the darkness of the modern musical world'. (Note the conventional use of the Dobrolyubov quotation – *cf.* p. 539, note 18.) He adds that, through meeting Yavorsky, he has realised that he is 'infected by conservatism' and is trying to rid himself of this. A typical adolescent reversal follows when Shostakovich (4 June 1925) meets Myaskovsky, whom he had previously disliked, and finds that he likes him after all, adding that 'the opposite happened' with Yavorsky; on 5 August 1925 he decides he likes Yavorsky again. Their friendship develops over the next year – on 31 December 1925 he tells Tanya he has received 24 letters from him since April – and in August 1926 he goes to Moscow where, briefly, he stays with Yavorsky. On 19 August 1926 he tells Tanya how comfortable Yavorsky's apartment is, adding that he locks his door at night and that Yavorsky keeps telling him that their relationship is not as close as he'd like: 'He's very nice, I love him very much, but alas (for him) it is purely platonic'. On 21 August Shostakovich tells Tanya that Yavorsky continues to talk suggestively about getting closer. He reports that Musenkin (Yavorsky's partner?) is away and describes not only locking his door but putting an armchair against it. Apart from a passing mention on 28 May 1927, no more references to Yavorsky occur in the Glivenko letters.

[41] Letter to Tanya Glivenko dated 13 July 1925.

[42] In a letter to Tanya dated 20 April 1927, he expresses a politically incorrect foreboding that the conductorless (i.e., 'democratic/popular') Persimfans orchestra will 'rape' his Second Symphony.

political passages – his clichéd reference to German Communism, the anti-NEP letter, the various (ultimately ambivalent) references to Lenin – belong to 1923–24. There is none at all in 1925.

In view of the publication (1994) by Elizabeth Wilson of testimonies from many of Shostakovich's old friends and acquaintances, there is now a robust case for presenting the young composer as largely apolitical, raised in a liberal tradition rather than a socialistic one, and, as such, interested neither in revolution nor ideology, but instead devoted more or less exclusively to the arts.[43] Writing to Yavorsky in 1925, Shostakovich confesses to a politically dangerous concentration on his individual creativity (as against the collective concern for the social good expected of all young Russians at the time): 'There are no other joys in life apart from music. For me, all of life is music'.[44] In confirmation, Boris Lossky, a pupil with Shostakovich at the Shidlovskaya School, opines, in an article written in 1989, that the Shostakovich family's liberalism was 'of a fairly conservative nature', adding that the *Funeral March in Memory of the Victims of the Revolution* was performed after the massacre of those protesting against Lenin's dissolution of the Constituent Assembly on 5 January 1918:[45] 'During the spring of 1918, Mitya never so much as hinted at any kind of sympathy with the "existing regime", and I can vouch that this was the case

[43] Speaking to Elizabeth Wilson some time between 1988 and 1990, Zoya Shostakovich insisted that the atmosphere in their house after the Revolution was 'very free and liberal', with 'no talk of politics'.

[44] Wilson, p. 30.

[45] On this day, around 50,000 students, civil servants and middle-class professionals marched towards Petrograd's Tauride Palace, protesting at Lenin's announced plans to dissolve the Constituent Assembly. Bolshevik troops machine-gunned the crowd from rooftops overlooking the Liteiny Prospekt, killing between ten and twenty and wounding as many more. These were buried on 9 January 1918, the thirteenth anniversary of Bloody Sunday, next to the victims of that massacre in the Preobrazhensky Cemetery. Maxim Gorky angrily pointed out the historical parallel in his column in *Novaya Zhizn* (*New Life*; No. 6, 220) for 9 January, describing the Constituent Assembly as the century-old goal of progressive intellectuals, works, and peasants, castigating Lenin's 'People's Commissars' for destroying this ideal by brute force, and accusing *Pravda* of systematically misrepresenting the truth of events. (*Cf.* Gorky, *Untimely Thoughts:*

until 1922'.[46] In this perspective we face a straight choice over whether Shostakovich's ostensibly pro-Lenin letters to Tanya of 1923–24 represented a genuine change of outlook, or were merely part of an attempt to portray himself as in step with the Revolution at a time when his position at the Conservatoire was ideologically precarious.[47] (The fact that the Glivenko letters show him abandoning all such political statements in 1925 points strongly to the second of these options.) Thereafter, contact with new acquaintances in Moscow seems to have broadened his mind and loosened his attitudes – to the point where it is legitimate to infer an active enjoyment of the relative freedom of life under NEP by 1926–27. This, of course, coincided with his meetings with such influential figures as Sollertinsky, Zoshchenko and Zamyatin, and his encounters with the satirical plays and stories of Mikhail Bulgakov. In spite of these potent influences, Shostakovich may have juggled his internal contradictions without coming to any final conclusions for several years – indeed, his Second and Third Symphonies are arguably best understood as the ambiguous works such a theory would predict (though there is room, too, for maintaining that their revolutionary enthusiasm was entirely, rather than only partially, simulated). Elizabeth Wilson herself is quite clear that Shostakovich's ostensibly 'Red' compositions of the late '20s were motivated chiefly by a self-

---

Essays on Revolution, Culture and the Bolsheviks 1917–18, Garnstone Press, London, 1968, pp. 123–26; Orlando Figes, *A People's Tragedy: The Russian Revolution 1891–1924*, Jonathan Cape, London, 1996, pp. 513–16.)

[46] Wilson, pp. 12–13 and 30. Also *cf.* Yevgeny Chukovsky's contention that Shostakovich was horrified by the publicly posted lists of those 'liquidated' as enemies of the People in the years immediately after the Revolution (Wilson, p. 19).

[47] The article quoted by Elizabeth Wilson (pp. 20–23) as being by Lev (Leo) Arnshtam is an obviously ghostwritten propaganda piece published in 1976. Its claims that Shostakovich was filled with revolutionary enthusiasm at the Conservatoire, or that his rhythmic sense was inculcated by 'the rhythm and pace of the Revolution', are Socialist Realist clichés and emphatically not to be trusted. Similarly, the letter by Andrey Balanchivadze, published in 1967 (Wilson, pp. 79–80), is an Aesopian construction written under Soviet censorship and, as such, to be read 'the other way up'.

protective wish to appear to conform.[48] On this view, the 'October' tag briefly attached to his First Piano Sonata may have been an attempt at making a nonconformist work appear politically palatable (and, as such, the first instance of this tactic in a career subsequently full of similar devices). In any case there would have been small chance of him maintaining an intellectual compromise – supposing him ever to have required one – during the Cultural Revolution of 1929–32, a crucial period in his life about which we have little documentation. (Unfortunately, the Glivenko letters peter out over a year before the onset of this tumultuous event.)

As for so many idealists of the period, Shostakovich's dilemma in the '20s took the form of an irreconcilable clash between his individualistic sensibility and his faith in the feasibility of benevolent collectivism. The intensity of this clash and the concrete reality of the issues involved must have been so crucial to his creative evolution that ignoring their influence can only prevent understanding of the music he was then writing. Inevitably somewhat theoretical to free western democrats, the conflict between individualism and collectivism was in no way an abstract issue to citizens of Stalin's Russia – and especially not to Soviet intellectuals. During the first years of the dictator's rule, what I have called Communism's 'abolition of the soul'[49] was accompanied by an enforced de-individualisation of the country's artists involving their 'remaking' into cultural technicians. For writers, this process was heralded by such slogans as 'The Book Is An Instrument of Production!' and 'For Coal! For Iron! For Machines! Each Literary Group Must Work For These!' (not to mention the bluntly candid 'We Must Break The Writer's Individualism!'). In place of the pre-Revolutionary concept of the ensouled individual with personal thoughts and feelings, the theorists of the new society imposed a behaviouristic vision of an ultimately

[48] Wilson, pp. 71 and 78. Valerian Bogdanov-Berezovsky, writing under constraint in 1976, remarks that 'an outstanding feature of the young Shostakovich was his early independence of thought and behaviour' – reliable Aesopian for 'He wasn't a Communist' (Wilson, p. 26). Also *cf.* Wilson's subsequent evidence that Shostakovich was contemptuous of the propagandist scenarios of all three of his ballets.

[49] *The New Shostakovich*, pp. 38–40.

mechanical human being whose so-called inner life was not just an anachronistic delusion but an active drag on the efficiency of social development.[50] Those conscripted to churn out 'Five-Year-Plan literature' were accordingly instructed to emphasise the motif of the 'remaking' of the individual through his or her willing (indeed ecstatic) self-synchronisation to the rhythm and 'tempo' of industrial machinery. Hand in hand with this went the notorious metaphor of the 'social machine' whereby every citizen was paradoxically ennobled by being degraded to the status of a disposable cog.[51]

Taking all this into account, it is clearly no accident that Shostakovich's music of the late '20s and early '30s is uniquely headlong, his recurring musical image one of mass hysteria – of a situation accelerating and running away with

[50] Such thinking was prefigured a decade earlier in the mystical vision of universal robotisation propounded by certain Proletkult writers – a vision epitomised in the following meditation on 'proletarian culture' published by the poet Aleksey Gastev in 1919:

> The mechanisation, not only of gestures, not only of production methods, but of everyday thinking, coupled with extreme practicality, characterises the psychology of the proletariat to a striking degree. The manifestations of such mechanised collectivism are so depersonalised that the function of their 'collective-complexes' resembles the movement of industrial parts – to the point where individual human beings cease to be recognisable behind drilled steps, blank faces, dry souls, and feelings so imperceptible that they cannot be measured by outward signs like tears or laughter, but only by manometer and taxometer [. . .]. As this psychological trait spreads in massive waves around the world, a single world mind will replace what formerly were millions of minds. In the end individual thinking will be impossible, and thought will become instead an objective cerebral process, regulated by systems of psychological switches and locks.

Such passages had a formative influence on Zamyatin's *We* and hence on Orwell's *Nineteen Eighty-Four*.

[51] During the Cultural Revolution, the 'bourgeois' sciences of social psychology and neurophysiology, whose representatives held that human 'mechanisation' could be achieved only at the cost of a massive eruption of neuroses and psychoses, were, like many other pre-Revolutionary scientific research endeavours, silenced and suppressed. Under the Second Five Year Plan, experts unable to support the government line on 'remaking' were replaced by practitioners of Pavlov's conditioning theory which promised the infinite adaptability of the human being.

itself. Indeed by the early '30s, he seems – to judge by his creative motto 'Thinking slowly, writing fast' – to have been consciously slowing his mind in order not to be swept away in the shallow rapids of Stalin's 'hyperindustrial' machine civilisation. It is against this monstrous background of a state-sponsored assault on individual feeling and integrity that the contradictions – real or only apparent – in both Shostakovich's contemporary music and his letters to Tanya Glivenko have to be weighed and understood.

UNIVERSAL BECAUSE SPECIFIC

Arguments for a Contextual Approach[1]

Ian MacDonald

'A composer must be local before he can be universal.'
– *Ralph Vaughan Williams*

In *The New Shostakovich*, I indicated some of the ways in which the modern tendencies to elevate abstraction and formal beauty conspire to create an atmosphere in which music with specific inner significance, such as Shostakovich's, is reduced or glossed over in both performance and analysis. I would like here to amplify this with reference to the dogmatic subjectivism associated with these trends, inasmuch as this critical stance has become something of a fallback position for those once happy to accept the Soviet line on Shostakovich yet now unwilling to adopt the contrary position.

To take a typical example, Nicholas Kenyon has dismissed my account of Shostakovich's historical context as irrelevant, 'undervaluing a composer whose musical genius, as someone said of Mozart's, was to suggest an infinite number of possibilities at once'.[2] This statement neatly encapsulates the paradox of the aesthetic ideal of 'universality' in music – which is that, to be 'universal', a given composition must not

[1] Versions of this piece appeared in *DSCH*, No. xix, Autumn 1991, pp. 38–45, and *Southern Humanities Review*, 26/2, Spring 1992, pp. 153–67. Also *cf.* a friendly rejoinder by Philippe Vandenbroek, 'Universal Because Philosophic', *DSCH*, No. xx, Spring 1992, pp. 78–81, followed by MacDonald's reply, 'Universal Because Human', in the same issue, pp. 82–83. –EDS.

[2] *The Guardian*, 20 May 1990.

(as one might expect) signify more or less the same thing to all men, but rather mean different things to everyone who hears it. The oddity of this notion, with its overtones of Doublethink, is clear from the fact that, in language, a statement which suggested an infinite number of possibilities at once would certainly be meaningless.

Having fixed his standard of musical sublimity and qualified Shostakovich for assessment by it, Kenyon rejects the idea that an artist so 'neurotically unsure of himself' – 'Did he ever know what he really thought? Did his frequent verbal betrayals of himself mean anything?' and so on – could ever be specifically interpreted. In other words, having been asked to accept one dizzy paradox, we are additionally required to believe in a stupid and self-doubting ditherer mysteriously capable of the loftiest ineffability once confronted with score-paper. Surely this quaint academic notion of Shostakovich as an *idiot savant* has been allowed to misdirect Western studies of the composer for long enough? How, for example, can those who maintain this theory acknowledge the Preludes and Fugues, Op. 87, as the product of a sophisticated intellect whilst otherwise maintaining that intellect to be basically muddled and naïve? As it happens, conjecture on this question is obsolete since Shostakovich's colleagues have witnessed in chorus that he was every bit as intelligent as his music suggests; yet the subjectivists, regarding such contextual material as an irrelevant intrusion on their private response, choose to ignore this.

To refuse to acknowledge Shostakovich's intelligence is, inevitably, to refuse to recognise the crucial satirical strand in his art – to see him, instead, as a confused introvert wallowing in tragic grandiloquence (what I have called the 'Hamlet' theory). However, it is not, as the subjectivists insist, merely a matter of taste as to which option one selects. It is not even a question of probability (i.e., that while a 'tragic-satiric' analysis of Shostakovich creates no contradictions, the 'Hamlet' theory breeds paradoxes within paradoxes, and yet still makes no sense). It is that the evidence of the historical record has entirely destroyed one of these rival positions, leaving us no fundamental interpretive dilemma over which to hesitate. Shostakovich was *indisputably* a tragic-satiric observer, not an introspective or bewildered Hamlet figure.

If the abstract, non-contextual, and aesthetic approaches to Shostakovich are discredited, what of the alternative? Why should a contextual approach be more appropriate?

It has been argued (for example, by F. R. Leavis and W. H. Auden) that, so far as literature goes, authorial biography and the wider historical, social and cultural context are distractions to our engagement with the timeless 'universality' of the text. I have characterised the similarly score-centered concern for 'universality' in music criticism, with its key concepts of 'pure music' on the one hand and the 'extra-musical' on the other, as subjective. Where music criticism of this kind differs from the sort of literary criticism advocated by Leavis and Auden (rendering it even more subjective) is that it lacks the moral dimension unavoidable in a linguistic medium, instead confining itself to aesthetic criteria. What is crucial to observe, however, is that this aestheticism is compromised wherever words are added to music in the form of a text, a libretto, a programme or an exegesis sponsored or written by the composer in question. When this happens, the division between 'pure music' and the 'extra-musical' element attached to it (in this case, language) becomes blurred in such a way as to point to an underlying philosophical misconception about music best illustrated by means of a simple example.

Interviewed recently,[3] Daniel Barenboim spoke derisively of the third movement of Shostakovich's Eighth Symphony, describing it as 'pages of violas playing crotchets – for hours it goes on'. When Barenboim took this up with some Soviet musicians, he received a reply that only deepened his irritation: 'They said that it symbolized the crushing of the Russian people or something – and I think that's a load of rubbish. When you need non-musical explanations like that to see the value of it – this I can't come to terms with'.

Postponing the issue of what, if anything, the passage in question 'means' and whether this 'meaning' should be allowed to alter our perception of its composer's methods in writing it, it seems reasonable to deduce from Barenboim's description that he finds the music boring or inadequate

[3] Stephen Johnson, 'Barenboim in Berlin', *Gramophone*, Vol. 68, No. 809, October 1990, p. 720.

because formally simple and repetitious. This being so, we can presumably further deduce that he would feel the same about the 34 common chords spaced evenly between Scenes 2 and 3 of Act III of Britten's opera *Billy Budd*. Or can we? One would, on the contrary, expect a musician of Barenboim's sensitivity to see that, at this point in his opera, Britten's simplicity and repetition are sufficiently apt that any formal reservation is obliterated by the emotional effect they produce. Billy Budd has just begged Captain Vere to save him, but being (to coin a phrase) trapped in formalities, Vere must condemn him. Britten's plain sequence symbolises the agony of Vere's mind, the awe of his power to ordain life or death, the implacability of fate, the insignificance of human endeavour. How do we know this? Because the music has words attached to it. Elsewhere in the same interview, Barenboim declares that *Così fan tutte* represents 'beauty married to falseness'. How does he know this? Because the music has words attached to it. Yet, according to Barenboim's definition with respect to Shostakovich, words are 'non-musical' things. How is it that he can 'come to terms' with Mozart's music via Da Ponte's words, but cannot do the same with Shostakovich's music via the words of his colleagues (or even, presumably, Shostakovich's own words in *Testimony*)?

Had Mozart left an account of his intentions in *Così fan tutte*, Barenboim would surely try to incorporate his understanding of these into his performance so as not to travesty the composer's meaning. By reading the libretto of *Billy Budd*, he would see why Britten uses simplicity and repetition. Similarly, by listening to Shostakovich's colleagues or by reading *Testimony*, he might see that, in many places (the Scherzo from the Piano Quintet, the march of the 'Leningrad' Symphony, the third movement of the Eighth Quartet, and so on) Shostakovich uses simplicity and repetition as satirical devices, mocking vulgarity by impersonating it. As with Mozart, 'non-musical explanations' would thus have helped Barenboim to see why Britten and Shostakovich chose to express themselves in certain ways. Whether he nonetheless still found their methods in so doing inadequate or uninteresting is another matter; at the very least, should he wish to conduct their music, he would now stand a fair chance of not making a mess of it.

Barenboim's philosophical misconception is the very simple – and common – one of confusing music with notation. Were music identical with notation, no problems of interpretation would ever arise. Robots could play it. But music is something larger: *thought and feeling expressed as sound represented in notation.* In this perspective, it is clear that no music is 'pure' and that there is no 'extra-musical' (or 'non-musical') element which contaminates it. Music, like the other arts, is part of life – life, as it were, expressing itself in an aural symbology. As the poet Wallace Stevens says, 'music is feeling, then, not sound'[4] – which is why it makes us think and feel (and value it).

Since no music can be divorced from the human context which gave birth to it, it follows that understanding the context in which Shostakovich composed is directly relevant to the performance and audition of his compositions. Once this is allowed, the issue becomes merely one of degree. In the case of most composers, the relationship of context and composition is gentle since the forces acting upon them or arising from within them are/were relatively moderate. In the case of Shostakovich and his contemporaries in the USSR during the Stalin period, the relationship was harsh – literally a matter of life and death. Theirs was a time and place in which millions died or disappeared into slave camps; in which fear and betrayal were institutionalised; in which natural morality and normal social relationships were virtually annihilated. This was, furthermore, a time and place in which the arts were dragooned, deformed and all but destroyed in what the radical Hungarian architect Imre Makovecz has called a process of 'cultural genocide'. Arguably, no more intense context for the production of art has ever existed – yet, despite this, subjective Western commentators on Shostakovich remain unwilling to admit that objective knowledge of this context has any legitimate role to play in understanding his music. Where reason alone is apparently insufficient, one can only fall back on commonsense. For example, I have in front of me a record of songs by the National Dance Company of Cambodia, the first lyric of which runs as follows:

[4] 'Peter Quince at the Clavier', from *Harmonium*, 1923.

Sleep well, my child.
We have gone through three fields:
The field of death, the field of chains and prisons
And the field of remembrance . . .
My child, you should remember this:
The regimes of separating and killing.
You should remember and must never forget
If you want your country to live . . .

Can anyone seriously maintain that an understanding of the context of such a song is irrelevant to its performance and audition? Of course not. And the same obviously applies to the music of Shostakovich.

This much at least is incontestable to those who knew the composer. For Kirill Kondrashin, Shostakovich's work is 'inseparable from the events of his life'.[5] 'His music', insists Vladimir Ashkenazy, 'was totally connected with personal experiences within the Soviet totalitarian system, the horrors of war, etc. From the 1930s to 1960s he lives through the tragedy of the nation, expressing it through the medium of his music.'[6] Daniil Zhitomirsky concurs: 'It was by the light of Shostakovich's music that we, his contemporaries, survived our special and indescribable hell, through whose circles he led us like some latter-day Virgil'.[7] Referring to the 'ideological darkness' which Shostakovich fought through his work, Sofiya Khentova states that 'everything he wrote was, in essence, a protest against slavery; music, the creative process, remained the last refuge of his free spirit'.[8] For Maria Yudina, the links between art and life are audible in the very forms the composer adopted: 'Shostakovich does not try to keep his work balanced; instead he invariably draws us into the catastrophe of contemporary reality'.[9] Indeed, to

[5] *Cf.* p. 519. –EDS.

[6] *Classic CD*, February 1991.

[7] Daniil Zhitomirsky, 'Shostakovich: The Public and the Private', English version by Tatjana M. Marovic (Norbury) and Ian MacDonald (originally in *Daugava*, 1990, No. 3). (Also *cf.* p. 419. –EDS.)

[8] 'Shostakovich and Rostropovich – 2', *DSCH*, No. xviii, May 1991, p. 24.

[9] Zhitomirsky, 'Shostakovich: The Public and the Private'.

Yuri Temirkanov, context is so vital as to be inexhaustible: 'I am always nervous when I conduct Shostakovich in the West because people know only superficially what happened; they don't know the real horror of the facts, and to understand Shostakovich fully you have to understand the extent of those horrors'.[10] As to the significance of *Testimony* in furthering such understanding, Maxim Shostakovich has observed: 'When we take this book in our hands we can imagine what this composer's life was like in this particular political situation – how difficult, how awful it was under the Soviet regime'.[11] In short, Russian musicians are unanimous in maintaining that a factual and imaginative grasp of the context of Shostakovich's music is not merely advisable but essential to understanding it.

What, then, is specifically to be gained from such a contextual approach? And how does approaching Shostakovich's music in this way affect its claim to 'universality'? To answer the first of these questions, what is to be gained from a contextual approach is (1) a clearer idea of Shostakovich's intentions in writing in certain ways, leading to (2) a sharper instinct for his 'tone' in general, leading further to (3) a more appropriate mode of interpretation (in both criticism and performance) than has been afforded his work in the West so far.

Since working thus from the specific to the general implies a quasi-programmatic treatment of many pieces by Shostakovich usually regarded in the West as 'pure music', it is necessary to know that such a treatment is, and has been for some time, standard practice among the composer's colleagues. For example, Kirill Kondrashin, who premiered Shostakovich's Fourth and Thirteenth Symphonies, described the concepts behind his own performances of the composer's music as follows:

> Not every work can be 'decoded' in detail, of course, but I feel that a conductor can better sense the form and significance of a work if he feels, behind the movements of musical thought,

[10] *CD Review*, June 1991.

[11] David Fanning, 'Always a Great Composer, Not a Papa', *Gramophone*, Vol. 68, No. 816, May 1991, p. 1992.

> emotions and feelings that can be put into words. *Sometimes he even finds a programmed logic that is close to a plot.* [. . .] The majority of Shostakovich's symphonies do not have titles and at first glance appear to be plotless. Nevertheless, contemporaries associate each of his symphonies with a specific period in the life of the composer, and this allows the listener to transform the development of musical thought into emotions close to the human heart *and into direct plot situations.* [. . .] The historical cataclysms that gave life to Shostakovich's music passed before my eyes as well, and they were part of my life, too. Several of his symphonies elicited such vivid associations with our reality that I developed them *to full programme detail.* Dmitry Dmitriyevich knew about my 'decodings'. He himself did not like to discuss the subtext of his music and usually said nothing, although he did not contradict me, either. Since he was usually pleased with my performances, I believe he had no objection to such an approach to his music.[12] [My italics. –IM]

The similar 'decodings' attempted in *The New Shostakovich* (published before I saw Kondrashin's statement) were naturally received with scepticism by Western advocates of 'pure music' and the subjective approach. In particular, it was argued that I had pursued too consistent a line in metaphor and in linking biographical and musical events. (Inconsistency is, of course, a virtual obligation for any philosophy of music which sees as its highest ideal the suggestion of 'an infinite number of possibilities at once'.) From the empirical point of view, it is thus worth pointing out that not only have several of the supposedly contentious commentaries on individual works in *The New Shostakovich* been confirmed since the book appeared,[13] but that Vladimir Ashkenazy,[14] Yuri Temirkanov,[15] Gennady Rozhdest-

[12] *Cf.* pp. 518–20. –EDS.

[13] Notably, Lebedinsky's observations concerning the Eighth Quartet and Seventh, Eleventh and Twelfth Symphonies (*cf.* pp. 472–82 –EDS.) and Maxim Shostakovich's description of the Fourth Symphony as 'a portrayal of the policies and apocalypses of the Soviet regime' (interview with Louis Blois, *DSCH*, No. xiv, November 1989, pp. 4–8).

[14] *Classic CD*, February 1991.

[15] *CD Review*, June 1991.

vensky,[16] Semyon Bychkov[17] and Kurt Sanderling[18] have all recently spoken of various Shostakovich pieces in terms similar to mine.

This is not to claim that absolute specificity of meaning is possible with any given bar Shostakovich wrote. Beyond a certain point, subjectivity comes back into play and we must each feel for ourselves the truth of what we hear. This, though, can only happen once contextual objectivity has narrowed our options from 'an infinite number' to something more realistic.

Just such a range of differing, yet closely related, interpretations have, for example, accumulated around the curious percussion passages in Shostakovich's Fourth Symphony (II), Second Cello Concerto (III), and Fifteenth Symphony (IV). I have suggested that the implied association is with marionettes and automata, both of which are known to have fascinated the composer and which arguably held sinister significance for him. For Yuri Temirkanov, however, the passages in the Fifteenth Symphony and Second Cello Concerto signify 'the ticking away of the hours' and symbolise the fear of death.[19] (Shostakovich was also, like Prokofiev, interested in clocks.) Speaking of the passage in the Fourth Symphony, Gennady Rozhdestvensky offers a third possibility: 'For me, and I think for Shostakovich, the association is prisoners tapping out messages to one another on the hot-water pipes in jail'.[20] All of these readings are justifiable by reference to context and therefore sufficiently appropriate to be taken on their merits. By comparison, the rare ventures into 'decoding' risked by aesthetically based commentators are nearly always vague (typically an allusion

[16] *The Independent*, 6 April 1991.

[17] *Cf*. pp. 589–96. –EDS.

[18] Norman Lebrecht, 'Sanderling's Summer' *Classical Music*, 18 May 1991.

[19] *CD Review*, June 1991.

[20] *The Independent*, 6 April 1991. An American orchestra with which Rozhdestvensky was rehearsing the work was bemused by this. One orchestra member dimly enquired: 'Why tap out messages when they can speak to one another on the telephone?' 'I realized', recalls the conductor, wearily, 'that there was no point in discussing the matter further'.

to the Russian landscape) or randomly inappropriate (usually a reference to the composer's music as involuntarily expressive of his own self-dramatised inner turmoil).

For my own part, I cannot, despite the independent confirmations of them, guarantee that my readings are absolutely reliable, let alone exhaustive. They were arrived at by a combination of contextual objectivity and intuition; those who knew and worked with Shostakovich will presumably continue to publish comparable accounts of his music which may be different from mine (although I confidently predict that the range of such differences will be narrow). For now, all that is crucial to grasp is that, in the case of Shostakovich, the objective focus of contextual understanding must precede and guide our individual subjective responses to his music. It could be argued that the same applies, in appropriately varying degrees, to all composers – indeed, I would make this argument. At present, however, it is enough to realise that there is no music more intensely conditioned by its context than Shostakovich's. Such realisation will of itself sweep away the sort of criticism that treats his works merely as formally determined and self-referential constructions of notes into which we may each randomly project our own private aesthetic and emotional concerns. It will also, by sharpening our sense of his intelligence, humour and propensity for satire, put an end to the tendency of Western performers to, as one British critic has rightly complained, 'Brahmsify Shostakovich'.

As to how approaching Shostakovich's music in this way affects its claim to 'universality', it is clear that universality is achieved not by art diffuse enough to mean different things to everyone it touches but, on the contrary, by art specific enough – in Ivan Bunin's terminology, 'stereoscopic' enough – to touch all of us in the same way. That is: the more sharply specific our perception of Shostakovich, the more universal he becomes. To grasp this, one need only refer to the comparable specificity and stereoscopic sharpness of the characters and situations presented in the works of his favourite authors (Gogol, Dostoyevsky, Chekhov) – or, in our own language, of Shakespeare and Dickens. It is not by idealisation or generalisation, but by focusing on specific characters in specific situations that universality is achieved. No accident, then, that Boris Tishchenko's description of

Shostakovich portrays a mind for which such focus was clearly an article of faith: 'What he said was concrete and specific: every thought was expressed in a strict yet ample literary form, sometimes it was even a short story. Shostakovich was hostile to diffuse, abstract discussions and platitudes. There was no magniloquence, no pathos, everything was specific and well-rounded.'[21]

Subjectivists often ask triumphantly how, if Shostakovich's music involves such specific and supposedly unsuspected significance, it has nevertheless managed to achieve 'universal' appeal. The answer is painfully simple: one does not have to understand something in order to enjoy it. In sex, attraction precedes penetration; the same goes for art. That Shostakovich's music should be popular in the West without being widely understood is surely a modest enough proposition.

[21] Dmitri and Ludmilla Sollertinsky, *Pages from the Life of Dmitri Shostakovich*, p. 184.

WRITING ABOUT SHOSTAKOVICH
The Post-Communist Perspective

Ian MacDonald

The appearance of *Testimony* in 1979 ignited a furious controversy which was still smoldering a decade later. Reduced to its basics, the argument consisted of two questions: had Shostakovich been a Communist or a secret dissident – and did it matter? The debate was pursued with some ferocity, Volkov's opponents effectively accusing him of charlatanry and dismissing *Testimony* as Cold War propaganda.

Since 1990 this controversy has subsided in synchronism with the collapse of Soviet power. With the withering of official restrictions, a wealth of material confirming the authenticity of *Testimony* has become available in both Russia and the West, the broad message of which is that Shostakovich was indeed a secret dissident and his former image as a Communist purely a contrivance of Soviet disinformation. The question of whether this affects appreciation of the composer's work has been answered equally categorically: every writer or interviewee to have endorsed *Testimony* is clear that the new view of Shostakovich in the book radically alters the understanding of his music. Moreover, some go further, claiming that the implications of the Shostakovich case call into question the basic assumptions of modern composition, criticism and performance. In short, the current changes in critical understanding of Shostakovich are central not only to the revaluation of his work which is already under way, but to the general contemporary reaction against the structural bias dominant in the arts throughout most of the present century.

Writing in 1989,[1] I argued that symbolic content was

[1] *The New Shostakovich.*

discernible in almost everything Shostakovich wrote and that, without recognising this, no real understanding of his music was possible. The same claim is repeatedly made by Russian commentators who have written or been interviewed about the composer during the last seven years – so insistently, in fact, that it seems fair to conclude that the case for it is now established beyond doubt. How far such an approach can be legitimately pursued is, of course, open to debate; all that has to be grasped at present is that the line of enquiry thus opened leads logically to revaluations of everything from individual passages in works by Shostakovich to the basic principles of music criticism in general.

To see how the Russian approach to Shostakovich's music carries implications affecting matters far beyond it, one has only to consider that staple of musicological studies, 'the finale problem'. Based on the feeling that, freed by Beethoven from classical formalities, the symphony had lost its predestined shape and become hard to conclude with its former inevitability, this notion has found much grist to its mill in Shostakovich's finales: hardly a single symphony by him convinces its critics that it ends properly. Often dismissed as 'not truly symphonic', the composer's efforts in the way of finishing many of his symphonies have struck most musicologists as bombastic or trivial or both. That he might have harboured ironic or satirical intent in writing these movements seems rarely to have occurred to them, for the simple reason that a composer's intentions have never played a major part in the study of the finale problem, which normally takes the form of a structural analysis of developing motifs and tonalities. Even if intentionality had been considered, it is unlikely that those dissatisfied with Shostakovich's finales would have detected any irony in them since, unfamiliar with the special conditions in which the composer was obliged to work, they would have had little idea what he might have intended to be ironic about.

A classic example of this is the finale of the Sixth Symphony – a short, manifestly vulgar and determinedly 'unsymphonic' *Presto* which not only fails to 'solve the problems' of the work's tragic opening *Largo* but also seems unrelated to it to the point of brusque indifference. Surely here, if anywhere, Shostakovich encounters 'the so-called problem of the finale' (as he once sardonically referred to it in

Rostislav Dubinsky's presence[2]) and dismally bungles its solution?

Some Russians, however, hear this music very differently. To Vladimir Ashkenazy, for instance, the finale of the Sixth is deeply ironic: 'Shostakovich despised the cheap "light entertainment" music, the propaganda marches, etc., that the Party so favoured. He wrote this movement with contempt for such music and everything it stood for'. What, for Ashkenazy, binds the searching *Largo* to its apparently superficial finale is not so much the play of abstract form as a shared sorrow and anger, expressed tragically in the former and satirically in the latter: 'I always see [the *Largo*] as the plight of the *individual* in Soviet society'.[3] This expressive link between the two movements is similarly characterised by the conductor Yuri Temirkanov, for whom the finale of No. 6, far from being trivial, is 'an incredibly tragic piece of music': 'First of all you sense there's a crowd, and when it's a crowd of that size, it's always frightening. Imagine being in Red Square and the people are made to "express joy"; it's like a sort of drug, they're all officially having fun, they're persuading themselves that they're enjoying themselves – and the artist is looking out of the window watching, completely horrified. That's the finale to the Sixth Symphony'.[4]

Since Shostakovich's Sixth has always been regarded as problematical in both Russia and the West, some may see Ashkenazy and Temirkanov as engaged in special pleading –

[2] *Cf.* Dubinsky, *Stormy Applause*, pp. 281 *et seq.*

[3] Edward Seckerson, 'Ashkenazy's Shostakovich', *Gramophone*, Vol. 67, No. 799, December 1989, p. 1116.

[4] *CD Review*, June 1991. Isaak Glikman's account of the Sixth Symphony, like most of his descriptions of Shostakovich's music, is vague and conventional. As he himself points out, Shostakovich rarely uttered an unironic word, a fact which renders his report of the composer's implausibly anodyne estimate of this movement all the more unconvincing: 'The most successful finale I've written. I think even the strictest critics will find it hard to fault' (*Lettres à un ami*, transl. Luba Jurgenson, Albin Michel, Paris, 1994, p. 23). In this connection, it is worth noting Ivan Sollertinsky's verdict on Glikman's description of the movement as the sort of finale Mozart and Rossini might have composed together had they lived in the twentieth century. 'You talk', he said, 'in high-flown phrases like a Roman rhetorician'.

yet such a conclusion is contradicted by the recent testimony of their Russian colleagues, wherein many comparable interpretations of Shostakovich's music are made. The example of the Sixth is, in any case, enough to show that the structural abstraction inherent in the concept of the finale problem often represents little more than subjective disappointment on the part of those used to hearing music as an art of formal design rather than of expression. It is, of course, legitimate, once having addressed it as an embodiment of its composer's thoughts and feelings, to conclude that Shostakovich's Sixth Symphony is nevertheless structurally unconvincing. What must be recognised, though, is that however technically sophisticated the principles by which such a conclusion is reached, they can never take precedence over the principles of *creative purpose* operative behind the form of the music being criticised. Without grasping a composer's intentions, one cannot judge his success in realising them. As the conductor Semyon Bychkov has pointed out, 'the important question for us is: what is it that he is trying to say in his music? Only after that can we look at *how* he is saying that'.[5]

As with criticism, so with composition. Led by the structural bias in music criticism, modern composers have gradually abandoned purpose, moving towards an ideal of 'pure' abstraction in which the score is its own justification and determining principle. Purposelessness of this kind reaches its extreme in the passages of effectively self-generating form to be found in total serialism, minimalism and some computer music – work in which a composer's personal presence, let alone any intention on his or her part, is barely detectable. This aside, a good deal of music composed less rigorously is nonetheless conditioned by the modern confusion of form with function; indeed, the modernist mainstream has so thoroughly cleansed itself of any concept of purpose beyond the notes that the success of a score is nowadays often judged more on the way it looks than on how it sounds (let alone on what it 'means'). Complaining of this recently, the Scottish composer James MacMillan described how a young 'generally tonal' composer friend of

[5] *Cf.* p. 593.

his had been told 'in headmasterly fashion' by a prominent figure in the modernist milieu that the trouble with his music was that 'it doesn't look good on paper'. For MacMillan, this was 'code for something else: music which, on paper, exhibits flashy notational complexities will more easily receive the imprimatur of the new-music establishment than a score where the beauties may lie hidden in tonal clarity and a perceptible pulse'.[6] Reading this another way, one might say that, having no concept of meaning in music, a modernist can conceive of no purpose in writing it other than the arrangement of notational devices in ingenious or pleasing patterns without regard to the way these may strike his listeners' ears, touch their emotions or change their thoughts. Although most recent Russian commentators would argue that no music could be further from this than that of Shostakovich, it is essentially by such principles that his output was, till quite recently, judged and found wanting in modernist circles. Through being misunderstood by it, Shostakovich's work can be said to have exposed the inadequacies of both modernist composition and the structural attitudes to music upon which it is based – and it may be this, rather than any consequent reassessments of his own significance and worth, which proves the longer-term influence on music history as a whole.

There is, in any case, a sense in which the example of Shostakovich challenges the very concept of 'music history' itself – for is it not the segregation of music from the rest of history that makes art as inescapably moral as Shostakovich's seem so perplexing in the modernist context? Yet Western music has harboured 'political' designs since the anti-papal satires of the *Roman de Fauvel*; indeed, such symbolism is ubiquitous in opera, a genre often devoted more to political ends than to its familiar themes of love and death.[7]

[6] *The Independent*, 5 October 1991.

[7] The reciprocal effect of taking the 'music' out of politics has been noted by Robert Conquest with reference to 'political science': 'a supposed discipline which, by concentrating on forms and structures, removes the essence of a given polity from active consideration' (*Tyrants and Typewriters: Communiqués in the Struggle for Truth*, Hutchinson, London, 1989, p. 93).

Structuralism aside, the main reason for the detachment of classical music from its historical context (and the consequent marginalisation of its political content) is that listening to it is largely the province of the comfortably-off. Generally approaching it in a spirit of escapism, such listeners rarely welcome the suggestion that their concepts of the music they enjoy are often ahistorical and hence, in effect, private fantasies bearing only coincidental resemblances to the formative urges of those who composed it. The usual riposte to this charge is the academic argument that music is a self-sufficient form appreciable on its own terms 'as music' and requiring no 'extra-musical' exegesis. Against this, I have argued[8] that music, far from being identical with the score, is instead 'thought and feeling expressed in sound represented as notation', and that consequently there can be no true performance of a score without reconstructing its formative expression from the context of its creation. In this sense, to refer to 'music "as music"' is meaningless. (Indeed, were such a thing possible, to perform it expressively would be illogical since expression, too, is strictly speaking 'extra-musical'.[9])

The defence of self-sufficient form is, in any case, only a smokescreen. Where 'extra-musical' considerations are overt (for instance, in Berlioz's *Symphonie fantastique*) only dogmatic structuralists refuse to recognise them. Indeed, even the supposedly controversial 'extra-musical' content of Shostakovich's music was happily accepted by Western classical audiences in the days when it was assumed to be Communist in tone and purpose. Why then do many members of this same, primarily middle-class, audience resent the new, anti-Communist Shostakovich? Apart from a residue of left-liberal revolutionary romanticism, the answer probably consists in what might politely be called inertia. Accepting the Communist Shostakovich required no effort; it was a 'given' of 'music history', much like the Smithson-smitten

[8] *Cf.* pp. 555–65.

[9] As previously noted, some music approaches this state when its score determines itself through the workings of a self-generating system. Unfortunately, the operator of such a system has to feed some minimally original musical material into it in order to set it in motion, thereby polluting its

Berlioz of the *Symphonie fantastique*. In a rudimentary political sense, it was as comfortable as the myth of 'Uncle Joe' Stalin to the war generations of Britain and America. The Communist Shostakovich, in other words, did not interfere much with the average listener's private response to his music. The anti-Communist Shostakovich, on the other hand, is annoying because he has to be thought about – and this threatens the cherished right to a private response.

Some assert this right on principle, regardless of how inappropriate their responses may be compared with the composer's formative intentions. To do this, they invoke the defence of self-sufficient form; portray Shostakovich as impenetrably inconsistent; even question the notion of objective truth itself. What they are really doing, however, is something all too human and thus easily understandable: they are trying to avoid confronting the misery of other people. For the 'new' Shostakovich is essentially confrontational – in Solomon Volkov's words, a composer who leaves one thinking of others instead of oneself. Worse still, the 'others' in this case are the helpless victims of an immense political catastrophe demanding not merely the reflex of pity but the exercise of a comprehending intellect.

A Shostakovich concert series given in London during 1989 was entitled 'Music from the Flames'. The lack of focus was characteristic. One may, after all, privately emote to one's heart's content over something so portentously vague while safely avoiding being touched by it. Calling it 'Music from the Communist Dystopia', on the other hand, would have made such self-indulgence rather difficult. At the very least it would have forced audiences to listen to familiar music in an unfamiliar way; at worst, it would have acknowledged the presence of political and ethical considerations in a pastime to which many turn in the explicit hope of escaping such things.

This reluctance to be confronted by art, particularly when one has repaired to it for solace in a trying world, is natural enough. Yet the fact remains that Shostakovich wrote from a

---

'purity' with human expression. (A computer would, of course, avoid this – though only if it also designed its own, non-human, composing system.)

world in which very little solace existed, and to deny that this experience forms the expressive heart of most of his work – to invoke instead that debatable entity 'pure' or 'absolute' music – is no longer an honest option. In the words of the inaugural declaration of the Shostakovich Academy, co-founded by the composer's third wife Irina in 1992, 'during the hard and cruel era of Stalinism, he had the courage to express in his music the misery of his people by means of an extraordinary dramatic feeling, and to denounce the hidden forces that were then eliminating millions of human lives'.[10] Likewise for Vladimir Ashkenazy, Shostakovich 'honours everywhere he can the Soviet individuals who stand up against the omnipresent powers – that, basically, is the theme and the context of his work'.[11] Many similar statements from other Russians have appeared in the last few years.[12] There is, in other words, no evading the issue: to approach Shostakovich in any sort of spirit of escapism (including that of imagining him to have been either a Communist 'populist' or an impenetrable enigma) is, in the post-*Testimony* era, simply inadmissible. On the contrary, listening to Shostakovich compels the listener willy-nilly out of the safety of the private response and into spiritual membership of the world community – a world of, among other things, tyranny, terror, hunger, disillusion and despair.

Inevitably, this makes much of the composer's music especially challenging – in a way which renders the largely methodological 'challenges' of most modernists childish by comparison. That is not, however, the sole cause of the suspicion in which the Western classical community holds the anti-Communist Shostakovich; there is also a widespread feeling that to hear Shostakovich as an artist battling against a specific political system is to diminish his claim to universality. As it happens, although they underline the importance of understanding the nature of the forces acting upon the composer during his career, Russian commentators are careful to frame this stipulation within the wider claim that his

[10] *Cf.* p. 294, note 26.

[11] Seckerson, 'Ashkenazy's Shostakovich', p. 1116.

[12] *Cf.* Wilson, *passim.*

work nevertheless holds permanent significance for humanity in general. (Vladimir Ashkenazy: 'In the end it really doesn't matter what society and what injustices we are talking about – music like his communicates a message so powerful, so important and so direct that people everywhere understand it'.[13]) Yet no matter how reassuring this confirmation of the general and permanent significance of Shostakovich's music may be, it should not divert our attention from serious contradictions in the prevailing concept of musical universality itself.

I have argued elsewhere[14] that, as used in modern criticism, 'universality' is an extremely relativistic term indicating music perceived as being sufficiently free of 'extra-musical' content to mean different things to everyone who hears it (as distinct from meaning one thing – or at least a cohesively limited number of things – to all of us). Clearly this paradoxically subjective notion of universality is related to the similarly subjective notion of 'pure' or 'absolute' music. Equally clearly, whether considered as specifically anti-Communist or as a generalised protest against tyranny, Shostakovich's music can never qualify as universal by such a definition – for to do so it would have to rid itself of all political associations, specific or general, and become interpretable in a limitless number of different ways. In effect, those deploring the more specific (symbolic or 'programmatic') approach of much post-Communist writing about Shostakovich's music are not so much objecting to its politicisation as demanding its 'return' to a virgin state of ultimate generality in which it can once again be all things to all men.[15] Applied pejoratively to Shostakovich the anti-Communist – though not, for some reason, to Shostakovich the Communist or Shostakovich the enigmatic introvert – this paradoxical concept of universality, logically pursued, would of course

[13] Seckerson, 'Ashkenazy's Shostakovich', p. 1116.

[14] Pp. 555–65.

[15] It is crucial to grasp that the 'politicisation' and 'political content' of Shostakovich's music discussed, for example, by Semyon Bychkov, Vladimir Ashkenazy and Maxim Shostakovich refers to its representation by Communist, rather than the post-Communist, commentators.

exclude any stable interpretation of the composer beyond the structural analysis of his scores.

Theoretical considerations aside, it remains popular to suppose that treating Shostakovich as an anti-Communist diminishes him; that this diminution is the consequence of interpreting him 'too specifically'; that he becomes more 'universal' if approached in a more generalised way; and that such universality is self-evidently virtuous and therefore to be preferred. This alleged equivalence of 'universal' and 'generalised' is, however, demonstrably foreign to art – most nakedly in the field of literature where the concepts are anything but synonymous. No writer, however bad, believes that describing something in a generalised way confers universality on it; on the contrary, literary universality is achieved by close observation of particular characters in specific situations. All the more significant, then, that several of the Russians to have written or spoken about Shostakovich since 1989 indicate that his scores contain a precision of image, character and situation directly comparable with that of the nineteenth-century literature he loved (and reputedly knew large tracts of by heart).

Examples of such 'literary' images were recently given by Norman Lebrecht in an account of a rehearsal with the Los Angeles Philharmonic conducted by the former East German conductor Kurt Sanderling. A Jew, Sanderling fled the Nazis in 1936, taking refuge with relatives in the USSR where he worked for twenty years as an assistant to Mravinsky at the Leningrad Philharmonic before being summoned to East Germany to found the Berlin Symphony Orchestra. 'Sanderling', insists Lebrecht, 'is prepared to assert that everything Shostakovich related from his own experience in the disputed Solomon Volkov memoir is essentially accurate'. In Lebrecht's view, the conductor's authority in such matters is of the highest kind:

> There is reason to suspect that Sanderling came closer to the tormented composer than the lofty Mravinsky, who directed the prestigious symphonies but let his colleague take over subsequent performances. He refuses to discuss his relationship with Shostakovich or write about it, unwilling to exploit something that was precious and private. Only in the seclusion of his green room and the creative furnace of the rehearsal hall will he recall personal and musical encounters,

> the acute memory of Shostakovich looking over both shoulders to see no one else was around before daring to utter a comment about his own work [. . .]. At one point, Sanderling tells the orchestra that the piccolo solo in the second movement of Shostakovich's Eighth Symphony represents a young army officer who has been given an unexpected week-end pass and goes whistling away down the road. A bassoon solo is a puffed-up party *apparatchik* swaggering off on his first trip abroad [. . .].[16]

In a similar deposition, made in an interview with Elizabeth Wilson in 1989, the former Leningrad Philharmonic violinist Yakov Milkis recalls Mravinsky himself scolding his players for poor *tremolo* in the slow movement of the Fifth Symphony: 'You haven't got the necessary intensity. Have you forgotten what this music is about and when it was born?' Moreover, in a certain passage in the finale of the Ninth Symphony, Mravinsky (claims Milkis) demanded 'the sound of the trampling of steel-shod boots'.[17]

From these and other examples, it is clear that Shostakovich, like the authors he revered, often wrote with a vivid specificity which can fairly be described as theatrical. This in itself serves to refute the notion that treating him 'too specifically' diminishes his claim to universality, for to ignore it is to miss a crucial element in his expression, rendering lofty Western claims about his universal significance somewhat premature. The missing element in question is the composer's satirical streak, arguably coequal with his tragic gift and, by virtue of its neglect, the key to much of the misunderstanding his music has so far met outside Russia and eastern Europe. Not that Shostakovich's specificity is exclusively satirical, his tragic expression frequently being just as vivid (for example, the 'weeping child' high-register cello

[16] *Classical Music*, 18 May 1991, p. 15. Interviewed by Hans Bitterlich for the sleevenote of his 1992 recording of Shostakovich's Eighth (Berlin Classics BC 2064-2), Sanderling dismisses the official Soviet view of the work (a meditation on 'the horrors of war' mitigated by 'the bright vision of a world of peace') as 'sheer nonsense': 'The theme was not the horrors of war, but the horrors of life, the life of an intellectual of his day'. Vladimir Ashkenazy shares this concept.

[17] Wilson, p. 315. Milkis adds: 'We knew that he wasn't referring to ordinary soldiers, but to the KGB forces'.

solos at the start of the Second Piano Trio and in the slow movements of the First Cello Concerto and Fifteenth Symphony). Yet there can be no doubt that the chief casualty of Western concentration on his structural design – and consequent neglect of his theatrical precision of utterance – has been the composer's rarely silent current of satire.

Audible in the solo voices and chamber groupings within his orchestra, Shostakovich's ironic and often grotesque theatricality is essentially Mahlerian, it being almost certainly this aspect of Mahler's genius which he found most compelling. There again, it is unlikely that he would have felt this affinity had not the trait been part of his own make-up, as is evident from an account by the novelist Konstantin Fedin of one of Shostakovich's boyhood recitals: 'He played his own works, clearly influenced by new music: unexpected pages which make one interpret the sounds like a theatrical performance wherein everything becomes tangible and obvious – laughter as much as tears'. (Here, it is worth noting, is a description not only of a precocious theatrical talent but of the double-aspected satiric-tragic approach characteristic of the composer's mature music.) That this theatricality was not merely a temperamental reflex but a conscious part of Shostakovich's expressive repertoire is deducible both from his stage-works and from the fundamentally dramaturgical design of orchestral pieces like the Eleventh Symphony. Writing of the Eleventh,[18] Lev Lebedinsky notes that the various revolutionary songs deployed throughout the Symphony develop 'as though representing the main protagonists in a drama [. . .] a *dramatic* development of extremely concrete vividness'.[19]

The quasi-operatic Mahlerian aspect of Shostakovich's theatricality – distinguished by its use of instruments, often beyond their natural registers, to mimic voices or impersonate characters – interacts throughout his music with a

[18] 'Letters', *Novy Mir*, 1990, No. 3.

[19] Solomon Volkov once told the Finnish musicologist and critic Seppo Heikinheimo that the pianist mentioned in *Testimony* as having been helped by Shostakovich to play more personally was probably Emil Gilels – and that the composer's help consisted of advising Gilels to think of the various themes and voices in a piece as 'different characters in a play' (letter from Heikinheimo to the author dated 29 December 1991).

Beethovenian use of motives, mostly of a rhythmic kind and usually very brief. However, as with the composer's Mahlerian voices and impersonations, his Beethovenian motives are by no means neutrally structural, being instead essentially theatrical and symbolic – an idiom characterised by Lebedinsky as 'programmes of dramatically conflicting ideas'. That is to say: political, moral and philosophical principles fight it out in Shostakovich's music much as they do in Mahler and Nielsen (and, arguably, in Beethoven). Yet there is a crucial difference in Shostakovich's case, for here the governing power, which so often imposes a *deus ex machina* 'triumphant' solution upon unanswered questions, is not the composer himself but rather the dictatorship (personified by Stalin) under which he was condemned to live.[20] The shadowy theatre in which the composer's mimicked voices and motivic principles interact owes its symbolic force as much to the fearful secrecy of its operations as to conventional notions of tension and development. Indeed, it is arguably this secrecy, more than any purely formal interest in extreme concentration, which caused Shostakovich's symbolic language to develop to such a pitch of refinement and intensity during the course of his fifty-year career. Alexander Ivashkin, artistic director of the Bolshoi Soloists' Ensemble from 1978 to 1991 and author of the first English-language biography of Alfred Schnittke,[21] explains:

> For many years we weren't allowed to speak or show what we thought. Consequently [. . .] when something came into the open, part of it stayed hidden, like an iceberg with only a small part above water. So, symbolism became very characteristic of Russian music – symbolism of the simplest kind. An

[20] Under Stalinism, every composer in the USSR felt obliged (or sometimes was forced) to produce such 'triumphant' conclusions. Prokofiev's Seventh Symphony offers one notable example, the composer having been obliged by official pressure to alter its originally downbeat ending. The finale of Myaskovsky's 27th, while composed as is, incorporates its own inbuilt *deus ex machina* coda-solution. Gavriil Popov's Sixth devotes its last ten minutes to a satirical eruption of megalomanic triumphalism outdoing the 'bombastic' conclusions of Shostakovich's Fifth, Seventh and Twelfth, and approaching the sustained *fffff* climax of the finale of Shostakovich's Fourth.

[21] *Alfred Schnittke*, Phaidon, London, 1996.

> interval, sound or rhythm became a symbol which the listener could identify. Music became the bridge to a thought or philosophical concept rather than an end in itself. It was never a mere sound construction.[22]

Ivashkin here gives an apt description of the motivic working discernible in most of Shostakovich's scores – yet his description points to an intent on the composer's part so far from the structural abstraction assumed of him by modern Western musicologists as to be diametrically opposed to it.[23] Moreover, that intent is detectable only through the process of locating his music in its very particular context – a process which, in practice, conclusively demonstrates the fallacy of imagining that specificity diminishes and de-universalises Shostakovich. To ignore that context as irrelevant to his universality is to preclude anything but a vague and diluted experience of his creative expression. One might as well argue that to reduce a work of literature to its structure,

[22] From Gerard McBurney's and Barrie Gavin's 'Think Today, Speak Tomorrow', BBC2, 27 May 1990.

[23] In *Alfred Schnittke* Ivashkin writes: 'Shostakovich gave unique expression to the thoughts and feelings of those generations of Russian people whose fate it was to live under the yoke of totalitarian power' (p. 217) Ivashkin adds (p. 61):

> Two events which made the greatest of impressions on Schnittke were the first performances of Shostakovich's Tenth Symphony in 1953 and of his First Violin Concerto in 1955. He remembers the official discussion after the Tenth Symphony, when everybody (except the composer Andrey Volkonsky, a student at that time) criticized Shostakovich. The Violin Concerto made a great impact on Schnittke's music. He has admitted that all his own violin concertos have been written under its influence. There is the same feeling of drama, the same sharp, even exaggerated, contrasts between the movements, and the same freedom and space for the cadenza, a monologue of the soloist 'hero'. For many years the concerto concept, inherited from Shostakovich, was most important in Schnittke's music. His numerous concertos and concerti grossi represent symbolically the typical Schnittkean idea of conflict between the individual (the soloist) and the collective (the orchestra). This type of drama is hidden in Shostakovich's music, which in many respects reflects the drama of Soviet life under the harsh political pressure of the Soviet regime. In Schnittke's music, too, there is always something extra-musical which needs to be deciphered, explained or resolved. Although his music is much more varied and wider in scope, in terms of its historical and multi-

concepts and theoretical significance is to render its characters, dialogue and circumstantial detail superfluous – whereas the latter are precisely what give the former life and meaning, differentiating art from abstract philosophy.

To grasp how such reductive schematicism prejudices the listener's chances of understanding Shostakovich's intentions, we need only consider the 'puffed-up party apparatchik' swaggering off on his diplomatic trip in Kurt Sanderling's disclosure about the Eighth Symphony. Clearly, a conductor working from the presumption that this score is a generalised lament over war and brutality is unlikely to phrase such a passage with much insight, leaving it to pass meaninglessly while players and audience drum their fingers waiting for the next obviously sad or brutal bit to turn up. Such a method accounts for the tragedy but leaves the satire unvoiced, smoothing the music into pseudo-universal generalisation. Yet this specificity, far from detracting from the composer's universality, is actually the very basis of it – as it is for Shakespeare and Dostoyevsky and every opera ever staged. It

---

> cultural orientation, it still refers, more or less, to the same type of direct relationship between art and reality, between the individual's mental organization, personal spirituality, and social entropy. Shostakovich, under the burden of Stalin's dictatorship, was much more cautious, preferring to speak indirectly and symbolically. Schnittke's generation grew up in a different situation and wanted to speak more openly and more directly – especially in the late 1950s and early 60s, the time of Khrushchev's 'thaw' – but it was still Shostakovich who made that kind of musical expression feasible [. . .]. The concerto is Schnittke's favourite type of composition not only because he had been constantly asked to write concertos for his friends, famous Russian soloists, but because the musical language of all his concertos is indissolubly connected with the personalized and profoundly individual statement of the soloist, who stands in opposition to a featureless and satanic social situation. This undoubtedly reflects the highly paradoxical role of personality and its connections with the social situation in the era of the Communist dictatorship. It is no secret that it was the personal, the individual, the unique, which formed the core of the extremely intensive development of Russian culture under the oppression of Communist ideology.

It is worth adding that this is equally true of Shostakovich's concertos, as well as of Prokofiev's 'Soviet' concertos and of the concertos of (for example) Myaskovsky, Vainberg and Boris Chaikovsky. Indeed there is no

goes without saying that Shostakovich's Eighth Symphony is ultimately for all times and all people – but this judgment should be achieved, not presumed. To begin from such a pious assumption is virtually to guarantee vague and pompous results.

The focus of context is vital in illuminating Shostakovich's satire. So awful was the socio-cultural background to much of his art that omitting irony and humour from his outlook would have rendered his work nearly as intolerable as the conditions determining it. In fact, his music is as full of derision as of compassion, and appreciating the former without reference to context is almost impossible. As for the sheer courage embodied in Shostakovich's satirical initiative, that will necessarily remain obscure to anyone unfamiliar with what he and his fellow artists in the USSR were up against during Stalin's dictatorship. Handicapped in just this way, many Western critics continue to judge the composer by wholly inappropriate ethical standards, travestying his achievements by grossly underestimating his heroism in accomplishing them. Between the end of the Cultural Revolution in 1932 and Stalin's death in 1953 he was the only artist of any kind in the USSR consistently doing truthful and consequently controversial work – hence his starring role in the 'formalist' crackdowns of 1936 and 1948. Far from avoiding moral responsibility, Shostakovich was nearly always, whether through choice or circumstance, alone in the front line against Socialist Realism (and thus against the Communist system itself). Seen in context, his Fifth Symphony is by far the most courageous gesture made by a Russian artist under Stalin. Indeed, apart from the writings of Alexander Solzhenitsyn – committed to paper long after the dictator had gone, but nonetheless heroic for that – Shostakovich's music was consistently the most subversively liberal influence in Russian life during the Soviet era. Solzhenitsyn aside, no writer (and certainly no painter, film-maker or theatre director) can compare with him in this. Anna Akhmatova's observation that, during the middle years

---

obvious difference in directness here between Shostakovich and Schnittke, Shostakovich being every bit as explicit in using the concerto in this way.

of this century, Russian culture existed 'under the sign of Shostakovich' is no exaggeration.[24]

There will, of course, be those who see this over-arching role in twentieth-century Russian history as irrelevant, or even as an obstacle, to the composer's claim to universality. Implicit in such a judgment is the sheltered Western belief that liberal democracy, far from a local and recent phenomenon, is the eternal condition of civilised society. In truth, the twentieth century, in macro-historical terms, has chiefly been the story of the rise and fall of Communism – with Fascism as an off-shoot and reaction to it – while, far from central, Western democracy is an historical anomaly peripheral to the ancient lineage of despotism in the majority of the world. The tradition of masked resistance to tyranny – which Solomon Volkov identifies as *yurodstvo* and Czesław Miłosz calls *ketman* – has existed in Asia from the earliest times.[25] Objectively speaking, autocracy is the historical mainstream, and democracy a late and limited experiment which, unless defended and disseminated, may not long outlast this century. In the widest perspective, then, Shostakovich has a serious claim to be considered the most universal composer in history.

If the tragic component of Shostakovich's style is unappreciable without some grasp of the scale of the internal mortality rate of Soviet Communism,[26] his satirical impulse depends similarly on understanding the endemic falsehood, cynicism and corruption of the Soviet system (attributes

[24] Quoted in *The New Shostakovich*, p. 274.

[25] An Iranian critic of my acquaintance prefers the Arabic word *tashbih*, seeing the phenomenon as inseparable from that of oriental despotism, a political form founded on autocratic control of irrigation systems: 'This despotism [he writes, in a letter to the author] exists in the "spirit" of nations like Russia, China and Iran, irrespective of historical period, viz., Stalin, Khomeini, or the political happenings in China in 1989. The reaction of artists has always been connected with *tashbih* and is still usual in contemporary Iranian poetry'.

[26] Recent estimates range from 'at least' 40 million (several authorities quoted by Hedrick Smith in *The New Russians*, Hutchinson, London, 1990), to 38–50 million (Igor Bestuzhevlada in the weekly *Nedelya*, April 1988) and 60 million (Vitaly Vitaliev of *Ogonyok*, quoted in *The Guardian*, 5 June 1990, and Gennady Rozhdestvensky, quoted by Jonathan Swain in 'A Golden Age', *Gramophone*, Vol. 71, No. 852, May 1994, p. 20).

satirised by Russia's 'individualist' artists of the '20s and documented from as early as the '30s by such independent-minded Western observers as Max Eastman, Eugene Lyons, Malcolm Muggeridge, André Gide, Arthur Koestler and George Orwell). It is no doubt easier, now that it has been overthrown, to accept that Marxism-Leninism was an evil farce, but it is nonetheless hard, without a minimum of background reading, to appreciate the extent to which, notwithstanding its prominent Western apologists, it deserved the bitter rejection meted out to it by the citizens of Russia and Eastern Europe during 1989–91. The blistering condemnations of Communism expressed by most of the recent Russian commentators on Shostakovich may surprise those whose view of him was formed by books like Christopher Norris's *Shostakovich: The Man and His Music* (1982) or programmes like *Shostakovich: Propagandist!* on BBC Radio 3.[27] Unfortunately, there is no 'short course' of enlightenment in this subject – though any collection of modern Russian jokes will provide a working outline. Suffice it here to consider an aphorism coined by the dissidents of Ceaucescu's Romania: 'It is impossible to be honest, intelligent and a Communist – one can be any two of these, but not all three'. The contempt readable between these bare lines is as sure a key to Shostakovich's satire as their deadly implication of moral compromise and spiritual paralysis.

The truth is that interpreting the composer's music becomes vastly simplified once context is allowed to guide our responses. Ridding our ears of inappropriate expectations is half the battle. Once we have given up dutifully persuading ourselves to hear bombs falling in the fourth movement of his Eighth Quartet, we stand a chance of recognising that the figure in question actually represents a fist pounding peremptorily on a door in the middle of the night. Likewise, by ignoring the discredited 'Nazi invasion' connotation of the march in the first movement of the Seventh Symphony, it becomes possible to appreciate the composer's extraordinary variety of satirical expression (in

[27] Broadcast between 12 and 16 February 1990 in the series 'Composer of the Week', these programmes took the form of playing Shostakovich's 'official' works without sceptical comment, as if he had intended them to be taken seriously.

particular his gift for mimicry). More generally, insights like these should help to expose the inadequacies of purely structural criticism – showing, for example, that whereas the 'standard' articles in English on the Fourth Symphony tell us almost nothing important about that controversial work, a film like Andrzej Fidyk's documentary on the personality-cult of Kim Il Sung, *The Parade*, tells us virtually everything.

In the future, writing about Shostakovich – and, for that matter, any other 'Soviet' composer – will clearly be an intensively cross-referential pursuit. Everything composed between 1917 and 1991 will have to be treated as a potential repository of highly specific meanings, and pushing the boundaries of the conceivable in this way is certain to produce angry disputes about 'over-interpretation'. Some of these objections will, of course, be sensible and just – yet it is far too soon, particularly for Western musicology in its present state of abstract ahistoricism, to prescribe limits to such contextual analysis.

One precept which will have to be accepted early in this endeavour is that Soviet sources are not only unreliable but often deliberately misleading about the artists they purport to represent.[28] Less obvious but equally true is that comparable caution should be exercised in approaching post-Communist Russian writing on the same subjects. In Shostakovich's case, some of the disagreements about him within this milieu stem from not entirely honourable hidden agendas. There is no reason to distrust any of the contributions from Russia in *Shostakovich Reconsidered*, but future researchers should remember that there is money in art and that motives associated with this fact may operate in disguise outside the publishing house and courtroom.[29]

[28] A striking instance of this is provided by Myaskovsky's Twelfth Symphony, the 'Collective Farm', described by his Soviet biographer as a harmonious model of socially optimistic art, but which, issued on compact disc in 1992 (Marco Polo 8.223302), proved to be as grimly disaffected as its companion-piece, the Eleventh.

[29] For example, the disputed authorship of *Rayok* involves an issue of royalties. The late Lev Lebedinsky's claim to have written part of the libretto placed him in dispute with the Shostakovich estate (i.e., the composer's third wife Irina); hence the suspicion that Yury Levitin, in

Another rule of thumb for future Shostakovich interpreters should be that, unless specifically indicated, the autobiographical reflex (assuming that the artist is talking about himself) does not apply in his case; that, on the contrary, he usually refers to the world around him, often in a spirit of impersonation. The point is made in 'To A Critic', first of the five *Satires* on poems by Sasha Chyorny:

> When the poet, describing a belle,
> Begins 'As I walked down the street,
> My corset was giving me hell',
> One shouldn't, quite obviously, treat
> This statement the way it appeared,
> Thinking poet and lady the same.
> Allow me, tactfully, to explain:
> The bard is a man. With a beard.

Regular applications of this principle in discussing Shostakovich's output would clearly be advisable, but perhaps particularly so where the products of his 'late' period are concerned. It is all too easy to read the dominant motifs of death and decay in this music as purely personal and without significance beyond the composer's private life. Yet there are good reasons to believe that these apparently self-absorbed expressions are as much concerned with the failing spirit of Russian culture as with the dwindling powers of their author. As his son Maxim has observed: 'Father wasn't conveying his personal health [in the works of the "late" period] but the health of an era, of the times'.[30]

---

attempting to discredit Lebedinsky (*Pravda*, 11 November 1990), was acting on Irina's behalf. Nor should pure mischief be overlooked. For instance, the claims by the late Michael Goldstein (Mikhail Gol'dshtein) of a previously unsuspected close relationship between Shostakovich and Zamyatin (in Leonid Heller, *Autour de Zamiatine*, L'Âge d'homme, Lausanne, 1989) are almost certainly baseless. (*Cf.* Ian MacDonald, 'Shostakovich and Zamyatin: A Seminal Influence?', *DSCH*, No. xxi, Summer 1992, pp. 2–6, and 'Shostakovich, Zamyatin, Goldstein and *The Bolt*: A Hoax Unmasked' on the website *Music Under Soviet Rule*: http://www.siue.edu/~aho/musov/zamyatin/zamyatin.html.)

[30] Maxim Shostakovich and Solomon Volkov, 'On "Late" Shostakovich – A Conversation' (included as programme notes to Maxim's performance of Shostakovich's Fourteenth Symphony with the New York Chamber Symphony, 17 January 1988, then reprinted in *DSCH*, No. xiii, August 1989, pp. 35–38. –EDS).

Inevitably, musicology will soon reclaim Shostakovich for formal analysis in hugely intensified detail – but it will be a different kind of musicology, steeped in the atmosphere of the composer's times, and thus able to match his formative purpose with a genuine analytical purposiveness of its own. The studies written from this ethos will, one hopes, not only render obsolete all existing commentaries on Shostakovich but challenge the musical world in general to abandon the empty structuralism – the separation of musical fact from human value, of expressive technique from creative intention – which has so reduced the scope of the art in recent decades.

Variation IV

THE LEGEND OF THE EIGHTH QUARTET

Ian MacDonald

It was once a standard component of the Shostakovich-as-Communist myth that his Eighth Quartet was a protest against war and (Nazi) fascism provoked by its composer's shock at seeing the ruins of Dresden in July 1960. Although still peddled in sleeve-notes, this idea seems increasingly dubious. Writing in 1989, I suggested that the Quartet was indeed a piece of protest music, but a protest instead against the Communist Party into which Shostakovich was then in the process of being forcibly enrolled.[1] This guess was confirmed in 1990 by the composer's colleague Lev Lebedinsky.[2] The Eighth Quartet, wrote Lebedinsky, was meant as a last testament, following which Shostakovich had intended to kill himself rather than face the shame of being misrepresented to the world as a Communist. Only the urgings of his friends dissuaded him from suicide.[3]

Clearly, this new explanation of the Eighth Quartet makes better sense than the old one, accounting, as the latter did not, for the pointedly autobiographical content of the work. As for its subtitle, this, too, conceals another meaning. For years before the slogans and placards against 'fascism' (i.e.,

[1] *The New Shostakovich*, pp. 221–24.

[2] 'Letters', *Novy Mir* (*New World*), 1990, No. 3. (Also *cf.* pp. 476–77. –EDS.)

[3] Also *cf.* Wilson, pp. 332–41.

Communism) appeared during the coup of August 1991, Soviet Communists had been called fascists by their dissident opponents. Following the 'bodyguard of lies' method employed by him to protect the hidden agenda of several earlier works, Shostakovich seems to have invoked the standard post-War East-European formula of a 'Memorial to the Victims of Fascism' to cover himself against Soviet reprisals whilst indicating his true intentions to his fellow dissidents. Possibly this idea occurred to him while he was in Dresden in July 1960, perhaps after visiting such a memorial. But there is no need to believe that the Quartet was composed (as distinct from being merely written down) in those legendary three days. If the new explanation of the genesis of the work is correct, Shostakovich must have been thinking about it for some time – indeed, if his usual practice is anything to go by, he had almost certainly composed most of it in his head before arriving in Dresden.

If this is true, why did he choose that time and place in which to write it down? It is conceivable that this much of the old legend of the Eighth Quartet is authentic: that though the music itself had already been composed, it was the sight of Dresden in ruins that galvanised Shostakovich into committing it to paper. On the other hand, there is the more prosaic possibility that staying at the ministerial guest-house at Göhrisch merely offered the composer a convenient break in which to do some writing and that the sight of Dresden played no part either in the conception of the music or in spurring it to be set down. Evidence to support this alternative conclusion is provided by an article in *Sachsische Neueste Nachrichten*[4] in which the newspaper's music critic, Hermann Werner Finke, asserts that Shostakovich first visited Dresden while in East Germany for the Bach Festival held at Leipzig during the week of 23–29 July 1950. During this stay in the city, according to Finke, Shostakovich amongst other things attended a concert by the Oborin-Oistrakh-Knushevitsky trio at Dresden's Great Hall and visited the Academy of Music and Theatre on Mendelssohn Avenue. As to how much of the city he saw, the itinerary sketched by Finke implies at least a day's activity – and since

[4] 13 August 1975.

the round trip from Leipzig to Dresden is 150 miles (suggesting that the composer must have stayed in Dresden overnight), the likelihood that Shostakovich's East German hosts could have spirited him in and out of the city without letting him see the state it was in (or, indeed, that they had some motive for doing so) seems small.

Having in all probability seen the full extent of the ruination of Dresden in 1950, it seems unlikely that Shostakovich would have found a similar experience in 1960 traumatic in itself, let alone the shocking stimulus to creation crucial to the old legend of the Eighth Quartet. What may actually have happened is that Dresden in 1960 reminded Shostakovich of Dresden in 1950 – and hence of himself in 1950, arguably the loneliest, most politically repressed period in his life. Since such an explanation accords convincingly with the autobiographical and anti-Communist nature of the quartet, I would suggest that it is true.[5]

[5] On 7 September 1960, a week before the ratification of Shostakovich's candidate membership of the Communist Party, an article 'by' him appeared in *Pravda* welcoming Suslov's redefinition of the theory of Socialist Realism and condemning twelve-tone music as formalist. Couched in the usual faceless officialese, the piece included a curious digression about the theatre-director Konstantin Stanislavsky (1863–1938) who, in old age, allegedly displayed his customary unquenchable thirst for knowledge by teaching himself 'the philosophy of dialectical materialism' and 'the laws governing the development of society'. Like Gorky *vis à vis* prose and Mayakovsky *vis à vis* verse, Stanislavsky was chosen by Stalin during the '30s to be a figurehead of Soviet orthodoxy in the theatre, by whom all other theatrical practitioners might be judged (and, where necessary, condemned). In order to qualify for this role – what Mikhail Heller (*Cogs*, p. 96) describes as a 'mini-leader' – it was necessary that Stanislavsky be presented as definitively orthodox; hence the edifying fiction that he devoted his final years to studying Marxism-Leninism. Evidently this loaded reference was included in 'Shostakovich's article' in order (1) to project him as an equivalent official 'mini-leader' in music, and (2) to justify his peculiar sudden interest in the Communist Party after having had nothing to do with it during his previous 54 years – 'just like Stanislavsky'! (A similar official legend was created around the aging Myaskovsky during the late '40s.)

THE SEVENTH SYMPHONY
Truth and Legend[1]

Semyon Bychkov

Semyon Bychkov was interviewed by Henrietta Cowling, Assistant Producer, BBC Music and Arts, in July 1991 for a short documentary feature broadcast during a live transmission from the Proms of Shostakovich's Seventh Symphony.

What is your reaction to the theories of Volkov and Lebedinsky that Shostakovich began composing the Seventh Symphony before the war broke out, and that the theme in the first movement describes Stalin rather than Hitler?

I think it is totally convincing as an explanation. First of all, we know that, physically, Shostakovich composed the first movement in one month and this took place very soon after the war had started. And knowing also that he would first compose the music in his mind before he put down anything on paper, then it's no wonder he would make a statement like that. Also, it will certainly answer many other questions about the significance of the piece and the meaning of it, and whether the fact that the march is Hitler's theme, as it has been called many times, or if it's Stalin's theme, or if it's an 'evil' theme. But the question of the date of the composition is only important so far as it allows a listener to get rid of the [Communist] politicisation of the piece that took place early on when it was only beginning to be performed. Throughout the years, the legend has grown and the piece has been covered with various explanations and theories, and after that we were stuck with the music alone and concerned ourselves with various ideological and political statements that suit various people.

[1] A version of this piece appeared in *DSCH Journal*, No. 5, Summer 1996, pp. 47–51.

Do you feel that propaganda has got in the way of this symphony?

Yes, I think that is the case with the Seventh Symphony, as it is the case with a lot of music of Shostakovich. You see, first of all you are dealing with a composer who lived in a very particular society, a very particular time of the life of his country, which is very different to the way of life and sense of values of the Western world. So one needs a lot of explanation. And secondly, a lot of statements about his music have been attributed to him which, taken at face value, would lead towards misunderstanding and [Communist] politicisation of his music. The Seventh Symphony is a typical example.

Do you feel there is a problem in the way that the West appreciates his music?

I think that if one thinks of the way the public responds to the music of Shostakovich in Western Europe and in America, you would see how clear people are about his music. They respond to it for what it gives them. They are not trying to politicise his music. They feel that this is a work of art that touches them very profoundly, and after hearing it they're able to imagine the music being written in the kind of country they have read or heard about. So today, in a way, it's an example of a work of art produced in a particular place and a particular time. I think what hurts the image of this music is the intellectualising of the so-called experts that has gone on for decades and that takes either the words of Shostakovich at their face value or tries to interpret the music by forgetting its meaning. I mean that these experts try to interpret this music without having known the life of those whose life is addressed and expressed in this music. You see, in a way Shostakovich is a spokesman for his people and for their life. He is also a historian. He observes what happens and he records it in musical sounds. He's not a politician and his great gift was being able to associate himself with the pain and with the suffering of millions of people who have either perished or were persecuted physically, emotionally, spiritually, in many different ways. And he's someone who has the talent not only to identify with that suffering but also to be able to express it in his chosen field, which happens to be music.

Can you tell us more about how important his music was for his people and how he was able to identify with them?

Well, the interesting thing is that all these misunderstandings about his music among music writers in the West never existed in the Soviet Union. His music was always understood by his public there, precisely what it was trying to tell them, because they all spoke the same language. In a way, one could compare his music to street music because it is so tied to life. And one could almost put the words behind the music and know exactly what it is trying to say. For example, they used to talk in that country about creating *Homo Sovieticus* – that's a famous expression. They made it known at the outset of the Soviet Union after the revolution of 1917 that they wanted to create 'a new type of man'. And they certainly have succeeded in many ways. The only thing they couldn't succeed in is completely destroying human nature. So the Russian language itself had suffered tremendously, as well as the people who had spoken it. It became full of various slogans and simplifications. So the music of Shostakovich is very clear to the [Russian] public because, as one would use a slogan in a very serious way and everyone will understand that that person doesn't believe one word of what he is saying, in the same way the public would respond to the sounds of Shostakovich's music knowing full well what he's really trying to say.

Going back to the ideas put forward in Testimony, *do you feel that it's possible to draw a parallel with Akhmatova's* Requiem, *which she wrote in a similar context and at a similar time? Do you think, in other words, that the Seventh Symphony is a work in which he expressed his grief for his friends who had been killed under Stalin?*

One can see a parallel in the idea of Akhmatova writing her *Requiem* to the victims of inhumanity, of Stalin's regime, and Shostakovich writing his requiems. According to *Testimony*, he said that his requiems were in the Seventh and Eighth Symphonies, but in hindsight we can see that in fact he wrote more than one requiem. One can think of the Fifth Symphony. Its slow movement is also a requiem. One can think of the Fourteenth Symphony. In a sense, most of his music is a requiem, only of course it doesn't necessarily mean that the mood is always mournful. But there is this theme that goes throughout the great tradition of art in Russia, which goes back centuries: the tradition of compassion, of sympathy for suffering – the tradition of remembrance of suffering and of those who suffered. Shostakovich is in direct line of that tradition. There are the famous words of Dostoyevsky, who said something to the effect of 'How can I ever feel totally happy knowing that there is still a suffering soul in this world?' And I feel Shostakovich identified with that as much as Dostoyevsky, as Akhmatova. The way he expressed it was through music and I think that brings us to another important aspect of looking at his music. Sometimes people ask what it is he wrote that is really new. What kind of new techniques, in which way did he advance the art of music? I think the question in itself is a very empty one, because the Slavic culture, Russian culture in particular, be it music or literature or any other form of art, has rarely concerned itself with the technique of expression. It always emphasised the inner life of the work of art. The inner process, the spiritual, the spirituality of art. Rather than art for its own sake. So for Shostakovich, for example, the play of sounds did not interest him. It did not interest him to create in new ways *per se*. He found them in order to satisfy what he was trying to say in music. He always regarded the rules of composition as simply the means. And in that sense he had total mastery of craft. His music is so well crafted. He practically never miscalculates and I can say that as a performer. We know that he was a very meticulous man and really prided himself on craftsmanship. But in the end the important question to us is: what is it that he is trying to say in his music? Only after that can we look at *how* he is saying that.

Do you think it's possible to link the Seventh Symphony with his Eighth Quartet where he also uses fascism as a mask for him to express all sorts of other things that were burning in his inner being?

But, you see, all of his music is totally connected. One can make a parallel with the Eighth Quartet. One can make a parallel with the Eleventh Symphony. One can make a parallel with the Eighth Symphony. One can go back and make a parallel with the Fifth Symphony. With a very few exceptions – where he simply had to write music to satisfy the government so that they would leave him alone and allow him to survive physically in those conditions – his entire output is about the same theme. It's about remembrance. It's about human suffering. It's about the genocide of a nation, of which he was one of the victims and which he shared with his people. So in that sense the Seventh Symphony corresponds to the quartets and it corresponds to most of the other things that he wrote.

What would you say is the universal significance of the Seventh Symphony?

You know in this century, like in every other century, we have known evil. We have known Hitler, we have known Stalin, we have known Lenin, we have known people like this that brought an unbelievable destruction and suffering to humanity – usually under the guise of great ideals, the guise of humanity and humanism. And so, in that sense, I think the Seventh Symphony has universal significance in two ways. It has significance as a work of art that can stand on its own. Because if you don't know anything, if you just listen to that music and don't know history or when it was written or any of the explanations of the piece, you still cannot fail to hear that this music talks. And if you are open enough, if you're really trying to hear what the music says, you will hear it vividly. He also wrote a lot of music for films and sometimes people make derogatory remarks to the effect that his music is film music. Well, there are some great films, there is nothing wrong with that. And, yes, this music contains the kind of sounds that one can visualise. One can see them. And this music talks. For example, in the first movement of the Seventh Symphony when the famous, infamous march starts, in one of the variations there is a theme that's played by an oboe and then, just after the oboe has played, the bassoon starts it and repeats everything that the oboe has just said. Now imagine two human beings, one in a position of absolute power and the other one who is the humble servant whose life can be taken at any whim of the master. And whatever master says, the servant will parrot. That is the way in which this music talks – and that is its significance as a pure work of art. And, in another sense, it's important to us in the same way as the works of great writers are important to us. We cannot live without Shakespeare. We cannot live without the great writers of the twentieth century. And what do they concern themselves with? The human condition. So Shostakovich, too, concerns himself with the human condition.

Do you feel that the war was an opportunity for Shostakovich, having been persecuted under the Terror in the thirties, to express himself in a freer way?

I think that the war was a mechanism which allowed people to release what was stored inside them over the years prior to it. Then the government and the people were too busy fighting a common enemy to think about ideology. They just stopped thinking about all that. They just had to survive. And I'm convinced that, as for many people, it was for Shostakovich a chance to open up and express what was stored there for such a long time. And of course there's always a question: how does one survive what he went through? How did people manage to survive and still preserve their integrity? Because, you see, they didn't have many choices. Either they were persecuted and killed or imprisoned without any reason, or they would have to be very careful – which, in fact, they were, so as not to create the slightest pretext for being suspected, arrested and terrorised. Shostakovich himself was viciously attacked in the press in 1936 and one can imagine what kind of situation he was in, not knowing whether he would live to see another day. And the war itself was felt even before it started. Everywhere in Europe, people who were tuned-in to what was happening felt that war was coming and I don't think someone like Shostakovich – a man of great intellect and a very astute person of tremendous intelligence – was surprised when the war started. And I think that prompted the release of the thoughts and emotions that had been in him for years prior to that.

What do you say to those who have not been able to see the Seventh Symphony as a great work of art?

I suppose I'm the wrong person to answer this question because I'm committed to the entire music of Shostakovich.

It is deeply important to me. Obviously, neither I nor anyone else can force another person to respond to a piece of music, to like it, to appreciate it. Everyone has simply to make a choice and it cannot be forced, cannot usually even be persuaded. It's something one either feels or one doesn't. To me, such questions simply don't exist, because to me Shostakovich is one of those composers that will stay for as long as human beings need to have music. In the same way Beethoven stays, in the same way Mozart stays, and Brahms and Mahler and all the other great composers. So I don't need to be persuaded that Shostakovich's Seventh Symphony is a great work of art. I take his entire creative output and there are some pieces to which I would feel especially attached to. There may be others that take me a longer time to have the same kind of affinity for. But it usually comes. It just takes time because he's a little bit forbidding sometimes. But as long as you realise that he says what he says with great wit, with great sarcasm, and with total honesty, and often tenderness, then you begin to relate to it. To me personally, the Seventh Symphony is a great masterpiece and I think the way the public responds to it when they hear it is the true judge. Who is there to play God, to say this is good and this is not so good, it's a little bit weak? No one can or should be in a position to do that. The fact that the piece is played and heard means that there are musicians who believe in it and who feel it must be expressed and there are audiences that share the same commitment and the same curiosity and the same willingness to open themselves to what the piece is trying to say.

DMITRY SHOSTAKOVICH: THE COMPOSER AS JEW[1]

Timothy L. Jackson

with an Appendix by Klaus Meyer

For Solomon Volkov

er pfeift seine Juden hervor
läßt schaufeln ein Grab in der Erde
er befiehlt uns spielt auf nun zum Tanz . . .
Er ruft spielt süßer den Tod
der Tod ist ein Meister aus Deutschland
er ruft streicht dunkler die Geigen
dann steigt ihr als Rauch in die Luft . . .

Paul Celan, *Todesfuge* [*Death Fugue*], 1952[2]

[1] I wish to thank Solomon Volkov, Dmitry Feofanov, Allan B. Ho, Joshua Koenigsberg and Klaus Meyer for many helpful comments and suggestions. I am especially indebted to Klaus Meyer, who first pointed out the citation of the 'Amen' cadence in the *Largo* of the Fifth Symphony and who kindly provided the appendix to this article. A Senior Fulbright Teaching and Research Fellowship to Germany (1994–95) held at the Institut für Musikwissenschaft at the Universität Nürnberg-Erlangen facilitated completion of this article. An earlier version of the article was read at the Israel Festival, 10 June 1996, and at Oxford University, 22 October 1997.

[2]
he whistles his Jews out in earth
has them dig for a grave
he commands us strike up for the dance . . .
He calls out more sweetly play death
death is a master from Germany
he calls out more darkly now stroke your strings
then as smoke you will rise into air . . .
Paul Celan: Poems. A Bilingual Edition, selected, translated and introduced by Michael Hamburger, Persea Books, New York, 1980, pp. 50–54.

Many of my works reflect my impressions of Jewish music.
Dmitry Shostakovich[3]

Shostakovich-as-Jew

In a recent article, 'Anne Frank: The Girl, Not the Icon', Edward Rothstein resisted the temptation to 'generalise' the Holocaust, to regard it simply as one barbaric act motivated by racial prejudice among many in the distant and recent past. Rothstein observed that

> from the very beginning, it was Otto Frank's goal that the diary shed its particularity and become a call for universal tolerance. In fact, in his first edition of Anne's diary, he deleted details that made Anne's references to her Jewishness seem too pronounced [...]. This is an attitude that also appears in the latest official Anne Frank literature, a study guide prepared by the Anne Frank Center U.S.A. for the new edition of the diary. The guide is so preoccupied with the universalist message that it is willing to turn what Lucy S. Dawidowicz, the historian, called Hitler's 'war against the Jews' into one skirmish among many.[4]

In Communist countries this universalising tendency was elevated to official policy; the fact that the Holocaust was primarily a Jewish tragedy was obfuscated and denied; those memorials which were erected remembered 'the victims of Fascism', without recognising that it was the Jews who were the primary target. But the systematic, industrial murder of six million Jews by gassing and other means is an unparalleled event in the history of man; no massacre of a civilian population before or since has surpassed this act of genocide either in scale or in method. Dmitry Shostakovich recognised the uniqueness of both the Holocaust and the Jewish experience. Furthermore, against official Soviet policy, he identified the Holocaust as a particularly Jewish catastrophe: the Jews were the primary victims and it was

[3] *Testimony*, p. 119/156.

[4] Edward Rothstein, 'Anne Frank: The Girl, Not the Icon', *The New York Times*, 25 February 1996, Section 2, p. 23.

they who would henceforth bear the scars of this experience in their collective psyche.

Shostakovich does not merely sympathise with the Jews or pity them. He is not just solicitous or generous. He is not a generalist but a particularist. In his Eighth String Quartet, he combines his anagram D-Es-C-H (D-E flat-C-B) with the 'Jewish' theme from his Second Piano Trio. The meaning is unequivocal; in this 'autobiographical' work, he identifies himself as a Jew, and as a Jew who expresses his Jewishness in his music. In the final analysis, the fact of this irrational self-definition by a non-Jew as a Jewish composer remains; Shostakovich believed himself to participate in the collective Jewish psyche. But while we cannot fully explain or even understand Shostakovich's motivations rationally, we can investigate the consequences of his self-identification as Jew.

In a study of citations, Günther von Noé carefully distinguishes citation from other forms of borrowing, namely association, the working out of a pre-existent theme, and plagiarism:

> What is a true citation? [. . .] there is one fundamental distinction between the citation and all other kinds of borrowing. This becomes clear when we enquire as to the *reason* for the citation. It has three main purposes: 1) establishing the time and local colour of a particular milieu, 2) making explicit very serious intellectual contents [*ernster gedanklicher Inhalte*], [or] 3) a cheerful point, musical humour, frequently is intensified by travesty (parody, caricature). All of these basic reasons [for the citation] have one thing in common: the listener is supposed to make an association. Therefore, the citation serves as the bearer of particular semantic contents [. . .].[5]

As is well known, Shostakovich employs citations for all three of Noé's purposes, but the quotation from and the allusion to Jewish music, both sacred and secular, invariably conveys 'very serious intellectual contents': it associates the composer with the Jews, both in his own mind and in the mind of the informed listener. Surprisingly, the non-Jewish Shostakovich's self-portrayal as a Jew is not entirely unique

[5] Günther von Noé, 'Das Zitat bei Richard Strauss', *Neue Zeitschrift für Musik*, cxxv/6, 1964, p. 234.

in the annals of twentieth-century music. In 1933, four years before Shostakovich's first reference to Jewish music in his Fifth Symphony,[6] the non-Jewish German composer Karl Amadeus Hartmann similarly identified himself with the Jews by quoting the Jewish liturgical song *Elijah the Prophet* in the main theme of the second movement of his First String Quartet.[7] This Jewish tune is also cited in the third movement of the Quartet and in the anti-war opera *Simplicius Simplicissimus* (1934), and Jewish-sounding intonations also loom large in Hartmann's symphonies. In Shostakovich, the Jewish element is a semantic key, which unlocks the meaning of further interrelated citations of Bach, Tchaikovsky, Wagner, Debussy and of his own works. In the following paragraphs, I shall propose that the Jewish element is nothing less than the rosetta stone to intertextuality in Shostakovich.

Once one fully recognises the deep-rootedness of the composer's 'Jewishness', one can understand why Yevtushenko's original text for *Babi Yar* so fired Shostakovich's imagination: it clearly and unequivocally articulated his own feelings:

Now I seem to be a Jew [my emphasis].
Here I plod through ancient Egypt.
Here I perish crucified on the cross.
And to this day I bear the scars of nails.
I seem to be Dreyfus . . .

Shostakovich's identification of Jesus as the quintessential persecuted Jew – and of himself as 'a Jew crucified by the authorities' – dates back at least to the Fifth Symphony (1937).[8] Perhaps nowhere is this self-portrait of the composer as Christ-like Jew drawn more clearly than in the 'autobiographical' Eighth String Quartet. Although the Jewish element dominates the quartet in the climax of the terrifying second movement, where Shostakovich combined his anagram D-Es-C-H (D-E flat-C-B) with the 'Jewish' theme

[6] *Cf.* pp. 609–17.

[7] Albrecht Dümling, 'Musikalischer Widerstand', in *Entartete Musik, Zur Düsseldorfer Ausstellung von 1938*, ed. Albrecht Dümling and Peter Girth, Landeshauptstadt, Düsseldorf, 1988, pp. 171–72.

[8] *Cf.* p. 609.

from his Second Piano Trio, there are, of course, many other references as well. These are identified by Shostakovich in a letter to his friend Isaak Glikman written shortly after the Eighth Quartet was finished:[9]

> When I die, it's hardly likely that someone will write a quartet dedicated to my memory. So I decided to write it myself. One could write on the frontispiece, 'Dedicated to the author of this quartet'. The main theme is the monogram D, Es, C, H – that is, my initials. The quartet makes use of themes from my works and the revolutionary song 'Tormented by Grievous Bondage'. My own themes are the following: from the First Symphony, the Eighth Symphony, the Piano Trio, the [First] Cello Concerto and *Lady Macbeth*. Wagner's Funeral March from *Götterdämmerung* and the second theme from the first movement of Tchaikovsky's Sixth Symphony are also hinted at.[10] And I forgot – there's also a theme from my Tenth Symphony. Quite something – this little miscellany! The pseudo-tragedy of the quartet is so great that, while composing it, my tears flowed as abundantly as urine after downing half a dozen beers. On arrival home, I have tried playing it twice, and have shed tears again. This time not because of the pseudo-tragedy, but because of my own wonder at the marvellous unity of form.

References to himself, Wagner, Tchaikovsky and Bach should not obscure the fact that this Quartet is engaged in a

[9] Letter of 19 July 1960, transl. in Wilson, p. 340.

[10] That Shostakovich should have had Tchaikovsky's Sixth Symphony in mind while composing the Eighth Quartet is unsurprising. As I have argued elsewhere (*Tchaikovsky's Sixth Symphony*, Cambridge Handbook, Cambridge University Press, Cambridge, forthcoming), Tchaikovsky also employs the 'cross' motive in this symphony to activate the 'Ecce homos' topos. The iconography derives from John 19: 4–7, where Christ is mocked as 'King of the Jews', crowned with thorns, and made to hold a reed sceptre in his bound hands. In this pitiable condition, he is exhibited to the contemptuous horde. The idea that the artist could 'crucify' himself in an autobiographical work reaches back at least to Dürer's self-portraits of himself as Christ. Dürer's self-identification with Christ was not considered blasphemy; rather, it was regarded as an act of homage: by assuming Christ's identity and suffering, the artist also partook of the ultimate redemption effected by His sacrifice. In the *Pathétique*, the composer plays upon this iconographic tradition, making the 'cross'-motive emblematic of himself as 'Man of Sorrows' – but also as an anti-Christ who remains unredeemed.

profound and wide-ranging dialogue with Beethoven's Quartet in C sharp minor, Op. 131. Like the Beethoven, the Shostakovich is in five unbroken movements (in Op. 131, the third and sixth movements are simply introductions to the fourth and seventh); both quartets open with slow fugues based on tetrachordal motives and are 'haunted' by the Neapolitan (♭II/♭$\hat{2}$). The largest-scale background harmonic progression in both works is the same. The Beethoven moves from C sharp (in the first movement) to D (in the second) to G sharp (in the sixth), and back to C sharp in the seventh (I–♭II–V–I), while the Shostakovich similarly moves from C (in the first movement) to C sharp/D flat (in the fourth movement) to G and back to C (in the fifth movement, again I–♭II–V–I).

The fugal opening of the Shostakovich, based on the composer's 'signature' tetrachordal motive D–E flat–C–B (0–1–3–4), is not only derived from Bach's C sharp minor Fugue[11] but also refers to the opening tetrachordal motive of Beethoven's opening fugue, G sharp–B sharp–C sharp–A (0–1–4–5), which is the same tetrachord but with the boundary major third expanded by a semitone to a perfect fourth. In the Bach fugue and in the Beethoven and Shostakovich quartets, the tetrachordal motive with its connotations of voice-crossing evokes the 'crucifixion'; in each of the three confessional works, the 'suffering' artist activates the 'Ecce homo' tradition to portray himself as 'Man of Sorrows', that is, as crucified Christ. But Shostakovich also brutally deforms his model; in a 'Jewish' reading of the Beethoven informed by the experience of the Holocaust, Beethoven's classical language is given a bitter 'Jewish' twist. The genial, motoric clockwork of the Beethoven Scherzo mushrooms in the *Allegro molto* of the Eighth Quartet into the hysterical industrial death-machinery of the Holocaust. Ostinato-like motivic figures become the inexorable wheels of the Nazi death-factory grinding up the Christ-like protagonist Shostakovich-as-Jew (represented by the 'signature' combined with the 'Jewish' motive from the Piano Trio). In the following Scherzo, the composer-as-Jew is resurrected, not triumphantly, as in a Baroque 'et resurrexit', but pitifully,

[11] *Cf.* the discussion of Exx. 2(a)–(d) on pp. 612–13.

wraithlike, like the souls of Celan's dead Jews ('He calls out more sweetly play death death is a master from Germany / he calls out more darkly now stroke your strings then as smoke you will rise into air').

In order to get the Thirteenth Symphony (1962) performed and published, Yevtushenko and Shostakovich were forced by the Communist authorities to 'generalise', to eulogise the Russian and Ukrainian, and not only the Jewish, victims; but the original conceptions of both the *Babi Yar* poem and symphonic poem, with their focus on the Jews and Jewish experience, were true to Shostakovich's view of the uniqueness of the Holocaust, of the Jewish experience, and of himself as Jew.

While composing the *Babi Yar* Symphony, the intensity of Shostakovich's self-identification as Jew may have led him to 'Judaise' his dead first wife, Nina, by associating her with Anne Frank. This hypothesis is supported by an allusion to the second song of the *Six Romances on Verses by Raleigh, Burns, Shakespeare* (1942) in the Anne Frank episode of the *Babi Yar* Symphony (rehearsal figure 13 *et seq.*) pointed out by Bernd Feuchtner. As Feuchtner observes, 'the Anne Frank *Allegretto* episode is feverishly and longingly illuminated by the celesta and reminiscences from the song dedicated to his wife Nina "Oh wert thou in the cauld blast"'.[12] We can be quite certain that Shostakovich had the English songs in mind while composing the *Babi Yar* Symphony because of the explicit quotation of the third song 'McPherson's Farewell' in the second movement ('Humour') of the Symphony. The connection between the second song and the 'Babi Yar' episode is more subtle. Here we are concerned not so much with quotation but allusion created by musical commonalities: both the song and the excerpt from the Symphony feature an extremely sparse texture of three low-tessitura obbligato voices (bass plus two independent accompanying voices), triple metre and a lilting emphasis on the neighbour-note figure. The textual association of Anne with Nina – the dedicatee of the Burns setting – is especially striking. In the Burns, the poet imagines his

[12] Bernd Feuchtner, '*Und Kunst geknebelt von der groben Macht*'*: Dmitri Schostakowitch, künstlerische Identität und staatliche Repression*, Sendler, Frankfurt am Main, 1986, p. 232.

beloved standing in an empty field, buffeted by the wind, and attempts to shield her from 'misfortune's storms':

> Oh wert thou in the cauld blast,
> On younder lea, on younder lea,
> My plaidie to the angry airt,
> I'd shelter thee, I'd shelter thee.

Similarly, at Babi Yar, as 'the wild grasses rustle', the poet appears at the edge of the ravine trying to summon the dead Anne and, through the power of love, protect her from the catastrophe:

> Don't be afraid, those are the booming sounds
> Of spring itself. It's coming here.
> Come to me,
> Quickly, give me your lips!

The assertion that the Jewish element in Shostakovich's music is but one of many ethnic influences understates its importance. To be sure, Shostakovich could write, for example, an overture incorporating Russian and Kirghiz folk tunes (Op. 115, 1963). But here, as elsewhere in his music, the references to popular and ethnic musics occur in very different contexts and with varied significances; they are certainly not autobiographical in nature. Symbolising Shostakovich's 'Jewishness' and his preoccupation with Jewish destiny, the references to Jewish music hold a privileged place in Shostakovich's work. In this article, we shall expose many of these allusions – some for the first time – and speculate as to their wider implications.

Posterity owes *Testimony*, arguably the most important primary source on Shostakovich, in part, to the composer's self-identification with the Jews. In 1968, Solomon Volkov attempted to stage *Rothschild's Violin*, an opera based on Chekhov's story, ostensibly composed by the Jewish composer Veniamin Fleishman and edited and orchestrated by Shostakovich. Volkov showed considerable courage in daring to produce an opera on a Jewish theme at a time when anything remotely Jewish was discouraged if not forbidden by the authorities.[13] This opera is intimately connected with

[13] *Testimony*, p. x/xiii. The production was immediately stopped by the authorities. Volkov has informed me that a recording of the staged performance made by the secret police may now be available.

the early formation of Shostakovich's Jewish identity and, by staging it, Volkov touched a chord in Shostakovich's innermost being.[14] Thus, he began to earn the trust which later made *Testimony* possible.

The common wisdom is that the Jewish idiom symbolising the 'composer as Jew' first appeared in Shostakovich's own work in 1943–44. For political or anti-Semitic reasons, the Soviet literature is either silent about or downplays the importance of Shostakovich's self-definition as a Jew. Thus, it has fallen to Western students of Shostakovich's music (especially the Israeli musicologist Joachim Braun) to expose systematically the Jewish aspect of Shostakovich's life and work. Braun's tables of Shostakovich's works containing Jewish motives begin with the 'edition and orchestration' of Fleishman's opera *Rothschild's Violin*, which he dates to 1943, and end with the song collection *New Jewish Songs* published in 1970 (Shostakovich served as editor-in-chief).[15] Ian McDonald claims that the Trio (1944) is 'the first of

[14] Some of Volkov's critics have suggested that Volkov exaggerated Shostakovich's Jewish persona because he himself is Jewish. Writing in *The New Yorker*, 24 March 1980, p. 132, George Steiner complained that 'there are very troubling points about the book [*Testimony*] as we have it. The uniformity of scorn and self-loathing is one; the emphasis on the Jewish question and on Shostakovich's purported involvement in this question is another. It is very difficult to escape the impression that Volkov has colored or arranged the conversations he set down – has added bile from his own incensed spirit'. The reviewer for *Music and Musicians*, 28 March 1980, p. 32, doubted that Shostakovich was so emphatic about anti-Semitism and suggested that 'perhaps the fact that his interlocutor was Jewish has coloured this as well as other matters'. This article not only corroborates Shostakovich's remarks concerning Jews and Judaism in *Testimony*; it also asserts that the Jewish element in Shostakovich's compositional persona is more significant than even Volkov realised.

In a private communication to me in June 1996, Volkov observed that Shostakovich continually returned to the Jewish theme in their conversations, and that, to avoid redundancy, he was, in fact, compelled to reduce the number of references to it in *Testimony*.

[15] *Cf.* Joachim Braun, 'The Double Meaning of Jewish Elements in Dmitri Shostakovich's Music' *Musical Quarterly*, lxxi, 1985, pp. 70–71; *Jews and Jewish Elements in Soviet Music*, Tel Aviv, 1978, pp. 72–76; and 'Shostakovich's Vocal Cycle *From Jewish Folk Poetry*: An Attempt in Interpretation of Style and Meaning', *Russian and Soviet Music: Essays for Boris Schwarz*, ed. Malcolm H. Brown, UMI Research Press, Ann Arbor,

Shostakovich's "Jewish" pieces'.[16] However, this study will advance the hypothesis that the Jewish element occurs considerably earlier in Shostakovich's music than these writers have suggested and is even more important than has been generally recognised – at least in the published literature.

Two men closely connected with the Jewish motive in Shostakovich's music were Ivan Sollertinsky and Fleishman. The musicologist Sollertinsky (1902–44), whom Shostakovich first met in 1927 at the age of 21, encouraged Shostakovich's intense study of Mahler's music. Since references to Jewish popular music initially entered Shostakovich's musical language via Mahler, it may not be coincidental that the Piano Trio, Op. 67 (1944), with its Jewish dance tunes, was dedicated to Sollertinsky's memory. The composer Fleishman (1913–41), who began studying with Shostakovich in 1937 and worked with him until he was killed in the defence of Leningrad in 1941, also seems to have played a crucial part in sensitising Shostakovich to Jews and Jewish plight.

This article re-examines the meaning and the chronological 'endpoints' of Shostakovich's self-identification as a Jew, asserting that Shostakovich began to identify with the Jews as early as 1936 – almost a decade earlier than is commonly believed. Referring to those works by Shostakovich which contain Jewish elements, Braun has claimed that 'it is the fate of Soviet Jewry that is symbolised in this music'.[17] This study presents a rather different view, suggesting that Shostakovich's Jewish references are first and foremost autobiographical in nature, symbolising his own fate as parallel to that of the Jews. Alienated and fearing for his life as a result of the editorial 'Muddle Instead of Music' (attributed to Stalin, published 28 January 1936), Shostakovich felt himself to be 'like a Jew', since 'in this most

---

1984, pp. 259–86. Also *cf.* Günter Wolter, '"Ein Lachen durch Tränen", Jüdische Musik bei Mahler und Schostakowitsch', *Das Orchester*, 41, 1993, pp. 672–74.

[16] MacDonald, *The New Shostakovich*, p. 73.

[17] Braun, 'Double Meaning', p. 72.

Christian of worlds, all poets are Yids'.[18] It should be pointed out that the composer's self-definition as a Jew did not entail belief in the specific tenets of the Jewish religion; however, Shostakovich's music and memoirs contain distinctly 'Jewish' ideas and emotions. In *Testimony*, Shostakovich declares that his pieces are tombstones for millions of innocents murdered by Stalin and Hitler and his obsession with the Holocaust is characteristically Jewish. The quotations from Jewish cantorial song or *davening* suggest that Jewish ideas of the Covenant – the Jews' recognition of God and God's reciprocal promise to protect them as His Chosen People – inform some of his most important works. Furthermore, distinctly 'Jewish' longing for an ideal state of being, the same Messianism that made loyal Communists of many Jews in the 1910s and '20s, fires Shostakovich's early Communist enthusiasm. But a typically 'Jewish' disillusionment also sets in early; the Messiah has not yet come. Misdeeds prevent man from attaining his highest potential in the image of God and Shostakovich contrasts glimpses of the promised Messianic epoch with bitter realisations of real-life oppression and evil.

The Jews are a distinct ethnic group – 'outsiders' in every host culture; despite centuries of persecution, they have nonetheless refused to assimilate completely. Shostakovich was a Russian of Polish descent without a drop of Jewish blood in his veins. For Shostakovich, 'being like a Jew' did not entail formal conversion to the Jewish religion; rather, 'being like a Jew' was symbolic. It meant being an outcast and doing what was necessary to survive while inwardly attempting to remain true to himself. As he says in *Testimony*, 'The Jews became the most persecuted and defenceless people of Europe. It was [in the '30s] a return to the Middle Ages. *Jews became a symbol for me.*'[19] Perhaps

[18] From 'The Poem of the End' by Marina Tsvetayeva. This poem was cited by Solomon Volkov in his lecture 'The Jewish Motive in Shostakovich', delivered in Toronto, Canada, for the Jewish Music Society, March 1991. I have used the term 'Yid' to translate Tsvetayeva's original term 'Zhids'. 'Zhid' in Polish means 'Jew', but when translated to a Russian context it gains derogatory and demeaning connotations (I am grateful to Eliezev Elper of Jerusalem for this information).

[19] *Testimony*, p. 119/157; emphasis added.

misinterpreting the *symbolic* meaning of the Jewish element in Shostakovich's music, Lev Kopelev states in his memoirs 'Shostakovich is naturally a Jew. Shostakovich-Rabinovitch . . . No, perhaps he was baptised. But his music is not at all Russian. It is cosmopolitan. We all know that.'[20]

There are two distinct phases in Shostakovich's assimilation of 'Jewish' elements into his own language. In the first (late '20s to 1936), Shostakovich imported Jewish idioms directly from Jewish popular culture (e.g., 'Kozelkov's Dance with Friends' in *The Bolt*) and indirectly via Mahler. During this period, the Jewish element is both satirised and celebrated. At the same time, Shostakovich assimilated Mahler's Jewish *Angst*, irony, humour and subtle allusions to *Klezmer* music along with a host of other distinctly Mahlerian stylistic traits. But from 1936 on, the composer's attitude towards the Jews changed profoundly. In this second phase of 'Jewish identity', the references to Jewish music were no longer simply exotic flavouring, satirical commentary or references to Mahler (as in the first phase). Rather, in this period of fear and mass terror, secret references to Jewish music assumed a new symbolic and autobiographical significance. Allusions to Jewish music referred not merely to the Jews, but pointed to 'Shostakovich-as-Jew' – to the artist as outcast, whose life, like that of a Jew, could be snuffed out any minute at the whim of the tyrant or hostile populace.

There are strong indications that Shostakovich's interest in Jews and Jewish music *antedated* both Russia's war with Germany and the reports of the Holocaust. His self-definition as a Jew may well have predated his relationship with Fleishman; indeed, he may well have been attracted to Fleishman precisely because of Fleishman's Jewishness. Significantly, the first Jewish quotation in Shostakovich's music (in the *Largo* of the Fifth Symphony) coincides with the beginning of Fleishman's study with Shostakovich in 1937. The impulse to compose an opera on the 'Jewish' subject of Chekhov's *Rothschild's Violin* came not from Fleishman but from Shostakovich himself, presumably in the years

[20] Quoted by Detlef Gojowy, *Dimitri Schostakowitsch mit Selbstzeugnissen und Bilddokumenten*, Rowohlt Taschenbuch Verlag, Hamburg, 1983, p. 140.

1937–41, and how much of this opera in its final form is actually by Fleishman remains an open question. Braun reports that Shostakovich's anagram DSCH 'already appears (albeit in transposed form)' in the opera.[21] This association of the composer's personal anagram with the 'Jewish' element suggests that Shostakovich both 'signed' the opera and secretly identified himself as being 'like a Jew' in 1943, if not earlier. Fleishman's work on *Rothschild's Violin* was also contemporaneous with composition of the Seventh Symphony, inspired by the (Jewish) Psalms of David and conceived earlier than generally believed (1938?–41).[22] If this reconstruction of chronology is correct, Shostakovich had already identified himself as a persecuted Jew – approximately seven years before news of the Holocaust was publicised in Russia in 1944.

The 'Amen' Cadence, the 'Crucifixus' Motive and the Third Symphony Citation in the *Largo* of the Fifth Symphony

The first direct reference to Jewish music is to synagogue chant (*hazanut*) in the *Largo* of the Fifth Symphony, Op. 47 (1937): the first theme of the second group (rehearsal 84, Ex. 1(a)) quotes the 'Amen' cadence from Jewish liturgical chant.[23] Shostakovich could have heard this cadence in the

[21] Braun, 'Double Meaning', p. 76. Braun attributes (mistakenly, in my view) the DSCH anagram to Fleishman, claiming that 'Shostakovich himself first used the DSCH formula (also transposed) in the Scherzo of the Violin Concerto'.

[22] In *Testimony*, Shostakovich asserts that 'the Seventh Symphony had been planned before the war' (p. 118/155); the present author has been told that a newly discovered sketch of the 'invasion theme' of the Symphony proves that contention. (*Cf.* p. 157. –EDS.)

[23] This quotation was first pointed out in print by Klaus Meyer in his M.A. dissertation, *Analytische Betrachtungen an Leonard Bernsteins Symphonie No. 1 'Jeremiah' und dem Ballett 'Fancy Free'*, Universität Erlangen-Nürnberg, 1988, p. 92. Joshua Koenigsberg, a cantor in New Haven, Connecticut, discovered the quotation independently. Presently completing his doctorate on the music of Leonard Bernstein, Meyer was alerted to the quotation because the 'Amen' cadence is also the principal subject of Bernstein's First Symphony, *Jeremiah* (Exx. 1(b), (c) and (d)).

Ex. 1
(a) Fifth Symphony, *Largo*, second theme, 'Amen' from Jewish liturgy

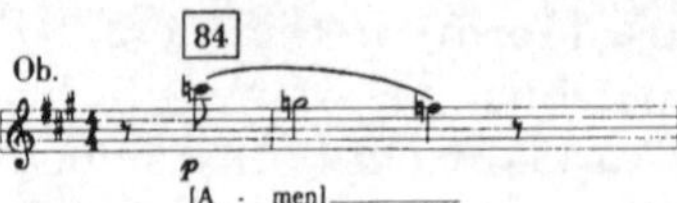

(b) Leonard Bernstein, *Jeremiah* Symphony, first movement, introduction, 'Amen' cadence

main synagogue in St Petersburg, which is only three blocks from the Conservatory. The cadence is, without doubt, very prominent in the Jewish service, being sung to various words on the holidays of Rosh Hashana (the Jewish New Year), Passover, Shavuoth and Succoth, and also on the Sabbath at the beginning of the month (Rosh Hodesh). This reference to Jewish prayer is the first of a number of allusions in Shostakovich's music to cantorial *hazanut* (see also the 'recitative' in the second movement of the Second Quartet (1944)[24] and the ninth fugue in the *Twenty-four Preludes and Fugues* (1950)).

One could argue that, in the *Largo* of the Fifth Symphony, this 'Amen' cadence is derived, on strictly musical grounds, from the first three notes of the opening theme as its retrograde (Ex. 1(e)). However, it is certainly possible that the first theme of the second group engendered the first theme (which never recurs in its original form), and not the other way around. Significantly, the character of Jewish synagogue chant is preserved at rehearsal 84 and 86. Like the Jewish chant, the melody in its entirety is monophonic and constructed from small motivic elements, which are repeated

---

Meyer believes Bernstein's use of the 'Amen' motive to be a quotation both from the Jewish liturgy and the *Largo* of Shostakovich's Fifth (*cf.* pp. 638–40). The 'Amen' cadence in Bernstein is discussed by Jack Gottlieb, 'Symbols of Faith in the Music of Leonard Bernstein', *Musical Quarterly*, lxvi, 1980, pp. 287–95.

[24] Curiously, the Second Quartet is not included in Braun's lists. It is, however, identified as a 'Jewish' work by MacDonald.

(c) *Jeremiah* Symphony, first movement, conclusion

with slight variations (centonisation). The tremolo pedal tone, which accompanies the melody, imparts to it a feeling of anguished isolation and vulnerability – especially 'Jewish' emotions.

This quotation from the Jewish liturgy occurs in the *Largo* in conjunction with a double quotation from Bach's C sharp minor Fugue (from the first book of *The Well-tempered Clavier*[25]) and from Shostakovich's own Third Symphony

[25] Shostakovich had memorised all of Bach's '48' by the age of fifteen, and they continued to fascinate him throughout his life.

Ex. 1 (cont.)
(d) Jeremiah Symphony, finale, conclusion

(e) **Fifth Symphony, *Largo*, first theme**

Ex. 2: Shostakovich's motivic references to Bach
(a)

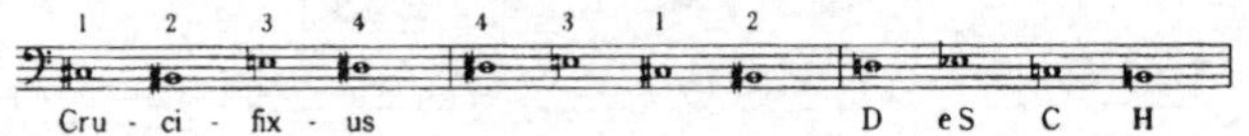

(b) Bach, *St Matthew Passion*

(c) Bach, *St John Passion*

('First of May'). The self-quotation was first identified by Karen Kopp, who calls attention to motive 'x' (Ex. 2(f)) in the Third Symphony at rehearsal 26+4, observing that

> as a citation in the *Largo*, [the motive] assumes an entirely different character: there in the *Allegro* [of the Third Symphony], it is scherzo-like, and part of an intensifying phrase; here, by contrast [in the *Largo*] (*Marcato*, high register), it takes on the resigned character of the 'sighing' motive. The expression of the swinging, rhythmically powerful effect of the May Day celebration of the Third Symphony is transformed into its opposite.[26]

In my view, however, Kopp locates the quotation too early in the Third Symphony; rather, the *Largo* quotes the very last statement of 'x' in the Third Symphony (at rehearsal 45a, Ex. 2(f)). Not only is it highlighted in the high register of the first violins; the correspondence is almost note-for-note (which is not the case at rehearsal 26+4 cited by Kopp). Indeed, at this quiet, retrospective point in the Third, 'x' has almost the same resigned, 'sighing' character as in the Fifth Symphony.

The theme stated at rehearsal 78 in the *Largo* (Ex. 2(e)) – and again at rehearsal 89 (Ex. 2(h)) – is simultaneously an almost literal quotation of the 'crucifixion' theme from Bach's Fugue in C sharp minor (Ex. 2(d) and (i)); in the following discussion I shall therefore refer to it as 'the crucifixion theme'. The anacrusis figure is taken from Bach's own transformation of the 'crucifixion' theme in the countersubject, which first appears in bar 49 (Ex. 2(i)). The climax of the *Largo* quotes this initial entry of the countersubject virtually note-for-note (Ex. 2(g), (h) and (i)). The specific association of this theme with the crucifixion is supported by its two other striking appearances in Bach's music: in the *St John* and *St Matthew Passions* at the point where the Jews demand the crucifixion of Christ (Ex. 2 (b) and (c)).[27]

The *combination* of these quotations in the *Largo* (pointed out for the first time here) sheds new light on this movement,

[26] Karen Kopp, *Form und Gehalt der Symphonien des Dmitrij Schostakowitsch*, Verlag für systematische Musikwissenschaft, Bonn, 1990, p. 201.

[27] Also *cf.* the fourth movement of Schumann's Third Symphony, 'The Rhenish', where the 'crucifixion' motive represents Cologne Cathedral.

Ex. 2 (cont.)

(d) Bach, *The Well-tempered Clavier*, Fugue in C sharp minor

(e) Shostakovich, Fifth Symphony, *Largo*

(f) Shostakovich, Third Symphony

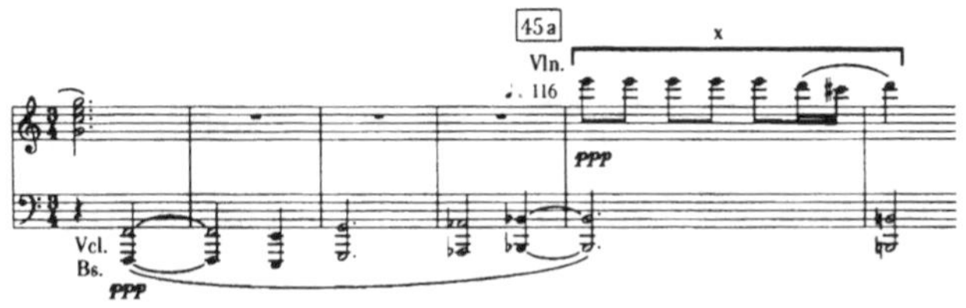

on the Fifth Symphony, and on Shostakovich's subsequent work. Indeed, this concatenation of citations discloses Shostakovich's covert response to Stalinism. Although the Fifth Symphony conforms outwardly to Stalinist aesthetics, through the concealed reference to Jewish prayer or *davening* Shostakovich reaffirms his own Covenant and prays, 'like a Jew', for God's protection of His Chosen One. 'Like a Jew', he will do what is necessary to survive, but he will never inwardly 'convert'. If the Third Symphony depicts the Proletariat's colossal struggle to attain Socialism, within the context of the Third, the statement of 'x' at rehearsal 45a functions as a reminiscence, perhaps of destroyed ideals. In the *Largo*, then, Shostakovich simply transferred the epithet for 'wistful reminiscence of destroyed ideals' from the newly banned Third to the Fifth Symphony.

The 'crucifixion' theme graphically suggests that Shostakovich-as-Jesus has been brought before Stalin-as-Pilate, and stands accused of heresy by the Party 'high priests'. In *Testimony*, Shostakovich recalls how his 'friends' withdrew from him as a marked man[28] – denying him, indeed, as Peter denied Christ. The *Largo* of the Fifth Symphony is Shostakovich's self-representation both as 'Jew' *and* as 'crucified Christ'. The DSCH anagram, which first appears in Shostakovich's work in the early 1940s, is clearly a transformation of the 'crucifixion' theme (Ex. 2(a) and (b)). In the second movement of the 'autobiographical' Eighth Quartet (1960), Shostakovich again represents himself both 'as Jew' and 'as crucified Christ' by combining his anagram (with its connotation of the 'crucifixion' *à la* C sharp

[28] P. 211/271–72.

(g)

(h) Shostakovich, *Largo*

(i) Bach, C sharp minor Fugue

minor Fugue of Bach) with the quotation of the 'Jewish' theme from the Second Piano Trio.

The 'Klezmer' Theme in the Seventh Symphony

Another important early Jewish reference occurs in the first movement of the Seventh Symphony (the composition of which was contemporaneous with the 'Jewish' opera project). The close connection of the Seventh Symphony with Jewish suffering is revealed in *Testimony*, where Shostakovich observes that

> I began writing it [the Seventh Symphony] having been deeply moved by the Psalms of David; the symphony deals with more than that, but the Psalms were the impetus. I began writing. David has some marvellous words on blood, that God takes revenge for blood, He doesn't forget the cries of the victims, and so on. When I think of the Psalms, I become agitated.[29]

Shostakovich probably had in mind Psalm 79, which contains the following verses:

> 2 The dead bodies of thy servants have they given to be meat unto the fowls of heaven, the flesh of thy saints unto the beasts of the earth.
> 3 Their blood have they shed like water round about Jerusalem; and there was none to bury them [. . .].
> 10 Wherefore should the heathen say, Where is their God? let Him be known among the heathen in our sight by the revenging of the blood of thy servants which is shed.

Thus, as in the *Largo* of the Fifth Symphony, Jewish ideas of the Covenant – God protecting the Chosen People and revenging His martyrs – also inform the Seventh Symphony. But in this work, Jewish popular rather than synagogue music, namely the 'klezmer' idiom, represents God's 'martyred servants' and the mechanistic ostinato, the fascist 'heathen', who 'have shed [their blood] like water round about Jerusalem'. The 'klezmer' dance melody erupts at the climax of the March in the opening movement (Ex. 3(a),

[29] P. 140/184.

Ex. 3

(a) Seventh Symphony, first movement, 'Klezmer' dance melody

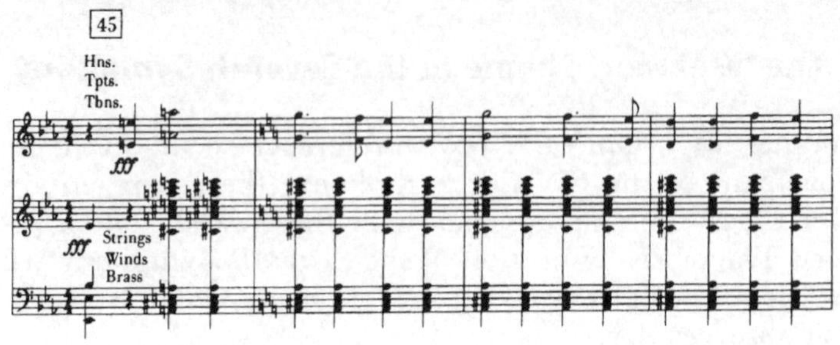

(b) Second Piano Trio, finale, 'Jewish' melody

rehearsal 45) and the music suddenly lurches upward to #IV (A is #IV in the context of E flat) in a klezmer-like modulation. This klezmer passage is strikingly similar to the 'Jewish' music in the Finale of the Piano Trio, bars 29 *et seq*. (composed in 1944, Ex. 3(b)).

In the first movement of the Seventh Symphony, the development (rehearsal 45–52) presents a colossal struggle between the 'fascist' march and the 'klezmer' melody, both themes being distorted in the course of the conflict before they are dissipated by the 'tragic-heroic' theme, which initiates the recapitulation (rehearsal 52 *et seq*.). As Shostakovich finished the work in 1941, perhaps the 'klezmer' theme, which is broken by the march, came to signify the martyred defenders of Leningrad and in particular, among them, his martyred Jewish friend Fleishman. Later (1944), when composing the Trio, Shostakovich may also have associated the 'tragic heroic' theme of the Seventh Symphony (Ex. 4(b), the minor mode reincarnation of the 'resolute heroic' melody of the opening) with his fallen Jewish friend by transforming this theme – which shapes the bass of the entire first movement of the Seventh (Ex. 4(a)) – into the 'Jewish' theme of the Trio (Ex. 4(c)).

Ex. 4
(a) Seventh Symphony, first movement, bass graph

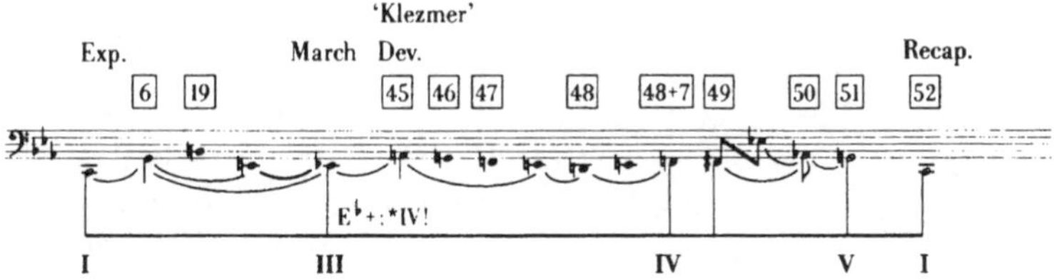

(b) Seventh Symphony, first movement, 'tragic-heroic' theme

(c) Second Piano Trio, finale, 'Jewish' melody

The Enharmonics of Despair and 'Jewish' Chromaticism

The organic connection Shostakovich forged between his own and Jewish music depends, in part, upon parallelism between the musical-poetical connotations of chromaticism in Shostakovich's and Jewish music. Let us first consider the symbolic implications of Jewish chromaticism. The characteristic Jewish *Steiger* (the Yiddish term for scales) may be analysed as chromatically distorted Western (Church) modes. In the *Freigish* ('Phrygian', Ex. 5 (a)), G sharp represents a displacement of G (#$\hat{3}$ displaces $\hat{3}$). In my study of the religious implications of enharmonicism, I proposed that, in Western-Christian religious music, sharps may represent the 'risen' or 'resurrected' and flats the 'fallen' and the 'unredeemed' states.[30] In the Jewish *Freigish*, the upward displacement of G to G sharp, which ascends as a leading tone to A ($\hat{4}$), may correspond to Jewish yearning for redemption, the messianic dream of a persecuted people. By contrast, F ($\flat\hat{2}$), which can be understood as a downward displacement of F sharp to F (in diatonic E minor), may signify the 'fallen', 'unredeemed' status of the Jewish people in exile. The striking dichotomy of descending $\flat\hat{2}$–$\hat{1}$ and ascending $\sharp\hat{3}$–$\hat{4}$, emphasised by the augmented second between $\flat\hat{2}$ and $\sharp\hat{3}$, seems to embody the typically Jewish *Weltanschauung* of 'laughter through tears', which Shostakovich found so attractive. In the 'altered Dorian', displayed in Ex. 5(b), the same augmented second occurs, now between $\hat{3}$ and $\sharp\hat{4}$. Here, the augmented fourth between $\hat{1}$ and $\sharp\hat{4}$, which seeks to resolve to the perfect fifth between $\hat{1}$ and $\hat{5}$, may also represent Jewish longing for redemption.

Ex. 5
(a) 'Jewish' Phrygian or Freigish (b) 'Jewish' altered Dorian
(c) Flatward enharmonic transformation in 'despair metaphor'

In the enharmonic model for redemption employed in Western religious music, the 'fallen' flat or natural is reinterpreted as its 'risen' enharmonically equivalent sharp or natural. The process of redemption through faith is then represented by the upward (i.e., sharpward) direction of the enharmonic transformation. But the model shown in Ex. 5(c) reverses the direction of the enharmonic transformation so that it 'collapses' flatwards from a 'higher' to a 'lower' state, i.e., from a state of elevation to depression, from faith to

[30] Timothy L. Jackson, 'The Enharmonics of Faith: Enharmonic Symbolism in Bruckner's *Christus factus est* (1884)', *Bruckner Jahrbuch 1987–88*, Akademische Druck- und Verlagsanstalt, Linz, 1990, pp. 4–20; also *cf.* my article '"Schubert as John the Baptist to Wagner-Jesus" – Large-scale Enharmonicism in Bruckner and his Models', *Bruckner Jahrbuch 1991–93*, Akademische Druck- und Verlagsanstalt, Linz, 1995, pp. 61–107.

despair. In some works, Shostakovich employs this 'enharmonic collapse-metaphor for despair' in conjunction with the Jewish chromaticism of the *Steiger*. The scale degrees of the *Steiger*, which were displaced sharpwards ($\#\hat{3}$ and $\#\hat{4}$), are enharmonically transformed flatwards ($\#\hat{3} = \flat\hat{4}$ and $\#\hat{4} = \flat\hat{5}$) within the despair metaphor to represent the tragic destiny of the Jews. In other words, characteristic ascending leading tones of the *Freigish* and the altered Dorian are crushed by their enharmonic equivalents in the flatward direction; by denying the Jews' chromatic longing for transcendence, Shostakovich discovers a potent tonal symbol for Jewish martyrdom and, by extension, for totalitarian destruction of man's spiritual life.

Let us turn, now, to Shostakovich's own characteristic enharmonic despair metaphor and see how it relates to chromaticism in the *Steiger*. The chromaticism in the *Largo* of the Fifth Symphony (as in many other Shostakovich works) results from a combination or mixture of modes. With its emphasis on B sharp (spelt C, $\#\hat{4}$), the following passage from the *Largo* (Ex. 6(a), rehearsal 77–78) strongly suggests the altered Dorian. Yearning for transcendence is represented not only by the upward chromatic displacement of $\hat{4}$ to $\#\hat{4}$ (B to B#), but also by the displacement of $\hat{3}$ to $\#\hat{3}$ (A to A sharp (spelt B flat)), as in the *Freigish*. Ex. 6(b) presents a middle-ground view of the *Largo* in its entirety, calling attention to enlargements of the neighbour-note motive 'x' from bar 3 (Ex. 1(e)) composed out over the course of Part 2 (rehearsal 87–end). The transformation of the original form of 'x', A–B–A, into A–B flat–A is responsible for the B flat minor of the 'crucifixus' section (rehearsal 89 *et seq*., Exx. 2(h) and 6(b)). Here, the emphatic assertion of the B flat violently negates the earlier ascending 'redeemed' A sharp, which now reveals its true 'fallen' nature as B flat. As shown in Ex. 6(b) and (c), this enharmonic collapse is played out in the final descent of the *Urlinie*. Instead of representing ultimate triumph, the *tierce de Picardie* in the final measures is to be understood as a bitter reminiscence of A sharp which, in the course of the movement, was undermined and ultimately overwhelmed by B flat within the enharmonic despair metaphor.

In 'O, Abram, how can I live without you?', the fourth song from Shostakovich's cycle *From Jewish Folk Poetry*,

Ex. 6

(a) Fifth Symphony, *Largo* – $\hat{4}$ displaced by $\sharp\hat{4}$ and $\hat{3}$ displaced by $\sharp\hat{3}$

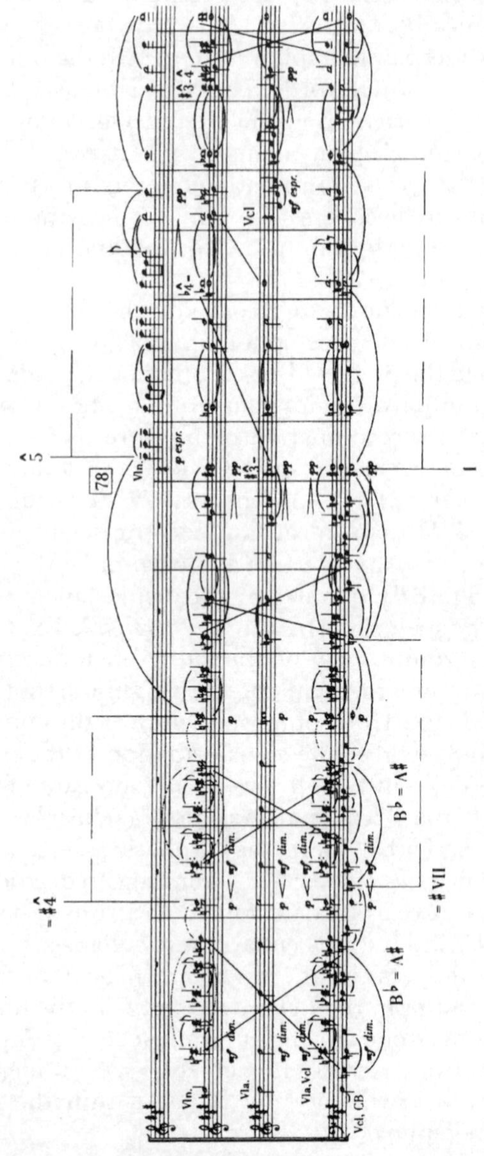

(b) Fifth Symphony, *Largo* – middle-ground graph showing A sharp/B flat enharmonic 'despair metaphor'

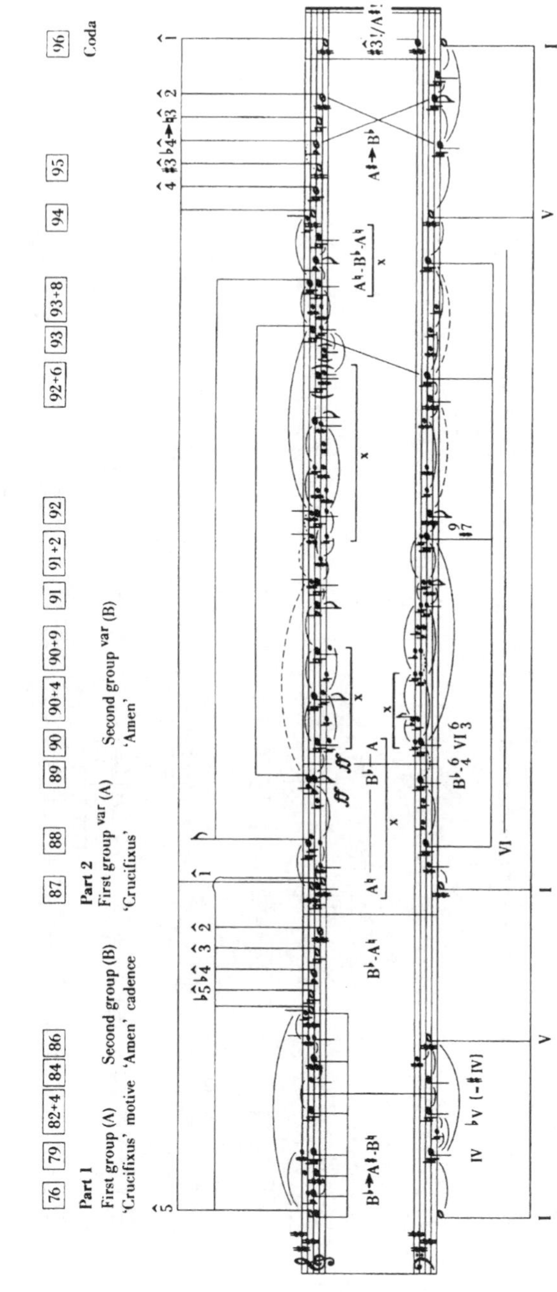

Ex. 6 (cont.)

(c) Fifth Symphony, *Largo* – enharmonic 'despair metaphor' ($\sharp\hat{3} = \flat\hat{4}$–$\hat{3}$) in the final *Urlinie* descent

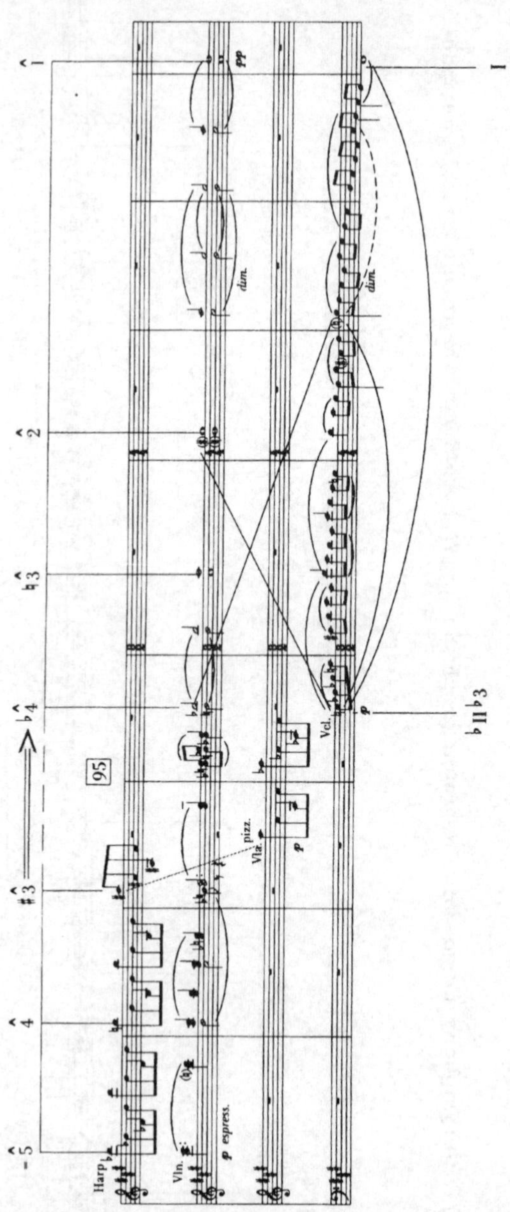

Aeolian built on A serves as the tonal background.[31] In this piece, the modes are also mixed: the chromatic tones D sharp ($\#\hat{4}$), C sharp ($\#\hat{3}$) and B flat ($\flat\hat{2}$) are borrowed from the Altered Dorian and the *Freigish*. In the course of the song, C sharp ($\#\hat{3}$) is compelled to function as enharmonically equivalent D flat ($\flat\hat{4}$). This idea, first suggested in bars 5–7 (Ex. 7(a)), is realised at the conclusion of the song (Ex. 7(b)). Thus, this song provides an especially clear example of Shostakovich's synthesis of the enharmonic despair metaphor with Jewish chromaticism: just as the lovers are overcome by the pain of separation, within the enharmonic collapse metaphor, the 'hopeful' C sharp ($\#\hat{3}$ of the *Freigish*) is converted into its 'despairing' enharmonic equivalent D flat ($\flat\hat{4}$).

Ex. 7
(a) *From Jewish Folk Poetry*, No. 4, $\flat\hat{4}$–$\hat{3}$ in bars 6–7

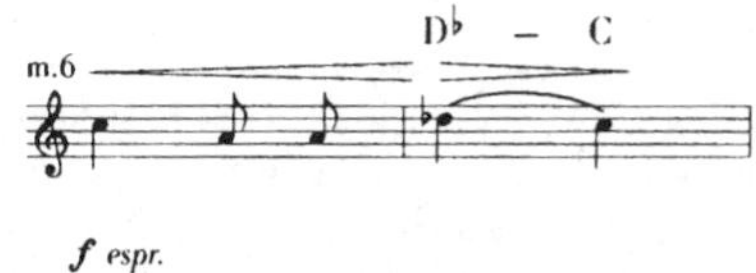

Flatward enharmonic transformation coincides with the mass murder of Jews by the SS *Einsatzgruppen* in the Finale of the Trio, the 'Jewish Dance of Death'.[32] In front of their

[31] Braun (incorrectly, in my view) asserts ('Shostakovich's Song Cycle', p. 277) that the tonal centre of the fourth song is E, not A.

[32] Shostakovich composed the Finale of the Trio upon hearing reports that the Germans had forced their Jewish victims to dance before murdering them; this is the source of the compositional idea. Shostakovich's music is programmatic, representing the Jews' Dance of Death and their apotheosis. In order to co-ordinate the programme with the music, it is helpful to outline the rather complicated sonata-form of the movement. The recapitulation is reversed (i.e., with second group material recapitulated before the first group) and an extensive cadenza with new melodic material inserted between the two groups as follows:

- Exposition (bars 1–132)
  - First Group (bars 1–97)
  - Second Group (bars 98–132)
- Development (bars 133–244)
- Recapitulation (bars 245–407)
  - Second Group (bars 245–81)

freshly dug graves, the Jews are at first reluctant, hesitant dancers; but then they become caught up in the dance as a vehicle for redemption (as in Hasidic tradition). In *Exodus* (XIX, 20), God had warned Moses that, were the people to look directly upon Him, they would all die; no one but Moses can survive the divine presence. The Torah relates that when Moses descended from Mount Sinai, the Israelites could not bear to look upon him because his face glowed so brightly from reflected radiance (*Exodus* XXXIV, 30–35). Shostakovich's dancing Jews must perish not only because they are shot by the Germans but because, in their triumphant moment of religious ecstasy achieved through dance, God is revealed to them in His unbearable majesty.[33] Over the course of the movement, the bass presents a massive enlargement of the opening dance motto (E–D sharp–E–F–D sharp,

---

Cadenza (bars 282–329)
New Melody (bars 286–329)
First Group/Coda (bars 330–407)

In the exposition, the slow, hesitating and stumbling beginning can be understood to represent the Jews' reluctant compliance with the bizarre command; however, as they become caught up in the dance, their music becomes increasingly impassioned. The climax of the dance (the end of the development and beginning of the recapitulation, bars 225–81) can be understood to represent the instance of both the Jews' spiritual triumph and their physical death. A programmatic reason for the injection of new material in the cadenza (bars 282–329) now suggests itself: the rising piano arpeggios and upward spiralling canonic melodies in the strings evoke the Jews' apotheosis (they rise, as in Celan's *Todesfuge*, 'as smoke into air'). The recapitulation of the first group (from bar 330), which might also be understood to function as a coda, is especially chilling: the Jews are now all dead; all that persists is the empty echo of their dance.

For a detailed discussion of the metaphorical significance of the reversed recapitulation, *cf.* my 'The Tragic Reversed Recapitulation in the German Classical Tradition', *Journal of Music Theory*, Vol. 40, No. 1, 1996, pp. 61–112, and 'The Finale of Bruckner's Seventh Symphony and Tragic Reversed Sonata Form' in *Bruckner Studies*, ed. Timothy L. Jackson and Paul Hawkshaw, Cambridge University Press, Cambridge, 1997, pp. 140–208.

[33] The same idea underpins Schoenberg's *A Survivor from Warsaw* (*cf.* Timothy L. Jackson, '"Your Songs Proclaim God's Return" – Arnold Schoenberg, the Composer and His Jewish Faith', *International Journal of Musicology*, VIII, 1997, pp. 277–316). At the end of *A Survivor*, the *Shema*-singing Jews must die, not merely because they are murdered by the Nazis, but because, in the ecstatic moment of redemption, they have looked upon God.

Ex. 7 (cont.)

(b) ***From Jewish Folk Poetry*, No. 4, enharmonic 'despair metaphor' ($\sharp\hat{3} = \flat\hat{4}$–$\hat{3}$)**

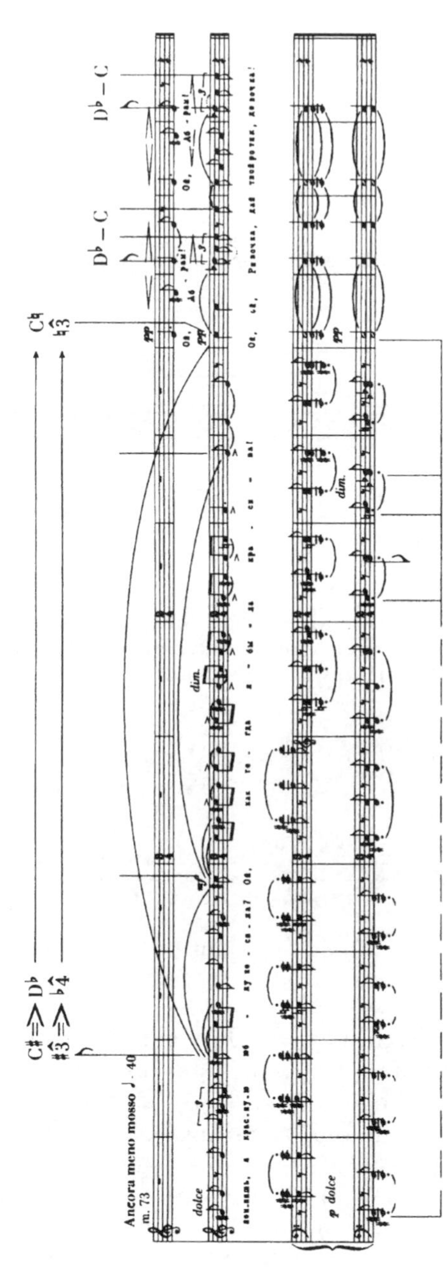

bars 5–6, Ex. 8(a)) enharmonically reinterpreted as E–E flat–F–F flat–E flat, Ex. 8(b)). Flatward transformation of E ($\hat{1}$) into F flat (♭♭$\hat{2}$) and D sharp (#$\hat{7}$) into E flat (♭$\hat{1}$) at the climax of the development coincides with the actual shooting (bars 225–230). The apotheosis of the Jewish martyrs is then celebrated in the reversed recapitulation and coda (bars 245–end).

Ex. 8
(a) Second Piano Trio, finale, dance motto

(b) Second Piano Trio, finale, bass graph showing massive enlargement of dance motto enharmonically transformed flatwards (enharmonic 'despair metaphor')

The Eighth String Quartet is dedicated 'To the victims of fascism and war', the quintessential 'victims of fascism' being, of course, the Jews. Two fundamental enharmonic issues in the Eighth String Quartet – is G F## and is A flat G sharp? – are taken note-for-note, like the 'Jewish' melody (Trio, Finale, bars 31 *et seq.* = Quartet, rehearsal 21 *et seq.*) from the Finale of the Trio. The opening of the Trio motivically associates F## with G in the linear strand G

Ex. 9
(a) Second Piano Trio, finale, motive G sharp–F double-sharp–G sharp sets up G sharp–G false relation

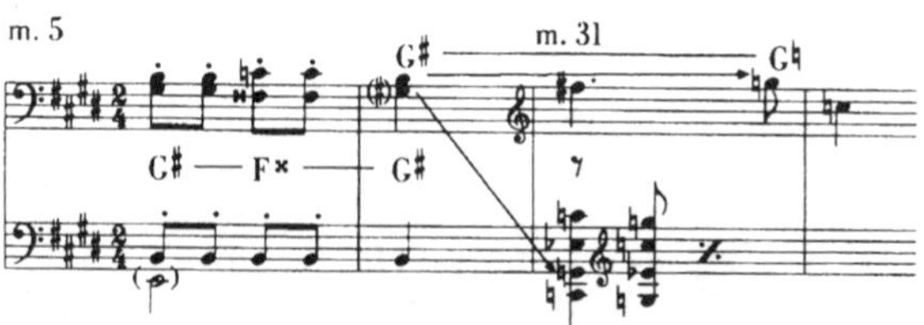

sharp–F##–G sharp (bars 5–6) and the false relation G–G sharp as E major moves to C minor (bars 1–31 *et seq.*, Ex. 9(a)). Since the C minor 'Jewish' theme from the Trio is restated literally in the G sharp minor second movement of the Quartet, its G (rehearsal 21) functions as an 'optimistic' F## leading tone ascending to G sharp (rehearsal 27, Ex. 9(b)). The restatement of the 'Jewish' melody of the Trio (rehearsal 32+19), re-establishes G. This time, G simply picks up the primary tone $\hat{5}$; the preceding G sharp (rehearsal 27) now functions as A flat, that is, as an upper neighbour descending to G (rehearsal 35, Ex. 9(b)). Thus the middle ground (in the transition from the second to the third movement) experiences a 'despairing' enharmonic reversal whereby G is prevented from functioning as an 'optimistic' leading-tone F## 'yearning' for G sharp and G sharp is reinterpreted as a 'pessimistic' A flat 'collapsing' to G. The 'optimistic' F## emphatically tries to re-assert itself in the fourth movement (rehearsal 53 *et seq.*); however, in the transition from the fourth movement into the fifth (rehearsal 58 *et seq.*), the earlier 'despairing' flatward enharmonic transformations are played out once again; this time, F## remains 'frozen' – frustrated – as G and G sharp is 'beaten down' as A flat resolving to G (Ex. 9(b)). In this way, the G–A flat/F##–G sharp dichotomy of the 'Jewish' melody from the Trio is integrated into the enharmonic despair metaphor spanning the entire Quartet. The tragic destiny of the Jews (the enharmonic negation of F## by G and G sharp by A flat) becomes synonymous with – in this 'autobiographical' quartet – the tragic destiny of 'Shostakovich as Jew'.

Ex. 9 (cont.)

(b) Eighth String Quartet, deep middle-ground graph showing definitive flatward enharmonic transformation in the 'despair metaphor' (F double-sharp = G, G sharp = A flat, C sharp = D flat)

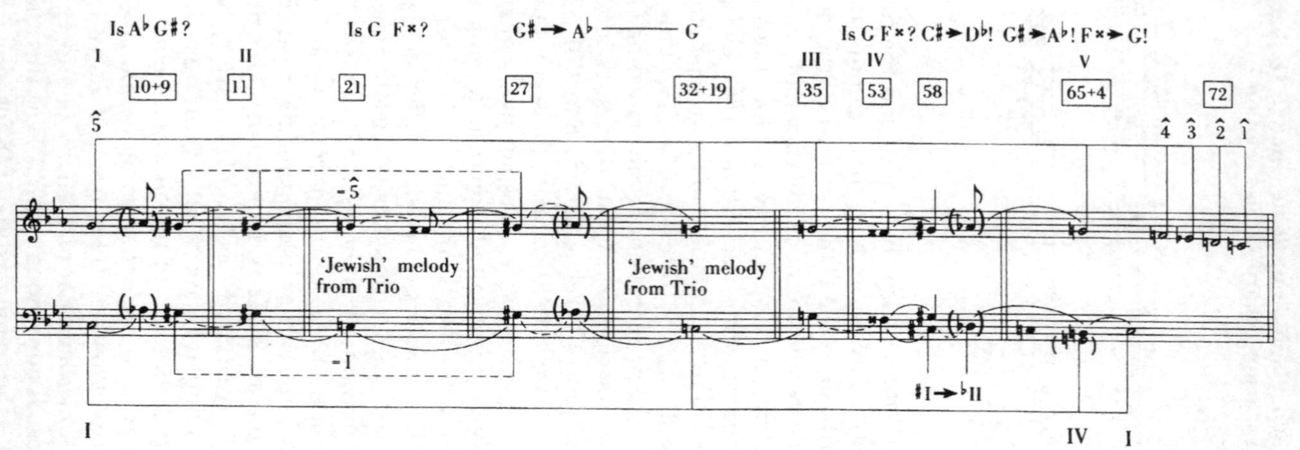

It is my contention that Shostakovich's 'Jewish' enharmonics should not be played 'straight', that is, eliminated through equal temperament, but should be 'bent' as they are in Jewish religious and folk music. In other words, in Shostakovich's 'Jewish' works, there is a special kind of 'Jewish' *musica ficta* whereby the 'enharmonics of despair' should be made audible. The extent to which in the Eighth Quartet, for example, G sharp should be audibly distinguished from the A flat into which it is ultimately transformed in the enharmonic despair metaphor (one could make analogous distinctions between the motivic-enharmonic strands F## versus G and E versus F flat) depends upon the performers. However, my point is that the players should not simply assume equal temperament; rather, they ought to consider the possibility of sonically distinguishing enharmonics. To be sure, equal temperament could be preserved and enharmonic distinctions be made mentally; but, in my view, enharmonic identities should be actualised physically through subtly different tunings of enharmonically equivalent sharps and flats. Furthermore, sonic interpretations should not depend solely upon Shostakovich's notation but rather upon a careful determination of the function of particular pitches in context, that is, according to their voice-leading functions.

Let us consider an example from the beginning of the first movement of the Eighth Quartet (bars 13–17, reh. 1−1 to reh. 1+5). In bars 13–14, Shostakovich's voice-leading implies a chromaticised voice exchange between C in the cello and e♭2 in the first violin (bar 13) and E in the cello and c♭2 spelled b1 in the first violin (bar 14). If the cellist 'bends' the B to make it sound as C flat, then the chord on the downbeat of bar 14 is not heard as a 'consonant' E minor triad but rather as a 'dissonant' triadic sonority E-G-C flat. Since the E in bar 14 ultimately falls as if it were an F flat to the E flat on the downbeat of bar 17, it is also possible to construe the cello's E as an F flat. Interpreted in this way, the sonority would be the even more 'dissonant' cluster F flat-G-C flat. The motive F flat–E flat in the cello would then be imitated by the first violin (bar 34, reh. 2+5) and the 'fallen', 'dissonant' F flat contrasted with its 'pure', 'consonant' alter ego, the E in bars 56, 64, 72, 88 and 91 (reh. 4, 4+8, 5, 7+1, 7+4). If one makes such distinctions of intonation, these give the

Eighth Quartet a different, much more 'dissonant' and plaintive sound than if it were played in strictly equal temperament, as was demonstrated by a recent performance, which realised the 'secret chromatic art' of Shostakovich's 'Jewish' enharmonic despair metaphor.[34]

'Death is a master from Germany': A 'Jewish' Reading of the the Finale of the Fifteenth Symphony

From 1944 on, the Jewish motif in Shostakovich's work evokes the Holocaust; the annihilation of the Jews by the Nazis becomes a paradigm for mass murder and criminality in the Soviet Union and elsewhere. The Fifteenth Symphony (1971), like the Thirteenth Symphony (1962), is Holocaust-haunted music. Surely, the death camps were still very much on Shostakovich's mind in his last years when, at the end of *Testimony*, he speaks of his dead friends and 'corpses, mountains of corpses'.[35]

In his memoirs, Shostakovich remarks that the Fifteenth Symphony is 'based on motifs' from Chekhov's short story *The Black Monk*, although 'it is a thoroughly independent work', and he associates it with the 'Jewish' opera *Rothschild's Violin*, also based on a Chekhovian theme.[36] Sequential presentation of the 'fate' theme from *Die Walküre* at the beginning of the Finale of the Fifteenth Symphony refers not simply to Brünnhilde's mortal summons to Siegmund (which parallels the ultimately fatal appearance of the Black Monk in Chekhov's story), but also to Death – because of the Wagnerian connotations – as Nazi-German:

[34] The performance was given by the 'Party of Four' (Malcolm Lowe and Ian Swensen, violins, Steven Dann, viola, and Kenneth Slowik, cello) on Stradivari instruments at the Smithsonian Institute, Washington, D.C., 10–11 May 1997.

[35] *Testimony*, p. 174/276.

[36] *Ibid.*, p. 173/275.

Sieh auf mich!
Ich bin's, der bald du folgst . . .
Nur Todgeweihten taugt mein Anblick,
Wer mich erschaut,
Der scheidet vom Lebens Licht.[37]

The *Leitmotiv* conjures up Death as a Nazi Brünnhilde summoning the doomed Jew Shostakovich. This association is supported by re-enactment, in the development of No. 15, of the confrontation in the Seventh Symphony between the 'fascist' mechanistic ostinato march theme (derived from the previously discussed ostinato march in the Seventh Symphony) and a 'Jewish' melody (Ex. 10(a)). At the climactic moment where the ostinato march is transposed from G sharp to C (rehearsal 134), Shostakovich introduces a new 'Jewish' melody (as at rehearsal 45 in the Seventh Symphony) characterised by a descending chain of 'iambic primas'. (As Joachim Braun has observed, this device is particularly common in Jewish folk melodies, suggesting that 'its distinctive structure, with the double accentuation of each scale degree [. . .] is of decisive semantic significance' – compare, for instance, Ex. 10(a) and (b).[38]) Here in the Fifteenth, as in the Seventh, the 'Jewish' melody is consumed in its struggle with the 'fascist' march. The *Allegretto* (rehearsal 138), which follows the ostinato episode, begins with a quotation of the BACH motive (Ex. 10(c)), this reference to the final, incomplete fugue from Bach's *Art of Fugue* suggesting that Brünnhilde-Death is about to remove the pen from the Jew Shostakovich's hand (just as Death stole the pen from Bach before he could complete his fugue).

In *Testimony*, Shostakovich calls attention to the uniquely tragic-comic quality of Jewish music: 'I think, if we speak of musical impressions, that Jewish folk music has made a most powerful impression on me. I never tire of delighting in it; it's multifaceted, it can appear to be happy while it is tragic.

37

Look upon me!
I am the one you will soon follow . . .
Only those destined to die can see my gaze,
He who beholds me
Departs from the light of life.

38 Braun, 'Shostakovich's Song Cycle', p. 280; 'Double Meaning', p. 72.

Ex. 10
(a) Fifteenth Symphony, finale 'Jewish' melody with iambic primas at the climax

(b) *Twenty-four Preludes and Fugues*, No. 8, Prelude, 'Jewish' melody with iambic primas

(c) Fifteenth Symphony, finale, BACH motive

It's almost always laughter through tears'.[39] Shostakovich goes on to observe that 'there should always be two levels in music', presumably the tragic and the comic superimposed. This remarkable 'Jewish' effect of 'laughter through tears' is achieved in the Fifteenth Symphony's *Finale* through far-reaching tragic-comic parody of the *Tristan* Prelude. Shostakovich's *Tristan* parody is also a double quotation (again, a *double* quotation, as in the *Largo* of the Fifth Symphony); not only does he parody *Tristan*, but Debussy's parody of *Tristan* in 'Golliwogg's Cakewalk' from *Children's Corner*.[40] Like the *Tristan* Prelude, the Finale is in A minor moving to A major. Ex. 11(a) shows the opening of *Tristan* with the characteristic motif of the rising sixth A–F followed

[39] *Testimony*, p. 118/156.

[40] Perhaps Shostakovich's comment that the first movement represents a toy shop also refers, in view of this quotation from *The Children's Corner*, to the last movement as well.

Ex. 11
(a) Wagner, *Tristan*, Prelude, opening

by the descending diminished third F–E–D sharp (labelled 'x'). When the *Tristan*-motive 'x' first appears in Shostakovich's Finale (rehearsal 112–13, Ex. 11(b)), the last tone is comically displaced from D sharp to D. 'X' is again humorously distorted – in conjunction with the 'fate' motive 'y' from *Die Walküre* – in the insouciant melodies that follow (rehearsal 113–16, Ex. 11(b)). In the recapitulation (rehearsal 143-3, Ex. 11(c)), there is another amusing displacement within 'x'; this time the anticipated F is unexpectedly changed to F sharp. Notice, for example, that 'x' also occurs in sinister contexts. In the ostinato, overlapping statements of 'x' are combined with references to the 'fascist' march ostinato of the Seventh Symphony (motif 'z', Ex. 11(d)). Furthermore, transposition of the ostinato melody from G sharp to C in the development (rehearsal 134) yields a note-for-note restatement of the original Wagnerian pitches (rehearsal 134+9, Ex. 11(e)). Indeed, massive enlargement of 'x's' neighbour-note motif (E)–F–E (Ex. 11(a)) in the bass in the Finale (rehearsal 120–42, Ex. 12(b)) seems to parody the bass of the *Tristan* Prelude (bars 63–84, Ex. 12(a)).

The Jewish people are strengthened by their ability to laugh at their troubles. It is their sense of humour – in conjunction with their faith – which has sustained them through the kind of trials that have broken the collective will of virtually every other ancient people. Through its superposition of tragic-comical musical references to Wagner's *Die Walküre* and *Tristan*, Shostakovich's own Seventh Symphony, and Jewish folk music, the Finale of the Fifteenth Symphony may be considered Shostakovich's quintessentially Jewish composition. Perhaps the humour of the Finale of No. 15 is even more 'Jewish' than the presentation of Jewish-sounding melodies in his other, more overtly Jewish

Ex. 11 (cont.)

(b) Fifteenth Symphony, finale, quotations from *Tristan* and *Die Walküre* in the exposition

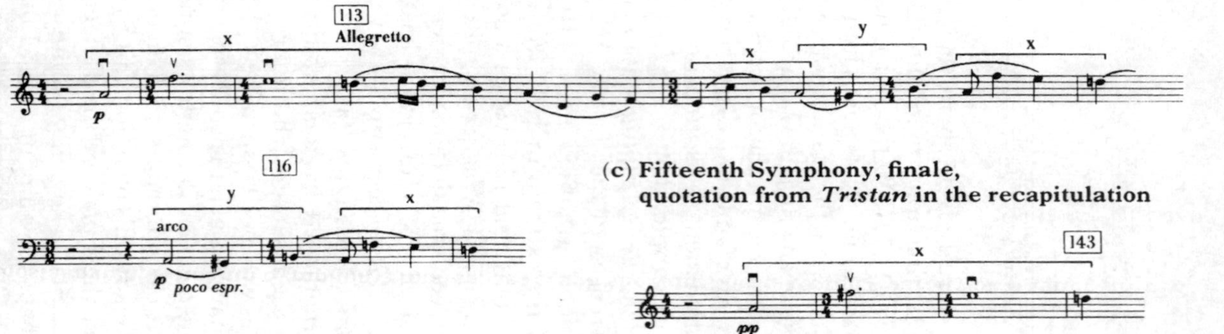

(c) Fifteenth Symphony, finale, quotation from *Tristan* in the recapitulation

(d) Fifteenth Symphony, finale, quotations from *Tristan* and the Seventh Symphony in the ostinato

(e) Fifteenth Symphony, finale, ostinato transposed recreates *Tristan* motive note-for note

Ex. 12

(a) Wagner, *Tristan*, Prelude, bass graph showing enlargement of the neighbour-note motive E–F–E

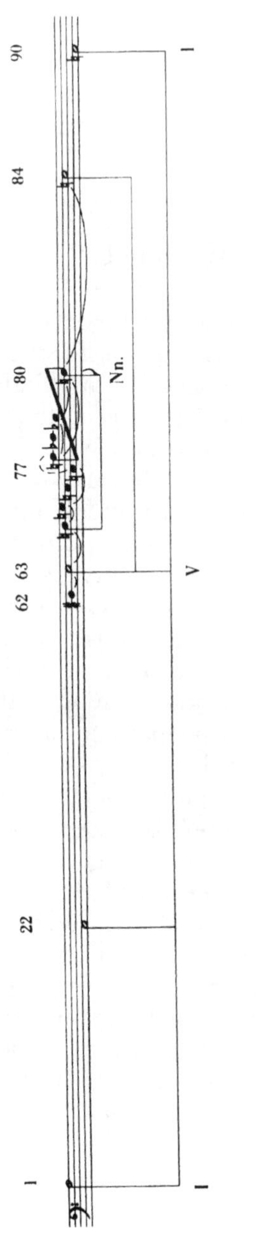

(b) Shostakovich, Fifteenth Symphony, finale, bass graph showing Shostakovich's parody of Wagner's E–F–E

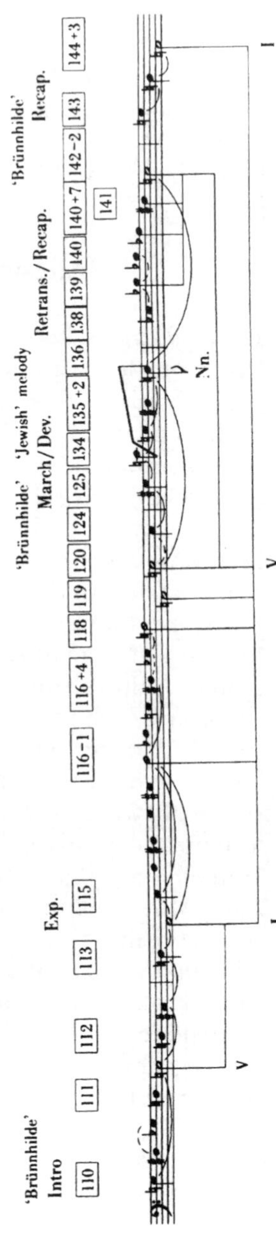

works. Like Jewish music and humour, the Finale is able to 'laugh through its tears', to poke fun at the German-Wagnerian death motives while, at the same time, weeping for 'the mountains of corpses'. In this last movement of his last symphony, Shostakovich-as-Jew laughs at Brünnhilde; humour enables him to resist demagogues, tyrants, regimes with their Auschwitzes, gas chambers, Babi Yars and Gulags. As eternal Jew, Shostakovich outlasts his enemies and even triumphs over Death.

Appendix by Klaus Meyer[41]

In the *Largo* of the Fifth Symphony, the entrances of the 'Amen' cadence are 'staged' in such a way as to suggest that it is a quotation. The motivic statements are highlighted texturally and orchestrally, thus sounding as if they emanate from another sphere. The first (rehearsal 84, oboe), second (rehearsal 86+1, flute) and fourth (rehearsal 96, harp and celesta) entrances are realised *pianissimo* by solo instruments, each time accompanied by a 'shimmering' violin tremolo on a single note. In the third entrance, the motive is pronounced *fortissimo* and *espressivo* by the cellos (rehearsal 90) in their high register against a tremolo major third, which immediately follows the climax of the movement. The passages preparing each presentation of the motive suggest that something important and meaningful is about to be articulated. The first entrance is anticipated by a concealed motivic statement of the 'Amen' cadence (within the portentous Bach 'crucifixus' motive (E flat–B flat–A flat, rehearsal 83+1)). Immediately before the second appearance of the 'Amen' motif, the opening neighbour-note motif (bar 3) is stated over a (G sharp) major triad (rehearsal 86), which casts a new light upon what follows. The 'crucifixus' motif prepares the third statement (as it did the first), however considerably intensified through its presentation in a powerful three-octave unison of xylophone, woodwinds, and strings (rehearsal 89). The fourth and last entrance (in the coda) is

[41] Translated from the German by Klaus Meyer and Timothy L. Jackson.

prepared by a collapse into the lowest register of the lower strings (rehearsal 95), and the motive coalesces out of the ascending F sharp minor harp triad. The pedal tremolo in the violins is a reminiscence of the 'shimmering', single-note tremolos of the earlier entrances.

Considering the significance of this cadential formula for Jewish cantorial music – well known to every religious Jew – it is not surprising that it has assumed an important role in compositions influenced by Jewish religious music. In *Schelomo*, the 'Hebraic Rhapsody for Cello and Orchestra' (1915–16) by Ernest Bloch, the 'Amen' cadence appears in the opening measures enlarged to a four-tone motive by a further falling fourth. Jack Gottlieb has pointed out the prominent role played by the cadential motive in Leonard Bernstein's compositions, where it appears in virtually all of his religiously inspired works.[42] Bernstein initially used the 'Amen' cadence in his First Symphony, *Jeremiah*, completed at the end of 1942, a three-movement work with a finale setting selected verses from Jeremiah's Lamentations. For this concluding movement, Bernstein returned to an earlier *Lamentation for Soprano and Orchestra*, which was already sketched in the summer of 1939. For a composition competition sponsored by the New England Conservatory, Bernstein completely revised the sketch in the latter part of 1942, changing the soprano to mezzo-soprano and adding the first two movements. The idea of using the 'Amen' cadence as the foundation of his symphony may have been inspired – consciously or unconsciously – by Shostakovich's Fifth, which Bernstein may have already known in 1939 and which he certainly encountered at the very latest in the summer of 1942, conducted by Serge Koussevitzky in Tanglewood.

The cadential formula functions in the *Jeremiah* Symphony as a 'Grundgestalt' from which nearly all motivic elements are derived. In its original form (falling fourth plus major second) it opens and closes the first movement ('Prophecy', bars 2 and 80–90; Ex. 1(b) and (c)), appears at the centre of the Scherzo ('Profanation', bar 230), and is presented near the conclusion of the third movement ('Lamentation', bar 106; Ex. 1(d)) at the end of the verse 'Lead us

[42] Gottlieb, 'Symbols of Faith'.

back to you, O Lord', setting 'elecha' as the last three notes of the mezzo-soprano part. While in the first and second movements the 'Amen' cadence represents God's voice articulated through Jeremiah's Prophecy, at the end of the work it symbolises the longing of the people of Israel for restoration of the Covenant with God and return to His leadership and protection.

After the devastating attacks in *Pravda* ('Muddle Instead of Music' and 'Ballet Falsehood'), which were part of the new rigid cultural politics of the Stalin administration, Shostakovich feared being declared 'an enemy of the people' and liquidated. It must have been especially irritating and painful that included among his forbidden works were the Second and Third Symphonies ('To October' and 'The First of May'), and the ballets *The Golden Age, The Bolt*, and *The Limpid Stream* (which provoked the second *Pravda* attack), all works which were revolutionary and progressive in two senses: first, in a compositional sense in their use of clusters (these clusters anticipate the techniques of the 1960s), collage techniques, noise-instruments, the integration of *Agitprop* intonations (in the symphonies), and the synthesis of high and low stylistic voices (in the ballets); and second, in political terms in their enthusiasm for the ideals of the October Revolution and the socialist utopia, which Stalin and his followers trampled under foot. Out of favour and singled-out for persecution, he suddenly found himself in a situation not unlike that experienced by the Jews for centuries in the ghettos of the diaspora. On account of its special presentation in the *Largo* of the Fifth Symphony, the 'Amen' cadence sounds like a revelation – for Shostakovich the perception that, from now on, he must inhabit an 'artistic diaspora' – and experience the kind of isolation which has been called 'inner emigration'. The *Largo* might be said to define 'inner emigration' in Jewish terms.

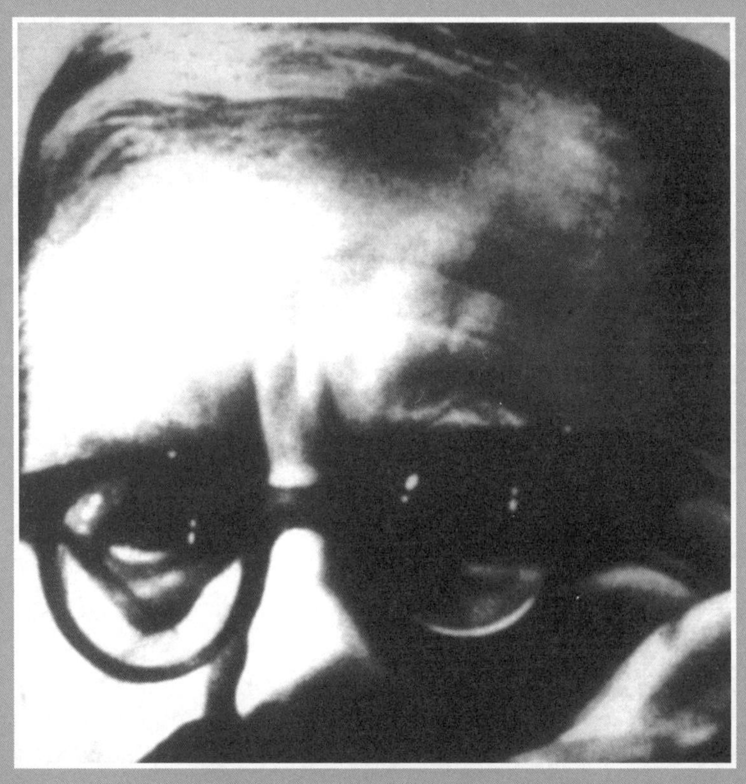

CODA

NAIVE ANTI-REVISIONISM
The Academic Misrepresentation of Dmitry Shostakovich[1]

Ian MacDonald

Can a score be said to be pointing at anything? I would suggest that what it points at is the music it partially represents through the medium of notation and, further, that the 'location' of the music chiefly determines the disposition of the pointing finger of the score – and not the other way around. Of course, not everyone in our era of cultural pseudo-science agrees that score and music are not identical. Scores being elaborate symbolic systems in their own right, many musicians naturally don't see that a score, however detailed, does not indicate music in itself but only the adjacent presence of music. Yet merely playing the notes is obviously no guarantee of performing the music. A would-be 'interpreter' must also divine the nature of the music by deciding what the score is pointing at. This, though, happens only gradually and interdependently – the interpreter shifting to and fro between the tangible form-world of the score to the intangible expression-world which hangs, penumbra-like, around it (and which, removing music from the realm of mathematical logic and thus from the purview of scientific analysis, to a large extent determines the form of notes we see on paper).

Did Shostakovich ever say anything – apart from hinting that a performance didn't match what he'd had in mind – which would lead us to believe that he held his scores to be at best partial representations of his music? He did. Referring

[1] An excerpt from this article was published in advance as 'Fay versus Shostakovich: Whose Stupidity?', *East European Jewish Affairs*, 26/2, 1996, pp. 5–26.

to a sparse passage in his score for Kozintsev's film of *King Lear*, he remarked, in that gnomic fashion for which creative persons are notorious, 'There may be few notes, but there's lots of music'.[2] Like Mahler, who observed that 'what is best in music is not to be found in the notes', Shostakovich meant to suggest that the notes of a score, however ingeniously constructed, are only pointers to the music they represent. A computer 'sequencer' could be programmed to perform the notes of Shostakovich's Fifth Symphony, but it could not play the music. That requires the participation of 'interpreters' who inhabit the culture of the symphony (and arguably of this symphony in particular) – which, at a minimum, means humans (and arguably means humans formerly, or now, resident in what used to be the USSR).

Unfortunately, this raises some fundamental, if almost entirely neglected, questions. In 'Music and Culture', Charles Seeger writes: 'We must be careful to avoid the fallacy that music is a "universal language". There are many music-communities in the world, though not, probably, as many as there are speech communities. Many of them are mutually unintelligible'.[3] There are good reasons to suppose that music, so often represented as tolerating no frontiers, is, in fact, far more culture-specific than we prefer to admit. For example, it may be impossible for the average non-Russian to listen to Shostakovich's Eleventh Symphony, with its quasi-operatic *leitmotif* treatment of a set of genre-specific national songs, in anything remotely approaching the state of mind of the average Russian listener. Yet this 'translation problem' is likely to apply, less obviously but no less pervasively, to everything else he wrote.

Although there are only a few references to 'pure music' in David Fanning's recent scholarly anthology,[4] this misleading concept – with its corollary of 'extra-musical' elements which, when associated with music, supposedly adulterate it – nonetheless governs the thinking deployed in it. To

[2] Quoted by Kozintsev in Wilson, p. 425.

[3] *Proceedings of the Music Teachers National Association for 1940*, MTNA, Pittsburgh, 1941, pp. 112–22.

[4] David Fanning (ed.), *Shostakovich Studies*, Cambridge University Press, Cambridge, 1996 (hereafter Fanning).

Fanning's credit, there is no pretence that notes alone can tell us the truth of the music they symbolise; questions of 'craftsmanship' are, as the book's preface promises, for the most part interwoven with considerations of 'political and personal context'. Yet the belief in a notional divide between form and expression is ubiquitous here, either in unspoken assumption or in the pseudo-scientific guise of the primitive dichotomies of contemporary literary theory (introversive/extroversive, semantic/syntactic, heteronomous/autonomous, etc). Of course, 'pure music' seems such a simple concept that, like oxygen or water, we tend to treat it as a self-evident basic constituent. But when musicology tackles Shostakovich, it is bound to admit his local music-community: the Russian classical quotations, the folk melodies, the political songs. Moreover, if it permits itself to go that far, it must, presumably, also admit the culture of which these allusions are part and which arguably gives them meaning. And if it acknowledges that culture, it must surely recognise the ideological forces whose clashes with it provoked these allusions in the first place. And, by then, what is there left of 'pure music'?

The debate over the significance of Shostakovich's music raises fundamental philosophical issues which few commentators seem aware of, let alone incorporate in their arguments. Hardly surprising, then, that an atmosphere of tentative confusion permeates the assertions these arguments contain. Although qualified to make detailed judgments on matters of structure and design, Western musicologists studying Shostakovich have so far proved unable to move from close analysis to general assessment with any degree of logic or consistency – an inability based about equally on lack of historical awareness and absence of any realisation that music cannot be divorced from human expression (itself inextricably dependent on human culture). A few of the essays in David Fanning's anthology go far in surmounting these problems, notably Patrick McCreless's study of the Second Piano Trio[5] and Fanning's own examination of *leitmotif* in *Lady Macbeth*.[6] Yet when Fanning, in his Introduction to

[5] *Ibid.*, pp. 113–36.

[6] *Ibid.*, pp. 137–59.

this book, is called upon to shift from close analysis to a more synoptic outlook, he reveals himself beset by uncertainties. Some of these may only be apparent – in his role as editor, he must, of course, appear to stand aloof from the fray – yet others are clearly genuine and a few are unconscious (i.e., he is unaware of them). The trouble with unconscious uncertainties is that they lead to false assumptions, and beyond the strictly technical domain of the score, Fanning's awareness of the human context of this subject is only occasionally informed by historical fact.

For instance, speaking of Manashir Yakubov's disclosure of the 'success' of *The Golden Age*,[7] Fanning ventures that this 'might provoke an intriguing anti-revisionist reflection that in 1930 Shostakovich's commitment to a vulgarly pro-Communist line may have been more whole-hearted than is often thought'.[8] It might indeed – but only from a commentator whose grasp of the Soviet background is weak enough to confuse a popular success with a work that succeeds in achieving an ideological target which the composer takes seriously. Only in the fevered imagination of academics do the masses voluntarily seek out art in which entertainment is an optional complement to the 'correct' expression of a political line. The plays of Bulgakov were huge popular successes in Russia during the 1920s (not least with Shostakovich[9]) precisely because they were so outrageously politically incorrect. The reason Russian audiences would have enjoyed *The Golden Age* in 1930 was not because it satirised fascists and NEPmen – although doubtless this would have made some among them feel pleasantly self-righteous – but because it entertained them with daring Western dances and quasi-capitalist fun and games at a time when Stalin's political-correctness squads were trying to impose a didactic theatre repertoire comparable with that foisted on the Chinese thirty years later by Madame Mao's fanatical cadres. Judging by his letters to Tanya Glivenko[10]

[7] *Ibid.*, pp. 189–204.

[8] *Ibid.*, p. 14.

[9] *Cf.* my 'Shostakovich and Bulgakov' (p. 541, note 23).

[10] *Cf.* pp. 530–54.

and the testimonies to his youthful 'apoliticalness' in Elizabeth Wilson's book,[11] Shostakovich is unlikely to have had any serious interest in fulfilling political quotas. We know, for example, that he despised the propagandist scenarios of his ballets as much as he disliked Bezymensky's propagandist verses for the Second Symphony and the texts of the TRAM plays for which he churned out incidental music.[12] As for how seriously he took the composition of *The Golden Age* and *The Bolt*, all we presently have to go on are a few letters and some eyewitness accounts which show him wearing the poker-face he appears to have adopted following the effective banning of *New Babylon* and *The Bedbug*. No doubt he did the best work his interest in these projects permitted, but the quality of their scores testifies that this interest was, at most, scant. Indeed, he reveals as much in unpublished letters to Shebalin dated 28 and 29 September 1931[13] where, berating his friend for defending Aleksandr Davidenko's vulgar propagandist music, he concedes that '*The Bolt* is shit, but compared to Davidenko it is Beethoven'. In other words, the idea – which, at a minimum, depends on the composer's demonstrable aesthetic commitment – that, in *The Golden Age*, Shostakovich harboured any kind of allegiance to 'a vulgarly pro-Communist line', is a long way wide of reality.

Lest it be imagined that I am manufacturing a mountain out of a molehill here, it is worth quoting David Fanning in less academically circumspect mood, in the review pages of *Gramophone*,[14] hotly admonishing the young Shostakovich for having perpetrated *The Bolt*:

[11] *Cf.* also Wilson, pp. 6, 13, 29, 30, 62, etc., and my 'Witness for the Defence' at the website *Music under Soviet Rule* (http://www.siue.edu/~aho/musov/witness/wit.html).

[12] TRAM was the Leningrad Workers' Youth Theatre, a Brechtian agit-prop company run by Mikhail Sokolovsky at a former cinema on the Liteiny Prospekt in Leningrad. Shostakovich was house composer from 1929 to 1931, a position he assumed in order to shield himself from criticism by Left proletarian art groups during the Soviet Cultural Revolution.

[13] *Cf.* p. 221, note 392.

[14] David Fanning, 'Shostakovich: *The Bolt*', a review of Chandos CHAN 9343/4, *Gramophone*, 73/865, June 1995, p. 58.

> How would you feel if in your rash youth you had composed two-and-a-half hours of music for a spectacle propagandizing on behalf of Stalin's First Five-Year Plan and scapegoating wreckers, all at a time (1931) when show trials and denunciations were laying the foundations for the murder of millions of your fellow citizens? In a word, I would suggest, embarrassed. It is not enough to say that no one in their right mind could have refused such a commission, or that Shostakovich carried out much of it with a slapdashness which amounted as near to contempt as he could dare, or that the Soviet critics condemned the results with a barrage of pejoratives (though I would agree that all those things have to be given due weight). No, *The Bolt* can be neither laughed nor shrugged off. It is a disturbing symptom of a very sick society, and it is surely no wonder that Shostakovich was noticeably less keen to see it restaged than *Lady Macbeth* or *The Nose*.

The passion in this passage is welcome, since it is appropriate, yet its internal contradictions suggest that its author, overtaken by a sudden revelation[15] of how hideous Stalinist society was even at this early stage, has here temporarily forfeited the 'judicious balance between stylistic and ethical questions' which he advances as his ideal in the Introduction to *Shostakovich Studies*.

Accusing Shostakovich of having approved the foul sentiments propagated in the scenario to *The Bolt*, Fanning suggests that the composer must in retrospect have felt 'embarrassed' about doing so. One might have thought 'anguished', 'horrified' or 'conscience-stricken' more appropriate for a man as hypersensitive as Shostakovich. Yet when, towards the end of his life, it was mooted that *The Bolt* be revived, he was merely dismissively discouraging (just as he was about the Second and Third Symphonies). No horror, no anguish, not even much embarrassment – only the awareness, as clear to him then as it seems to have been in 1931 when he was commissioned to compose the ballet, that it was 'shit'. Presumably, then, the rest – the hell of the First Five-Year Plan – had been as tangible to Shostakovich during 1928–32 as it obviously was in the 1970s.

[15] Perhaps brought on by reading Richard Taruskin's account of Russia in the early 1930s (Taruskin, 'Lies'), compiled for *Shostakovich Studies* (pp. 17–56) early in 1995. *Cf.* pp. 652 *et seq.*

Seemingly late on the uptake about what Shostakovich and his fellow artists had been faced with around 1931, Fanning is right to be shocked but wrong to place the blame for his outrage on the composer. The mitigating circumstances he lists – and which he admits should be given 'due weight' – could only be employed to 'laugh or shrug off' *The Bolt* by someone of shallow sensibility and sketchy historical awareness. They are very serious factors indeed and together constitute a strong case for believing Shostakovich's later attitude to the ballet to have reflected a similar, if not identical, attitude to it at the time of its composition. David Fanning's final judgment – 'a disturbing symptom of a very sick society' – is sufficiently neutral to offend no one, whatever their view. But Shostakovich can hardly be blamed if the ballet he was forced to write (or risk being hounded by RAPM and classified as 'unreliable' by the GPU[16]) should be symptomatic of that frightful situation. How could it not be?

The inevitable concomitant of suggesting that, in *The Bolt*, Shostakovich effectively upheld the purges of Russia's technical intelligentsia in the Shakhty and 'Industrial Party' show-trials, is that, in his exactly contemporary opera *Lady Macbeth*, he must also have been supporting Stalin's genocidal campaign against the peasants. This is the thesis propounded by Richard Taruskin, an American musicologist who, in the words of David Fanning, possesses 'a scholarly grasp of Russian music in all its aspects unrivalled outside Russia (and possibly within Russia too)'. 'No one', Fanning continues, 'is better placed to turn back the "torrent of romantically revisionary, sentimental nonsense" which Taruskin finds characteristic of writing on Shostakovich in the eras of glasnost' and post-Communism'.[17] If this is true, it says more about the regrettable condition of present Shostakovich musicology than about Taruskin's supposed eminence within it. For example, one might expect of a scholar that he argue his case without losing his temper (in

[16] On RAPM, *cf.* pp. 340 and 543, note 27; the GPU (Gosudarstvennaya Politicheskaya Administratsiya, or State Political Administration), later replaced by the NKVD, was, of course, the secret police.

[17] Fanning, p. 3.

Fanning's book Taruskin manages to call me a 'McCarthyite', a 'Stalinist' and a 'vile trivialiser' within the space of one page).[18] What is more serious – and a matter of interest, one trusts, to his academic peers in America – is his apparent willingness to bend the entire framework of the subject to accommodate his own viewpoint.

Richard Taruskin boasts a peculiar pedigree in the Shostakovich debate. Beginning as a supporter of Solomon Volkov, he turned on him when, in 1980, Laurel Fay published an essay purporting to demolish the integrity of *Testimony*.[19] Stung by this implied affront to his dignity, Taruskin has since fiercely opposed all attempts to interpret Shostakovich with any reference to *Testimony* which is not outright dismissive. In this, he has been buttressed by Fay and a third American academic, the Prokofiev specialist Malcolm Hamrick Brown. Taruskin, though, is first among equals, the bell-wether of Shostakovich anti-revisionism. Until recently Taruskin's main contribution to the Shostakovich debate was his article 'The Opera and the Dictator: The Peculiar Martyrdom of Dmitri Shostakovich'.[20] Here, he argues that *Lady Macbeth*, far from a tale of individual passion in a proto-collectivist society, is instead an apologia for Stalin's genocidal campaign of 1930 against the *kulaks*. To Taruskin, the opera is 'a profoundly inhumane work of art' in which its composer ('perhaps Soviet Russia's most loyal musical son') by various means 'dehumanizes' his heroine's persecutors and victims so as to 'perpetrate [the] colossal moral inversion' of legitimising her murders. *Lady Macbeth*, he claims, is a politically motivated travesty which presents all of its cast except Katerina as 'class enemies' to be despised and

[18] Reviewing Taruskin's recent book on Stravinsky in *Tempo*, No. 200, April 1997, pp. 36–39, English composer-musicologist and Shostakovich specialist Gerard McBurney reported that 'Taruskin writes (and indeed talks) with the unmistakably ungentlemanly air of a bully'. Initially overawed by Taruskin's loutish demeanour ('the splendid leer of a prosecution lawyer scenting the blood of his cowering opponents'), McBurney eventually tired of it ('just too much irritation and scorn'). I leave the reader to judge from subsequent excerpts from Taruskin's writings as to whether the cap fits.

[19] *Cf*. pp. 7–8 and 117.

[20] Taruskin, 'Dictator' pp. 34–40.

destroyed. 'Its chilling treatment of the victims', he concludes, 'amounts to a justification of genocide'.

Taruskin's view of Shostakovich as 'perhaps Soviet Russia's most loyal musical son' is an extreme version of the image familiar from the days when (in Taruskin's words) 'the old official view (of) the composer as an unwavering apostle of Soviet patriotism and established ideology' was still in force. That official view began to crumble with the appearance of *Testimony*, was given a little help on its way by myself a decade later,[21] and has since been almost entirely destroyed by the many testimonies of the composer's former friends and colleagues, enabled to speak freely by the collapse of the Soviet Union in 1991. Although Taruskin's theory predates this collapse, he has since repeated it in full and with no substantial changes.[22] It is as if, by having posthumously exposed Taruskin to the possibility of ridicule, Shostakovich (not only Volkov) must be counter-exposed by Taruskin as a thoroughgoing rogue. Yet theories, however outré, must be taken on their merits. Is Taruskin's plausible?

I have argued[23] that on half-a-dozen grounds Taruskin's analysis of *Lady Macbeth* fails to add up. The most obvious objection, however, is the fact that the opera, written between the ages of 23 and 25, continued to mean something deeply special to Shostakovich for the rest of his life. In the words of his son Maxim, it was 'his child which he loved a lot'. In terms of Taruskin's hypothesis, this allows only two conclusions: either Shostakovich did mean to suck up to Stalin by 'dehumanising' the peasants in *Lady Macbeth*, and, for some reason (amorality? senility? stupidity?) saw no cause to be troubled by this attitude thirty years later; or that he harboured nothing remotely approaching the ideas Taruskin proposes – in which case Taruskin's thesis becomes, at best, unconscionably irresponsible.

How, for example, are we to understand the climactic quotation from *Lady Macbeth* in the Eighth Quartet – a work dedicated (ambiguously, in the revisionist view) to 'the

[21] In *The New Shostakovich*.

[22] *Cf*. p. 172, note 204.

[23] 'Arena', *DSCH Journal*, 2, Winter 1994, pp. 37–40. Also *cf*. pp. 531–34, note 6 and p. 534, note 9.

victims of Fascism'? Is this Shostakovich's confession of complicity in genocide? (After all, according to Lev Lebedinsky, his intended next act was suicide.[24]) If we ignore the extensive testimony in Elizabeth Wilson's book to the effect that Shostakovich was a humane, highly intelligent, acutely sensitive man – and Taruskin is anxious to rubbish as much of this as he can – we might, at a very long stretch, conclude that the composer was a dim, indecisive, morally obtuse Soviet collaborator whose ostensibly anti-Stalinist and anti-anti-Semitic works are in truth expressions of guilt instilled in him by a vague awareness that his life had consisted of a series of catastrophic misapprehensions. ('What a dismal surprise awaited them!' Taruskin jeers, describing the supposed fumbling attempt by Shostakovich and his librettist to curry favour with Stalin by writing *Lady Macbeth*. 'How completely they had misunderstood the nature of Stalinism', etc.[25]) Of course, even this strained hypothesis would not explain why, having made his 'confession' about *Lady Macbeth* in the Eighth Quartet, Shostakovich went on to adapt the opera for further performances and even connived at making a film of it. What an unprincipled scoundrel he must have been! With what diabolical ingenuity must he have faked the strength of mind and character which we gullible souls hear in his symphonic works and chamber music and on which all his acquaintances remark!

It appears that something more than the old academic superiority-complex about Shostakovich's intelligence drives Taruskin's theory of him. In a sense, his view amounts to a duel to the death wherein one or other, Shostakovich or Taruskin, must perish ignominiously. Yet, coherent or not, Taruskin's thesis is toughly argued and reinforced with historical references. To lay readers, this display may seem authoritative. Is it? Let us examine his essay on the Fifth Symphony, given pride of place by Fanning in *Shostakovich Studies* by being positioned first.

Taruskin opens with a spectacular assault on those who falsify the past, although the novelty here is that he attacks

[24] *Cf.* pp. 476–77.

[25] Taruskin, 'Abominable', p. 25.

not the erstwhile Soviet regime but those who take a revisionist, post-*Testimony* view of Shostakovich's life and music:

> *Poshlost'* – smug vulgarity, insipid pretension – has always lived and thrived in such accounts. Risking nothing, we excoriate the past to flatter ourselves. Our high moral dudgeon comes cheap. It is sterile. In fact it is nostalgic. We look back upon the Stalin period romantically, as a time of heroism. We flay the villains, *as we define them*, and enjoy an ersatz moral triumph. We not only pity the victims, *as we define them*, but envy them and wishfully project on to them our own idealized identities. Nor have we even given up our investment in personality cults, it seems; all we have done is install new worshipped personalities in place of the old. The new idolatry is as blinding as the old, just as destructive of values, just as crippling to our critical faculties. Shostakovich remains just as hidden from view as he was before, and efforts to make him visible are still roundly denounced, if from the other side.[26]

Taruskin's style in this passage indicates a mood of fury hardly suited to persuading his reader that existing definitions of villainy and victimhood vis-à-vis Soviet history are self-flattering misconceptions. The paradoxical trick of presenting the likes of Stalin, Yezhov and Beria as victims of their situation can indeed almost be brought off – as in the final chapter of Chris Ward's *Stalin's Russia*,[27] which commences under the genuinely self-flattering inscription *Tout comprendre, c'est tout pardonner* – but to do so requires a low-key actuarial stance which elevates political theory and demographical statistics over 'anecdote' and 'circumstance'. By contrast, Taruskin here attempts to cudgel the reader into believing that including context and probable intention in our account of Shostakovich is 'as destructive of values, as crippling to our critical faculties' as Stalin's monstrous 'personality cult'. If proposing an equivalence between Stalinism and revisionism in Shostakovich studies is positively surreal, the rest of Taruskin's disquisition, with its quaint attempts at

[26] Taruskin, 'Lies', p. 18; emphasis added. In a footnote to this last statement, Taruskin refers to his article on *Lady Macbeth*, 'The Opera and the Dictator', and to my comments on it in a letter to *The Times Literary Supplement* (28 September–4 October 1990, p. 1031).

[27] Edward Arnold, London, 1993, p. 228 (hereafter Ward).

insight into the minds of his enemies, merely seems morally deficient. It is astonishing that one should have to point out that Stalinism happened within our lifetimes and that, unless continuously investigated and explained to future generations, could recur in some modified form in the near future. Is Taruskin urging total moral relativism? Would he wish us to forgive Hitler's SS and stop bothering our heads with what went on at Auschwitz on the grounds that such concern is 'romantic', 'nostalgic' or 'self-flattering'? Has he noticed what's been going on in Bosnia and Chechnya and China recently?

Resuming a semblance of academic probity, Taruskin proceeds to a brief account of the Soviet Cultural Revolution and the subsequent imposition of Stalin's cultural bureaucracy in 1932. So far as it goes, this is useful scholarship, especially since Taruskin is unusual among musicologists in describing the era of the First Five-Year Plan at all, let alone accurately portraying it as 'an orgy of totalitarian coercion [. . .,] a time of unprecedented political and economic violence, replete with show trials, mass arrests and punitive mass starvation, ceaselessly accompanied by a din of mass indoctrination that included the hardening of the Stalin personality-cult'.[28] Although Taruskin makes no deductions

[28] Perhaps he arrived at this picture via his own studies; perhaps his attention was drawn to it by the only music book ever to have focused on it before: *The New Shostakovich*. Or perhaps he was provoked into researching the subject by my contention, made in my aforementioned letter to *The Times Literary Supplement*, that his 'contorted reading [of *Lady Macbeth*. . .] makes nonsense of the wider context of Shostakovich's life in the early Thirties'. Whatever the truth, the awkwardness with which this section joins the main body of Taruskin's essay is, in effect, acknowledged by its author: 'That is enough about phoney *perestroyka*. It is an ugly word and a much-rehearsed (if still under-documented) one, and I have recalled it only as a preface to the *perestroyka* that is my subject, Shostakovich's own'. This sentence conceals some curious sleight-of-hand. The *perestroyka* (literally, 'restructuring') of the Cultural Revolution, far from 'much-rehearsed', as Taruskin claims, is as under-investigated as it is under-documented. So far but one book – Sheila Fitzpatrick's *Cultural Revolution in Russia 1928–31* (Indiana University Press, Bloomington, 1978) – has examined the phenomenon as a whole, and then merely provisionally. Indeed, more research is required into this cultural period, if only because the current partial understanding of it makes it hard to arrive at firm conclusions about Shostakovich's outlook in the music he composed under its auspices. But if this is so, why Taruskin's pose of

about how this ghastly era is likely to have affected the outlook of musicians and composers at the time, at least he mentions it, which is more than can be said of most of his colleagues in musicology. He is also – scandalously – unique among musicologists both in acknowledging the 'mortal duress to which artists in the Soviet Union were then subjected' and in pointing out that Shostakovich's Fifth Symphony was 'first performed' – performed, the reader will note, as distinct from composed – 'at the very height of [. . .] perhaps the bloodiest political terror the world has ever seen'. Nor do these examples represent the only contributions which Taruskin makes to our understanding of the Fifth Symphony in this essay. His discussion of the work's reception is relatively calm, his assertion that the Symphony is 'a richly coded utterance, but one which can never be wholly encompassed or defined' is close to the truth,[29] while his identification of 'the "intonations" and the "imagery" of leave-taking and of funerals' in the *Largo* is revelatory. Relaxed in his expertise, he can even make us smile, describing Nikolay Chelyapov's attempts to distinguish the Composers' Union's programme from that of RAPM as 'no mean task, actually'. In short, there is enough here to show that a less intemperate Richard Taruskin might have been the definitive Shostakovich expert David Fanning supposes he is. Unfortunately, this impression is not maintained.

Having discoursed sensitively about the *Largo* of the Fifth as an expression of literally unspeakable grief – 'every member of the symphony's early audiences had lost friends and family members during the black year 1937, loved ones whose deaths they had had to endure in numb horror'[30] – Taruskin arrives at the work's finale, where he must confront

---

familiarity with the allegedly plentiful 'rehearsing' of a topic which has, in reality, barely reached the audition stage?

[29] Although it roundly contradicts his own confident assertion elsewhere ('Who Was Shostakovich?', *Atlantic Monthly*, 275/2, February 1995, p. 71; hereafter Taruskin, 'Who') that the Eighth Quartet represents the only 'explicit note [in a bottle]' in Shostakovich's career.

[30] This included Shostakovich. In 1937, his mother-in-law Sofiya Varzar, his uncle Maxim Kostrikin, and his brother-in-law Vsevolod Frederiks were all arrested. Frederiks subsequently died in the Gulag. Meanwhile Shostakovich's sister Mariya was internally exiled to the city of Frunze.

the question of whether it 'fails on purpose'[31] or merely because the composer, for some reason, could not write his way out of a compositional *impasse*. Here, seemingly infuriated by the idea that Shostakovich might have been the sardonic, critical observer of *Testimony*, Taruskin summons a display of coercive bluster so misrepresentative of historical fact as to undermine his claim to be a serious commentator on Soviet affairs:

> If we claim to find defiant ridicule in the Fifth Symphony, we necessarily adjudge its composer, at this point in his career, to have been a 'dissident'. That characterization has got to be rejected as a self-gratifying anachronism. There were no dissidents in Stalin's Russia. There were old opponents, to be sure, but by late 1937 they were all dead or behind bars. There were the forlorn and malcontented, but they were silent. Public dissent or even principled criticism were simply unknown. Dissidence began under Khrushchev. It is natural that latter-day dissidents would like [Shostakovich] for an ancestor. It is also understandable, should it ever turn out that Shostakovich was the author of *Testimony*, that he, who though mercilessly threatened never suffered a dissident's trials, should have wished, late in life, to portray himself in another light. The self-loathing of the formerly silent and the formerly deluded has long been a salient feature of Soviet intellectual life.[32]

Taruskin dismisses as 'a self-gratifying anachronism' the idea that Shostakovich could have had any 'dissident' agenda in a work as early as the Fifth Symphony on the grounds that 'there were no dissidents in Stalin's Russia' – i.e., Shostakovich wasn't a 'dissident' because he didn't publicly dissent (until, one presumes, the Thirteenth Symphony). As a proposition, this is tautological; as a general view of Stalinist Russia, it is, frankly, preposterous.[33] Of course there were no

[31] Taruskin, 'Lies', p. 46.

[32] Taruskin, 'Lies', pp. 46–47.

[33] Apparently embarrassed by the crassness of Taruskin's contentions, Fanning, p. 3, attempts to soften the impact by claiming that their purveyor 'urges us, in effect, to distinguish between dissidence and nonconformism'. Fortunately the concept of 'nuance' is sufficiently alien to the full-tilt Taruskin that we can declare, without fear of contradiction or prevarication, that he 'urges' nothing of the kind.

public dissenters against Stalin's regime; anyone under the illusion that public dissent was then feasible – as Eric Roseberry seems to be[34] – is either naïve or new to the subject. By choosing an expression ('dissidence') applicable only after 1956, Taruskin erects a meaningless Aunt Sally. No one who claims to detect signs of anti-Stalinism in Shostakovich's Fifth Symphony has ever referred to the composer as a 'dissident' in post-1956 terms. My own preference is for the phrase 'secret dissident', following (for example) Mstislav Rostropovich, who conceives Shostakovich's symphonies as 'a secret history of Russia',[35] and Nadezhda Mandelstam, who documented what she called Russia's 'secret intelligentsia'[36] – those who privately dissented with the regime from the early days of the Revolution and continued to do so until the public idiom of dissidence emerged under the milder conditions of the 1960s. Among Madame Mandelstam's associates in this milieu was the poetess Anna Akhmatova who secretly wrote the sequence *Requiem*, concerning Stalin's Terror (while this process was going on), whispering it to friends in case of hidden microphones.

[34] Roseberry (author of *Ideology, Style, Content, and Thematic Process in the Symphonies, Cello Concertos, and String Quartets of Shostakovich*, Garland, New York, 1989) has voiced doubt about the post-*Testimony* concept of the finale of the Fifth Symphony as expressive of a forced rejoicing. 'After all', he writes (in 'Some Thoughts After a Re-reading of *Testimony*', in *Melos*, 1/4–5, Summer 1993, p. 24), 'Shostakovich's original pronouncements on this symphony at the time of its Moscow première made no mention of such a hidden agenda'. To anyone even vaguely familiar with the situation in Russia in 1937–38, the assumption behind this sentence – that no hidden agenda Shostakovich might have had at that time could have been serious enough to hide – will seem ludicrous, as will the idea that he could have openly confessed such an agenda during Stalin's Terror (or, indeed, at any time before the 'thaws' of the '60s). Russians to whom I have read this passage have been amazed that an 'expert' on Shostakovich could have so little comprehension of the general subject-area of which the composer was a part.

[35] Quoted in MacDonald, *The New Shostakovich*, p. 6. In an interview for *BBC Music Magazine* (February 1995, pp. 16–20), Rostropovich called Shostakovich 'the uncapped historiographer of our lives', adding that, had this been apparent to the Soviet authorities, he would have ended up behind bars – 'but music is too abstract, especially for idiots'.

[36] Nadezhda Mandelstam, *Hope Against Hope*, Collins Harvill, London, 1971, pp. 318–19.

Requiem contains details about the Terror (interrogation procedures, transit prisons, the extent and location of the Gulag) which were likewise whispered amongst the Soviet populace as the Terror proceeded. Such instances gainsay Taruskin; yet the naivety of his conception – dead or jailed Old Bolsheviks on the one hand and the empty-minded (if sometimes 'forlorn and malcontented') masses on the other – requires closer consideration if it is to be thoroughly discredited.[37]

Elsewhere,[38] Taruskin has contended that Shostakovich was not a dissident but an *intelligent:* 'He was heir to a noble tradition of artistic and social thought – one that abhorred injustice and political repression, but one that also valued social commitment, participation in one's community, and solidarity with people. Shostakovich's mature idea of art, in contrast with the egoistic traditions of Western modernism, was based not on alienation but on service'. It is hard to see how Taruskin can reconcile his nobly unalienated Shostakovich with the lackey who, he claims, tried to curry favour with Stalin by demonising the peasants in *Lady Macbeth* (let alone with the tragi-satirist who lambasted the Soviet state in the Thirteenth Symphony). More to the point is that this portrait of the Soviet *intelligenty* is wildly inaccurate; indeed,

[37] Taruskin's idea that Stalin's purges liquidated his 'old enemies' and froze the rest of Soviet society into a general state of hypnotised terror is a crude version of the 'totalitarian' model of Stalinist repression current in Western Soviet studies during the 1950s and '60s. Yet, as Merle Fainsod suggested in *How Russia Is Ruled* (Harvard University Press, Cambridge, Massachussetts, 1963), Stalinist totalitarianism was 'inefficient', i.e., not totally controlled through a vertical chain of command, but rather by an overlapping agglomeration of competing power centres within the Stalinist system. Recent scholarship on the purges of the 1930s (e.g., J. Arch Getty and Roberta T. Manning (eds.), *Stalinist Terror: New Perspectives*, Cambridge University Press, Cambridge, 1993) has confirmed this looser, less predictable model in some detail, including the finding that the Old Bolsheviks, whom Stalin is supposed to have wiped out during the late 1930s, were not targeted as such, although the mortality rate of a particular stratum of membership within this group was unusually high (J. Arch Getty and William Chase, 'Patterns of Repression Among the Soviet Elite in the Late 1930s: A Biographical Approach', in Getty and Manning, pp. 225–46). Taruskin's conception is not only simplistic even by earlier standards but now empirically refutable and thus obsolete.

[38]. Taruskin, 'Who', pp. 70 and 72.

contemporary Russian intellectuals would probably call it (to borrow Taruskin's own unfortunate phrase) 'romantic [. . .] sentimental nonsense'.

Russia's intelligentsia, a social stratum which much exercised Lenin (who on one memorable occasion informed Maxim Gorky that its members represented, not the nation's brains, but shit[39]), was, from the October coup in 1917, almost entirely opposed to the Bolshevik government. These people, representing both the scientific-technological world and that of the arts and humanities, were generally speaking liberal democrats and, as such, supporters of the Constituent Assembly. Thus, when Lenin dissolved this elected body (in which the Bolsheviks were in a minority), the intelligentsia began to resist.[40] According to Zhores Medvedev, 'The larger part of the senior research and academic personnel backed the anti-Bolshevik forces, and during the first waves of Red Terror "professors" and "academicians" were almost automatically considered to be enemies of Soviet power'.[41] Indeed, Richard Pipes records that Lunacharsky 'virtually had to beg students and teachers to end their boycott of the new regime'.[42] This did not mean that the intelligentsia were necessarily conservative. Writing in 1919, the agrarian socialist Vladimir Stankevich noted, among the Moscow *intelligenty*, 'a fanatical hatred of the Bolsheviks' together

[39] *V. I. Lenin i A. M. Gorky* (*V. I. Lenin and A. M. Gorky*), Academy of Sciences Publishing House, Moscow, 1961, p. 263.

[40] *Cf.* p. 550, note 45.

[41] Boris Kagarlitsky, *The Thinking Reed: Intellectuals and the Soviet State from 1917 to the Present*, Verso, London, 1988, p. 48 (hereafter Kagarlitsky).

[42] *Russia Under the Bolshevik Regime*, Harvill, London, 1995, p. 286. 'In time', continues Pipes, 'many intellectuals made their peace (or, rather, truce) with the regime, often to escape death from starvation, but even they proved grudging collaborators at best. The "creative intelligentsia" whom the regime succeeded in winning over were mostly hacks and daubers unable to make it on their own, who, like similar mediocrities in Nazi Germany, flocked to the party in power in quest of patronage'. Nadezhda Mandelstam confirms that starvation was often the lot of 'secret intellectuals' (*sic*) who were unable to come to a working accommodation with the authorities under Stalinism (*Hope Against Hope*, p. 319).

with not a trace of sympathy for the Whites.[43] The truth is that the Russian intelligentsia were mostly cautiously progressive, and hence as disinclined to revert to a former autocracy as to embrace a future one. They represented the central majority of Russian political sentiment and, but for Lenin's ruthlessness, which simply annihilated thousands of them, they might have offered a viable alternative to Stalinism.[44]

The 'problem of the intelligentsia' continued to be a bane to Bolshevism after the Civil War. In 1925, Bukharin acknowledged that 'in the initial period of the October Revolution it was the worst section of intelligentsia who came over to us', whereas 'the majority of the honest intelligentsia were against us'. Indeed, he admitted that the *intelligenty* were still a problem which required solution: 'We need standardised intellectuals, as if from a factory'.[45] Not that the intelligentsia could publicly dissent even in 1925, for the labour camps created by Lenin in 1918 to accommodate the Left opposition were already filling with intellectuals deemed generally 'unreliable'.[46] Dissent had to be private or oblique. Roy Medvedev: 'Many of the old intelligentsia took an ironic or frankly contemptuous attitude to the Bolshevik leaders, Stalin among them. For these people Lenin was no idol. *They expressed such attitudes only among themselves, however, not in public*'.[47] Such were those whom Stalin sought to quell with his 'wrecking' trials of the technical (scientific and engineering) intelligentsia and with the Cultural Revolution against the arts and humanities intelligentsia. Medvedev and Robert

[43] Kagarlitsky, p. 48.

[44] Christopher Norris, reviewing my book *The New Shostakovich* as a revival of Cold War attitudes ('Shostakovich and Cultural Politics', *Melos*, 1/4–5, Summer 1993, p. 37), has suggested, astonishingly, that the 'only alternative' to Communism in the 1920s was 'some form of minimally liberalized quasi-Tsarist autocracy'.

[45] Moscow Communist Party conference on the question of the intelligentsia, February 1925.

[46] *Cf.* Alexander Solzhenitsyn on the policy of 'social prophylaxis' in *The Gulag Archipelago*, Collins Harvill, London, 1974, Vol. 1, pp. 42 *et seq.*

[47] Roy Medvedev, *Let History Judge: The Origins and Consequences of Stalinism*, rev. edn., Oxford University Press, London, 1989, p. 285 (my italics; hereafter R. Medvedev).

Conquest supply long lists of liquidated *intelligenty*, indicating that, as well as these 'names', thousands of lesser-known figures, from university academics to school teachers, were similarly done away with. When Stalin attacked in 1928–29, the proportion of 'counter-revolutionaries' among the intelligentsia was officially put at 'between 90 and 95 percent'.[48] As it happens, this was a gross oversimplification made for the express purpose of facilitating a purge. Most of the intelligentsia, although acutely aware of the baleful illiberality of the Soviet regime, had no alternative but to work for it – and did so, so far as they were able, conscientiously. Far from wishing to eradicate 'wreckers' (a category of dissenters which amounted to a figment of propaganda), Stalin simply meant to crush the liberal intelligentsia's will to resist.[49]

In the early days of Stalin's assault on the nation's brains, the brunt of it fell on the 'technicians' – people of a scientific or engineering background shared by Shostakovich's father (a histologist), first wife (a physicist), mother-in-law (an astronomer, arrested in 1937), and brother-in-law Vsevolod Frederiks (a physicist, also arrested in 1937). Wits then referred (among themselves, of course, not in public) to the holding jails of major Soviet cities as the 'engineer-technician vacation homes'.[50] Those arrested, moreover, were far from bewildered by what was happening to them. D. Vitkovsky, a chemical engineer 'picked up' in 1931, recalls: 'Everyone had learned the lessons of the Shakhty and Ramzin ['Industrial Party'] trials very well: you could save your skin only by denouncing yourself and others. No one had any illusions about the real aim of these confessions'.[51] Nor was cynicism the prerogative solely of the arrested. In spite of government endeavours to manage events, rumours ran through Soviet

[48] Kagarlitsky, p. 89.

[49] Robert Conquest: 'The Russian intelligentsia had for over a century been the traditional repository of the ideas of resistance to despotism and, above all, to thought control. It was natural that the Purge struck at it with particular force' (*The Great Terror: A Reassessment*, Hutchinson, London, 1990, p. 291; hereafter Conquest).

[50] R. Medvedev, p. 286.

[51] R. Medvedev, p. 286. For more on the Shakhty and Industrial Party trials, *cf*. MacDonald, *The New Shostakovich*, Chapter 2, *passim*.

society like wildfire (for example, the 'bush telegraph' transmission of news of the suicide of Stalin's wife in 1932, reported in the press as a case of fatal illness). Indeed private dissent was rife even beyond the privileged *intelligenty*, and, in 1932, at the end of the First Five-Year Plan, during which the peasants of the Ukraine had been in open revolt, the general mood in the country was resentful and rebellious.

A bout of politico-cultural *perestroyka* curbed this incipient mutiny: the bureaucracy of control evolved under the aegis of Socialist Realism, backed up by the machinery of surveillance and terror developed by Yagoda, muzzled even the obliquest public expression of dissent among Russia's surviving intellectuals.[52] 'During the 1930s', writes Fyodor Druzhinin, 'fear became the uppermost emotion for Shostakovich and for our intelligentsia. It was a fear not only for their personal existence, though that was real enough, but a fear for their families, their work, and their whole country.'[53] To such fear was added perpetual propaganda designed to confuse and delude. 'Only a boss should have time to think', was the line sent out to the country in Afinogenov's Stalin-edited play *The Lie* in 1933. Should one have been unused to thinking, or tired of it, or aware that it was dangerous, here was a ready-provided excuse to give it up and become a 'cog'. Many Soviet citizens were poorly educated and simple-minded; they easily acquiesced. Others, mesmerised by ideology, were already robots. But to conclude from this – as Taruskin apparently does – that, somewhere between 1932 and 1937, the entire populace of the USSR, including the historical awkward-squad of its specialist intelligentsia, completely ceased to have any private thoughts, is to take behaviouristic contempt for the individual mind to an absurd extreme.

In the first place, we know that not only Akhmatova and Nadezhda Mandelstam but virtually every writer of note, from Maxim Gorky downwards, either had serious doubts

[52] *Cf.*, for example, Mikhail Heller and Aleksandr Nekrich, *Utopia in Power: The History of the Soviet Union from 1917 to the Present*, Hutchinson, London, 1986, pp. 262–76 (hereafter Heller and Nekrich); Conquest, pp. 291–307.

[53] Wilson, p. 390.

about the regime or, in private, harboured some form of dissenting sentiment.[54] The reason so many of these people lived in nerve-corroding fear of arrest was that they knew that, by the state's definition, they warranted it. Secretly they questioned or disagreed: that made them 'counter-revolutionaries'. Nor, except in brief exchanges with trusted colleagues (such as Babel's with Ehrenburg[55]), could the extent of their secret dissidence be intimated, let alone openly expressed. Thus they went on thinking, observing and, so far as possible feeling, while at the same time delivering manuscripts and speeches which denied their inner world.

Richard Taruskin would have us believe that throughout Stalin's dictatorship such astute men and women had only a blank space in their skulls – not a single sceptical impression from which to fashion a critical thought. He thinks they fell victim to 'kidnap syndrome', whereby a captive is psychologically remade as an admirer of his captor: 'The nearest parallel in today's world is the case of Salman Rushdie, whose response to dire death threats has included reconfirmation in the faith of his oppressors'.[56] But only fragile minds succumb so easily. Even after weeks of grotesque torture and sleep-deprivation, men like Babel and Meyerhold (and many others among the show-trial casts of 1936–38), reverted from confession to denial. As for Salman Rushdie, does not Taruskin realise that the author's 'reconfirmation' as a Moslem was a transparent ploy which no one, least of all himself, took seriously? Furthermore, does he not think that Rushdie's desperate strategy to get his persecutors off his back, however ignominious, is justified by his continued production of literature which resists illiberality and is still greeted by critics as among the finest fiction currently being written in Britain? And does he spy here no parallel with Shostakovich?

Taruskin suggests that Shostakovich was like the mass of Soviet society in being bamboozled by Stalinist propaganda. As for 'masses', one should be wary of sweeping judgments.

[54] Vitaly Shentalinsky, *The KGB's Literary Archive*, transl. John Crowfoot, Harvill, London, 1995, *passim* (hereafter Shentalinsky).

[55] *Cf. The New Shostakovich*, pp. 117 and 121–22.

[56] Taruskin, 'Lies', p. 24.

To claim, on the basis of probability, to be privy to the minds of hundreds of millions of people is a large claim indeed, from whatever point of view. Yet even 'ordinary' people deprived of privileged information will not long succumb to propaganda which finds no confirmation in everyday life. The inability of Soviet manufacturing industry to deliver the goods it incessantly boasted of 'overproducing' was a bad joke to its weary consumers[57] long before Stalin died. Power-cuts, shortages and all-round shoddiness were as endemic as 'disappearing' neighbours and diametrical turn-arounds in the daily decrees of official truth from the state media. (By all accounts, Iranian citizens are equally cynical about their own 'revolutionary' state.) One must assume that Taruskin's occupation allows little commerce with 'ordinary' people.

In this respect, he resembles a British academic specialist on North Korea who appeared on television during the week of mourning for Kim Il Sung – an epic display of such apparently unfeigned grief that the reporter who interviewed this specialist wanted to know if it could possibly be genuine. Of course it was, the latter confidently replied. He had visited North Korea regularly for the last twenty years and could assure us that the people loved their Leader with a deep devotion. Sadly his confidence, like that of rather too many academic 'experts' on totalitarian regimes before him, was soon scuppered by a pair of detailed reports by the British journalist Terry McCarthy in *The Independent*.[58] Travelling around North Korea, snatching brief conversations with 'ordinary' people, most of whom were still too frightened by their brutal regime to voice their feelings in anything but hurried asides and oblique comments, McCarthy discovered a populace 'soaked in cynicism' about its insane political system and longing for freedom and change. An almost identical state of affairs obtains in the quasi-Stalinist 'People's Republic' of China. John Simpson, chief foreign correspondent for the BBC, writes:

[57] *Cf.* Sarah Davies, *Popular Opinion in Stalin's Russia: Terror, Propaganda, and Dissent: 1934–41*, Cambridge University Press, Cambridge, 1997.

[58] 21 and 22 November 1994.

> [Among the] different processes going on at the time of the Tiananmen demonstrations of 1989 [. . .] was a fullscale rebellion by the Beijing working-class. I saw a little of this myself, and was shaken by the sheer hatred ordinary people had for Communism and for everyone who worked for it. Driving through Beijing a couple of days after the massacre, I saw dozens of police stations and party offices wrecked, and the burned bodies of policemen, soldiers, and party officials left in the streets.[59]

So much, one might think, for the empty-minded masses. Yet Taruskin's view of Shostakovich's degree of awareness becomes the more absurd when one considers that the composer was anything but part of mass society; rather, he belonged to an intellectual community almost all of which was covertly anti-Bolshevik, let alone anti-Stalinist, and which had possessed a privileged, if partial, view of what was happening in Russia from 1917 onwards.[60] To posit that anyone as intelligent and individual as Shostakovich could have been fooled in isolation would be far-fetched enough; to maintain as much of a man who was incessantly at the fulcrum of Soviet cultural politics from the age of nineteen, had so many friends and colleagues in the arts world that his lists of people to 'say hello to' in any Soviet city amounted to miniature directories, and who numbered among his contacts several of the country's most important disaffected writers – not to mention Marshal Tukhachevsky[61] – is to abandon

[59] *The Sunday Telegraph*, 29 June 1997.

[60] After the purges of the early 1930s, a significant new recruitment to this intelligentsia was Jewish, which accounts in large part for Stalin's anti-Semitic policies from 1936 onwards. *Cf.* Kagarlitsky, pp. 128–29. Also *cf.* pp. 221–28 and 686–708 on Laurel Fay's eccentric assertions about Soviet anti-Semitism.

[61] Shostakovich's link with Tukhachevsky was probably the most important of all such relationships in terms of providing him with up-to-date information on the inner workings of the USSR. Stalin had a long-standing jealousy and suspicion of his generals and of Tukhachevsky in particular. Hence purges within the Soviet military continued at relatively low intensity throughout the '30s, a situation of which Tukhachevsky was fully aware. He therefore lived in constant anticipation of what eventually befell him in 1937 and was not surprised when it finally came to pass. *Cf.* Harold Shukman (ed.), *Stalin's Generals*, Weidenfeld & Nicolson, London, 1993, pp. 255–73.

credibility. To Taruskin, Shostakovich's links with men like Zoshchenko, Bulgakov, Zamyatin and Olesha – rather than, say, with Gorky, Fadeyev, Nikolay Ostrovsky and Aleksey Tolstoy – hold no significance. To suggest otherwise, according to Taruskin, is 'sinister' and Vyshinsky-like: the 'rank tactic' of 'the very model of a Stalinist critic' (he means me).[62] It has been said that one cannot be honest, intelligent and a Communist; one can be any two of these, but not all three. When I point out that Shostakovich was on friendly terms with what Taruskin calls 'a few anti-Utopian writers of the 1920s' (satirists, actually), I do so not to prove 'guilt by association', or even innocence by association, but rather intelligence by association. However, I concede that this point is probably lost on Richard Taruskin.[63]

The recurrent theme of Russian testimony on Shostakovich to have emerged since Dzerzhinsky's detested statue in Lubyanka Square was toppled is that the composer was a long-standing secret dissident able to voice dissent where others could not by expressing it obliquely via instrumental music. 'Shostakovich could say in music what could not be said in words.' We read and hear this statement repeatedly from his former friends and colleagues. Indeed, Elizabeth Wilson's book *Shostakovich: A Life Remembered* (which Taruskin, in 'Public Lies and Unspeakable Truth', does not even mention) is crammed with such affidavits.[64] Are we to reject all of this as special pleading, as Taruskin directs us to and as David Fanning seems half-inclined to? Taruskin

[62] In Fanning, p. 53.

[63] Stalinism was a crudely anti-intellectual system run by NCO-level cadres drafted in by Stalin from the provinces to replace the high-grade Leninist Bolsheviks he liquidated. Robert Conquest makes this point in his review of Robert W. Thurston's *Life and Terror in Stalinist Russia, 1934–41*, where he deplores Thurston's 'honest naivety' in 'praising the "upward social mobility" found under Stalinism, while omitting the downward mobility into the execution cellars of the Lubyanka and the gravepits of Lelashevo that accompanied it; and, even more importantly, neglecting the nature of those promoted – the "negative selection", as they now say in Moscow, of the "morally and intellectually crippled", as Alexander Weissberg put it' ('Stalin: The Revised Edition', *National Review*, 15 July 1996, pp. 45–48).

[64] *Cf.* my 'Witnesses for the Defence', (*cf.* Bibliography, p. 744).

asserts that Rudolf Barshai, Isaak Glikman, Georgiy Gachev and twenty or so Russian commentators he fails to acknowledge are merely 'egoistically trivializing the agonies of the Stalin years' in claiming to detect signs of secret dissidence in Shostakovich's music of this era. I would suggest that, on the basis of what is generally accepted in all adjacent fields of Soviet study, this statement represents at best a flagrant ignorance of the facts; a less charitable view might suspect a deliberate attempt to mislead lay opinion.

In his discussion of Shostakovich's Fifth Symphony, Richard Taruskin raises legitimate questions about my interpretation. Far from being defensive about this, I welcome the fact that musicologists are thinking along these lines.[65] As for diversity of interpretation, this is inevitable (though not to the extent of giving up interpretation itself simply because not all of us hear everything the same way). Yet the terms of the debate remain strangulatingly narrow. One of the half-dozen ideas I attempted to introduce into the Shostakovich debate in *The New Shostakovich* (written in 1988–89) is that the composer was as much a satirist as a tragedian. During the 1980s, under the influence of the rather straightfaced recordings of the Symphonies by Bernard Haitink, Shostakovich's music had been routinely interpreted as nobly tragic. The innocent assumption then, as we have to recall less than a decade later, was that Shostakovich's melancholy was almost entirely provoked by anguish over Russia's war casualties.[66] Anything too brashly or bitingly disruptive to

[65] For example, Patrick McCreless, in his essay on the Second Piano Trio (Fanning, pp. 113–36), offers a sensible interdependent examination of form and expression. McCreless defines his aim as the interrelation of 'what we might call the "cycle of structure" (the network of thematic and tonal development and return across movements) with what we might call the "cycle of meaning" (the way that the multi-movement work as a whole makes a coherent extra-musical statement)'. In spite of his uncritical adoption of the philosophical solecism of 'extra-musicality', McCreless is precisely on target here and his essay, which intelligently takes issue with my interpretation (offering a finer reading of the climactic transition in the finale), is a model of what Shostakovich musicology, at a minimum, should be.

[66] E.g., David Pownall's naïve play *Master Class*, Faber and Faber, London, 1983.

this edifying agenda was assimilated as irony – though the issue of what the composer might have intended to be ironic about was never broached. Consequently Shostakovich's music began to be spoken of with a solemn face similar to that adopted by politically unenlightened literary critics vis-à-vis Orwell's *Nineteen Eighty-four*, a book customarily discussed as a relentlessly grim (and speculatively futuristic) anti-Utopia. What I proposed in 1989 was that – like *Nineteen Eighty-four*, which, when grasped as a satire on Stalinism circa 1948, becomes, in its first half at least, bitterly funny[67] – much of what Shostakovich wrote, heard in the context of his socio-political background, is as blackly humorous as the social satires of his favourite authors.

My thesis that Shostakovich was partly a satirist received support in 1994, when we discovered from several of Elizabeth Wilson's witnesses that he loved Russian literary satire so much that he knew reams of it by heart. Yet so far no musicologist has taken up this idea with any certainty (if at all) – all except Richard Taruskin, who, with his 'No Dissent' theory of Stalinism, attempts to exclude even the possibility that Shostakovich might have had hidden, let alone satirical, purposes in his work. In this connection it is worth observing that Taruskin's reading of the Fifth Symphony differs from mine chiefly in refusing to concede Shostakovich any active intention in it beyond that of carrying on to the next bar. Taruskin allows his 'little puppet Mitya'[68] passively to vent 'suppressed grief' in the *Largo* but not to express anything in the way of considered thought about the cause of this grief. He cannot, in other words, be allowed to be actively critical of

[67] *Cf.* MacDonald, *The New Shostakovich*, pp. 265–70. The error of not 'placing' *Nineteen Eighty-Four* in a Soviet context is still being made, with the usual misdirecting consequences, e.g., W. J. West (in *The Larger Evils. Nineteen-Eighty-Four: The Truth Behind the Satire*, Canongate, London, 1992, p. 2): 'It would be a strange reader who could find something to laugh at in Orwell's masterpiece in any chapter, let alone on every page. The book resembles far more strongly a deliberate cold warning'. To put it simply: without knowledge of the context Orwell is satirising, his jokes cannot be appreciated. The same goes for Shostakovich. *Cf.* Robert Conquest, 'Orwell: *1984*' (in *Tyrants and Typewriters. Communiqués in the Struggle for Truth*, Hutchinson, London, 1989, pp. 86–96).

[68] Taruskin, 'Lies', p. 31.

anything, let alone harbour satirical intentions. Why? Because he would start to look like the sardonic Shostakovich presented by Solomon Volkov in *Testimony*.

Taruskin seems to come to no conclusion as to whether the coda of the finale of the Fifth is ambiguous in tone or structure, let alone in being so on purpose. As for the pregnant quotation from 'Rebirth', the first of Shostakovich's *Pushkin Songs*, Op. 46, he concludes only that 'the image [conveyed in the words attached to the musical passage in question] suggests not the promise of a bright future but an escape into the past' – an interpretation consistent with a dissenting ('counter-revolutionary') outlook. Although this contradicts Taruskin's thesis that Shostakovich could have had no 'dissident' intent in his music of this period, he ventures no further opinion.

Nor does he mention Gerard McBurney's observation[69] that the first four notes of the finale are also the first four notes of the song, and, as such, correspond to the words 'A barbarian artist' in Pushkin's text:

> A barbarian artist, with sleepy brush
> Blackens over a picture of genius
> And his lawless drawing
> Scribbles meaninglessly upon it.
>
> But with the years, the alien paints
> Flake off like old scales;
> The creation of genius appears before us
> In its former beauty.
>
> Thus do delusions fall away
> From my worn-out soul,
> And there spring up within it
> Visions of original, pure days.

McBurney's thesis is that Shostakovich used Pushkin's poem, itself an Aesopian text written under Tsarist censorship, as a way of encoding the true meaning of the otherwise inevitably debatable finale of the Symphony. Stalin – or his cultural *apparat* – is the 'barbarian artist' who blackened over

[69] 'A Hidden Agenda', BBC Radio 3, 26 February 1993. Elizabeth Wilson (p. 125) paraphrases the essence of McBurney's talk, a passage which Taruskin must have read in 1994 (ample time for him to have incorporated this information into his essay for Fanning's 1995 anthology).

Lady Macbeth in the *Pravda* editorial of 28 January 1936 and in 1937 forced Shostakovich to veil his own intentions in the Fifth Symphony. In other words, the first statement of the finale, erupting brutally from the hypersensitive hush of the *Largo*, conjures precisely the 'external, elemental, subjugating force' (Georgiy Khubov's words[70]) which revisionist commentators identify as driving the coda. Moreover, Pushkin's lines offer multiple resonances for Shostakovich's predicament: the 'lawlessness' of the barbarian artist's drawing corresponds to the indifference of the Stalinist justice system to legal process; 'original, pure days' suggests a yearning allusion to the pre-Communist era; 'thus do delusions fall away' anticipates both the misunderstanding the finale is bound to evoke and its eventual correct explanation once the Pushkin allusions are grasped. (It is worth noting, too, that the word *chisti* – meaning 'pure' in the sense of having been cleaned and restored to its original state, thus completing Pushkin's painting metaphor – is directly related to the Russian word for 'purge', *chistka*, now infamous in the term 'ethnic *cleansing*'.) The Pushkin reference thus allowed Shostakovich to have his cake and eat it: he could leave it as a clue to his true intentions – and, if put on the spot about it by the authorities, he could maintain that the poem referred to himself as a 'restructured' personality embracing Communist anti-individualism. The code was deniable, as it had to be.

If this argument is accepted, we are bound to conclude that Shostakovich's outlook throughout the Fifth Symphony was one of dissent amounting to muted protest. Whether the coda of the finale is tragic or satirical then becomes a matter of opinion; it can be heard either way. (Certainly the scherzo becomes arguably satirical, as Maxim Shostakovich and Kurt Sanderling have recently asserted.[71]) Without splitting hairs over the difference between irony and satire, it is clear that, contrary to Taruskin's contentions, there is a *prima facie* case to be made for a dissenting tone and intent in the Fifth. Why, then, despite the fact that they were made public more than

[70] Taruskin, 'Lies', p. 38.

[71] *Cf*. p. 408, above, and the notes to Sanderling's recording of the Fifth Symphony, Berlin Classics BC 2063-2.

three years earlier, does Taruskin disregard McBurney's suggestions? Is he simply omitting any data which does not redound to his advantage? And is this why he makes no mention of the testimonies in Elizabeth Wilson's book? These suspicions increase when we examine his account of the reception of the Fifth Symphony.

Taruskin begins by tacitly excluding any possibility of dissent or satire. Shostakovich, he claims, was unpersoned in 1936 not because Stalin or his cultural *apparat* sensed anything intrinsically suspect in his music (beyond its refusal to abide by the optimistic folk-nationalism of the prescribed style) but 'as a demonstration of the might of Soviet power [and] because his precocious fame and his phenomenal talent had made him the object of the greatest envy'. In other words, it happened to be time to stamp on a famous composer and the envy of Shostakovich's less talented colleagues had made him a target. At present we lack the data with which to speculate on the complex question of what really transpired between Shostakovich and the Soviet authorities in 1936–37, beyond observing that Taruskin's assertion that the composer voluntarily withdrew the Fourth Symphony is contradicted by Isaak Glikman (who reports it as a decision forced on Shostakovich from 'on high'[72]), and suggesting, in a spirit of truce, that, until the Stalin Archive is opened, we lack the materials from which to form a judgment.[73]

More to the immediate point is the general thrust of Taruskin's narrative, which suggests that the affair was almost entirely a question of Socialist Realist aesthetics: the Fourth Symphony, he asserts, failed to conform to official prescription by being formally unruly, whereas the Fifth 'amounted to a paradigm of Stalinist neoclassicism'. Here, we might be tempted to pursue a diversion: the contemporary Socialist Realist ideal in symphonism. For instance, can it possibly be true that the cloth-eared Stalin and his *lumpen* art stooges desired 'neoclassical' symphonies in 1937? Was this not a counter-revolutionary bourgeois idiom which only

[72] Wilson, p. 119.

[73] Some documents from the Stalin Archive have been used by Edvard Radzinsky in his recent (and scathing) biography *Stalin*, trans. H. T. Willetts, Hodder & Stoughton, London, 1996.

came into demand in 1938–39 when the USSR suddenly needed to cozy up to the West, fearing the breakdown of its clandestine arrangement with Nazi Germany?[74] Did not the Soviet authorities in 1936–37 actually want more tub-thumping 'song-symphonies' of the sort dutifully churned out by Lev Knipper?[75] But such questions, though interesting, are beside the point at hand – which is that, having ruled out anything more serious than musical style as an issue in the Shostakovich Affair of 1936–37, Taruskin needs to show that the Soviet system assimilated the Fifth Symphony without any ideological difficulty as part of a predetermined Pavlovian process of public reward and punishment.

Auditioned in a piano-duet reduction by the composer and Nikita Bogoslovsky at the Leningrad Composers' Union early in autumn 1937, Shostakovich's Fifth was available to the cultural *apparat* at least three months before its Leningrad premiere. From this, Taruskin concludes: 'Shostakovich's work was known on high before its public unveiling. Its status as apology and as a promise of personal *perestroyka* was a conferred status, bestowed from above as if to show that the same power that condemned and repressed could also restore and reward'.[76] In other words, the Soviet assimilation of the Fifth Symphony was instant: the state welcomed it from the outset with the smooth smile of one who has had time to prepare a watertight alibi.

Suggesting that Shostakovich's 'forgiveness was surely just as foreordained as his fall', Taruskin claims that the composer's remuneration for fulfilling the Socialist Realist requirements of 'heroic classicism' was 'the immediate reward [of] an orgy of public praise [which] went on for months, to the point where Isaak Dunayevsky, the songwriter who was then president of the Leningrad Composers' Union, tried to put on the brakes [with] a memorandum comparing the Fifth's reception to a stock speculation, a

[74] *Cf.* Stephen Koch, *Double Lives: Stalin, Willi Munzenberg and the Seduction of the Intellectuals*, HarperCollins, New York, 1994, *passim*.

[75] *Cf.* Boris Schwarz, *Music and Musical Life in Soviet Russia 1917–1970*, London, 1970, pp. 160–61 (hereafter Schwarz).

[76] Taruskin, 'Lies', p. 24.

ballyhoo, even a psychosis that threatened to lead Soviet music into a climate of "creative *laissez-faire*" in which the Union might not be able to exercise its police function'.[77] The date of Dunayevsky's memorandum was 29 January 1938, the day of the Moscow premiere. The performance at which the Fifth Symphony had first been unveiled to the public was the Leningrad premiere on 21 November 1937, two months earlier. If official praise of the Fifth Symphony had been going on 'for months' by the time Dunayevsky took up his poison pen, this approval must certainly have been 'fore-ordained' and 'immediately' expedited. Indeed, Taruskin supplies one example of such instant response: a 'groveling civic panegyric' (*sic*) printed in *Muzyka* on 26 November 1937, in which the authors call Shostakovich's new symphony 'a work of such philosophical depth and emotional force [as] could only be created here in the USSR'. Aside from this, the only reviews praising the Fifth which Taruskin brings to our notice date from 1938–39 – with one exception: Aleksey Tolstoy's *Izvestia* piece which appeared four days from the end of 1937.

Tolstoy (observes Taruskin) in this article assimilated the symphony to a contemporary Soviet literary genre which concerned 'the formation of new consciousness – personal *perestroyka* – on the part of "searching heroes", honest blunderers whose life experiences teach them to embrace revolutionary ideals'. From Tolstoy's article came the prefabricated catchphrase 'the formation of personality (within a social environment)' which, absolving the *Largo* of Shostakovich's Fifth Symphony from the charge of tragic individualism, became the basis of the official Soviet view of the work as embodying 'the (re)making of a man'.[78] Dismissing the view, voiced in *Testimony*, that Tolstoy's piece was ghost-written by musicologists, Taruskin presents it as if it were the initiative of its author alone, rather than part of an official campaign to assimilate the Fifth Symphony initiated a full month after the Leningrad premiere. Yet we need only read the article to see that it *was* ghost-written: 'Our audience

[77] *Ibid.*, pp. 26–27.

[78] *Ibid.*, p. 32.

is organically incapable of accepting decadent, gloomy, pessimistic art. Our audience responds enthusiastically to all that is bright, clear, joyous, optimistic, life-affirming [etc., etc.]'. This passage – taking the (*de facto*) enthusiasm of the People as proof that Shostakovich's *perestroyka* was genuine (and thus officially condonable) – is expressed in standard Socialist Realist officialese which the authorities could have obtained from any retained hack without troubling Count Tolstoy, whose participation was clearly required solely for the sake of his name and who, only two years earlier, would have been replaced by Gorky. That the 'Tolstoy' article became the matrix for the official terminological assimilation of the Fifth can have been no accident. It was clearly written as such and must therefore have been deemed necessary by Stalin's *apparat*.

But if the 'Tolstoy' article was deemed necessary on 28 December 1937, there must have been something the authorities considered awry with the general reception of the Fifth before that point. That this was purely a question of diversity of expressed opinion is vanishingly unlikely in that such diversity was designedly forbidden by the prefabricated phraseology of Socialist Realism, which all published writers were then obliged to use like pieces of verbal Lego. What, on the face of it, appears more likely is that an undertow of jealous grumbling from Shostakovich's rivals in the Composers' Union had, by mid-December 1937, coincided with a basic uncertainty among the cultural *apparat* over what to make of the Symphony, thereby creating a need for a fully considered official position on the work.

In other words, Taruskin's 'immediate' praise was not, as he claims, 'foreordained' and pre-scheduled by Stalin's arts watchdogs, still less 'policed' by editors primed to censor and rewrite along a precisely prescribed political line. Instead, and within the necessary limitations of Socialist Realist newspeak, it was an unpoliced – and hence entirely unofficial – expression of genuine front-line critical feedback.[79] It was precisely this unofficial enthusiasm for Shostakovich's Fifth

[79] The authors of the aforementioned 'groveling civic panegyric' in *Muzyka* were two obscure Moscow composers, neither of whom ever held any rank in the Composers' Union.

against which Dunayevsky was delegated to register an official warning. Taruskin has it backwards.[80]

Isaak Glikman – whose testimony Taruskin insinuates (on no given grounds) is somehow questionable – records that, far from assimilated and contextualised by the Soviet authorities soon after its audition in early autumn 1937 (i.e., in preparation for the critical D-day of its Leningrad premiere), the Symphony was still undefined and the subject of pessimistic speculation during rehearsals. He and Shostakovich 'remembered how, during the rehearsals of the Fifth Symphony, certain people had doubts about the work; there was nothing extraordinary in their trepidation. Only after the premiere, did I tell Dmitry Dmitriyevich how some of the orchestral musicians warned me that the Symphony would definitely be torn to shreds by the critics [. . .]. This was said without a trace of malice on their part, but rather with regret'.[81]

The fact that there was no sense of officially prefabricated triumph among the orchestra as they rehearsed the Symphony suggests that there was likewise none among the *apparatchiki* who would have hung around the hall while the rehearsals were under way. Indeed, this is confirmed by the then-director of the Leningrad Philharmonic, Mikhail Chulaki (no friend of Shostakovich), who wrote about the bureaucratic reaction to the Fifth Symphony in *Zvezda* in 1987.[82] Far from being a 'foreordained' and 'immediate' success in official circles, the Fifth, insists Chulaki, was received at first with surprise and then with suspicion among the *apparat*, the official belief being that the enthusiastic reactions the work was drawing must somehow have been 'fabricated' by 'wreckers' out to sabotage the People's music. Chulaki quotes the conductor Aleksandr Gauk who heard

[80] Dunayevsky, an eminently disposable cog, would never have had the temerity to criticise an 'officially-sanctioned orgy of praise' unless, having tired of life, he wished to quit it forthwith by means of a bullet-hole in the back of the neck. Supposing him, on the other hand, to have had a normal desire to go on breathing, he would have dared publicly to deplore only something which the *apparat* likewise deplored (i.e., something out of its ken and its control).

[81] Wilson, pp. 129–30.

[82] *Ibid.*, pp. 132–38.

Shatilov, the director of the Musical Department of the Repertoire Committee in Moscow, seriously telling another official the day after the Leningrad premiere that the popular success of the Fifth Symphony had been 'a put-up job arranged by Shostakovich's Moscow friends, who had gone to Leningrad for this very purpose'. Accordingly, two senior officials from the Central Arts Committee, Surin and Yarustovsky (later satirised by Shostakovich in *Rayok*) were immediately dispatched to Leningrad 'to find out how it was that the concert organisers had managed to inspire such a loud and demonstrative success'. At the next performance of the Symphony, this gruesome twosome surveyed the wildly cheering audience. Chulaki heard Surin 'shout' over the applause: '"Just look, all the concert-goers have been handpicked one by one. These are not normal concert-goers. The Symphony's success has been scandalously fabricated", and so on [. . .]'.[83]

Secure in this surrealistic conclusion, Surin and Yarustovsky returned to Moscow, where they trumpeted it around official circles. Chulaki continues:

> *For some time*, echoes of the 'symphonic scandal' stirred up by the two officials continued to reach Leningrad. I had to write explanations, fill in questionnaires and prove the absence of the criminal. [. . .] And in the meantime the Symphony continued its life, and was widely performed, invariably exciting a lively and enthusiastic response from its audiences. But what was to be done about the 'official opinion', which would *at some point in time* have to be formulated by the big-wigs so that it could filter downwards? *At last* the Leningrad District Party Committee showed interest in the Symphony [emphasis added].

Chulaki describes how he was required to stage a special audition of the Symphony for the Leningrad Party Aktif. His Party liaison ('a very decisive, butch lady') took one look at

[83] Their reaction (and subsequent initial report to Moscow by telephone) is apparently alluded to in the libretto to *Rayok*, where they are referred to as 'the employees of the Department of Musical Security of the MIP (Ministry of Ideological Purity), B. M. Yasrustovsky and P. I. Srulin' and described as calling 'the district Sewage Disposal Unit' which arrives without delay at 'the scene of the accident' (the 'accident', in this case, being the far from officially 'foreordained' Fifth Symphony in D minor).

Chulaki's suggested programme and replied: 'What's all this, symphonies and more symphonies? We need something for the People'. (Evidently not an *aficionada* of 'Stalinist neo-classicism'!) In spite of a sticky moment when Chulaki narrowly escaped social reclassification as a 'saboteur', the concert went ahead and, according to Sofiya Khentova,[84] led to the official Soviet definition of the Symphony as 'an optimistic tragedy'. Richard Taruskin does us the honour of mentioning this last fact but otherwise says absolutely nothing about the attestations of Glikman, Gauk and Chulaki, which, to say the least, bear crucially on his supposedly scholarly account of the reception of the work.

Far from being the 'foreordained' redemption of a temporarily disgraced artist, the evidence (and any sensible deduction) suggests rather that the response of the *apparat* to Shostakovich's Fifth was a hasty botch designed to make a world-famous composer (upon whom they could not then lay a finger) seem part of their stupid world of bumpkin ideology – pure *Testimony*, in other words. No wonder Taruskin cannot stomach it.

If the officially defined approval of the Fifth dates from 1938 and 1939, there clearly can have been no planned reception of the sort Taruskin wishes us to believe in. This, in turn, implies (as does Chulaki's account) that the rank-and-file official view of Shostakovich's music was, at best, obtuse and, at worst, totally uncomprehending. In other words, there was plenty of room for Shostakovich not only to have entertained satirical thoughts but also to have secreted them in his symphonies.[85]

One of the tools of satire is impersonation, which necessarily involves a specific focus on individual personages, real or imagined. Taruskin refers scornfully to a passage in my description of the Fifth Symphony in which I see, in a dialogue between solo flute and horn, the image of 'two dazed delegates agreeing that the rally had been splendid and the Leader marvellous'. To debunk this notion, he calls upon

[84] Taruskin, 'Lies', p. 34

[85] Such a looser, less efficiently 'totalitarian' situation in the policing of Soviet music under Stalin would be consistent with recent historical findings (*cf.* Getty and Manning).

'Shostakovich', in his guise as a piece of journalism bearing his byline and printed in the March 1933 issue of *Sovetskaya Muzyka*: 'When a critic writes that in such-and-such a symphony Soviet civil servants are represented by the oboe and the clarinet, and Red Army men by the brass section, you want to scream!' Taruskin adds: 'I don't imagine he would have felt any differently were the civil servants represented by the flute and the horn'. One infers that Taruskin believes impersonation of personages by musical instruments to be either impossible in itself or, within the magnificent precincts of a symphony, too vulgar to be admissible.

Let us address the 'impossibility' option first. Consider 'Samuel Goldenberg and Schmuyle' from Musorgsky's *Pictures At An Exhibition*; then ponder the fourth variation in the march from the *Leningrad* Symphony. Consider, too, Mahler's satirical song 'In Praise of Lofty Intellect' in the context of the 'braying donkey' effects in the finale of Shostakovich's First Piano Concerto, the scherzo of his First Violin Concerto, and at the start of the second movement of his Sixth Symphony. As for whether certain passages in Shostakovich's symphonies, as in Mahler's, entail instrumental impersonations, one can, in the absence of words-of-one-syllable confirmation from the composer, argue only on the basis of probability. That Russian symphonism admitted such literalness is shown, for example, by Alexander Tcherepnin's Fourth Symphony (1957), which contains a passage where violin phrases 'name' the streets during an evocation of a carriage drive through St Petersburg. In a similar vein, an important theme in Nikolay Myaskovsky's Sixth Symphony (1923) is a 'musicalisation' of the words 'Death, death to the enemies of the Revolution!' which he heard shouted by the state prosecutor Nikolay Krylenko.[86]

Although Shostakovich's ballets are full of such stuff – and, as such, hardly distinguishable from similar passages in

[86] In the opinion of Nikolay Korndorf, co-founder of the modern Association for Contemporary Music, Myaskovsky's Sixth Symphony is 'about' (*sic*) a specific aspect of the October Revolution: 'I think it describes the destruction of culture, the death of creators including writers, composers, and artists'. He adds: 'For me, this is real music in that it is nonconformist' (Anne Ferenc, 'The Association of Contemporary Music in Moscow: An Interview with Nikolai Korndorf', *Tempo*, No. 190, September 1994, p. 3).

(for instance) his Fourth Symphony – Taruskin, like Malcolm Brown, rejects the suggestion that the composer was capable of stooping to such vulgarly 'illustrative' means. Yet we know that Shostakovich did, on occasion, think musically along these very lines. In a passage from her war-time diary in Kuibyshev (supplied in Elizabeth Wilson's book[87]), Flora Litvinova describes Shostakovich as reciting from memory a passage from Gogol's *Dead Souls*:

> He ordered that the washing utensils be brought up to him, and for an excessively long time he scrubbed both his cheeks with soap, inflating them from inside his mouth with his tongue; then taking the towel from the shoulders of the inn servant, he dried his fleshy face on all sides, starting from behind his ears, snorting first a couple of times in the servant's face. Can you imagine this scene? Here I would use a bassoon, trumpet, and drum. Then when he puts on his shirt-front, 'having plucked two hairs from his nose', I'd use the piccolo [. . .].

Litvinova adds: 'When Gogol goes on to describe the Governor's party, Dmitri Dmitriyevich *gave each personage a musical characterisation*' (emphasis added).

Many witnesses have described Shostakovich's talent for satirical impersonation; indeed, Marina Sabinina has shown that, given the chance, he would satirically impersonate Soviet officials 'by quota' in batches of a dozen at a time.[88] Moreover, all of the major conductors who worked closely with Shostakovich are known to have conceived passages in his symphonies in precisely this way. Kurt Sanderling, for instance, hears a piccolo solo in the second movement of the Eighth Symphony as representing 'a young army officer who has been given an unexpected weekend pass and goes whistling away down the road', while a bassoon solo is 'a puffed-up party *apparatchik* swaggering off on his first trip abroad'.[89]

[87] Wilson, p. 166.

[88] Wilson, p. 225. According to his close friend Isaak Glikman, Shostakovich 'always spoke with a nuance of irony' (Glikman, *Lettres à un ami*, Albin Michel, Paris, 1993, p. 9).

[89] *Cf.* pp. 575–76.

Similar observations are on record by Mravinsky, Kondrashin, Rozhdestvensky and Maxim Shostakovich.[90]

What, then, of the comment 'by' Shostakovich in *Sovetskaya Muzyka*? If it indeed represents his opinion in March 1933, it appears to be one of those views of his which were true at one time of the day, or in one context, and untrue in another. At best, it is an attack, not on musical impersonation itself, but on the dull interpretation of it by dimwits. It may even have been a double-tongued hint that his music did, in fact, contain such material. This sort of deviousness was scarcely unknown.

For example, apparently intending to show that the authorities had some inkling of what was going on in Shostakovich's Fifth Symphony, Taruskin quotes from a commentary, made in February 1938, by the Marxist critic Georgiy Khubov in which the latter manages to hint that the Symphony is subversive while at the same time suggesting that this subversion is inadvertent: that the composer stands betrayed by his recalcitrant bourgeois individualism and that his symphonic *perestroyka*, while he may in some part of himself have wished it to be sincere, is nevertheless not so (i.e., he does not truly love Big Brother). Taruskin senses this ambiguity: 'Khubov, writing from the depths of the Stalinist freeze, leads his "perceptive, attentive listener" to all the unmentionable truths [about the work's alleged hidden agenda] adumbrated after the thaw [. . .] all the while stating their falsehood'. But why, one is bound to ask, should Khubov have done this? Was he, in some obscure way, simultaneously a perceptive critic and an obtuse zealot? Had he perhaps been officially mandated to aim a shot across Shostakovich's bow? Or was he a covert admirer of Shostakovich, trying Aesopically to draw attention to the secret dissidence in the Symphony while simultaneously heading off retribution for this error by describing it as a regrettable but unintentional by-product of the composer's still untranscended social limitations?

Georgiy Khubov was exactly the sort of ambiguous figure to fit the more devious hypothesis. He maintained an orthodox face throughout the 1940s and 1950s, and, with

[90] Wilson, p. 315; Kondrashin, pp. 519–20; *The Independent*, 6 April 1991; Albert, pp. 400–18.

Kabalevsky, was one of the chief critics of the resubmitted *Lady Macbeth* at the Ministry of Culture audition in March 1956. (Here, he reiterated the *Pravda* attack of 1936.) Yet Khubov was also an advocate of Shostakovich's rehabilitation after 1953 and was early in criticising the stereotyped products of Socialist Realism. His paper of February 1953, delivered while Stalin was still alive, can be read both ways: on the one hand, as a plea for fewer bureaucratic restrictions on music and an end to the so-called 'no-conflict theory'; on the other, as an expression of nostalgia for the heyday of Socialist Realism. (His speech to the Second Congress of the Composers' Union in 1957 is similarly hedged with suggestive ambiguities.) In the long run, Khubov either altered his Marxist views or let his mask slip. Dismissed from the editorship of *Sovetskaya Muzyka* for 'revisionism', he became a friend of Shostakovich and was at his Moscow flat along with Irina Antonovna in 1974 when the Taneyev Quartet first played the composer his Fifteenth Quartet. These facts raise questions about what Khubov was really driving at in his 1938 observations on the Fifth Symphony, not the least of which is: did Shostakovich grasp what he was up to? (Isaak Glikman recalls that the composer's expression, on reading Khubov's description of the *Largo*, was one of 'bewilderment'.[91] Could it, instead, have been one of alarm mingled with a twinge of excitement at being understood, even by an apparent enemy?) Taruskin tells us nothing about any of this, and one is forced to ask why. Perhaps looking too closely at someone like Khubov, whose real opinions were so difficult to pin down, might have made a remark like 'There were no dissidents in Stalin's Russia' seem overbearingly simplistic? After all, why venture (shrewdly) that Khubov's analysis contains 'a rich vein of rhetorical ambiguity inviting readerly irony, in short, of doublespeak as classically defined'[92] only to dismiss it by describing its apparent perspicacities as arrived at 'wittingly or unwittingly – it matters not'? The crux of this discussion is intention; treating it as immaterial takes us back to square one.

Even if we refuse to concede satire as one of Shostakovich's intentions in the Fifth Symphony – despite the fact that in

91 *Lettres à un ami*, p. 20.

92 Taruskin, 'Lies', p. 38.

Russia during 1927–34 it was as a musical satirist that he was primarily considered – it should be clear at least that, short of jeopardising his family, he was prepared to resist the demands of the regime as far as he could. As Boris Schwarz wrote in 1972:

> It is often overlooked that [the Fifth Symphony] *could have been* the Fourth Symphony, had [Shostakovich] so desired [. . .]. In the four months that elapsed between the first article in *Pravda* and the completion of the Fourth Symphony, Shostakovich could have reshaped the Fourth Symphony to make it more acceptable in terms of the official criticism. Shaken though he was by the criticism, he followed his artistic conscience and left the Fourth intact.[93]

What Schwarz misses is that Shostakovich could have presented the Fifth Symphony as his Fourth, thus kowtowing even lower to the authorities by dropping the Fourth from his symphonic canon altogether, instead of leaving an intriguing gap which must have caused endless speculation among Soviet concertgoers. Not to have done so is, at the very least, suggestive of a mind with thoughts of its own.

Richard Taruskin's essay on the Fifth Symphony is, it seems, not a work of scholarship, which requires a certain dispassion, but a polemic. There is nothing wrong with polemics if they are announced as such. If, on the other hand, they are presented as academic studies which weigh all points of view and take account of all the data on offer and yet are nothing of the kind, we may justifiably feel deceived. The *modus operandi* of this particular deception is misrepresentation by omission. Taruskin, for example, is content offhandedly to dismiss as special pleading the sort of testimony Elizabeth Wilson has patiently amassed in her indispensable book. Fanning, by contrast, appears to be unable to choose between such differing accounts because everyone might be lying. Yet this is true of every other subject-area within the overall scope of 'Soviet culture'. And why? Because the USSR was a totalitarian entity in which truth was perverted at source by the state and in which paranoid rumour consequently ran riot. Lamely to excuse oneself from coming to any 'probable'

[93] Schwarz, p. 172.

conclusions on local details when the general nature of Soviet life between 1917 and 1991 is now so copiously documented is intellectual helplessness of the first order.

Where this academic disinclination to pass judgments results in mere vagueness, the harm is mild, if nonetheless misleading; where it involves casting aspersions on the credentials of witnesses in order to make failing to come to a judgment seem a positive virtue, the damage is less readily forgivable. For instance, Fanning refers slightingly to Lev Lebedinsky and Daniil Zhitomirsky as 'apostates of the proletarian line', drawing no distinction between the status of their testimony and the contrary contentions of Yury Levitin. In fact, Lebedinsky and Zhitomirsky were among the first free-thinkers in the realm of Soviet musicology after the War and, as such, staunchly anti-Stalin – attitudes upon which were founded their post-war friendships with Shostakovich. Because of his nonconformity, Lebedinsky was for many years obliged to work mostly in the field of 'folklore', confining his dissent to cryptic journalistic references to Shostakovich's 'resistance to authority'. Similarly, Zhitomirsky (like Georgiy Khubov) was banned from the pages of *Sovetskaya Muzyka* as a revisionist during 1963–65. By contrast, Levitin, their opponent in the 1990 Russian-language revisionism debate, became a Party member in 1947 and thereafter remained, to all intents and purposes, a supporter of the official line. Nor, contrary to Fanning, is the musicologist Leo Mazel' neutral as between Lebedinsky and Levitin in their rival views of the Seventh Symphony; instead, whilst rebuking Lebedinsky for his 'one-dimensional' interpretation, Mazel' confirms his claims about the Seventh Symphony, admonishes Levitin for 'ungentlemanly' misstatements and intemperate language, and goes on to propose his own revisionist interpretation of Shostakovich.[94] Here, Fanning allows disinterest to degenerate into outright misrepresentation.

Indeed, misrepresentation emerges as a central theme of academic anti-revisionism. For example, Malcolm H. Brown, attacking the present writer in 1993,[95] refers to

[94] *Cf.* Mazel', pp. 489 *et seq.*

[95] '*The New Shostakovich*: A Review', *Melos*, 1/4–5, Summer 1993, p. 30 (hereafter Brown).

Maxim Shostakovich's 'long-standing and outspoken skepticism about [Solomon] Volkov', claiming that 'the composer's son has complained about *Testimony* from the time of his defection to the West in 1981'. The lay reader would naturally conclude from this that Maxim has repudiated both *Testimony* and its editor continuously from 1981 to the present day. In fact, the truth, as Brown well knows, is that in 1981 Maxim spoke under the duress of possible Soviet reprisal against the Shostakovich family in the USSR;[96] that he substantially modified his views in favour of *Testimony* over the next four years, concluding with a full endorsement of it on television in 1986;[97] that he has since spoken of the book with, significantly, an approval matched in enthusiasm by that of his sister Galina;[98] and that, from 1989 onwards, he has publicly acknowledged his friendship with and respect for Volkov, an acknowledgment confirmed by a published interview[99] and an appearance together at a Shostakovich symposium in New York in 1992.[100]

Brown's apparent willingness to overlook these objections to his position is, to say the least, regrettable.[101] Nor is it the only instance of this sort of thing. In the same article, for example, he attempts to represent Shostakovich's acquiescence in being drafted into the Communist Party in 1960–61 as the cynical manœuvre of 'a sometime closet dissident and a sometime collaborator'.[102] Brown makes no mention of the testimony of Shostakovich's colleague Lev Lebedinsky that the composer was so upset by this episode that he planned to kill himself, leaving his Eighth Quartet as a suicide note.[103]

[96] *Cf.* pp. 59–60.

[97] Interview with Michael Berkeley, BBC2, 27 September 1986.

[98] *Cf.* pp. 83–84 and 111–14.

[99] 'On "Late" Shostakovich', interview with Solomon Volkov, *DSCH*, No. xiii, August 1989, pp. 35–38.

[100] *Cf.* pp. 373–99.

[101] *Cf.* also pp. 242–43.

[102] Brown, p. 32.

[103] Lebedinsky, 'Letters', *Novy Mir*, 1990, No. 3; *cf.* p. 476 and *The New Shostakovich*, pp. 221–24. For a rebuttal of Brown's case on this point, *cf.* Ian MacDonald, 'A Reply To Messrs Norris and Brown', *Melos*, 1/4–5, Summer 1993, pp. 45–46; also *Notes*, 50/3, March 1994, pp. 1207–10. Anyone requiring help in judging between the contenders

This claim, later amplified by Lebedinsky,[104] was effectively confirmed by Isaak Glikman in 1993.[105] In 1960, Glikman and Lebedinsky were Shostakovich's closest intimates – yet Brown continues to evade their evidence on this score, presumably because it contradicts what he prefers were true.

The same appears to be true of Richard Taruskin, not least because of his extraordinary refusal so much as to mention the mass of testimony provided by Elizabeth Wilson (testimony through which, in the view of Calum MacDonald, 'the relationship of individual works to the life is graphically brought out [allowing Shostakovich's] works [to] be read as coded protest and denunciation of Soviet misrule, infusing the melodic commonplaces and rhetorical vocabulary of musical "Socialist Realism" with transcendent ambiguity').[106] More extraordinary yet are Taruskin's continued attacks on Volkov as a purveyor of bogus goods without mentioning that Galina Drubachevskaya, a former colleague of Volkov at *Sovetskaya Muzyka*, has explicitly confirmed Volkov's story of how the interviews for *Testimony* came about.[107] This omission does not appear to be mere oversight: Taruskin cites Drubachevskaya's interview with Volkov in *Muzykal'naya Akademiya* (which starts with her aforementioned statement) in his review of the facsimile of Shostakovich's Seventh Symphony, published in 1993.[108]

---

may find instructive the spluttering incoherence of Brown's presumably discomfited response (*ibid.*, pp. 1210–11). Note, too, Maxim Shostakovich's statement (p. 398): 'My father cried twice in his life: when his mother died and when he came home to say "They've made me join the Party". [. . .] This was sobbing, not just tears, but sobbing. It was in the 1960s that he was forced to join the Party. There was simply no other way for him at that time'.

104 Wilson, pp. 335–38 and 340–41.

105 Glikman, *Lettres à un ami*, pp. 160–61; Wilson, pp. 338–39. To the contrary, Marina Sabinina claims that Shostakovich joined the Communist Party because 'membership would allow him to play a more active part in social and musical life', explaining: 'He had a very strong feeling to defend a right cause and innocent suffering people' (*Melos*, 1/4–5, Summer 1993, p. 68).

106 *Tempo*, No. 191, December 1994, pp. 42–44.

107 *Muzykal'naya Akademiya*, 1992, No. 3, pp. 3–14. *Cf.* pp. 315–16.

108 *Notes*, 50/2, December 1993, p. 759.

Indeed, turning a blind eye to Drubachevskaya's unequivocal and reiterated[109] support for Volkov is becoming something of an academic habit. Even David Fanning, who refers to *Testimony* as 'a curious mixture of rumour, fact and slanted reminiscence' and speaks (as from the moral high ground) of Volkov's 'well-known dishonesty', cites Drubachevskaya's interview,[110] though only to quote Volkov's frank admission that 'there's much we don't know about Shostakovich'. Fanning remains shamefully silent about Drubachevskaya's inconvenient testament to Volkov's probity.

Much of the misrepresentation perpetrated by anti-revisionists is inadvertent and can be ascribed to straightforward ignorance of the historical background. Eric Roseberry's remarkable solecism has been noted;[111] many similar instances casually bestrew record and CD sleeve-notes.[112] Yet anti-revisionist unfamiliarity with history often seems perversely willful. For example, in a recent article[113] about the song-cycle *From Jewish Folk Poetry*, Laurel Fay

[109] *Cf.* p. 255, note 46.

[110] Fanning, p. 4, note 11.

[111] *Cf.* pp. 166–67 and 657, note 34.

[112] E.g., the sleevenote to a Chandos disc (CHAN 9131) which manages half-a-dozen fundamental errors about the Soviet background in as many lines, including the claims that Stalin was in power at the time of the composition of Shostakovich's *Prelude and Scherzo*, Op. 11, and that NEP was Stalin's repressive invention (rather than Lenin's detour into liberalisation to avoid national economic collapse in 1921). Almost exactly the same muddle is made by Stephen Jackson in his 'Classic FM Lifelines' booklet on the composer (*Dmitri Shostakovich: An Essential Guide to his Life and Works*, Pavilion, London, 1997, p. 19), where he claims that Stalin took over from Lenin in 1924, immediately set about creating 'socialism in one country', founded the NKVD in 1926, and 'a couple of years later' inaugurated Socialist Realism. In fact, Stalin did not achieve his dictatorship nor begin to shape Soviet policy until the end of 1927, Socialist Realism was not enforced until 1932, and the Soviet secret police – created (not by Stalin but by Lenin) as the Cheka in 1917 – did not become the NKVD until 1934.

[113] 'The Composer Was Courageous But Not As Much as in Myth', *The New York Times*, 14 April 1996, Section 2, pp. 27, 32 (hereafter Fay, 'Myth').

has claimed that Shostakovich's ostensible courage in composing this work between 1 August and 21 October 1948 is an illusion of hindsight on the grounds that Stalin's anti-Semitic policies did not come into effect until a month after it was finished. To buttress this thesis, she observes that, far from writing *From Jewish Folk Poetry* 'for the drawer' in the knowledge that it could not then be performed, Shostakovich did not conceal the fact of its composition and expected to 'demonstrate' it early in 1949; that, in May 1948, Stalin ensured that the Soviet Union was the first country to recognise the state of Israel; that a contemporary *Pravda* editorial hailed the Soviet Union's policy of equality and mutual respect between the ethnic cultures of the country's constituent minorities; that, in September 1948, 50,000 Soviet Jews were allowed to greet Golda Meir as the first Israeli ambassador to the USSR; and that anti-Semitism did not officially appear until the liquidation of the Jewish Anti-Fascist Committee (20 November 1948). From this, Fay deduces that Shostakovich harboured no dissident intent in writing *From Jewish Folk Poetry* which was, instead, an earnest attempt to supply the contemporary demand of Socialist Realism for music in popular style based on folk-national themes. Shostakovich, argues Fay, was merely trying to fulfill his quota. 'It was his rotten luck', she concludes, 'that of all the available nationalities, great and small, he just happened to pick the wrong "folk" as his inspiration.'[114]

[114] In making this particular claim, Fay adds to the litany of anti-revisionist misrepresentation by selective quotation, in this case concealing the manœuvre by means of paraphrase: 'As Joachim Braun, the leading authority on the "Jewish" facet in Shostakovich's music, has pointed out, *From Jewish Folk Poetry* is an example of stylized urban folk art. It uses genuine folk texts. Its melodic and harmonic style is simple and accessible. Everything is in complete accord with the aesthetic precepts handed down by the Central Committee and ratified at the Composers' Congress' (Fay, 'Myth', p. 32). This appears to be a paraphrase of a passage in Braun's essay 'Shostakovich's Song Cycle *From Jewish Folk Poetry*: Aspects of Style and Meaning', in Malcolm H. Brown (ed.), *Russian and Soviet Music: Essays for Boris Schwarz*, UMI Research Press, Ann Arbour, 1985, p. 263. This same passage is itself a paraphrase by Braun of a paragraph in his earlier essay 'The Double Meaning of Jewish Elements in Dmitri Shostakovich's Music', a paper read at the XIII Congress of the Inter-

To take Fay's points in reverse order, she gives us to believe that official anti-Semitism was not operative in the

---

national Musicological Society (Strasbourg, August 1982) and subsequently printed in *Musical Quarterly*, lxxi/1, 1985, p. 75:

> *From Jewish Folk Poetry* was withheld by Shostakovich from publication and performance until Stalin's death in 1955 [*sic*]. How should this be explained? The cycle was precisely the kind of music required at this time (1948) by Soviet official aesthetics. It was written in a democratic form, using simple traditional musical language based on folklore and was easy for the listener to understand. The text was folk art. But we are confronted with a paradox: a work in complete agreement with the musical and artistic requirements of the Party is concealed by the author. However, even in an artistic and musical form acceptable to officialdom, the Jewish subject matter was, by its mere existence, provocative. At a time when Jewish culture was under fire, the performance of such a work would have been dangerous.

Braun goes on to refer to 'the more or less obvious dissidence of the text' of *From Jewish Folk Poetry* which he describes as starting a new trend in Soviet music 'notable for its anti-establishment [. . .] overtones' and use of 'Aesopian language' (pp. 78–79). Braun concludes:

> The use of Jewish elements in Shostakovich's music reaches far beyond their specific and 'colorful' Jewishness. The intrinsic meaning of these elements is of a socio-symbolic nature and may be interpreted as concealed dissidence. *It is in fact a hidden language of resistance communicated to the aware listener of its subtle meaning.* Dissidence and opposition are here represented by the Jewish element which, because of its special place in Soviet culture, served as a perfect vehicle and 'screening device' for the expression of 'symbolic values' consciously and, in part, unconsciously employed by the artist [emphasis added].

Lest it be imagined that Braun's unequivocal view of *From Jewish Folk Poetry* as a dissident work did not survive into his later essay, 'Shostakovich's Vocal Cycle *From Jewish Folk Poetry*: Aspects of Style and Meaning', it is necessary only to quote from the latter, a mere three pages before the passage Fay seems to have paraphrased (Braun, p. 260): 'The cycle is one of Shostakovich's most beautiful and richly symbolic compositions, a masterpiece of the composer's "secret language" of dissent. From the very hour of its creation, it was embroiled in controversy'. The rest of Braun's essay takes the form of a detailed literary and musicological justification of these views, concluding with a reiteration of his description, in 1982, of the work as an 'Aesopian' utterance constituting a '"screening device" for the composer's artistic and ethical self-expression' (p. 281). Fay's paraphrasal use of Braun's words in her *New York Times* piece clearly constitutes another sort of screening device – one intended to give the illusion of conferring on her claims the imprimatur of an authority whose view of the work is, as she certainly knows, diametrically opposed to hers. (*Cf.* Braun's own response to Fay on pp. 288–89, note 418. –EDS.)

USSR until, at the earliest, late 1948.[115] This opinion is wildly erroneous. Unofficial anti-Semitism has been indigenous in Russia throughout the century, regardless of the declared policy of the ruling group; indeed, anti-Semitic sentiments and policies permeated Soviet circles from the 1920s onwards.[116] Lenin, for example, made no attempt to curb anti-Semitism in the Red Army during the Civil War, as a result of which Jewish village life was all but wiped out.[117] During the 1920s, NEPmen were often popularly assumed to be Jewish, a prejudice which remained conspicuously undiscouraged by the Communist Party.[118] Official discrimination against Soviet Jews began in 1932 with the introduction of the internal passport system, which effectively prevented Jews integrating into Soviet society. ('Point 5' disclosed the passport-holder's ethnicity and, in practice, was used to discriminate against Jews in housing and employment.[119])

[115] She writes ('Myth'): 'If Stalin's minions were already implementing their scheme for the eventual containment or eradication of Soviet Jewry, Shostakovich and the vast majority of his compatriots were obviously not privy to the plan. By the autumn of 1948, they could have received few hints'.

[116] *Cf.* Nora Levin, *The Jews in the Soviet Union since 1917. Paradox of Survival*, New York University Press, New York, 1988, Vol. 1 (hereafter Levin); Yaacov Ro'i, ed., *Jews and Jewish Life in Russia and the Soviet Union*, Frank Cass, Ilford, Essex, 1995; Benjamin Pinkus, *The Jews of the Soviet Union: The History of a National Minority*, Cambridge University Press, Cambridge, 1988 (hereafter Pinkus); Lionel Kochan (ed.), *The Jews in Soviet Russia from 1917 to the Present*, Oxford University Press for Institute of Jewish Affairs, Oxford, 1972; Gennadi Kostyrchenko, *Out of the Red Shadows: Anti-Semitism in Stalin's Russia*, trans. H. T. Willetts, Prometheus Books, Amherst, New York, 1995.

[117] Dmitri Volkogonov, *Lenin: Life and Legacy*, HarperCollins, New York, 1994, pp. 203–4.

[118] Geoffrey Hosking, *A History of the Soviet Union*, rev. edn., Fontana, London, 1985, p. 258 (hereafter Hosking). When the OGPU (as the Bolshevik secret police, formerly the Cheka, were then called) searched Bulgakov's flat in May 1926, the writer's landlord told a joke about a Jew standing in Lubyanka Square who was asked where the State Insurance company's offices were. Since the premises were now occupied by the OGPU, the Jew punned: 'I don't know where Gosstrakh is now, [State-Insure or, as it also sounds to Russians, State-Fear], but Gosuzhas [State-Horror] is over there' (Shentalinsky, p. 72.)

[119] Ward, p. 205; Hosking, p. 258.

When, during the early 1930s, Jewish intellectuals reinforced the progressive, westernising wing of the Soviet intelligentsia, they became a prime target of Stalin's purges, many of the arrests and trials of 1936–38 being specifically aimed against Jewish organisations in the Soviet Union.[120] Stalin himself, in August 1936, described the so-called United Centre of Trotsky, Kamenev and Zinoviev as a conspiracy of 'three frustrated Jewish intellectuals'. (The anti-Semitic impulse within the Terror even applied to the secret police themselves. During 1936–37 nearly all NKVD leaders with Jewish names were shot.[121]) After the signing of the non-aggression pact with Germany in August 1939, Jews were excluded from the Soviet foreign affairs department, the foreign trade commissariat, the navy, TASS, administrative posts in ports, airlines, railways, and all the main Soviet publications.[122] During the War, Stalin closed the Soviet-Polish border to Jews fleeing the Nazis, vetoed Jewish candidates for front-line newspapers, and restricted the rights of Soviet Jews.[123] After the War, any Jew who had managed to survive the Holocaust in the Ukraine, Byelorussia or the Baltic states was automatically treated by the Soviet authorities as a German spy.[124]

[120] Kagarlitsky, pp. 128–29; R. Medvedev, p. 803.

[121] R. Medvedev, p. 562.

[122] Heller and Nekrich, p. 364.

[123] R. Medvedev, p. 804. The most overt instance of official Soviet anti-Semitism during the War was the liquidation, in 1941, of Henryk Erlich and Victor Alter, two Polish Jews who had fled to the USSR ahead of the Nazi invasion. Recent research (Shimon Redlich, *War, Holocaust, and Stalinism: A Documented Study of the Jewish Anti-Fascist Committee in the USSR*, Harwood Academic Publishers, London, 1995, pp. 9–19) has shown that, despite their anti-Soviet record, Erlich and Alter were groomed by Beria to be founders of a planned forerunner to the Jewish Anti-Fascist Committee: the Jewish Anti-Hitlerite Committee. Stalin, however, suspected that the pair were spies investigating the disappearance of 15,000 Polish officers in Spring 1940 (the Katyn Forest massacre; e.g., Heller and Nekrich, pp. 403–7). Erlich and Alter were arrested in December 1941 to prevent them reporting to General Sikorski during his visit to Moscow. Erlich hanged himself in an NKVD jail; Alter was shot in 1942.

[124] Heller and Nekrich, pp. 486–87.

Although conceived and sanctioned at the highest stratum of government, such policies were rarely announced. According to Roy Medvedev, 'most anti-Jewish measures were not given publicity; they were usually carried out on oral instructions. But the anti-Semitic feelings of Stalin and his retinue, including Kaganovich, a Jew, were no secret to the party apparatus'.[125] During the 1980s, Western scholars were accustomed to date the start of official Soviet anti-Semitism to 1945,[126] but since the opening of the Central Committee Archives it has become clear that the concerted Stalinist policy of anti-Jewish discrimination and harassment began at least three years earlier.[127] A memorandum from the head of the Central Committee Propaganda and Agitation Department, to the secretariat of the Central Committee (17 August 1942) draws attention to the fact that 'the heads of the institutions of Russian art are not Russian (primarily Jews)'.[128] Attached to this document is a long list of non-Russians with a stress on the 'unacceptable clogging' of the Bolshoi Theatre (by such 'primarily Jewish' aliens) and a

[125] R. Medvedev, p. 804.

[126] E.g., Hosking, p. 258.

[127] Arkady Vaksberg, *Stalin Against the Jews*, Alfred A. Knopf, New York, 1994, p. 134 (hereafter Vaksberg). 'It is impossible not to conclude that 1942 marked the start of the sharp change in Stalin's already revealed policy toward Soviet Jews. The subtle signals he sent out were picked up by the sensitive radar of the *apparatchiks* and influenced the position of the major and minor *nomenklatura*, which shamelessly began a hue and cry about Jewish preponderance, without bothering to find euphemisms for their vicious anti-Semitism' (*ibid.*, p. 138). *Cf.* Nadezhda Mandelstam: 'Anti-Semitism is propagated from above and brews in the cauldron known as the *apparat*' (*Hope Abandoned*, Collins Harvill, London, 1974, p. 272).

[128] Vaksberg, pp. 135–36. *Cf.* Kostyrchenko, pp. 15–20. The author of this openly anti-Semitic memorandum, Georgy Aleksandrov, was head of Agitprop from 1940 to 1947. An ambitious young Marxist theoretician, he advanced his career in the upper echelons of the Communist Party by espousing Russian chauvinism and elements of Nazi racialism. Between 1947 and 1952, Aleksandrov waged fierce battles on several fronts with his rivals in the *apparat*, all sides accusing one another of 'cosmopolitanism'. After Stalin's death, he briefly became minister of culture in 1954 before being thrown out of office (ostensibly for sexual misdemeanours) and exiled to Minsk, where he died in 1961 (Kostyrchenko, pp. 24–29 and 209–18).

similarly specific focus on 'the Jews' (*sic*) in the Moscow and Leningrad Conservatories, and in the theatre and music press corps.[129] Among those named are the soprano Nina Dorliak, a lifelong friend of the Shostakovich family who later married Sviatoslav Richter. (As a member of the composer's inner circle, Dorliak was privately asked by him to rehearse *From Jewish Folk Poetry* in 1948.[130]) According to the journalist Arkady Vaksberg, the Party archives for 1942–44 contain many similar memoranda listing dozens of names of Jewish cultural figures 'to be replaced by persons of Russian nationality'.[131] These include the pianist Aleksandr Gol'denveizer [Goldenweiser] and the cinema director Sergey Yutkevich, with whom Shostakovich worked on the films *Golden Mountains* (1931), *Counterplan* (1932) and *Man with a Gun* (1938), and the 'concert spectacles' *Native Leningrad* (1942) and *Victorious Spring* (1945).[132] Nor was the tone of official Soviet anti-Semitic prejudice noticeably different from the contemporary Nazi kind. In 1943, the head of Soviet cinematography notified the Central Committee that Sergey Eisenstein, then preparing *Ivan the Terrible*, had chosen for his leading lady the actress Faina Ranevskaya, 'whose Semitic features', wrote the official, 'are blatantly obvious in close-up'. (He added a request for official help 'to force Eisenstein not to accept this actress'.[133]) It was once thought that the first round of officially engineered anti-Semitic dismissals was the removal of Jews from the army

[129] The latter are (absurdly) accused of 'hushing up the concerts of the Russian pianist [Vladimir] Sofronitsky' and 'producing extended articles on Emil Gilels, David Oistrakh, and others'.

[130] *Cf.* Wilson, pp. 234–37. In fact, Dorliak was not Jewish and featured on this list solely because of her foreign-sounding name. Others named included Lev Tseitlin, Abram Yampolsky, Aleksandr Gedike, Mikhail Pekelis, Arkady Ostrovsky, Maximilian Steinberg, Semyon Ginzburg, Aleksandr Rabinovich, Moisey Grinberg, Grigory Kogan, Semyon Shlifstein, Daniil Zhitomirsky, Viktor Zukkerman, Konstantin Galkovsky, Abram Goltzman 'and their like'.

[131] Vaksberg, p. 136.

[132] For some details on Shostakovich's relationship with Yutkevich, *cf.* John Riley, 'From the Fifth Symphony to *Man With A Gun*', *DSCH Journal*, No. 3, Summer 1995, pp. 31–36.

[133] Vaksberg, p. 138.

apparat (and their replacement by Russians) in 1943.[134] Vaksberg shows otherwise:

> It was in the field of culture that the expulsion of Jews from management and administrative posts began, for the moment camouflaged each time (out of a desire to maintain good relations with their allies, the Americans and British) with some decent excuse (age, illness, 'transfer to other work', 'necessity', etc.). But the real reasons for the firings were not a secret.[135]

Because of the unusual extent of his contacts among Soviet Jews, the primacy of culture as a focus for official anti-Semitism would have been manifest to Shostakovich almost as soon as the 1942–43 campaign got under way (or, at the latest, by 1944, when he wrote the Second Piano Trio and Second Quartet). Indeed we know this to be so from the fact that in September 1943 Shostakovich signed a petition protesting the sacking on racial grounds of Yevgeny Guzikov, a professor at the Moscow Conservatory.[136] In any case, this state-directed racial prejudice became inescapably obvious in 1945 when some twenty Jewish violinists were 'swept out' of the Moscow Music Competition after the first round.[137]

[134] Heller and Nekrich, p. 486: 'In the Soviet army and in the rear, rumors intentionally were spread about cowardice and desertion on the part of the Jews'. Such officially inspired rumours – which became the basis of the much-circulated anti-Semitic jibes mentioned by Shostakovich in *Testimony* – were protested against by the writer Ilya Ehrenburg at the second plenum of the Jewish Anti-Fascist Committee in February 1943 (Kostrychenko, pp. 20–21).

[135] Vaksberg, p. 136.

[136] Kostyrchenko, p. 18.

[137] *Cf.* Dubinsky, p. 3. Stalin concealed much of this by distributing Stalin Prizes to prominent Soviet Jews. Vaksberg (pp. 137–38):

> The Stalin Prize – the state's highest and most desirable award – served as a shield, guaranteeing the safety of the laureate, and the number (quite high) of Jews in the list of recipients lulled naive simpletons, desperate for a ray of hope, into thinking that there could be no further persecution [. . .]. Conductor Samuil Samosud, given the Stalin Prize back in 1941 and then fired from the 'government' Bolshoi Theatre in 1943, received two more Stalin Prizes after that – both from the hands of the tyrant [. . .]. So there was no need to rebut the rumors of sanctions against people of Jewish descent. The resolutions on conferring the Stalin Prize, signed by Stalin and published in all the newspapers and solemnly read over the radio,

Soviet Jews now began to be depicted as agents of American imperialism and alluded to as the main exponents of a phenomenon referred to as 'cosmopolitanism'.[138] Such 'anti-patriotic elements' were contrasted with the wholesome native sons and daughters of the Motherland, their feet planted firmly in the soil of Russian tradition and folkloric conservatism – a racialist vision disseminated by a new party magazine, *Culture and Life*. In May 1946, the painter Aleksandr Gerasimov attacked 'cosmopolitan' (Jewish) art critics whom he portrayed as polluting the clear stream of Russian national art with their 'alleluia-ising' of allegedly inferior work.[139] During Summer 1946, the Zhdanovshchina took 'an explicitly anti-Jewish turn'[140] when a distinguished Soviet Jewish cultural figure and member of the Jewish Anti-Fascist Committee (JAFC), Professor Yitzhak Nusinov, was severely criticised at the eleventh plenary session of the Soviet Writers' Union. (Nusinov was referred to in press reports as 'a vagabond without a passport' – a standard Soviet anti-Semitic insult.[141]) In September 1946, the journal of the

---

were visible, weighty, and irrefutable rebuttals. Any foreign slanderer who would dare mention signs of anti-Semitism in the USSR could be shut up with a look at the list of recipients.

[138] Defined in the *Smaller Soviet Encyclopedia* (1930) as the belief of 'a person who considers the whole world to be his fatherland and does not recognise himself as belonging to a particular nationality', by 1946 cosmopolitanism had become code for the culturally internationalist disposition of the post-1930s Soviet intelligentsia (in practice, more often than not, meaning Jewish intellectuals). As such, it figured in various phases of the Zhdanovshchina during 1946–48. (In 1948, for example, Georgi Rublyov, head of the Moscow Artists' Union, was sacked for allowing two Jewish art critics to state their 'cosmopolitan' views during a discussion on naturalism.) The anti-Semitic campaign against 'rootless cosmopolitans', initiated by *Pravda* in January 1949, differed from previous examples of this phenomenon chiefly in its violence, vulgarity and shameless concertedness.

[139] Matthew Cullerne Bown, *Art under Stalin*, Phaidon, London, 1991, pp. 207–9. In February 1948, Gerasimov's committee dissolved the Moscow Union of Soviet Artists, sacking its chairman, Abram Efros, a Jew.

[140] Redlich, p. 121.

[141] Levin, Vol. 1, p. 468. Arrested as an American spy, Nusinov died in the Lefortovo prison in Moscow in 1950 (Kostyrchenko, p. 137).

JAFC, *Eynikayt*, was obliged to carry an article announcing the inception of a campaign against Jewish 'cultural nationalism' and attacking Soviet Yiddish writers for concentrating on 'undesirable' themes such as the Holocaust and 'adoration' of the Jewish past.[142] Following a report into the alleged 'counter-revolutionary international Zionist' activities of the JAFC submitted to him by Mikhail Suslov in November 1946, Stalin moved to exclude Jews from the Party and government *apparat*.[143]

A Politburo plot to liquidate the JAFC was formulated at the beginning of 1947.[144] Later that year, Moscow University began applying a rigid entry quota on Jews, and refusing Jewish 'medal-winners' (those who had achieved top placings in the All-Union entrance exams).[145] Further to the anti-'alleluia-ising' drive of Summer 1946, press attacks on the 'toadying' and 'bowing and scraping' of Jewish literary critics were stepped up through the second half of 1947.[146] In a parallel to the 1946 attack on Nusinov, the Yiddish writer Itzik Kipnis was attacked in the Ukrainian press throughout the middle of the year. Persecution of leading Jewish representatives of the Soviet medical profession commenced that summer.[147] Finally, in December 1947, Beria's agents began arresting and torturing members of the JAFC.[148]

Anti-Semitism was not merely endemic in the USSR before 1948 – it was systemic.

Laurel Fay's naive trust in the editorial integrity of *Pravda* appears to have led her into mistaking the camouflage of

[142] Redlich, p. 121.

[143] Dmitri Volkogonov, *Stalin: Triumph and Tragedy*, ed. and transl. Harold Shukman, Weidenfeld and Nicolson, London, 1991, p. 567; R. Medvedev, p. 804; Redlich, p. 123.

[144] Central Committee recommendations to close the JAFC were 'close to being implemented' in early 1947 (Redlich, p. 124).

[145] Hosking, p. 258.

[146] Pinkus, p. 153. Ilya Ehrenburg cautiously defended Jewish critics, asking how it was possible to 'toady' to, for example, Shakespeare.

[147] Yakov Rapoport, *The Doctors' Plot*, Fourth Estate, London, 1991, pp. 244–45.

[148] Redlich, p. 128.

Soviet officialese for actual Soviet reality. Stalinist policy towards the 'nationalities' (regarded by the Politburo as innately treasonable) was always repressive.[149] In fact, at the very moment that *Pravda* was proclaiming sweetness and light among the peoples of the Union in 1948, a massive deportation of Lithuanians was under way, followed in 1949 by a further flood of 'Baltic *kulaks*' from Latvia and Estonia.[150] In all, 3,500,000 ethnic-minority citizens were exiled or resettled during the 1940s.[151] Naturally, the Soviet media sought to ensure that neither the West nor the bulk of the Russian and Ukrainian populace of the USSR knew much about this, a strategy expedited by publishing the usual blatant lies in *Pravda* and by conjuring up a constant parade of pseudo-nationalistic cultural diversions (notably the Kazakh 'minstrel' Dzhambul Dzhabayev, amusingly recalled by Shostakovich in *Testimony*[152]). Laurel Fay is not the only one to have been fooled; they ran into millions. Yet her claim is that Shostakovich was one of these – that he stupidly believed government propaganda about the nationalities, hopefully embarked on his own (uncommissioned) Socialist Realist venture in musical solidarity with this false representation, and that he 'just happened to pick the wrong "folk" as his inspiration'. The idea that the author of this statement is presently engaged in producing what her publisher, Oxford University Press, trusts will be a definitive

[149] Anything *Pravda* happened to claim about tolerating the Soviet Union's nationalities in 1948 must be set against the ferocious purges conducted against them during the early 1930s and again during 1937–40, not to mention Stalin's wholesale war-time deportations (often directly into the Gulag) of Balkars, Chechens, Ingush, Kalmyks, Karachai, Khemshins, Krymchaks, Kurds, Meskhetians, Volga Germans, Crimean Tatars and Caucasian Greeks. These peoples' lands were usurped by Russian and Ukrainian emigrants, an outrage which, of course, remained in force in 1948 when *Pravda* was engaged in deceiving gullible Westerners into believing otherwise. *Cf*. Robert Conquest, *The Nation Killers: The Soviet Deportation of Nationalities*, Macmillan, London, 1960; Aleksandr Nekrich, *The Punished Peoples: The Deportation and Tragic Fate of Soviet Minorities at the End of the Second World War*, W. W. Norton, New York and London, 1978.

[150] *Cf*. Solzhenitsyn, *The Gulag Archipelago*, Vol. 3, pp. 385–405.

[151] Ward, p. 160.

[152] Pp. 160–62/209–11.

biography of Shostakovich would be comic were there not so many dead bodies involved.

As I have emphasised,[153] Shostakovich was utterly unlike the average Soviet citizen in occupying an informationally privileged position in Soviet society. Apart from his contacts within the *intelligenty* and the *nomenklatura* – which were, to say the least, extensive – he had experience of regional politics among the nationalities which would have opened his eyes to aspects of Soviet life opaque to most of his fellow citizens.[154] More importantly, he had cultivated a special interest in Jewish art and custom for five years (possibly ten years[155]) before the events of 1948. How much of Shostakovich's fascination with Jewish culture derived from his friendship with Moisei Vainberg (Mieczyslaw Weinberg) is, at present, hard to gauge – although it is clear that the two composers were closely and continuously influential on each other.[156] What is certain is that this liaison – together with his

[153] *Cf.* pp. 665–67.

[154] *Cf.* p. 268, notes 59 and 60.

[155] *Cf.* pp. 608–9. In *Testimony*, pp. 97–99/128–31, Shostakovich remarks on the impact of anti-Semitism in Soviet cultural circles consequent upon the Molotov-Ribbentrop Pact of 1939.

[156] Theirs was a unique compositional relationship in which, thanks to living in the same Moscow block, influence ran to and fro between them on a daily basis. Vainberg revered Shostakovich for showing him 'a new continent' in music and called himself his mentor's 'flesh and blood'. He performed the four-hand piano reductions of Shostakovich's Tenth and Twelfth Symphonies (with the composer and Boris Tchaikovsky respectively) at their auditions in the Composers' Union, acted as consigliere in the behind-the-scenes manœuvring before the premiere of the Thirteenth, and deputised for Sviatoslav Richter at the first outings of the *Seven Romances on Poems of Aleksandr Blok* and the Violin Sonata. In return, Shostakovich dedicated his Tenth Quartet to Vainberg and unfailingly enthused about his music (especially his 1968 opera *The Passenger*, which he called 'an amazing work'). Vainberg's Fifth Symphony (1962) adopts the two-note motif of Shostakovich's Fourth (premiered just before it was written), acknowledging the debt with an allusion to that work's eerie celesta-led coda. In fact the 'influence' seems to have been mutual, the dotted duple rhythm in Vainberg's finale turning up at the climax of Shostakovich's 'Babi Yar', written later in the same year. The second and fifth movements of Vainberg's Sixth Symphony (1963) parallel their equivalents in Shostakovich's Thirteenth Symphony closely. Likewise, Vainberg's subject (Nazi massacres of Jewish children) derives – if only in the most immediate sense – from 'Babi Yar'. (His family was burned alive

friendships with Leo Arnshtam, Isaak Glikman and Daniil Zhitomirsky, not to mention the scores of Jewish musicians with whom he worked throughout his career (especially Veniamin Fleishman) – would have ensured that Shostakovich, whether he wished to or not, must have known about the perennial systemic anti-Semitism of Stalin's dictatorship.

Vainberg moved to Moscow in 1943 at Shostakovich's behest, having sent him his First Symphony (1942) from Tashkent. According to Vainberg's wife Natalya Vovsi-Mikhoels, they and Shostakovich thereafter 'met often, at

---

by the Nazis in Warsaw.) On the other hand, the brutally peremptory timpani of Vainberg's Sixth (III) seem to have come to Shostakovich's mind while writing his Second Cello Concerto and Second Violin Concerto a few years later. Similarly, the skirling 'Malagueña' in Shostakovich's Fourteenth Symphony appears to be based on the central $\frac{3}{4}$ passage in Vainberg's tumultuous scherzo. In fact, he may have been moved to orchestrate *From Jewish Folk Poetry* by Vainberg's score (which, like the ninth movement of Shostakovich's cycle, ironically subverts the lie of Socialist Realist optimism in its finale). Vainberg's Seventh Symphony (1964) is a fascinating instance of himself and Shostakovich treading so closely in each other's footsteps that it is hard to distinguish who is following whom. It appears to have been written during the summer of 1964 between the composition of Shostakovich's Ninth Quartet (May) and Tenth Quartet (July), perhaps overlapping the completion of one and the start of the other. (On 21 July, Shostakovich wrote to Isaak Glikman that he'd finished his Tenth and dedicated it to Vainberg. He was particularly pleased with this because, in 1963, Vainberg had 'overtaken' him by writing a Ninth Quartet and now, with his own Tenth, he'd regained the lead!) Steeped in the language of Shostakovich's quartets, Vainberg's Seventh Symphony is cast in a continuous sequence of five movements, of which the last is an extended finale which mirrors the lay-out of Shostakovich's Ninth Quartet, quotes obliquely from the passacaglia theme of Shostakovich's First Violin Concerto (III), and provides Shostakovich with some cues for his Tenth Quartet. While Bartókian in some aspects, Vainberg's stark, dissonant and emotionally ferocious Tenth Symphony (1968) was probably inspired by the republication in 1967 (after being out of print for twenty years) of Shostakovich's *Prelude and Scherzo*, Op. 11 – and perhaps, too, by the appearance, in 1968, of Barshai's arrangement of Shostakovich's Tenth Quartet (*Symphony for Strings*, Op. 118a). The violent cadenzas in Shostakovich's Second Violin Concerto are likewise suggested by Vainberg's solo interludes; yet his score transcends the derivative by virtue of its sheer intensity, while its limping Jewish 'Burlesque' hints that Shostakovich's similar themes of the late 1940s were influenced as much by listening to Vainberg as by studying Jewish popular music in the raw.

friends' houses and at concerts and restaurants' over the next five years.[157] More significantly, Madame Vainberg was the daughter of the head of the JAFC – the actor Solomon Mikhoels, then the most prominent Jew in the USSR. Mikhoels, who had spoken in defence of Shostakovich's Eighth Symphony in 1943,[158] was killed in a car accident in Minsk shortly before the start of Zhdanov's January 1948 'conference of musical activists' in Moscow (in which a concerted attack on Shostakovich's Eighth functioned as centrepiece). Whether or not this was a coincidence, Mikhoels was, in fact, murdered by agents of Beria's MGB.[159] Yet according to Laurel Fay, 'the true circumstances of his murder, let alone its pivotal significance [in heralding the naked anti-Semitism of 1948–53], eluded even suspicious family members for some time'.[160] Fay implies that the Vovsi family did not grasp that Mikhoels had been murdered (and thus could not have surmised by whom) 'for some time'. Her purpose here is to suggest that Shostakovich – who, through Vainberg, was close to the Vovsi family – had no reason to suppose that Mikhoels had been done away with by the secret police; that, suspecting nothing sinister about Mikhoels' death, neither could he have perceived its 'pivotal significance'; and, hence, that *From Jewish Folk Poetry* could not have come about, as (for example) Elizabeth Wilson assumes, as 'his immediate response [. . .] to aid the repressed, irrespective of race or creed'.[161]

The indefinite phrase 'for some time' thus assumes a crucial significance. Shostakovich began composing *From Jewish Folk Poetry* around eight months after Mikhoels'

[157] Wilson, p. 228.

[158] Also *cf*. p. 693.

[159] In the plain words of Nikita Khrushchev, 'they killed him like beasts' (*Khrushchev Remembers*, André Deutsch, London, 1970, p. 261). Mikhoels' murder was officially acknowledged fifteen years after the event in *Sovetskaya Byelorossiya*, 13 January 1963.

The MGB (Ministerstvo Gosudarstvennoy Bezopasnosti, or Ministry of State Security), run by Lavrenti Beria and Viktor Abakumov, succeeded the NKVD in 1946, subsequently becoming the KGB in 1954.

[160] Fay, 'Myth', p. 32.

[161] Wilson, p. 227.

assassination. Had Shostakovich or the Vovsi family put two and two together by then? Did he (or they) manage this only after he had finished *From Jewish Folk Poetry* – for example, following the liquidation of the Jewish Anti-Fascist Committee (20 November)? Or did they simply remain unenlightened long enough for the question to have become academic (i.e., until the outbreak of the declared campaign against 'Zionist infestation' in 1949)? Clearly Laurel Fay wishes to imply that 'for some time' at any rate means sufficiently long to support her claim that, *pace* Elizabeth Wilson, there was no 'enormous selflessness and courage'[162] in Shostakovich's impulse to compose *From Jewish Folk Poetry*.

Unhappily for Fay, we have Natalya Vainberg's own account of this episode[163] in which she states that she had suspected her father had been murdered almost from the very beginning, and that by March 1948 (four to five months before Shostakovich began composing *From Jewish Folk Poetry*) she had received unofficial confirmation.[164] In an article commissioned for Wilson's book,[165] Mikhoels' daughter describes 13 January 1948 – the day of the

[162] *Ibid.*, p. 227.

[163] Natal'ya Vovsi-Mikhoels, 'Moi otets – Solomon Mikhoels: Vospominaniya o zhizni i gibeli' ('My Father – Solomon Mikhoels: Reminiscences of Life and Death'), *Novy Mir*, 1990, No. 3, pp. 226–48.

[164] In fact, she received oblique confirmation much earlier than this when Yulia Kaganovich, niece of Lazar Kaganovich, came to the Vovsi-Mikhoels apartment on the day of Mikhoels' funeral (16 January 1948): 'She led us to the bathroom, the only room where we could have privacy, and said quietly, "Uncle sends his regards . . . and he told me to tell you never to ask anyone about anything". In fact, it was not so much a warning as an order' (Vaksberg, pp. 170–71). Joachim Braun, in his essay 'Shostakovich's Song Cycle *From Jewish Folk Poetry*' in Brown (ed.), *Russian and Soviet Music* (hereafter referred to as Braun, 'Aspects'), p. 261 – which Fay has certainly read (*cf.* p. 687, note 114) – writes: 'Ludmila Poliakova has argued convincingly that composition [of *From Jewish Folk Poetry*] took place in the summer of 1948, while the testimony of Natalia Mikhoels [. . .] seems to advance the date to the spring of 1948. According to Natalia Mikhoels, it was May 1948 when Shostakovich raised questions about the rhythmic flow of the original folk texts, which Shostakovich knew only in Russian translation'.

[165] Wilson, pp. 227–32.

announcement of her father's death and also the first meeting of Zhdanov's conference (which ran from 1 p.m. to 6 p.m.):

> As soon as [the meeting] was over Dmitri Dmitriyevich came straight to see us. We ourselves had been living on another plane for the last seven hours; the news of Father's death earlier that day had left us completely devastated. The doors of the flat were open and a stream of people came and went in silence – an endless stream of stunned and frightened people. We wandered amongst them, without lingering or talking to any of them. Suddenly I heard my name called out; on seeing Dmitri Dmitriyevich, I went up to him. Silently he embraced me and my husband, the composer Moisei Weinberg, then he went over to the bookcase and, with his back to everyone in the room, pronounced quietly but distinctly and with uncharacteristic deliberation, 'I envy him . . .'. He didn't say another word, but stood rooted to the spot, hugging us both around the shoulders.

For the purposes of her thesis, Laurel Fay requires us to picture a scene of natural grief and mourning with no suspicion of anything sinister or menacing. Yet 'an endless stream of stunned and frightened people' came and went in the Vainbergs' apartment that day. Of what were they frightened, if not of an imminent, officially sponsored pogrom? The most prominent Soviet Jew – a man active in both the JAFC and the Jewish-American Charitable Organisation (JOINT) – had, at the age of 58 and the height of his powers, been 'killed in a car accident' (a well-established euphemism, in the case of prominent or troublesome people, for 'murdered by the security organs'). Are we to believe that, after sixteen years of institutionalised anti-Semitism under Stalin, those who came to the Vainbergs' apartment on 13 January 1948 were 'stunned and frightened' merely by the fickle caprices of a life in which one might stroll the quiet backstreets of Minsk and find oneself crushed to death under the wheels of a lorry?

Rostislav Dubinsky recalled a fellow musician, Lisa, who, after the anti-Semitic 'fixing' of the 1945 Moscow Music Competition, shouted a protest ('Lenin is dead, but his deeds live on!'). At a vigil for Mikhoels on Herzen Street on 14 January 1948, this same Lisa was arrested (and later sent to the Gulag for fifteen years) for saying that he could not have died 'without help'. According to Dubinsky, 'all Herzen

Street from the conservatory to the Jewish State Theatre was packed with people [. . .] thousands of silent people, caught by one disaster and fearing another'.[166] Of what 'disaster' were these thousands afraid? Laurel Fay wishes us to believe that Soviet Jews, nominally protected from discrimination by the legal code, were then in a placid condition of comfortable unawareness. Yet Yakov Rapoport, one of the nine physicians later arrested in the so-called Doctors' Plot of 1952–53,[167] recalls that 'no one had any doubts that the murder [of Mikhoels] was somehow connected with the terror emanating from the MGB building in Dzerzhinsky Square (formerly Lubyanka)'.[168] Dubinsky offers confirmation. To Lisa's cry that she didn't believe Mikhoels had died without help, his whispered response was: 'Nobody believes that, but be quiet'.[169] Far from calm, the atmosphere among Soviet Jewry in the aftermath of Mikhoels' death is portrayed by Dubinsky and Rapoport as tense with anxiety.[170]

Only someone ignorant of the predicament of Soviet Jews during the 1940s would be naive enough to expect anything

[166] Dubinsky, pp. 4–6.

[167] *Cf.* p. 695, note 147.

[168] Rapoport, p. 68. Also *cf.* Vaksberg, p. 169: 'Anyone with even a remote connection to Moscow's Jewish circles was in on the secret: there had been no car accident, Mikhoels had been murdered'.

[169] Dubinsky, p. 4. As always, word of mouth ran ahead of official truth in the USSR. In May 1948, JAFC leader Itzik Fefer quietly informed Alec Waterman, a British-Jewish communist then visiting Moscow, that Mikhoels had been murdered (Redlich, p. 129).

[170] Historian Nora Levin confirms this mood among Soviet Jews in January 1948 (Levin, Vol. 1, p. 494). Gennadi Kostyrchenko, on the other hand, claims (without citing any source) that, unlike those close to Mikhoels who uniformly assumed that he had been murdered, 'the majority of [ordinary] Jews believed what was written in the newspapers' (*op. cit.* p. 97). This, though, was clearly not true, for example, of the ordinary Jews in Minsk. Soon after Mikhoels' death, Itzik Fefer went there and met the writer Itzik Platner who told him that 'none of the Jews in [Minsk] believed that the artist's death was accidental, but rather saw it as a planned murder intended to "cut the head of the Jewish community"' (*ibid*, p. 95, n. 185). Nor, as Kostyrchenko himself shows, can Ilya Ehrenburg's later statement (made for Soviet publication in 1967) that 'the official version seemed to be the convincing version in the spring of 1948', be taken at face value (*ibid.*, p. 97, n. 192; pp. 106–12; p. 106, n. 228).

but tense anxiety from them in January 1948. By then the Jewish community in the USSR was, socially and culturally, under siege. To appreciate the intensity of this state of affairs, one has only to read the following letter from Yakov Grinberg, of the Moscow Arts Department, pleading to Stalin about the condition of Soviet Jewish intellectuals as early as May 1943:

> Dear leader and teacher J. V. Stalin! How can it be explained that in our Soviet land in such harsh times the murky wave of repulsive anti-Semitism has been reborn and has penetrated into individual Soviet apparats and even Party organizations? [. . .]
>
> In the organs supervising the arts, people whisper about it with enigmatic expressions. This then breeds hostility towards Jews working in that field. [. . .] Any qualified Jew can no longer count on getting independent work even of the most modest scope. This policy has loosened the tongues of many ignorant and unstable elements, and the mood of many Communist and non-Party Jews is very bleak. [. . .] I know that People's Artist of the USSR Comrade Mikhoels, People's Artist of the RSFSR Tairov,[171] and many rank-and-file workers have spoken of this with great anxiety. We know that a number of representatives of the artistic intelligentsia (Jews) appealed to writer [Ilya] Ehrenburg to raise this issue [. . .] *It is becoming unbearable! It is no longer random, it is planned. Once again the terrible Jewish question has arisen.*[172]

A full five years before Shostakovich wrote *From Jewish Folk Poetry*, the situation for the Soviet Jewish intelligentsia was not only 'unbearable' but perceived by them as 'planned' as such. Nor, as we have seen, did the predicament of Soviet Jewry ameliorate; instead, it got steadily worse after 1943. This evidence speaks for itself.

Since Shostakovich and Solomon Mikhoels admired each other's artistry, it is safe to assume that the composer would have been unusually interested in Mikhoels' fate, particularly in view of the fact that the actor had been the father-in-law of his special friend Moisei Vainberg. Laurel Fay simply violates commonsense when she implies that a man as close to

[171] Aleksandr Tairov (1885–1950), creator and director of the Moscow Chamber Theatre.

[172] Vaksberg, pp. 136–37; emphasis added.

Mikhoels as Shostakovich would not have been aware of the extent of officially engineered anti-Semitic persecution in January 1948. According to historian Shimon Redlich, 'an increasingly tense and oppressive atmosphere was felt within the [Jewish Anti-Fascist] Committee' in August 1947.[173] The reason was that Stalin was then closing in on the JAFC, which he paranoiacally suspected of harbouring a plot against him. Stalin, it now appears, feared that the family of his late second wife, the Alliluyevs, were using the JAFC (and chiefly Mikhoels) to submit incriminating data on his private life to American intelligence agents.[174] 'What remained to be done', observes Redlich, 'was to find the guilty, extract confessions, and stage a trial. Mikhoels [. . .] was the perfect culprit. Arrests of those slated to play roles in the "plot" started in December 1947.'[175] Under the supervision of Abakumov, certain key JAFC members were quickly beaten into incriminating Mikhoels.[176] Did Mikhoels know they had been arrested? He did.[177] Is this likely to have gone unnoticed by his colleagues in the top echelon of the Soviet Jewish community? Hardly. Would his daughter, Natalya Vovsi-Mikhoels, and her husband, Moisei Vainberg, have known about it? Almost certainly. And would Shostakovich, who then met the Vainbergs 'often, at friends' houses and at concerts and restaurants', have been aware of it? This, at the very least, is highly probable.

In the end, Stalin decided to dispense with putting Mikhoels on trial, fearing that the actor would blurt out something embarrassing in front of the foreign press corps. Issuing the order to kill Mikhoels and selecting the MGB agents involved, the dictator personally designed the murder scenario, in which a drugged Mikhoels was dragged out of a car and driven over by a lorry till his skull was crushed

[173] Redlich, p. 126.

[174] *Ibid.*, p. 127; Kostyrchenko, p. 83–84.

[175] Redlich, p. 128.

[176] Gennadi Kostyrchenko gives appallingly graphic details of the MGB's interrogation methods (*op. cit.*, pp. 85–88).

[177] Redlich, p. 129.

beyond recognition.[178] Not that this brutal expedient deflected Stalin from his obsession with punishing the JAFC, arrests of whose members continued during the weeks after Mikhoels' death, under the hypocritical cover of a lavish state funeral for this very popular actor.[179] As in the case of the NKVD plot against Tukhachevsky and the sordid destruction of the Tukhachevsky family in May-June 1937,[180] Shostakovich was here but a heartbeat away from a business not merely vile but actively dangerous to him. Again, Fay strains credulity well beyond breaking point by suggesting that all this passed blithely over his head. Nor is it remotely conceivable that Shostakovich remained unaware of the attacks on 'Jewish national exclusiveness' and 'bourgeois nationalism' which subsequently intensified throughout 1948.[181]

What, then, of Stalin's decision, in May 1948, to recognise Israel, and of Golda Meir's civic reception as Israel's first ambassador to Moscow? Taking official appearances for reality, Laurel Fay assumes that these events confirm the absence of official anti-Semitism before November 1948 and support her idea that Soviet Jews were unaware of any impending trouble until then. In fact, Stalin's recognition of Israel was entirely unrelated to the predicament of Soviet Jews, being instead part of the USSR's opening strategy in the Cold War, following the completion of the Soviet Bloc and the founding of Cominform. During the final stages of the Second World War, Stalin had taken a decision to support a Jewish homeland in Palestine on the dual assumption that such a state would (a) be socialist and (b) weaken Britain's influence in the Middle East.[182] His sanctioning of the Jewish Anti-

[178] *Ibid.*, pp. 130–31. This is the official version. A conflicting account is given by a witness quoted by Rostislav Dubinsky, p. 6.

[179] Redlich, p. 132.

[180] *Cf.* Ian MacDonald, 'You Must Remember! Shostakovich's Alleged Interrogation by the NKVD in 1937', *DSCH Journal*, 6, Winter 1996, pp. 25–27; this article can also be consulted at the website *Music under Soviet Rule*, at http://www.siue.edu/~aho/musov/basner/basner.html.

[181] Levin, Vol. 1, p. 495. Braun, 'Aspects', p. 262 (*cf.* p. 687, note 114).

[182] Ward, p. 205; Hosking, pp. 258–59; Heller, *Cogs*, pp. 130–35; Kostyrchenko, pp. 101–5.

Fascist Committee was part of this strategy.[183] Having in 1947 signed treaties with the former European allies of Germany (notably Italy), Stalin implemented his Middle Eastern policy by attempting to obtain a trusteeship over the former Italian colony of Libya, and by conceding *de jure* recognition of Israel (going one better than Truman, who had stopped at *de facto* recognition).[184] As it turned out, Stalin's probe in Israel's direction brought no result other than to convince him that Israel, far from a potential socialist Trojan horse, was in reality an American-backed capitalist-imperialist plot. Worse, so far as Soviet Jews were concerned, their high turn-out for the reception they were allowed to give to Golda Meir infuriated Stalin and his minions, who immediately began planning the crackdown against Zionism launched later that year. Throughout all this, Stalin's true murderous intent towards Soviet Jewry remained completely unaffected by what, for him, was a mere diplomatic speculation. 'While publicly showing sympathy for Jewish causes, including the foundation of the state of Israel', writes the Kremlin historian Dmitri Volkogonov, 'behind the scenes the Politburo was rewriting its script.'[185] This script was, in effect, creeping genocide by stages, climaxing five years later with what would probably have been a full-scale quasi-Nazi Holocaust.

If Stalin's recognition of Israel and the reception for Golda Meir muddied the water for Soviet Jews during Summer 1948, the intensifying Soviet domestic policy of anti-Semitic discrimination and harassment would have set strict limits on wishful thinking. By virtue of his link with the Vovsi family, Shostakovich was then at the very heart of the ferment of Soviet Jewish anxiety.[186] Indeed, he had been in such a

[183] Redlich, p. 9. The JAFC was organised by (and thus reported to) Sovinformburo. After Israel came into being, it was officially regarded as a centre of Zionist agitation and marked for liquidation. *Cf.* Kostyrchenko, pp. 30–132.

[184] Stalin's moves in the Middle East coincided with his initiation of the Berlin Blockade.

[185] Volkogonov, *Stalin: Triumph and Tragedy*, p. 315.

[186] After Mikhoels' death, Jews stopped attending his Jewish State Theatre because it was rumoured that the MGB were shadowing and arresting all who did so (Rapoport, pp. 67–68).

position for well over a year by then. Flora Litvinova claims that, in December 1946,[187] she found Dmitry and Nina Shostakovich 'despondent', having just read the *Pravda* attack on 'The Anti-Party Group of Theatre Critics', whom the paper vilified as 'advocates of a rootless cosmopolitanism, so despicable to Soviet Man'. 'A "rootless cosmopolitan"', explains Litvinova, 'was synonymous with the word "Jew". The hostile nature of the "cosmopolitans" was now revealed; the pseudonyms they hid behind were being exposed.'[188] To contend that *From Jewish Folk Poetry* had nothing to do with any of this – that it was merely 'Shostakovich's rotten luck that of all the available nationalities, he just happened to pick the wrong "folk"' – grotesquely distorts historical reality. As with Richard Taruskin's indefensible claims about *Lady Macbeth* and misleading account of the reception of Shostakovich's Fifth Symphony, Laurel Fay's fictional redaction of the history of Soviet Jewry flows from a determination to report matters not as they are but in any manner which contradicts *Testimony*.[189] Yet the ahistorical assertions of Taruskin and Fay are contradicted repeatedly and in depth

[187] The date mistakenly given in Elizabeth Wilson's book is December 1947. The *Pravda* attack on 'The Anti-Party Group of Theatre Critics' appeared on 2 February 1949. However, a similar attack on Jewish critics was published on 14 December 1946, and it would seem that this is the one to which Litvinova refers (although the phraseology she records is that of the later, more famous, *Pravda* attack).

[188] Wilson, p. 202.

[189] As has been shown above (p. 687, note 114), Fay is certainly familiar with Joachim Braun's articles on the context of *From Jewish Folk Poetry* published in 1983 and 1985. Yet she writes as if she has never come across Natalya Vovsi-Mikhoels's report, given to Braun in a personal interview, that, while visiting Mikhoels's apartment on the day after the actor's death, 'Shostakovich spoke at the gathering of how "this" had started with the Jews but would end with the entire intelligentsia' (Braun, 'Aspects', p. 261; *cf.* Wilson, pp. 227–28). This remarkable statement shows that the composer was clear from the start that Mikhoels had been murdered and that this was part of the ongoing official campaign of persecution of Soviet Jews. Further, it shows him cynically critical of the Soviet authorities, which he evidently expected were then about to broaden their target to include the entire Soviet intelligentsia as they had in 1928–32 and 1935–39. This statement is sufficient by itself to discredit Fay's quaint conception of Shostakovich as a blundering innocent abroad. 'Shostakovich was not a lost sheep', insists Andrey Bitov (p. 524). 'He knew.'

by the vast majority of those close to Shostakovich in place or spirit during the Soviet era. One such, Natalya Vovsi-Mikhoels (Madame Vainberg), is categorical. Far from a chance collision with historical forces of which its composer was oblivious, *From Jewish Folk Poetry*, she insists, was 'an open protest by Shostakovich against the hounding of the Jews in this last five-year plan of Stalin's'.[190]

Laurel Fay's misapprehension that *From Jewish Folk Poetry* has nothing to do with the predicament of Soviet Jews at the time it was written depends primarily on a willful ignorance of history.[191] Yet there is a second strand to her thesis. She contends that the relative openness with which Shostakovich went about creating *From Jewish Folk Poetry* can only mean one thing: that he feared no consequences because he harboured no dissident intent in composing it. She argues this not because of the rampancy of Soviet-instigated anti-Semitism (which she assumes not to have existed until the work was finished), but because Shostakovich was 'petrified with fear' after being publicly pilloried in February and April. 'He had', she hazards, 'ample inducement to contemplate suicide, but surely courting martyrdom by means of his music would have been an unnecessarily gruesome way to go about it.'[192]

Since, notwithstanding Laurel Fay, the broad external facts of Shostakovich's life in 1948 are as indisputable as those of contemporary Stalinist anti-Semitism, we (like Fay) are here obliged to speculate on the composer's state of mind – an

[190] Wilson, p. 229. The Fourth Five-Year Plan ran from 1946 to 1950. When asked to respond to Laurel Fay's allegation that anti-Semitism was little known in the USSR before the writing of *From Jewish Folk Poetry*, Vovsi-Mikhoels stated, 'that is incorrect'. She also disputed Fay's contention that Shostakovich 'just happened to choose the "wrong" folk for his inspiration': 'That choice was no accident. This topic concerned him' (*cf.* p. 226, note 411).

[191] Dr Harold Shukman, head of the Russian and East European Centre at St Antony's College, Oxford, writes (letter to the author, 17 July 1996): 'I can barely believe Laurel Fay's position. That anyone with minimal access to published sources on the Soviet period of Russian history could be unaware of some of the most infamous events experienced by Soviet Jews is amazing'.

[192] Fay, 'Myth', p. 27.

enterprise, at best, of probability. To grasp the tentative nature of such speculation, we need only examine the opening sentence of Fay's article: 'Nineteen forty-eight was the worst year of Dmitri Shostakovich's life'. On what basis can such a statement be made? Certainly, the external events of his life in 1948 were harsh, but were they any harsher than the external events of his life in, say, 1936? As for his inner reactions to these external events, how, in the absence of a detailed autobiographical account, can anyone know how he felt or thought? The inner life is a delicate thing not so easily measured by the crude test of what happens to be synchronous in the external world. How can anyone be sure that 1953, when Shostakovich appears to have loved and lost Elmira Nazirova, was not, subjectively, more difficult for him? How can we presume to say how much Shostakovich suffered from the loss of Ivan Sollertinsky in 1943, or of his wife Nina in 1954, or of his mother in 1955? We cannot. A certain caution is necessary here.

As for Shostakovich being in a suicidal state following the January 1948 conference, there is (should we wish to take any notice of it) his own word for it in *Testimony*: 'At the time it seemed as though my end had come'.[193] The composer Yury Levitin confirms that Shostakovich was indeed suicidal in the immediate aftermath of the conference (in fact so disturbed that he reduced his wife to tears with his inconsolable urge to do away with himself).[194] How long, though, can anyone remain in such an extreme state of mind? We know that Shostakovich had extricated himself from it by, at the latest, the winter of 1949–50, when, in a 'jolly' and 'mischievous' mood, he made Marina Sabinina laugh by impersonating members of the Academic Council of the Moscow Conservatoire.[195] Yet how can we be sure that he did not emerge from it considerably earlier, if not within days of Levitin witnessing his 'terrible state' after the January 1948 conference? A key element in this question is the origin of Shostakovich's scurrilous satire on the 1948 conference:

[193] *Testimony*, p. 111/146.

[194] Wilson, p. 211. Rostropovich describes Levitin, Vainberg, Lebedinsky, Ustvolskaya and Glikman as among those closest in offering their support to Shostakovich at this time (Wilson, p. 216).

[195] Wilson, pp. 225–26.

Rayok. If *Rayok* could be at least partly dated to Summer 1948 – as Isaak Glikman is supposed to have stated,[196] and as Manashir Yakubov has since affirmed (insisting that Shostakovich played over the original sketch 'to his closest friends already in 1948')[197] – then there would be good reason to suppose that Shostakovich more than recovered his equilibrium that year; indeed, that he swung from anguished self-destruction all the way across the emotional spectrum to bitter self-assertion. However, the date of *Rayok* is in dispute.[198]

For now, in the absence of further information which might put these issues beyond reasonable doubt, we are reduced to speculating on Shostakovich's inner world during the period of the composition of *From Jewish Folk Poetry* (1 August to 21 October 1948). All that we can be sure of from the external point of view is that he seems to have been sufficiently calm not to have made any sustained effort to keep the existence of the work concealed; indeed, Laurel Fay's apparent trump card is a letter from Shostakovich to 'a former student' dated January 1949 in which he mentions that he expects to 'demonstrate' the songs within ten days at the Composers' Union (from which she concludes that he had no fear about doing so, and that this fearlessness must betoken a clear conscience based on an earnest wish to appease the *apparat*).[199]

Those familiar with suicidal behaviour will know that the basic condition – a desire not to exist at all, which is actually

[196] Andrey Aleksandrov, 'Juvenilian Lash', *Sovetskaya Kul'tura*, 20 January 1989.

[197] Calum MacDonald, 'The Anti-Formalist 'Rayok' – Learners Start Here!', *Tempo*, No. 173, June 1990, p. 29 (hereafter C. MacDonald).

[198] C. MacDonald, pp. 28–30; Wilson, pp. 296–99; p. 272, note 7.

[199] Fay, 'Myth', p. 27. This letter appears to be that of 22 January 1949 to Kara Karayev, first mentioned in 1985 by Joachim Braun (Braun, 'Aspects', note 26a, p. 283): 'Shostakovich is probably speaking about a presentation at the Composers' Union. Did this take place or not? In any case the letter confirms that the composer thought about going ahead with the performance of op. 79. The revision of this decision indeed came only in late January or February 1949, at the height of the anti-Semitic wave, perhaps in connection with the attack on musicologists in February.' Fay uses Braun's discovery but makes no mention of his exegesis (*cf*. Braun, 'Aspects', p. 263)

a fear of life itself – can swing over to a mood of nothing-left-to-lose bravado in which the prospect of death becomes a matter of indifference.[200] This may not persist for very long before swinging back into the basic state of fearful depression; yet, while it lasts, it can produce acts of self-regardless (to the onlooker, 'near-suicidal') courage.[201] Under Stalinism, the lives of poets like Mandelstam, Pasternak and Akhmatova were marked by precisely such oscillations between interludes of selfless bravery and sudden collapses into fear and self-doubt (moments during which each wrote what Richard Taruskin would presumably deride as 'groveling civic panegyrics'). Shostakovich toyed with suicide from his teens to his last days,[202] and it is legitimate to suggest that his life and career shows the same oscillating pattern under stress as the lives and careers of Mandelstam, Pasternak, and Akhmatova. On his own admission, he could, at times, be scared into a condition of near-robotic compliance with external demands (relieved, in rare moments, by childlike tears or outbursts of self-loathing). At other times, he could, it seems, swing over to the associated state of reckless bravado and, under a compulsion – come what

[200] *Cf.* Gavin J. Fairbairn, *Contemplating Suicide: The Language and Ethics of Self Harm*, Routledge, London, 1995, pp. 87–92 ('cosmic roulette'), 111–14 ('dangerous pursuits'), 114–16 ('heroic actions'); R. M. Martin, 'Suicide and Self-Sacrifice', in M. P. Battin and D. J. Mayo (eds.), *Suicide: The Philosophical Issues*, Peter Owen, London, 1981; K. Lebacqz and H. T. Englehardt, Jr., 'Suicide', in D. J. Horan and D. Mall (eds.), *Death, Dying, and Euthanasia*, Aletheia, Frederick (Maryland), 1980.

[201] Like many creative people (e.g., Mahler), Shostakovich was prone to sudden mood-swings. Mikhail Druskin describes these and the discipline with which Shostakovich suppressed them: 'Already in his youth, Shostakovich was unpredictable and given to sudden vacillations [*sic*] of mood; at one moment, jolly and easy, the next pensive; then suddenly he would switch off altogether. And as the years went by these changes intensified. [. . .] But he also had remarkable self-possession, and however difficult the circumstances, he was always able to contain himself; for his deep sense of responsibility towards life and art was an organic constituent of his make-up, and he totally accepted the moral principles behind these concepts' (Wilson, p. 42. *Cf.* the testimony of Arnold Ferkelman, Wilson, p. 105). Tatyana Glivenko likewise reports Shostakovich's 'fluctuating' moods (*ibid.*, p. 84).

[202] *Cf.* MacDonald, p. 545, note 31; Lebedinsky, p. 476; *Testimony*, p. 89/118.

may – to tell the truth in his own way (i.e., in music), commit himself to acts of self-regardless courage (of which the Fifth Symphony is, arguably, the prime example).[203] If Lev Lebedinsky[204] is to be believed, the Twelfth Symphony was planned as a work of comparable bravery until the composer's nerve failed. Yet, having humiliated himself by scribbling a compromised rewrite of the Twelfth at the last minute, Shostakovich swung back into self-regardless resolve in his next opus: the Thirteenth Symphony – his most obviously dissident work.

It is arguably no coincidence that Shostakovich went back onto the attack in his Thirteenth Symphony. This is a composition which sprang from his electrifying encounter (in *Literaturnaya Gazeta*) with Yevgeny Yevtushenko's 'Babi Yar', a poem that draws its power from direct identification with the Jewish experience under Nazism. This identification is embodied in the line 'I feel myself to be a Jew', which Timothy L. Jackson suggests was an emotional flashpoint for the composer.[205] Jackson's speculation is, of course, of the kind we must be cautious about, yet its probability is significantly enhanced by Yevtushenko's report that Shostakovich wept as he sang his setting of the similar line 'It seems to me that I am Anne Frank'.[206] If, as appears more than possible, Shostakovich identified his own beleaguered situation with that of the Jew in the Soviet Union (or any alien society), it is unsurprising that Yevtushenko's public voicing of this identification should have overwhelmed him.

Given Shostakovich's personal identification with the Jewish predicament, wrongs done to Jews must have functioned as an external analogy of wrongs done to himself – in

[203] I refer to the stages of conception and creation. Clearly Shostakovich reverted to discretion in both the Fifth Symphony's finale and his subsequent attributable remarks about the work as a whole.

[204] Wilson, pp. 346–47.

[205] *Cf*. p. 600. According to Kirill Kondrashin, a district Party secretary complained of the Thirteenth Symphony, 'This is outrageous, we let Shostakovich join the Party, and then he goes and presents us with a symphony about Jews' (Wilson, p. 359).

[206] Wilson, p. 364.

which case, such external wrongs would presumably have been a major cause of his swings into self-regardless courage. It is conceivable that, when isolated in suffering, his resistance became low because of underlying doubts about his own worth[207] or because of the conviction that he was a coward (instead of naturally being very afraid during such interludes).[208] Yet once this state was forgotten, he was able to find courage in anger over the suffering of others, and of Jews in particular – an indignation he could not, when solitary and

[207] As 'a frail boy' (Flora Litvinova; Wilson, p. 308), Shostakovich had probably been bullied at school – a possible spur to the development of his talent for mimicry, which he may have used as a protective device. He seems to have avoided confrontations with those stronger than himself by not resisting, a trait mentioned several times in his letters to Tanya Glivenko (p. 542, note 25). (According to Litvinova, he was 'incapable of resisting any form of force and boorishness. When pressure was exerted on him, he was ready to compromise himself, read out or sign anything, so long as he would be left alone' (Wilson, p. 308). 'From childhood', he told Lev Lebedinsky, 'I have been doing things that I wanted not to do' (Wilson, p. 337). Although doubtless effective as strategy, this tendency to bend in the presence of brute force is bound to have damaged his self-esteem. Indeed, it could, at times, reduce him to hysteria. Marina Sabinina records him telling her how he had been obliged to read a piece of 'idiotic, disgusting nonsense' at the 1948 Moscow conference: 'I read like the most paltry wretch, a parasite, a puppet, a cut-out paper doll on a string!!' Sabinina adds: 'This last phrase he shrieked out like a frenzied maniac, and then kept repeating it. I sat there completely dazed' (Wilson, pp. 294–95. *Cf.* Isaak Glikman, Wilson, p. 338).

[208] According to Edison Denisov, Shostakovich confessed to him in 1957 that he had 'always been a coward', adding that if Denisov had seen the things he had, then he too would have become a coward. 'For instance, he told how during the period of the purges he would go to visit a friend, only to discover that this friend had disappeared without trace, and nobody knew what had happened to him. His possessions had been bundled up and thrown out on to the street, and strangers were occupying his flat. Another reason for his cowardice was his profound and obsessive love for his children' (Wilson, p. 304). Flora Litvinova concurs: 'Shostakovich was quite simply afraid. He feared for his children, his family, himself, and his neighbour. [. . .] Then perhaps it was the terror of seeing so many people disappear, the mass of people who were arrested and perished in the camps' (*ibid.*, p. 308). Lev Lebedinsky records Shostakovich sobbing hysterically at being forced to join the Party in 1960: 'I will never forget some of the things he said that night: "I am scared to death of them." "You don't know the whole truth." "I'm a wretched alcoholic." "I've been a whore, I am and always will be a whore." (He often lashed at himself in strong words.)' (Wilson, p. 337).

under stress, muster on his own behalf.[209] Rostislav Dubinsky recorded a telling incident at a Moldavian restaurant in 1956 when a loutish anti-Semite joined Shostakovich's company: 'There was a heavy silence around the table. How often, in the presence of rudeness, cultured people are petrified!' Pouring a drink with hands trembling so violently that vodka spilled on the table-cloth, Shostakovich exclaimed 'What filth!' The lout turned out to be violent and had to be ejected by waiters. Here, Shostakovich's fear of brute force was momentarily forgotten in a spontaneous swing into self-regardless courage.[210] In a comparable incident during rehearsals for the Thirteenth Symphony in 1962, the singer Vitaly Gromadsky stupidly suggested that there was no anti-Semitism in the USSR. According to Kirill Kondrashin, who was on the podium, Shostakovich 'blew up', exclaiming 'No, there is, there is anti-Semitism in the Soviet Union. It is an outrageous thing, and we must fight it. We must shout it from the roof-tops'.[211]

Valentin Berlinsky has said of Shostakovich that, while basically mild, 'he hated injustice, malice, pettiness – and when somebody of quality, somebody he valued, was humiliated, he became very angry'.[212] Similarly, Flora Litvinova takes pains to put the composer's dread-filled depressions in the perspective of his 'courage and nobility': 'Despite his fear, I know how many people he helped, and how often he

209 As a form of disinterest, self-regardless behaviour is related to moral altruism, the ardent belief in natural justice, and – significantly – the trait of self-denial, a characteristic which marked Shostakovich in his more balanced moods (in the form of extreme self-control, self-reserving formality, or self-effacing modesty) and also in his periods of isolated suffering (in the form of lacerating self-contempt).

210 Dubinsky, p. 119.

211 Wilson, p. 358–59. Elsewhere (*cf. DSCH*, No. xviii, p. 9) Kondrashin writes of this incident: 'I realized that this was a sensitive subject. Jewish melodies occur in many of his works. Personally, there was nothing Jewish about Shostakovich, as regards nationality, culture, or terms of upbringing. But I see in his Jewish motifs a manifestation of his subconscious, or perhaps even conscious, protest. *His Jewish songs were written at the height of the anti-Jewish campaign in the late 1940s*' (emphasis added).

212 Interview with Michael Oliver, *Music Magazine*, BBC Radio 3, 1983.

interceded for people'.[213] There is no need to retail the innumerable testimonials to Shostakovich's generosity and determination in pleading for and supporting the victimised. What is, however, worth noting is how many of those he felt impelled to help in this way – even to the extent of risking his life – happened to be Jewish.

The high proportion of Jews among those whom Shostakovich especially favoured and aided is partly an artifact of his unusually large number of Jewish friends of all ages (who, at times, functioned as a protective inner circle round him). Consequently it might be argued that since, by the 1940s, Jews bulked disproportionately large in the intelligentsia,[214] neither the overall quantity of Shostakovich's Jewish friends nor the number he specially favoured and aided are of any statistical significance. But this argument fails on the demonstrable fact that anyone befriending Jews in the USSR after 1942 could have done so only in the knowledge that such friendships made them an inevitable target of suspicion for the Soviet security organs. Shostakovich's liberal befriending of Jews cannot have been accidental. Hence the quantity of his Jewish friends is, statistically and otherwise, highly significant.

So committed was Shostakovich to his Jewish friends that he stood virtually *in loco parentis* to some of them. Isaak Schwartz testifies to the composer's fatherly interest in his upbringing and education;[215] in the same way, Shostakovich and his wife Nina were fully prepared to adopt the Vainbergs' seven-year-old daughter Vitosha had her parents fallen victim to Stalin's planned pogrom in 1953.[216] Indeed, this latter incident constitutes one of the most outstanding examples of the composer's self-regardless, 'near-suicidal' courage on behalf of those whose victimhood incensed him.

[213] Wilson, p. 308.

[214] Kagarlitsky, pp. 128–29.

[215] Wilson, p. 220. When Schwartz's father was arrested in 1936, Isaak, then fourteen, was exiled with his mother to Frunze, Kirghizia. Here he was taken under the wing of Shostakovich's sister Mariya, herself exiled to Frunze after her husband Vsevolod Frederiks was arrested in 1937.

[216] Wilson, p. 232. Also *cf.* the case of Rafiil Khozak (Wilson, pp. 234–35).

When Vainberg was arrested in February 1953 – at the height of the anti-Semitic media furor over the so-called Doctors' Plot[217] – Shostakovich (records Kirill Kondrashin[218]) 'inundated' Stalin and Beria with letters pleading for his release. Vainberg's wife Natalya Vovsi-Mikhoels, describes these terrifying events as follows:

> To be arrested in those times meant departure forever. The families of those arrested were ostracized. I rushed between the Moscow prisons, the Lubyanka and the Butyrka, and didn't know whom to approach. A few days after his arrest, a great friend of ours rang me and suggested we met [*sic*]. While we paced the dark and narrow Moscow lanes, he told me that Shostakovich was writing a letter to Beria and needed me to come and help him edit it. It was sheer lunacy to go to Shostakovich in my situation! But I went and read the letter in which he, Shostakovich, vouched that Weinberg was an honest citizen and a most talented young composer, whose chief interest in life was music. I understood how dangerous it was for Shostakovich to vouch for an enemy of the people, a Jew, and furthermore, Mikhoels' son-in-law [...]. I felt stunned, grateful, and terrified all at the same time. I expressed these emotions as best I could to Dmitri Dmitriyevich, but he, shy of being thanked, just continued to repeat, 'Don't worry, don't worry, they won't do anything to me'.[219]

Shostakovich's avowed disregard of the possibility of reprisal over his intercession for Vainberg should not be allowed to mislead us into imagining that what he did then was anything other than extraordinarily risky.[220] By means of his famous

[217] *Cf.* p. 226, note 412.

[218] 'Shostakovich by Kondrashin', *DSCH*, No. xiii, August 1989, p. 20.

[219] Wilson, p. 231.

[220] Vainberg's position was indeed perilous. According to papers formerly in the Central Party Archives and now held in the Russian Centre for the Preservation and Study of Documents of Modern History in Moscow, Vainberg ('under the investigators' pressure') confessed that, at the order (*sic*) of his father-in-law Solomon Mikhoels, he had from 1944 onwards propagated within the Composers' Union the idea of creating a Jewish republic in the Crimea: 'For this purpose, in 1945 and 1946 Vainberg vainly insisted on creating a Jewish section within the Composers' Union, on the basis of which he planned to create a Jewish conservatory in the Crimea. He even asked A. M. Veprik for two volumes of synagogue music. Vainberg was also accused of composing two cycles of Jewish songs

phone-call to the composer around the end of February 1949,[221] Stalin had signalled that Shostakovich was, for the moment at least, 'not to be touched'; yet such was the dictator's unpredictability that this order could have been rescinded at any time, as were similar orders concerning Isaak Babel', Osip Mandelstam and Vsevolod Meyerhold.[222] (This was especially true in 1953, when Stalin was in the final stages of paranoid megalomania and, more particularly, since the issue touched upon his by-then almost insane loathing of Jews.) By 1953, Shostakovich had seen too many of his friends, relatives and colleagues arrested to be under any illusion of the danger of bothering monsters like Stalin and Beria about one victim out of millions. Yet he did so – and the presumption must be that he acted, firstly, because a wrong had been done to someone he valued; and, secondly, because that person, as a Jew, stood as a symbol of his own solitary victimhood. As in other cases, Vainberg's misfortune jolted Shostakovich out of the helplessness of his own isolation and swung him into a mood of self-regardless courage.

Laurel Fay's contention is that Shostakovich made no sustained secret of composing *From Jewish Folk Poetry* because he had no fear of being punished for it. Yet time and again he committed himself to courageous acts on behalf of others in the full knowledge that he had no reliable way of estimating the risks he took in so doing. Reduced to suicidal hysteria by the Zhdanov conference, he was, within months, hiding a condemned Jew in his Moscow flat: Moshe Beregovsky, a musicologist specialising in precisely the kind of Jewish folk music which Shostakovich turned to that summer in *From Jewish Folk Poetry*.[223] Since Beregovsky was on

---

employing lyrics by Isaac Peretz and Samuil Galkin, as well as of giving Ya. A. Shaporin the idea of writing *Vokaliz*, based on a Jewish melody' (Kostyrchenko, p. 196, n. 67.) The charges against Vainberg were equivalent in gravity to those made against other Jewish intellectuals repressed during 1946–53.

221 Wilson, pp. 212–13.

222 *Cf*. Shentalinsky, pp. 22–71 and 170–91.

223 Testimony of Thomas Sanderling in Wilson, p. 234. (*Cf*. p. 222, note 398.) Beregovsky's troubles stemmed from his work as a publisher of Eastern European Jewish *shtetl* village songs (*shtetl* is Yiddish for 'little town'). His activities having been curtailed by Stalin's *apparat*, Bere-

the run from the Soviet authority in Kiev, Shostakovich was violating the legal code by harbouring an enemy of the People. Does this resemble the act of one fearless because self-convinced that his honest intent to regain favour with the *apparat* would protect him under any circumstance, however perilous? Or is it, rather, the impulsive courage of an often terrified man, moved to a potentially suicidal act by the misfortune of a fellow victim?

If Shostakovich could occasionally be as self-regardlessly brave[224] as he was sometimes ignominiously crushed and frightened, then the act of composing *From Jewish Folk Poetry* without sustainedly concealing it from the Soviet authorities is, at worst, nothing like the cast-iron guarantee of conformism proffered by Laurel Fay, and, at best, a typical piece of near-suicidal bravado on the part of an artist who, stung by injustice inflicted on others, could become extremely resolute in the face of retribution from above. All accounts of Shostakovich's demeanour during the manœuvres before the premiere of his Thirteenth Symphony in 1963 show him gripped by just such bloody-minded determination. Perhaps, then, in 1948, he simply snapped and got angry? Perhaps, in persecuting the Jews he saw as external symbols of his own woe, the Soviet state pushed Shostakovich too far and he came out fighting, as he later did in 1963? Questioned in 1962 about his disinterred yet still controversial Fourth Symphony, he replied 'Let them eat it'. Could this not have been his feeling whilst writing and rehearsing

---

govsky was working on an anthology of klezmer music when he became close to Shostakovich. The composer Gerard McBurney (letter to the present writer dated 19 February 1997) conjectures that Shostakovich may also have known of Beregovsky's collection of Jewish songs without words, recently published in Russia under the editorship of M. Goldin. McBurney (who regards the proposition that Shostakovich was unaware of the extent of official anti-Semitism in Stalin's USSR as absurd), believes that *From Jewish Folk Poetry* is, in essence, an *hommage* to the fatalistic spiritual resilience expressed in the *shtetl* idiom as the composer discovered it through Beregovsky's work (commentary on BBC Radio 3, 4 May 1997).

[224] *Cf.* pp. 219–33. For anyone who understands the conditions of post-Stalinist repression, Vladimir Zak's account of Shostakovich's astounding *yurodivy* performance on the podium at the opening of the Fifth Congress of Soviet Composers (1972) is proof alone of the composer's occasional departures into reckless self-exposure.

From Jewish Folk Poetry? Such an explanation has the merit of according with the other evidence, personal and historical, marshalled here.[225]

Laurel Fay presents Shostakovich as earnestly labouring to placate the authorities with a simple piece of Socialist Realist folk-national kitsch. Yet Shostakovich would have had to have been absurdly stupid not to have realised that *From Jewish Folk Poetry* was almost certainly too hot to handle even in Summer 1948, let alone during Winter 1948–49. Why, then, did he not place it straight in his drawer, as he appears to have done with other 'Jewish' works like the First Violin Concerto and Fourth Quartet? Why, on the contrary, did he hold private performances of the cycle and even express a belief that it might be officially auditioned in early 1949? Apart from the fact that, as yet, we have an inadequate picture of how the First Violin Concerto and Fourth Quartet came to be held back, there is no necessary mystery about Shostakovich's attitude to *From Jewish Folk Poetry*. That it was something he strongly believed in, and was therefore prepared to fight for, is clear from the testimony of Abraam Gozenpud, a mutual friend of Ivan Sollertinsky and Vissarion Shebalin:

> Shostakovich first showed his cycle *From Jewish Folk Poetry* at the Moscow Union of Composers early in 1953, just after the news bulletin in the press had appeared denouncing the [Jewish] Doctors. [. . .] the performance of this cycle at that time was an act of great civic courage.[226]

If submitting *From Jewish Folk Poetry* was severely inadvisable in January 1949, it was suicidally dangerous in January 1953, a time when Stalin was about to launch an all-out campaign to exterminate Soviet Jewry under cover of a

[225] Shostakovich was not alone in displaying such suicidal courage. Rostropovich records that Sviatoslav Richter refused to give concerts (*went on strike!*) until he was allowed to perform Prokofiev's Ninth Piano Sonata (composed 1947, premiered in Moscow in 1951). Rostropovich likewise 'despised' David Oistrakh for not similarly demonstrating on behalf of Shostakovich's First Violin Concerto, which consequently remained unheard until 1955 (Wilson, pp. 218–19). Rostropovich himself harangued Khrennikov when, in 1950, a helpless Prokofiev confessed that he had no money to buy food.

[226] Wilson, p. 238.

further general purge. If Laurel Fay had read and understood Gozenpud's affidavit, she might not have allowed her thesis into print. With the knowledge now available, there is no impugnable mystery about why Shostakovich told himself, and others, that *From Jewish Folk Poetry* would go before the examining board early in 1949. At times like those of the Doctors' Plot and of the premiere of the Thirteenth Symphony, he must simply have put his head down and butted the gate of state censorship without looking too closely where he was going. After all, to gaze straight at danger is virtually guaranteed to give it the power to frighten you. Under certain circumstances, it is wiser to act as if everything is quite normal and destined to finish happily, even if objective evidence is to the contrary. Perhaps Shostakovich even managed to convince himself that, once he had brought *From Jewish Folk Poetry* before the panel of the Composers' Union, he could bluff them into accepting it as a straightfaced sacrifice to Socialist Realism. After all, unlikelier bluffs had worked in the past, and the Soviet cultural *apparat* was not staffed by geniuses. Clearly Laurel Fay would have been easily enough deceived had she been on the panel. The final nail in the coffin of Fay's interpretation is, of course, the music itself, which, with the exception of Shostakovich's Thirteenth Symphony, is about as far from innocuous, Party-pleasing oatmeal as any Soviet composer ever ventured.[227]

Fay's historically illiterate interpretation of *From Jewish Folk Poetry* depends, in the end, on an estimate of Shostakovich's intelligence which is frankly insulting.[228] Yet this assumption is a central tenet of anti-revisionism, obtruding also in the

[227] Mud, unfortunately, sticks. Gennady Rozhdestvensky's recording of Shostakovich's *From Jewish Folk Poetry* (RCA Victor Red Seal 09026-68434-2) was issued late in 1996 with a sleevenote written in good faith by RCA editor Emily King on the basis of Fay's article in *The New York Times*. As a result, Shostakovich finds himself portrayed in Emily King's commentary as a frightened conformist with no interest in the Jewish question, anxious only to rehabilitate himself with the *apparat* by concocting a piece of randomly selected folk-nationalism which coincidentally featured Jewish subject matter. Emily King cannot be condemned for this; she had no reason to suspect that Fay's claims were spurious.

[228] *Cf. The New Shostakovich*, pp. 247–53.

writings of Taruskin, Brown and Norris. Again and again we run up against their indefensible contention that Shostakovich was no brighter than the average, supposedly utterly bamboozled, Soviet citizen. The only way to justify such a view is to resuscitate the old 'official' version of Shostakovich – an imaginary figure once naively assumed to have been the sincere author of the ridiculously inept articles which appeared over his signature in Soviet publications. Indeed, in his description of the composer as 'perhaps Soviet Russia's most loyal musical son', Richard Taruskin has attempted just such a nightmare resurrection. Yet the testimony of Shostakovich's friends and colleagues to the contrary is overwhelming. Nowhere in the anti-revisionist portrayal of the composer is there any glimpse of 'those frightened, very intelligent eyes' observed (among many others) by Robert Craft;[229] no hint of the brilliant mimic, the deadpan ironist, the scalpel-sharp raconteur, the faultless memoriser of enormous tracts of music and literature, the speed-reader who could take in musical scores or pages of prose at a glance.[230] Yet this insensitivity (or willful blindness) to Shostakovich's extraordinary mind is as nothing beside the pitiful inability of the anti-revisionists to appreciate the composer's extraordinary moral stature, whether from testimony or by direct intuitive contact with his music.

The efforts of a small coterie of academics to put the lid back on the possibility that Shostakovich may have been anything other than an 'honest blunderer' or a Communist stooge will, I believe, strike most fair-minded readers as an insult to their intelligence. Indeed, the extent to which some members of this coterie are prepared to misrepresent the composer suggests a wish, at all costs, to detach Shostakovich

[229] Craft, *Stravinsky: The Chronicle Of A Friendship 1948–1971*, Victor Gollancz, London, 1972, p. 194. *Cf.* Glikman, p. 12: 'His magnificent grey eyes which shone behind his glasses, intelligent and perspicacious, now meditative, now laughing'.

[230] As such, he was a match for his closest friend, the polymath Ivan Sollertinsky, who spoke at least two dozen languages (32, counting dialects). Like Shostakovich, Sollertinsky had a photographic memory and allegedly knew by heart the works of Shakespeare, Pushkin, Gogol, Aristotle and Plato (Solomon Volkov, *St Petersburg: A Cultural History*, p. 408).

from a highly charged political background which they do not understand or fear to get involved with. The constant complaint of anti-revisionists is that revisionism 'trivialises' Shostakovich. This charge would be easier to treat seriously were those making it to demonstrate a more coherent grasp of the intellectual issues this subject raises; yet unhappy confusion reigns. 'It is time', declares David Fanning in his introduction to *Shostakovich Studies*, 'to let all who care about Shostakovich's music speak for themselves and in their own way'. Who, it is fair to enquire, has ever prevented this? The closest thing to a dominant line on Shostakovich so far has been that of Western academic anti-revisionism. (Taruskin, whom Fanning presents as a saviour figure, is actually part of a long-established academic incumbency in the United States.) If, Fanning continues, *Shostakovich Studies* 'does not at least succeed in proving that musicologists have a role to play in enhancing the understanding of his message, then it will truly have earned the composer's scorn from the grave'. Again the assumption is false and incongruous. No one has ever claimed that musicology is irrelevant to the study of Shostakovich; that would be madness. What I propose is that 'pure' musicology – the value-free examination of that limited portion of the music which is representable by the score – cannot, as logic predicts and practice confirms, by itself tell us anything of real consequence about this composer's music (or, indeed, of any other composer's music).

Attempts to understand Shostakovich's work as 'pure music' are doomed from the outset, not merely because it is dependent on context but because the idea of 'pure music' is, in itself, an illusion. Nor is this contextual dependence anything to fear. Universality emerges from local specificity and Shostakovich's work, at root, is very specific. Equally, at its highest reach, it is as universal as any other great music; indeed it can fairly be said to be *more* universal than most other great music.[231] What ultimately makes it universal is the blend of its composer's near-supernatural giftedness with his obstinate fidelity to the truth as he experienced it in all its local and specific vividness, absurdity and horror. Elizabeth

[231] *Cf.* pp. 555–65.

Wilson has written that Shostakovich in his symphonic works 'spoke from a moral stand as the voice of civic conscience'. The composer's lifelong creative colleague Grigory Kozintsev goes further: 'In Shostakovich's music I hear a virulent hatred of cruelty, of the cult of power, of the persecution of truth . . . Music is not a profession for Shostakovich, it is the necessity to speak out and to convey what lies behind the lives of people, to depict our age and our country'.[232] Clearly, music like this exists far beyond the compass of mere technical analysis. In order to grapple productively with Shostakovich, critics must not only take the fullest possible account of context in their assessments; they must also consider his music in its ethical aspect. It was the conviction of John Ruskin that we should apprehend art 'with our whole moral being'. If doing so requires a fundamental redefinition of musicology, so be it.

[232] Wilson, pp. 371 and 374.

BIBLIOGRAPHY

1. Books

ALDISERT, RUGGERO J., *The Judicial Process*, West Publishing Co., St. Paul, 1976.

ANON, *A Chronicle of Current Events*, Khronika Press, New York, 1976.

——, *Materialy soveshchaniya. Stenografichesky otchyot* (*Materials of the Conference. Stenographic Account*), 1948.

——, *Merriam-Webster's Collegiate Dictionary*, 10th edn., Merriam-Webster, Inc., Springfield, Massachusetts, 1993.

——, *Smaller Soviet Encyclopedia*, 1930.

——, *Sovetskaya Muzykal'naya Entsiklopediya* (*Soviet Musical Encyclopaedia*), Sovetskaya Entsiklopediya, Moscow, 1982.

——, *The 20th Century, An Almanac*, World Almanac Publications, New York, 1985.

——, *V. I. Lenin i A. M. Gorky* (*V. I. Lenin and A. M. Gorky*), Academy of Sciences Publishing House, Moscow, 1961.

ANTSIFEROV, NIKOLAY, *Dusha Peterburga* (*The Soul of Petersburg*), Brokgauz-Efron, Petersburg, 1922; reprinted Kniga, Moscow, 1991.

BANICHENKO, D. L., *Pisateli i tsenzory* (*Writers and Censors*), Rossiya Molodaya, Moscow, 1994.

——, (ed.), *'Literaturny front': Istoriya politicheskoy tsenzury 1932–1946* (*'Literary Front': History of political censorship 1932–1946*), Entsiklopediya Rossiyskikh Dereven', Moscow, 1994.

BERNANDT, B., YAMPOL'SKY, I. M., and KISELYOVA, T. YE., *Kto pisal o muzyke, Bio-bibliografichesky slovar' muzykal'nykh kritikov i lits, pisavshikh o muzyke v dorevolyutsionnoy Rossii i SSSR* (*Who Wrote About Music, a Bio-Bibliographical Dictionary of Music Critics and People Who Wrote About Music in Pre-Revolutionary Russia and the USSR*), Sovetsky Kompozitor, Moscow, 1989.

BLYUM, A. V., *Za kulisami 'ministerstva pravdy': Tainaya istoriya sovetskoy tsenzury, 1917–1929* (*Backstage at the 'Ministry of Truth'. Secret History of Soviet Censorship, 1917–1929*), Akademichesky Proekt, St. Petersburg, 1994.

BOBROVSKY, VIKTOR, *Kamernyye instrumental'nyye ansambli D. Shostakovicha: issledovaniye* (*Chamber Instrumental Ensembles of D. Shostakovich: A Study*), Sovetsky Kompozitor, Moscow, 1961.

BOGDANOVA, ALLA VLADIMIROVNA., *Muzyka i vlast'* (*Poststalinsky Period*) (*Music and the Regime* (*Post-Stalin Period*)), Naslediye, Moscow, 1995.

BONOSKY, PHILLIP, *Two Cultures*, Progress Publishers, Moscow, 1978.

BOWN, MATTHEW CULLERNE, *Art Under Stalin*, Phaidon, London, 1991.

BOYD, BRIAN, *Vladimir Nabokov*, Chatto & Windus, London, 1990.

BRAUN, JOACHIM, *Jews and Jewish Elements in Soviet Music*, Tel-Aviv, 1978.

BROWN, MALCOLM H., (ed.), *Russian and Soviet Music: Essays for Boris Schwarz*, UMI Research Press, Ann Arbor, 1984.

—— and WILEY, ROLAND JOHN, (eds.), *Slavonic and Western Music: Essays for Gerald Abraham*, UMI Research Press, Ann Arbor, 1985.

CELAN, PAUL, *Poems. A Bilingual Edition*, selected, translated and introduced by Michael Hamburger, Persea Books, New York, 1980.

CHEREPNIN, NIKOLAY, *Vospominaniya* (*Reminiscences*), Sovetsky Kompozitor, Moscow, 1979.

CHICAGO-KENT COLLEGE OF LAW, *Ethics Guidelines For Legal Writing Classes*.

CHUKOVSKY, K., *Dnevnik, 1901–1929* (*Diary, 1901–1929*), Sovetsky Pisatel', Moscow, 1991.

——, *Dnevnik, 1930–1969* (*Diary, 1930–1969*), Sovremenny Pisatel', Moscow, 1994.

CLARK, KATERINA, and HOLQUIST, MICHAEL, *Mikhail Bakhtin*, Harvard University Press, Cambridge, 1984.

CONQUEST, ROBERT, *The Great Terror: A Reassessment*, Hutchinson, London, 1990/Oxford University Press, New York, 1991.

——, *The Nation Killers: the Soviet Deportation of Nationalities*, Macmillan, London, 1960.

——, *Tyrants and Typewriters: Communiqués in the Struggle for Truth*, Hutchinson, London, 1989.

CRAFT, ROBERT, *Stravinsky: The Chronicle of a Friendship 1948–1971*, Victor Gollancz, London, 1972.

DANILEVICH, LEV, *Shostakovich: zhizn' i tvorchestvo* (*Shostakovich: Life and Works*), Sovetsky Kompozitor, Moscow, 1980.

——, (ed.), *Dmitry Shostakovich*, Sovetsky Kompozitor, Moscow, 1967.

DAVIES, SARAH, *Popular Opinion in Stalin's Russia: Terror, Propaganda and Dissent, 1934–1941*, Cambridge University Press, Cambridge, 1997.

DERIABIN, PETER, and GIBNEY, FRANK, *The Secret World*, Doubleday and Co., New York, 1959; revised edition, Ballantine Books, New York, 1982.

DUBINSKY, ROSTISLAV, *Stormy Applause: Making Music in a Worker's State*, Hutchinson, London/Hill and Wang, New York, 1989.

FADEYEV, ALEKSANDR, *Za tridtsat' let* (*During Thirty Years*), Sovetsky pisatel', Moscow, 1957.

FAINSOD, MERLE, *How Russia Is Ruled*, revised edition, Harvard University Press, Cambridge, 1963.

FAIRBAIRN, GAVIN J., *Contemplating Suicide: The Language and Ethics of Self Harm*, Routledge, London, 1995.

FANNING, DAVID, (ed.), *Shostakovich Studies*, Cambridge University Press, Cambridge, 1995.

FEUCHTNER, BERND, *'Und Kunst geknebelt von der groben Macht': Dmitri Schostakowitch, künstlerische Identität und staatliche Repression*, Sendler, Frankfurt am Main, 1986.

FIGES, ORLANDO, *A People's Tragedy: The Russian Revolution 1891–1924*, Jonathan Cape, London, 1996.

FISK, JOSIAH, (ed.), *Composers on Music*, Northeastern University Press, Boston, 1997.

FITZPATRICK, SHEILA, *Cultural Revolution in Russia 1928–31*, Indiana University Press, Bloomington, 1978.

FRISHMAN, DMITRY, *Georgy Sviridov*, Muzyka, Moscow, 1971.

GERSHKOVICH, ALEKSANDR, *Teatr na Taganke, 1964–1984* (*Taganka: The Rebellious Soviet Theatre, 1964–1984*), Chalidze Publications, Benson (Vermont), 1986.

GETTY, J. ARCH, and MANNING, ROBERTA T., (eds.), *Stalinist Terror: New Perspectives*, Cambridge University Press, Cambridge, 1993.

GILBOA, YEHOSHUA A., *The Black Years of Soviet Jewry, 1939–1953*, transl. Yosef Shachter and Dov Ben-Abba, Little, Brown, Boston, 1971.

GLEASON, ABBOTT, KENEZ, PETER, and STITES, RICHARD, (eds.),

Bolshevik Culture: Experiment and Order in the Russian Revolution, Indiana University Press, Bloomington, 1985.

GLIKMAN, ISAAK, *Lettres à un ami*, transl. Luba Jurgenson, Albin Michel, Paris, 1994.

——, *Pis'ma k drugu: Dmitry Shostakovich Isaaku Glikmanu* (*Letters to a Friend*), DSCH, Moscow/Kompozitor, St Petersburg, 1993.

GOJOWY, DETLEF, *Dimitri Schostakowitsch mit Selbstzeugnissen und Bilddokumenten*, Rowohlt Taschenbuch Verlag, Hamburg, 1983.

GORKY, MAXIM, *The Autobiography of Maxim Gorky*, transl. Isidor Schneider, Citadel Press, Secaucus (New Jersey), 1949.

——, *Untimely Thoughts: Essays On Revolution, Culture and the Bolsheviks 1917–18*, Garnstone Press, London, 1968.

GRIGOR'YEV, LEV, and PLATEK, YAKOV, *Sovetskiye kompozitory i muzykovedy, spravochnik v 3 tomakh* (*Soviet Composers and Musicologists, Dictionary in Three Volumes*), Sovetsky Kompozitor, Moscow, 1981.

——, (compilers), *Shostakovich: About Himself and His Times*, transl. Angus and Neilian Roxburgh, Progress Publishers, Moscow, 1981; a slightly modified version of Yakovlev's compilation, 1980.

HEIKINHEIMO, SEPPO, *Mätämunan muistelmat*, Otava, Helsinki, 1997.

HEINLEIN, ROBERT A., *Expanded Universe*, Ace Books, New York, 1980.

——, *Friday*, Ballantine Books, New York, 1982.

——, *Stranger in a Strange Land*, 1961; reprinted by Ace Books, New York, 1991.

HELLER, LEONID, *Autour de Zamiatine*, L'Âge d'homme, Lausanne, 1989.

HELLER, MIKHAIL, *Cogs In The Soviet Wheel: The Formation of Soviet Man*, transl. David Floyd, Collins Harvill, London, 1987.

——, and NEKRICH, ALEKSANDR, *Utopia in Power: The History of the Soviet Union from 1917 to the Present*, Hutchinson, London, 1986.

HO, ALLAN B., and FEOFANOV, DMITRY, (eds.), *Biographical Dictionary of Russian/Soviet Composers*, Greenwood Press, Westport, 1989.

HOSKING, GEOFFREY, *A History of the Soviet Union*, revised edition, Fontana Press, London, 1985.

HULME, DEREK C., *Shostakovich: A Catalogue, Bibliography and Discography*, second edition, Oxford University Press, Oxford, 1991.

IPPOLITOV-IVANOV, MIKHAIL, *50 let russkoy muzyki v moikh vospominaniyakh* (*50 Years of Russian Music in my Reminiscences*), Muzgiz, Moscow, 1934.

IVASHKIN, ALEKSANDR V., *Alfred Schnittke*, Phaidon, London, 1996.

——, (compiler), *Besedy s Al'fredom Shnitke* (*Conversations with Alfred Schnittke*), RIK Kul'tura, Moscow, 1994.

JACKSON, TIMOTHY L., *Tchaikovsky's Sixth Symphony*, Cambridge Handbooks, Cambridge University Press, forthcoming.

JOSEPH, FRANK, *Dostoevsky: The Seeds of Revolt, 1821–1849*, *Dostoevsky: The Years of Ordeal, 1850–1869*, *Dostoevsky: The Stir of Liberation, 1860–1865* and *Dostoevsky: The Miraculous Years, 1865–1871*, Princeton Univ. Press, 1976, 1983, 1986 and 1995/Robson, London, 1977, 1983 and 1987.

KAGARLITSKY, BORIS, *The Thinking Reed: Intellectuals and the Soviet State from 1917 to the Present*, Verso, London, 1988.

KAPLAN, LANCE (ed.), *Mudrik Transcribed: Classes & Talks by Marvin Mudrik*, University of California Press, Santa Barbara, 1989.

KASPAROV, GARRI, *Unlimited Fight*, Fizkul'tura i Sport, Moscow, 1989.

KHACHATURIAN, ARAM, *Stranitsy zhizni i tvorchestva. Iz besed s G. M. Shneyersonom* (*Pages of Life and Work. From conversations with G. M. Shneyerson*), Sovetsky kompozitor, Moscow, 1982.

KHENTOVA, SOFIYA, *D. Shostakovich v gody Velikoy Otechestvennoy voiny* (*D. Shostakovich in the Days of the Great Patriotic War*), Muzyka, Leningrad, 1979.

——, *Shostakovich v Petrograde-Leningrade*, Lenizdat, Leningrad, 1979.

——, *Shostakovich. Tridtsatiletiye 1945–1975* (*Shostakovich. Thirty Years 1945–1975*), Sovetsky Kompozitor, Leningrad, 1982.

——, *Shostakovich. Zhizn' i tvorchestvo* (*Shostakovich. Life and Work*), two vols., Sovetsky Kompozitor, Leningrad, 1986.

——, *Udivitel'ny Shostakovich* (*Amazing Shostakovich*), Variant, St Petersburg, 1993.

KHODASEVICH, VLADISLAV, *Derzhavin*, Sovremennyiye zapiski/Annales contemporaines, Paris, 1931; reprinted Kniga, Moscow, 1988.

KHRENNIKOV, TIKHON, *Pervy vsesoyuzny s'yezd sovetskikh kompozitorov. Stenografichesky otchyot* (*First All-Union Congress of Soviet Composers. Stenographic Account*), Moscow, 1948.

——, *Tak Eto Bylo: Tikhon Khrennikov o Vremeni i o Sebe* (*The Way It Was: Tikhon Khrennikov About the Time and Himself*), as related to and edited by V. Rubtsova, Muzyka, Moscow, 1994.

KHRUSHCHEV, NIKITA, *Khrushchev Remembers*, André Deutsch, London, 1970.

KOCH, STEPHEN, *Double Lives: Stalin, Willi Munzenberg and the Seduction of the Intellectuals*, HarperCollins, New York, 1994.

KOCHAN, LIONEL, (ed.), *The Jews in Soviet Russia from 1917 to the Present*, Oxford University Press for Institute of Jewish Affairs, Oxford, 1972.

KOPP, KAREN, *Form und Gehalt der Symphonien des Dmitrij Schostakowitsch*, Verlag für systematische Musikwissenschaft, Bonn, 1990.

KOSTYRCHENKO, GENNADI, *V plenu u krasnogo faraona* (*In the Captivity of the Red Pharaoh*), transl. H. T. Willetts as *Out of the Red Shadows: Anti-Semitism in Stalin's Russia*, Prometheus Books, Amherst, New York, 1995.

KREMLYOV, YU., *Esteticheskiye vzglyady S. S. Prokof'yeva* (*Aesthetic Views of S. S. Prokofiev*), Muzyka, Leningrad, 1966.

LANE, MARK, *Rush to Judgment* (a critique of the Warren Commission's inquiry into the murders of President John F. Kennedy, Officer J. D. Tippit, and Lee Harvey Oswald), Holt, Rinehart and Winston, New York, 1966.

LEVIN, NORA, *The Jews in the Soviet Union Since 1917. Paradox of Survival*, New York University Press, New York, 1988.

LUKYANOVA, NATALIYA VALERIEVNA, *Shostakovich: His Life and Times*, transl. Yuri Shirokov, Paganiniana Publications, Inc., Neptune City, New Jersey, 1984.

MACDONALD, IAN, *The New Shostakovich*, Fourth Estate, London/Northeastern University Press, Boston, 1990; Oxford University Press, Oxford, 1991.

MALKO, NIKOLAI, *A Certain Art*, W. Morrow, New York, 1966.

MANDELSTAM, NADEZHDA, *Hope Abandoned*, Collins Harvill, London, 1974.

——, *Hope Against Hope*, Collins Harvill, London, 1971.

MARCUS, RICHARD L., REDISH, MARTIN H., and SHERMAN, EDWARD F., *Civil Procedure – A Modern Approach*, West Publishing Co., St. Paul, 1995.

MAREK, GEORGE R., *Toscanini*, Atheneum, New York/Vision Press, London, 1975.

MAZEL', LEO, *Simfonii D. D. Shostakovicha – Putevoditel'* (*Shostakovich's Symphonies: A Guide*), Sovetsky Kompozitor, Moscow, 1960.

MEDVEDEV, ROY, *Let History Judge: The Origins and Consequences of Stalinism*, rev. edn., Oxford University Press, Oxford, 1989.

MEYER, KLAUS, *Analytische Betrachtungen an Leonard Bernsteins Symphonie No. 1 'Jeremiah' und dem Ballett 'Fancy Free'*, Universität Erlangen-Nürnberg, M.A. dissertation, 1988.

MEYER, KRZYSZTOF, *Dimitri Chostakovich*, Fayard, Paris, 1994.

NABOKOV, NICOLAS, *Old Friends and New Music*, Little, Brown, Boston, 1951.

NAYMAN, ANATOLY, *Remembering Anna Akhmatova*, transl. Wendy Roslyn, Peter Halban, London, 1989.

NEISSER, ULRIC, *Memory Observed: Remembering in Natural Contexts*, W. H. Freeman, San Francisco, 1982.

NEKRICH, ALEKSANDR, *The Punished Peoples: The Deportation and Tragic Fate of Soviet Minorities at the End of the Second World War*, W. W. Norton, New York and London, 1978.

NORRIS, CHRISTOPHER, (ed.), *Shostakovich: The Man and His Music*, Marion Boyars, London, 1982.

OLKHOVSKY, ANDREY, *Music Under the Soviets: The Agony of an Art*, New York, 1955; reprinted by Greenwood Press, Westport, 1975.

ORLOV, GENRIKH, *Simfonii Shostakovicha* (*Shostakovich's Symphonies*), Gosudarstvennoye Muzykal'noye Izdatel'stvo, Leningrad, 1961.

PANKIN, BORIS, *100 Oborvannykh Dney* (*100 Days That Were Cut Short*), Sovershenno Sekretno, Moscow, 1993.

PARROTT, JASPER, with VLADIMIR ASHKENAZY, *Beyond Frontiers*, Collins, London/Atheneum, New York, 1985.

PINKUS, BENJAMIN, *The Jews of the Soviet Union: The History of a National Minority*, Cambridge University Press, Cambridge, 1988.

PIPES, RICHARD, *Russia Under the Bolshevik Regime*, Harvill, London, 1995.

——, *The Russian Revolution 1899–1919*, Collins Harvill, London, 1990.

PLISETSKAYA, MAYA, *Maya Plisetskaya*, Novosti, Moscow, 1994.

POWNALL, DAVID, *Master Class*, Faber and Faber, London, 1983.

PROKOFIEV, SERGEY, *Avtobiografiya*, ed. M. G. Kozlova, Sovetsky Kompozitor, Moscow, 1973.

——, *Avtografy S. S. Prokof'yeva v Fondakh Gosudarstvennogo tsentral'nogo muzeya muzykal'noy kul'tury im. M. I. Glinki, Spravochnik* (*S. S. Prokofiev's Autographs in the Fonds of the State Central Museum of Culture, named after M. I. Glinka, Catalogue*), Sovetsky Kompozitor, Moscow, 1977.

——, *Prokofiev by Prokofiev*, ed. David H. Appel, transl. Guy Daniels, Doubleday, Garden City, New York, 1979.

—— and Myaskovsky, Nikolay Ya., *Pis'ma* (*Letters*), Sovetsky Kompozitor, Moscow, 1977.

Pylyayev, Mikhail, *Stary Peterburg* (*Old Petersburg*), 2nd edn., A. S. Suvorin, St Petersburg, 1889.

Rabinovich, D., *D. Shostakovich*, Foreign Languages Publishing House, Moscow, 1959.

Rachmaninoff, Sergei, *Rachmaninoff's Recollections told to Oskar von Riesemann*, transl. Dolly Rutherford, Macmillan, New York, 1934.

Rapoport, Yakov, *The Doctors' Plot*, Fourth Estate, London, 1991.

Reddaway, Peter, (ed. and transl.), *Uncensored Russia. Protest and Dissent in the Soviet Union*, American Heritage Press, New York, 1972.

Redlich, Shimon, *War, Holocaust, and Stalinism: A Documented Study of the Jewish Anti-Fascist Committee in the USSR*, Harwood Academic Publishers, London, 1995.

Rimsky-Korsakov, Nikolay, *Chronicle of My Musical Life*, St. Petersburg, 1909; transl. J. Joffe, Alfred A. Knopf, New York, 1942.

——, *Polnoye Sobraniye Sochineny* (*Complete Works*), State Music Publishers, Moscow, 1955.

Ro'i, Yaacov, (ed.), *Jews and Jewish Life in Russia and the Soviet Union*, Frank Cass, Ilford, Essex, 1995.

Robinson, Harlow, *Sergei Prokofiev: A Biography*, Viking, New York, 1987.

Roseberry, Eric, *Ideology, Style, Content, and Thematic Process in the Symphonies, Cello Concertos, and String Quartets of Shostakovich*, dissertation, Garland, New York, 1989.

Rostropovich, Mstislav, *Mstislav Rostropovich and Galina Vishnevskaya: Conversations with Claude Samuel*, translated by E. Thomas Glasow, Amadeus Press, Portland, 1995.

Rubinstein, Anton, *Autobiography of Anton Rubinstein, 1829–1889*, Little, Brown, Boston, 1890.

Rudnitsky, K., *Rezhissyor Meierkhol'd* (*Meyerhold the Stage Director*), Iskusstvo, Moscow, 1969.

SABININA, MARINA, *Dmitry Shostakovich*, Znaniye, Moscow, 1959.

——, *Shostakovich – simfonist* (*Shostakovich – The Symphonist*), Muzyka, Moscow, 1976.

SACHS, HARVEY, *Toscanini*, J. B. Lippincott Co., New York, 1978.

SADOVNIKOV, YE., (ed.), *D. Shostakovich. Notografichesky i bibliografichesky spravochnik* (*D. Shostakovich. Musical and Bibliographical Dictionary*), Muzyka, Moscow, 1965.

SALEHIEH, VAHID, (ed.), *Special Issue on Shostakovich*, a collection of articles in *Melos*, 1/4–5, Stockholm, 1993.

SCAMMELL, MICHAEL, *Solzhenitsyn: A Biography*, W. W. Norton and Co., New York, 1984.

SCHILLINGER, FRANCES, *Joseph Schillinger: A Memoir*, Greenberg, New York, 1949; reprinted by Da Capo Press, New York, 1976.

SCHONBERG, HAROLD C., *Horowitz: His Life and Music*, Simon and Schuster, New York, 1992.

SCHWARZ, BORIS, *Music and Musical Life in Soviet Russia 1917–1970*, Barrie & Jenkins, London, 1970/W. W. Norton, New York, 1972.

——, *Music and Musical Life in Soviet Russia, 1917–1981*, enlarged edn., Indiana University Press, Bloomington, 1983.

SHEBALIN, VISSARION, and SABININA, MARINA, *Literaturnoye naslediye* (*Literary Heritage*), Sovetsky Kompozitor, Moscow, 1975.

SHENTALINSKY, VITALY, *The KGB's Literary Archive*, transl. John Crowfoot, Harvill Press, London, 1995.

SHLIFSTEIN, SEMYON, *S. S. Prokof'yev: Notografichesky Spravochnik* (*S. S. Prokofiev: Catalogue of Works*), Sovetsky Kompozitor, Moscow, 1962.

SHNEYERSON, GRIGORY, *O Muzyke Zhivoy i Myortvoy* (*On Music Alive and Dead*), Sovetsky Kompozitor, Moscow, 1960.

——, (ed.), *D. Shostakovich: stat'i i materialy* (*D. Shostakovich: Articles and Materials*), Sovetsky Kompozitor, Moscow, 1976.

SHOSTAKOVICH, DMITRI, *Testimony: The Memoirs of Dmitri Shostakovich, as related to and edited by Solomon Volkov*, transl. Antonina W. Bouis, Hamish Hamilton, London/Harper and Row, New York, 1979.

SMITH, HEDRICK, *The New Russians*, Hutchinson, London, 1990.

SOLLERTINSKY, DMITRI and LUDMILLA, *Pages from the Life of*

Dmitri Shostakovich, Harcourt Brace Jovanovich, New York, 1980/Robert Hale, London, 1981.

SOLZHENITSYN, ALEXANDER, *The Gulag Archipelago*, Collins Harvill, London/Harper & Row, New York, three vols. 1974, 1975 and 1978.

STARR, S. FREDERICK, *Red and Hot: The Fate of Jazz in the Soviet Union 1917–1980*, Oxford University Press, New York, 1983.

STEPANOV, NIKOLAY, *Ivan Krylov*, Twayne Publishers, New York, 1973.

STOLPYANSKY, PYOTR, *Muzyka i muzitsyrovanye v starom Peterburge* (*Music and Music-making in the Old Petersburg*), Mysl, Leningrad, 1925; reprinted Muzyka, Leningrad, 1989.

STRAUSS, LEO, *Persecution and the Art of Writing*, The Free Press, Glencoe, Illinois, 1952.

STRAVINSKY, IGOR, *Igor Stravinsky, Selected Correspondence*, Alfred A. Knopf, New York, three vols., 1982, 1984 and 1985.

STRAVINSKY, VERA, and CRAFT, ROBERT, *Stravinsky in Pictures and Documents*, Simon & Schuster, New York, 1978.

SZAMUELY, TIBOR, *The Russian Tradition*, Secker and Warburg, London, 1974.

TARUSKIN, RICHARD, *Text and Act*, Oxford University Press, Oxford, 1995.

TAUBMAN, HOWARD, *The Maestro: The Life of Toscanini*, Simon and Schuster, New York, 1951.

TERRAS, VICTOR, *Handbook of Russian Literature*, Yale University Press, New Haven, 1985.

TILL, NICHOLAS, *Mozart and the Enlightenment: Truth, Virtue and Beauty in Mozart's Operas*, Faber and Faber, London, 1992.

TISHCHENKO, BORIS, *Pis'ma Dmitriya Dmitriyevicha Shostakovicha Borisu Tishchenko* (*Letters of Dmitry Dmitriyevich Shostakovich to Boris Tishchenko*), Kompozitor, St Petersburg, 1997.

TODD, ALBERT C., (ed.), with YEVTUSHENKO, YEVGENY and RAGAN, JAMES, *Yevgeny Yevtushenko: The Collected Poems, 1952–1990*, Henry Holt and Co., New York, 1991.

TOLSTOY, LEV NIKOLAYEVICH, *Sobraniye Sochineniy* (*Complete Works*), Vol. 12, Gozlit, Moscow, 1948.

VAKSBERG, ARKADY, *Stalin Against the Jews*, Alfred A. Knopf, New York, 1994.

VASILENKO, SERGEY, *Vospominaniya muzykanta* (*Reminiscences of a Musician*), Muzyka, Leningrad, 1976.

VISHNEVSKAYA, GALINA, *Galina. Istoriya Zhizni* (*Galina. Life History*), La Presse Libre/Kontinent, Paris, 1985.

——, *Galina: A Russian Story*, transl. Guy Daniels, Harcourt Brace Jovanovich, New York, 1984/Hodder and Stoughton, London, 1985.

VOLKOGONOV, DMITRI, *Lenin: Life and Legacy*, HarperCollins, New York, 1994.

——, *Stalin: Triumph and Tragedy*, ed. and transl. Harold Shukman, Weidenfeld and Nicolson, London, 1991.

VOLKOV, MARIANNA and SOLOMON, *Iosif Brodsky v N'yu-Yorke* (*Joseph Brodsky in New York*), Cultural Center for Soviet Refugees, Inc., New York, 1990.

VOLKOV, SOLOMON, *Balanchine's Tchaikovsky*, transl. Antonina W. Bouis, Simon and Schuster, New York, 1985.

——, *Brodsky ob Akhmatovoy: Dialogi s S. Volkovym* (*Brodsky on Akhmatova: Dialogues with S. Volkov*), Nezavisimaya Gazeta, Moscow, 1992.

——, *Conversations with Joseph Brodsky: A Poet's Journey through the Twentieth Century*, transl. Marian Schwartz, The Free Press, New York, 1998.

——, *Molodyye Kompozitory Leningrada* (*Young Composers of Leningrad*), Sovetsky Kompozitor, Leningrad, 1971.

——, *St Petersburg: A Cultural History*, transl. Antonina W. Bouis, The Free Press, New York, 1995; Sinclair-Stevenson, London, 1996.

—— and MILSTEIN, NATHAN, *From Russia to the West*, transl. Antonina W. Bouis, Barrie & Jenkins, London/Henry Holt and Co., New York, 1990.

WARD, CHRIS, *Stalin's Russia*, Edward Arnold, London, 1993.

WERTH, ALEXANDER, *Musical Uproar in Moscow*, Turnstile Press, London, 1949.

WEST, W. J., *The Larger Evils. Nineteen-Eighty-Four: The Truth Behind the Satire*, Canongate, London, 1992.

WILSON, ELIZABETH, *Shostakovich: A Life Remembered*, Faber and Faber, London/Princeton University Press, Princeton, 1994.

YAKOVLEV, MIKHAIL MIKHAILOVICH, (compiler), *D. Shostakovich o vremeni i o sebe, 1926–1975* (*D. Shostakovich About His Time and Himself, 1926–1975*), Sovetsky Kompozitor, Moscow, 1980.

YAKOVLEV, NIKOLAY, *CIA's Target – The USSR*, 2nd edn., Progress Publishers, Moscow, 1984.

YAKUBOV, MANASHIR, *Dmitry Shostakovich, String Quartets*, Moscow Philharmonic Orchestra, Moscow, 1986.

YARUSTOVSKY, B. M., (ed.), *I. F. Stravinsky: Stat'i i materialy* (*I.

F. Stravinsky: Articles and Materials), Sovetsky Kompozitor, Moscow, 1973.

YEVTUSHENKO, YEVGENY, *Fatal Half-Measures: The Culture of Democracy in the Soviet Union*, ed. and transl. Antonina W. Bouis, Little, Brown, Boston, 1991.

——, *Precocious Autobiography*, Collins Harvill, London/E. P. Dutton, New York, 1963.

2. Articles

ABRAHAM, GERALD, 'The Citizen Composer', *The Times Literary Supplement*, 4 June 1982, p. 609.

——, 'Discordant Realities', *The Times Literary Supplement*, 23 November 1979, Section 6C, p. 23.

ALEKSANDROV, ANDREY, 'Juvenilian Lash', *Music in the USSR*, January–March 1990, pp. 42–43; reprinted as 'The Scourge of Juvenal (*Rayok*)' in *DSCH*, No. xii, pp. 3–4.

ANON, 'Arestovannaya literatura' ('Arrested Literature'), *Gosudarstvennaya bezopasnost i demokratiya* (*State Security and Democracy*), Moscow, 1992.

——, 'Baletnaya fal'sh' ('Ballet Falsehood'), *Pravda*, 6 February 1936, p. 3.

——, 'Court Cuts Sentence on Writer Who Linked Greek Paper With KGB', *Reuters North European Service*, 26 May 1984.

——, 'A Cry from the Tomb', review of *Testimony*, *The Economist*, 273, 27 October–2 November 1979, pp. 120, 123.

——, 'Klop' ('The Bedbug'), *Literaturnaya Gazeta*, 14 November 1979, p. 8. Translated in *BBC Summary of World Broadcasts*, 16 November 1979, SU/6273/A1/1; available in LEXIS, News Library, Archiv file.

——, '"Klop" Lopnul' ('The "Bed-Bug" Blew Up'), *Literaturnaya Gazeta* (*Literary Gazette*), 19 December 1979, p. 9.

——, 'Moy tvorchesky otvet' ('My Artistic Reply'), a review of Shostakovich's Symphony No. 5, *Vechernyaya Moskva* (*Evening Moscow*) No. 19/4249, 25 January 1938, p. 3.

——, 'Notes for *Notes*', *Notes*, 51/4, June 1995, p. 1277.

——, 'Ofitsial'noye dos'ye', *Literaturnaya Gazeta*, 14 November 1979, p. 8.

——, 'Revelations – the 10th Symphony', *DSCH Journal*, 1, Summer 1994, pp. 24–25, summarising Nelly Kravetz's paper of 28 January 1994.

——, review of *Testimony*, *Music and Musicians*, 28, March 1980, pp. 20–23.

——, review of *Testimony*, *The New Republic*, 181, 10 November 1979, p. 34.

——, 'S. S. Prokof'yev glazami sovremennikov: "Etot balet budet zhit' . . .". Stenogramma obsuzhdeniya Zolushki. Stenogramma zasedaniya Khudozhestvennogo soveta po teatru i dramaturgii Komiteta po delam iskusstv pri SNK SSSR. 16 Nov. 1945' ('S. S. Prokofiev in the Eyes of His Contemporaries. Minutes of the Discussion of Cinderella'), *Sovetskaya Muzyka*, 1991, No. 11, p. 81.

——, 'Shostakovich's Son Says Moves Against Artists Led to Defection', *The New York Times*, 14 May 1981, p. A18.

——, 'A Soviet Mouthpiece or a Part of the Free Press?', *The Economist*, Vol. 303, No. 7494, 18 April 1987, pp. 19–22.

——, 'Sumbur vmesto muzyki' ('Muddle Instead of Music'), *Pravda*, 28 January, 1936, p. 3.

——, 'Velikaya missiya sovetskoy muzyki. Shestoy s'yezd kompozitorov SSSR. Iz vystupleny delegatov' ('Great Mission of Soviet music. The Sixth Congress of Composers of the USSR. From Speeches of the delegates'), *Sovetskaya Muzyka*, 1980, No. 3, p. 71.

——, 'Zhalkaya Poddelka. O tak nazyvayemykh "memuarakh" D. D. Shostakovicha' ('Pitiful Forgery. Concerning the So-called "Memoirs" of D. D. Shostakovich'), *Literaturnaya Gazeta*, 14 November 1979, p. 8. Excerpts translated in *BBC Summary of World Broadcasts*, 16 November 1979, SU/6273/A1/1; available in LEXIS, News Library, Archiv file.

ASHKENAZY, VLADIMIR, comments in *Classic CD*, February 1991.

——, 'Shostakovich Was Not an Enigma', *DSCH*, No. xx, Spring 1992, pp. 4–14.

AVERINTSEV, SERGEY, preface to MANDELSTAM, OSIP, *Sochineniya v dvukh tomakh* (*Works in Two Volumes*), Khudozhestvennaya Literatura, Moscow, 1990, pp. 5–64.

BENEDETTI, CARLO, article about Vasily Sitnikov, *l'Unità*, 20 October 1979.

BOGDANOV-BEREZOVSKY, VALERIAN, '*Ledi Makbet Mtsenskogo Uyezda*. Prem'yera v leningradskom Malom opernom teatre' ('*Lady Macbeth of the Mtsensk District*. Premiere at the Leningrad Maly Opera Theatre'), *Sovetskoye Iskusstvo* (*Soviet Art*), 11 February 1934.

BONOSKY, PHILLIP, 'Defaming the Memory of a Famous Composer', *Daily World*, 10 November 1979, p. 12.

BORDEWICH, FERGUS M., 'Democracy Adrift', *Atlantic*, 256/6, December 1985, pp. 38, 40, 42, 44–45.

BOULT, SIR ADRIAN, 'Toscanini's Secret' and 'Toscanini's Technique', in Martin Anderson (ed.), *Boult on Music*, Toccata Press, London, 1983, pp. 86 and 93.

BRAUDO, E., 'Pobeda sovetskoy muzyki' ('The Victory of Soviet Music'), *Literaturnaya Gazeta* (*Literary Gazette*), 30 January 1934.

BRAUN, JOACHIM, 'Shostakovich's Vocal Cycle *From Jewish Folk Poetry*: An Attempt in Interpretation of Style and Meaning', in Malcolm H. Brown (ed.), *Russian and Soviet Music: Essays for Boris Schwarz, q. v.*, pp. 259–86.

——, 'The Double Meaning of Jewish Elements in Dmitri Shostakovich's Music', *The Musical Quarterly*, lxxi/1, 1985, pp. 68–80.

BROWN, DAVID, 'Glinka', *The New Grove Dictionary of Music and Musicians*, ed. Stanley Sadie, Macmillan, London, 1980, Vol. 7, pp. 434–47.

BROWN, MALCOLM H., 'Communications', *Notes*, 50/3, March 1994, pp. 1210–11.

——, 'Letters: Shostakovich', *The New York Times Book Review*, 9 December 1979, Section 7, p. 37.

——, review of Ian MacDonald's *The New Shostakovich*, *Notes*, 49/3, March 1993, pp. 956–61; reprinted as ' "The New Shostakovich": A Review', *Melos*, 1/4–5, Summer 1993, pp. 28–33.

——, 'Shostakovich', *The 1995 Grolier Multimedia Encyclopedia*, CD-ROM.

CANNING, HUGH, 'Scores to Settle', *The Sunday Times*, 7 August 1994, Section 7, p. 5.

CRAFT, ROBERT, 'Testaments from Shostakovich and Prokofiev', in *Present Perspectives*, Alfred A. Knopf, New York, 1984, pp. 76–87; reprinted from Craft, 'Notes from the Composer', *N. Y. Review of Books*, 24 January 1980, pp. 9–12.

CRUTCHFIELD, WILL, 'Music: Shostakovich 14th', *The New York Times*, 19 January 1988, Section C, p. 17.

DAVIES, HUGH, 'Shostakovich Score Inspired by Stalin Era', *The Daily Telegraph*, 12 January 1989, International Section, p. 10.

DUNNING, JENNIFER, 'Nijinsky Diaries: A Giant's Ardent Effusions', *The New York Times*, 7 September 1995, pp. C15, 17.

DÜMLING, ALBRECHT, 'Musikalischer Widerstand', in *Entartete*

Musik, Zur Düsseldorfer Ausstellung von 1938, ed. Albrecht Dümling and Peter Girth, Landeshauptstadt, Düsseldorf, 1988, pp. 171–72.

Evans, Robert, 'Moscow', *Reuters Ltd.*, 7 November 1979; available in LEXIS, News Library, Archiv file.

——, 'Moscow', *Reuters Ltd.*, 16 November 1979; available in LEXIS, News Library, Archiv file.

Fanning, David, 'Always a Great Composer, Not a Papa', *Gramophone*, 68/816, May 1991, pp. 1991–92.

——, 'Introduction. Talking About Eggs: Musicology and Shostakovich', in David Fanning, *Shostakovich Studies*, *q. v.*, pp. 1–16.

——, 'Shostakovich: *The Bolt*', a review of Chandos CHAN 9343/4, *Gramophone*, 73/865, June 1995, pp. 56, 58.

Fay, Laurel E., 'The Composer Was Courageous, But Not As Much as in Myth', *The New York Times*, 14 April 1996, Section 2, pp. 27 and 32.

——, 'From *Lady Macbeth* to *Katerina*: Shostakovich's Versions and Revisions', in David Fanning, *Shostakovich Studies*, *q.v.*, pp. 160–88.

——, 'Musorgsky and Shostakovich', in Malcolm H. Brown (ed.), *Musorgsky: In Memoriam 1881–1981*, UMI Research Press, Ann Arbor, 1982, pp. 215–26.

——, 'The Punch in Shostakovich's *Nose*', in Malcolm H. Brown (ed.), *Russian and Soviet Music: Essays for Boris Schwarz Essays for Boris Schwarz*, *q. v.*, pp. 229–43.

——, 'Shostakovich versus Volkov: Whose *Testimony*?', *The Russian Review*, 39/4, October 1980, pp. 484–93.

Ferenc, Anne, 'The Association for Contemporary Music in Moscow: An Interview with Nikolai Korndorf', *Tempo*, No. 190, September 1994, pp. 2–4.

Finke, Hermann Werner, writing about Shostakovich's first trip to Dresden, 1950, *Sachsische Neueste Nachrichten*, 13 August 1975.

Gavrilov, Andrey, 'Feeling of Regained Freedom', *Ogonyok*, 49, December 1989, pp. 5, 26.

Genina, Liana, 'Razbeg pered propast'yu' ('Running Start to an Abyss'), *Muzykal'naya Akademiya*, 1992, No. 3, pp. 13–14.

Gershov, Solomon, 'Remembering D. D. Shostakovich: 1 – Early Days', *DSCH Journal*, No. 2, Winter 1994, pp. 3–6.

——, 'Remembering D. D. Shostakovich: 2 – Final Sketches', *DSCH Journal*, No. 3, Summer 1995, pp. 6–11.

GETTY, J. ARCH, and CHASE, WILLIAM, 'Patterns of Repression Among the Soviet Elite in the Late 1930s: A Biographical Approach', in J. Arch Getty and Roberta Manning, *Stalinist Terror: New Perspectives*, Cambridge University Press, Cambridge, 1993, pp. 225–46.

GLIKMAN, GAVRIIL, 'Shostakovich As I Knew Him', *Kontinent*, 37–38, 1983.

GOJOWY, DETLEF, 'Dmitry Schostakowitsch: Briefe an Edison Denissow', *Musik des Ostens*, 10, Bärenreiter, Kassel, 1986, p. 202.

GOLDSMITH, SIR JAMES, 'Soviet Active Measures v. the Free Press', *Heritage Foundation Reports*, 465, 28 October 1985, pp. 43 *et seq.*; available in LEXIS, News Library, Archiv file.

GOLOVINSKY, G., 'S lubov'yu k cheloveku' ('With Love toward Men'), *Sovetskaya Muzyka*, 1962, No. 5, pp. 28–34.

GOTTLIEB, JACK, 'Symbols of Faith in the Music of Leonard Bernstein', *The Musical Quarterly*, lxvi, 1980, pp. 287–95.

GRINBERG, M., '*Katerina Izmailova*. Opera i spectakl' ('*Katerina Izmailova*. The Opera and the Production'), *Sovetskoye Iskusstvo*, February 1934.

HEIKINHEIMO, SEPPO, 'Kymmenen Vuotta Aitouskiistaa' ('A Decade of Struggle about Authenticity'), typescript in English provided courtesy of the author; published in Finnish in *Dmitri Šostakovitšin muistelmat* (the 2nd Finnish edn. of *Testimony*), Kustannusosakeyhtiö Otava, Keuruu, 1989, pp. 351–57.

——, 'Shostakovich's Memoirs: The Party Line', *Musical America*, November 1981, pp. 20–22.

——, 'Tikhon Khrennikov in Interview', *Tempo*, No. 173, June 1990, pp. 18–20.

HENAHAN, DONAL, 'Did Shostakovich Have a Secret?', *The New York Times*, 10 July 1983, Section 2, p. 21.

——, 'How Time Alters Our Views of Music', *The New York Times*, 1 August 1982, Section 2, pp. 1, 17.

——, 'Music View: Myths Just Keep Coming Back', *The New York Times*, 15 February 1981, Section 2, pp. 17, 27.

HO, ALLAN B., and FEOFANOV, DMITRY, 'Shostakovich and the "*Testimony* Affair"', *DSCH Journal*, No. 8, Winter 1997, pp. 42–46.

HOCHSCHILD, ADAM, 'Cleaning Up Stalin's Act', *The New York Times*, 8 May 1996, p. A23.

HUNTER, IAN M., 'An Exceptional Memory', *British Journal of Psychology*, No. 68, 1977, pp. 155–64; abridged reprint in Ulric Neisser, *Memory Observed*, *q.v.*, pp. 418–24.

——, 'Lengthy Verbatim Recall (LVR) and the Mythical Gift of Tape-Recorder Memory', in *Psychology in the 1990's*, ed. Kirsti Lagerspetz and Pekka Niemi, Elsevier Science Publishers, Amsterdam, 1984, pp. 425–40.

JACKSON, TIMOTHY L., 'The Enharmonics of Faith: Enharmonic Symbolism in Bruckner's *Christus factus est* (1884)', in *Bruckner Jahrbuch 1987–88*, Akademische Druck- und Verlagsanstalt, Linz, 1990, pp. 4–20.

——, 'The Finale of Bruckner's Seventh Symphony and Tragic Reversed Sonata Form', in *Bruckner Studies*, ed. Timothy Jackson and Paul Hawkshaw, Cambridge University Press, Cambridge, 1997, pp. 140–208.

——, ' "Schubert as John the Baptist to Wagner-Jesus" – Large-scale Enharmonicism in Bruckner and his Models', in *Bruckner Jahrbuch 1991–93*, Akademische Druck- und Verlagsanstalt, Linz, 1995, pp. 61–107.

——, 'The Tragic Reversed Recapitulation in the German Classical Tradition', *Journal of Music Theory*, 40/1, 1996, pp. 61–112.

——, ' "Your Songs Proclaim God's Return" – Arnold Schoenberg, the Composer and His Jewish Faith', *International Journal of Musicology*, VIII, 1997, pp. 277–316.

JARMAN, DOUGLAS, ' "Man hat auch nur Fleisch und Blut": Towards a Berg Biography', in David Gable and Robert P. Morgan (eds.), *Alban Berg: Historical and Analytical Perspectives*, Clarendon Press, Oxford, 1991, pp. 11–23.

JOHNSON, STEPHEN, 'All in a Life', *Gramophone*, Vol. 72, No. 857, October 1994, pp. 31–32.

——, 'Barenboim in Berlin', *Gramophone*, Vol. 68, No. 809, October 1990, pp. 719–21.

KARLINSKY, SIMON, 'Our Destinies are Bad', *Nation*, 24 November 1979, pp. 533–36.

KENYON, NICHOLAS, writing in *The Guardian*, 20 May 1990.

KHENTOVA, SOFIA, 'A Russian Love Story', transl. Katya Vinogradova and Ian MacDonald, *DSCH*, No. xxi, Summer 1992, pp. 18–21.

——, 'Shostakovich i Khachaturyan: Ikh sblizil 1948-y god' ('Shostakovich and Khachaturian: They Were Drawn Together by the Year 1948'), *Muzykal'naya Zhizn'*, 1988, No. 24, pp. 10–11.

——, 'Shostakovich: Legendy i Pravda' ('Shostakovich: Legends and the Truth'), *Novoye Russkoye Slovo* (*New Russian Word*),

7 July 1989, p. 6; reprinted from *Vecherny Leningrad* (*Evening Leningrad*), 15–19 May 1989.

——, 'Shostakovich and Poetry', *DSCH*, No. xx, Spring 1992, pp. 64–73.

——, 'Shostakovich and Rostropovich – 2', *DSCH*, No. xviii, May 1991, pp. 20–26.

——, 'Zhenshchiny v zhizni Shostakovicha' ('Women in Shostakovich's Life), *Vremya i My* (*Time and We*), 1991, No. 112, pp. 277–78.

KHRENNIKOV, TIKHON, Speech to the Sixth Congress of Composers, in 'Muzyka prinadlezhit narodu' ('Music Belongs to the People'), *Sovetskaya Kul'tura*, 23 November 1979, p. 4.

——, 'Velikaya missiya sovetskoy muzyki' ('The Great Mission of Soviet Music'), *Sovetskaya Muzyka*, 1980, No. 1, pp. 27–28.

KING, EMILY, notes to Gennady Rozhdestvensky's second recording of Veniamin Fleishman's opera *Rothschild's Violin*, RCA 68434-2 (1996).

KOLODIN, IRVING, 'Music to My Ears: Open Door to a Closed Society', *Saturday Review*, 10 November 1979, p. 50.

KONDRASHIN, KIRILL, *DSCH*, No. xviii, pp. 9–12; from *Muzykal'naya Zhizn'* (via *Sputnik*).

——, 'Shostakovich by Kondrashin', *DSCH*, No. xiii, August 1989, p. 20.

KOVAL', MARION, attack on Shostakovich's Symphony No. 9, *Sovetskoye Iskusstvo*, 28 February 1948.

——, re-assessment of Shostakovich's music, *Izvestia*, 8 December 1951.

KUCHINKE, NORBERT, and SCHMIDT, FELIX, 'Shostakovich: Why I Fled From Russia', transl. Gillian Macdonald, *The Sunday Times*, 17 May 1981, p. 35A.

LEBACQZ, K., and ENGLEHARDT, H. T., JR., 'Suicide', in D. J. Horan and D. Mall (eds.), *Death, Dying, and Euthanasia*, Aletheia, Frederick (Maryland) 1980.

LEBEDINSKY, LEV, 'O Chesti Mastera' ('The Master's Honour'), *Pravda*, 19 March 1991.

——, 'The Origin of Shostakovich's *Rayok*', *Tempo*, No. 173, June 1990, pp. 31–32.

——, 'Pis'ma' ('Letters'), *Novy Mir* (*New World*), 1990, No. 3.

——, 'Some Musical Quotations of Shostakovich', *DSCH*, No. xvii, December 1990, pp. 5–12; from *Novy Mir*, 1990, No. 3, pp. 262–67.

LEBRECHT, NORMAN, 'Sanderling's Summer', *Classical Music*, 18 May 1991, p. 15.

LEDEEN, MICHAEL, 'The New Cold War Revisionism', *The American Spectator*, 28, June 1995, pp. 28–32.

LEVITIN, YURY, 'Fal'shivaya nota, ili grustnyye mysli o delakh muzykal'nykh', ('A False Note: Some Sad Reflections on Musical Matters'), *Pravda*, 11 November 1990, p. 3.

LIBBY, THEODORE W., JR., 'I Bring the Blood of Shostakovich to Freedom', *Musical America*, November 1981, pp. 18–22.

LITTLER, WILLIAM, 'Editor of Shostakovich Book Talks About the Man', *Toronto Star*, 19 February 1991, p. D4.

LITVINOVA, FLORA, 'Vspominaya Shostakovicha' ('Remembering Shostakovich'), *Znamya*, 12, December 1996, pp. 156–77.

LIVSHITS, A., preface to V. I. FLEISHMAN, *Skripka Rotshil'da*, ed. Georgy Kirkor, Muzyka, Moscow, 1965.

MACDONALD, CALUM, 'The Anti-Formalist "Rayok" – Learners Start Here!', *Tempo*, No. 173, June 1990, pp. 23–30.

——, review of Elizabeth Wilson's *Shostakovich: A Life Remembered*, *Tempo*, No. 191, December 1994, pp. 42–44.

MACDONALD, IAN, 'Arena', *DSCH Journal*, No. 2, Winter 1994, pp. 37–40.

——, 'Common Sense About Shostakovich: Breaking the "Hermeneutic Circle"', *Southern Humanities Review*, 26/2, Spring 1992, pp. 153–67.

——, 'Communications', *Notes*, 50/3, March 1994, pp. 1207–10.

——, 'Fay Versus Shostakovich: Whose Stupidity?', *East European Jewish Affairs*, 26/2, 1996, pp. 5–26.

——, letter about Taruskin's article on *Lady Macbeth*, *The Times Literary Supplement*, 28 September–4 October 1990, p. 1031.

——, *Music Under Soviet Rule*, Internet Website, http://www.siue.edu/~aho/musov/musov.html.

——, 'A Reply to Messrs Norris and Brown', *Melos*, 1/4–5, Summer 1993, pp. 42–49.

——, review of Elizabeth Wilson's *Shostakovich: A Life Remembered*, *DSCH Journal*, No. 2, Winter 1994, pp. 17–21.

—— 'Shostakovich and Bulgakov: A Significant Affinity', *DSCH*, No. xviii, May 1991, pp. 54–58; also on the Internet at http://www.siue.edu./~aho/musov/bulgakov/bulgakov.html.

——, 'Shostakovich and Zamyatin: A Seminal Influence?', *DSCH*, xxi, Summer 1992, pp. 2–6.

——, 'Shostakovich, Zamyatin, Goldstein and *The Bolt*: A Hoax

Unmasked', *Music Under Soviet Rule* (Internet http://www.siue.edu/~aho/musov/zamyatin/zamyatin.html).

——, 'A Soviet Propaganda Play about the Downfall of Shostakovich in 1948', *DSCH*, No. xix, Autumn 1991, pp. 48–9.

——, 'The Turning Point', *DSCH Journal*, No. 9, forthcoming; also on the Internet, http://www.siue.edu/~aho/musov/turningpoint.html.

——, 'Universal Because Human', *DSCH*, No. xx, Spring 1992, pp. 82–83.

——, 'Witnesses for the Defence', *Music under Soviet Rule* (Internet: http://www.siue.edu/~aho/musov/witness/wit.html).

——, 'You Must Remember! Shostakovich's Alleged Interrogation by the NKVD in 1937', *DSCH Journal*, No. 6, Winter 1996, pp. 25–27.

MacDonald, Ian, and Feofanov, Dmitry, '"Do Not Judge Me Harshly": Anti-Communism in Shostakovich's Letters to Isaak Glikman', *DSCH Journal*, No. 8, Winter 1997; also on the Internet at http://www.siue.edu/~aho/musov/doubletalk.html.

Macdonald, Hugh, review of *Testimony*, *Books and Bookmen*, April 1980, pp. 55–56.

Mackenzie, Jean, and Bershidsky, Leonid, 'Analysts Fear KGB Comeback', *Moscow Times*, 9 April 1995, international edition, p. 12.

Macmillan, James, comments in *The Independent*, 5 October 1991.

Malko, Nikolai, *A Certain Art*, W. Morrow, New York, 1966.

Martin, R. M., 'Suicide and Self-Sacrifice', in M. P. Battin and D. J. Mayo (eds.), *Suicide: The Philosophical Issues*, Peter Owen, London, 1981.

McBurney, Gerard, 'Dear Shostakovich . . .', *BBC Music Magazine*, April 1995, pp. 9–10.

——, review of Richard Taruskin's *Stravinsky and the Russian Traditions*, *Tempo*, No. 200, April 1997, pp. 36–39.

Mercer, Alan, '*Testimony* – A Film: Based on a Conversation with the Producer', (interview with Tony Palmer), *DSCH*, No. iii, September-October 1987, pp. 17–21.

Meyer, Krzysztof, 'Recollection of a Man', *Melos*, 1/4–5, Summer 1993, pp. 52–64.

Mitgang, Herbert, 'Shostakovich Author Responds to Criticism', *The New York Times*, 22 November 1979, Section 3, p. 21.

——, 'Shostakovich Memoir, Smuggled Out, Is Due', *The New York Times*, 10 September 1979, p. C14.

MRAVINSKY, YEVGENY, 'Tridsat' let s muzykoy Shostakovicha' ('Thirty Years With Shostakovich's Music'), in Gili Ordzhonikidze (ed.), *Dmitry Shostakovich*, Sovetsky Kompozitor, Moscow, 1967, pp. 103–16.

NEST'YEV, IZRAEL, 'Zametki o tvorchestve Shostakovicha. Neskol'ko mysley, vyzvannykh Devyatoy simfoniyey' (Notes About Shostakovich's Works. Some Thoughts Provoked by the Ninth Symphony), *Kul'tura i zhizn'* (*Culture and Life*), 30 September 1946.

NICE, DAVID, 'The Welsh Shostakovich', *Gramophone*, 75/891, August 1997, pp. 20–22.

NIKOLAYEV, ALEKSEY, 'Eto byl zamechatel'ny drug' ('He was a wonderful friend'), letters from Shostakovich to Vissarion Shebalin, *Sovetskaya Muzyka*, 1982, No. 7, pp. 75–85.

NIKOLSKA, IRINA, 'Dmitry Shostakovich', interviews with Marina Sabinina, Izrael Nest'yev, Valentin Berlinsky, Ivan Martynov, Lev Lebedinsky, Boris Tishchenko, Vera Volkova, and Manashir Yakubov, *Melos*, 1/4–5, Summer 1993, pp. 65–87.

NOÉ, GÜNTHER VON, 'Das Zitat bei Richard Strauss', *Neue Zeitschrift für Musik*, cxxv/6, 1964, pp. 234–38.

NORRIS, CHRISTOPHER, 'The Cold War Revived: Shostakovich and Cultural Politics', a review of Ian MacDonald's *The New Shostakovich*, *Melos*, 1/4–5, Summer 1993, pp. 35–41.

——, 'Shostakovich: Politics and Musical Language', in Christopher Norris (ed.), *Shostakovich: The Man and His Music*, pp. 163–87.

——, *The Times Literary Supplement*, 5 June 1986, p. 606.

NORRIS, GEOFFREY, *The Daily Telegraph*, 11 November 1991.

——, 'Bitter Memories, the Shostakovich Testimony', *The Musical Times*, 1980, pp. 241–43.

PANN, LILI, 'Muzyka prosvechivayet vsego cheloveka naskvoz'' ('Music Shines through the Man'), interview with Solomon Volkov, *Literaturnaya Gazeta*, 27/5659, 2 July 1997, p. 14.

PANTIELYEV, GRIGORY, 'Prokof'yev: Razmyshleniya, Svidetel'stva, Spory. Beseda s Gennadiyem Rozhdestvenskim' ('Prokofiev: Thoughts, Testimonies, Arguments. A Talk with Gennady Rozhdestvensky'), *Sovetskaya Muzyka*, 1991, No. 4, p. 12.

PERLE, GEORGE, 'The Secret Program of the *Lyric* Suite', *International Alban Berg Society Newsletter*, June 1977, pp. 4–12.

PROKHOROV, VADIM, 'A Conversation with Maxim Shostakovich', *American Record Guide*, 60/2, March/April 1997, pp. 24–28.

——, 'A Personal View of Shostakovich: Son Reflects on Shostakovich before Friends of Music Concert', *Fairfield Minuteman*, 4 April 1996, pp. B16, 19.

PROKOFIEV, OLEG, 'To the editor ... Shostakovich's Memoirs', *The London Times Literary Supplement*, 14 December 1979, p. 134.

PROKOFIEV, SERGEY, 'Yunyye gody' ('Years of Youth'), in *Leningradskaya konservatoriya v vospominaniyakh 1862–1962* (*Leningrad Conservatory in Reminiscences 1862–1962*), Gosudarstvennoye muzykal'noye izdatel'stvo, Leningrad, 1962.

RABINOVICH, D., and SHLIFSHTEIN, SEMYON, 'Poema o nashikh dnyakh' ('Poem about Our Days'), *Literatura i Iskusstvo* (*Literature and Art*), 4 April 1941.

RAKHMANOVA, MARINA, 'Poslesloviye' ('Afterword [to Prokofiev's Report, on p. 100]'), *Sovetskaya Muzyka*, 1991, No. 4, p. 101.

RAMEY, PHILLIP, 'Do They Prove a Case?', *Ovation*, 1/1, February 1980, pp. 22–24 and 76.

REDEPENNING, DOROTHEA, 'And Art Made Tongue-Tied by Authority', in David Fanning, *Shostakovich Studies*, *q. v.*, pp. 205–28.

RIBKE, JULIANE, 'From a Conversation with Mstislav Rostropovich', notes accompanying Deutsche Grammophon 410 509-2.

RILEY, JOHN, 'From the Fifth Symphony to *Man With A Gun*', *DSCH Journal*, 3, Summer 1995, pp. 31–36.

ROBINSON, HARLOW, 'His Music Never Lied', *The New York Times*, 25 November 1990, Section 7, p. 16.

ROCKWELL, JOHN, 'Rostropovich to Conduct Premiere of Unpublished Shostakovich Work', *The New York Times*, 11 January 1989, p. C17.

——, 'Shostakovich Finds Many Advocates, No Great Champion', *The New York Times*, 19 April 1992, Section 2, p. 28.

RODRIGUEZ, NATALIA, and BROWN, MALCOLM H., (transl.), 'Prokofiev's Correspondence with Stravinsky and Shostakovich', in Malcolm H. Brown and John Riley (eds.), *Slavonic and Western Music: Essays for Gerald Abraham, q. v.*, pp. 271–92.

ROSEBERRY, ERIC, 'Some Thoughts After a Re-reading of Testimony', *Melos*, 1/4–5, Summer 1993, pp. 24–25.

ROSTROPOVICH, MSTISLAV, comments in *The Independent*, 6 April and 5 October 1991.

——, comments in *The New York Post*, 11 July 1978, p. 1.

——, interview in *BBC Music Magazine*, February 1995, pp. 16–20.

——, 'Plachu nalog Bogu' ('I Pay My Due to God'), *Izvestia*, 64, 6 April 1994.

ROTHSTEIN, EDWARD, 'Anne Frank: The Girl, Not the Icon', *The New York Times*, 25 February 1996, Section 2, pp. 1, 23.

——, 'Musical Freedom and Why Dictators Fear It', *The New York Times*, 23 August 1981, Section 2, pp. 1, 20.

ROZHDESTVENSKY, GENNADY, comments in *The Independent*, 6 April 1991.

——, 'My Work on Symphony No. 4', Melodiya A10 00319 000.

——, notes to his first recording of Veniamin Fleishman's opera *Rothschild's Violin*, Melodiya A10-00019 (1983).

——, 'O sud'be baleta S. Prokof'yeva Romeo i Dzhul'yetta' ('On the Fate of S. Prokofiev's Ballet *Romeo and Juliet*'), *Sovetskaya Muzyka*, 1973, No. 12, pp. 56–58.

RUBINSTEIN, ANTON, with SEMEVSKY, M., '"Avtobiografichiskiye rasskazy" Antona Rubinshteyna' ('Autobiographical stories of Anton Rubinstein'), *Literaturnoye naslediye v tryokh tomakh* (*Literary Works in Three Volumes*), Muzyka, Moscow, 1983.

SAFFORD, EDWIN, 'Shostakovich: Rise and Fall', *The Providence Sunday Journal*, 3 February 1980, p. H16.

SAHAKIAN, WILLIAM S., and LEWIS, MABEL, 'Material Fallacies of Reasoning', in *Ideas of Great Philosophers*, Harper and Row, New York, 1966.

SALEHIEH, VAHID, interview with Detlef Gojowy, *Melos*, 1/4–5, Summer 1993, pp. 50–51.

——, interview with Torsten Ekbom, *Melos*, 1/4–5, Summer 1993, p. 26.

SANDERLING, KURT, comments in notes to his recording of Shostakovich's Symphony No. 5 (Berlin Classics BC 2063–2).

——, interviewed by Hans Bitterlich for the notes to his 1992 recording of Shostakovich's Symphony No. 8 (Berlin Classics BC 2064–2).

——, 'Performers on Shostakovich: Kurt Sanderling', interview in Lyon, France, October 1996, *DSCH Journal*, No. 6, Winter 1996, pp. 11–14.

SCHAEFFER, PETER, 'Shostakovich's *Testimony*: The Whole Truth?', *Books & Arts*, 7 March 1980, p. 29.

SCHNEERSON, GRIGORY, 'At the Birth of Dmitri Shostakovich's Eighth Symphony', transl. Laurel E. Fay in Malcolm H. Brown (ed.), *Russian and Soviet Music: Essays for Boris Schwarz, q. v.*, pp. 253–57.

SCHONBERG, HAROLD C., 'A Hero of the State', *The New York Times*, 21 September 1980, Section 7, p. 12.

——, 'Words and Music Under Stalin', *The New York Times Book Review*, 21 October 1979, Section 7, pp. 1, 46–47.

SCHÖNBERGER, ELMER, 'Dmitri Shostakovich's Memoirs: Testimony', *Keynotes*, 10, 1979, No. 2, pp. 55–58.

——, '"Er is niets dat mij ook maar enigszins aan de authenticiteit van het boek doet twijfelen": Mark Lubotski over de memoires van Dmitri Sjostakovitsj' ('There is nothing which makes me doubt at all the authenticity of the book: Mark Lubotsky about the Shostakovich memoirs'), *Vrij Nederland*, 40/50, 15 December 1979, p. 21.

SCHWARZ, BORIS, 'Shostakovich', *The New Grove Dictionary of Music and Musicians*, Macmillan, London, 1980, Vol. 17, pp. 264–75.

SCHWARZ, BORIS, and FAY, LAUREL E., 'Shostakovich', in *New Grove Russian Masters 2*, W. W. Norton, New York, 1986, pp. 173-231.

SECKERSON, EDWARD, 'Ashkenazy's Shostakovich', *Gramophone*, Vol. 67, No. 799, December 1989, pp. 1115–16.

SEEGER, CHARLES, 'Music and Culture', *Proceedings of the Music Teachers National Association for 1940*, MTNA, Pittsburgh, 1941.

SHAFAREVICH, IGOR' R., 'Shostakovich i Russkoye Soprotivlenye Kommunizmu' ('Shostakovich and the Russian Resistance to Communism'), in *Sochineniya v tryokh tomakh* (*Works in Three Volumes*), Feniks, Moscow, 1994.

SHAGINYAN, MARIETTA, 'Fifty Letters from Dmitri Shostakovich', *Soviet Literature*, 1984, No. 1, pp. 68–99.

SHCHEDRIN, RODION, letter in *Gramophone*, Vol. 75, No. 894, November 1997, p. 8.

SHOSTAKOVICH, DMITRY, 'Avtobiografiya' ('Autobiography'), *Sovetskaya Muzyka*, 1966, No. 9, pp. 24–25.

——, 'Kak rozhdayetsya muzyka' ('How Music is Born'), *Literaturnaya Gazeta*, 21 December 1965; reprinted in Lev Danilevich (ed.), *Dmitry Shostakovich*, Sovetsky Kompozitor, Moscow, 1967, p. 36.

——, 'Nasha rabota v gody Otechestvennoy voiny' ('Our Work During the Years of the Patriotic War'), in *Raboty kompozitorov i muzykovedov Leningrada v gody Velikoy Otechestvennoy voiny*

(*Works of Leningrad Composers and Musicologists During the Years of the Great Patriotic War*), 1946.

——, 'O moyey opere' ('About My Opera), in the collection *Katerina Izmailova*, Leningrad, 1934, p. 11.

——, *Rayok*, notes and libretto accompanying Erato ECD 75571, adapted André Lischke and transl. Stuart Walters and Jan Butler.

——, 'Sovetskaya muzyka v dni voiny' ('Soviet Music During the Days of the War'), *Sovetskaya Muzyka*, 1975, No. 11, pp. 64–77.

——, 'V dni oborony Leningrada' ('During the Days of the Defence of Leningrad'), *Sovetskoye Iskusstvo*, 8 October 1941.

SHOSTAKOVICH, DMITRY (actually by Daniil Zhitomirsky), 'O nekotorych nasushchnykh voprosakh muzykal'nogo tvorchestva. Zametki kompozitora' ('About Certain Vital Questions in Musical Creativity: A Composer's Remarks'), *Pravda*, 17 June 1956.

—— (actually by Daniil Zhitomirsky), a speech for the Second Congress of Composers, *Pravda*, 27 March 1957.

SHOSTAKOVICH, IRINA, 'Remembering Shostakovich', interview in France, October 1996, *DSCH Journal*, No. 6, Winter 1996, pp. 2–5.

SHOSTAKOVICH, MAXIM, interview with Louis Blois, *DSCH*, No. xiv, November 1989, pp. 4–8.

—— and SOLOMON VOLKOV, 'On "Late" Shostakovich – A Conversation', included as programme notes to Maxim's performance of Shostakovich's Fourteenth Symphony with the New York Chamber Symphony, 17 January 1988; reprinted in *DSCH*, No. xiii, August 1989, pp. 35–38.

SIMPSON, JOHN, writing in *The Sunday Telegraph*, 29 June 1997.

SMITH, DINITIA, 'Scholar Who Says Jung Lied Is at War With Descendants', *The New York Times*, 3 June 1995, Section 1, pp. 1, 9.

SMITH, PATRICK J., review of *Testimony, Musical America*, March 1980, pp. 12–13.

——, review of Wilson's *Shostakovich: A Life Remembered, Opera News*, 59/6, 10 December 1994, p. 67.

SOKOL'SKY, M., 'Katerina Izmailova', *Sovetskoye Iskusstvo*, 1934, Nos. 4–5.

SPIEGELMAN, JOEL W., 'The Czar of Soviet Music', *High Fidelity*, 36/3, March 1986, pp. 54–55, 76.

SPINELLI, OLIVIERO, 'Alla Scala sale al podio il Maestro Kgb', *L'Europeo*, 35, 13 December 1979, 134–41.

STARR, S. FREDERICK, 'Private Anguish, Public Scorn', review of *Testimony*, *Books & Arts*, 7 December 1979, p. 4.

STEINER, GEORGE, 'Books: Marche Funebre', review of *Testimony*, *The New Yorker*, 24 March 1980, pp. 129–32.

STEVENS, WALLACE, 'Peter Quince at the Clavier', from *Harmonium*, 1923.

STEWART, ROBERT, 'I Am Not That Psychoanalytical Superman', *The New York Times*, 6 March 1994, Section 7, pp. 1 and 22–23.

STRADLING, ROBERT, 'Shostakovich and the Soviet System', in Christopher Norris (ed.), *Shostakovich: The Man and His Music*, *q. v.*, pp. 189–217.

STREL'NIKOV, NIKOLAY, 'Pamyati Al'bana Berga' ('In Memory of Alban Berg'), *Rabochy i teatr* (*The Worker and the Theatre*), 1936, No. 2, pp. 22–23.

SUPLEE, CURT, 'The Anatomy of a Defection: Maxim Shostakovich's Lifelong Quest for the Music of Freedom', *The Washington Post*, 24 April 1981, p. F1.

SWAIN, JONATHAN, 'A Golden Age', *Gramophone*, Vol. 71, No. 852, May 1994, pp. 20–21.

SZERSNOVICZ, PATRICK, and THOMAS, GRÉGORY, 'Prénom Maxime', *Le monde de la musique*, 118, January 1989, supplement, pp. xiv–xv.

TAL'NIKOV, A., 'Katerina Izmailova', *Vechernyaya Moskva* (*Moscow Evening Paper*), 26 January 1934.

TARUSKIN, RICHARD, 'A Martyred Opera Reflects Its Abominable Time', *The New York Times*, 6 November 1994, Section 2, pp. 25 and 35–36.

——, 'The Opera and the Dictator: the peculiar martyrdom of Dmitri Shostakovich', *The New Republic*, 200/12, 20 March 1989, pp. 34–40.

——, 'Public Lies and Unspeakable Truths: Interpreting Shostakovich's Fifth Symphony', in David Fanning (ed.), *Shostakovich Studies*, *q. v.*, pp. 17–56.

——, review of the facsimile of Shostakovich's Symphony No. 7, *Notes*, 50/2, December 1993, pp. 756–61.

——, 'Who Was Shostakovich?', *The Atlantic Monthly*, 275/2, February 1995, pp. 62–72.

TEACHOUT, TERRY, 'The Problem of Shostakovich', *Commentary*, February 1995, pp. 46–49.

TEMIRKANOV, YURI, comments in *CD Review*, June 1991.

TISHCHENKO, BORIS, 'Briefly on Important Issues', *Music in the*

USSR, July/September 1989, p. 35; a translation of 'Velikiye khudozhniki' ('Great Artists'), *Sovetskaya Kul'tura*, 15 October 1988, p. 8.

VANDENBROEK, PHILIPPE, 'Universal Because Philosophic', *DSCH*, No. xx, Spring 1992, pp. 78–81.

VIDAL, PIERRE, 'Shostakovich by Kondrashin' (interview), *DSCH*, No. xiii, August 1989, pp. 9–23.

VOLKOV, SOLOMON, 'Darf ich Ihnen die "Wolke" widmen?', interview with Lilya Brik, *Die Zeit*, 30, 22 July 1983, pp. 29–30.

——, 'Dmitri Shostakovitch and "Tea for Two"', *Musical Quarterly*, lxiv/2, 1978, pp. 223–38; an abbreviated reprint of his article of the same title in *Slavica Hierosolymitana*, Vol. 3, The Magnes Press, The Hebrew University, Jerusalem, 1978, pp. 264–71.

——, 'Dmitri Shostakovich's "Jewish Motif: A Creative Enigma"', 1985, included with the programme of the US premiere of *From Jewish Folk Poetry*, Op. 79a (23–24 November 1985, New York) conducted by Maxim Shostakovich.

——, 'In Venedig an die Newa denken: Gespräch mit Joseph Brodsky', *Die Welt*, 13 November 1982, p. 13.

——, interview with Leonid Kogan, *Sovetskaya Muzyka*, 1975, No. 1, p. 76; reprinted in Leonid Kogan, *Vospominaniya. Pis'ma. Stat'i. Interv'yu* (*Reminiscences, Letters, Articles, Interview*), Sovetsky Kompozitor, Moscow, 1987, p. 204, but without mention of Volkov.

——, 'Mysli o Muzykal'nom Ispolnitel'stve' ('Thoughts on Musical Performance'), interview with Mariya Yudina, in *Muzyka i Zhizn'. Muzyka i Muzykanty Leningrada* (*Music and Life. Music and Musicians of Leningrad*), Sovetsky Kompozitor, Leningrad, 1972, pp. 202–6; reprinted in Mariya Veniaminovna Yudina, *Stat'i, Vospominaniya, Materialy* (*Articles, Reminiscences, Materials*), Sovetsky Kompozitor, Moscow, 1978, p. 299, but without mention of Volkov.

——, 'Novy kvartet D. Shostakovicha' ('New Quartet of D. Shostakovich'), *Smena* (*Change*), 7 October 1960, p. 4.

——, 'O neizbezhnoy vstreche: Shostakovich i Dostroyevsky', ('On the Inevitable Meeting: Shostakovich and Dostoyevsky'), in *Rossiya/Russia, Studi e ricerche*, No. 4, ed. Vittoria Strada, Giulio Einaudi, Torino, 1980, pp. 199–222.

——, 'Peizazh poeta' ('Poet's Landscape'), interview with Joseph Brodsky, *Chast' rechi* (*Part of Speech*), Vol. 1, New York, 1980, pp. 27–36.

——, 'Questo Boris è uno specchio oscuro', *L'Europeo*, 35, 13 December 1979, p. 137.

——, 'Razgovor s Iosifom Brodskim: U. H. Odin' ('Conversation with Iosif Brodsky: W. H. Auden'), chapter from the book *Conversations with Iosif Brodsky, Novy Amerikanets* (*New American*), New York, 1982, No. 186, 5–11 September, pp. 25–27; No. 187, 12–18 September, pp. 23–25; No. 188, 19–25 September, pp. 24–26; and No. 189, 26 September–2 October, pp. 24–26.

——, 'Requiem for a Friend', *Ovation*, 1/6, July 1980, p. 15.

——, 'Souchastiye voobrazheniya. Razgovor s Iosifom Brodskim' ('Participation of Imagination. A Conversation with Joseph Brodsky'), *Ogonyok*, 1991, No. 7, pp. 7–11.

——, 'Soviet Schizophrenia toward Stravinsky: Razing His House at Centennial Time', *The New York Times*, 26 June 1982, Section 1, p. 25.

——, 'Universal Messages: Reflections in Conversation with Günter Wolter', *Tempo*, No. 200, April 1997, pp. 14–19.

——, 'Venetsiya: glazami stikhotvortsa. Dialog s Iosifom Brodskim' ('Venice in the Eyes of a Poet. Dialogue with Joseph Brodsky'), *Chast' rechi*, 2–3, New York, 1981–82, pp. 175–87.

——, 'Vspominaya Annu Akhmatovu. Razgovor s Iosifom Brodskim' ('Remembering Anna Akhmatova. A Conversation with Joseph Brodsky'), *Kontinent*, 53, 1987, pp. 337–82.

Vovsi-Mikhoels, Natal'ya, 'Moi otets – Solomon Mikhoels: Vospominaniya o zhizni i gibeli' (My Father – Solomon Mikhoels: Reminiscences of Life and Death'), *Novy Mir*, 1990, No. 3, pp. 226–48.

Wang, Dajue, 'Shostakovich: Music on the Brain?', *The Musical Times*, 124, June 1983, pp. 347–48.

Warrack, John, review of *Testimony*, *Opera*, 31, March 1980, pp. 245–46.

Whitney, Craig R., 'Shostakovich Memoir a Shock to Kin', *The New York Times*, 13 November 1979, p. C7.

Witonski, Peter T., 'Traitor to Art', *The National Review*, xxxi/45, 9 November 1979, p. 1410.

Wolter, Günter, ' "Ein Lachen durch Tränen", Jüdische Musik bei Mahler und Schostakowitsch', *Das Orchester*, 41, 1993, pp. 672–74.

Yakubov, Manashir, 'Dmitri Schostakowitschs "Antiformalistischer Rajok"', in *Sowjetische Musik im Licht der Perestroika*, ed. Hermann Danuser, Hannelore Gerlach and Jürgen Köchel, Laaber, 1990, pp. 171–91.

——, 'Istoriya, Sud'by, Mify i Real'nost' ('History, Fates, Myths and Reality'), *Muzykal'noye obozreniye* (*Musical Review*), 18 October 1992, pp. 4–5.

——, 'Preface to the Facsimile Edition of Shostakovich's Seventh Symphony ("Leningrad")', Zen-On Music Co., Tokyo, 1992, pp. 7–10.

ZAGORSKY, WILLIAM, 'From Moscow to Montréal in Pursuit of Music: An Afternoon with Yuli Turovsky', *Fanfare*, 14/2, November-December 1990, pp. 524–30.

ZHITOMIRSKY, DANIIL, review of Shostakovich's Symphony No. 8, *Informatisionny sbornik Soyuza kompozitorov* (*Informational Booklet of Soviet Composers*), 1944, Nos. 5–6.

——, 'Iz razmyshleniy o stile Shostakovicha' ('Reflections on Shostakovich's Style'), *Sovetskaya Muzyka*, 1976, No. 9, pp. 55–62.

——, 'Nos – Opera Shostakovicha') ('The Nose – Opera by Shostakovich'), *Proletarsky Muzykant* (*Proletarian Musician*), 7–8, Moscow, 1929.

——, notes on Shostakovich's Quartet No. 2, *Moskovskaya gosudarstvennaya filarmoniya, 1944–45* (*Moscow State Philharmonic, 1944–45*), Moscow, 1945.

——, 'Shostakovich Ofitsial'ny i Podlinny' ('Shostakovich: Official and Real'), *Daugava*, 1990, No. 3, transl. Tatjana M. Marovic (Norbury), Katia Vinogradova and Ian MacDonald as 'Shostakovich: The Public and the Private' (Internet http://www.siue.edu/~aho/musov/zhito/zhito. html). For an earlier translation *cf. DSCH*, No. xviii, May 1991, pp. 45–51; *DSCH*, No. xix, Autumn 1991, pp. 4–15; *DSCH*, No. xx, Spring 1992, pp. 40–42; and *DSCH*, No. xxi, Summer 1992, pp. 12–16.

3. Papers and Programmes

ABC NEWS, *Rush to Judgment*? (Anita Hill vs. Clarence Thomas: The Untold Story; originally telecast on the program 'Turning Point'), Films for the Humanities, 1994.

BARSOVA, INNA, 'Between "Social Demands" and the "Music of Grand Passions" (the years 1934–37 in the life of Dmitry Shostakovich)', paper, University of Michigan, 28 January 1994; typescript, transl. Karen Rosenflanz, provided courtesy of the author.

Berlinsky, Valentin, interview with Michael Oliver, *Music Magazine*, BBC Radio 3, 1983.

Brown, Malcolm H., 'Shostakovich: Expropriated and Exploited', paper, Shostakovich conference, California State University, Long Beach, 17 February 1996.

Dubinsky, Rostislav, 'The Interior Shostakovich', statement read at a conference organised by Bucknell University, New York, 9 September 1980, typescript.

Fay, Laurel E., paper, meeting of the American Musicological Society, New York, 3 November 1995.

——, paper, Shostakovich symposium, Hunter College, New York, September 1996.

Heikinheimo, Seppo, 'A Decade of Struggle About Authenticity', typescript (in English) provided courtesy of the author.

——, 'Shostakovich: The Official Version', typescript (in English) provided courtesy of the author.

Kondrashin, Kirill, 'The Interior Shostakovich', statement read at a conference organised by Bucknell University, New York, 9 September 1980, typescript.

Kravetz, Nelly, 'A New Insight Into the Tenth Symphony of Dmitri Shostakovich', paper, University of Michigan, 28 January 1994.

Lien, Molly Warner, and Feofanov, Dmitry, 'One Step Ahead, Two Steps Behind, and Who is to Blame? Extraconstitutional Apologetics and the Russian Experiment', unpublished typescript on file with the authors.

McBurney, Gerard, 'A Hidden Agenda' (on the Fifth Symphony), BBC Radio 3, 26 February 1993.

——, 'What's in a Name?' (on the Tenth Symphony), BBC Radio 3, 4 May 1997.

——, and Gavin, Barrie, 'Think Today, Speak Tomorrow', BBC2, 27 May 1990.

Robinson, Harlow, 'And Art Made Tongue-Tied By Authority: The Dialogue Between Shostakovich and Shakespeare', paper, Brown Symposium XVII, Southwestern University, 23 February 1995; typescript provided courtesy of the author.

Shostakovich, Irina, comments at the Shostakovich conference, California State University, Long Beach, 18 February 1996; transl. by Sofiya Krapkova.

Shostakovich, Maxim, interview with Michael Berkeley, BBC 2, 27 September 1986.

Todd, Albert C., 'The Many Literary Worlds of Babi Yar',

paper, Brown Symposium XVII, Southwestern University, 25 February 1995.

VOLKOV, SOLOMON, 'The Jewish Motif in Shostakovich', paper, Jewish Music Society, Toronto, March 1991.

YAKUBOV, MANASHIR, 'Musorgsky's *Rayok*, Shostakovich's *Anti-Formalist Rayok*, and the Traditions of Russian Musical Satire from Alexander II to Stalin and Brezhnev', paper, University of Michigan, 28 January 1994; typescript, transl. Elizabeth Wilson, provided courtesy of the author.

INDEX

Figures in italics refer to illustrations;
DDS = Dmitry Dmitrievich Shostakovich.

Press Comment on *Shostakovich Reconsidered*

'or 20 years the composer's memoirs, *Testimony*, have been ttacked as fraudulent, and the composer maligned as a man who ave in to Soviet pressure and compromised his art. The present uthors wish to defend Shostakovich's reputation, conducting, in n entertaining trial format, a passionate defence of the book. 'here are also numerous other musicological and cultural essays – splendid celebration of this sublime musician.

Stephen Poole, *The Guardian*

shkenazy has contributed the introduction to a retaliatory misile by Allan B. Ho and Dmitry Feofanov, titled *Shostakovich Reonsidered* and published this week by Toccata Press. Bulky but bsorbing, this devastating counter-attack exposes levels of acalemic self-delusion that might be condonable under North Corean water torture but seem a tad contorted in the cathedra of vy League colleges and the columns of the *New Grove Dictionary*.

Norman Lebrecht, *The Daily Telegraph*

Ho and Feofanov's defense of *Testimony* is] couched deliberately n courtroom terms, cross-examining and painstakingly disrediting objections one by one. This is so thoroughly done it urely puts the onus on *Testimony's* detractors to return to the tand [. . . .I] will be putting references to Volkov's dishonesty on ce until that happens. [. . .] read their book and enjoy the frisson f its TV-courtroom-drama-style presentation.

David Fanning, *BBC Music Magazine*

t's very rare to come across a book that's so readable. [. . .] What it loes set up, without much doubt, is Solomon Volkov's essential robity – that he's done what he's done honourably. I think he omes out of this very well all round, I have to say.

Stephen Johnson, *BBC*

The 'Terrible Trio' – namely Fay, Brown and Taruskin (but not necessarily in that order) – are about to have the wind taken out of their academic sails, are about to see their respective ivory towers crumble to nought: but above all are about to acquiesce – Volkov wasn't at all a 'liar' and what's more he and Shostakovich *did* indeed meet more than three times over a glass or two of *kvas*, and that all those unpleasant things about Prokofiev and others might well have come from Dmitri Dmitrievich's own lips.

[...] One thing is crystal clear: [*Shostakovich Reconsidered*] will be one of those 'indispensable' books on your shelf – like *Testimony*, like *Shostakovich Remembered* (by Elizabeth Wilson) and *Lettres à un Ami* (Glikman, in French) and Derek Hulme's Second Catalogue.

In this Trial by Jury, only one course of action is possible, Ladies and Gentlemen – read Ho and Feofanov's determined tome, it *will* add to your perception of the Shostakovich debate and may well lead to a moral, if not a circumstantial acquittal.

Nigel Papworth, *DSCH Journal*

There are just *too* many people who knew the composer, shared sometimes drunken conversation with him, and who have sufficiently little of an axe to grind, who believe the book genuine. [...] Taking all such indicators together [the evidence presented in *Shostakovich Reconsidered*], I think it is fair to conclude that *Testimony* is authentic as an expression of the composer's views and should probably also be thought of as verbatim.

John Shand, *Tempo*

The book, organised like a court case where the memoirs stand on trial, is extremely easy to read, set in a language that is readily understood by those who are invited to act as jury. The footnotes and cross references are thorough to the point of providing substantial commentary on the side, allowing one to follow the logic of the cross examination and defence. There is extensive rebuttal of the studies of the anti-revisionists that leaves the misleading claims of these scholars bare to ridicule, warranted as they are by such preposterous papers such as Laurel Fay's on Shostakovich's song-cycle *From Jewish Folk Poetry*. In short it is ruthless, but deservedly so in light of such published scholastic deceptions that revolve around selective representation and deliberate misinterpretation of material, dependency on outdated material and on splitting hairs with Volkov and MacDonald.

The climax of this intensive trial and the ultimate test of the trength of this book lies in the treatment of *Testimony's* biggest iddle: the 8 passages from the memoirs allegedly plagiarised from ear-identical sources previously published in the Soviet Union. Vhile at first encounter this evidence looks to be Volkov's un-oing, Ho and Feofanov in masterly fashion make a convincing ase for the composer's well-documented capacity for self-quota-ion. Backed by well-rounded in-depth research, it is the centre-iece of an exhaustive defence that will leave little doubt in the eaders' minds of the authenticity of *Testimony* and the portrait ithin. [...]

Shostakovich Reconsidered thus acts like a ray of sunshine through he stormy clouds of these past decades of controversy over who he real Shostakovich was. More than just closing the case on *'estimony*, as one must after going through the book, it provides he much needed all-round perspective of a composer who was ot only a commentator and a critic of his times, but also a sharp nd colourful satirist whose outlook on life and music far ex-eeded what we thought we knew of him.

C. H. Loh, *The Sun* (Kuala Lumpur)

s there still someone in Finland suspecting that Solomon Volkov, ditor of 'The Memoirs of Dmitri Shostakovich', distorted the ords of the composer? Suspicions can now be discarded. Allan Io and Dmitri Feofanov testify in their new book called *Shosta-ovich Reconsidered*, with an immense torrent of facts, that the iemoirs are, in all essential parts, discourse which the composer ad partly related to people other than Volkov, too.

[...] One almost feels sorry for the scholars who mocked 'olkov – such as Malcolm Brown, Richard Taruskin, and Laurel ay. Ho and Feofanov show with direct quotations that these holars, opponents of Volkov, separated sentences from their ictual context when they judged the book to be a forgery. They lso show that these scholars do not know or at least have not ommented upon the latest research which supports the au-ienticity of Volkov's book.

Vesa Sirén, *Helsingin Sanomat* (Finland);
transl. by Markus Lång

'his intriguing book tackles one of the hottest musico-political ontroversies of the past 20 years: a web of alleged deceit involving iusical masterworks, top-of-the-range academic reputations and old-war politics. Was *Testimony*, purportedly the authorised memoir of a great Soviet composer, Dmitri Shostakovich, 'as related to and edited by Solomon Volkov', a fake?

[...] Some western musicologists accused Mr Volkov of rewriting parts of *Testimony* from press cuttings, of tricking Shostakovich into signing the first page of each chapter and of getting his wife to put him in the front row at Shostakovich's funeral for a photograph. Most seriously, Shostakovich's political disavowals in *Testimony* were challenged.

Now the author-editors of *Shostakovich Reconsidered,* a useful collection of essays and documents, have mounted a forensic rebuttal of all these charges against the Volkov book (Dimitry Feofanov is both a musician and a lawyer). Despite the book's relentless courtroom tone, a good case is made out, built on Russian sources. ***The Economist***

[...] the variety of opinions and styles is one of the things that make this thick volume so readable. In their 300 page defence of *Testimony,* Ho and Feofanov adopt something close to a courtroom style, which holds the attention to the end, and makes the case for the memoirs seem virtually unassailable. [...] Read *Shostakovich Reconsidered* by all means; marvel at its breadth of reference, the force of the writing, and ultimately at the power of this music to stir up such intensity of feeling, such aggression.

Stephen Johnson, *Times Literary Supplement*

It has taken nearly 20 years of close collaboration for Allan B. Ho, also a musicologist, and Dmitry Feofanov, a music-loving bilingual attorney, to accumulate the formidable wealth of data that jampacks the 787 pages of their new book *Shostakovich Reconsidered* (Toccata Press, London; with an 'overture' by Vladimir Ashkenazy). They energetically set out to do to Brown, Fay, & Taruskin what a sledge-hammer customarily does to a tent-stake. They conclude by issuing not only Shostakovich but also Solomon Volkov – who has for years suffered in dignified silence – an unconditionally clean bill of political, ethical, and moral health. [...] Rarely have musicologists – ordinarily rather mild-mannered denizens of the groves of Academe – come in for such an all-out demolition job as is delivered by this book.

Paul Moor, *American Record Guide*